Discovering God's Word

◆ AN INTRODUCTION TO SCRIPTURE ◆

Teacher's Manual

Marilyn Gustin, Ph.D.

Benziger Publishing Company

Mission Hills, California

Send all inquiries to:
BENZIGER PUBLISHING COMPANY
15319 Chatsworth Street
P.O. Box 9609
Mission Hills, CA 91346-9609

ISBN 0-02-662334-X (Student's Edition)
ISBN 0-02-662335-8 (Teacher's Wraparound Edition)

Printed in the United States of America.

1 2 3 4 5 6 7   RRW   99 98 97 96 95

Acknowledgments ◆

There is no adequate way to express all my gratitude as I look back over the creation of "Discovering God's Word" and its accompanying teachers' materials. In a work such as this, always there are contributors and influences which are unnamed, yet happily remembered. Then, too, there are mentors and guides, helpers and critics along the way whose contribution must be mentioned. Three of these I want to mention.

First, deep thanks goes to my father, Harry E. Thomas, a retired minister in the Church of the Brethren, who taught me to love ideas and who brought me up in a home filled with Bible stories. I am extremely grateful for his willingness always to discuss any question from a dozen viewpoints, and especially in recent years, to encourage my every project.

Then my gratitude goes to John Herbert Otwell, my first professor of Scripture at Pacific School of Religion. He taught us the Old Testament with a passion akin to the prophets' own and challenged us to go beyond what we thought we ever could do in biblical scholarship. He is no longer living on this earth, except in the hearts and memories of many students who will always be grateful to him.

Words cannot adequately express my immense gratitude and affection for Wayne R. Rood, Professor Emeritus of Religious Education at Pacific School of Religion. Everything I know about teaching, every success I have ever had in teaching, every talk I've ever given, and my approach to every piece I've ever written are rooted in what he so beautifully taught and exemplified. His insight that teaching is fundamentally relational, his ever-open door that welcomed us all, his persistent gentleness and openness to our growth—and much more—have been the major influence in all my professional life. And he's topped it all off by being kind enough to write the Foreword to this book.

Others have made specific contributions to this book. To them, particular thanks:

To Father William Hogan, C.Ss.R., without whose insistence I might never have written anything;

To Francine O'Connor, an editor at Liguori Publications, for thinking I could do this and saying so;

To Virginia Allen, retired teacher par excellence, for the help on choral reading;

To Wayne Rood's book, *The Art of Teaching Christianity*, for specific help with dramatization;

And to John Allen, MA, for countless suggestions and changes on behalf of the students he knows so well.

Particular and everlasting gratitude goes to my husband, John. Every writer says that the work could not have been completed without the support of a loving and supportive spouse, and only writers, perhaps, understand how true this statement is: without him, not only this work but none of my work in the last thirteen years would have been possible.

To all of these and to the Lord, thank you, thank you, thank you!

Foreword ◆

This book will lead you into the Bible, that ancient holy book that has formed cultures, led nations, and transformed individual lives for two thousand years. In a thousand pages the Bible spans sixteen centuries of spiritual adventure—about 1,500 years before Jesus and 100 after. Your guide in this adventure, the author of this textbook, is a master teacher.

People often say that the best teachers are born. I've known a few. They sail effortlessly through a class session. They do everything right. They know what questions to ask. They sense when the time has come to give answers. Intuitively they know when a short answer is enough and when a longer answer is needed. Marilyn Gustin is a born teacher.

In classes I taught at Pacific School of Religion in Berkeley, we thought a lot together about the skills of classic teachers and the philosophies of modern educators, and noted that the Master Teacher was himself *The Lesson*. We found that effective teachers make the most of their natural gifts—humor, patience, honesty, interests, hobbies. They like pupils, their subject, the energy of classroom give-and-take. We talked about how to encourage teachers to be their own best selves on behalf of their pupils.

There's another thing. Marilyn grew up with the Bible. She knows and loves it. She has written a series of valuable guides for studying the Bible. She went on to the Graduate Theological Union in Berkeley for more graduate work in Biblical Studies. Trust her when she doesn't give a date for Noah and the Flood: nobody knows or needs to know. Trust her when she says that some letters that bear Paul's name were probably not written by him. She is telling you the best anybody knows.

There's one thing more, maybe the most important. Marilyn believes what she tells you. "The Bible is," she says on page 6, "a unique place to meet God." That's what it means to her, personally. So when she invites you to pray 1 Corinthians 13, try it. She has.

This is an excellent book. Study it. Enjoy it. May the Lord lead you. May the Lord walk beside you. May the Lord dwell within you.

Wayne R. Rood
Professor Emeritus of Religious Education
Pacific School of Religion
Berkeley, California

Components

Discovering God's Word consists of the following components:
- Student Text
- Teacher's Wraparound Edition
- Teacher's Resource Book
- Transparency Packet

The Student Text

There are fifteen chapters in *Discovering God's Word*, divided into two units.

- Chapter 1 serves as an introduction to the text and teaches students the basic skills that they need to use the Bible.
- Unit One contains eight chapters that examine the history of the people of Israel and the various types of literature found in the Old Testament.
- Unit Two introduces students to the New Testament in its five chapters, focusing on the four accounts of the Gospel, Acts, Paul's letters, and the catholic letters. Chapter 15, serving as a conclusion to the entire text, reviews with students the skills that they have learned during the course and encourages them to continue to read and study the Bible on their own.

Discovering God's Word is designed to be used side-by-side with an open Bible. *Discovering God's Word* provides students with the skills they will need to understand what they read in the Bible. Although written as an introduction to the Bible, *Discovering God's Word* provides students with the solid foundation they need to develop a life-long love affair with God's word.

Discovering God's Word Unit and Chapter Titles

Chapter 1	What Is the Bible?
Unit One	Original Covenant
Chapter 2	Moses and the Covenant
Chapter 3	David, Dedicated to Yahweh
Chapter 4	Genesis: At the Beginning
Chapter 5	Elijah and the Divided Kingdom
Chapter 6	Isaiah and Jeremiah
Chapter 7	Exile: An Ending and a Beginning
Chapter 8	Return and Rebuilding
Chapter 9	Wisdom
Unit Two	New Covenant
Chapter 10	Jesus' Life and Message
Chapter 11	Responding to Jesus
Chapter 12	Acts of the Apostles
Chapter 13	The Teaching of Paul
Chapter 14	Christianity Develops Roots
Chapter 15	You and the Bible

Student Text Structure

Each unit contains the following elements:

Unit Opener: A brief introduction to the books of the Bible found in that chapter.

Unit Review: Study questions from all of the chapters found in that unit along with selected Bible activities and suggestions for praying with the Bible.

Chapter Organization

In each chapter you will find:

Chapter Opener: A brief story that introduces students to the major theme to be considered in the chapter.

Within the Chapter:

- There are two sections in each chapter, each section beginning with a short, introductory paragraph about the topic of the section and learning objectives for the section. Section One of each chapter establishes the historical, theological, or theoretical context of the material to be studied. Section Two leads students on an in-depth investigation of important biblical books.
- There are two or three main teaching concepts in each section around which the lessons in the Teacher's Wraparound Edition are based. Each of these main divisions concludes with a set of discussion and application questions under the heading, "Have You Considered?"
- Several features regularly appear in each chapter . They are:
  1. *Learn from the Map*: Maps are provided to help students establish the historical and geographical context of events described in the Bible.
  2. *The Bible in Context*: This feature explains how the Bible uses various words and phrases.
  3. *In the Spotlight*: Ideas mentioned in the text narrative are further developed.
  4. *Scripture Workshop*: This feature appears in each section. Students are directed to work with the Bible and practice the skills that they have learned.
  5. *People of Note*: There are many people whose lives are connected to the Bible in some way. This brief feature investigates a few of these people.
  6. *Spiritual Reflection*: People have used the Bible as a source of prayer for 2,500 years. Students are exposed to various ways of praying with the Bible.
- Photos with captions are placed throughout the text to help students visualize ideas and events that happened within the Bible.
- Each chapter ends with a two-page Review that includes:
  1. *Q/A*: Study questions related to each section of the text.
  2. *Bible Activity*: Opportunities for students to work with the Bible in greater detail.
  3. *Glossary*: New words and definitions found in that chapter.
     A complete glossary for the text can be found in the Teacher's Resource Book.
  4. *Understanding More About*: Bible scholarship speaks in a language all its own. This feature helps students "crack the code" so that they, too, can better understand the Bible.

The Teacher's Wraparound Edition

The Teacher's Wraparound Edition (TWE) provides a detailed lesson plan for introducing students to the scriptures using the Bible and *Discovering God's Word* together. The comprehensive lesson plan is placed in the columns beside the pertinent student text page.

The lessons are developed around the following format:

1. *Welcome*: An opening activity that invites students into that day's lesson.

2. *Introducing the Lesson*: A brief overview of key concepts is presented, along with teaching objectives for the lesson and several activities to involve the students.

3. *Development*: Step-by-step instructions for teaching the lesson are listed under the subhead "What to Do."

4. *Recall*: The teacher is provided with a brief exercise to review what students have learned during the lesson.

5. *Connect*: The Bible is a living instrument that affects our lives today. Students are challenged to make the connection between what they have learned and events affecting the world.

6. *What's Next?*: Students are given a glimpse of the material that will follow in the next lesson.

Answers to every question presented in the student text are provided in the TWE under the heading with which they appear in the text. So answers to the questions asked in "Learn from the Map," "Scripture Workshop," or "Have You Considered?" will appear in the TWE under the same headings.

At the bottom of each page of the TWE are teacher enrichment opportunities titled "More about the Text" and "More about the Lesson." These features provide additional information the teacher will find helpful in expanding a lesson or an idea presented in the text.

While the Teacher's Wraparound Edition for *Discovering God's Word* provides the teacher with a detailed approach for teaching a lesson, the author presumes that teachers will develop their own specific lesson plans for each class. The lesson ideas and resource suggestions presented in the TWE cannot replace teachers' active participation in designing effective lessons for their students. There is no one *best* way to teach any lesson; the best way is the one that works most effectively with your students.

The Teacher's Resource Book

The Teacher's Resource Book (TRB) provides materials teachers will find useful. The pages are three-hole punched and perforated so that individual pages can be easily removed from the book for reproduction or inclusion in a binder.

Many of the resources in the TRB are correlated to the lesson plans found in the TWE by chapter number and letter; thus, the first resource in Chapter 1 will be listed 1A, the second 1B, and so on. All of the pages in the TRB may be used as blackline masters and reproduced for student use.

Each chapter of the TRB contains the following:

- An outline of the learning objectives and main themes of the chapter.

- An abridged lesson plan.

- Resources for teaching the lesson. These will include resources mentioned in the TWE along with others that the teacher might find useful in teaching the subject matter.

- Enrichment articles, to provide teachers with additional information that they might need to teach a particular idea or concept.

- Chapter tests and answers.

- Both students and teachers are encouraged to keep a journal during this class. A form for each type of journal is provided.

When you teach Scripture, are you merely exposing students to information? Of course, you hope to interest them in it, even awaken their fascination. Is that all? Is there something more?

Yes, there is something more. This "more" is the most important aspect of your classroom experience. It is what makes teaching Scripture different from teaching any other subjects: *Scripture is the Word of God.* When teachers and students study Scripture, they become points of a living triangle. It is as if the teacher is one point on

Our Lord, active in the Word

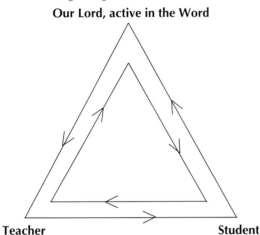

Teacher   **Student**

the base, the student is the other, and the Lord—the Word of God—is the apex. The Spirit of God flows along all sides of the triangle, in all directions, bringing each point into a living relationship with the other points.

While we might assume that the teaching of Scripture originates with us or with the designers of school curriculum, it does not. The teaching of Scripture is an aspect of the Lord's gracious initiative, reaching out to all of us, teachers and students alike. God invites us to meet in the beauty of the divine Word.

Because of this truth, we are not initiators of the teaching process, nor of the students' learning process. Neither are we responsible for the fulfillment of learning that takes place in the students. That is truly between the Lord and each learner.

When we undertake to teach Scripture, therefore, we do so in response to the Lord's invitation. A foundation for our effort is already laid in the action of the Spirit toward us and within us. The flow of grace has awakened in us (perhaps recently, perhaps long ago) love for the Scripture and love for the students. Such love will indeed feel like our own love, and so it is. It is ours, however, only because it is given to us by the action of the Spirit in our hearts.

Thus opens the pathway, as it were, of the Spirit from the Lord to the teacher, and the response of the teacher to the Lord within. While this is occurring, the Lord is also speaking to the heart of the student. God's gracious invitation to relationship, to a meeting in the Word, is extended deep within every student. Who can say for sure whether the invitation is consciously recognized by a young person?

In this process, the teacher has no direct part. It occurs in the secret spirit of the student, just as it occurs in the secret spirit of the teacher. Yet the teacher knows that the Spirit is active within each student. That knowledge affects the teacher's attitude toward each student and is the basis of the classroom relationship between teacher and students. The teacher recognizes that what happens in the classroom participates in a holy event in the student's heart. The teacher views each student in light of this truth, with reverence and care. The relationship between teacher and students becomes the sacred space within which the Spirit can deepen her work in each one.

The relationship enjoys several levels. The Spirit is one, active both in teacher and student, so there is a bond between them, recognized or not. Of course, love springs into consciousness all the more when it is recognized. The student can hardly avoid responding to this love. When it is expressed in the context of the Word of God, the student will be open to the Word within. The teacher, of course, will foster this relationship in a mature way. The teacher-student relationship becomes a matrix within which the Word of God can come alive for the student, can become conscious in the student's mind and heart. Teacher and students learn to appreciate each other simply and freely. They like each other. They can laugh together.

As the class days pass, students and teacher alike may become aware of the living presence of the Word in the classroom with them. While it is a spontaneous presence, the "place" for it has been prepared by the quality of the relationships already occurring in the triangle of Lord, teacher, student. The teacher also does very well to point out his or her awareness of the Lord's presence and to invite the students to recognize and acknowledge it. Perhaps most precious of all, there will always be at least one student who says (within the heart if not aloud), "Oh, that's what I have felt!"

When Scripture is taught in this vital awareness, it has every opportunity to capture the hearts of the students. Scripture then becomes itself the living Word to the students, the ground of their own relationship with the Lord, the soil in which they may sink deep roots for this current week and for the rest of their lives.

St. John Baptist de la Salle, a teacher of youth and a teacher of teachers, puts it differently, and beautifully:

> Paul testifies . . . that there are different kinds of ministry and work, and that the same Holy Spirit is manifested in a variety of gifts. . . . Therefore you should not doubt that you have been given the grace to teach [students], to instruct them in the Gospel, and to form them in religion. This is a great gift which God gave you when he called you to this holy work. In your teaching, the [students] in your charge must see by the way you teach that you are true ministers of God, full of true charity and sincere in carrying out your task. . . . Be driven by the love of God then, because Jesus Christ died for all, that those who live may live not for themselves but for him who died and rose for them. Let your students be moved by your untiring care for them and feel as though God were encouraging them through you. . . . See to it that the abundant grace God has given [your students] may be shown in the years to come.

Teaching with Open Bibles

Because of the power of the Spirit found in Scripture itself, it is good to teach with open Bibles. The students will have a textbook in front of them. All students should also have a Bible in front of them, preferably their own, but if this is not possible, then certainly a Bible belonging to the school or parish. (It is wise to have a couple extra Bibles on hand for forgetful students.)

The Bible should remain open during the whole class session, even if it just lies there unused. The open book communicates to the students that the Bible is as important as the text. They will, of course, come to know that it is much more important.

The Pupil Edition and the lessons in this Teacher's Wraparound Edition are designed to give the students the maximum possible experience using the Bible. Just mechanically, it is simpler if the Bible lies open and ready, next to the textbook.

Extensive quotations from the Bible have been avoided in the Pupil Edition for a simple reason: too many teachers and students may not "trouble themselves" to do hands-on work with the Scripture if all they need is found on a textbook page. If this happens, the students will not build the skills or a solid foundation for their own future use of the Scripture. The Bible itself must become familiar to them in this course of study. The best way to help that happen is to have them working in the Bible constantly.

If this approach is new to you, you will probably benefit as much from it as your students will. Many Catholic adults are not yet comfortable finding their way through the Bible. Teaching Scripture from this perspective means teaching mostly information, history, ideas, doctrine, and tradition. These are all valuable, but they remain external to the teacher and the students.

Inspiration and Revelation

Probably any of us could easily say, "The Scripture is the inspired, revealed Word of God." While the statement is true enough, it tells us little about the meaning of inspiration and revelation.

The most important aspects of inspiration and revelation for you and your students to understand are included in the text. But as the class studies further, you will probably have other questions and so will your students. The question that most often arises is the question of "inerrancy" or being error-free. Our modern, fact-oriented mentality automatically assumes that the inerrancy of the Bible means freedom from errors of fact. We expect that an inerrant writing has its facts right, its events accurately described, and that it is free from anything that even vaguely seems like a contradiction. In this understanding, diversity is not valued.

The biblical writers, however, were not twentieth century Westerners. They valued other aspects of truth besides mere fact. Most of all, they valued the significance of events viewed in terms of the people's relationship with Yahweh, the Lord. These writers seldom lost sight of meanings, though they did not always keep the facts intact.

Apparently this was all right with God. Why else would God have chosen to reveal the divine self to a people with this kind of mentality? And if God has overseen the process (whether we can fully imagine the mechanics or not), then we want to take the result with utmost seriousness, on its own terms. We want to avoid as much as possible imposing our own mentality on the Scripture.

In regard to revelation, another frequent question is about the words that follow the declaration, "Thus says the Lord." Were those words (to prophets and others) dictated by God? Scholars are prone to doubt it, but that may be a limitation in their own scholarly method as much as a restriction on the ways God can act in people's lives. Scholarship has no logical way to determine what the Lord actually does. Faith, especially faith living in intimacy with God, will experience God in many ways. If scholarship cannot say with certainty that the Lord did dictate the poetic passages in the Old Testament, for example, neither can it say with certainty that the Lord did not do so. Catholic teaching today says basically that God's full intention is accomplished in Scripture, expressed through the fully human minds, personalities, and culture of the biblical writers.

If you would like to ponder more about inspiration and revelation, you may study the quotations in the TRB taken from the Jerome Biblical Commentary, or you can look up "inspiration" and "revelation" in a Bible dictionary.

The Attitude of Students toward the Bible

Obviously, most teen students have an unformed attitude toward the Bible. They have heard things, perhaps from peers. They have vague opinions or feelings. They know the Bible is important. That may be all.

They are also, however, largely products of their culture. So they will have lots of questions and be quite ready to challenge certain conventional views of the Bible. Here are some suggestions for your responses.

1. **Do not be afraid!** Your job is not to prove anything about the Bible. Let them play safely with their opinions of it. You do not have to defend the Scripture from any question, even if it feels to you like an attack. The Bible is quite big enough and solid enough to defend itself if given a little time and attention. The Bible is, after all, an adult book that has challenged the understanding of the best mature minds across the centuries. We need not worry about keeping everything tidy in a teen's mind!

2. **Respect the questioning mind of the student.** You can always say, "I don't know. Let's look it up. Let's think more about it." You do not have to have answers for everything. In fact, a vivid question left open and frequently recalled may do more for a student's long-term learning than any other teaching method! If your students want logic and concrete information, give them as much as you can. But you need not force material that is neither logical nor concrete into a pre-fabricated pattern in the teenager's mind. Point out as often as you need to that a lot is unknown, a lot is not logical. Today's questions would not have interested many of the biblical writers and editors. Many questions cannot be answered except by educated (sometimes highly educated) conjectures. You may wish to suggest that your students keep a list of unanswered questions. They would not be the first to want to take such a list to heaven one day and quickly corner someone there who knows!

3. The most important factor is your own attitude. If you respect the Bible and can live with open questions, your students will know that they can, too. Questions left honestly open now will enable students to enter young adulthood without having to throw out everything they have learned or believed when they discover other and still deeper questions. So you can peacefully let them exercise their full mental capacities on the Bible right now, without anxiety.

Standard Resources

Ideally, every classroom where the Scripture is taught would have certain research resources available to both teacher and students. If not available in your classroom, check for their availability in the school library. These basics are frequently used in this study.

- **Bible Dictionary:** A Bible dictionary lists important words and topics alphabetically and provides detailed explanations, including Bible references when relevant. The topics include items that appear in the Bible, themes related closely to the Bible or Bible study, and often themes related to other works (like the Dead Sea scrolls) from biblical times which have some relevance for understanding the Bible. The Bible dictionary usually includes quite extensive illustrations, maps, and timelines. If a question begins with "what" or "who," it's a good question for the Bible dictionary. (An excellent resource is Harper's Bible Dictionary.)

- **Concordance:** A concordance is an alphabetical listing of the words used in the Bible, with all the verses in which a particular word appears. Some concordances are "complete," that is, they do list every word. Others are abbreviated, the editors having chosen to omit words that are too common. A concordance allows a student to find Bible references for any name or topic, and to locate verses they only half-remember. If, for example, you wanted to know everything the Bible says about Melchizedek, you would look up the word in the concordance and find its list of references by the biblical book, with all the phrases in which Melchizedek appears. Then, you could look up all related references in the Bible itself. If you partly remembered a verse—say, something about a deer and water—you would look up "deer" and find the phrase that you need, with its reference. Perhaps you would want to know where the "Our Father" is found; pick a word and look it up in a concordance.

It is handy to have a concordance designed to match the version of the Bible you are using, because translations vary and specific words may be different (like "reign of God" or "kingdom of God"). But usually this is not an insurmountable problem, if you are at all familiar with the Bible.

- **Bible Atlas:** A Bible atlas is primarily about biblical geography and history. A good atlas has both political and topographical maps so that places can be found easily. A Bible atlas will usually include many pictures and artifacts of the Middle East, along with sketches of historical events. A Bible atlas adds immeasurably to understanding and to a feeling of the reality of the events and personalities, as well as the lands, of biblical history. (Nelson has long published good Bible atlases.)

  Along with an atlas, a set of wall maps, or large maps on a stand, is a valuable asset to a Bible classroom. These should include maps of Palestine in different time periods, with changes clearly delineated; maps of the Mediterranean area in Old Testament times and in New Testament times, with major empires clearly shown. The *Map Transparency Packet* available for use with *Discovering God's Word* provides these resources for you.

- **Bible Commentary:** A Bible commentary sets forth scholarly information about the Bible, including questions of date, authorship, political and religious circumstances, and other pertinent data. The commentary will then move through a book, verse by verse, and explain its content, or give interpretive information about it. Full-volume commentaries have been written on every book in the Bible. Several one-volume commentaries, covering all the biblical books and adding articles about Bible-related topics, have also been published. The most familiar one is the *New Jerome Biblical Commentary.* Commentaries are essential for the serious student, but are not always easy to read or understand.

This textbook does not make much use of Bible commentaries, because they tend to be too detailed and dense. A nice exception to this is the *Jerome Bible Handbook* which is designed for the student who wants a quick picture of any book of the Bible. It is attractively laid out and easy to use.

Prayer and Teaching

Because multi-faceted relationships between us and God (remember the triangle) develop when teacher and students meet in the Word of God, prayer is the next most important thing to encountering the Bible itself. Prayer both expresses our relationship with God and helps to improve that relationship.

For the teacher, prayer is vital. It keeps one consciously connected with the Spirit's purposes in biblical study. It keeps the teacher's heart open for personal growth, as well as for insights into helping students.

For the student, prayer is vital for similar reasons. It opens a new recognition of the Spirit in the class work and gives them a chance to express their own experience of God in the Scripture. Most importantly, it opens their hearts to the direct action of the Spirit within them. Prayer draws students and teachers together before the Lord.

We are all beggars before God. That makes us sisters and brothers, regardless of our age or experience. The teacher of Scripture is also a student of Scripture. The adolescent students of Scripture can also teach each other and sometimes even teach the teacher as well. The Spirit's gifts are greater than the teacher's knowledge.

Praying for yourself is always important. Praying for yourself as teacher of Scripture is specifically important. The needs you feel in relation to the Bible as well as the students are welcomed by the Lord in prayer. Responses are given and can be counted on. The Lord is at least as vitally interested in this enterprise as is the teacher. So be sure, before every lesson at the very least, to open your heart to the Lord, so you may be supplied with whatever God knows you will need.

Praying for your students is equally vital, because your relationship with them is so central to their initial relationship with Scripture. Those for whom we pray regularly, and by name, become unexplainably precious to us. We respond to them differently than those for whom we do not pray. Moreover, mystery though it may be, praying for your students will make them better learners.

Praying with your students is essential. You are all pilgrims together, journeying into the living center of God's Word. This mutuality expresses itself beautifully and naturally in shared prayer. Ideally, as much as possible, your prayer with your students would be spontaneous, from the heart at the moment. It can come from your mouth, or the mouths of your students. In the beginning, you and they may feel a bit shy about this. Practice is everything. More than one class of students has been drawn into Christian love by sharing their prayer. It's a wonderful opportunity.

Some people prefer to plan their prayer with students and to give students an opportunity to plan their prayer with each other. This, too, is good. Avoid a constant emphasis on rote prayers, learned long ago. Such memorized prayers are sometimes suggested for closing more spontaneous prayer times.

Sometimes you will express the class prayer yourself, and sometimes you will ask students to do it. Sometimes the prayer will be planned in advance and sometimes it will be spontaneous. You may also ask students to say what they are grateful for, or what they need, and weave these into a class prayer with a response. Whatever the forms of prayer you use (and variety is good), encourage your students to forget about what is right or what sounds good. There is only one real requirement for prayer: it must be honest.

The importance of prayer to your class experience cannot be overemphasized. The more you can share it with your students, the more powerful it will be.

The "Spiritual Reflection" feature offered in each chapter (with a few added in the Teacher's Wraparound) is intended to draw the student and the Scripture together in prayer. They will be nice experiences for you as well. Sometimes they are to be done in class, but more often they are to be done in private. Although these form an intimate space, intended for the private meeting of the individual heart and the Lord, your students may be glad, in time, to share their experiences. In the beginning, assure them that these reflections are for them alone. Periodically it would be good to give them an opportunity to share, though always as a volunteer exercise. This is not reiterated in the Teacher's Wraparound, because its usefulness will depend on your own sensitivity to your students and their life of prayer.

Keeping a Journal

As an on-going exercise in prayerful reflection, keeping a journal is recommended for you and for your students during this Bible study. For the teacher, three kinds of prayerful reflections are suggested and forms for these are given in the TRB:
- Reflection before a chapter
- Reflection after each lesson, plus
- A "Bonus Focus for You"

These reflections are for and about you. They are your chance to grow along with your students.

At the close of each lesson plan, you will find a "Bonus Focus for You." This feature will point you to a Scripture passage not used in the lesson, but which offers a deeper reflection on one of the lesson's topics. This feature is intended for your own enrichment, although of course, the richer you feel, the better you teach. After each lesson is completed, you are invited to reflect about your classroom experience.

Evaluation is as necessary as any other part of your planning. It keeps you growing as a teacher, helps you see students' needs, and provides insights for the next lesson plan. Questions and suggestions are offered for your evaluations in the Evaluation Journal forms in the TRB.

For the students, a variety of prayer forms and reflections are suggested throughout the course. Many of these appear in the "Spiritual Reflection" feature; some do not. Students are to be encouraged to write whatever they think, feel and experience in their journal. It is not for your eyes unless they want them to be. Occasionally, it would be good to find out if they are actually writing in their journals. Essentially, however, this is not a course requirement as such. It is

an explicit chance for the student to encounter the Lord in and through the Scripture lessons.

Keeping a journal involves a skill which may be new to teens (or to you), but it is a wonderful tool for growth and awareness: expressing one's feelings and thoughts in words, just as they are. This is not about learning to be "a writer" with perfect grammar and syntax. It is an opportunity to grow in self-expression, so that awareness is heightened and one's experience remains available later. Writing in a journal keeps one's thoughts and memories alive for future reference.

Journals can be a rich form of prayer and deepening experience of God. As such, they belong with Scripture study and will enhance it. You are encouraged to help your students discover how valuable such reflection can be—and the best way to do that is to discover it for yourself (if you haven't already).

Both your journal and those of the students can be easily set up at the beginning of each class, by using the journal forms provided in the TRB. Each student's journal should be kept in a separate folder or binder. Your journal, too, should have its own holder.

Here are a few general tips for using the lesson materials provided in the Teacher's Wraparound Edition. You will see that each chapter in the student text has common features and each lesson is planned according to this common pattern.

Nevertheless, there are differences. Ideally, a teacher would read all the materials at least one full chapter ahead. Begin by reading two or three chapters to get started. Looking ahead in this way helps you help your students keep the contents of the lessons integrated and connected.

Moreover, a few of the lesson plans include activities that need to be planned well in advance. Some ask for student volunteers to do special projects and they, too, will need to prepare. Keeping at least a chapter ahead of your students will give you a comfortable margin.

Homework assignments are suggested at the end of each lesson. Plan to review the homework from the previous lesson at the beginning of each session. How you will handle homework is left entirely to your discretion. Sometimes you may wish to collect it, sometimes not (especially if it is journal writing). Sometimes all you need to do is check to see whether the students completed the assigned task, while other times the assignment is perfect for group sharing and could be used to start off a new lesson.

Preparing the Lesson

When you begin a chapter, make full use of the "Preparing Yourself" and "Preparing the Lessons" heads which begin each lesson plan. Read all the materials thoroughly, including the student text, lesson plan, and all the enrichment and suggestions included in the TRB.

Of special importance—and delight, one hopes!—is that you read the Scripture references mentioned. Read more than the reference cited to enrich yourself. By being familiar with the verses prior to and after those cited, you will feel well acquainted with the students' assignments. Even if you are already a devoted Scripture student yourself, your own life will be continuously enhanced by knowing the Scripture passages shared with your students. Your teaching will be more effective, too.

Each lesson also includes a map, a glossary and special features. It is good to familiarize yourself well with these. As you examine the lesson materials (text and TWE) you will see particular features that have little explanation, but are important to the triangular relationships you are building.

Environment

The environment of your classroom should be conducive to the study of Scripture. The room itself should be a warm and welcoming place. The lighting can be used to create a happy kind of space for your exploration of God's word. The quality of the space in which you invite your students will influence how they feel, work, laugh, pray, and learn together. That quality should be expressive of the beauty and importance of the content of your lessons: the Word of God itself.

An environmental feature recommended in this plan is a Bible table. On it, the Bible—open to that day's lesson—is displayed and honored. The appearance of the Bible table can be enhanced with a candle, flowers, pictures, or other symbols relating to the lesson or chapter. The Bible table should stand in a prominent place in the room. On occasion it can be moved, to emphasize the importance of a prayer ceremony or other special event. The contents on the table will be changed at least for every chapter. Some suggestions are made in "Preparing the Lessons," but you can use other ideas as well.

Remember: your room says what value you place on the events that happen within it. Help it to say what you want the students to hear.

Welcoming

Every lesson opens with a "Welcome" activity. When you welcome your students explicitly and warmly you are offering them an expression of love. Such a gesture sets a caring tone within which the work of Scripture study can flourish. A warm welcome communicates the love of God for each of your students. They will feel glad to be with you again and comfortable in your classroom. That's a wonderful atmosphere to help bring the Word of God to life.

Welcoming the students involves your willingness to look at them with respect, because you see the Spirit present in them. The same Christ who came to live in their hearts with their baptisms looks back out at you (a little disguised, perhaps) and smiles. See Christ in your students and they will see him in you.

Helping the students to welcome each other is also a wonderful gift to them. At first they may feel a little odd, but encourage them to say warm and welcoming greetings to each other, to join in welcoming activities, and to learn to welcome the group as a whole. Several opportunities are given in the lesson plans for students to plan and carry out the welcoming activities.

All of this special welcoming is a particularized way of helping to form your class into a Christian community, a group of followers with Christ at the center of their learning. Such a community is important for your students; it will influence them for the rest of their lives.

Have You Considered?

This feature, which closes each lesson, is designed to help the students think about what they are learning, usually in relation to their own lives and their view of the world's events. You will handle this most effectively if you have thought through your own answers to these questions. Possible answers are included in the TWE.

Right from the beginning, help your students to know that these are not questions with right or wrong answers. They are "thought" questions, designed to open avenues of exploration with your students. If the exploration goes off in a slightly different direction than you might have considered, you decide whether it is worthwhile to let it follow its own way.

Review Questions

Although answers to review questions are given for your convenience, it is good to answer them yourself before you use the provided answers. The better you know your own material, the more flexible you will be in class, and the more freedom the Spirit will have to move you all in an unexpected direction if it is best for the students.

Lesson plans have been included in the TWE so you do not need to start from scratch. But every teacher has various gifts and different students learn better from other teachers. Use your own talents; tailor the lesson plans to the students you have. If the lesson plan contains more than what you or your students can handle on a given day, omit what is least useful. If you have time and interest for doing more, be as creative as you can, using the suggestions as springboards for your own gifts.

Do not feel that you have to rush the students through every point of the lesson agenda you bring to class. In fact, effective teachers generally come to each session over-prepared on purpose. If you are over-prepared, you will be confident. If you are confident, you can change direction for the benefit of your students' immediate needs and interest. Use the teachers' materials provided, but give yourself the freedom and fun of going beyond them, branching out in your own way.

What's Next?

The function of "What's Next?" which appears at the end of each lesson, is to build a bit of interest in the next lesson. Of course, the best way to do that is to have a wonderful class this time! Still, it is always interesting to take a peek at what's coming up, without giving away just how it is to be handled. Suggestions are made, but be as creative as you can about this and intensify your students' interest from one lesson to the next. If you can invent sharper questions and issues to tantalize, by all means do so and enjoy them!

Special Resources

Bringing in special resources can spark renewed interest in your classroom. Videos and other presentations are widely available. One unusual resource is a portable exhibit of genuine archaeological artifacts from an ancient city in Palestine. The Bade Institute of the Pacific School of Religion has for years made available boxes of genuine artifacts (a 5,000 year old cup, an ancient safety pin, a stone for slinging like David used, oil lamps you can light), with helpful explanations and pictures. For a nominal sum, these exhibits are mailed on loan to you. Complete instructions are included in the package. The students can read about these articles as they would in a museum, but they can also handle them—carefully! Scripture verses are provided which correlate with the ancient items. Students always enjoy these exhibits, because they are concrete and easily relate to the Bible. They are best used about half way through the Old Testament study. For more information contact:

The Bade Institute, Pacific School of Religion,
1798 Scenic Ave., Berkeley, CA 94709.

The teaching plan provided in the Teacher's Wraparound Edition of *Discovering God's Word* fits comfortably into many different time frames and catechetical settings. Suggestions for teaching this text in most common settings are listed below; however, you are encouraged to adapt the material in any way that best meets the needs of your students.

The most familiar model is based on a 14-week semester course. Models are also provided for using *Discovering God's Word* in courses of three times a week, once a week, workshop series, over two or three weekends, and a full year (28-week).

Model 1:
Semester Course—Five Days a Week

This model will be used most commonly in a one-semester course in a Catholic high school setting. All of the chapters (except 1 and 15 which are each meant to be taught over three days) fit neatly into the following five day approach:

- **Day 1:** Introduce the chapter, begin Section One.
- **Day 2:** Conclude the first section.
- **Day 3:** Begin Section Two.
- **Day 4:** Conclude the second section.
- **Day 5:** Review the chapter, share student activities, and have the chapter test.

This model builds upon the lesson suggestions presented in the TWE and expects that students will read much of the text in the classroom. Extra days are provided for the teacher to expand the lesson with field trips and guest speakers.

Model 2:
Semester Course—Three Days a Week

Discovering God's Word can also be taught in a setting meeting three days a week over a semester. The flow would be as follows.

- **Day 1:** Introduce the chapter, study the material presented in Section One.
- **Day 2:** Present Section Two and work on student projects.
- **Day 3:** Review the chapter, share student activities, and conduct the chapter test.

Consult the Abridged Lesson in the TRB for ways to teach using this model. Students will read most of the material at home, with class time used for discussion, activities, and comparisons.

Model 3:
One Day a Week

This model will be used most commonly in a parish youth ministry, Confirmation, or religious education setting. The material from one chapter can form the framework for the one-night session. The Abridged Lesson in the TRB provides ideas for teaching a chapter in one session.

Model 4:
Workshop or Retreat

To cover the material in *Discovering God's Word* as part of several workshops or retreats requires added planning time. The emphasis must be on creative activities that actively involve the students. Here is a suggested outline for a five retreat or workshop process:

- Introducing the Bible and Bible history
- Prophecy in the Bible
- Wisdom Literature
- Jesus and his Teachings
- Acts and the Letters.

Model 5:
One Year Course—Five Days a Week

This model will be used in some Catholic high school settings. Typically, these classes will study the Old Testament during the first semester and the New Testament during the second semester. To use this model with the first nine chapters (introduction and first unit), one to two days would be spent on each lesson. In addition, at least one day each week would be set aside for student dramatic presentations and reports. A full day would also be used to review the chapter completely before taking the chapter test.

The final six chapters (Unit Two), would be taught by allocating ten class sessions to each chapter, along with a day for student projects and a day for tests. With the one year model, students would have adequate time to read much more of the Bible itself, returning to the text for support and guidance.

The following teaching suggestions are strongly recommended for use to enhance *Discovering God's Word* in a course of study.

Teaching Students with Special Needs

Students with special needs are often included in regular religion classes or parish ministry programs. These students are learning the same information and skills, competing for the same grades, and thinking of future jobs, careers, and vocations like any other students. Because students with special needs are often slower to respond to questions, it is tempting to skip their responses when trying to meet class objectives. This deprives special needs students of equal opportunities.

In some cases you'll need to alter your teaching methods when working with these students. The important thing is that if an activity requires students to write on the board or share a journal entry, these students should be required to do so also as long as they are physically and mentally capable. Students in wheelchairs may require a lowered writing board or the use of an overhead transparency. For the visually impaired, an oral response is appropriate. Hearing impaired students may need the assistance of an interpreter to help with journal sharing or in other class discussions.

The following suggestions can help your classroom or adapt your teaching methods to create a positive learning environment for all your students.

The Physically Challenged

- Adjust the room arrangement to students' needs.
- Encourage verbal activities and small group participation.
- Encourage these students to participate in physical activities within their capabilities.

The Learning Disabled

- Focus on the positive; point out students' strengths.
- Avoid assigning these students to seats around distracting students.
- Encourage small group participation.
- Encourage students to express themselves verbally.
- Be very clear in the directions you provide.
- Adapt lessons to fit the needs of these students; for example, you may need to provide them with a greater amount of time for an assignment.
- Provide an organized environment in which expectations are clear and realistic.
- Provide positive feedback whenever possible.

The Visually Impaired

- Seat the students in good light near the area where the main presentation will be given.
- Whenever possible, provide hands-on experiences.
- Assign another student to assist the visually impaired student.
- Allow students to record assignments or complete them verbally.
- Tape-record each chapter of the textbook.
- Encourage verbal participation.
- Administer tests and quizzes orally.
- Allow students to move about freely so they can get close to charts or displays.

The Hearing Impaired

- Seat students near the area where the main presentation will be given.
- Use the board to highlight key terms and phrases.
- Guide students to the appropriate text page during discussions.
- Ask a good student to make copies of his or her notes for the hearing impaired students.
- Provide written copies of tests, assignments, and discussion questions.
- Look directly at hearing impaired students when speaking. Talk at your normal volume and in your normal tone of voice.
- Learn sign language or provide an interpreter who knows sign language.
- Write directions for activities on the chalkboard.
- Encourage as much verbal interaction as possible.

Teaching Students from Various Cultural and Ethnic Backgrounds

Because one's understanding of the Bible is influenced by one's culture, ethnicity, and socioeconomic background, it is important that teachers be sensitive to these differences in students.

Parents, grandparents, other relatives, or members of a particular cultural, ethnic, or socioeconomic group may have passed on long-standing beliefs about the scriptures. While in practice, some of these beliefs ultimately may be part of a person's experience, they must not interfere with the students ability to dream openly and freely.

If students are willing to share practices and beliefs unique to their culture, it may help other students better understand the culture and the cultural influence that are present in the Bible.

Teaching Students with Limited English Proficiency

Students with limited English proficiency may not have trouble mastering the content. Their difficulty may be only with the language. With these students it is important to remember that requiring tasks before a student is ready for them can slow down the learning process. The following guidelines can help you pace and reinforce the instructions for these students:

1. *Allow time for students to become familiar with the structure of English.* Some students may know many English words but have difficulty with word order. For example, adjectives often precede the nouns they modify in English: "That is a yellow pencil." But in Spanish, the usual order would be "That is a pencil yellow." By accepting mistakes and praising students' efforts, you will provide an atmosphere in which students can experiment with English.

2. *Remember that students can often understand more than they can express.* Students may be able to use simple, direct English sentences but have trouble with figures of speech, idioms, and words with multiple meanings. Further development of their oral language, along with written English forms, can help these students develop more sophisticated English language skills.

3. *As students begin to develop writing skills, they may mix English with their native language.* Accept these language mixtures. At this stage, confidence and enjoyment of writing are the most important goals. Students who feel comfortable with English will be more motivated to write in English.

4. *Provide peer learning by grouping English proficient students with students with a limited proficiency.* Encourage students working in pairs or small heterogeneous groups to teach one another skills.

Helping students think should be a primary goal of all education. Learning only easily testable facts is inadequate preparation for living in the twenty-first century.

Definitions of Thinking

Critical thinking can be defined as the process of reasonably or logically deciding what to do or believe. It is a process that is made up of many considerations. The learner needs to:

1. understand his or her own and other's meanings and views;
2. look for relationships, causes, inferences, theories, patterns;
3. look for alternatives; and
4. make judgments, choices, or decisions based on the information.

Creative thinking requires the ability to identify and formulate problems, as well as the ability to generate alternative solutions. Fluency (quantity of ideas), flexibility (variety of ideas), originality (unusual or unique ideas), and elaboration (details for the implementation of ideas) are necessary components of creative thinking.

Assumptions for Teaching Thinking

These assumptions underlie the teaching of thinking:
• All students are capable of higher level thinking.
• Thinking skills can be taught and learned.
• Thinking can be effectively taught within any content area.
• Appropriate expectations for logical thinking are based on physiological maturation, social experiences, and the knowledge level of the students.
• Learners can be taught to transfer thinking skills from a specific content area to an internalized process applicable to a variety of new learning.

Actions for Teaching Thinking

How then do we teach thinking? Doesn't all learning require thinking? What is meant by higher level thinking? These questions and questions like them require teachers to reflect upon the instructional strategies used in daily lessons and to include opportunities for students to reason and think about what is being learned. All learning does require thinking. Benjamin Bloom's *Taxonomy of the Cognitive Domain* is probably the most widely recognized schema for levels of thinking. Questions, statements, and activities can be designed based on the taxonomy that will elicit the complexity of thinking congruent with the lesson's objective(s). Here are some examples:
• **Knowledge:** define, recognize, recall, identify, label, understand, examine, show, collect.
• **Comprehension:** translate, interpret, explain, describe, summarize, extrapolate.
• **Application:** apply, solve, experiment, show, predict.
• **Analysis:** connect, relate, differentiate, classify, arrange, check, group, distinguish, organize, categorize, detect, compare, infer.
• **Synthesis:** produce, propose, design, plan, combine, formulate, compose, hypothesize, construct.
• **Evaluation:** appraise, judge, criticize, decide.

Certain misunderstandings need to be cleared away if Bloom's *Taxonomy* is to be used successfully:
• The levels of taxonomy build, one on the other. Students cannot be expected to operate at a higher level of thinking without the necessary foundation. For example, a student cannot plan and participate in a pro-life campaign without understanding the entire spectrum of life issues affecting all those from the unborn to the aged.
• The level of complexity (from knowledge to evaluation) is not equal to the level of difficulty. For example, listing the prerequisites for various jobs and careers is a difficult task, but it remains a task at the lowest level of the taxonomy, knowledge.
• All students at any age and any ability level can experience thinking at each of the levels of taxonomy.

Questions and Activities

Examples of questions that promote thinking at various levels are shown below.
Knowledge—the identification and recall of information:
• Who, what, when, where, how?
• Describe . . .
Comprehension—the organization and selection of facts and ideas:
• Retell in your own words
• What is the main idea of . . . ?
Application—the use of facts, rules, principles:
• How is . . . an example of . . . ?
• How is . . . related to . . . ?
Analysis—the separation of a whole into component parts:
• What are the parts or features of . . . ?
• Classify . . . according to . . .
• How does . . . compare/contrast with . . . ?
Synthesis—the combination of ideas to form a new whole:
• What would you predict/infer from . . . ?
• What might happen if you combined . . . with . . . ?
Evaluation—the development of opinions, judgments, or decisions:
• What do you think about . . . ?
• Prioritize

Not all questions or interactions need to move from teacher to student. Dialogue among peers is an effective technique to use when teaching thinking. When students discuss, explain, debate, decide, or solve problems together they increase their thinking and learning. Asking students to generate their own questions and activities is another strategy that encourages student thinking.

Responses

Responses to student interaction can be crucial. Dialogue and thinking can be readily turned off by criticism or praise. It is easy to recognize that such responses as "Wrong," "Who has the right answer?" or "Oh no!" are obvious turn-offs. But so are responses that praise: "That's right!" "Exactly," or "What a great answer." After hearing responses like these, students will consider the dialogue closed and be reluctant to add alternative ideas or contribute new thoughts.

By using silence (wait time) you demonstrate to students that you expect answers and have faith in the students' ability to provide those answers. Given sufficient time, students will respond with more complete thoughts, show evidence of more creative thinking and exhibit an increased speculation in their thinking.

Your accepting responses can provide a psychologically safe climate in which students can take risks and time to explore their own thinking. When using passive types of responses, you simply receive the student's input with such phrases as "I see," "That's one idea," or "Um hmm." More active kinds of responses allow you to rephrase, translate, or summarize the input: "You say that . . .," "Your point then is that . . ." Emphatic acceptance lets you show feeling as well as understanding: "I can see why you would violently disagree . . . ," "That would certainly make us all feel safer . . ."

Use clarifying strategies when you need more information so that the student's point of view can be understood. It requires the student to give more information and to talk about his or her thinking.

Classroom Climate and Structure

The classroom climate and structure or meeting format provide further opportunities to foster thinking among students. If thinking is the objective, students need to interact and be in decision-making roles. They need to feel responsible for their learning.

Recognize Special Issues and Needs

Resource and media aids need to be ordered in advance. Materials needed for projects and activities also need to be at hand. If guest speakers or panelists are to come to class, they need to be invited and the time arranged well in advance. Speakers and panelists should always be prescreened to see what they plan to say. Plan ahead!

The Importance of Stories

Discovering God's Word features many real-life stories of people who faced the issues presented in the text. The value of such stories should not be diminished. It is through the telling and retelling of stories that the aims of the lesson become a part of the students' own lives. The stories may be presented in a variety of ways; the students may read them individually, or with a partner or small group. Allow time for the students to comment on the situation presented and share their own similar experiences. In some cases, you may have the students role-play the story that is presented in the text, an extension to the story, or a similar story from their own experience.

Working with a Partner or in a Small Group

Questioning, discussing, and sharing comments on any lesson is important. An easy and immediate way to accomplish this is to have the students work through all or part of a lesson with a partner or in a small group of five or six students. This concept also encourages the students to learn as much as they can from the lesson, and then present their ideas to their classmates for discussion.

The Have You Considered? ideas at the end of each lesson are discussion starters. Also, certain journal entries may be shared. Projects may be completed with a partner or with several others in a small group. The more familiar everyone is with a topic, the more lively and focused the discussion can be. It is often helpful to choose one person to moderate the discussion in small group settings. It is the moderator's responsibility to make sure that everyone has a chance to be heard.

Projects and Activities

Discovering God's Word works best in a hands-on environment. Class time should be made available for the students to be introduced to, plan for, and, in some cases, work on projects and activities. In most cases, it is best to allow the students to choose their own projects. The Bible Activity section of the Chapter Review lists several ideas related to the material. Also, refer to the suggestions found in the TWE. In addition, there are several different activities per chapter in the student text. Give the students the freedom to use these projects as starting points and to develop them in creative new directions.

Role Plays

For role plays, it is wise to set the specific scene and explain the characters before assigning roles. If the students have developed their own role play idea, ask them to at least follow this common format. Leave time for the students to prepare their roles (at least part of a class period). Allow the scenes to go no longer than four to five minutes. Always include a follow-up discussion for comments and questions. Several groups can act the same scene and the class can discuss the differences.

Debate

Present the students with a strongly sided issue. For example, you may use this format: "Do you agree or disagree with the proposition that ..." The aim is to provide students with direct experience in taking positions on issues and defending them. After the class receives the statement or the case, groups can be formed to discuss reasons for one position or the other.

Brainstorming

Brainstorming is a form of free association used to generate ideas. There are no right or wrong answers in a brainstorming session. Rules for brainstorming sessions might include:

1. No commenting on anyone else's suggestion.
2. Raise your hand and wait to be called.
3. If your idea is on the board, please don't repeat it; think of a new idea instead.

Allow the students time to offer their ideas. Record their ideas, as they are mentioned, someplace where all can see. After the brainstorming session, examine the ideas more closely. Ask the students to look for commonalties and differences in what they have suggested. Evaluate the ideas and narrow the choices to those acceptable to the whole class. Use the ideas throughout the lesson.

Journal Writing

Each student should have his or her own personal journal. Journal writing entries should remain private, unless specified. The TWE provides regular opportunities for writing in a journal. Allow the students frequent opportunities to write. Journal writing may be used to:

1. clarify ideas and feelings;
2. trace growth in prayer life;
3. voice opinions privately.

Media

Augment your lessons with various forms of media: videos, music, magazine, and newspaper articles help to keep the lessons relevant and breaks up the usual format. Help your students develop critical thinking skills by having them critique the media you use.

Prayer

Prayer communication with God—should be a primary activity of the class. Recognizing that God is present in the class dynamic is crucial. Begin and end class meetings with a prayer. Look for ways to help the students pray, and live out their prayer, in new ways (see "Spiritual Reflection" in each chapter).

Discovering God's Word

◆ AN INTRODUCTION TO SCRIPTURE ◆

Marilyn Gustin, Ph.D.

Benziger Publishing Company
Mission Hills, California

Cover Photo by Garo Nalbandian

Ainari/Art Resource 64, 153; Bill Aron/Photo Edit 21; Art Resource 10, 14, 168, 62, 67, 77, 86, 87, 90, 116, 239; Leslye Bordon/Photo Edit 257; Robert Brenner/Photo Edit 11; Bidgeman Art Library/Art Resource 18, 28; Buck Campell/FPG International 122; Comstock 274; Culver Pictures 19, 45, 149, 248; Dennis MacDonald/Photo Edit 242, 273; Mary Kate Denny/Photo Edit 223, 277; Ectra/Photo Edit 185; Myrleen Ferguson/Photo Edit 200, 206, 280; FPG International 210; Tony Freeman 8, 132, 278; Giraudon/Art Resource 150, 224, 230, 264; Jeff Isacc Greenberg/Photo Edit 212; Jewish Museum/Art Resource 44, 120; Lessing/Art Resource 6, 20, 29, 41, 48, 56, 80, 94, 105, 118, 156, 162, 190, 191, 235, 254, 255, 268, 272; Stephen McBrady 4, 5, 281; Stephen McBrady/Photo Edit 188, 194r; National Museum of American Art/Art Resource 197; National Portrait Gallery/Art Resource 180; Richard Nowitz 16, 23, 25, 26, 38, 101, 123, 133, 139, 175, 193, 198, 258, 259; Alan Oddie/Photo Edit 275; Photo Edit 36, 138; Zev Radovan 52, 70, 72, 82, 95, 98, 100, 114b, 130, 216, 241, 260; Scala/Art Resource 22, 27, 30, 39, 43, 47, 54, 57, 61, 83, 96, 103, 104, 106, 112, 121, 135, 143, 144, 151, 157, 172, 179, 181, 194L, 196, 199, 205, 215, 218, 219, 221, 232, 238, 243, 244, 250, 251, 262; Rhoda Sidney/Photo Edit 148, 170; Taposchaner/FPG International 228; Tate Gallery/Art Resource 176, 183; Vanni/Art Resource 114t, 146, 237, 271; Wayne State University/Archives of Labor and Urban Affairs 276; Wide World Photos 60, 74, 76, 81; David Young-Wolff/Photo Edit 92, 140, 160, 161, 186, 270

High School Consultant
John Allen, MA
Notre Dame High School, Sherman Oaks, CA

Censor Librorum
The Reverend Michel J. St. Pierre

Imprimatur
The Most Reverend Kenneth A. Angell, D.D.
Bishop of Burlington
Given at Burlington, Vermont on the 24th of January, 1994.

The nihil obstat and imprimatur are official declarations that a book or pamphlet is free of doctrinal or moral error. No implication is contained therein that those who have granted the nihil obstat and imprimatur agree with the contents, opinions, or statements expressed.

Send all inquiries to:
BENZIGER PUBLISHING COMPANY
15319 Chatsworth Street
P.O. Box 9609
Mission Hills, California 91346-9609

ISBN 0-02-662334-X (Student's Edition)
ISBN 0-02-662335-8 (Teacher's Wraparound Edition)

Printed in the United States of America

2 3 4 5 RRW 99 98 97 96 95 94

Table of Contents

What Is the Bible?

Chapter Overview

This chapter introduces students to the Bible. They will learn how to find passages in the Bible and see the Bible as God's word revealed to us.

Teaching Objectives

By the end of this chapter students will be able to:
• Explain the difference between the Old and New Testaments.
• Find Bible passages using reference numbers.
• Define "salvation history" and "religious truth."
• Demonstrate how the Bible is both revealed and inspired.

Welcome

What to Do

Greet the students as they arrive. Give each student 20 seconds to tell you something about his or her background. Use this time to take roll and to learn the names students prefer to be called.

Introducing the Chapter

What to Do

• Begin the class with prayer. Since this is probably your first session with these students, be prepared to lead them in prayer. As the year progresses, turn responsibility for class prayer over to the students.
• Give each student a pencil and a piece of paper. Start promptly. Have the students ask others, "What do you know about the Bible?" See who can get the longest list in 5 minutes. Then have volunteers read their lists, with all the other students crossing off duplications. Do this until a single list is obtained. Compliment the students on how much they already know about the Bible.
• Ask if they have any questions they would like answered about the Bible; list these on the board.

CHAPTER 1

What Is the Bible?

1000	**1000 B.C.E.** ● Rule of King David ● Beginnings of Pentateuch
	726 ● Fall of Northern Kingdom
	600 ● Rise of Babylonian empire
	587 ● Fall of Southern Kingdom ● Deuteronomic history, Pentateuch
500	**500** ● Confucius discusses "right living"
	300 ● Writings
30	**33 C.E.** ● Death of Jesus
	51 ● First letter of Paul
	150 ● Close of New Testament
1000	**1000** ● Middle East ruled by Byzantium
	1500 ● Middle East ruled by Ottoman Turks ● Protestant Reformation
	1850 ● Industrial Revolution
1900	
	1948 ● Modern State of Israel
	1965 ● Second Vatican Council calls for return to Scripture

Legend

● General History
● Biblical History
● Jewish History
● Books written

S hannon walked into the first religion class of the year a little worried; she knew nothing about the Bible. Would she end up behind everyone else and feel left out? Nervously, she pulled her Bible out of her book bag, waiting to see what would happen.

Mr. Martinez introduced himself to the class, took roll, and then said, "Let's get started right away." He handed Shannon's friend, John, an open Bible and asked him to read aloud from the Gospel of Matthew. After helping John find the right page, Mr. Martinez waited.

"Take this and eat it, this is my body," John read.

Mr. Martinez interrupted, "Anybody recognize those words?"

Hands shot up immediately, including Shannon's. "The priest says those words at Mass," she said.

MORE ABOUT THE TEXT

What Is the Bible

The stories in the Bible have many facets, but they are always about the relationship between God and people, and their way of life as viewed through that relationship. The Covenant was offered first to a people called the Israelites who, eventually, came to be called Jews. Their understanding of God's free gift of choice and relationship included the recognition that God's treatment of people was based on compassion.

Yet the people were always free to reject or ignore the Covenant, and they often did. Thus, the drama of biblical history arises: God seeks a people to teach how to live in God's love, but the people are not responsive to God's offer. This theme carries into the New Testament, where Jesus continues to offer ultimate love and guidance, yet is rejected by many. To those who accept, a new quality of life is given.

"Very good," Mr. Martinez replied, smiling. "Let's try something a little more difficult." He handed the Bible to Sophia and asked her to read the marked passage. Sophia read about two people named Moses and Aaron who went to talk to somebody called the pharaoh. "Anybody know what a pharaoh is?" Mr. Martinez asked.

Suddenly Shannon remembered studying Egypt in middle school. "The king of Egypt," she said.

"Excellent!" responded Mr. Martinez. "I wanted to make a point with these questions. I wanted to show you that you all know more about the Bible than you think. Shannon, here, is already on her way to being a Bible expert!"

Shannon smiled and felt her nervousness going away. "Maybe the semester won't be so bad after all," she thought.

Whether you're aware of it or not, you probably already have some knowledge of the Bible that you learned from church and from school. In this book, you will build upon what you already know, and also learn to understand the Bible in a variety of new ways. In the process, you will also discover that the Bible is a book that can entertain you, educate you, inspire you, and most importantly, involve you in a conversation with God, who speaks through its pages.

Whether or not you establish a conversation with God during this course of study is up to you. As with any relationship, developing a closeness and dialogue with God requires a great deal of effort and attention. The more time you spend speaking with God, the better able you will be to communicate with God. The more time you spend reading the Bible in order to understand God's word, the better able you will be to understand it.

Development

What to Do

• Distribute Bibles and textbooks (if necessary).

• Have students turn to page 4 and read the opening story to themselves. How does this story supplement the student's lists that are on the board? Give them an opportunity now to expand their list.

• Here are some of the answers students might include: the Lord's Prayer (*Matthew* 6:9–13); the "Holy, Holy, Holy" from the Mass (*Isaiah* 6:3 and *Matthew* 21:9); the Sign of Peace (1 *Corinthians* 16:20 and 1 *Thessalonians* 5:26). They might know the names of biblical characters: David, Bathsheba, Samson, Zacchaeus, the Good Samaritan, Paul, Adam and Eve, and so on. Have them look up doubtful names in a Bible dictionary.

Using the Timeline

Introduce students to the timeline on page 4. Tell them that each chapter begins with a timeline. Ask: "Why do you think a book about the Bible includes a timeline?" (Answer: Because the Bible must be understood in its historical context to be understood at all.) The Bible is, in a sense, a history of a people of faith. This group of people lived its life in history and were influenced by the events that happened around them. These historical events shaped the content of the Bible.

Review the timeline with the students so that they understand the importance of each event and what influence they might have had on the Bible.

MORE ABOUT THE TEXT

The Timeline

• 1000 B.C.E. The first books of the Bible were written. Prior to this date, the Scriptures of the Israelites (Hebrews) were transmitted orally.

• 726 The nation of Israel is destroyed.

• 600 and 587 The destruction of Judah.

• 500 Much of the Old Testament is older than Confucius's writings.

• 300 The final books of the Old Testament were written around this time.

• 33–150 C.E. The New Testament was written after Jesus' death.

• 1000 Visits to the Holy Land became nearly impossible. Biblical archaeology ceased for many years.

• 1500 Protestant Reformation led to a renewed interest in biblical scholarship and personal study.

• 1850–Present Modern influences on Scripture study.

LESSON ONE (pages 6–9)

◆ Introducing the Bible

Teaching Objectives

By the end of this lesson students will be able to:
• Explain the differences between the Old and New Testaments.
• Find passages in the Bible on their own.
• Define what is meant by "canon" and the "oral tradition."

Development

Outcome

• Students will consider reasons for studying the Bible.
• Students will understand how the Bible is organized.
• Students will study the map of ancient Israel and will be able to find places on it.
• Students will learn how to find passages in the Bible.

What to Do

Read "Introducing the Bible" and "Why Study the Bible." Discuss with students the six reasons presented for studying the Bible. Have students offer their own reasons for engaging in this study.

Look at "Learn from the Map." Have the students locate the main features of Israel. Be sure they include the Dead Sea, the Jordan River, the Sea of Galilee, the Mediterranean coast, the various mountain ranges, and Jerusalem. The length of Israel as shown on this map is approximately 170 miles.

Read "How the Bible is Organized," both Old and New Testament sections. Have the students open their Bibles to the Table of Contents and identify its parts. Have them locate in the list the uniquely Catholic books of the Old Testament. Open the Bible to the first page of the Old Testament and the first page of the New Testament. Students may wish to mark these two places for easy reference.

Read "How the Bible Was Written." Form groups of five. Give one person a short passage to read. (Easy passages for this include Acts 9:1–9; Genesis 37:1–11; Genesis 11:1–9; Daniel 14:1–22.) That student secretly tells the passage to a second student who tells it to a third,

---

Getting Started

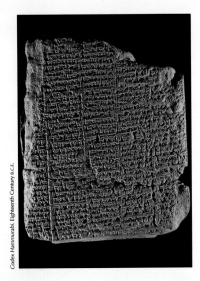

Codex Hammurabi, Eighteenth Century B.C.E.

Within each chapter of this book there are two sections. The first section provides the background you need to understand a part of the Bible. It always illustrates how God's Word has been shaped by the circumstances in which it was written.

For both sections in each chapter, you'll be given a set of "learning objectives." These identify what you should know by the end of the section. In this first section of the book you will consider how the Bible is organized, how it came to be written, and why there is diversity in the Bible.

Learning Objectives for Section One

By the end of this section, you will be able to:

• Explain the difference between the two testaments.
• Look up Bible references by chapter and verse.
• Define "canon" and "oral tradition."
• Explain why there is diversity in the Bible.

◆ Introducing the Bible

As you would with any book, you need to know your way around the Bible to make the best use of it. First, however, you need to decide that learning about the Bible is worth doing. As you'll see, there are a variety of reasons why learning more about the Bible is a valuable thing for you to do.

Why Study the Bible?

There are several reasons why knowledge of the Bible should be important to you.

1. The Bible is a unique place to meet God. Through prayer and reflection, you can grow in your appreciation of what God has to say to you.
2. The Bible is the "book of the Church." It tells the story of the people of God, and therefore connects us to our ancestors in faith.
3. The Bible can help you solve the problems you meet in ordinary life, especially ethical and moral dilemmas. The Bible presents ways that other people in God's family were confronted with problems, the choices they made, and the results of those choices.
4. Because the Bible is so often used in social debate today, a familiarity with Scripture will help protect you from being manipulated by politicians and people using the Bible to accomplish their own ends.
5. Because the Bible is cherished by many different religions, knowing the Bible helps us build relationships with people of other faiths.
6. Bible study builds solid academic skills. It requires you to learn to read literature carefully, and to place it in historical context.

MORE ABOUT THE TEXT

Going Deeper

(1) Being able to meet God through the Bible requires a familiarity with it. (2) The "book of the Church" was produced, protected and preserved by people of faith. It grew out of the community life of the Israelites and the early experiences of Jesus' followers. (3) Sometimes the Bible gives direct instruction on these issues. Sometimes we must draw our own conclusions. (4) We are not always able to prove a case against those who misuse the Bible. (5) In the past, disagreements about biblical interpretation have troubled inter-faith relationships as much as helped them. It is important to acknowledge that our interpretations are not always the same. We can then seek out common appreciation and understanding on which to build relationships. (6) Placing biblical references in historical context requires learning history well enough that the correct placement comes easily.

LEARN FROM THE MAP

Ancient Israel

Once in each chapter, you'll have a chance to explore the geography of the Bible. Here, you see ancient Israel, the land that was promised by God as part of the Covenant. Take a minute now to become familiar with the lay of the land. Notice how small the area is—so much history in so little space! Using the scale given, can you figure out how long Israel is?

© 1994 Magellan Geographix℠ Santa Barbara, CA.

Area: *Approximately 8,000 square miles*
Elevation–Highest Point: *3,962 feet*
Lowest Point: *1,292 feet below sea level*
Physical Features: 1) *Coastal Plain—117 miles along Mediterranean Coast;* **2)** *Western Mountains—extending from Galilee to Jerusalem;* **3)** *Negev—the triangularly shaped southern half of the country;* **4)** *Rift Valley—the land along the Jordan River*

How the Bible Is Organized

There are two main divisions in the Bible: The Old Testament and the New Testament. The word "testament" means "covenant." The theme of the Covenant between God and humanity is central to both sections of the Bible. The Bible is, in fact, the story of God's Covenant with humanity. In the Covenant, God offers to bless and protect us in exchange for obedience to the path God marks out for us.

The Old Testament　The first two-thirds of the Bible is the story of ancient Israel. It begins with the creation of the universe and follows the story through the rise and fall of the Israelite kingdom. The Old Testament is divided into four sections:

- **Pentateuch.** This section includes the first five books of the Bible, called "Torah" by the Jews. These books include the stories of the creation of the world and of the nation of Israel, as well as the law given by God to the Israelites.
- **Historical Books.** These books tell the story of the nation of Israel from the Hebrew's entry into the promised land until the Exile.
- **Writings.** This section includes religious poetry and essays about God's relationship with humanity.
- **Prophets.** These are the words of the people God inspired to present messages to Israel.

You'll learn from the Old Testament that God chose Israel to be a special nation. God made a Covenant with Israel: if Israel would accept God's law, God would bless and protect it. The Old Testament tells the story of Israel's struggle to be faithful to the Covenant, and to understand the God who had chosen it.

Most of the books of the Old Testament are also sacred to Jews, who call their collection the "Tanakh." A few books from the ancient Greek version of the Old Testament are accepted by Catholics, but not by Jews or some other Christians, who accept only the books from the ancient Hebrew version. The list of accepted books in the Bible is called the "canon."

The New Testament　Christians believe that through Jesus, God made a new Covenant with humanity. Based on the earlier Covenant with Israel, this new arrangement invites all humanity to become part of God's Chosen People through faith in Jesus.

and so on around the group. When everyone has had a chance to tell the passage, read the original aloud to the whole group. Ask them what they now think about oral tradition.

After the exercise, the students may at first think oral tradition is unreliable. But you can guide them to see that this is not necessarily so. The Israelites (and other oral cultures) have talents that we modern folks have forgotten, especially the ability to listen well and repeat accurately. Help the students to see that the Israelites were not so primitive mentally. You may want to tell the story in Teacher's Resource 1B.

Practicing the Skills

Read "Diversity in the Bible." Form three small groups and divide the following passages equally among them: *Story* (Luke 16:1–8); *Poem* (Job 38:2–7); *History* (2 Kings 24:1–7); *Legend* (Genesis 25:24–34); *Myth* (Genesis 2:4b–9); *Song* (Judith 16:1–6); *Wise sayings* (Proverbs 10:20–24); *Prophecy* (Isaiah 5:11–16); *Laws* (Leviticus 11:1–8); *Letters* (Philippians 1:1–8).

Each group can choose one person to read the passages to everyone, so that the students can hear the difference between types of literature. Discuss the different feel, sound, rhythms, and any other characteristic differences noted by the students. Then, have the whole class look at Amos 5:4–9, each one reading aloud, but softly to himself. Can they find the break between two types of literature? If so, compliment them: "You have just begun to do real biblical scholarship!"

Extending the Activity　Have each group take turns reading their passages aloud to the class. Have everyone else try to guess what type of writing the passage is.

MORE ABOUT THE TEXT

Scriptural Books

Note that "Writings" is the Hebrew name for those books sometimes called in modern editions of the Bible "The Wisdom Books." The students can read the names of the books aloud, section by section, beginning to become familiar with them.

The "uniquely Catholic" books of the Old Testament are sometimes called the "apocrypha" (from the Greek for "hidden"), and are often included in a separate section in Protestant editions of the Bible. These books are Tobit, Judith, 1 and 2 Maccabees, Wisdom, Sirach (also called Ecclesiasticus), Baruch, and parts of Esther and Daniel (those parts designated by letters instead of chapter numbers).

For the story of how different groups came to have different Bibles, see Teacher's Resource 1A. Teacher's Resource 1A explains how different groups came to have different Bibles.

Recall

Turn to the Review questions on page 14. Present the Section One questions to students as a way to review the text material: students should recall the answers if they can, and look them up again if they do not remember.

Connect

What to Do

Homework Assignment: (a) Write out your own answers to Section One Review questions. (b) Answer this question: If you were going to explain to a friend what you have learned so far in this chapter, what would you give as the most important things to know?

What's Next

Tell the students that during the next session they will explore how the Bible is the revealed, inspired "Word of God."

---

in the Spotlight

Discuss with students the importance of recognizing that the Bible was written in different languages. They should recognize that any English version of the Bible is a translation (which explains why there are so many different versions of the Bible), and that scholars can roughly tell when a book was written by its original language.

The New Testament consists of:

- **Gospel accounts.** Four collections of stories and sayings of Jesus.
- **Acts of the Apostles.** The story of the early Christian Church after the Ascension of Jesus.
- **Letters.** Letters written by early Christians that show us the problems and concerns of the early Church.
- **Revelation.** A book which offers comfort to oppressed Christians, promising future salvation.

How the Bible Was Written

The stories now found in the Bible were told for many centuries before they were written down. They were memorized by professional storytellers and passed along by word of mouth. This is called the "oral tradition."

Eventually, people preserved these traditions in writing. The earliest writings probably date from 1000 B.C.E. For the most part, we don't know who the authors were, because ancient people weren't interested in the identity of the author. For them, the content mattered, not who wrote it. As a result, different works by different authors often got combined into new works, a process called "editing."

The Old Testament was reedited and put into its final form after the destruction of the nation of Israel by the Babylonians in 587 B.C.E. The priests who put it together wanted to make sure that the sacred traditions of the nation didn't perish.

The New Testament was written during a much shorter period of time, approximately a hundred years: 40–110 C.E. It, too, began with oral stories about Jesus, and then was put on paper to preserve these traditions for later generations. For a while, the Church argued over which books should be in the New Testament, reaching a general consensus around 300 C.E. The Bible was finalized only at the Council of Trent in 1543.

Diversity in the Bible

As we've seen, the Bible is not one big book, but a collection of smaller books. The Bible is, in fact, a small library: 73 separate titles, with 46 in the Old Testament and 27 in the New Testament. The word "bible" comes from a Greek term which means "the books."

As you would expect to find in any library, there are many different kinds of writing in the Bible.

---

in the Spotlight
Biblical Languages

"In the Spotlight" is another feature that will appear in each chapter. This "In the Spotlight" deals with the languages of the Bible.

The ancient Israelites spoke *Hebrew,* and most of the Old Testament is written in this language. Around 500 B.C.E., however, they started to speak *Aramaic,* another Middle Eastern language, and some portions of the Bible were written in it. Finally, after 300 B.C.E., Greece dominated the Middle East, and a few Old Testament books were written in that language.

The New Testament was written entirely in Greek. The early Christians lived in the eastern Roman empire, where Greek was the international language. Although Jesus knew Greek, his primary language was Aramaic, since he was a part of Jewish culture. There are also some hints that he may have known Latin.

Think of the Bible as a library with many different types of books to explore.

MORE ABOUT THE TEXT

The New Testament

In the New Testament section, the Letters may be divided into two sections: the New Testament Letters and the Catholic Letters. When this division is made, the Book of Revelation is usually included in the Catholic Letters, even though it is written as an apocalypse (a form of visionary writing with an encoded message) in literary form. Other than how the books are categorized, there are no differences between the Catholic and other editions of the New Testament.

Scripture Workshop

Chapter and Verse

Twice in every chapter, you'll find a "Scripture Workshop." These exercises are intended to give you hands-on experience in working with the Bible.

In order to use the Bible, it is important to be able to look up references in the way they are usually given. For example, Chapter 10, verses three to five of the First Book of Kings would be written like this:

1 Kings 10:3–5

When searching for a biblical reference, first locate the book, then turn to the chapter. Most Bibles put the chapter numbers as headings on each page. Make sure you are at the beginning of the chapter. Then, search for the first verse listed in the reference. Read the *passage* through the last verse listed.

Finding Bible passages can be fun. How fast can you look up these references? Write the first word of each passage. Then read the completed sentence.

Tobit 8:6	Genesis 31:15
Hebrews 4:12	Proverbs 29:17

Stories and histories, legends and myths, poetry, songs, wise sayings, prophecies, laws, letters—all of these types of writing are included in Scripture. Although at times the Bible may seem like a slow-moving sermon or history book, it's really a record of the ways people in ancient Israel experienced God. The Bible is actually alive with the excitement and astonishment they felt.

Because the Bible is a "library" consisting of different books, written by different people at different times and in different styles, it is hardly surprising that these books exhibit different points of view on

---

The Bible in Context

Dating History

"The Bible in Context" will examine specific biblical issues in detail. This one describes how dates are identified in this textbook.

Traditionally, dates were given using B.C., meaning "before Christ," and A.D., meaning "anno Domini" (Latin for "in the year of the Lord"). These abbreviations have been in use since the Middle Ages.

Although these abbreviations work as well as anything else for dividing time, they are specifically Christian designations. Jews, Muslims, and members of other religions based on the Bible may feel uncomfortable referring to the "year of the Lord," when they do not share the belief that Jesus is the Lord of humanity.

For that reason, biblical scholars have substituted the terms B.C.E., meaning "before the common era," and C.E., meaning "in the common era," as a neutral means of dating historical events.

many subjects. These are not "contradictions," but simply different human beings responding to their experience of God in different ways. Consider this example: A newscaster reports, "An earthquake struck Northern India killing over 20,000." A person who survived the quake said, "Buildings fell around our heads. Why did God save my family instead of my neighbors'?" The same truth, different expressions.

The Bible records the efforts of many holy people, who, over thousands of years, attempted to express the truth about God. Those efforts have to be read in the light of much study and prayer before we can come to our own conclusions about their meaning.

Have You Considered?

These questions appear regularly throughout the chapter to help you think about the issues raised in that part of the book.

1. Which reason for studying the Bible seems most important to you? Why?
2. Why do you suppose Jews don't like to use the term "Old Testament" to refer to their Scriptures? What does this phrase suggest which they might find objectionable?
3. If there are many different people who contributed to the Bible at different times, why does it follow that we should expect to find different points of view?

◆ Biblical Truths

Welcome

What to Do

Form groups of three. One student will ask the other two, "Explain to me whether or not the Bible is true." The asking students will report their answers to the whole class. If this leads to a desire for more discussion, good! Tell them that is the point of today's lesson.

Introducing the Lesson

Teaching Objectives

By the end of this lesson students will be able to:

• Explain the meaning of the terms "salvation history" and "religious truth" as applied to the Bible.

• Discuss what is meant by the terms "inspired Word of God" and "revealed truth" as applied to the Bible.

• Demonstrate how the Bible is the Church's book.

What to Do

• Pray with the class. You should be prepared to lead the class in prayer. You may wish to use Romans 13:12–14 (see "People of Note" on page 12). Ask the students how they can "put on Christ."

• Recall the last lesson by asking volunteers to read their answers to the Review Questions. If other students have points to add, they may do so, but this is simply recall-time, not discussion. Spend only a few minutes on it.

• Connect the ideas of diversity in the Bible and oral tradition (from Section One) with today's interest: how is the Bible true? Suggest that a seventh good reason to study the Bible is simply that it contains truth.

Development

• Read aloud the overview and learning objectives for Section Two. Ask for any questions. Then, have the students read silently "Biblical Truths," "A Book of Religious Experience," "Salvation History," and "Religious Truth."

• Discuss how people share experiences with each other. How do the students tell their best friend about what happened on a date? Do they

---

Understanding the Bible

Playfair Book of Hours, *St. Jerome in his Study*, Fifteenth Century.

The second section in each chapter of this book focuses on a specific part of the Bible, and studies how that part helps you learn about God and yourself. In order to do this, it applies what you learned in the first section.

In the first section you learned about what the Bible is, how it came to be written, and how knowing how to read the Bible can be an asset for you. In this section you will come to understand the Bible as the story of human salvation. The Bible is God's Word, inspired through human authors and revealed over many centuries.

Learning Objectives for Section Two

By the end of this section, you should be able to:

• Define "salvation history" and "religious truth."

• Explain what is meant by the phrase "Word of God."

• Explain the idea that the Bible is "revealed" and "inspired."

• Discuss why the Bible is the Church's book.

◆ Biblical Truths

Both through study and prayer, our goal is to understand the truth of the Bible. The word "truth," however, can be used in many different ways. What are the different kinds of truth found in these statements:

• "My mother loves me."
• "$2+2=4$"

The first statement is just as true as the mathematical equation but you can prove that "4" is the answer to the math problem using logic. Could you prove your mother's love in this way? The point is, two statements can both be true, but in different ways. In this section, you will learn what the statement "the Bible is true" means.

The Bible Is a Book of Religious Experience

The Bible does not pretend to be based on totally objective history. The biblical writers and

editors wanted to use history to teach about God. When they wrote about the past, therefore, they had several preconceived notions about what had happened. They believed that the most important goal was understanding God, not objectivity about the past.

In our day, we think of historical truth in scientific terms: "What are the facts about how something happened in the past?" But ancient history-writers conceived of truth differently. They thought of history in moral terms, and a historian's job was to assign credit and blame for the events of the past. The specific details of what happened were not very important.

They wrote with what we would call a "bias," that is, an idea of why things happened based on a careful judgment. A history lacking such a bias would, by their standards, be considered incomplete.

Salvation History

The nature of ancient history-writing means that the biblical authors were interested not so much in

---

◆ MORE ABOUT THE LESSON

Preparing the Role-Play

Before beginning the skit, the teacher is to explain to the mother (whispered so that no one else can hear) that she (the mother) has already planned a surprise party for the daughter, but has not told the father. The mother doesn't want to reveal this surprise in the middle of the conflict.

The students are likely to report different views and different experiences of the skit. The

two observers may not agree either. Then, tell everyone the whispered instructions that were given to the mother. Ask if that knowledge changes anyone's experience of the skit. Discuss how our understanding of context can affect the way we experience things. A viewpoint without full understanding sees differently than one with full understanding.

Learning about the Bible requires effort on your part, just as you must study to master mathematics.

Scripture Workshop

Be open to questions and discussion, because the relationship of factuality to experience, especially in the telling of it, is problematic for our culture as a whole. As they work with more of the Scripture, they will understand better and become more comfortable with the nature of biblical truth.

The answers to the questions are:

1. Herod the Great
2. Quirinus

Have the students read and discuss "Understanding More About:" on page 15.

history itself, but how the events of the past could be seen in relation to their faith. For them, all of history was religious history.

Religious history is often referred to as *salvation history*. The history of salvation recounts God's unending love for the Chosen People. The Bible constantly reminds us of how God is with us. The history of salvation is fulfilled in the life, death, and resurrection of Jesus Christ.

Religious Truth

From a strictly factual standpoint, one part of the Bible may not agree with another part. There are instances of geographical error and numbers are often used as symbols. For example:

- In Mark's Gospel account, the author explains how Jesus traveled south from Galilee to Jerusalem through Tyre and Sidon. These two cities, however, are actually north of Galilee, and therefore Mark's geography is confused.
- Numbers were certainly used differently than they are today. In the Bible, numbers are often exaggerated or used as symbols, rather than used literally. The Book of Exodus says that 600,000 men left Egypt when Moses led the Jewish slaves to freedom. But if there really had been that many Israelites in Egypt, they could have conquered Egypt rather than flee from it. Since women and children accompanied

---

Scripture Workshop

Historical Dates

The Bible's focus on religious history often means that minor historical details are left out or confused. The following exercise will illustrate this point.

Open your Bible to Chapter 2 of Matthew. Keep that place, and also turn to Chapter 2 of Luke. Both Gospel accounts tell the story of the birth of Jesus. Now, answer the questions below:

1. According to Matthew, who was king when Jesus was born?
2. According to Luke, who was the governor when Jesus was born?

We know from historical records that Herod the Great died in 4 B.C.E., while Quirinius was not sent to Syria until 6 C.E. Knowing this, is it possible that both Matthew and Luke could be right?

When we get to the New Testament, you'll see that both Matthew and Luke have reasons for dating the birth of Jesus as they do, but these reasons have to do with religious truth, not historical fact.

---

describe only events, or do they also mention feelings and what it meant for them personally?

- Read "The Bible and the 'Word of God'," "The Bible Is Inspired," and "The Bible Is Revealed." Consult a Bible dictionary or *The New Jerome Biblical Commentary* for more information on inspiration and revelation.

Extending the Lesson   Role play this situation: A mother and father are in the living room. The teenage daughter enters, goes directly to the mother and begs to take the car on her birthday. Mother says no, but can't give any real reason. Father jumps in to support Daughter's request. Mother gets totally upset and stubborn. Daughter yells. Father puts his arms around her and takes her out of the room, Daughter resisting all the way. Mother then storms off.

Have two other students watch as "objective observers." You can substitute a son for the daughter, if you wish.

When the skit is over, ask each student participant to describe his or her experience of what happened and what was it like for them? Then ask the objective observers to tell what they saw. For more about role-playing, see Teacher's Resource 1C.

MORE ABOUT THE TEXT

Significant Beliefs

No historical writing will ever be totally objective. In all cultures, what comes down to us as history is actually a fabric of facts, memories, reflections on the past, and beliefs about the significance of events. As soon as people ask, "Why did that happen?" or "Exactly what did happen?" or "What did that event really mean?" we enter the subjective realm of interpretation.

At some times in American history, for example, southerners experienced almost everything differently from northerners, blacks from whites, and Catholics from Protestants. Each of these groups had a bias about what was significant and what was not, and this bias affected the way they experienced every event. The Bible is no different. Its biases are on the side of truth about living and truth about God. These biases shape its message to us.

Practicing the Skills

Complete the Bible Activity on page 14 as a class. Help the students apply what they have learned to these instances in the Bible. Their "answers" need not be correct, but encourage them to think logically about them.

| People of Note | Have the students form small groups. |

Explore these questions: "What is your reaction to this incident?" "What do you think happened to Augustine?" "Why do you think these words had such a big effect on him?" "How might something in the Bible affect you as if it were a direct message to you from God?" "If you did experience God speaking directly to you, how do you think you might react?"

Recall

Review the Glossary on page 15 with the class. Ask them to write out their own individual answers to the Review Questions for Section Two.

Connect

What to Do

Discuss how to pray with the Bible as presented in "Spiritual Reflection." Introduce the students to the idea of keeping a journal.

Homework Assignment: Have students complete the Spiritual Reflection experience and write about it in their journal. Assure them that this will not be shared with anyone except on a voluntary basis. You will ask whether or not they did the Reflection, and give them an opportunity to share what they wrote.

What's Next

Introduce students to the general theme for the next lesson.

What to Do

Say, "Now that you have the basic skills necessary to work with the Bible, we will begin a study of the Old Testament. Before the next class, ask several adults what questions they have about the Old Testament. Bring their questions (and yours) for your consideration."

12

| People of Note | ### Saint Augustine |

"People of Note" will appear in the second section of each chapter. It will focus on some person (or group of people) important for understanding the Bible.

Though a brilliant man, Augustine had lived a carefree life. He enjoyed a good party, and he lived with his mistress for 16 years. Prior to becoming a bishop and great thinker in the Church, Augustine converted to Christianity with the help of the Bible.

In July of 386, Augustine heard a voice cry out, *"Tolle, lege,"* which means, "take and read." Augustine randomly opened the Bible to the Book of Romans. He read:

Let us throw off the works of darkness and put on the armor of light; let us conduct ourselves properly as in the day, not in orgies and drunkenness, nor in promiscuity and licentiousness, not in rivalry and jealousy. But put on the Lord Jesus Christ, and make no provision for the desires of the flesh.

Romans 13:12–14

Augustine was to turn to the Bible as his source of inspiration for the rest of his life. Reflecting on Psalm 36 Augustine wrote, "There is obviously some kind of blissful vision reserved for us; . . . It is for this that our hearts are being trained in all the hardships and trials of this life. . . . you are being schooled for a wonderous destiny." For Augustine, the Bible was the text for this school.

---

the men on their journey, a conservative figure would put the total number at 1,500,000. Such a multitude would have difficulty being fed by all the fields and pastures in the promised land, let alone the desert they crossed!

The reason for these "inaccuracies" is that biblical authors were mainly concerned with presenting religious truth about God and God's relationship with them.

Biblical authors also knew that what they understood could be expressed in ways other than factual reporting, such as poetry and tall tales. For example, the account of Jonah being swallowed by a big fish (*Jonah* 2:1–2) seems unlikely to be fact, though many ancient people believed in the mysteries of the deep. But it does communicate in a very dramatic way the truth of God's persistence and saving power.

Religious truth—the truth of God's love and care for humanity—is preserved in the Bible, whether buried beneath factual inaccuracies or not.

The Bible and the "Word of God"

The Bible is often called the "Word of God." This phrase refers, first of all, to the experience of people in the Old Testament, to whom God spoke quite directly. God placed the Word, or message, into the hearts and minds of those who heard it and felt it. They, in turn, passed it along to others in their preaching and writing. By passing on God's Word,

"the works performed by God in the history of salvation . . . clarify the mystery" (*Dei Verbum*, #2).

The Bible Is Revealed

Revelation means "the uncovering of something that was previously not known." From a personal standpoint, such a revelation may simply come from a thought that pops into your head or the reception of some words of advice from another.

Revelation can come directly from God. Married people often reflect back on how it was "revealed" to them that a person they were dating was the "right one" for them. God is certainly revealed to us in such personal ways. God speaks to us in personal revelation—sometimes even directly—through our relationships, our daily experiences, natural and historic events, and in prayer.

The Bible is a book of such revelations. Although we can never be completely sure if a personal revelation comes to us from God, we are sure that the Bible is a direct communication of truth from God. Our certainty comes from the tradition of the Church, as well as the evidence of the millions of lives over time which have been touched and healed by prayerful reading of Scripture.

The divine revelation, as presented in the Bible, continues to have power today. The message of the Bible is not limited to a certain time or to a select few.

MORE ABOUT THE TEXT

An Adult Book

When you consider the meaning of inspiration and revelation, you recognize that the Bible is clearly an adult book. Exactly how inspiration and revelation work is still disputed by scholars. The students need to learn the difference between these two words and when to use them. In addition, it is important for the students to understand that the Bible

expresses what God wants us to have. Finally, it is essential that the students recognize that the authors neither merely wrote whatever they wanted nor did God give them every word to say. Somehow, God was involved with the authors as they wrote, providing guidance and encouragement. The Bible is considered a sacred collection of writings because we recognize God's involvement in it.

The Bible Is Inspired

When we say the Bible is inspired we mean that it was written by human authors under the **guidance and protection** of the Holy Spirit. Catholics believe that the Holy Spirit teaches "that truth which God, for the sake of our salvation, wished to see confided to the sacred Scriptures" (*Vatican II, Dei Verbum,* III.11).

Because the Scriptures were written by humans, they contain all the biases, mistakes, and points of view common to people of a particular time in history. But, because they are also divinely inspired, the writings of the Bible are free from error involving anything that God wanted to express.

Exactly how inspiration works is not fully known. But through our own experiences, we can gain some idea of how God's Word is communicated through the written words of Scripture.

Have you ever been called to the front of the classroom to give an oral presentation? Even though you may have spent hours and hours preparing, you were still nervous and not sure of what you would say and how you would say it. As you relaxed and your presentation went on, you were amazed at how easily the words came out. You might ask, "Is *this really me* speaking?" That's an example of how inspiration operates.

Jesus explained inspiration in more detail just prior to his arrest. Speaking to his disciples, he said:

> *When they lead you away and hand you over, do not worry beforehand about what you are to say. But say whatever will be given to you at that hour. For it will not be you who are speaking but the Holy Spirit.*
>
> Mark 13:11

Have You Considered?

1. What would be a helpful definition of the term "Word of God"?
2. How is religious history different from other forms of history?
3. What different kinds of truth are there? For example, how is moral truth (how you know something is right or wrong) different from scientific truth?

Spiritual Reflection

Praying with the Bible

Praying with Scripture has been mentioned several times in this chapter. Here's a way to begin:

- Find a place where you can be alone for a while, without any time limit, uninterrupted and quiet.
- Settle yourself comfortably and become very still. Breath softly.
- After you are relaxed, open your Bible to Psalm 103. (Psalms can be found almost in the middle of your Bible; look it up in the table of contents.)
- Pray in your own words. Ask the Lord to be with you and to help you be aware of God's love.
- Think about the words as you read the psalm very slowly. Let yourself **feel** their meaning.

- When one line seems finished to you, go quietly to the next and repeat what you have just done.
- Pray for as long as you feel good about what you are doing. (You don't have to pray the whole psalm, or you could repeat it several times.)
- When you are finished, take two extra moments to thank God for this quiet time. Thank God for the qualities described in this psalm. Ask God to help you remember what you have prayed. Then, take a deep breath, get up, and go your way!

Have You Considered?

Form three small groups, one for each question. Encourage the groups to write down and share with each other their own ideas, exploring beyond what the text gives them. They can add what they think. Everyone in the small group must agree on the final written answer. Then each group reads their results to the class. Possible answers:

1. The message placed by God into the hearts and minds of the people would be a helpful definition for "Word of God."
2. Religious history differs from other types of history because it looks at how the events of the past can be seen in relation to religious faith.
3. Moral truth is different from scientific truth in that it does not deal with observable events.

MORE ABOUT THE TEXT

Saint Augustine

This experience did not come to Augustine suddenly. As a young man he had truly struggled to find truth. Augustine's father had been a pagan. His mother was a Christian, Saint Monica. She tried for years to convince the young man of the error of his way, but only after his conversion experience did her words make sense to him. He studied many philosophies. He did not like the behavioral and moral rules of Christianity, because he preferred to live as he pleased—rakishly. He had a mistress and a son, Adeodatus (meaning "gift of God"). Of the mistress, little is known except that Augustine discontinued the relationship, but did provide financially for her. His son was baptized at the same ceremony as Augustine and lived with his father for many years.

Q/A

Section One

1. "Tanakh" is an acronym for Law, Prophets, and Writings—the three components of the Jewish Bible.

2. The covenant is an agreement or promise between God and humanity.

3. The Old Testament is the story of the people of ancient Israel and God's relationship with them. The New Testament concerns Jesus and the birth of Christianity.

4. In the oral tradition, stories and sayings are preserved and passed down by word of mouth, often by storytellers.

5. A canon is an authoritative list of books which are considered scripture.

6. There is diversity in the Bible because it is the product of many different authors.

7. Reasons for studying the Bible include: Because it is a unique place to meet God; Because it is the book of the Church; Because it can help solve moral and ethical dilemmas; Because it is often used in social debates; Because the Bible is cherished by many different religions.

Q/A

Section One
1. What does "Tanakh" mean?
2. What is the meaning of the term "covenant"?
3. What is the difference between the Old and New Testaments?
4. Describe the process known as "the oral tradition."
5. Define the term "canon."
6. Why is there diversity in the Bible?
7. List four reasons to study the Bible.

Section Two
1. Define the term "salvation history."
2. Define the term "religious truth."
3. How is the Bible a book of revelation?
4. Explain how the Bible is divinely inspired.
5. Why are there inaccuracies in the Bible?
6. Who was Saint Augustine and what was his connection with the Bible?

BIBLE ACTIVITY

1. Open your Bible to Chapter 5 of the prophet Isaiah (find it in the table of contents if you need to). Look at the verse numbers in this chapter. What do you notice? Based on what you now know about how the Bible was put together, what problem do you think the publisher of this Bible was trying to correct?

2. Read Chapter 5 of Genesis. Notice the ages of the people in this chapter. Based on what you learned in this chapter, do you think these ages should be taken literally? If not, what do you think the author might have intended to symbolize by using such high numbers?

Loeb ben Elhanan, *Hebrew Prayerbook*. Eighteenth Century.

BIBLE ACTIVITY

1. Isaiah 5 is printed as it is to show that the verses as preserved are not all in numerical order. The order of these verses probably became confused as manuscripts were copied and recopied over the centuries. The publisher is trying to restore the original sequence although they are numbered strangely.

2. The ages of the people listed in Genesis 5 should not be taken literally. The great life span of these people was in contrast to the average (but much shorter) lifespans of people in the authors day (forty to sixty years of age). The author wanted to suggest that the farther people strayed from obedience to God, the more the human life-span shrank.

GLOSSARY

- **Canon:** The list of books accepted for the Bible.
- **Inspiration:** The idea that God assisted the authors in writing the Bible.
- **Old Testament:** The first two-thirds of the Bible which tells the story of ancient Israel's covenant relationship with God.
- **Oral Tradition:** The process of storytelling and word of mouth circulation that occurred before any of the biblical books were written down.
- **Pentateuch:** First five books of the Bible.
- **Religious Truth:** The truth of what the Bible tells us about God's love and desire for our well-being.
- **Revelation:** The idea that the Bible shows us something of God.
- **Salvation History:** The idea that God is involved with the events of history, directing them for our salvation.
- **Tanakh:** Word used by Jews to refer to their holy Scriptures.
- **Testament:** Another word for "covenant," which refers to a promise made by God to humanity.
- **Word of God:** A term for the Bible; it refers to the inspiration of the biblical authors by the Holy Spirit.

UNDERSTANDING MORE ABOUT:

Ancient Manuscripts

This is the final feature you'll find in each chapter. It's a chance to introduce some issue or aspect of Bible studies that will help in your understanding the Bible.

All the books of the Bible were written before printing presses, so copies were made by hand. A handmade copy of something is called a "manuscript."

Biblical scholars translate the Bible from ancient manuscripts. This process is complicated, however, by four facts about ancient Hebrew manuscripts: (1) they have no punctuation, (2) they are written entirely in capital letters, (3) no spaces are placed between letters, and (4) Hebrew was written without vowels until about 700 C.E.!

How can anyone read such a mess? Actually, it's not as hard as you may think. Try this one for starters:

YOUCANREADTHIS.

When written in your native language, you can generally recognize the different words and easily decide where punctuation should go. Now try this one without vowels:

THBBLSGDBK.

For people who study the Bible, it takes years to acquire the kind of familiarity with the original languages needed to make translations easily. Even then, there are cases where it's difficult to tell what is meant. Try this:

GODISNOWHERE.

Did you get "God is now here" or "God is nowhere?" In cases such as these, biblical scholars have to trust their skill and instincts, as well as the context in which the phrase appears.

By the way, the answer to the example above without vowels is "The Bible is a Good Book."

Section Two

1. The term "salvation history" means that God has shaped the events of history to bring people to salvation; it also is used to express the story of salvation as recorded in the Old Testament and New Testament.

2. The term "religious truth" means that in the Bible, we find all the truths necessary for our salvation.

3. The Bible is "revealed" because it is a direct communication of truth from God.

4. The Bible is divinely inspired because it was written by human authors under the guidance and protection of the Holy Spirit.

5. There are inaccuracies in the Bible because its authors were more interested in communicating truths about God and human life than in meeting modern historical standards.

6. Augustine was an important philosopher, writer, bishop, and theologian, who took the Bible as the basis for his life.

The Original Covenant

Unit Overview

This unit looks at the books of the Old Testament.

• In Chapter 2, students are introduced to Moses and God's Covenant with the Hebrew people.

• Chapter 3 presents the formation of the nation of Israel, looking particularly at how its leadership evolved. David is the key figure in this chapter.

• Chapter 4 explores the formational stories of the Israelites, looking at the myths of creation and the legends of the patriarchs.

• Chapter 5 considers the further development of the nation of Israel and how it divided into two nations, Judah and Israel, following the death of Solomon. The prophetic voice of Elijah establishes the focus for this chapter.

• Chapter 6 looks at the role of the prophets in the history of the Jews. The messages of Isaiah and Jeremiah are given special prominence.

• After the Exodus experience and God's Covenant with Moses, the Babylonian Exile had the greatest impact on the faith of the Jewish people. Chapter 7 examines the Exile and shows how this period changed the Jewish faith.

• Following the Exile, the Jewish people returned to Judah and rebuilt their lives. The history of this struggle is addressed in Chapter 8.

• Every Middle Eastern culture had its own Wisdom tradition, and the Jewish culture was no exception. Chapter 9 looks at the importance of the Wisdom literature to the Bible.

Introducing the Lesson

What to Do

• Bring a family album to class (or have students bring family albums to class). Look through the album(s) and have students identify the various types of material found there. Emphasize that this album tells the story of a particular person's or family's life. Have students discuss the importance of such records.

• Then, have the students read "The Original Covenant" two-page spread (up to "Why Read the Old Testament?") to themselves.

The Original Covenant

Chapter Listings

The first part of the Bible is called the "Old Testament." The word "testament" means "covenant." In this case, covenant refers to the special, unbreakable agreement between God and humanity. The Old Testament is the story of God's original Covenant made with Israel. Catholics consider this part of the Bible to be "Scripture," or "holy writings," just as much as the New Testament. In order to understand it, there are a few basic things about the Old Testament you should know.

A Family Story

The stories in the Old Testament are about the people we look to as our ancestors in faith. As such, the Old Testament resembles a family scrapbook. It contains historical records, just as a

---

MORE ABOUT THE TEXT

Divisions of the Old Testament

The "Pentateuch" section of the Bible includes the legendary patriarchs of Israel, the delivery from Egyptian slavery, the conquering of Palestine and the first couple hundred years of life there. The books of Leviticus, Numbers, and Deuteronomy contain the Jewish law.

While tradition attributes the Pentateuch to Moses, it was clearly written much later in the history of the Jewish people.

The "Writings" include large collections of proverbs and sayings which do not speak at all of God's relationship with people, but offer observations about human life and how to live it wisely and well. Here are liturgical songs for groups and individuals, as well as love poetry and an early novel (Job).

The "Prophets" section is usually divided into the "major" prophets (the longer books, Isaiah, Jeremiah, Ezekiel) and the "minor" prophets.

scrapbook might have birth certificates and wedding licenses. The Old Testament also has essays and stories, like a scrapbook might have letters and other writings. The Old Testament has no photographs, of course, but it does have vivid descriptions of people, so real you can almost see them. The Old Testament also has its share of legends and tall tales, like exaggerated stories about family members.

When you read a scrapbook, you expect to see something different on every page. You will also find many different kinds of writing in the Bible. You shouldn't expect everything to read the same way or share exactly the same ideas, just as you wouldn't expect that from a scrapbook.

Finally, just as you wouldn't hold a scrapbook to the same standards of historical and scientific accuracy as you would a textbook, you should expect to find factual mistakes and exaggerations here and there in the Old Testament. The authors, inspired by God, were trying to tell their family story, not write an error-free research paper.

Why the "Old Testament"?

Why is the first part of the Bible called the "Old" Testament? Christians use this word to signify that God has made a more recent covenant with humanity through Jesus, which is described in the "New" Testament. Jews, however, believe that the first covenant is still in effect. They don't think of it as "old," since to them there isn't a "new" one. For this reason, Jews don't use the term "Old Testament" for their Scripture. They call it the "Tanakh," a Hebrew word which stands for the three parts of the Jewish Bible: law, prophets, and writings.

The Old Testament has four basic divisions:

1. The Pentateuch (Greek for "five books") are the first five books in the Old Testament: *Genesis, Exodus, Leviticus, Numbers* and *Deuteronomy*. Judaism knows these five books as the "Torah." Sometimes Jewish people refer to their whole Bible as "Torah."

2. The Historical Books are *Joshua* and *Judges*, books which tell of Israel's entry into the promised land and her first years there; *Samuel, Kings*, and *Chronicles*, records of the rise and fall of the monarchy of Israel; *Ezra* and *Nehemiah*, stories of the return to Jerusalem after 538 B.C.E. and the rebuilding of the nation and the Temple; and *Maccabees*, the story of Jewish rebellion against Greek influences.

3. The Wisdom Books include the *Psalms, Job, Ecclesiastes, Proverbs, Wisdom, Sirach*, and *Song of Songs*. These books suggest how people should live, and why there is evil in the universe. They are reflections about life, justice, choice and behavior, and love. They are collections of advice, reflections and sayings about love, human as well as divine.

4. Prophets include the three major (or longer) prophetic books and the twelve minor (or shorter) books. The major books are *Isaiah, Jeremiah*, and *Ezekiel. Daniel* includes legends and predictions, visions and symbols. If the reader understands the historical situation in which each prophet lived, he or she can then understand the meaning of the prophecy offered in the books.

Why Read the Old Testament?

Since the Catholic Church teaches that we have a new Covenant with God through Jesus, you may be wondering why we bother with the Old Testament at all. Although it is a logical question, there are several reasons why neglecting the Old Testament would be a tragic mistake.

1. The Second Vatican Council (1962–65), declared that the Old Testament has permanent value and is an important witness to God's revelation.
2. The actions and attitudes of our ancestors in faith can be examples for us.
3. Reading the Old Testament prepares us to understand the New.
4. The Old Testament forms a link between the three major western religions: Christianity, Judaism, and Islam.
5. The final reason for studying the Old Testament is because it introduces us to the story of salvation.

By reading the Old Testament, we are able to locate ourselves as members of a faith community involved in an ongoing relationship with God. We can face the challenges life gives us, knowing that God has a plan for our salvation. We can face the future with confidence, anchored in a covenant relationship that spans 3,000 years, and that is founded upon God's ultimate gift: the power of love.

• Have the students open their Bibles to the table of contents for the Old Testament and find the names of the books listed in "Why the Old Testament?" and then locate each of its books.

• Help students come to a comfortable recognition of each of the divisions of the Old Testament. See what questions they may have about the books of the Old Testament at this time. Answer clarification questions at this time. Write down any questions that need further development and refer back to them when you reach the appropriate chapter.

• Using a brainstorming approach, have students give reasons why the Old Testament should or should not be studied. List all reasons on the board. After a few minutes call time. As a class, examine the students' reasons and cross out those that are frivolous or totally inappropriate. (Let the students help make this decision.) Then, have several students read aloud "Why Read the Old Testament." Compare the students' reasons to the five provided here.

Connect

What to Do

Homework Assignment: Have students write a paragraph expressing what they hope to gain from the study of the Old Testament. Collect their work at the next session. Save them for review at the end of Chapter 9.

What's Next

Have the students find the Book of Exodus in their Bibles. Say: "The Exodus experience is the most important event in Jewish history. Through God's intervention, people who had been slaves were given their freedom. God formed a covenant with them."

◆ MORE ABOUT THE LESSON

Shaping the Old Testament

The Bible is a collection of revered, sacred writings, much of which were gathered, modified, and put into order during and after the Exile. The process continues well past 400 B.C.E. The priests who did this vital work wanted to preserve their great heritage, applying the ancient understandings to the problems and challenges of their own time.

The editing that took place here does not make the old documents inauthentic. Rather, editing helped to deepen the ancient content to make it understandable for later times. The writings we call "biblical" were fluid and changing until the end of the first century C.E.

When Jerusalem was destroyed and Judah no more, Judaism established a set Torah in order to survive without a Temple and without a country of its own.

Moses and the Covenant

Chapter Overview

This chapter introduces the students to Moses, the Exodus experience, and the importance of God's Covenant with the Hebrew people and, ultimately, with all of us.

Teaching Objectives

By the end of this chapter students will be able to:
• Recognize the importance of relationships and how they are formalized (and sometimes legalized) by agreements.
• See that their lives are full of agreements of many kinds.
• Begin to consider the value of a covenant with God.

Welcome

Demonstrate that you and your students are in this process of learning together, with shared interests and concerns.

What to Do

Greet as many of the students by name as you can. Mention, with thanks, a few of their contributions from the previous class.

Introducing the Chapter

What to Do

The main idea of this chapter, covenant, will be connected to common student experiences.
• Begin the lesson with prayer.
• Ask the class: "What do you mean when you say, 'Let's make a deal?' When do you want to make deals? How do you affirm your agreement? What do you think of people who don't keep their deals?"
• Offer the students a "deal" between you and them: for example, "I promise to prepare well and try to be the best teacher I can, and help you learn; you agree to study and do your assignments and try to be good learners." Help them work out their part. To seal your deal you may wish to shake hands all around or ask students for their suggestions on how to "seal the deal."

Moses and the Covenant

1450	**1450 B.C.E.** ● Beginning of Hittite Empire
1300	**1304–1237** ● Reign of Ramses II in Egypt **1300** ● Mycenaean-Minoan culture begin civil wars **1300–1280** ● Likely date for the Exodus **1288** ● Battle of Kadesh; Egypt and the Hittites make peace
	1250 ● Greek settlers found a colony in Etruria (Italy); basis for Etruscan civilization ● Tribal life in Canaan; Judges
1200	**1212** ● Merneptah stele, commemorates victory of Egypt over Israel **1200** ● Migration of "Sea Peoples" into the Middle East—later called Philistines
550	**1000** ● Exodus story first written **550** ● Book of Exodus completed

Legend

● General History
● Biblical History
● Jewish History
● Books written

Chagall, *Exodus.* Twentieth Century.

R elationships with people you love are different from relationships with people in movie theaters or video arcades. When you buy a movie ticket or change a dollar for video game tokens, you form a "contract" with the owner of the theater or arcade. Your ticket or token entitles you to a service, namely a movie or video game. If the machine breaks down or the game doesn't work, you get your money back. You also hold the owner responsible if anything happens to you or your possessions while you're on the premises.

With people you love, you have a different kind of relationship, one we call a "covenant." Let Karen, age 26, explain. She recently married Patrick, her college boyfriend. Here's what she has learned about a covenant relationship after 11 months of marriage:

◆ MORE ABOUT THE LESSON

"Deals"

"Deals" can be formal or informal, legal or illegal, personal or national. In this lesson, students learn about a very formal, yet intensely personal "deal" between God and people— a covenant. Your "deal" with them is a kind of informal covenant, for right now, on their own level.

In the discussion, guide the students to understand that "deals" are made when people want common qualities in life (as in a marriage) or work toward common goals; or when different people each have something the other wants; or when some people are needy and others are benefactors. Some ways to "seal the deal" might include: sharing food, special handshakes, signing a legal paper, taking an oath, or making shared vows.

I have found that one of the strengths of our relationship is freedom. My goal has always been to study law. Patrick knew that our finances would be tight while I went to law school and yet he supported me in all ways. Through our relationship, I feel like I am blossoming into the person that God intends for me to be.

Our marriage grows, in part, due to the support we receive from our family, friends, and Church. To have the people we love and care about at our wedding to share and witness our love was a great gift.

Most importantly, God is a part of our relationship. The faith that Patrick and I share has been the foundation of our marriage. Most nights we talk about our day and then we pray together before going to sleep. We believe that our marriage is modeled on the relationship that God has had with humanity since the beginning of time.

God's faithfulness throughout history is an inspiration to us. We expect to receive many blessings in married life, especially children. We know that our love will survive and last forever!

Loving Relationships   Contracts are legal agreements which protect rights. They are written in technical language that can feel very cold. Covenants, however, bind people together in a warm, loving relationship. Although you can form a contract just by buying a ticket, a covenant takes a lot of time, effort, and trust to build.

In this chapter, you will read about how God began the Covenant with the people of Israel. This Covenant is still alive today in the lives of Jews and Christians throughout the world. You will also see how God built a relationship with the Hebrew people, freeing them from slavery in Egypt and leading them safely across the desert to the promised land. We call this event the "Exodus" (exit) from Egypt. Finally, you will discover how God cemented the Covenant by giving the Israelites the law through their great leader, Moses.

The story of the Exodus has been expressed in many artistic media, including this filmed version called The Ten Commandments.

MORE ABOUT THE TEXT

Covenant

There is no exact modern parallel to the Covenant between God and Israel. It is unique just as the relationship between them was unique in their world. But the qualities of their Covenant are the qualities of relationship that God still offers to all people, including Christians. Love and self-giving on God's side, with acceptance, love, and following the teachings of God on our side build a strong relationship with God today, just as they did in early times.

• Explain that the Bible is the story of a special kind of deal, a particular relationship that exists between God and humanity. This relationship began with the Hebrews in ancient times and extends all the way to us.

• Have the students read the opening two pages. Ask them how a marriage agreement is the same or different from the "deal" you just made with them. Is your classroom "deal" closer to a contract or a covenant? Why?

Extend the Activity   Develop a written agreement—a class covenant—that spells out some aspects of how you will treat students and how students will treat each other. Set up your agreement along the lines of the covenant model described in this chapter. See the Teacher's Resource 2A for a possible agreement. Have all students sign the agreement and post it for everyone to see.

Development

Using the Timeline

Students will understand that God's choice of the people Israel happened in history, through a definite divine act at a definite time.

What to Do

Turn the students' attention to the timeline. Remind them of the purposes of the timeline (as explained in Chapter 1). Explain that the Covenant with the people of Israel was a definite event, that happened at a definite time, coinciding with the Exodus. Have the students find the Exodus on the timeline.

Point out the other events that were happening in the Middle East in the decades surrounding the Exodus/Covenant: Egypt tended to other international interests; new civilizations were blooming; older civilizations were fighting; people were migrating. Have them find examples of each of these events on the timeline.

How do they expect God to act definitely in the middle of today's history? What does God have to do with other kinds of agreements today, like the "deal" you just made as a class or with international treaties.

LESSON ONE (pages 20–22)

◆ A Covenant People

Teaching Objectives

By the end of this lesson students will be able to:
• Understand the concepts of "election" and "covenant."
• Make connections between what the ancient Hebrews understood about God and what we understand about God today.

Development

Outcome

• The students will understand that "election" is God's free and loving choice to be in active relationships with people, seen especially in the Covenant with the Hebrews.
• Students will understand different kinds of treaties and how one kind was used in the Bible to express the Covenant relationship with God.
• Students will compare loving covenant relationships to modern agreements.

What to Do

1. Have the students read the opening paragraph (page 20) and the "Learning Objectives." Explain that the first two objectives are related to this lesson. Suggest that they watch closely to find these objectives and understand them well enough to describe in their own words.

2. Have the students read "Covenants in the Ancient Middle East." Discuss with the students which kind of treaty—parity or vassal—would be the most binding. Why? Would they rather make a deal today with their peers or with an authority figure? Why?

3. Ask the students which covenant would be stronger: one made with God or one with people? Why?

Practicing the Skills

This skill is a beginning ability to find biblical references.

What to Do

1. Have the students open their Bibles to Exodus 1 and put a marker there. Then have them mark Deuteronomy 1. Leave the Bibles open on the tables, so that they are easy to glance at.

Forming a Covenant

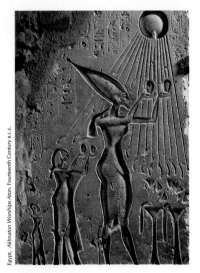

Egypt. *Akhnaton Worships Aton.* Fourteenth Century B.C.E.

One of the most important themes in the Old Testament is the special relationship that exists between God and the people of Israel.

This special relationship did not happen immediately. The people of Israel grew into it over the course of many hundred years. Yet, from the beginning of the Covenant, God's love for the Hebrew people is clearly evident. Before looking at the story of how this Covenant began, we will consider how people living in the ancient world would have understood the idea of a "covenant." In addition, we will find out who the ancient Hebrews were and how they thought about God.

Learning Objectives for Section One

By the end of this section, you will be able to:

• Explain the idea of God's "election" of Israel.

• Describe the variety and elements of ancient covenants.

• Compare the Bible to writings from a similar time and place.

• Define "monotheism" and place it in its historical context.

◆ A Covenant People

For Jews, the most important story of the Tanakh is found in the Book of Exodus. *Exodus* comes from a Greek word meaning "to exit." The story of the Hebrews' exit and liberation from slavery in Egypt is told in chapters 1–15 of the Book of Exodus. It is the story of how, from all the people on earth, God chose the Hebrews, offering them freedom from slavery, rules to live by, and the blessing of a permanent homeland.

Election

The covenant agreement in the Book of Exodus is understood as a fulfillment of the promises made to the Hebrews' ancestors, particularly the patriarch, Abraham. The agreement also made new promises, since the land of Canaan, which had first been promised to Abraham, would be a lasting gift from God to the Hebrew People. You will study more about Abraham in Chapter 4.

The Covenant bound the people in a loving relationship with God. They were a people especially chosen from among all the other races and nations on earth. They had been "elected" by God, not because of anything that they had accomplished, but because of God's love for them:

> It was not because you are the largest of all nations that the Lord set His heart on you and chose you, for you are really the smallest of all nations. It was because the Lord loved you and because of His fidelity to the oath He had sworn to your fathers.
>
> (Deuteronomy 7:7–8)

The election of the Hebrew people reveals most clearly God's saving power. God freely chose the Hebrews because God loved them, and for no other reason. Think about that for a moment; what does it mean that someone is chosen strictly out of God's love? What would it mean to you to know that God will love you and be with you no matter what you may do? Such an act of generous love is hard to understand, yet that is how God is.

◆ MORE ABOUT THE LESSON

Biblical References

The main sections of Exodus which you will briefly point out to the students begin at these verses: Exodus 1:1 describes the early Hebrew existence in Egypt; Exodus 2:1 begins Moses' own story; Exodus 5:1 begins the negotiations with Pharaoh; Exodus 11 tells about the last plague; Exodus 12 is ritual law; Exodus 13–15 is the departure and triumph of the Hebrews.

The Sh'ma

The Covenant between God and the Hebrews, described in the Book of Exodus, remains the basis of life for modern Judaism. Today's Jews stand in a tradition that is over 3,200 years old!

Jews have a special prayer which expresses this relationship with God, called the "Sh'ma" (from the Hebrew word meaning, "hear.") The first line reads: "Sh'ma Yisrael: Adonai Elohenu Adonai Echad!" ("Hear O Israel: The Lord our God, the Lord is One!") The words of the prayer are taken from the Book of Deuteronomy.

According to the Jewish "rabbis," or teachers, when Jews say the first verse of this prayer, they renew their acceptance of the Covenant. This act is called "accepting the yoke of the kingdom of Heaven." Traditionally, Jews cover their eyes when saying the first verse, and stretch out the word "echad" ("one") as they think about God's oneness.

Another custom related to this prayer is the *Mezuzah*, a container with a scroll inside with the words of the Sh'ma written on it. Jews place the Mezuzah on their doorposts, because the last line of the Sh'ma instructs them to keep the words of the prayer "on the doorposts of your house and upon your gates." (Interestingly, the Mezuzah is always hung at an angle. It seems that two great rabbis in the Middle Ages argued over whether the Mezuzah should be placed horizontally or vertically. Eventually, they reached this compromise.)

These customs, and many others like them, remind the Jews of their special relationship with God, formed by the Covenant of Exodus.

Covenants in the Ancient Middle East

The ancient Israelites who wrote the Book of Exodus needed a set of terms to describe this special relationship between God and Israel. The closest parallel they could find was the treaties formed between two nations. Therefore, they used the language and even the format of international treaties to describe the bond that existed between God and Israel. They called this agreement a "*b'rith*," or "covenant," the same word they used for alliances between groups and nations.

Most of our information about these ancient treaties comes from the study of the Hittite Empire (1400–1200 B.C.E.; the area is now part of modern Turkey), although other nations of that time also made formal agreements with covenants. (The Hittite covenants were based upon the code of law developed in Babylon.)

In form, the covenant treaty consisted of three parts: (1) the agreement itself, (2) witnesses, and (3) a ritual act. The witnesses were not only other humans, but also the Hittite gods.

The two sides bound themselves to their agreement through an act of ritual. For example, they would kill an animal, cut it in half, and walk between the halves. This ritual symbolized that they should be killed and cut into pieces if they broke their word. For a description of a similar ritual involving Abraham, see Genesis 15.

Each year Jewish families remember God's Covenant with them by celebrating Passover with the Seder meal where the story of the rescue from Egypt is remembered.

Explain that the first 15 chapters of Exodus tell the traditional story of the Hebrews and their condition in Egypt, of Moses' early life and of the long period of failed negotiations with Pharaoh, before the Hebrews actually departed from Egypt.

Briefly take the students through Exodus 1–15, pointing out the main sections.

Explain that the Book of Exodus was not all written at once. Exodus reached its final form at least 700 years after the event (examine timeline).

2. Have the students read "Election" (page 20). Then give them a chance to ask questions about this reading. Let them think about what God's love and God's choice might mean to them. Ask them to jot down their ideas in their journals.

Recall

Ask volunteers to name the most important single thing they have learned today. Individual answers will differ, so continue until you get a good overall review.

Connect

What to Do

Homework assignment: "Ask your family and friends about agreements they have made. List them and answer these two questions for each one: Was the agreement based on love, legality, or something else? How binding do you think each agreement is? How is this agreement like or unlike the Covenant?"

Have the students read "The Bible in Context." Then have them look up and read silently the whole "Sh'ma" and instructions in Deuteronomy 4:6. Ask for a volunteer to stand up and read these verses aloud, dramatically, as a real proclamation.

Ask for their reactions to this exercise. Show them the mezuzah you borrowed (or the picture).

◆ MORE ABOUT THE LESSON

Development

The most important point to make or to emphasize to the students is that a Covenant, as understood in the Bible, is based on love and freedom. Once agreed to, it is binding on both God and people. Keeping the Covenant is an act of love. Because almost immediately the Covenant is ignored by the Hebrew people (as you'll see in "The Making of the Nation," this chapter), and they will continue to ignore it periodically throughout the national history, it is important to see in the very beginning that a Covenant is meant to be kept by both parties to it. In Israel's ongoing history, God keeps promises out of love for Israel and because of integrity. The people have to grow into such integrity and it will take centuries of experience to master it.

What's Next?

What to Do

Prepare for the next lesson. Say something like "The Hebrews were real people, like us. They had ideas about life, relationships with each other, problems and joys. Like us, they had ancestors and neighbors; they shared beliefs with other people, too. In our next lesson we will learn more about the Hebrew people."

Have You Considered?

1. A covenant requires a greater giving of self, and therefore probably occurs more rarely than a contract.

2. Ideally, a marriage would most closely resemble a parity treaty. The family experience of students will influence their response.

3. Encourage students to explore possible examples of God calling people today. You may want to introduce the concept of vocations or explore the parallels between the Church today and the ancient people of Israel.

Bonus Focus for You

Read Deuteronomy 26:5–10. It describes a ritual for harvest offering. Read it aloud to yourself. Imagine yourself offering a portion of your own "harvest" (be it paycheck or other goods) and repeating these verses to express your own deep thanks to God. You, too, are rooted in the Covenant. Experiment with it and ponder what it means to you.

Scripture Workshop

Have the students look up Deuteronomy 5:1–33. Ask a few students to share what they have written.

Answer

The four elements of the vassal treaty are: Deuteronomy 5:6—Description of the greatness and kindness of the king; 5:7–21—List of rules and regulations; 5:1–5—Naming witnesses to the treaty; and 5:32–33—Blessings and Curses.

Scripture Workshop

Elements of the Vassal Treaty

The vassal treaty:

- Described the greatness and kindness of the king.
- Listed rules and regulations.
- Named the witnesses and enforcers of the treaty.
- Identified the blessing and curses that would follow either obedience or disobedience.

To become familiar with this format, do the following:

1. Find each of the four elements of the vassal treaty in Deuteronomy 5:1–33. This passage is a version of the giving of the Ten Commandments to Moses.
2. List the verse numbers where each of the elements occur.
3. Write 1 or 2 sentences for each, explaining how you recognize these particular elements in the verses.

Over time, two major types of covenants became prevalent in the ancient Middle East. One was a *parity treaty*, an agreement entered into by equal parties. A second type of covenant was a *vassal treaty*, that is, a powerful king would gain power over a weaker one.

The Covenant given by God to the Hebrews was a very formal treaty. It was not an agreement between equals. It was more like the agreement between a conquering king and his new subject. Therefore, it was closest in form to the vassal treaty. Yet, this Covenant agreement was also quite different from any other that existed at that time.

Have You Considered?

1. Which do you think is more rare, contracts or covenants? Why?
2. Which type of covenant (parity treaty or vassal treaty) does a marriage most closely resemble? Explain your answer.
3. The Bible says that God chose the Hebrews to make them into a special nation. Do you think that God continues to choose people today for special purposes? Explain your answer.

These lion gates continue to guard the remains of the Hittite city of Hattusas, the ancient capital of the Hittite empire. The Hittite nation lasted from the sixteenth to the seventh century B.C.E.

◆ MORE ABOUT THE LESSON

Recall

At least these points should emerge in your class review: people make different kinds of agreements; God and the Hebrews made a Covenant; God offered it to them as the basis for a loving relationship; this Covenant was special because God designed it and gave it freely; the Covenant was binding on both God and the Hebrew people.

For the Hebrew people who followed Moses out of Egypt, the destination was the land of Canaan.

◆ The Early History of the Chosen People

Most scholars agree that the people of God did not think of themselves as a nation until after they had made it out of Egypt and into the promised land. In other words, they did not become a nation until after the Exodus. Before this time, they existed as various tribes and clans who shared a language and some cultural traditions. In order to understand the importance of the Exodus, we need to look at this earlier period.

The Hebrews

Before you continue, take a moment to understand a few names.

- An **"Israelite"** was someone who was a citizen of the nation of Israel. Since Israel did not exist as a nation until after the Exodus, there were no "Israelites" in Egypt.
- A **"Hebrew"** was someone who spoke the Hebrew language and was born into the Hebrew culture. This cultural group was organized into tribes, shared a language and traditions (including stories and songs), served as slaves in Egypt, and formed the basis for the nation of Israel.
- **The word "Semite,"** is often used in place of the word "Hebrew." Semite, however, refers to a much larger group of people that includes Hebrews, Arabs, Canaanites, Babylonians, Assyrians, and other people who live in Palestine and Mesopotamia. Each of these peoples speaks a related language.

The Hebrews probably were originally a group of "nomads," people who wander around following a flock or herd of animals rather than living in one settled location. They roamed the Middle East, merging with various groups as they went along. Eventually, they became farmers and settled down.

The Hebrews probably came to Egypt, along with many other smaller cultural groups, attracted by the higher standard of living to be found there. Over time, these groups were reduced to slavery. In the next section, we will take up the story of the Exodus, as God delivers the Hebrews from their slavery and leads them to a homeland.

MORE ABOUT THE TEXT

Monotheism

Practically everyone in the ancient Middle East believed there were many gods and goddesses and that each had certain functions to perform in nature, in politics, or in people's lives. When a person needed help with one of these areas of life, he or she would appeal to the proper deity. (A fertility god/goddess was offered sacrifices asking for a good crop or for the birth of a healthy child.)

Moses and the Hebrews were the first (after Akhenaton) to single out one god and worship that god only. This was the beginning of long experience, which seems designed by God to show the Israelites that Yahweh was the only God.

Be sure the students grasp the difference between monotheism (there is only one God) and henotheism (polytheism, but worshipping only one God).

SECTION ONE

LESSON TWO (pages 23–25)

◆ The Early History of the Chosen People

Welcome

What to Do

Watch for one or two students with whom you might chat as they enter the room. When everyone has gathered, say "Welcome back! I'm glad to see you." Make a little welcoming small talk.

Remind the students of your class covenant. Tell them you are prepared; ask if they are (have they done their homework, for example).

Form small groups. Each person is to ask the person on his or her left to "name one thing you know about God." Each person in the group is to come up with something different from the others. Everyone is to have a chance to answer.

Ask, "How many gods are there? Did anyone mention this obvious point in the group?"

Introducing the Lesson

Teaching Objectives

By the end of this lesson students will be able to:

- Demonstrate a knowledge of what "monotheism" means and how this belief developed in historical time.
- Explain the meaning of the four basic words necessary for all Bible study: Israelite, Hebrew, Semite, and nomad.
- Show a basic familiarity with the general features of the ancient Middle East and other points important for their continuing study.
- Explain what monotheism means and how it differs from polytheism. Students will know that monotheism developed over time for the Israelites and was influenced by connections with other cultures.

What to Do

Have the students read the opening paragraph and "The Hebrews" on page 23 quietly. What questions do they have? Ask them to explain the differences between the terms in this passage.

Development

What to Do

"Learn From the Map." First notice what familiar terms are on the map. Help the students locate any areas or peoples mentioned in the paragraphs they've just read. Using an atlas, encyclopedia, or a Bible dictionary, have them look up places not seen on this map including Arabia, Canaan, Babylon, Assyria, Palestine, and Mesopotamia. Some of these sites will be noted on maps in later chapters. Have the students locate on the map each place or area. Point out that though the geography remains the same, political situations and boundaries have changed again and again over time, and are still not settled today. Remind the students to keep their eyes open to changes in the map as the class continues.

Have the students read "How the Israelites Thought about God." Ask: "From the description in the text, was Akhenaton a true monotheist?" Discuss. Share with the students the material in "More about the Text," below. Be certain they understand this concept before you go further.

Practicing the Skills

Reading comparatively to see that the Bible did not arise in isolation, but in conversation with other cultures.

What to Do

Have the students find in their Bibles and read Psalm 19 and Psalm 104:1–23. Ask whether there is any indication that these psalms could have been influenced by Egyptian hymns or by Akhenaton? Have students explain their answers. Now pass out copies of Akhenaton's hymn (See Teacher's Resource 2B). Have them compare it with these two psalms. What similarities are there? What differences?

Ask what the students conclude from this practice. Help them to see that although influenced by others, the Israelites changed the other cultures' ideas, adapting them for their own use.

Recall

Turn to Chapter Two Review, page 38. Ask the students to write down their answers to "Q/A" Section One. Encourage them to use their text to find answers. A review is not a test.

24

LEARN FROM THE MAP

The Ancient Middle East

Notice that ancient Israel was near to several larger, more powerful empires. Through trade, immigration, and political ties, Israel's culture was strongly influenced by the cultures of these surrounding nations. Each time Israel was conquered, its culture and religion was affected. For this reason, it's not surprising that the biblical authors modeled their description of the relationship between God and Israel on the covenant formulas used by surrounding nations to make treaties.

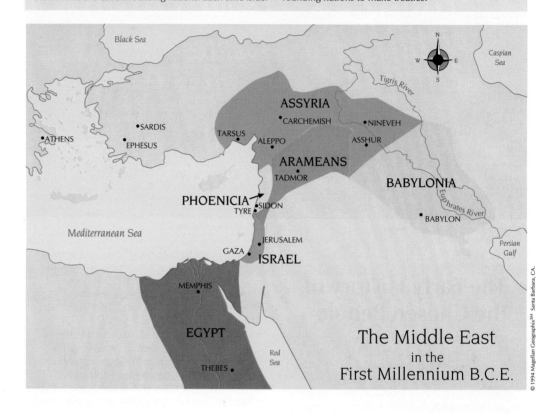

The Middle East
in the
First Millennium B.C.E.

© 1994 Magellan Geographix℠ Santa Barbara, CA.

How the Israelites Thought about God

The Israelites were unusual in the ancient world because their Covenant said that they worshipped only *one* God, although all of the surrounding cultures worshipped a wide variety of gods and goddesses. Moses may have recognized that this Yahweh whom he worshipped exclusively was the only God, but that's not true for the rest of the Hebrews. The Bible records an ongoing battle that raged over the people's worship of many gods, even in the Sinai while on the Exodus!

There is a major difference between the idea that Yahweh is the first among many gods, and the idea that Yahweh is the **only** God. It took the Hebrew people many years to come to this complex understanding. Their awareness grew with experience and especially with the insights of the prophets.

Moses told the people that the God who delivered them from Egypt and the Sinai was "a jealous God," who insisted that they "have no other gods besides Me." This God was different from the gods worshipped by other people. This God demanded an exclusive right to the people's allegiance. This teaching, however, did not deny the *existence* of other gods. It was, instead, the first step toward that realization.

◆ **MORE ABOUT THE LESSON**

The Map

The better the students know the map of the ancient Middle East, the easier it will be for them to understand the history and relationships of Israel to other nations. Take as much time as necessary to explore the map, according to what the students already know. Point out the Mediterranean Sea, the Jordan River from the Sea of Galilee to the Dead Sea (Salt Sea), Egypt, the Red Sea and the Reed Sea, the area of Palestine/Canaan, the Tigris and Euphrates Rivers, the general area of Mesopotamia (which includes Babylon and Assyria), and the area that is now Turkey (Hittite territory). Let the students search for as many of these as are in their text map. You can then add the rest.

The Middle East has always been in political flux and has usually been in conflict. Despite this, three of the world's great religions were born here: Judaism, Christianity, and Islam.

Toward Monotheism   Belief in the existence of only one God is called *monotheism*. Ironically, the foundations of monotheism may have begun in Egypt itself.

From 1364–1347 B.C.E., the Egyptian pharaoh was Akhenaton. Unlike his forefathers, he worshipped only one god, the Solar Disk or Sun God. Akhenaton's name means "Glorious Spirit of Aten," referring to the sun god, Aten. He forced this belief on the nation and did his best to eliminate all other religious views. After his death, Egypt returned to the practice of worshipping many gods (*polytheism*). During his reign, however, the Israelite slaves in Egypt would certainly have been exposed to Akhenaton's monotheism. We know that they were moved by Akhenaton's religious poetry, because his "Hymn to the Sun" influenced many of the psalms.

The Hebrew Difference   The Hebrews did not simply take over Akhenaton's ideas, however. Always when the Hebrews (or Israelites) were influenced by religious ideas other than their own, they reshaped them to express their unique experience and understanding of God. Even in the beginning, they did not see Yahweh as part of nature, as Egyptian myth tended to do. Yahweh was, instead, separate from and above nature.

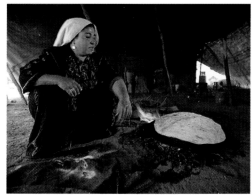

Nomadic people still wander across the Middle East, leading their animals to water and better pastures. Their lives have changed little over the centuries.

in the *Spotlight*

The Armarna Letters

There are very few records outside the Bible that help us understand these events which happened over 32 centuries ago. Within the last 100 years, however, archaeologists have discovered a series of writings which are as old or older than the Bible, and which help us understand the Bible in new ways.

One such text is a collection known as the Amarna letters, which date from the time of the pharaoh Akhenaton (between 1400 and 1350 B.C.E.). In several of the letters, the rulers of Palestine and Syria write to the pharaoh in Egypt, asking for military assistance. Wandering groups of attackers called the *'Apiru'* were attacking small walled cities and could not be defeated.

Some scholars have suggested that these 'Apiru' are the same as or related to the 'Ivri,' or 'Hebrews.' It's not really certain that these two people are the same group, but it does show that many peoples were wandering in search of a home at the time the Israelites made their journey from Egypt into the Promised Land.

Today, belief in the existence of only one God is so common that it may be hard to imagine anything else. But in the time when Israel was finding its identity as a people, monotheism would have been almost unimaginable.

Yahweh demanded exclusive worship and loyalty of his people, who were not inclined to speculate about (for them) all the details of divine nature. They wanted to know whose power was available to them and how they should live in relationship with that god. For the early Israelites, Yahweh was the one.

Have You Considered?

1. Why do you think the Hebrews could not form a nation while living as slaves in Egypt? What prevented this from happening?
2. The Amarna letters and the religious policies of Akhenaton help us understand the historical context of the Bible. Give an example of how knowing the context of something today helps you understand it.
3. What difference does it make whether there *is* only one God or if there were many gods, but you worshipped only one?

MORE ABOUT THE TEXT

In the Spotlight

Tel el Amarna—the ruin of Akhenaton's capital city, built in honor of the sun—is in Egypt about halfway between Thebes and Memphis, on the east side of the Nile River. A beautiful city, it was abandoned by the next pharaoh because of its associations with Akhenaton's religious convictions. Many significant archaeological items have been found there, including letters from biblical cities like Jerusalem, Shechem, and Megiddo. This evidence shows that the "Promised Land" was fully occupied long before the Hebrews began to live there.

Connect

Students will have an opportunity to personalize their new thinking about monotheism.

What to Do

Ask the students to write a few lines in their journals about believing in one God as opposed to believing in many gods, even if worshipping only one. It can be a statement of personal faith or an imagined statement by an ancient Hebrew.

What's Next?

What to Do

Tell the students that Israel's roots with Egypt were even deeper than Akhenaton or their life in Egypt. Their leader, law-giver, and the molder of the new people was raised in the Egyptian palace, probably as a prince. But his Hebrew heritage proved to be stronger than his upbringing—and God had special plans for him.

---

in the Spotlight

Have the students read "In The Spotlight." Discuss Amarna and point out the general location of Tell el Amarna on the map (along the Nile River in Egypt).

Have You Considered?

1. Many answers are possible here, but students should observe that the Israelites did not have the necessary political freedom to form a nation while in Egypt.
2. Many answers are possible. One is the use of the word "bad," which has one meaning in certain contexts and the opposite meaning in others.
3. In the second case, you are a polytheist (one who believes in many gods), but you choose to be loyal to only one.

Bonus Focus for You ———

Read and ponder Psalm 96. Can you find the mixture of strict monotheism with the older acknowledgment of many gods?

◆ The Story of Moses

Welcome

What to Do

1. Place yourself in a different part of the classroom today and as the students come near you, speak quietly but personally with a few of them. Then, welcome them all.

2. Pantomime for them a short, familiar scene from the story of Moses. Make it like a charade; they can ask 10 yes-or-no questions to help them guess. If they don't guess the answer, tell them to remember what you've done and speak up when they figure it out during the lesson.

Introducing the Lesson

Teaching Objectives

By the end of this lesson students will be able to:

• Become familiar with the background of the Hebrews in Egypt. They will see how this is an example of biblical writers presenting a religious rather than a factual viewpoint.

• Learn the story of Moses' youth and the importance to Moses of learning God's name.

• Become familiar with the story of the Exodus from Egypt.

What to Do

Have the students read the objectives and the first paragraph of "The Story of Moses" on page 30. Then, have them find and read Exodus 1:8–22. Discuss with the students the biblical viewpoint here: the authors are interested in telling the religious story as seen through a later perspective. Lead them to question the story and participate in the discussion.

Development

What to Do

1. Have the students read Exodus 2:1–15 aloud. Several students can read a paragraph each, either as volunteers or at your request. Help them enjoy the story for its own sake—it's a good tale! Next, have them read to themselves "Moses' Birth and Early Years," which summarizes the story.

Israel Becomes a Nation

Few characters in the Bible rival Moses in importance:

• He was the person who introduced the Hebrews to Yahweh and served as God's voice.

• He was the leader who brought the Hebrews out of slavery in Egypt to freedom in the promised land of Israel.

• He was the one who received the Law, the code which God gave to the people of Israel as a sign of their election.

In this section, we'll see how God forms Israel into a nation.

Learning Objectives for Section Two

By the end of this section, you will be able to:

• Describe the importance of Moses in the story of Israel.

• Explain the idea of "formation" and how the wilderness experience of Israel was as an example of formation.

• Identify the Ten Commandments and explain their significance.

◆ The Story of Moses

The witness, mediator, and key figure in the covenant between God and the Hebrews was Moses. Even today, Moses is generally considered the most important figure in Jewish history. Moses is the person appointed by God to deliver the Hebrews from slavery in Egypt and to lead them to the promised land of Canaan. Most importantly, Moses was the one who received the Law from God and promised obedience on behalf of the people. In this way, it was Moses through whom the Covenant between God and Israel was made. The story of the Covenant, therefore, begins with his life story.

Moses' Birth and Early Years

According to the story in the Book of Exodus, the pharaoh began to fear the Hebrews because

the more they were oppressed, the more they multiplied and spread.

(Exodus 1:12)

The Pharaoh issued an edict (royal order) to kill all the baby Hebrew boys in order to stop the Hebrew population from growing.

Exodus tells how the infant Moses was spared when his mother set him afloat in the Nile River in a basket made of papyrus. He was found by a royal princess and his life was spared. The name Moses is similar to an Egyptian word, *Mosheh*, which means "to draw out."

The story of Moses' rescue is the type of story that is quite common in ancient literature. It was a sign of divine favor when a child survived a brush with death in order that he might grow into a great leader and deliverer of his people. Early Christians even had a similar story about Jesus (see *Matthew* 2).

As a young man, Moses was forced to leave Egypt because he killed an Egyptian who was striking a Hebrew. When the event became known, Moses fled for his life to Midian, an area including the eastern side of the Sinai peninsula. There, Moses was taken into the clan of the priest, Jethro, given a wife, and became a shepherd.

◆ MORE ABOUT THE LESSON

Welcoming Activity

You might want to enlist the secret help of one or two of the students and plan this activity before class so the scene would be more complete. Some of the possible scenes are: Baby Moses is saved; the burning bush (a student could be the bush!); a confrontation with Pharaoh; the parting of the Reed Sea. Some students will know something about these most famous scenes from Exodus. Others will not. Regardless, the whole class can enjoy the guessing game and it will encourage them to focus on the lesson.

It was while Moses was living in the desert of Midian that the knowledge of the "greatness and kindness" of Yahweh was revealed to him.

"I Am Who I Am"

God's introduction to Moses and the Hebrew people is described in Exodus 3:1–4:17. In the desert Moses encounters a burning bush that is not consumed by the fire. From this bush Moses hears the voice of God.

The story of the burning bush reveals God's concern and action on behalf of the Hebrew People. God has seen their suffering in Egypt, and God intends to deliver them from slavery. God tells Moses that he will be the one to lead the Hebrew people out of Egypt. Moses' first response is to refuse:

> Who am I that I should go to the Pharaoh and lead the Israelites out of Egypt?
>
> (Exodus 3:11)

God answers: "I will be with you" (Exodus 3:12).

Moses then attempts to find out God's name. To most ancient people, a person's name was the expression of who he or she was. Names were not given by accident, a name expressed a person's character. Parents carefully named their children. After major events, people would often adopt new names to reflect who they were now. In addition, ancient magic spells were based on the power of knowing the secret names of angels and spirits. For a Hebrew to know someone's name, therefore, meant that he or she held some type of power over the other.

God refuses to be possessed. Instead of giving a name to Moses, God says, "I am" or "I am who I am."

Raphael, Moses and the Burning Bush. Sixteenth Century.

What does the artist, Raphael, do to capture God's power in the burning bush?

Scripture Workshop

The Burning Bush

The scene where Moses encounters God in the burning bush is called a "theophany," an appearance by a god to a human being. This experience is the key to Moses' later life and accomplishments. It is also the beginning of God's explicit action in the history of the Hebrew people. Read Exodus 3:1–4:17, where this story is told. Answer the following questions:

1. What did Moses see? What would you think of such a sight?
2. What did the voice in the bush say to Moses? List five separate points.
3. How did Moses react? (3:11, 4:1 and 4:10–14) Was his reaction justified?
4. Who was Aaron? What was his function to be?
5. What does God give Moses to take with him? What is Moses to do with God's gift?

The Hebrew word for "I am" is YHWH. (Remember, in Hebrew only consonants were written.) Today we write this Hebrew word "Yahweh."

From this statement, Moses learns that the essence of God is *being*. Whatever is, exists because of God. God brings all things to be. The name "I am who I am" also says that this God cannot be controlled by Moses or any other creature. Instead, it is Yahweh who will be in control. The Hebrews will learn time and time again that it is Yahweh who saves them, when God is ready to save them. Yahweh will not be forced into acting.

In the Jewish tradition, the name of God is so sacred that it is not to be spoken aloud. Conservative and Orthodox Jews today maintain the tradition of not pronouncing or even writing the name of God at all. This tradition springs from the idea that the name of God should not be manipulated for human purposes for any reason.

The Liberation from Egypt

There once was a fish who swam in a different direction from the other fish in her school. Another fish questioned her. "Where are you going?"

---

2. Form small groups. Each group should choose a scribe. Have all the students complete "Scripture Workshop" and report its answers.
3. Have the students read "I Am Who I Am." Ask them to look for an explanation of the importance of God's name as they read. Volunteers can share what they have found.
4. Form four small groups, each with a scribe (even if there are only two students in each group!). Have them turn to the "Bible Activity," page 38. Assign one question to each group. When they are finished with the work, have them report their findings to the class.
5. Read "The Liberation from Egypt" and "Final Plague." Ask how the ideas in these two sections enrich their understanding of the Bible.

Scripture Workshop

1. Moses saw a bush which was burning without being consumed.
2. Possible answers—God . . .
   a. tells Moses to come nearer.
   b. tells Moses to remove his sandals because he stood on holy ground.
   c. tells Moses that God has seen the suffering.
   d. promises to rescue them.
   e. says that God will send Moses.
   f. says that the people will worship God on Mt. Sinai.
   g. reveals the divine name: Yahweh, or I AM.
   h. sends Moses to inform the people.
   i. promises to smite Egypt through wonderful deeds.
   j. gives miraculous powers to Moses.
   k. assigns Aaron as an assistant to speak for him.
3. Moses was skeptical and overwhelmed.
4. Aaron was Moses' brother. His function was to speak for Moses and be his assistant.

◆ MORE ABOUT THE LESSON

Scripture Workshop

Some of these questions are not about fact, but are asking the students to think about what they are learning. Encourage them to speak honestly and commend them for sharing their sincere reactions and opinions. This helps create an open atmosphere and teaches that the Bible is both worthy of their thoughts and can stand up to their honest reactions.

MORE ABOUT THE TEXT

I Am Who I Am

The four letters of the name of God have been used in many ways over the centuries. Since they did not include vowels, exact pronunciation is unknown. See Teacher's Resource 2C for a sample of the Hebrew tetragrammaton (the "four-lettered word"). If you can't enlarge the Hebrew for the class, you can write it on the chalkboard. It reads from right to left.

Practicing the Skills

What to Do

Have the students read Exodus 15:1–13 and compare it with the versions of the story they have just read. What is similar? What is different? Does this sound like a factual recounting? Ask the students what kind of a poem this seems to be.

Recall

Have the students, in their own words, retell the story of Moses. Write (or have a student write) the ideas on the chalkboard, leaving room so you can fill in details.

Connect

What to Do

Homework Assignment: the students are to ask a parent or other adult whether he or she felt called to a (a) profession, (b) family life, (c) participation in the church or community.

What's Next?

Call attention to the picture on page 33. "What would it be like to live here?" Then, read Exodus 16:2–3 aloud.

Have You Considered?

1. Focus students on the question of how a "call" from God might be received. How are we aware that God is calling us?

2. Allow for many possible answers. Historically, the answer is probably connected to the Israelite struggle to overcome the temptations of idolatry and polytheism.

3. Connect responses to Moses' reaction upon meeting Yahweh, and the pharaoh's stubbornness in seeing the hand of God in the plagues.

Bonus Focus for You

Psalms 111 and 114 are later songs praising God, but both are rooted in the memory of the Exodus, the Covenant, and the events in the Sinai desert. Read them several times to yourself, preferably aloud. See if you can capture something of the feeling of praise and gratitude that motivated the composer. Can you allow the wonder of God's actions to touch your own heart? If so, you have another richness to share.

Poynter, *Israel in Egypt.* Nineteenth Century.

The Hebrew people were the slaves of the Egyptians, and provided the manual labor for building cities for Ramses II.

The counter-cultural fish responded, "Leave me alone. I am looking for the ocean."

"Ocean? You are swimming in the ocean at this very moment," the other fish said.

"This is not the ocean. This is only water," the first fish responded, and continued on her way.

The point of the story is that sometimes we may have trouble recognizing or seeing something clearly, even though it is right before our eyes. This failure to see clearly was the problem the Pharaoh had with Moses' and Aaron's demand from Yahweh to "Let my people go to worship me in the desert" (*Exodus* 7:16).

Several times, Moses brought God's word to Pharaoh, commanding him to let the Hebrews go. Each time, Pharaoh refused, and so God sent down a series of "plagues." In spite of the plagues—water filled with blood, influx of frogs, flies, and gnats—that befell Egypt, Pharaoh remained stubborn and refused to release the Hebrews from slavery.

While these plagues did not convince Pharaoh or Egypt of God's power, they do reveal to us Yahweh's authority over all people, events, and gods, along with Yahweh's determination to deliver the Hebrews to freedom. God was drawing the Hebrews into a new venture that would be forever binding. The plagues were signs to Israel of God's commitment to them. Through the plagues, Israel learned that God can be trusted.

Final Plague

The final plague is known to us as the "death of the first born":

At midnight the Lord slew every first-born in the land of Egypt, from the first-born of Pharaoh on the throne to the first-born of the prisoner in the dungeon, as well as all the first-born of the animals.

(Exodus 12:29)

Whereas the first-born of the Egyptians were killed, the lives of the Hebrews were spared because of their participation in the rituals of an ancient festival known as the *Pesach.* (Originally a celebration of the birth of the new lambs in spring.)

Following God's command, the Hebrews, on the night of the tenth plague, smeared the blood of slaughtered lambs over their doorposts. Putting blood on the doorpost was an ancient practice to avert evil and call down divine protection.

Seeing the blood on the lintel and the two doorposts, the Lord will pass over that door and not let the destroyer come into your houses to strike you down.

(Exodus 12:23)

The results of this final plague were devastating: the first-born children of the Egyptians died while the first-born children of the Hebrews lived. Following the finality of the tenth plague, the Hebrews were permitted to leave Egypt.

Their departure from Egypt was accompanied by amazing events: a pillar of cloud and fire led their way through the desert, (*Exodus* 13:21), and the Reed Sea parted and drowned the pursuing Egyptian army (*Exodus* 14:19–28).

Today, the Jewish feast of Passover celebrates when the Lord "passed over" their homes. It is one of the most holy festivals of the Jewish year. The ritual meal which Jews eat on this night is called the "seder."

Moses introduced the Hebrews to the "God of your fathers, the God of Abraham, the God of Isaac, the God of Jacob" (*Exodus* 3:15). The Exodus from Egypt proved to the Hebrews that Yahweh was indeed their God and that they were Yahweh's People.

Their joy is expressed by the hymn Miriam sang after the Hebrews crossed the Reed Sea to the freedom of a new life in the desert:

◆ MORE ABOUT THE LESSON

How to Review

Their story, when complete, should include all they can recall about the following points: Hebrew life before Moses, the threat to Hebrew babies, the birth, rescue, and adoption of Moses, the murder and Moses' flight, his marriage and occupation, the burning bush, God's message and Moses' reaction, receiving the name of God, the plagues, the magic tricks by Moses and the Egyptians, the last plague and Passover, the crossing of the Reed Sea and destruction of the pursuing soldiers, and Miriam's victory song of celebration.

I will sing to the Lord, for He is gloriously triumphant; horse and chariot He has cast into the sea. My strength and my courage is the Lord, and He has been my savior.

(Exodus 15:1–2)

The story of the Hebrew's salvation from Egyptian slavery demonstrates the power of Yahweh. The Hebrews were powerless; their deliverance was accomplished by the deeds of Yahweh alone. The story of Yahweh's compassion, guidance, and deliverance shaped the Hebrew people into God's people.

Have You Considered?

1. Moses was called by God for a special and unique task. What does it mean to be called by God today? What might a person be called to do?
2. From God's point of view, explain to Moses why you refuse to reveal more of your identity.
3. Describe an event when you had difficulty recognizing something that was "right before your eyes."

The Sinai Desert is a wild and barren land. The Hebrews' journey through it could not have been easy.

◆ The Making of the Nation

When Moses brought the Hebrews out of Israel, they brought with them all their differences. The common experience of slavery in Egypt had made them one people, but they were not yet a nation.

The bond between Yahweh and the Hebrews was further formed in the desert wilderness. After leaving Egypt, the Hebrew people crossed to the other side of the Reed Sea. Their journey was long and difficult. Though their exact route cannot be determined, they eventually reached Mount Sinai, where God's Law was given to them.

Years in the Desert

A prophecy recorded in the Book of Hosea sums up Yahweh's relationship with the Hebrews in this opening stage of their desert journey:

When Israel was a child I loved him, out of Egypt I called My son.

(Hosea 11:1)

◆ MORE ABOUT THE LESSON

Wilderness Journey

The map on page 24 and Map Transparency "Chapter 2" show the "Wilderness Journey" including the locations mentioned here, plus a possible "route." This is, at best, an attempt to join together the places mentioned in the biblical story. The Hebrews' precise route is unknown, but pointing out even a few specific places will make the events more concrete for your students. Supplement this map, if desired, with a biblical atlas. If you do not have a classroom map, learn the locations from an atlas or Bible dictionary and point them out on the map in the text.

Exodus 16 and 17 aloud. Then have the students quietly read "Yahweh Provides" and compare it with Exodus 16 and 17. Ask them to identify by chapter and verse number each of the events discussed in the text.

2. Form small groups, each choosing a speaker. Each group is to discuss: "What do you think about the 'miracles' and the probable 'natural' explanations? Do you think a miracle teaches more about God than a natural event? Would you listen more to a 'miracle story' than to a story you could easily explain? Why?"

3. Each group's speaker shares the group's findings with the class. Note: this is to encourage students to think for themselves and is not a test with right or wrong answers.

4. You can help by introducing the ideas below, if the students don't think of them. Ask the students to find the places in Exodus 16–17 where the Lord taught the people something specific about their relationship (16:4, 16:12, 17:5). Ask them to put into their own words the lesson Yahweh wanted them to learn.

5. Have the students find and read silently Exodus 19–20. Give them a little background.

6. Have them read "The Giving of the Law" and "The Ten Commandments." Ask, "What difference does it make if the Commandments are just a set of rules instead of the basis for a Covenant relationship with God?"

7. Have the students read "A Covenant People" carefully. Have the students perform an impromptu dramatization of how the Covenant was made and then betrayed.

8. When finished with the impromptu dramatization, ask the students how it has affected their view of the ratification of the Covenant and the first betrayal.

9. Next, have the students read "God's Involvement" as a basis for discussion and review.

Raphael, Water from the Rock. Sixteenth Century.

Through the able leadership of Moses, God freed the Hebrews from slavery and formed a Covenant with them.

Yahweh molded the Hebrews by teaching them discipline and trust, in much the same way that a parent molds the behavior of a young child.

The Bible says the journey in the desert took 40 years. Why did it take so long? Not because the distance was long; it wasn't, as you can see at a glance on your map. The number 40 probably stands for a generation, not an exact length of time. This number suggests that:

- Most of the adults who had lived in Egypt died in the desert.
- Many of the people who eventually entered the promised land were born in the desert.

Whether it was 40 years or a generation, it's clear that the journey took a long time to complete; much longer than the distance involved warranted. Exodus makes it clear that the journey was long because Yahweh was forming the Hebrews into a new people focused on the life God wanted to give them.

So, in the beginning years of the desert experience, the Hebrews were like babies who needed a new kind of care, new obstacles to overcome, and new challenges to strengthen them. Gradually, the character of this people was oriented to their identity as the people of Yahweh.

Yahweh Provides

The Hebrews persevered for a long while in the desert because they believed that the experience was a transition to a better life to come. Yahweh had promised them freedom and a land that they could call their own. Nevertheless, they had to survive while

in the desert. It was in that experience of day-to-day living that they learned total dependence on Moses—and Yahweh.

The major hardships of the desert were a lack of food and water, and the threat of attack by enemies. In each of these cases, Moses provided the leadership necessary for the Hebrews to move forward, while God provided the food, water, and protection.

The People Are Hungry   The people complained to Moses and Aaron about their hunger and thirst. God told Moses: "I will now rain down bread from heaven for you" (*Exodus* 16:4). This bread, known as manna, supplemented a diet of quail meat.

Although these events are presented in the Bible as supernatural miracles, there are possible natural explanations for them:

- **Manna.** The term is connected with the Hebrew expression for "What is this?" It may refer to the small honeydew pellets that are produced by the excretions of scale insects that suck the sap of the tamarisk plant. It is often found in the morning hours before it is eaten by ants, and it resembles white bread.

- **Birds.** There is an annual migration of birds from Europe to the south in September and October. During this time, quail fly over the Sinai Peninsula in great numbers. When they lie down to rest, they can easily be gathered for food.

The People Are Thirsty   When the people were thirsty, Moses prayed to God, who told him, "Strike the rock, and the water will flow from it for the people to drink" (*Exodus* 17:6). Moses did this in the presence of the Hebrew leaders and water flowed readily.

Actually, this event can also be explained by natural causes. When water flows slowly it often leaves lime deposits. Sometimes, water flows so slowly through certain kinds of rocks that large lime deposits form, blocking the flow of water completely.

A person familiar with the desert, as Moses was, would have learned how to recognize such places. When he knocked off the lime deposit, the water would run freely once again. To people unacquainted with desert life (such as the Hebrews out of Egypt), this "miracle" would surely seem extraordinary!

The People Are Attacked   While traveling, the Israelites were attacked by a people from southern Palestine called the *Amalekites*. Moses inspired the Israelites to do battle. The story is told in Exodus 17:8–13. While his assistant, Joshua, led the fight, Moses stood on a hill with his arms outstretched to

---

◆ MORE ABOUT THE LESSON

Teaching with the Bible

This lesson gives an excellent opportunity to use the text and the Bible side by side. Notice that each instruction includes both the text and the Bible. The events in the text with references are: lived 40 years in the desert (*Exodus* 16:35); people complain (*Exodus* 16:2–3); Yahweh responds with manna (*Exodus* 16:4–12) and quail (*Exodus* 16:13a);

Yahweh gives water (*Exodus* 17:1–7); Yahweh protects from attack (*Exodus* 17:8–13).

Use the Bible itself as much as possible. Read verses aloud. Have students role-play or dramatize a story. Use their artistic abilities to bring the passages to life. By having them work directly with the Bible, they gain a love for the book.

heaven. Moses' witness provided inspiration and helped to lead Israel to victory. Moses built an altar there in remembrance. Unlike the examples mentioned above, there are no natural occurrences to explain this phenomenon.

Through these actions, Moses and God won greater respect and trust from the people. God's hand was seen in every occurrence. The people had gained more strength and a faith to follow.

The Giving of the Law at Mount Sinai

Recall the four elements of a vassal covenant mentioned earlier:

1. The greatness and kindness of the king is highlighted.
2. Rules and stipulations are included.
3. Witnesses and enforcers of the treaty are stipulated.
4. Blessings and curses are stated dependent on how the rules of the covenant were followed.

By the time the Israelites reached Mount Sinai, Yahweh was ready to enter into the Covenant with them. But this relationship would not be a covenant of parity, as equals trade favors between themselves. Yahweh's power and faithfulness were proved to the Hebrews in the Exodus from Egypt and through their time in the desert. Now, the Hebrews would be offered a chance to become a Covenant people, Yahweh's chosen ones for all time.

When they arrived in the desert of Sinai, Moses went up to the mountain to speak with God. These were Yahweh's words:

> You have seen for yourselves how I treated the Egyptians and how I bore you up on eagle wings and brought you here to myself. Therefore, if you hearken to my voice and keep my covenant, you shall be My special possession, dearer to Me than all other people, though all the earth is mine.
>
> (Exodus 19:4–6)

While God made the Covenant with Moses, the Hebrew people were ordered to remain at the foot of the mountain with only Moses and Aaron climbing to the top. Sinai was "wrapped in smoke, for the Lord came down upon it in fire" (*Exodus* 19:18). Yahweh then delivered the Law to Moses and Aaron for the sake of all the people.

The Ten Commandments

The heart of the Covenant is known as the *Decalogue* or *Ten Commandments*. They parallel the elements of the vassal treaty. First the announcement on the king's qualifications to receive homage:

> I, *the Lord, am your God, who brought you out of the land of Egypt, that place of slavery.*
>
> (Exodus 20:2)

Next, the rules and stipulations. In vassal covenants, the first condition was always a pledge of loyalty to the king. The first condition of Israel's Covenant is no different:

> *You shall not have other gods besides Me.*
>
> (Exodus 20:3)

In the Book of Exodus, three chapters of lesser regulations follow the Decalogue. Most of these later laws reflect the circumstances after the Hebrews had settled in Canaan. According to Jewish tradition, there are 613 commands in the law.

While in the Hittite vassal treaties the gods themselves often served as witnesses to the agreement, here the Hebrew people are referred to as witnesses, as are heaven and earth:

> He summons the heavens from above, and the earth, to the trial of His people: "Gather My faithful ones before Me, those who have made a covenant with Me by sacrifice."
>
> (Psalm 50:4–5)

Hittite treaties concluded with a list of blessings and curses that spelled out the consequences of faithfulness or disobedience to the covenant. In the Ten Commandments, there is a suggestion of punishments after the second and fifth commandments. For example, after the fifth commandment, the ruling is "For the Lord will not leave unpunished him who takes His name in vain" (*Exodus* 20:7).

The account of the giving of the decalogue in Deuteronomy Chapter 11 (a companion story to the one in Exodus), describes a ceremony of pronouncing blesses and curses, exactly as performed in the vassal treaties.

A Covenant People

When Moses came down from Mount Sinai, he heard the people make the pledge: "We will do everything the Lord has told us" (*Exodus* 24:3). According to the narrative:

Recall

With the students, turn to "Chapter 2 Review, Q/A" Section Two. First discuss question 1. Then tell the students that some of the questions involve readings in the text that have not yet been assigned, but they are to find them anyway.

Have the students write down their answers to questions 2–8, again using the text as needed.

Have the students read through the Glossary and ask for any clarification they may need. Encourage them to ask, because there are no "stupid questions," only sometimes people are too uncomfortable to ask what they want to know.

Connect

Students will consider the Covenant in relationship to themselves and people they know.

What to Do

Pray the Spiritual Reflection as a class. Have the students answer these questions in their Journal: "Do you think God's call to Covenant relationship is for you as an individual? for your whole family? for the church? What would you like to say to God about the call to Covenant?"

What's Next?

Students will begin to think about the next stages of Hebrew/Israelite development, both as a nation and in their relationship with God.

What to Do

Preview the coming chapter. Tell the students to come to the next class prepared to share whatever they already know and can remember about David, Joshua, or Samuel.

Pray with the students, thanking God for the class session and student contributions.

◆ MORE ABOUT THE LESSON

"Miracles"

Today, most people need to think about "miracles" because we have a cultural assumption that God is different from and separated from the natural world. Rational "explanations" seem to make "natural events" less wondrous than "miracles." You may suggest these ideas: seeming miracles may be a natural part of a yet unknown lawful realm (just as the desert events often were); God can and does respond to people through familiar events as much as through amazing events; all of nature is quite wondrous, and our scientific "explanations" do not take away the qualities of harmonious order, inter-connectedness, and intelligence that science can observe, but not fully explain.

Aaron and Joshua are key figures in the early history of the people of Israel. As is typical of stories in the Bible, Moses—the youngest and less able of the brothers—was chosen by God to lead the Hebrews from slavery. God worked amazing deeds through Moses. But God also used the gifts of Aaron and Joshua.

Aaron was the spokesman. He proclaimed God's message as given through Moses. Aaron also was the priest who gave in to the people's demand for a golden calf so that they could worship God in the desert (see *Exodus* 32).

Joshua was Moses' trusted military leader. The tactics used by Joshua to bring the Hebrews into the Promised Land are considered those of a great military mind. Even today, they are studied in military academies around the world.

People of Note

Joshua and Aaron

Joshua was Moses' assistant for politics and military battles. He is introduced in Scripture rather suddenly as a military leader in the first battle against the Amalekites (*Exodus 17:8–14*). In Numbers 11:28, it says that Joshua had been Moses' aide since his youth and that his father's name was Nun.

These few points are all that is known about Joshua's early life. Eventually, this man would become Moses' successor. When the time came for scouts to be sent to spy on the Promised Land, it was Joshua who led the first mission.

Frequently mentioned in the Pentateuch, Moses' older brother Aaron was the first priest of Israel, made one through the anointing of Moses (see: *Leviticus 8:1–8*). Aaron also filled other important roles in the Exodus and in the acceptance of the Covenant at Sinai. When Moses did not believe he was capable of speaking to the people, God made Aaron spokesman.

It is Aaron's role as priest that is of most lasting importance to the people of Israel. Centuries later, Israel's priests would become the political as well as religious rulers. This was the case in the time of Jesus.

- Moses arose early the next morning and wrote down all the words that God had spoken to him.
- He then built an altar at the foot of the mountain, with twelve pillars to represent the twelve tribes of Israel.
- Young men were sent out to offer the blood of young bulls as peace offerings to God.
- Moses took a cup filled with half of the blood and sprinkled it on the altar.
- Moses read from the Covenant and splashed some blood on the people, saying: "This is the blood of the Covenant which the Lord has made with you in accordance with all these words of His" (*Exodus* 24:8).

The ratification, or approval, of the Covenant in blood was very significant to the Hebrews. Because blood was what sustained life, a sacrificial offering of blood was thought to have the power to bind two parties together. The Israelites now shared a common life with God. They became blood brothers and sisters and established lasting family ties with Yahweh.

An Unworthy People   Of course, the fact that the Hebrews had a covenant with God did not mean that they somehow became perfect. Far from it. In fact, even while Moses was on Mount Sinai, they demonstrated their weakness and fear.

The Book of Exodus says that Moses was on Mount Sinai with Yahweh for 40 days receiving the Law. (Note that the number 40 is used here once again. What do you think this might mean?) While he was away, the people began to question whether Moses was ever going to return, and to doubt his leadership. They resolved to continue their journey without him, and decided to fashion images of God to carry with them as they moved forward.

The story tells us that they melted the gold they had taken with them from Egypt, known as the "spoils of Egypt," and used it to fashion a golden calf. The "golden calf" was probably an image of a bull that was commonly used in ancient Middle Eastern religions to represent powerful male gods. The same image was later used by the kings of the Northern Kingdom of Israel when they set up shrines to compete with the Temple in Jerusalem.

Moses Loses His Temper   When Moses returned, he was astonished. After only a few days without him to remind them, the Hebrews had abandoned Yahweh. Moses expressed his anger over this behavior by smashing the tablets of the Law. Although new tablets would be fashioned, and the Covenant sealed, Moses' action marked the beginning of Israel's struggle to become faithful.

This story shows us how difficult it often is to see God's involvement in our lives in the "heat of the moment." Lost in the desert, eager to reach their new home, the Hebrews behaved like spoiled children. They lost patience when they couldn't see immediate results or didn't receive what they wanted. Impatience is a powerful temptation we experience any time we find circumstances pressing down around us.

God's Involvement

The most important thing that the Hebrews learned through their experience of election, deliverance, and covenant was that Yahweh wanted to be involved in their lives. From all of their experiences,

---

◆ MORE ABOUT THE LESSON

Dramatization

For help with the impromptu dramatization, see "Dramatizing Bible Stories," Teacher's Resource 2D. As additional background for this dramatization, the students can read Exodus 24 and 32.

This activity is for fun and meant to involve the students directly with the story. Let students choose the character they wish to play. They may put on the dramatization any way they want to read and/or "translate" it. If some students cannot participate the first time as they would like, do it again, with them as the characters they'd like to try.

the Hebrews learned that God was not far away. Rather, they learned that God was a present, creative power who guided the affairs of nations, and showed deep care and concern for each individual person.

The Israelites marveled at God's involvement with their lives. They wondered why they had been chosen. The only answer they found was that Yahweh had freely chosen them. They had done nothing to merit the gift of the Covenant. In this favor, they discovered God's great mercy. They had been given a special relationship with God.

In the Covenant relationship, the Hebrews became Yahweh's special people. They acquired an identity in Yahweh's love for them and in God's wonderful deeds on their behalf. They were offered God's constant protection and were invited to always remain close to God. That they remained free to act against God's law is a part of the story.

From the first communication to Moses, Yahweh had promised them "a good and spacious land, a land flowing with milk and honey" (*Exodus* 3:8). In response, the people were to follow God's commands gratefully. The Hebrews had every reason to hope: Yahweh was their God and a land would be given to them.

The Old Testament recognizes God as the initiator of a kind, cherished relationship, and the one who was always faithful to that relationship, even when people did not respond with equal fidelity or love. Because people had lots to learn about love, God also taught them by discipline and consequences, just as good parents must sometimes teach their immature children.

The Old Testament traces God's invitation to eternal love that is open to all who wish to belong to the covenanted people.

Have You Considered?

1. How do scientific explanations threaten the idea that it was Yahweh who cared for the Israelites in the wilderness?
2. Explain how the wilderness experience was a time of "formation." Why is character so often formed through difficult situations?
3. The Israelites had to "ratify" the covenant with God. How can we indicate our acceptance of the Covenant today?

Spiritual Reflection

Praying with Exodus

Choose readers. Conduct this prayer service with your classmates on the theme of covenant and the sharing of God's Word.

Reader 1: Yahweh instructs us through the Living Word of Scripture. Let us prepare to receive God's Word by reciting from Psalm 18:

All: I love You, O Lord, my strength, O Lord, my rock, my fortress, my deliverer. My God, my rock of refuge, my shield, the horn of my salvation, my stronghold! Praised be the Lord, I exclaim, and I am safe from my enemies.

Reader 2: A reading from the Book of Exodus.
(Read Exodus 19:1–8. In this reading, the Bible tells us that the Israelites are the Chosen People.)

Reader 2: Let us respond from Psalm 99.

All: The Lord is king; the peoples tremble; he is throned upon the cherubim; the earth quakes. The Lord in Zion is great, He is high above all peoples. Let them praise your great and awesome name; holy is He!

Reader 3: A reading from the Book of Exodus.
(Read Exodus 24: 1–8. In this reading, the Bible tells us that Moses read the book of the Covenant to the Israelites, who promised to be obedient to Yahweh.)

Reader 3: Let us respond from Psalm 117.

All: Praise the Lord, all you nations; glorify Him, all you peoples! For steadfast is His kindness toward us, and the fidelity of the Lord endures forever.

Have You Considered?

1. By providing "rational" explanations for the miracles of manna and quail, among other things, the idea that God was caring for the Israelites appears in jeopardy. Ask students to consider: could God work *through* such rational processes?

2. In the wilderness, the various Israelite tribes united into a single nation, solidified by the receiving of the Covenant on Mt. Sinai. Allow for students to discuss difficult times in their own lives, and the character changes these produced.

3. Various answers are possible. Direct students to think about how we "accept" God's challenges to us through liturgies such as the Mass, as well as in our daily lives through our struggle to live the values of scripture.

Bonus Focus for You ――――――
What desirable leadership qualities have you seen in Moses during your preparation and teaching of this lesson? Where did Moses get his strength and his persistence? Reread Exodus 2:23–4:20. What do you think Moses' inner attitudes were like after all these experiences?

Spiritual Reflection

Pray the Spiritual Reflection as a class. Have the students answer these questions in their journals: "Do you think God's call to Covenant relationship is for you as an individual? for your whole family? for the Church? What would you like to say to God about the call to Covenant?"

MORE ABOUT THE TEXT

"God's Involvement"

These are the main ideas to be drawn about God from all of the material covered in this chapter about Moses and the Covenant: Yahweh wanted to be involved in the life of the Hebrew people; guide was present to them, working on their behalf; they were freely chosen by God through no effort of their own; their identity as a people was tied to this relationship with God.

These understandings are the foundation of all the rest of Israel's history—and the foundation of good Old Testament understanding, too. The New Testament does not refer to them so much, but without these understandings about God and people, Jesus would have no ground on which to build. Be sure the students grasp them well.

Q/A

Section One

1. Contracts are legal agreements which protect rights. Covenants bind people in warm, loving relationships.

2. A parity treaty was formed between equals. In a vassal treaty, a superior power dictated terms to an inferior one.

3. The Covenant between Yahweh and Israel had the three elements of a Hittite vassal treaty: (1) witnesses, (2) the covenant itself, and (3) a ritual act.

4. The Israelites were a people specially chosen by God from among all the nations of earth to receive the Covenant.

5. The 'Apiru were a band of wandering nomads who attacked and defeated many cities in Palestine and Syria around 1350 B.C.E. Some scholars believe that the 'Apiru may be related to the 'Ivri, or Israelites.

6. An Israelite was a citizen of the nation of Israel, which did not exist until the settlement in Canaan. A Hebrew was someone who spoke Hebrew and was born into the Hebrew culture.

7. Monotheism is the belief in the existence of only one God. This is different from professing loyalty to only one God, but believing in many.

8. Akhenaton was the Egyptian pharaoh from 1364–1347 B.C.E. who developed a monotheistic form of the Egyptian religion. The Hebrew slaves would have known of Akhenaton's monotheism from their time in Egypt.

Q/A

Section One

1. How is a covenant different from a contract?
2. What were the differences between a parity treaty and a vassal treaty?
3. How was the covenant God made with the Hebrews like a Hittite vassal treaty?
4. What is the meaning of election?
5. Who were the 'Apiru'?
6. What is the difference between an Israelite and a Hebrew?
7. Define "monotheism."
8. Who was Akhenaton and what is his significance to the Bible?

Section Two

1. Define "formation." How is the experience of the Hebrews in the wilderness an example of this?
2. What are the possible natural explanations for the miracles of the manna, the quail, and the rock water? What is meant by the number 40, as in "40 years in the desert," and "40 days on Mount Sinai"?
3. Who was Joshua? Who was Aaron?
4. How were the Hebrews spared the final plague, the death of the first-born?
5. What is one example of how the Hebrews were dependent on Yahweh in the desert?
6. What is the first commandment of the Decalogue?
7. Who were the witnesses of the covenant between Yahweh and the Hebrews?
8. How was the Covenant ratified?

BIBLE ACTIVITY

Pick two of the following references, read them, and answer the questions. Together, these references narrate the deliverance from Egypt.

1. Exodus 5:1–8:11
   a. Describe the work of the Hebrews in Egypt.
   b. How did Moses react? How did the Lord react?
   c. What magic did Moses perform? What did the Egyptian magicians perform?
   d. What are the first plagues?
   e. Could Moses do anything the Egyptian magicians couldn't?
2. Exodus 8:12–10:29
   a. What plagues does the Lord send by Moses' staff?
   b. What effect do the plagues have on Pharaoh?
   c. Who are the two main opponents seen in these stories?
3. Exodus 11:1–13:16
   a. What was the point of the death of the first-born Egyptians?
   b. Compare 12:1–27 with the rest of the passage. What changes if you leave this part out?
   c. List the similarities and differences in comparing 12:1–27 with 13:1–16.
4. Exodus 13:17–15:21
   a. Who arranged for the Egyptians to pursue the Hebrews?
   b. What exaggerations do you find in these stories? List specific verses and give reasons for your choices.
   c. How did the Hebrews escape from the Egyptian army?

BIBLE ACTIVITY

1. Exodus 5:1–8:11
a. The Hebrews were slaves, whose job included making bricks.
b. Moses was concerned that the Egyptians might not listen to him. The Lord answered by providing signs.
c. Moses had Aaron throw down a staff, which became a serpent. The Egyptian magicians did the same, but Aaron's serpent swallowed theirs.
d. The first plagues included the turning of water into blood, frogs, and gnats.
e. The Egyptian magicians were unable to produce gnats as Moses did.

2. Exodus 8:12–10:29
a. The plague of gnats.
b. Pharaoh remains obstinate despite the evidence of the plagues.
c. God, through Moses, and the pharaoh.

GLOSSARY

- **Armarna letters:** Letters from the princes of Palestine to the Pharaoh that describe a nomadic people that could be the Hebrews.
- **Contract:** A legal agreement establishing rights and responsibilities between two or more people.
- **Covenant:** A bond which unites two or more people in a loving relationship.
- **Decalogue/Ten Commandments:** The ten rules which form the basis of the Law.
- **Deliverance:** The act of God in freeing the Hebrews from captivity.
- **Election:** The idea that God has freely chosen to establish a covenant with the Hebrew people.
- **Exodus:** The Hebrew slaves leaving captivity in Egypt for freedom in the promised land.
- **Hebrews:** A group of nomadic peoples who settled in Egypt and later formed the nation of Israel; part of the "Semitic" cultural group.
- **Israelites:** The nation of people living in Israel under the covenant formed on Mount Sinai.
- **Parity treaty:** An ancient treaty made between two parties of equal social standing.
- **Manna:** A food which the Israelites found in the wilderness while traveling to the promised land.
- **Monotheism:** Belief in only one god.
- **Moses:** The leader chosen from birth to bring the Hebrews out of Egypt and into the promised land.
- **Passover:** The Jewish feast celebrating the "passing over" of their people by God on the night of the final plague in Egypt.
- **Pharaoh:** The king of Egypt.
- **Ratification:** The people's acceptance of the covenant given by God.
- **Theophany:** An appearance by a god to a human being.
- **Vassal treaty:** An ancient treaty made between two parties, one of which was more powerful or from a higher social class than the other; most often it was a treaty between a stronger king and a weaker one.
- **Yahweh:** A Hebrew expression which means "I am who I am;" it was the answer Moses received when he asked God's name.

UNDERSTANDING MORE ABOUT:

Different Bible Translations

As you learned in Chapter 1, the various books of the Bible were written in different languages, generally Hebrew for the Old Testament and Greek for the New Testament. Since you're now reading the Bible in English, you may wonder about how the translations happened.

Actually, there are many different English translations of the Bible. The most popular of all time has been the King James version, produced for James I of England in 1611. This translation is regarded as a masterpiece of English literature, rivaling Shakespeare in beauty of expression.

Because of conflict between Catholics and Protestants, however, Pope Paul V forbade Catholics to read this translation made for a Protestant King. Instead, Catholic scholars translated the Douay-Reims version, named for the towns in France where the translation was produced.

Despite the beauty of their language, both of these translations were made before modern biblical scholarship, and were therefore based on poor-quality manuscripts. Both Catholics and Protestants have since produced more accurate translations today.

The translation used in this book is called *The New American Bible*. The NAB is the translation approved by the American bishops for use in Catholic Churches. Protestant scholars worked with Catholics in putting it together, however, just as Catholics helped prepare the *Revised Standard Version*, the most commonly-used Protestant Bible translation.

Generally, Catholics and Protestants may use one another's Bibles today without fear of "getting something wrong." Differences of opinion, where they exist, are about how to interpret passages, not about what they actually say.

Section Two

1. "Formation" refers to God's shaping of the people into a nation. The long and difficult desert journey provided the setting for this to happen.
2. The manna may refer to small honeydew pellets produced by a scale insect. The quail may have been part of an annual migration which passes over the Sinai peninsula and provides a ready food source. In the miracle of the water, Moses may have removed a lime deposit from a rock, which had been blocking the flow of water. The number 40 probably stands for the generation that passed while the Israelites were traveling.
3. Joshua was the military figure who led the Israelites into the promised land after the death of Moses. Aaron was Moses' brother, whose eloquence was useful in his capacity as Moses' assistant.
4. By painting lamb's blood on their doorposts and lintels, the Israelites were passed over by the angel of death.
5. The Hebrews depended upon God for food, water, and direction.
6. You shall not have other gods besides Me.
7. The Hebrew people, as well as heaven and earth.
8. In a ceremony in which young bulls were slaughtered and blood splattered on the people.

3. Exodus 11:1–13:16
a. To compel pharaoh to allow the Hebrews to depart from Egypt.
b. There would be no reference to the lamb's blood on the doorposts and lintels.
c. The second passage refers to the sacrifice of all first-born male animals and the dedication of all first-born male sons. The first refers to the prescribed ritual for the sacrifice of the Passover lamb. Both place the festival in the month of A*bib*, and both understand Passover as a seven-day feast.

4. Exodus 13:17–15:21
a. God.
b. Many choices are possible. Among them: column of cloud/fire—13:21–22; parting of the sea—14:21–22; number of Egyptians pursuing the Israelites—14:6–9; drowning of the Egyptians—14:26–31; fear of the surrounding nations—15:14–16. Student responses will differ as to the reason for their choices. Direct students to consider what literary purposes are served by such exaggeration.
c. The Egyptians were drowned in the sea.

Chapter Overview

In this chapter, students will encounter the story of David, the greatest king in the history of Israel. As they study the way God led the people through David, students will consider the various ways God provides leadership to us today.

Teaching Objectives

By the end of this chapter students will be able to:

• Recognize the difference between ancient and modern history.

• Perceive the reality of God's guidance behind the story of Israel's entrance into Canaan.

• Be able to discuss the stories of Saul and David with understanding.

• See that real leadership begins with obedience to God's law.

Welcome

Remind the students that you are interested in them as persons. Try to greet all your students by name, letting them know that you care for them as individuals.

What to Do

Ask: "Name some famous people from ancient history." Write the names on the board as they are mentioned. Ask: "Why are these people remembered?" Then say, "What are the names of some of the famous people from the Bible?" Write the names on the board. Then say: "In the Bible, as in history in general, only the most important people are remembered by name." Put on the chalkboard three column titles: "I am Joshua," "I am Samuel," and "I am David." Ask the students what they already know about each of these people, and put their information in the proper column.

Introducing the Chapter

The central theme of this chapter, *leadership*, will be connected to the development of Israel as a nation, as well as the students' own ideas about leadership.

CHAPTER

3

David, Dedicated to Yahweh

1200	**1200 B.C.E.** ● Trojan War ● India: *Upanishads* written **1200–1000** ● Period of the Judges
1100	**1100** ● First Chinese dictionary ● Sun Pyramid built in Mexico **1100–1000** ● Philistines in Canaan **1050** ● Silk made in China ● Samuel **1020** ● Phoenicia imports tin from England ● Saul is king
1000	**1000** ● Nearby nations weak, conquered by David ● David is king ● Genesis begun **960** ● Solomon is king ● Judges written? **950** ● 1 and 2 Samuel begun
900	**900** ● Native Americans in California

Legend

● General History
● Biblical History
● Jewish History
● Books written

I n your many roles as a son or daughter, a friend, a student, and as a member of various clubs and organizations, you have already experienced many different styles of leadership. See if you can identify the leadership styles in the following examples.

• Sixth months before high school graduation, John's family moved 1500 miles to a new city. Although the family protested, his father said **he** would make the final decision.

• Adela loved being in Mr. Birmbaum's third period math class. Though he assigned homework, he never checked it! "High school students are responsible adolescents. If they don't understand a problem they can ask for help. I am not going to play policeman," he said. Adela used her freedom to skip homework assignments

---

◆ MORE ABOUT THE LESSON

Familiar Stories

Often students will be familiar with some of the stories about these characters. They may have seen these events portrayed in movies, paintings, or even as statues. Although they may have seen them, they may also need a little prodding to recall them.

Some of the pieces of art with which the students may be most familiar include: the hymn "Joshua fit the battle of Jericho and the walls came tumbling' down;" Samuel called by God when he was a child; David and Goliath; David and Bathsheba; David having written some psalms or played a harp. If the students remember little or nothing, that's okay. Use this exercise to arouse their interest in the topic.

regularly. Then, reality struck when she did poorly on Mr. Birmbaum's very difficult tests. Adela's grades sunk lower than ever before. Now she wished that Mr. Birmbaum had **forced** her to work.
- Down by 15 points at half-time, Wayne thought that Coach Klemm might really explode in the locker room. Instead, Coach simply noted a few points that needed improving, saying calmly, "If we can cut the lead in half by the start of the fourth quarter we can win." Then, he surprised Wayne and the other players by asking for their opinions. "What do you think we are doing wrong? How can we improve?" At first, the players didn't comment, but then, one by one, they began to suggest how they could play better.

How did these examples of leadership differ? How would you describe these forms of leadership? For the first example, did you choose hard-handed ruler? Dictator? "Do as I say" leadership is all too common. Mr. Birmbaum, in the second example, held people accountable for making responsible choices and bearing the consequences of their own behavior. How did you describe the final example? The coach offered his own opinions and then let the players share theirs. This is known as shared leadership.

Consider the following questions:
- How important is leadership to the success of an activity?
- Are there times when the leader is more important than the members of a group?
- What makes for a good leader?
- From your experience, how are leaders chosen by a group? Why does the group choose the leader that it does?

As you can see, there are a lot of pieces that go into being a leader. Think of these issues as you read about Israel's changing leadership.

A Time of Development

As the Hebrews moved from the desert to their promised land of Canaan, they were clearly under the leadership and rule of Yahweh. As they formed into a nation, they experimented with new forms of leadership.

In Chapter 3, you will see how Israel developed from a loosely confederated people into a unified nation under various types of leaders: from Moses' successor, Joshua, to the military leaders, (the Judges) and to the kings, Saul and David.

Dictators and rulers, hands-off and shared leadership. As you read about the leaders of Israel, take note of how they made use of various leadership styles. How can each be an effective form of leadership? How did each shape the future of the nation?

MORE ABOUT THE TEXT

Making Connections

Students generally enjoy forming connections between the Bible and history. When you introduce the issue of leadership, you may wish to refer to our own national story. In what way was the American revolution about replacing one kind of leadership with another? Why were people dissatisfied with the kind of leadership they had?

From this experience, students can form a hypothesis: leaders who place their own welfare before that of the people they lead will have problems. Keep this hypothesis current in the students' minds as you guide them through the stories of Saul and David.

What to Do

Students are frequently in the position of being led by others. This reality gives them a wide variety of experiences from which to draw as you introduce the subject matter of this chapter.
- Begin the lesson with a prayer, asking God to lead you as you begin a new chapter.
- Have the class reread the story which opens the chapter. Ask them how they have experienced leadership styles similar to those described here.
- In groups, have the class develop a profile of a good leader. Compare the qualities the groups identify.
- Explain that the Bible contains the stories of many different leaders, each with their own style. Despite their diversity as individuals, the Bible suggests that good leaders all share one characteristic—a trusting faith in God. In this chapter, we will consider the story of one of the greatest leaders in the biblical story, King David.

Extend the Activity   Have the students read the opening spread pages, including "A Time of Development." Questions are scattered through these paragraphs. Call on volunteers to respond to each of them.

Development

Using the Timeline

Ask the students to examine the timeline and find the three leaders mentioned in the welcoming exercise. Another Israelite leader is mentioned; can they find him? (It is King Saul.)

Ask the students to locate and mention any timeline information that is not related directly to Palestine. Do they know what these items are? If not, have them look them up in a dictionary or atlas. Point out that the story of ancient Israel is part of the story of human history, and that the people of Israel experienced the same forces as other ancient cultures (war, an agricultural-based economy, and limited literacy). In this way, students should come to see they already have a "head start" in understanding the biblical story.

LESSON ONE (pages 38–39)

◆ The Deuteronomic History

Teaching Objectives

By the end of this lesson students will be able to:
- Define the term "Deuteronomic," and explain why this portion of the Bible is called "Deuteronomic."
- Explain the difference in intent between ancient and modern history writers.
- Express how this difference between ancient and modern historians shapes their own understanding of past events.

Development

What to Do

Ask the students how they might go about writing a history of their town and the surrounding country. What would they do? Whom would they consult? Where would they get information? What questions would they ask their informants? What kind of information would they consider the most important? Why? List their responses on the chalkboard. Have the students read "The Deuteronomic History" and "The Bible in Context" feature. Discuss with them how the Deuteronomic history helped the Israelites understand the meaning of the Exile.

Practicing the Skills

What to Do

Explain to students that many mistakes can be made in reading the Bible if one does not understand what kind of literature is being read. As an illustration, bring a newspaper to class. Have students go through the paper to determine the different styles of writing they find there. Help them recognize the difference between hard news, sports, columnists, the comics, editorials (including the editorial cartoon), and the horoscope.

Have students read "Ancient vs. Modern History." When they're finished, have a class discussion to form a list on the board of the right expectations to have of these books, as well as some examples of wrong expectations.

Israel Enters the Promised Land

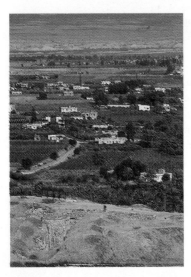

The books of Joshua, Judges, 1 and 2 Samuel, and 1 and 2 Kings record ancient Israel's national history. For this reason, they were very important to later generations of Israelites, who looked to them for inspiration and comfort. To understand them, we need to look at the circumstances in which they were written. Because they open with the entry into the promised land, we also need to see how that entrance happened in order to follow the rest of the story.

Learning Objectives for Section One

By the end of this section, you will be able to:
- Explain the importance of the Deuteronomic history.
- Explain the difference between ancient and modern styles of writing history.
- Describe how the Israelites gradually occupied Canaan.
- Recognize the structure of the tribal system in ancient Israel and describe how it worked.

◆ The Deuteronomic History

The events described in Joshua, Judges, and 1 and 2 Samuel took place between the years 1,200–900 B.C.E., although these books were not finalized until several hundred years later. To understand their message, we need to take a closer look at the circumstances in Israel when they were written into their final form.

We will see in Chapter 7 that around 587 B.C.E., the Babylonians became a strong military power in the Middle East, defeated the Israelites, and took them into "exile." This means that they took the Israelites as prisoners and forced them to live in Babylon. They destroyed all that the Israelites had built: the homes, businesses, and places of worship. This was a terrible blow to their faith because they believed they were God's Chosen People. How could God allow such a horrible thing to happen?

The authors and editors of Joshua, Judges, 1 and 2 Samuel, and 1 and 2 Kings thought they had the answer. This disaster had happened not because God forgot about them, or because God was not powerful enough to protect them, but because Israel had sinned and violated the Covenant. This understanding would explain how Israel could be the Chosen People and still suffer such a humiliating defeat.

The writers of these books drew on the memories of the various tribes and smaller groups that had come together to make up the nation of Israel, and put together its history. The writers designed this history to show that Israel's punishment in the exile was deserved because of its misbehavior, and that God is never unfaithful to the Covenant made with Moses. Even in the Exile, if the people were to turn their backs on their sinfulness, God would restore their hopes.

This understanding of Israel's history is what we see in Joshua, Judges, 1 and 2 Samuel, and 1 and 2 Kings. It's called the "Deuteronomic history" because the authors felt that Israel had sinned by not obeying the laws found in Deuteronomy.

◆ MORE ABOUT THE LESSON

Why Did it Happen?

Choose one or two recent major events (wars, natural catastrophes, or others). Make sure the students have heard of the event, or inform them of the events yourself. Be as detailed as you possibly can, offering interpretation as you see fit. Check to see that the students understand the implications and consequences of this event.

Then, have them restate the event as if they were the Deuteronomic historian. What viewpoint would this writer have applied to these events? Have several students read their explanations aloud. When each statement is made, ask the rest of the students whether they agree or disagree with it. They should provide an answer whichever side of the argument they might take.

The Bible in Context

Developing Traditions

The Deuteronomic history contains stories, legends, and historical records from a variety of Israel's ancient tribes and clans. How were all of these traditions combined into one?

Such a historical collections of stories is actually not so unique. The United States, for example, has a single history, yet, in the beginning, there were thirteen colonies with separate backgrounds and separate histories. People had come to the New World from different countries for different reasons. Later, the French traditions of the Louisiana Territory, as well as the Spanish traditions that had developed in the Far West, were added to the history of America.

In the same way, Israel's history is the collected stories of many different people who shared a common belief in God and an acceptance of the Covenant.

Ancient vs. Modern History

The history of Israel was not invented. The Deuteronomic historians (or "D") drew on much older sources in order to compile their history. They used the official records written down during the time when Israel had strong kings. For other periods, such as the time of Joshua and the Judges, they relied primarily on stories passed down by word of mouth.

The Deuteronomic account is historically accurate in general and can often be confirmed by sources outside the Bible. There are places, however, where mistakes were made, the roles of certain people are exaggerated, or the significance of events are either over emphasized or down-played. In other words, there are places where this record is not accurate by modern historical standards.

Like all ancient historians, the Deuteronomic authors did not view their task as "getting all the facts straight." This is a very modern idea. Instead, they felt their job was to communicate the meaning of their history, what it was "all about." In so doing, they felt free to edit their sources to make their point.

This approach to history is one of the basic differences between ancient and modern historians. Today, historians are criticized if they are inaccurate about dates and places. In the ancient world, historians were given a great deal of liberty with such matters. Their purpose was to explain what it all meant, what the inner purpose of the past had been.

By these standards, the Deuteronomic history is excellent history indeed.

As we read these books, then, we should not be surprised to see minor contradictions or misrepresentations of what "actually happened." These are to be expected because of the very nature of ancient history. Focus, instead, on the message the Deuteronomic authors try to communicate; it is their understanding of God's faithfulness to the Covenant made with Moses and ratified by the people of Israel.

Have You Considered?

1. Name an example of how the circumstances in which a book, movie, or television show is put together influence its message.
2. How can a story be made-up and yet still be true? Give an example with your answer.
3. The Deuteronomic historian's answer to the question "Why does God allow bad things to happen to people?" was that the people sinned. What's your answer to that question? Include the reasons for your answer.

Ancient historians like the famous Greek Thucydides, shown here, had a different approach to history than do modern historians.

Bust of Thucydides. Fifth Century B.C.E.

Recall

Ask students to compare the way an ancient historian would cover some modern event as opposed to the way a modern historian would cover the same event.

Connect

What to Do

Homework Assignment: Have the students look up and read Joshua 23:14–16, Judges 3:7–9, and 1 Samuel 2:9. Ask them to put in their own words the ideas expressed in these verses. If the students were to apply these ideas to modern events, what might they mean?

What's Next?

What to Do

Mention that Joshua is the main topic of the next class session, that he was a fine military leader, and that they will learn much more about him.

Have You Considered?

1. Many examples are possible here. Students may wish to consider how *Uncle Tom's Cabin* clearly reflects the context of black slavery in America, and how *Night* by Elie Wiesel comes out of the holocaust experience.
2. Many answers are possible. Consider books students may have read, such as *Catcher in the Rye*, and the "truth" about problems facing adolescents which this work of fiction contains.
3. Allow for a variety of answers to this question. Let students discuss how their experiences influenced their answers, and how this sheds light on points made in this section about how the experience of the Exile influenced the point of view of the Deuteronomic historian.

Bonus Focus for You ——

Read 2 Samuel 22 and 23:1–7. Assuming that David did in fact compose these songs, do you think King David would have agreed with the Deuteronomic historians' interpretation of history?

MORE ABOUT THE TEXT

Livy

The Roman historian Livy is a good example of how ancient history-writing differs from that composed by modern writers. Livy's history of the Julio-Claudian emperors of Rome emphasizes their personal and moral failings, and barely touches on the events modern historians would be interested in: the economy, trade, or political and social forces. Livy was convinced that the success of the nation depended upon the moral stature of the leader, and wrote his history from this point of view.

Livy wrote during a period of great moral decay in Rome and stressed that his purpose for writing was to tell a moral story. Livy considered Rome's greatness to be founded upon discipline, both personal and national. Rome began to decay, wrote Livy, when the nation's discipline began to fade.

◆ The Entry Into the Promised Land

Teaching Objectives

By the end of this lesson students will be able to:

• Recognize the differences between how the Book of Joshua describes the entry of the Hebrews into Canaan and how modern historians understand it.

• Understand how the system of governance through the 12 tribes developed and name some of the problems found in that system.

Welcome

Greet students, by name if possible. Remind them of what was accomplished during your last meeting, and ask them to recap what they learned.

What to Do

Form small groups. Ask the students to imagine that they are nomads, living in tents and pasturing animals. They want to conquer the towns in a settled land. What would they need to consider in order to accomplish their plan?

Introducing the Lesson

Teaching Objectives

By the end of this lesson students will be able to:

• Understand why the Book of Joshua describes the Hebrews' entry into Canaan in terms of a military conquest.

• Follow the story as presented by the archaeological record.

• Understand how the 12 tribes formed out of pledges of loyalty to the Covenant.

---

in the Spotlight

Have the students read "in the Spotlight." Make sure they can recognize the different ways the territory of the Promised Land is named, depending on the particular time in history. This will save much confusion as the land is called by these different names.

◆ The Entry into the Promised Land

The point made at the beginning of Joshua is clearly that Yahweh continued to lead the Israelites to the land that was promised to them even after Moses' death. Yahweh said to Moses' aide, Joshua: "As I promised Moses, I will deliver to you every place where you set foot" (Joshua 1:3). The Book of Joshua presents a record of Yahweh's faithfulness to this promise.

Joshua

In many ways, Joshua himself is portrayed as the ideal leader of Israel, one who keeps God's law in its entirety. In so doing, Joshua was promised that Yahweh would be with him "by day and by night." Yahweh told him: "Do not fear or be dismayed, for the Lord, your God, is with you wherever you go" (Joshua 1:9).

In the book that bears his name, Joshua is portrayed as a great general and military leader. Today, a statue of Joshua stands outside West Point, the Army's military academy, in recognition of his great leadership.

Israel's entry into the promised land is pictured as one great victory after another. Probably the best-known of these battles was at the city of Jericho.

When the Israelites attacked Jericho, Yahweh directed them to circle the city seven times as the priests led the Ark of the Covenant before them. According to Joshua, the priests blew the ram's horn after the seventh time around, and the walls of the city crumbled. The Israelites swarmed in and captured the city.

This episode is told in highly dramatic fashion by the Deuteronomic historian. It illustrates the author's total confidence that Joshua's victories happened through the power of Yahweh.

The Archaeological Record While the fall of Jericho's walls makes an interesting story, archaeological evidence suggests that the Deuteronomic historians may have exaggerated how things actually happened. While the land of Canaan was eventually won by the Israelites, the events of the conquest were far more complicated and took a much longer time than the first 12 chapters of Joshua suggest. Even though all the details of the settlement of Canaan are not known, a general picture can be pieced together.

---

in the Spotlight
Canaan

You may have noticed that we have used a variety of words to refer to the land where the Hebrews settled: Israel, Canaan, Palestine. All three of these terms refer to basically the same territory, a stretch of land along the eastern coast of the Mediterranean Sea. Generally, we call this place "Canaan" before the kingdom of Saul, "Israel" after that. "Palestine" refers to the whole territory after the kingdom of Israel split apart in 922 B.C.E. After that date, only the northern portion of the territory should technically be called "Israel."

The Situation in Canaan In Canaan, around 1200 B.C.E., when the Hebrews first entered the land, cities were self-governed; there was no national or larger government. They made their own laws and fought their own battles. The territory of a city also included the farmlands surrounding it, that were worked by the city's inhabitants.

Cities often fought among themselves for control of territory and resources such as water and wood. This conflict between cities explains why Canaan was so vulnerable to attacks by the Hebrews: it was divided against itself. In addition to this disunity,

• **There was no standing army.** Most Canaanites were farmers and traders, becoming soldiers only when necessary to defend their town.

• **Alliances between cities were rare,** and the defeat of a city was generally ignored by its neighbors.

This disunity also helps to explain why Canaan was so often ruled by foreign powers such as Egypt, the Hittites, and the Philistines.

The Canaanites did share a common fertility religion. This means that their myths and rituals were concerned with keeping the land and animals fertile, so that crops would grow and herds would have offspring. But even though the Canaanites held certain religious attitudes in common, there was wide variation in their practical understanding of religion, which intensified the disunity of their community and political habits.

A Gradual Conquest

Over a period of time, small groups of Israelites won small battles in the hills of Canaan. Military

---

MORE ABOUT THE TEXT

Joshua

The story of Joshua at Jericho appeals widely to the imagination. From a purely physical viewpoint, the events as described in this chapter may seem unlikely. Yet, the students will benefit from thinking about a couple of additional factors that are often not mentioned. What psychological effect would Joshua's actions have on the people of Jericho? Would this have changed the way they fought the people of Jericho.

A second factor to consider is the known power of rhythm: soldiers are not allowed to march in step across a bridge, because the rhythmic vibrations can damage the structure. Any steady rhythm applied to a physical object eventually affects it. Would the marching, horns and shouting possibly have affected Jericho? You will not be able to answer these questions, but discussing them is a way of taking the biblical text seriously, though not literally.

Scripture Workshop

Renewing the Covenant

The people of Israel renewed the Covenant with God regularly. It was not enough for the Israelites to express belief in the power of goodness of Yahweh. They also had to express their commitment to live as God directed. The Book of Joshua captures the power of this ceremony and its importance in the life of Israel.

Read about the annual Covenant renewal ceremony in Joshua 24:1–28. Compare this with Joshua 8:30–35. Then answer these questions:

1. What mighty deeds of Yahweh were retold at the ceremony?
2. What were the requirements for new members?
3. How did the people respond?
4. What, besides Covenant renewal, was done on that day?

individual towns and settlements as they were able in order to gain land on which to settle.

As they were victorious in these battles, additional towns and territories came under their control and the total number of people belonging to the people of Israel increased. Within a few years, the Hebrews were able to put together a large, well-trained, and battle tested fighting force that was able to defeat larger settlements in battle.

Pledging Allegiance to the Covenant   Not all of Israel's success came about through battle. Some opposing clans and towns probably joined with the Hebrews voluntarily because of the special covenant relationship they had with Yahweh. These people would hear of the Hebrews' deliverance from the Egyptians and the stories of God's love and care for them in the desert.

All who joined the Israelites did so by pledging their allegiance to Yahweh and by promising to keep the Covenant. For a town to join the already covenanted clans was a big step. It required the approval of all the clans when they gathered together at an annual, solemn ceremony in which the

successes in the hill country gave the core group of Hebrews a foothold in the new land. However, their first expedition could not have taken them much further than the rugged mountains for these reasons:

1. **The Egyptians controlled the major cities in the plains.** The Hebrew warriors were no match for the powerful Egyptian army.
2. **The Hebrews were guerrilla fighters.** They took advantage of the rough terrain to overcome their limited wood and stone weapons and their lack of horses. In the wide open areas of the plains, they were at a disadvantage.
3. **The Philistines.** A people who lived in the southwest coastal area—had iron tools, iron weapons, and they also used chariots. They held a long-lasting monopoly on the making of iron. The use of chariots with iron armoring and the use of iron tools became part of Israel's culture only in the time of King David.

Growing Town by Town   Israel could not have put together a large military effort. They did not have iron weapons and did not have a standing army. The Israelites did, however, continue military attacks on

Philistine spearhead. Twelfth Century B.C.E.

The Philistines used their control of iron making technology to build a strong army.

◆ MORE ABOUT THE LESSON

A Gradual Conquest

Limited evidence exists about the Hebrew's entrance into Canaan. Much of that comes from the study of small hillside farms and seaside communities. What evidence there is supports the idea of the Hebrews gradually establishing a community among the Canaanites and all of the other groups over a period of several hundred years. A close reading of the Bible itself shows that the Hebrews had to defend themselves constantly, so no decisive battle was ever won.

While it might be possible that everything happened as the Bible suggests—after all, everything is possible for God—archaeological evidence implies that the biblical account is more interested in God's mighty deeds than it is with historical, factual evidence.

What to Do

Have the students read Joshua 5:13–6:25 (the legend of Jericho's collapse) silently to themselves. Ask them to imagine the scenes as they read. What do they think of the story?

Development

What to Do

1. Have the students read the lesson's opening paragraph and "Joshua." Ask the students which they enjoyed the most, the dramatic story in Joshua or the textbook's explanation.
2. Have the students read "A Gradual Conquest." Using a topographical map or a Bible atlas, have the students locate (or point out and describe yourself): the southeastern hill country; the cities in the plains; the territory and cities of the Philistines on the coast. Remind the students of the opening exercise. What would aggressive nomads hiding in the hill country need to conquer the rest of Canaan?

Have the students read "Twelve Tribes." Look together at the map of the "twelve tribes" on page 42. Note the areas dominated by "northern" tribes, and the territory of the "southern" tribes.

Scripture Workshop

1. The ceremony described in Joshua 24:1–28 told of God's call of Abraham and his guidance of the patriarchs, his liberation of the Hebrews from slavery in Egypt, and his powerful help in settling the land of Canaan.
2. New members had to be willing to cast off their belief in foreign gods and worship Yahweh alone.
3. New members agreed to obey Yahweh in all ways.
4. Joshua set up a stone in the Shechem sanctuary as a sign of the people's commitment to obey Yahweh.

Practicing the Skills

What to Do

Have the students complete the second "Bible Activity" on page 52.

Recall

Have the students work in pairs to write their answers to "Q/A," Section One in the Chapter 3 Review.

Connect

What to Do

If possible, invite someone who was born and raised in another culture to talk with the students about his or her experience.

What's Next?

What to Do

Explain that securing land to live on was only one of many challenges faced by the Hebrews as they entered Canaan. One of the challenges they faced was forming a style of government. That is the subject of the next lesson.

Have You Considered?

1. The Deuteronomic historian emphasized the mightiness of Yahweh, as reflected in the military triumphs. This message would have been important to the recently conquered Jews. Allow students to discuss how similar self-doubts might lead people to exaggerate their own importance.

2. The concept of being "chosen" may lead people to think that they are superior to others, and therefore to think that it is okay to abuse others in order to achieve their own personal ends. Give students the freedom to discuss this with examples of their own.

3. A loose confederation makes it difficult to coordinate actions and resources, something especially important when the nation is facing a military threat.

Bonus Focus for You ───

Look again at Joshua 24:15. This choice to renew our faith in the covenant is faced not only at special times of recommitment (as in Covenant renewal), but during every day of our lives. Ponder the ways in which you make the choice to renew your relationship with God daily.

members renewed their allegiance to Yahweh. The new members would also recite these pledges. This ceremony occurred, at least for a while, in the town of *Shechem*. Eventually, Shechem became the religious center of the Covenant confederation. By joining the Covenant, people became "children of Israel," or Israelites. In time, no distinctions were made between those who professed the Covenant early and those who came to it later. Their common Covenant brought them a common historical tradition—roots for all of them together.

Twelve Tribes

As more groups joined or were conquered by Israel, a tribal system developed. There were ten northern tribes, the most powerful of which were *Ephraim and Mannaseh*. The two southern tribes were *Judah and Benjamin*.

Only commitment to the Covenant and Yahweh's leadership held these 12 tribes together. Each of the 12 tribes lived independently of the others, each had its own territory, life, and form of government. There was no one political system that united them, only the Covenant. It would be as if there were no federal government in the United States, only states.

They did, however, come to each other's aid in times of military crises. The tribes would band together to face the common enemy as needed. Afterwards, they would go their separate ways.

This sense of tribal independence never left the Israelites. As we shall see, it is a major reason why the unified kingdom of Israel lasted only 100 years.

Have You Considered?

1. Why do you suppose the Deuteronomic historian placed such emphasis on Joshua's military success? When are you tempted to over-emphasize your own accomplishments?
2. When Europeans colonized the Americas, many looked to the Book of Joshua to justify their behavior. How does this illustrate a possible misunderstanding of the idea that someone is "chosen" by God?
3. At first, the United States tried a system of government similar to that used by the 12 tribes. Under the Articles of Confederation, each state was almost totally independent from the others. Why do you think this system was abandoned? What would the problems with it be?

Israel's Twelve Tribes

Each of the 12 tribes had its own territory, as shown here. In addition, each tribe had its own collection of traditional legends and songs. Eventually, many of these legends and songs were combined into historical works such as the Deuteronomic history and into collections of reflections and observations like the Proverbs. Consult Joshua 13–21 to see how the land was divided between the tribes.

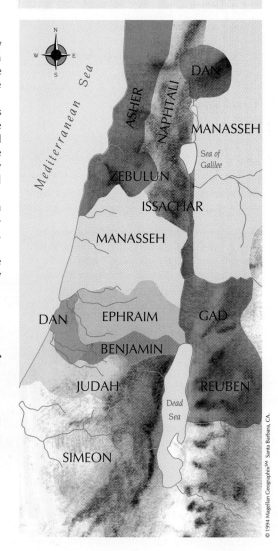

© 1994 Magellan Geographix℠ Santa Barbara, CA.

MORE ABOUT THE TEXT

The 12 Tribes

The number 12 is a special number in the Middle East. Although it was an ideal number among the Israelites, the naming of the 12 tribes developed much later. For this reason, the map of the tribal territories above is a much later reconstruction, projected back onto earlier events.

Every group that joined the covenant brought its own culture, customs and legends. The histories, when they were later written, found ways of including much of the collective beliefs and practices left after the new groups joined the covenant relationship. These differences in culture and background are the largest part of the reason that the "Twelve tribes" could not maintain a genuine unity: the Covenant was, in practical terms, not enough by itself to hold such widely divergent political and cultural groups together.

Israel Gets a King

Bernini, *David*, Seventeenth Century.

After the Hebrews moved into Canaan, each tribe went its own way, with its own laws and leaders. From time to time, a crisis would come along that required several tribes to work together. When that happened, God would inspire a temporary military leader called a "judge," to lead the tribe. Over time, however, the Israelites decided they didn't like this system, and they asked Samuel for a king. This began the monarchy that produced Israel's most famous leaders: Saul, David, and Solomon. We'll follow this amazing story in this section.

Learning Objectives for Section Two

By the end of this section, you will be able to:

- Define: judge.
- Explain the meaning of theology and how it is used in the Book of Judges.
- Identify: Samuel, Saul, David.
- Describe God's Covenant with David.

◆ The Judges

In ancient Israel the word "judge" meant something quite different from how the term is used today. In modern times, a judge is someone who rules in a court of law. When you hear the word judge you may imagine a person dressed in a black robe and called "your honor."

That's not what the word meant for the Israelites. For them, a judge was someone inspired by God to lead them in battle and govern them afterwards. In the Book of Judges we hear the stories of these inspired leaders.

Theological Ideas in Judges

A "theology" expresses one's understanding of God. In writing the Book of Judges, the Deuteronomic historians were clearly guided by certain beliefs about God and the Covenant. The writers make the following theological points:

- When Israel followed Yahweh and the Covenant, she lived in peaceful prosperity.
- When Israel lost the awareness that Yahweh, and only Yahweh, was in charge, suffering followed (usually at the hands of a foreign group that would threaten an Israelite area or town).
- The people would cry out to Yahweh for help, and help would be granted.
- After their rescue, they would resume their careful practice of the Covenant, at least for awhile.

This pattern which the Deuteronomic historian saw as prevalent during the time of the judges (B.C.E. 1200–1120) is summarized as:

1. Sin
2. Punishment
3. Repentance
4. Deliverance

The theology here is very simple: when Israel obeys the demands of the Covenant, God keeps it safe; when Israel disobeys, it suffers disaster.

MORE ABOUT THE TEXT

The Pattern

The students should see that the "sin" in the pattern of "sin, punishment, repentance and deliverance" was forgetting Yahweh and worshipping other gods; that the "punishment" was the serious threat to their lives that they experienced; that the "repentance" was when the people admitted their wrongdoings and begged Yahweh for help; and that the "deliverance" was Yahweh's saving action.

This pattern is consistent through each story of the judges. Look at how many of the stories begin:

- "Because the Israelites had offended the Lord by forgetting the Lord" (Judges 3:7).
- "Again the Israelites offended the Lord" (Judges 3:12).
- "After Ehud's death, however, the Israelites again offended the Lord" (Judges 4:1).
- "The Israelites offended the Lord" (Judges 6:1).

SECTION TWO

LESSON THREE (pages 43-45)

◆ The Judges

Welcome

What to Do

Express your pleasure in being with your students. Briefly remind them of what was learned during the previous class session.

Introducing the Lesson

Teaching Objectives

By the end of this lesson students will be able to:

- Learn the meaning of the term "judge."
- Understand how the Deuteronomic historian viewed the judges.
- Define "charismatic."
- Identify two major lessons to be learned from the judges.

What To Do

Find the Period of the Judges on the timeline, page 36. Have the students read the introduction to Section Two and the first two paragraphs under "The Judges." Then have them read Judges 1:10–20. Explain that this passage is the basis for understanding Israelite life according to the rest of the Book of Judges. Invite the students to ask questions. Be sure the students understand these basic paragraphs in Judges.

Development

What to Do

1. Explain that the Book of Judges is about what happened to a number of ancient clans or tribes after they had joined the Covenant people. They are not chronological or given in any special order. They are written so that the pattern of events is the same for each judge. Have the students read "Theological Ideas in Judges" and "Charismatic Leadership." Have the students name what the Israelites did to match steps 1–4.

2. Read "Lessons Learned from the Judges." See if students can give examples, either from history or their own experience, of leadership coming from an unlikely source.

Practicing the Skills

What to Do

Ask the students to complete Bible Activity number 1, on page 52. Form small groups. Students are to discuss how the pattern in Judges can be applied to life today, naming concrete events in their own life or that of their family, church, or city, which demonstrate this pattern.

Recall

Do an impromptu dramatic reading of Judges 6:1–7:22. Invite volunteers to make the reading "come alive."

Connect

What to Do

Homework Assignment: Ask the students to watch the news or read a newspaper to find stories which include one or more steps in the pattern of the judges they have discussed today.

What's Next?

Read Judges 8:22–23 aloud. Ask students what they think this passage means. Tell them, "This is a sign of things to come."

Have You Considered?

1. Allow for a variety of student responses. Possible examples include: Martin Luther King Jr., George Washington, Lech Walesa. Expect and even encourage sports figures to be mentioned.

2. Students should be encouraged to explore several possible ways in which God's faithfulness has been revealed to them.

3. Encourage students to think about examples they have personally witnessed, as opposed to historical events they know only from class work.

Bonus Focus for You

In the story of Gideon, especially 7:1–8, consider that God wanted Gideon and all the people to know that it was the Lord who was the conqueror of Midian, not Gideon. At some stage of spiritual growth, you may be "stripped" in a similar way to bring you to a deeper level of trust in the Lord's action in your life.

Tissot, *Jael Smote Sisera and Slew Him.* Nineteenth Century.

The Book of Judges retells the brave deeds of the Hebrew people as they fought to survive. This picture shows an event recorded in Judges 4:17–22.

Charismatic Leadership

When a tribe was faced with attack, the spirit of Yahweh would "fall upon" an individual, making that man or woman strong and full of initiative. That person would then rally soldiers from the nearby covenanted clans to help defeat the invader. These individual leaders, given their strength from Yahweh, are called the judges.

The style of leadership common to the judges is sometimes called "charismatic leadership." "Charismatic" means "empowered by the spirit." Today, we use this word to refer to any leader who has the power to move and inspire his or her followers to action.

Lessons Learned from the Judges

One lesson that can be learned from the Book of Judges is that our lives are better when we remember God and obey the teachings of the Covenant. It is not that God punishes us when we fail to live up to our promises, but rather that every action in life brings with it definite consequences. Actions that take people far from God have terrible consequences. But every time this happened to a clan in Israel, they were rescued from the crisis by Yahweh.

The Book of Judges also teaches the lesson that the people God chooses will often be the unexpected choice. One of the most powerful and important judges, Deborah, was a woman. She led Israel into battle when all the male generals lost their nerve. It may have shocked many Israelites to hear that Deborah (and not a man) was giving the orders. But then again, since Yahweh was in charge, whomever Yahweh chose would be followed into battle.

Each of the stories of the judges tells how Yahweh acted on behalf of the people. Each time some of the Israelites were in trouble because of their disobedience, Yahweh inspired a judge who saved them and led them to victory. Through each battle, Yahweh was with the people. Again and again, the Covenant with Yahweh was strengthened by God's faithfulness and the people were once again drawn to repentance and prayer, deliverance and victory.

Have You Considered?

1. Share an example of how a charismatic leader can lead people into a situation against overwhelming odds. The example may be historical or from current events.

2. How has God's faithfulness been revealed in your lifetime? Explain.

3. Describe an experience, similar to that of Deborah, where prejudice against a certain group has been challenged by dramatic action from a member of that group.

◆ MORE ABOUT THE LESSON

Charisma

As you develop this topic of charismatic leadership, you might wish to develop the root meaning of the word for the students. The English word "charism" comes from the Greek word meaning "gift." In a religious sense, all charisms are gifts from God. The word is variously defined as a special power, a personal magic for leadership that arouses loyalty, and a magnetic appeal.

Students should be able to distinguish "charismatic" leadership from "institutional" leadership. Have them apply the distinction to their own school, or to the local community. Charismatic leaders inspire people through the force of their own personality, or the ideas they represent, but such leadership is unpredictable and, in the long-term, undependable. Such considerations will help students to prepare for the issues raised in the next section.

Careers of the Judges

When you look at this chart, do not imagine that these careers should be added together or that they are in sequential order. Each judge's work (and the length of success) was for a certain local group—a clan within Israel—sometimes enlarged by contributions of warriors from other local clans. Later, when the stories were collected, they were all recognized to be Israelite judges, from whom all Israel had benefited and learned.

Name	Reference	Success	Result
Othniel	Judges 3:7–11	Defeated King of Aram	40 years of peace
Ethud	Judges 3:12–30	Defeated 10,000 Moabites	80 years of peace
Shamgar	Judges 3:31	Slew 600 Philistines	Unknown
Deborah and Barak	Judges 4:1–5:31	Defeated Canaanite army	40 years of peace
Gideon	Judges 6:1–8:35	Defeated legions of Midian	40 years of rest
Tola	Judges 10:1 and 2	Unknown	Led for 23 years
Jair	Judges 10:3–5	Unknown	Led for 22 years
Jephthah	Judges 11:1–12:7	Slew Ammonites, Amorites	Led for 6 years
Ibzan	Judges 12:8–10	Unknown	Led for 7 years
Elon	Judges 12:11–12	Unknown	Led for 10 years
Abdon	Judges 12:13–15	Unknown	Led for 8 years
Samson	Judges 13–16	Slew Philistines	Led for 20 years
Samuel	1 Samuel 1 and 25:1	Anointed Kings of Israel	Saul and the monarchy

◆ A King Is Anointed

Against enemies such as the Philistines, with their trained army, iron weapons, and chariots, Israel's way of waging war—a charismatic leader calling fighters together in a time of need—was not effective. Lacking a central organization, the Hebrews were no match for its neighboring nations, each ruled by a king.

Samuel

In approximately 1040 B.C.E., Samuel, the most influential of the judges, led the forces of Israel. Samuel was also a prophet. Samuel lived in Ramah, where he led a group of prophets dedicated to protecting Israel's traditional worship against pagan practices. Some of the elders (leaders) of Israel came to Samuel, asking him to anoint a king.

The Only King of Israel Samuel was not enthusiastic about the requests for a king. Yahweh was the one and only King of Israel for Samuel. For the people to want a human king seemed, to Samuel, a direct rejection of God. Yahweh had brought the people into the land and protected them in times of threat. Why should the people now reject Yahweh's protection and promise? Didn't they know that an Israelite king would be a tyrant, just like the neighboring kings?

Samuel warned them that any king he might appoint would:

- Take your sons and assign them to his chariots and horses.
- Set them to do his plowing and his harvesting.

Samuel, portrayed here in the movie, King David, was the last judge of Israel.

LESSON FOUR (pages 45–47)

◆ A King is Anointed

Welcome

Form the class into two "political parties." One group is the "we want the judges" party, while the other is the "we want a king" party. Each group is to come up with as many reasons as they can in five minutes to support their side and to argue against the other side. Record their findings on the chalkboard. Make it a contest to see who can think of the most and best arguments.

Introducing the Lesson

Teaching Objectives

By the end of this lesson students will be able to:

- Understand why the people wanted a king, and why Samuel resisted their demands.
- Identify Saul as the first king of Israel, and explain why he lost favor with the Lord.

What to Do

Ask the students to share their homework. Together, see if the class has found at least one contemporary instance of each step of the pattern of the judges.

Development

What to Do

1. Have the students read "Samuel." Discuss the reasons why the people wanted a king. Do the students agree that ancient Israel needed a king?

   Ask students to reflect on our own government in light of Samuel's reservations about the role of a king. Are his concerns basically on target for our own society? If so, would students agree that we would be better off without a strong central government? Have them connect their observations with what they know about ancient Israel.

2. Have the students read "King Saul" in their text. Ask them what they think of Saul from this description. Have the students imagine that they are Saul, and read 1 Samuel 12:6–25. Ask them: "If Saul heard all this today, how would he feel about being king?"

3. Today's scholars think Israel could not have survived under the leadership of the judges. What do you think might have happened if the Israelites had kept the charismatic leaders and held fast to Yahweh as their only "king"?

Practicing the Skills

What to Do

Form three small groups. Have Group One read 1 Samuel 8 and list the people's reasons for wanting a king. Have Group Two read 1 Samuel 9:1–10:16. If this were the only story about Saul becoming king, how would we think it happened? Have Group Three read 1 Samuel 10:17–11:15. Taken alone, how does this story suggest Saul became king? Ask the groups to share their results. Discuss with them the mixture of stories and see if the students can discover their common element.

Scripture Workshop

1. Five common elements are:

a. the barrenness of the wife

b. the wife prays for a child

c. an announcement to the wife that God will reward her faithfulness

d. the wife conceives a male child

e. the child is dedicated to God

2. Differences in the story between the two births:

a. Samuel's mother was reproached for her barrenness.

b. Samuel's mother begged God for a child.

c. An angel appeared to Samson's mother twice to tell her how to raise the child.

3. Allow for several possible responses. Historically, the most probable reason is to signify that this person was chosen from birth by God for a special task.

Scripture Workshop

Birth Stories

As you learned when you studied about the life of Moses, ancient literature concentrated much attention on the events surrounding a great leader's birth. The more unique the events surrounding a birth, the greater the leader. This is seen once again in the stories of the judges. Look up Judges 13:1–25 and 1 Samuel 1:1–28. The first reading is the story of the birth of Samson, and the second is the story of the Birth of Samuel.

1. Make a list of all the elements the two stories have in common (include at least five items).

2. How do these two stories differ? Make another list and include at least three differences.

3. Answer this question: Why do you suppose the Bible so often includes a story about the miraculous birth of an important character?

- Use your daughters as ointment makers, as cooks, and as bakers.
- Take the best of your fields, tithe your crops, and give the revenue to his eunuchs and his slaves.

When this takes place, you will complain against the king whom you have chosen, but on that day the LORD will not answer you.

(1 Samuel 8:10–18)

The people refused to listen and persisted with their demands:

There must be a king over us. We too must be like other nations, with a king to rule us and to lead us in warfare and fight our battles.

(1 Samuel 8:19–20)

There is an old saying, "Be careful when you ask God for something, for your wish might be granted." That is, you might get more than what you expected or wanted. That's exactly what happened to Israel in this case; God responded,

Grant the people's every request. It is not you they reject, they are rejecting me as their king. As they have treated me constantly from the day I brought

them up from Egypt to this day, deserting me and worshipping strange gods, so do they treat you, too.

(1 Samuel 8:6–9)

Samuel then ordered the men of Israel to report back to their own cities. The people of Israel had made their decision, they would have a king. The period of direct rule of Israel by Yahweh and through the judges was at its end. Today, historians question whether charismatic leadership could have continued to be successful in Israel. Most likely, Israel would never have achieved power and stability as a nation without a monarchy. Their society was simply not unified enough under the judges.

It is not known if Samuel's warnings of the corruptness and ineffectiveness of a monarchy were his own, or those of later editors who had experienced the effects of the monarchy. Regardless, the *ideal ruler* for Israel is clearly identified by the Deuteronomic historian as Yahweh.

King Saul

Saul was the king first chosen and anointed by Samuel as "commander over the Lord's heritage" and governor of Israel (*see 1 Samuel 9–10*). After leading the Israelites to a military victory over the Ammonites (1 Samuel 11), the people acclaimed Saul their ruler.

Saul was truly a tragic person (some people think that he was the inspiration for Shakespeare's "King Lear"). He was known as a handsome man, courageous, yet modest, and willing to admit his faults. He was, however, emotionally unstable. Apparently, he suffered terrible mood swings.

People Are Alienated Saul alienated the people close to him, including Samuel. Although Saul was a religious man, he did not appreciate the importance of religion. Twice, he disobeyed direct instructions from Samuel, and in so doing he offended God's prophet.

As Saul lost favor with Samuel and Yahweh because of his odd behavior, the spirit that had "rushed upon him" at his anointing, turned dark. Saul became even more depressed and moody. His fears of losing the kingship dominated his decisions. His response to seemingly unimportant matters bordered on craziness. Needless to say, his court and his army both began to lose their trust in his leadership.

To his credit, Saul kept his faith in Yahweh. When a battle turned against him, Saul would suspect that he or one of his men had done something to displease God. Nevertheless, Saul learned the hard way

---

MORE ABOUT THE TEXT

Saul

When psychologists today read the whole story of Saul, they suggest that he had always been emotionally unstable and that he eventually became mentally ill (manic-depressive). This illness shows most clearly in his relationship with David: sometimes loving him as a son and then threatening his life as a terrible enemy.

His behavior was clearly erratic. He could and did threaten his own son, Jonathan, with death

for disobeying an unknown order, yet Saul himself disobeyed Samuel when he found it expedient to do so. Such vacillation made his two main tasks almost impossible: he could neither be an effective commander against the Philistines, nor inspire firm loyalty.

In this way, Saul, too, was a transitional figure. Thus the whole period of Samuel and Saul was a transition between the leadership of the judges to that of the kings.

that Yahweh shaped the course of history and de-manded absolute faithfulness from those who fol-lowed the Covenant.

A Difficult Challenge Saul was faced with a dif-ficult task: to form a nation out of the loosely united tribes of Israel. People who had previously gathered only for religious ritual and for self-defense now were being asked to give up their tribal independence, form a standing army, pay taxes, and pledge allegiance to a king. Adding to Saul's other problems, he was at-tempting this while trying to fight off a powerful Philistine army.

Saul's fall from favor with Samuel (1 *Samuel* 15) foreshadows the trouble the nation would always have between political and religious leadership. Although Saul was the anointed king, Samuel still was the religious leader in Israel. When Saul failed to follow Samuel's instructions, he offended God by claiming power that was not properly his. Samuel had told Saul he must destroy his enemies completely, but Saul saved some treasure and spared the life of the king. As a result, Samuel rejected Saul. He said,

I will not return with you, because you rejected the command of the LORD and the LORD rejects you as king of Israel . . . The LORD has torn the kingdom of Israel from you this day, and has given it to a neighbor of yours, who is better than you.

(1 Samuel 15:26–28)

Saul's days as king were numbered.

Have You Considered?

1. Why do you suppose that religious and political leaders, such as Samuel and Saul, so often find themselves fighting with each other?
2. Put yourself in the position of one of the ancient Israelites. Do you think you would have wanted a king?
3. One of Saul's problems was insecurity about his position as king. Discuss an example of how insecurity can prevent us from making the right choices in difficult situations.

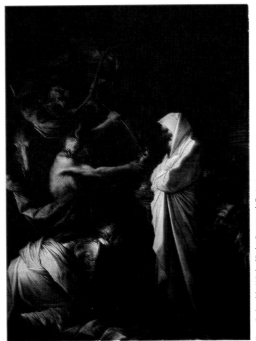

Rosa, Saul and the Witch of Endor. Seventeenth Century.

After Samuel's death, Saul asked a witch at Endor to call forth his ghost (1 Samuel 28:8–25).

◆ David: The Beginnings

David is the central character in the Deuter-onomic history, and one of the most important fig-ures in the entire Bible story. It was during David's rule that Israel truly became a nation. Under David, Israel secured peace with its neighbors and the na-tion prospered. The story of David is found in 1 and 2 Samuel.

Introducing David

David is introduced in three separate stories.

1. **1 Samuel 16:1–3.** David is first introduced during Samuel's visit to the sons of the shepherd, Jesse. Samuel said: "Do not judge from his appearance . . . Not as man sees does God see, because man sees the appearance but the Lord looks into the heart" (1 *Samuel* 16:7).

MORE ABOUT THE TEXT

The Witch of Endor

The picture on page 47 shows Saul consulting the witch of Endor to ask a question of Samuel after he had died. Yahweh had expressly ordered the Israelites not to engage in foreign religious practices such as conjuring spirits. What does it say about Saul that he would resort to this ac-tion? Note that this story does not question the reality of spirits or the ability of human beings to summon them. Rather, it condemns the prac-tice as being inconsistent with faithfulness to Yahweh.

Recall

Ask volunteers to list all they remember about the following:

a. The reasons the people wanted a king
b. Yahweh's and Samuel's reaction to the people's wishes
c. Characteristics and tasks of Samuel
d. Characteristics and tasks of Saul

Connect

What to Do

Ask the students to think of cur-rent events or historical people they know about who either were affected by transitions or who were mentally unstable.

What's Next?

What to Do

Say to the class: "One of the most fascinating people in all of the Bible is David. He was one of the great leaders of his time. He showed mu-sical talent, was a warrior and strate-gist, a man of profound faith, and a strong king. But he had his weak-nesses, which the Bible tells about as well. Next class we will begin to learn about David."

Have You Considered?

1. Political leaders are often tempted to compromise princi-ples for the sake of getting things done. Religious leaders have the responsibility of insisting that principles be upheld. This situa-tion often leads to conflict be-tween these two types of leaders.
2. Differing answers are possible. They should focus on the reasons the Israelites wanted a king: na-tional security, and the desire to be like other nations.
3. Many different examples are possible. Ask the students for sin-cere responses from their own experience.

Bonus Focus for You ————

Read 1 Samuel 2:1–10, a song at-tributed to Samuel's mother Hannah as a song of rejoicing over her son's birth. Compare it to Mary's familiar song of joy, the "Magnificat" in Luke 1:46–55. What do you think the Biblical writers saw in common be-tween Samuel and Jesus?

47

LESSON FIVE (pages 47–51)

◆ David: The Beginnings

Welcome

Welcome the students all together. Next, form three groups. One person in each group is to be the "stranger." The groups are to play at welcoming the stranger. Keep it light-hearted and fun. Expect giggles! Ask first the "strangers," then the "hosts," to express what this was like for them. Ask for two volunteers who will be willing to help you welcome the class members as they enter next time.

Introducing the Lesson

Teaching Objectives

By the end of this lesson students will be able to:
• Get a brief preview of David's early days.
• Learn about the qualities which made David unique.
• Follow the chain of events which led to David becoming king.
• Understand the aspects of David's rule that allowed him to build a strong monarchy.
• Identify the importance of God's covenant with David.

What to Do

Have the students read the first paragraph of "David: The Beginnings." Invite them to share with the class anything they may already know about David. Ask, "Why do you think David is considered the greatest king of Israel?"

Development

What to Do

1. Have students read "Introducing David" aloud, but stop them before they read the last paragraph. Form them into groups and ask each group to write 2 or 3 sentences explaining what we should make of the inconsistencies and contradictions we find in these three stories. Each group should share its work with the class. Then, turn to the unread paragraph on page 48, and see how close the class was to the explanation given in the textbook.

2. **1 Samuel 16:14–23.** David is brought to King Saul at Gibeah with the reputation of a gifted musician. Saul was "tormented by an evil spirit" and David was asked to play his harp to soothe the pain of his headaches.

David is known as a musician—he is credited with composing some of the psalms—and he also is recognized as a great military leader. He may well have developed some of his military skills while serving as Saul's armor-bearer.

3. **1 Samuel 17:1–18:5.** The third story is the famous incident with the Philistine, Goliath, and the slingshot.

Although the story may be legendary, there's nothing impossible about it; the slingshot was an accepted weapon of war, and in the right hands, it could be deadly. This story details the first of many military triumphs for David. Because of his success, the people exalted him over Saul: "Saul has slain his thousands, and David his ten thousands" (1 *Samuel* 18:7).

There are some inconsistencies in the David and Goliath story, however. For one, Saul had to ask who David was, although David had already been introduced to Saul in the earlier story (not to mention that 16:21 has Saul being very fond of David). Also, the story reports that "David took the head of the Philistine and brought it to Jerusalem" even though Jerusalem was not yet an Israelite city (1 *Samuel* 17:54). Finally, in 2 Samuel 21:19, another Israelite soldier, Elhanan, is said to have killed Goliath.

What are we to make of the contradictions in this story? Remember what you learned about the nature of ancient history. Because David had become a great king and Israel a great power, legends of his early strength would have been quite common. It would have certainly been possible for David, the famous and revered leader, to be credited for a lowly soldier's actions. The Deuteronomic historian is interested in the meaning of the story, that as a young man David showed the qualities that would make him a great king, even if the facts aren't quite accurate. To ancient peoples, this was how history should be written.

David's Early Career

However David is introduced, he is always pictured as being intensely loyal to King Saul, the anointed one of Yahweh. And although Saul is shown to be jealous of David and his popularity, David is never shown wavering in his respect for Saul.

David must have been a person of considerable political importance, for he married Saul's daughter, Michal, and he formed a lasting friendship with one of Saul's sons, Jonathan. Lofty accomplishments for a lowly shepherd!

Rembrandt, *David Playing the Harp before Saul.* Seventeenth Century.

David is remembered also for his love of music.

◆ MORE ABOUT THE LESSON

Introduction

David began as a shepherd, one of the lowest social situations in that time. He died as the king of a large and powerful empire, the founder of a royal dynasty that would last for over 400 years. He is remembered as an inspiring leader, an outstandingly successful warrior, a shrewd governmental administrator, a musician and composer, patron of liturgical arts, and a charismatic leader who won the loyalty of a diverse and quarrelsome group of clans. Most importantly for the Bible—and maybe for us, too—David was deeply devoted to Yahweh and remained Yahweh's servant even through his own times of weakness. David has been a hero for many generations of people. As we study David, see if you think he was heroic enough to imitate.

David was undoubtedly an important military leader in his own right. He most certainly had men who followed his leadership, and, probably, he was actively involved in politics, no matter how innocent the Bible makes him out to be. Saul, for all of his moods, was still an intelligent leader. Saul certainly considered David a political rival, because he openly declared war on David, driving him into hiding.

David with the Philistines David found shelter from Saul among the Philistines, in the "cave of Adullam." He was quickly joined there by a loyal group of his own followers, "all those who were in difficulties or in debt, or who were embittered, and he became their leader" (1 *Samuel* 22:1–2). Like Robin Hood in the Sherwood Forest, David formed these men into a superior fighting force.

Faced with Saul's hostility, David approached *Achish*, the Philistine king. He offered the king the services of his army and pledged to be Achish's vassal. Not only would David bring Achish the loot from his raids against the Amalekite villages in southern Palestine and the Negeb, but he would also strengthen Achish's position against Israel. David insisted, however, that he would not fight the Israelites directly. In short, David cut a deal with the Philistines to protect himself against Saul.

David Prepares By helping the Philistines, David and his army brought relief to the southern tribes, especially Judah, from the constant attacks they had faced from the Amalekites. David divided the loot, sharing with the people of Judah, gaining their gratitude and earning their trust. The people later rewarded David's generosity by making him king.

Saul and his son Jonathan were eventually killed in a battle with the Philistines at Gilboa. Afterwards, David moved to the town of Hebron, where the leaders of Judah came to him and declared him the king over the tribes living in southern Canaan.

Have You Considered?

1. What characteristics of leadership do you recognize in David? What kind of a leader would David have been?
2. David has been described as a resourceful person. In what ways do you find him to be resourceful?
3. It is possible that the story of Goliath had nothing to do with David, who was added to the story later as his popularity grew. Why do you think people like stories about the courage and goodness of their leaders? What other examples can you think of that fit this pattern?

◆ David Becomes King

David made Israel into a true power in the Middle East, and the kingdom would never again be as united as it was at the height of his rule. Forever after, when Israelites thought of their "glory days," it was David they remembered. Most importantly, David received a promise from Yahweh that a descendant would rule Israel forever.

David did not come to power miraculously, and he was not a perfect model of holiness. David's story is another example of how Yahweh chooses to work through imperfect human beings to achieve divine goals. In the end, however, David overcame his temptations and limitations to provide the classic model of a king who was faithful to God.

David Takes Over

Although accounts vary at times, 1 and 2 Samuel provide a fascinating story about the death of Saul, and about David becoming king. Here are the highlights as the Bible tells the story:

1. **The Philistines attack Israel** and kill Jonathan and several of Saul's other sons (1 *Samuel* 31:2).
2. **Saul is wounded** and begs for someone to kill him. When no one will, Saul falls on his own sword and kills himself. The Philistines find the body, mutilate it, and show it for all to see (1 *Samuel* 31:3–10).
3. **David learns of Saul's death.** 2 Samuel begins with David's hearing of Saul's Death. Here again we have a contradiction, because the messenger reports that he killed Saul "for I knew that he could not survive his wounds" (2 *Samuel* 1:10).
4. **David pays tribute to Saul and Jonathan** in 2 Samuel 1:17–27. David then is "anointed king of the Judahites" (2 *Samuel* 2:1–7) and "spent seven years and six months" (2 *Samuel* 2:11).
5. **Saul's son Ishbaal is made king** over the rest of Israel ruling for two years (2 *Samuel* 2:10).

   There followed a long war between the house of Saul and that of David, in which David grew stronger, but the house of Saul weaker.

   (2 Samuel 3:1)

Finally, Abner, Ishbaal's general, changes allegiance. He tells David, "Make an agreement with me and I will aid you by bringing all Israel over to you" (2 *Samuel* 3:12). Before he can complete the deal, Abner is murdered by David's general, Joab (2 *Samuel* 3:12–39).

2. Have the students read "David's Early Career." Half the students are to read 1 Samuel 20, the story of David's close friendship with Saul's son Jonathan. The other half of the class is to read 1 Samuel 24 and 26, stories of David's sparing Saul's life. What do students think of David thus far?

Practicing the Skills

Students will build skills of recognizing the differences in stories about the same or related events.

What to Do

Form the class into three groups. Have one group read section 1 and 1 Samuel 16:1–13; a second group read section 2 and 1 Samuel 16:14–23; and a third group read section 3 and 1 Samuel 17:1–18:5. In the groups, each student can read one or two verses aloud as the others follow, so everyone has a chance to read.

Ask each group to choose a spokesperson who will tell the group story to the rest of the class. Ask, "What contradictions do you find in these stories of how David enters Israelite history?"

Have You Considered?

1. Responses will differ. Some qualities include: David was loyal, brave, intelligent, willing to take risks, and a great fighter. In terms of what kind of leader he was, the teacher might direct students to compare him to modern leaders. Would he be like President Kennedy? General Schwarzkopf?
2. Ask students to point to incidents from David's life which demonstrate his resourcefulness. For example, David's ability to evade Saul when the king wanted to kill him.
3. For examples, students may mention traditional stories about George Washington: chopping down of the cherry tree, or throwing the dollar across the Potomac. The motive for such stories is probably to emphasize the greatness of a culture's heroes.

MORE ABOUT THE TEXT

The Slingshot

1 Samuel tells us that David killed Goliath with a slingshot. In the popular imagination, this has often been pictured as David using a child's toy to kill a powerful warrior. In fact, the slingshot was an effective and widely-used weapon of war in the ancient world. Ancient armies would form battalions of slingshot specialists, equivalent to medieval archers or modern sharpshooters.

◆ MORE ABOUT THE LESSON

A Small Kingdom

The approximate border between Judah and Israel runs east-west, a few miles north of Jerusalem. Hebron is a Judahite town. At this early date, Israel may have included land as far north as the Sea of Galilee; Judah extended south to the Negev Desert, but excluded the coastal areas and land east of the Jordan. It was a small kingdom!

◆ David Becomes King

Development

What to Do

Have a volunteer read aloud the first two paragraphs of "David Becomes King," as the rest follow along in their texts.

1. Have the students open their Bibles to 1 Samuel 31.

Walk them through "David Takes Over," by having them read the text paragraph and biblical references. One student will read aloud from the text, another from the Bible, and so on for each of the seven steps. Have them look at a map of Palestine in Old Testament times. Show the approximate borders of Judah and Israel when David became king. Note the location of Hebron and of Jerusalem.

Guide a student discussion on the question: If something is God's will, does it matter how it is accomplished?

2. Have the students read "David Builds a Strong Monarchy." Have them write down a list of all the accomplishments of David as king. Have the students debate the question: "Was David a great king?" Use points from "David Builds a Strong Monarchy" as well as "People of Note" in responding to this question.

Read "God's Covenant with David." Then, have a student read aloud 2 Samuel 7:11b–16. Ask whether this covenant with David is conditional or unconditional.

People of Note Have the students read "People of Note." Explain that this incident is more important than just an ordinary adultery and murder case, as bad as that may seem. An equally important character in this story is Nathan. Have them read the story in 2 Samuel 11:1–12:25.

Recall

Homework Assignment: Ask each student to choose the event or characteristic of David that he or she likes the best, and the event or characteristic he or she likes the least.

50

David and Bathsheba

Despite his greatness as a king, David was not a perfect person. Through much of his life he was troubled. The best example of this was his affair with Bathsheba.

One day, while David was standing on the roof of the palace, he saw a woman sunbathing. He was filled with lust for her, and he immediately sent someone to find out who she was. It turned out that she was the wife of Uriah, a Hittite who fought in David's army. Even though she was married, David decided to have an affair with her.

Before long, Bathsheba was pregnant. To conceal his crime, David tried to get Uriah to have intercourse with Bathsheba so he would think the child was his. Uriah, however, refused, because he didn't want to relax while his troops were still in combat. Thus, David felt he had no choice: he had Uriah killed in the next battle.

The prophet Nathan then approached David. He told him a story of a rich man who had stolen and killed the only lamb belonging to a poor servant. David said the rich man should be killed, and Nathan responded, "You are the man!" David wept with sorrow and begged forgiveness.

This story shows us that everyone, even God's anointed ones, experience weaknesses and temptations.

---

6. Ishbaal gave up hope when he heard of Abner's death. Ishbal was himself soon murdered by his own followers. (2 *Samuel* 4).

7. David was now king of all Israel.

After this, "When all the elders of Israel came to David in Hebron, King David made an agreement with them there before the Lord, and they anointed him king of Israel."

(2 Samuel 5:3)

He had proved himself in battle and had been accepted by the elders of the tribes. He had mourned the deaths of Saul, Jonathan, Abner, and Ishbaal. Now that he was king, however, David's problems really began. If he were to have a nation to rule, he first had to defeat the mighty Philistine army with its iron weapons and chariots.

David Builds a Strong Monarchy

The days of charismatic leadership—as in the time of the judges—ended completely when David took power. David came to power with an army of loyal soldiers hardened by their days among the Philistines. He had the blessing of the leaders of Israel to gather a more powerful army and use it to defend Israel. David took control of Israel's future and built it into a powerful nation. He was God's anointed and he would rule!

Military Victories The Philistines presented David with an immediate military problem:

When the Philistines heard that David had been anointed king of Israel, they all took the field in search of him.

(2 Samuel 5:17)

When David asked about the feasibility of battle Yahweh responded: "Attack, for I will surely deliver the Philistines into your grip" (2 *Samuel* 5:18). And attack David did. In two decisive battles, David's army drove the Philistines out of central Palestine and back to their territory on the southern plain. They would never again pose a major threat to Israel's security.

Statesmanship David next turned his attention to administering the unified nation. He moved the capital city from Hebron to Jerusalem. Jerusalem had been an independent Canaanite city, without allegiance to any tribe or to the Israelite covenant before David captured it (2 *Samuel* 5:6–9).

Jerusalem was centrally located to both the northern and southern halves of Israel, and, because it was built on a hill surrounded by three valleys, it was easily defended. Jerusalem came to be known as the "City of David," which is literally true. Jerusalem was captured by David and was never tribal property.

With relative peace at home, David expanded the kingdom. He conquered the territories of Edom, Moab, and Ammon. David also formed many alliances with other rulers, including one with Phoenicia that would last for centuries and greatly benefit Israel's economic life.

Religious Leader As a religious leader, David was very influential. Jerusalem became both the nation's political capital and its religious center. The Ark of the Covenant had been hidden for more than 20 years in fear of losing it to the Philistines. David brought it to Jerusalem with great celebration. David, who was

girt with a linen apron, came dancing before the Lord with abandon, as he and all the Israelites were

---

MORE ABOUT THE TEXT

The Moabite Stone

David's military victories allowed Israel to incorporate many non-Israelite territories into the nation. Countries such as Edom, Ammon, and Moab became part of "greater Israel." We know of Moab's later struggles with Israel from an inscription known as the "Moabite stone," discovered in the nineteenth century and dating from a period roughly a century after the rule of David. The stone describes the battles fought by the Moabite king Mesha against some of David's successors. The dates and names given in these descriptions, for the most part, confirm the general accuracy of the biblical narrative.

bringing up the Ark of the Lord with shouts of joy and to the sound of the horn.

(2 Samuel 5:14)

David had a special tent built, like the one that the Israelites believed had housed the Ark in the Sinai desert. Priests were appointed to serve in the sacred tent and oversee sacrifices and liturgies.

David also made a valuable contribution to liturgical music. Besides composing music himself, he encouraged choral music (songs sung by choirs) and hired musicians to perform it. He supported public worship of Yahweh and enriched it in every way he could, leaving a lasting legacy.

One thing that David did not do was to build a permanent temple for the Ark. Religious habits are slower to change than others, and the people were used to the Ark as a mobile symbol. The prophet Nathan discouraged him, reporting God's words that it would be David's son "who shall build a house for My name" (2 Samuel 7:13).

God's Covenant with David

From the experience of the Exodus, to the giving of the Covenant to Moses, to the military leadership of the judges, the Israelites understood that all leadership came from Yahweh. David took his place alongside Moses as a recipient of Yahweh's Covenant.

Under King David, a theology developed which said that the king ruled as God's appointed. Further, the Israelites believed that God had made a covenant with David which promised that David and his descendants would sit on the throne of Israel forever. As David himself said,

Is not my house firm before God? He has made an eternal covenant with me, set forth in detail and secured. Will He not bring to fruition all my salvation and my every desire?

(2 Samuel 23:5)

When the Israelite kingdom had been destroyed in the time of the Deuteronomic historian, the people questioned whether or not God had broken this promise. The Deuteronomic historian responded that God's word was unbreakable, and that in the future God would establish a "Son of David" on Israel's throne forever. Today, Christians see that promise fulfilled in the reign of Jesus.

Have You Considered?

1. When Abner decided to double-cross Ishbaal, David went along with the deal. Was he wrong to do so? Why or why not?
2. The ancient Israelites believed that God selected the king, and that political power came from God. How could this belief lead to abuses of power from corrupt leaders?
3. Read through the list of David's accomplishments above. Which do you consider to be the greatest? Why?

Spiritual Reflection

Praying the Psalms

Many of the psalms are attributed to David. Some of the psalms seem especially appropriate to David's life. Today, we continue to use the psalms in our public prayer. The response to the first reading at Mass is usually taken from the Book of Psalms. Develop your own psalm response to be used at liturgy. Follow these directions:

• Read Psalms 14, 15, and 16 in their entirety.
• Choose the psalm that appeals to you the most.

• Reflect on the words of the psalm in writing.
• Quietly pray, using the words of the Psalm to guide your thoughts.
• When you have prayed as long as you feel comfortable, use David's words in Psalm 16:8–11 as a promise to the Lord and as a thanksgiving.

Ask them to write a paragraph about each one in their journal, and explain why they made the choices they did.

Connect

What To Do

Have the students read the psalms mentioned in "Spiritual Reflection." Ask them to imagine the circumstances in David's life which might lie behind these psalms (even if they were not directly authored by David, they are intended to reflect his life story). Then, ask them to point out circumstances in their own lives which might parallel these experiences.

What's Next?

What to Do

Say: "In addition to what you have learned about David so far, scholars say that he sponsored many projects of cultural and religious importance. One of these was the writing down of many ancient traditions of the people of Israel. Some of these writings are included in the Book of Genesis. We'll explore some of their interests in the next chapter when we study the Book of Genesis."

Have You Considered?

1. Student responses will vary. Ask "yes" respondents to consider David's responsibility under the covenant to set a moral tone for the nation. Ask "no" respondents to consider David's political need to consolidate his rule, and to spare the nation further civil war.
2. Leaders who are regarded as "chosen" by God can easily abuse that power if they become corrupt or self-indulgent.
3. Allow responses to vary, but be sure that students have selected a specific accomplishment, and that they have good reasons for their selection.

Bonus Focus for You

Read King David's prayer in 2 Samuel 7:18–28. Ponder the humility and the strength that combine here. Notice how David attributes some of his great accomplishments to God's action. How can you develop more of these qualities and attitudes in your own life?

MORE ABOUT THE TEXT

The Psalms

The psalms in this reflection are attributed to David. For reading Psalms 14, 15, and 16, divide the class into two groups. Tell them that they will read these psalms in the way that Christians have read psalms in groups for at least 1700 years. One volunteer student announces the psalm number and title. Then each group reads a verse, alternating throughout the psalm. When this reading is completed, ask the students to identify any connections between David's life and the ideas in these psalms. Ask them to identify which ideas offer suggestions for their own living.

Then ask for a time of quiet in the room and direct the students to follow the rest of the instructions in "Spiritual Reflection." When they have finished, ask them to open their Spiritual Journal and write a little about this experience of praying with the psalms.

Q/A

Section One

1. The Deuteronomic history is a history of Israel from the entry into Canaan to the Exile. It was written during the Exile as a way to account for Judah's destruction.

2. The Deuteronomic historian answers that the people (through their leaders) had broken the covenant by worshipping foreign gods and abandoning justice.

3. Ancient historians regarded their task as recording the meaning of the past. They freely altered and exaggerated their records to bring out the themes they felt were important. Modern historians regard factual accuracy as their most important objective.

4. Canaan is the name used before the time of Saul for the land occupied by the ancient Israelites. The same land is called Israel after the formation of the kingdom. Palestine is the name for the entire territory after it split apart following the rule of Solomon.

5. Joshua is presented as one who kept God's law in its entirety.

6. Israel could not have conquered all of Canaan because: (a) The Egyptians controlled the major cities in the plains, (b) The Hebrews were guerrilla fighters, (c) The Philistines had a military advantage with their iron weapons.

7. The Israelites were members of a loose confederation, which came together in times of emergency, but otherwise allowed the individual tribes to set their own course. The major weakness in this system was the inability to coordinate policies.

8. To join the covenant, a clan needed the approval of all the other clans and had to pledge loyalty to the covenant at the sacred site of Shechem.

Q/A

Section One

1. What is the Deuteronomic history? Under what circumstances was it written?
2. What answer does the Deuteronomic history give to the question of why God would allow bad things to happen to the Chosen People?
3. What is the difference between ancient and modern approaches to writing history?
4. Define the following terms: Canaan, Israel, Palestine.
5. Why might Joshua be described as the "ideal leader of Israel"?
6. What are some reasons why Israel's initial military action in Canaan could not have taken them much farther than the southern hill country?
7. What was the system of government for the 12 tribes? What were the weaknesses in this system?
8. How did a clan join the Israelite covenant faith?

Section Two

1. Who were the judges and what was their role in Israel?
2. What are the four phases of Israel's behavior during the time of the judges?
3. Define: charismatic leadership, theology.
4. What is the basic theological idea in Judges?
5. Why did the Israelites want a king? How did Samuel respond to their request?
6. What was the significance of establishing Jerusalem as the capital city of the new nation?
7. What contributions did David make as a religious leader?
8. What was God's covenant with David?

BIBLE ACTIVITY

1. Read Judges 2:1–4 and Judges 3–4. Outline the four-fold pattern of sin, punishment, repentance, and deliverance as seen in these passages.
2. Read and summarize Joshua's final plea to the Israelites in Joshua 23, identifying his major concerns for Israel.
3. Write a dramatization of Samuel's call as described in 1 Samuel 3:1 and 21. Include these characters: narrator, Samuel, Eli, Yahweh.
4. Report on these incidents from Saul's life: (a) Saul is anointed by Samuel (1 *Samuel* 10:1–10), (b) Saul turns away from God (1 *Samuel* 15:22–35), and (c) Saul is jealous of David (1 *Samuel* 18:6–15).
5. Form debate panels to take positions on the different forms of leadership modeled in this chapter. Each group should defend one form of leadership as the ideal.

These ruins are believed to be the remains of King David's tomb.

BIBLE ACTIVITY

1. The four-fold pattern is as follows:
a. Sin: 2:1–4, failure to rid Israel of foreign worship
b. Punishment: 3:1–14, Yahweh allows foreign powers to dominate Israel
c. Repentance: 3:15, the Israelites cry out to Yahweh for help
d. Deliverance: 3:16–30, Ehud delivers the Israelites from subjection to Eglon

2. Joshua's major concern was that the Israelites should serve Yahweh loyally. He advised the Israelites not to worship foreign gods, mingle with foreign nations, or intermarry with foreign cultures.

3. Allow for student creativity in framing this scene. Insist, however, that the substance of Samuel's call be accurately depicted.

GLOSSARY

- **Ark of the Covenant:** A portable shrine originally constructed in the Sinai desert, believed to contain the tablets of the Law; a symbol of God's presence.
- **Canaan:** The area around the Jordan River and the Dead Sea. This is the term used before David's kingdom.
- **Charismatic leader:** A person upon whom the spirit of the Lord had come with power, thus enabling him or her to be a successful military leader and judge.
- **Confederation:** A league or alliance. In Israel, the confederation was based on the Covenant.
- **Deuteronomic History:** The history of Israel, written in 587 B.C.E., that includes the books of Joshua, Judges, 1 and 2 Samuel, and 1 and 2 Kings.
- **Israel:** The term used for the promised land (Canaan) after the kingdom is formed. Also used for the Northern Kingdom after 920 B.C.E.
- **Judah:** The southern part of Canaan.
- **Judge:** A charismatic leader and dispenser of justice among the Israelites from about 1200–1030 B.C.E.
- **Palestine:** Another term for the promised land, used to refer to the entire territory after the split between Israel and Judah.
- **Philistines:** A people who came from the Aegean area to the coast of Palestine around 1100 B.C.E.; rivals of Israel for control of the land of Canaan.
- **Theology:** The study of God. When talking about people's theology, the term refers to their ideas about God.
- **Tribe:** A group of people united by family ties and common interests; ancient Israel was divided into 12 tribes.
- **Vassal:** One who holds land given by a superior (e.g., a king), and who fights and/or farms for him in return.

UNDERSTANDING MORE ABOUT:

The Deuteronomic History

The Deuteronomic history received its name because its authors believed Israel had sinned by not following the laws in the Book of Deuteronomy. "Deuteronomy" is a Greek word meaning "second law." The fifth book of the Pentateuch, Deuteronomy has that name because it is a second version of the laws found in Exodus.

In 2 Kings 22, the Deuteronomic historians describe the reign of Josiah, one of the descendants of King David. The historians say that King Josiah found a book of law in the Temple while it was being renovated. The king was devastated, because he realized that the nation had not obeyed the laws of God as set forth in this book. Many scholars believe this book to be Deuteronomy.

About 100 years later, the Deuteronomic historians, living in exile, examined the history of Israel. The theme of their work was that Israel's disregard for the Law grew steadily worse after King David, until God allowed them to be defeated and humiliated. Through the promise of the Covenant with David, however, the Deuteronomic historians held out hope that things would improve and God would rebuild the people.

Section Two

1. A judge was a military leader inspired by God in times of crisis to help the Israelites defeat a common enemy, and then to govern them afterwards.
2. The four phases of behavior are: sin, punishment, repentance, and deliverance.
3. A charismatic leader is one inspired by the Spirit and who leads by the force of his or her personality. "Theology" means the study of God.
4. The basic theological idea in Judges is that when Israel obeys the covenant, God keeps it safe; when it disobeys, disasters follow.
5. The Israelites wanted a king to unite them against their enemies, and so they could be like other nations.
6. Jerusalem was centrally located, and it was built on a hill surrounded by three valleys, so that it was easily defended. Because Jerusalem had been an independent Canaanite city, it had no loyalty to any particular tribe.
7. David centralized religious observance in Jerusalem and established a system of worship. He also composed sacred music and supported public worship of Yahweh.
8. God's covenant with David was that descendants of David would sit on the throne of Israel forever.

4. Students should include three elements in their answers:
   a. the contents of each scene
   b. the motives for each character's action
   c. the consequences
5. The leadership styles the students debate should include:
   a. dictatorial leadership (Solomon)
   b. hands-off leadership (Saul)
   c. shared responsibility (David and Nathan)

Refer them back to the opening story of this chapter for further discussion. The debate should include references to the consequences of these leadership styles in the biblical story.

Chapter Overview

In this chapter, students will learn about the creation stories and legends of the patriarchs found in the Book of Genesis. These stories take us back to our origins, both as humans and as a faith community centered in loyalty to Yahweh. As such, they are the "family stories" of Christianity as well as Judaism.

Teaching Objectives

By the end of this chapter students will be able to:

• Recognize these stories as a medium for expressing the most basic identity and heritage of the religious family.

• Appreciate the stories in Genesis as important myths rather than as historical narrative.

• Value the patriarchal legends as witnesses to the origins of our faith tradition.

• See their own life stories as meaningful parts in the larger faith story.

Welcome

Show by your actions as well as your words that you are interested in the students as persons and want to share this learning experience with them.

What to Do

Make sure you greet at least a few students by name, and walk out from behind the desk or podium to talk with them. This conversation doesn't have to be about the lesson: talk about sports, the weather, or whatever is most likely to be on their minds. The point is to engage them "person to person."

Introducing the Chapter

What to Do

• Begin the lesson with a prayer, preferably one that draws upon some aspect of our common faith story.

• Begin the class by saying that in this chapter we will look at the stories about creation and the first people called by God. These stories are in a book called "Genesis," which

CHAPTER

4

Genesis:
At the Beginning

1900	**1900 B.C.E.** ● Japan settled by Jomon People ● Probable date for migration of Abraham
	1880 ● Egypt invades Canaan
	1830 ● Teutons settle in Norway ● Babylon and Egypt show highly developed astronomy
	1800 ● Stonehenge begun ● Egypt's first novel written
	1720 ● Egyptian alphabet
1700	**1700** ● Palace of Minos—first indoor plumbing ● Joseph in Egypt
	1670 ● Hyksos rule Nile Delta
	1650 ● India builds first water dam—of marble
	1600 ● Oral traditions about Patriarchs
1500	

Michelangelo, *The Creation of Adam*. Sixteenth Century.

Legend

● General History
● Biblical History
● Jewish History
● Books written

As a high school graduation present, George's father repaired the old family camper and gave it to him. Soon after graduation, George and his two older brothers took off from San Pedro, California, for a cross-country trip to New York state.

The drive took almost two weeks. The brothers camped at some pretty remote places along the way. They were able to take only two showers during the entire trip. The worst part about it was that none of them knew how to cook anything but scrambled eggs. Needless to say, they were all happy when they reached their Uncle Antonio's house in the Little Italy section of Manhattan. George thought, "A warm shower, a great Italian meal, and then . . . check out the night life in New York!"

After supper, Uncle Antonio had other plans. "Boys, boys, I have some things to show you and some things to tell you," he said.

◆ MORE ABOUT THE LESSON

Stonehenge

Stonehenge is a site in central England which dates back to a period roughly contemporary with Abraham. It is made up of a series of stone pillars, arranged so that they point to the rising of the summer solstice. Evidence indicates that the site was long used as a religious or ceremonial center.

Stonehenge is a testament to the fascination ancient peoples had with astronomy, a fascination which cultures surrounding Israel also developed.

The old man pulled out a worn photo album and an envelope of other equally tattered papers.

"This is our family story," he began, extending some old, faded photographs. "Here I am with your father and our parents at Ellis Island. We were so frightened; we were only babies, your father and I. He was three and I was six when we came here. The boat ride from Italy seemed to last a year, although it really only took ten days. Your grandmama and grandpapa were strong. When many of their friends fled back to their homeland because of the crowded living conditions here in the city, they decided they could make a better life for their children here. They would never have made it without their great trust in God to provide. Look here. This one shows the fish market where we worked and lived. At first the smell of fish was everywhere. But, as we got used to it, the smell didn't bother us. Did your father ever tell you about the first time he met your mother? Look, here are some of the love letters he wrote to her from the war."

George's brothers squirmed anxiously. George knew they were thinking about having fun in Times Square. George waved them on. "You guys go party without me. I'm a little tired. Besides, these stories are interesting!"

His uncle smiled and went on with his stories.

Cherished Family Stories

During George's visit to his uncle's home in New York he discovered a universal truth: people in all times and places have cherished their family story. It gives them some perspective on what's happening in their own lives. Being in touch with their roots gives people a better foundation for living in the present, because it helps them answer one of the basic human questions: "Who am I?"

People have always searched to discover their origins far beyond their own memory. The question "How did we begin?" comes up in every culture and in every generation. You may also be interested in your own origins: Where did you come from? Where did your parents, grandparents, and great-grandparents live and what did they do? How did your family customs get started?

The Israelites asked these same questions. Much of their early history was unknown. In order to explain their origins—and the origins of humankind—they developed more of their family story. In this chapter, you'll learn about that story as it's presented in the Book of Genesis.

means "beginnings." Ask students what they already know or have heard about these stories. At this point, it's not necessary to correct false impressions.

• Ask for volunteers to share a story with the class from their own family. To break the ice, you may want to share a story from your own family.

• After a few students have shared stories, ask them to think about what these stories have in common. Why is it so important for people to know about their ancestors?

• With this in mind, have the students read the opening two pages in the chapter (pages 54–55). Ask them to discuss why George found his uncle's stories so interesting, while his brothers did not.

Extend the Activity   Have your students develop a "family story" for the class. It should begin with a selection of stories from each of their backgrounds, and then include how they came to be part of this particular "learning family." It should also include a couple of stories about you.

Development

Using the Timeline

Point out that although the authors of the Book of Genesis were not very interested in providing exact dates for the events it describes, scholars date the period of Abraham at around 1900 B.C.E. This was a period of great migration and settlement all over the world. In this way, the story of Abraham is part of the larger "family story" of humanity from this time.

Ask the students if they can identify some of the items mentioned on the timeline. For example, do they know what or where Stonehenge is? Have they heard of Babylon, and can they locate it on a map? In this way, students can begin to develop a sense of what was happening in the world at the time the Biblical stories were taking place.

Finally, point out to the students that the date for the first oral traditions about the patriarchs is around 1600 B.C.E. In other words, at least 300 years passed between the events themselves and the beginnings of any attempt to collect these stories.

◆ MORE ABOUT THE LESSON

Story

For much of the Catholic Church's history, it was assumed that people learn morality as they learn geometry: by studying rules and doing proofs. As a result, the Catholic Church developed a long list of moral rules and regulations.

Today, we realize that people develop a moral sense through witnessing the examples of others, either in person or through media, such as oral tradition, books and film.

Rules help clarify values which already exist, but the basis of those values lies in our personal response to the conditions we encounter. This truth lies behind the Church's renewed effort to emphasize Scripture as a source of moral examples, and it also explains why the lives of the saints have always been such a source of inspiration and challenge to Catholics. As you share these stories with your students, be aware that you have the power to shape their lives.

LESSON ONE (pages 56–58)

◆ The Authors of Genesis

Teaching Objectives

By the end of this lesson students will be able to:
- Define the term "source" as applied to the Bible.
- Identify the three sources of the Genesis stories.
- Explain how the three sources were combined to form the biblical narrative, and connect this with their own experience of group projects.

Development

What to Do

1. Have the students write their first names and the names of the city and state (or country) where they were born on name tags. Find out how many were born nearby and how many were born farther away. Determine who was born the closest to your classroom. Who was born the farthest? How many duplications are there of city, state, or country? How many students know where their parents were born? their grandparents? Comment on the richness of the classroom's shared family backgrounds, traditions, and experiences. Point out the differences and commonalties you find.

2. Have the students read the opening paragraph and Learning Objectives for Section One. Briefly explain the Exile and its connection to these stories. Have the students read the opening two paragraphs of "The Authors of Genesis" and "Sources." Explain how scholars "discovered" the composite nature of Genesis.

3. Have the students open their Bibles to Genesis and put a marker at the end of both Chapter 11 and Chapter 36. Explain that the three sections of Genesis they just marked off reflect different content and types of writing. Each section will be used in this chapter's lessons. Have the students now read "The Three Sources."

Myth, Legend, and Story

Babylonian, *Goddess Gula with Her Dog.* Fourteenth Century B.C.E.

In Chapter 3, you studied a part of the Israelites' family story, the Deuteronomic history. But this part of the story wasn't enough. The Israelites wanted to examine their story as far back as the beginning of humanity, and also to their beginnings as a people. Of course, no historical records exist from that far back in time. The Israelites had to develop other kinds of stories about these ancient events. For the beginnings of humanity, they used the type of story called a myth, and for their origins as a people, they used legends. First, meet the people responsible for these stories: the authors of the Book of Genesis.

Learning Objectives for Section One

By the end of this section, you will be able to:

- Compare and contrast the three authors of Genesis.
- Explain the four functions of myth.
- Compare and contrast different ancient Middle Eastern "creation myths."
- Explain the nature of a legend.

◆ The Authors of Genesis

The Book of Genesis, as it is in the Bible, was finalized relatively late in the history of the Old Testament. It was probably finished a little later than the Deuteronomic history, sometime during the Babylonian Exile after 587 B.C.E. The Exile was a national disaster, so catastrophic that it threatened to bring Israel's family story to an end. This threat to the survival of the nation created an intense interest in the beginnings of the story.

The Book of Genesis was put together by people who combined and edited earlier sources in an effort to keep the nation together. By rallying its members around the story of their roots the writers and editors of Genesis hoped to help the exiled Israelites feel proud about who they were; they wanted the people to know their ancestors and to see God's blessings from the beginning of time. These efforts brought them a deeper understanding of God and God's purposes for the world and for humankind.

Sources

In modern times, we have a concept called "plagiarism." We regard it as immoral (not to mention illegal) to use someone else's words as our own. In the ancient world, however, this concept did not exist. *Scribes,* the people who were responsible for copying and taking care of a culture's literature, felt free to take the words of one author, mix them with those of other authors, to produce a new book, without giving credit to anyone.

Using written works in this way was accepted in the ancient world because people felt that literature belonged to the whole culture, not simply to the person who had produced it. An original work is known as a *"source."* Often books were produced by combining several original sources together. In most cases, the original authors have not been credited with their work.

MORE ABOUT THE TEXT

The Exile

About 400 years after King David died, Israel, as an independent nation, came to an end. We are jumping ahead now, because Genesis was partly written by a group working at that time. In 587 B.C.E., Babylon demolished Jerusalem and destroyed its beloved Temple. The Israelites were driven into exile in Babylon. There they had to face an altogether new life and a profound threat to their faith. It was a horrible time, but it became the crucible which purified and strengthened them, resulting in the vibrant faith of Judaism. Part of that transformation was accomplished by the "Priestly" writers and editors in their efforts to preserve Jewish identity without an independent government and without a central Temple. Their work eventually became the Pentateuch.

Since most biblical books have more than one source, we often find different points of view and different versions of the same event repeated within the text. Two or more sources have been combined into one version. This mixing of sources allows the insights and wisdom of many different people to contribute to the contents of the Bible. Nowhere is this variety more evident than in the first 11 chapters of Genesis.

The Three Sources

The earliest writings in Genesis come from three sources, or authors.

- **"J" Source.** The largest source is known as the *Yahwist* source. This author referred to God by the name "Yahweh." The Yahwist source is commonly referred to as "J" because in German (the people who first suggested this theory were German), J is the first letter of the name of God, Yahweh. The Yahwist author probably worked in the court of King David (1020–970 B.C.E.).

- **"E" Source.** The second early source is called the *Elohist,* derived from the way the author refers to God. "Elohim" is the generic Hebrew word for God. The Elohist source is found in bits and pieces throughout the Book of Genesis. It is known commonly as the "E" source. It is most likely that the "E" author wrote in the time of Solomon.

- **"P" Source.** Genesis was put into its final shape and form by the priestly authors. These authors are known as the "P" source. The priestly authors

The Bible in Context

Writing in the Ancient Middle East

When the authors of the Bible sat down to write, they couldn't simply boot up their word processors and type. The technology of writing then may have been primitive compared to our modern instruments, but the techniques developed by ancient people were fascinating.

The earliest writings—*cuneiform*—are dated prior to 4000 B.C.E. in Mesopotamia. Cuneiform writing was done with a wedge-shaped stylus (needle) on clay tablets. The tablets were then baked to make them hard so that they couldn't be erased. Cuneiform was a common form of writing for many centuries.

In Egypt, *hieroglyphs,* or picture writing was developed around 3000 B.C.E. The Egyptians wrote on *papyrus,* a kind of paper manufactured from the leaves of the papyrus plant. Strips would then be cut and glued together to form a scroll. The fibers of the plant provided horizontal lines to guide a scribe's writing.

Another common writing surface was stone, used for official decrees of the king and for national records. Animal skins, especially leather, were also used. For everyday needs, people would use easily erased wax tablets. In general, however, ordinary people didn't know how to write. When they needed something written, they would usually pay a highly respected "scribe,"—a professional trained to write and read well—to do the writing for them.

Brugel, J. *Earthly Paradise.* Seventeenth Century.

God's act of creation is celebrated in the Book of Genesis. It is a time of perfection and beauty, peace and harmony.

Practicing the Skills

What to Do

Have the students read Genesis 12:10–20. (See below, More about the Lesson, page 58.) Then, have the students read and compare Genesis 20:1–17. Ask students to find and name the differences and the similarities in these two stories. They should focus particularly on the different names used for God. Write their list of differences and similarities on the board under those headings. Finally, direct them to read Genesis 11:10–27. Ask them to guess the source of this passage. When someone finally says "P," ask: "How would you know this is from 'P'?"

Recall

Lead a discussion of "Have You Considered?" to review this lesson. Have the students write out their answers to "Chapter 4 Review Q/A," Section One, numbers 1–3.

Connect

What to Do

Homework Assignment: Have the students ask their parents and/or other relatives about the birthplaces of parents and grandparents, and about their jobs, their hobbies, and their moving around. The students should also ask for at least one story out of the lives of their grandparents. They are to enter this information in their spiritual journal.

What's Next?

What to Do

Say: "There are many kinds of family stories. Some of them are passed along by retelling, especially the funny ones or the ones that reveal the character of a person. Others may be in old letters or diaries. Some of these stories report exactly what happened, and some stories get embellished along the way. However, they all reveal something about the family and its tradition. We will study Israel's story at our next class."

◆ MORE ABOUT THE LESSON

Composite Character

Being aware of the composite nature of Genesis and other books is important because it helps us see that the Bible was not dictated by God in a tour de force of revelation. Rather, divine values entered human understanding through human experiences over a long period of time. In this way, Israel eventually came to know that God is involved in every part of human life, with great patience and compassion for our gradual learning.

Refer the students to the photo on page 6 of the text for an example of cuneiform writing. This tablet contains some of the laws from the famous "Code of Hammurabi," with which students may be familiar. For an example of how clay was used, see the picture on page 98, a cylinder which contains records of the Assyrian king Sennacherib. A recently made scroll can be seen on page 101. Ask the students to imagine the difficulties involved in writing on these various surfaces. That's one reason why a professional class of scribes existed!

LEARN FROM THE MAP

Discuss with the students the importance of Abraham's journey. What would it take to make students want to go on such a long trip, leaving family and friends behind? Abraham traveled approximately 850 miles.

Have You Considered?

1. Point out to students that most biblical books, such as the five which make up the Pentateuch, were written by groups of people over a long period of time. Similar projects of their own might be group assignments in school or a family scrapbook.

2. Allow students to bring up a variety of possibilities. Three good suggestions are: (a) we are able to get a broader perspective on the subject; (b) we get more information from a variety of authors; (c) we have more possibilities for making connections to our own lives and experiences.

3. During the Exile, the Israelites experienced defeat. If they were to survive, they had to find a way to preserve their traditions. Point out that in difficult times, people like to have the sense of security that tradition brings.

Bonus Focus for You

Consider the phenomenal dedication of the Priestly writers. You, as teacher, are part of this venerable tradition. Let it inspire you to greatness.

LEARN FROM THE MAP

Abraham's Journey

Many of the legends in Genesis concern Abraham, the person looked upon as the "father" of the Hebrew people. Originally from Ur in Mesopotamia, Abraham migrated into Canaan somewhere around 1800 B.C.E. in response to an invitation from God. Using the map's scale of one–quarter (1/4) inch equals 60 miles, calculate the approximate distance of this journey.

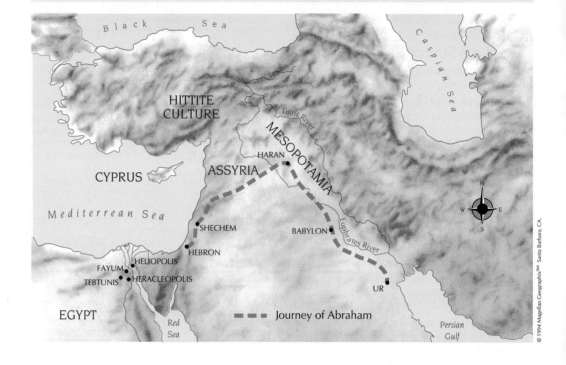

© 1994 Magellan Geographix℠ Santa Barbara, CA.

- - - Journey of Abraham

added to the "J" and "E" sources to give the story its final form.

How can you tell the material added by "P"? Look for:

- Chronological information, lists, and family trees.
- Laws like those having to do with the Sabbath and circumcision.
- Definitions of covenant, as in those between God and Noah or God and Abraham that can be understood only in the light of the Covenant given to Moses.

In the first eleven chapters of Genesis, the two main sources are the Yahwist and the Priestly writers (the Elohist references begin with Chapter 12). These chapters attempt to tell the story of creation and to answer some of the basic questions that the people of God had about their past.

Have You Considered?

1. Have you ever worked on a group project? What was it like putting all your contributions together? How might your experience be similar to how biblical books such as Genesis were put together?

2. List some advantages (at least three) that might result from having more than one author's point of view represented in the Bible.

3. The Babylonian exile, when the "P" source put Genesis together, was a time of great pain for Israel. Why do you suppose interest in their nation's past was so strong for the people at this time? Why do people in general find comfort in the stories about where they came from?

◆ MORE ABOUT THE LESSON

The Name of God

Explain that the first reference (*Genesis* 12:10–20) is from the Yahwist (or "J") source, as seen by the name of God, "The LORD." This is the usual translation of Yahweh. The second reference (*Genesis* 20:1–17) is from the Elohist (or "E") source, as you can tell from the name "God," which is the usual translation of Elohim. This passage is also a "doublet" or semi-duplicate of the first passage. By comparing them, students can see how one basic story was held in more than one tradition and came to have differing details. The third reference (*Genesis* 11:10–27) is from the Priestly (or "P") source. Lists like this abound in the Pentateuch, as do covenant and legal combinations as found in Genesis 17. (If you have time, you may have the students read this.)

◆ Mythology and Genesis

The first part of Genesis (chapters 1–11) are stories from the "J" and "P" authors about the origins of humanity. These are mythological stories rather than historical accounts, and therefore they're called "creation myths." To appreciate the beautiful stories "J" and "P" have contributed to Genesis, it's first necessary to focus on what's meant by the term "myth."

What Is a Myth?

A myth is an imaginative story which embodies the beliefs and values of a group of people. Myths tell about a culture's gods and heroes, and are usually set far back in the past, often at the beginning of time. These stories are not meant to be taken as historical records. Instead, myths communicate ideas and beliefs in story form.

A common misconception is that a myth is a story without truth. Some people fault myths for not having the same kind of truth found in historical, mathematical, or scientific works. This complaint misses the point. A myth contains a different kind of truth; it conveys meanings which are truthful, but which may or may not have a basis in historical fact.

The Earth Mother   Let's take an example. Native American creation myths often tell of an "earth mother" who gave birth to all living things at the beginning of time. Is this story true? Well, if by "true" you mean was the earth mother a historical or scientific fact, then probably not. But since the earth provides the food and water all things need to survive, don't we depend on it for our very lives as we do our mothers? Isn't it true that without the earth, nothing could exist? In this sense, then, the myth speaks a powerful truth.

This example shows the nature of myth. Myths are symbolic stories and can be understood in many ways. The purpose of a myth is to reveal many meanings, many levels of understanding through a simple story. Myths point beyond the obvious to more inward or spiritual realities.

Truths for Understanding God   In Genesis, the creation myths found in chapters 1–11 are full of important truths for understanding God, God's plan for humanity, and our common destiny. Sometimes,

however, these truths get lost when people try to read Genesis as if it were a history or science book.

People who argue "creationism" (God created all things as stated in Genesis) over the science of evolution, are misreading the Genesis story. Their argument is based on a mistake. Myth doesn't try to tell us "what actually happened." It uses stories to communicate ideas. Genesis is not interested in the scientific facts of creation, as long as we recognize that God is the Creator.

All Cultures Have Myths   All cultures have their own myths. Through myths, people learn about values, beliefs, and experiences. Myths, likewise, help individuals to find out how they fit into the group.

---

in the Spotlight
Middle Eastern Creation Myths

Myths about the beginning of the world and of humanity are called "creation myths." As you've learned, all cultures have myths, and the ancient Middle East was no exception.

Here are summaries of two creation myths from ancient Middle Eastern cultures. See how many similarities you can spot with the creation mythology in Genesis.

The "Enuma Elish" (Babylonian):

Marduk, a fierce warrior, fights with the goddess Tiamat for rule over the other gods. Marduk, who controls the winds, fills Tiamat with air and stabs her with his spear. After his victory, Marduk is the supreme god. He then orders a rival's throat slit. From the blood of his opponent, Marduk has human beings created. He decreed that humans are to serve as the slaves of the gods. Marduk was celebrated as a king who rules over the kingdom of heaven.

The Epic of Gilgamesh (Babylonian):

The hero Gilgamesh is one-third human and two-thirds divine. Nevertheless, he is a mortal man. He decides, therefore, to go on a quest for immortality. He searches for and finds Utnapishtim, a human being who survived a great flood by riding on a boat. The gods are so upset that a mortal has survived their flood, they turn Utnapishtim and his wife into immortals! Utnapishtim tells Gilgamesh where he can find the plant that will give him eternal life. Gilgamesh finds the plant, but he is so tired from his journey that he decides to sleep before he eats it. While Gilgamesh sleeps, a serpent steals the plant, and, therefore, denys Gilgamesh eternal life.

◆ MORE ABOUT THE LESSON

"The Creation" Reading

You may handle this in one of two ways: small groups can read the poem, rotating readers one stanza per person; or the whole class can divide into two "choirs," each reading an alternate stanza. The last stanza should be read by everyone together, or it can be dramatized: one student speaks God's words and a different narrator proclaims each stanza, reading to the rest of the class. The last stanza would be read by all. When you have chosen your method, have the class read the poem silently; assign parts to volunteers as needed; read the whole poem aloud.

LESSON TWO (pages 59–61)

◆ Mythology and Genesis

Welcome

What to Do

Ask students to volunteer the most interesting story they heard from their own family. Lead the class in applauding each story as it is told. Hear three or four of them.

Introducing the Lesson

Teaching Objectives

By the end of the lesson students will be able to:
• Define "myth" and describe its four functions.
• Explain the differences between myth and historical or scientific accounts.
• Define "legend" and "saga."
• Discuss the different kinds of truth contained in legends.

What to Do

Find out whether the students think the stories they heard from their families are totally accurate reports or not. Does it matter to them if the stories are entirely factual? What do they think about these stories about relatives? How do they feel connected to their families by the information they have gathered in their homework assignment?

Development

What to Do

1. Ask the students if they have heard of myths and what they already know about myths. Then have them open their Bibles to the first marker from the last class, at the end of Chapter 11. Say: "Everything that comes before this marker is mythological." Have them quickly look through the eleven chapters to find any words or scenes that are familiar to them. Or you may remind them of a few items.

2. Have the students read "Mythology and Genesis." Ask students to compare their earlier definition of myth with what they found in this section. Help them discuss the following main points to be sure they understand: myth is about

true meanings; it helps us understand the purposes of God; it helps us know what is good; every culture has its own myths (Genesis 1–11 are some of ours).

3. Read "The Creation" (Teacher's Resource 4A). Explain that this is a modern version of the first myth in Genesis.

4. Ask the students to pick one story or anecdote from the family stories they collected earlier. Then ask them to explain how this story shows how the world, family, and society works, and how people should behave.

Practicing the Skills

What to Do

Have your students read the "in the Spotlight" box on page 59. Then go over with them the four functions of myth listed on page 60. Ask them to apply these four functions to the Enuma Elish and Gilgamesh myths. What is the image of the gods projected in these myths? What sorts of human behavior are valued in them? Help them see that these myths do communicate beliefs and values to the people who embrace them.

Have You Considered?

1. Myths are stories which are not intended to be historically or scientifically accurate.

2. The Israelites always adapted the mythical traditions of other cultures to their covenant faith in Yahweh.

3. The myth of the "earth mother" comes from Native American culture. This myth embodies the truth that the earth provides for us and nurtures us.

◆ Legend and Genesis

Development

What to Do

1. Have the students read "Legend and Genesis." Ask them to explain, based on the definition given in this section, why this particular story qualifies as a legend. Most importantly, ask them to identify the important value or belief which is imbedded in this legend.

The most important beliefs of a culture or religion are included in these creation myths.

Myth fulfills four functions:

1. **Theological.** Myths tell us what God is like and how God relates with us.
2. **Cosmic.** Myths tell us how the world works and what its purpose is.
3. **Social.** Myths tell us how society should be organized and who should be in charge.
4. **Ethical.** Myths tell us what values human beings should have and how we should behave.

When myths are read or told, it is up to the individual listener to find the particular meaning in the story. If one is only interested in the literal facts of the story, the deeper significance of the myth is often missed or misunderstood.

The Oral Tradition

For generations, Israel's myths were kept orally—stories that were told and re-told, passed along from an elder to a younger person, and cherished for the understanding and stability they provided to the community. The passing of knowledge in this way is known as the *oral tradition*.

Eventually, by the time of King David, the nation of Israel had progressed to where it could capture the oral tradition in writing. "J" was the first author to write a creation myth based on the oral tradition. Later, "P" did the same thing. The fact that these stories survived so long in the memories of the people is proof of how important they were. Like all creation myths, they helped the people maintain their identity.

Have You Considered?

1. Given what you know about mythology, should "creation by God" be taught as a rival scientific theory to the hypothesis of evolution in science classes? Why or why not?
2. What was the main way the Israelites altered and changed the form of myths found in other ancient Middle Eastern cultures?
3. In this chapter, we said that all cultures have myths. What is an example of myth in American culture? Do you think this myth captures some truth? Why or why not?

◆ Legend and Genesis

Myth is not the only style of writing that "J" and "P" used to tell the family story of Israel. In Genesis 12–50, they move from telling the story of the creation of the world to telling the story of the Hebrew people's beginnings. To do that, they used the form of writing known as "legend."

What Is a Legend?

Babe Ruth was one of the greatest baseball players of all time. A famous story about the Babe illustrates the nature of a legend. According to the story, the Babe visited a dying boy in a hospital and promised to hit a home run for him in that day's game. During the game, the Babe stepped up to the plate, pointed to the outfield bleachers, and then hit the ball exactly where he had pointed. This homer is known as Babe Ruth's "called shot."

Babe Ruth is a legendary hero. While Ruth's records are factual, stories are told to emphasize his performance that may go beyond what actually happened.

Inside and Out

When discussing the meanings of myths, use this interesting quotation from an unknown ten-year-old: "A myth is a story that's not true on the outside, but is true on the inside." What does this mean to your students? Direct them to be specific about the ways in which myth is not true and the ways in which it is. The broader point which students must understand is that "truth" is not an either/or proposition: something may be true in some ways and not true in others.

This story illustrates the nature of a legend in two ways:

1. **It has been told and re-told countless numbers of times.** For those who hear the story, it helps bind them in a "family" of baseball fans by connecting them to the game's past.
2. **It may or may not be true.** There were no TV cameras present at that game, radio recordings are inconclusive, and people who were there are unsure about what happened.

A "legend," therefore, is an unverifiable story about some famous person or event of the past. Although legends are generally about actual, historical individuals, the purpose of the story is not to provide fact. Instead, legends illustrate principles and beliefs mixing fact with fiction.

The legends in Genesis are of this sort. The characters in these legends were real people: Abraham, Isaac, Jacob, and Joseph all really existed. There's no way to know, however, whether the specific stories told about them actually happened. Certainly there's some historical truth in these legends. The purpose of these legends, however, is not to record details accurately, but to connect the Israelites to their origins and their relationship with God.

Sagas

The specific kind of legend used in Genesis is called a *saga*. A saga is a tale—with both elements of legend and history—that describes a famous person of the past.

The sagas in Genesis 12–36 center primarily on three characters: Abraham, Isaac, and Jacob. From Genesis 37–50, the focus shifts to Joseph. Scholars disagree about exactly how much of these stories is legend and how much is based on historical truth, though they all agree that the stories contain a mixture of both. It is likely that the stories of Abraham, Isaac, and Jacob are part of Israel's earliest oral traditions.

Customs and legal items mentioned in these sagas date them to a definite time in history: between 1900 and 1700 B.C.E.

Have You Considered?

1. Give another example of a "legend" as defined in this section. How do you suppose this story got started?
2. Do you think it matters how much historical truth a legend contains? Why or why not?

Raphael, The Story of Joseph. Sixteenth Century.

The saga of Joseph serves as a transition from the patriarchal legends and the Exodus.

◆ MORE ABOUT THE LESSON

Legends

You will need to know some examples of additional legends. Here are a few possibilities: the pilgrims on the Mayflower; George Washington and the cherry tree; the shoot-out at the OK Corral; King Arthur and the Round Table; Merlin; or heroic stories from a war. Stories about Geronimo or Chief Seattle are often made into legends. There may be legends connected with your school or the town you live in, or other sports stars.

The important point here is to help the students see that legends are a part of our life, neither confined to the Old Testament nor at all peculiar. We do not require other legends to be absolutely accurate, so we need not require the biblical legends to be so either.

---

2. Have the students discuss the questions in "Have You Considered?" Add this question: "Do legends have the same four functions as myths? Explain the reasons for your opinion."

Practicing the Skills

What to Do

Form small groups of three or four students. Ask each group to write its own "legend." Their legend should meet these criteria: (a) be about an actual, historical person, (b) be unverifiable, (c) illustrate some value or belief shared by the group. Share the completed legends with the entire class.

Recall

Ask the students to write the answers to "Chapter 4 Review Q/A," Section One, numbers 4–8. They should try to answer them first without using the text, but may use the text if they have difficulty. Ask for volunteers to share their answers.

Connect

What to Do

Ask students to find a legend they haven't yet discussed in class. At the next class meeting, you can ask for volunteers to share their work.

What's Next?

What to Do

Tell the students that the next lesson will be about the myths in Genesis.

Have You Considered?

1. Allow students to present a variety of examples, drawn from various fields (sports, politics, the military).
2. The amount of historical truth found in legends is not all that important for perceiving the religious truth.

Bonus Focus for You ——————

Consider your personal reaction to the content of this lesson.

Take a few minutes to ponder your feelings about Genesis and how you feel about what you are teaching the students.

◆ Creation Myths in Genesis

Welcome

What to Do

Welcome early arrivals and ask them to assist you in greeting the rest of their classmates. Together, try to see that everyone is greeted personally.

Ask your students to talk about the "Adam and Eve" story. At this stage, don't correct any false impressions they might have formed; simply let them talk. At the conclusion of the discussion, point out that this story must be very important for us to know so much about it already, and for that reason, this section of Genesis is worth a deeper look.

Introducing the Lesson

Teaching Objectives

By the end of this lesson students should be able to:
- Identify the key differences between the "J" and "P" stories.
- Understand the connection between the "P" story and the circumstances in which it was written.
- Recognize the function of stories about how original perfection was corrupted.

What to Do

Have the students read the opening paragraph and Learning Objectives for Section Two (page 62), paying special attention to the four questions. Ask the students if they can remember the names of the four functions of myth reflected in these questions. Use this discussion to refocus the students on the importance of myth in expressing values and beliefs.

Development

What to Do

1. Have the students read Genesis 2:4–25 silently. Form four small groups. Each group will choose a scribe to record the result of their discussion. With their Bibles open to Genesis 2, each small group is to form an answer to the four opening questions. They should begin by reading the story again, this time aloud, and noting the

---

Israel Explores Its Roots

Bible of Souvigny, *Descendants of Abraham.* Twelfth Century.

Now that you know about myths and legends and who wrote the ones in Genesis, you're ready to encounter the stories themselves.

As you read through them, remember the four functions of myth, and ask:

1. What does this story tell me about God?
2. What does it tell me about the world?
3. What does this story tell me about my society, based on how it got started?
4. What does it tell me about how I should behave?

Learning Objectives for Section Two

By the end of this section, you will be able to:

- Compare and contrast the "J" and "P" creation stories.
- Discuss the following stories: Cain and Abel, The Flood, The Tower of Babel.
- Identify Abraham, Sarah, Isaac, Jacob, Esau, Joseph, and the 12 sons of Jacob.

◆ Creation Myths in Genesis

The earliest myths in Genesis were written by the Yahwist; the later materials were added by the Priestly writers. Remember that the Yahwist wrote under King David (approximately 1000 B.C.E.) while the Priestly authors wrote at the time of the Exile (around 550 B.C.E.).

Using the story forms of the Creation and the Flood common to the mid-East, the Israelite myths highlight Yahweh's presence in the world's beginnings and in the fall of humanity. The nature of God is revealed as just and forgiving. These two themes of creation and redemption found in the myths of Genesis 1–11 are repeated often through the rest of Hebrew Scripture.

The "J" Story

The Yahwist creation story in Genesis 2:4–4:16 describes both the creation of the world and of human beings. The Yahwist creation story also introduces a longer narrative that includes sections on the fall of humankind from grace and the loss of the privileges of paradise.

Imagine along with the writer of the story:

- Yahweh is intimately involved with creation—"hands on," so to speak.
- The first event is the creation of humanity: " . . . the Lord God formed man out of the clay of the ground and blew into his nostrils the breath of life, and so man became a living being" (*Genesis* 2:7).
- Everything else—the garden, and all other living things—was created for the man's benefit.

◆ MORE ABOUT THE LESSON

The Nature of Myth

Because the nature of myth allows for considerable variation of meanings, the discussion can thus be broad. The general meanings will be recognizable by most of the students, but some may also find personal, individualized meanings. Encourage students to personally interpret these stories, but caution them that "what it means to me" may not be exactly the same meaning another person will understand.

- God brings all the living creatures before the man to be named.
- When a suitable mate for the man is not found among the other animals, Yahweh created woman.

What do you notice about this story? What image of God does the writer offer us: an all-knowing, distant deity or one who is actively involved in creation and who learns by doing?

As you read the creation story, notice that God, at first, thinks the garden and other living things will make the man happy. Only when God finds out this was wrong is woman created. This is a very different understanding of God than that held by the "P" authors, as you will discover.

The "P" Story

The "P" story (*Genesis* 1:1–2:3) stands on its own. There is no doubt here that God is in control and that God knows what's what.

- God first creates the environment, and then its inhabitants, all in six days. An impressive feat, an act of a powerful God.
- Human beings are created last, the climax of all that went before: "God created man in His image; in the divine image He created him; male and female He created them" (*Genesis* 1:27).
- Because human beings are made like God in a mysterious and powerful way, they are responsible for the rest of creation.

The style of the Priestly authors follows a precise pattern in which the works of the three first days establish the conditions for the last three. Read Genesis 1:1–31 and look for this pattern:

- The created light of the *first day* is given form in the sun and the moon of the *fourth day*.
- The sea and sky of the *second day* are the habitats of the fish and birds of the *fifth day*.
- The earth and its vegetation created on the *third day* provide a home and food source for the animals and people of the *sixth day*.

This pattern was similar to a primitive three-tiered understanding of the universe—heavens above, earth below, and waters underneath.

In the Priestly story, Yahweh is understood to be in complete control of creation. Nothing happens that is not part of the divine plan. Also, Yahweh creates with the purpose of creating humankind in the divine image. You can notice here the differences between the Yahwist and Priestly understanding of God.

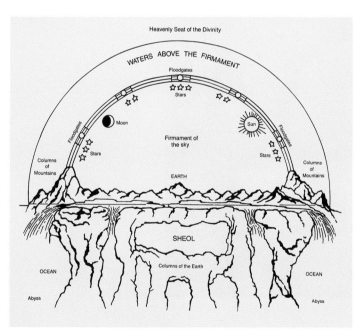

This illustration depicts the structure of the world as seen by ancient peoples. Compare this model to the story in Genesis 1–2:3.

order of events: What did God create first, second, and so on? The scribe should record the answers.

2. When all the groups have finished, ask one group's scribe to tell the answer to question 1. Then ask if the other groups agree. Using all answers, make as rich an answer to question 1 as possible. Follow the same procedure for the rest of the questions, giving each group a chance to be first to answer.

3. As a summary, have the students read the opening two paragraphs of "Creation Myths in Genesis" and all of "The 'J' Story."

4. In the same small groups, have the students read silently the "P" story in Genesis 1:1–2:3. With a different scribe in each group, have the students do the same things they did for the "J" story. Compare the two stories: What are the differences and similarities in order of events? in the answers to the four questions?

5. Have the students read "The 'P' Story" in their text, noting especially the comments about the Sabbath day. Ask if the students have questions about the "P" story.

6. Lead the students in their discussion of the questions in "Have You Considered?"

Practicing the Skills

What to Do

Ask students to study the chart of the ancient view of the universe on page 63. Explain that this was the way ancient peoples assumed the world was structured. What do students think about this cosmology? Have them compare it to our scientific view of the world.

Have the students read Chapter 1 of Genesis and describe the passages where they find references to this world view. Help them to "put the pieces together" from the reading and compare it to the chart.

Ask them to write in their Spiritual Journal which of the meanings of the two creation stories can be significant for them personally. Have them complete this sentence: "My own story begins in the creation stories because . . ."

MORE ABOUT THE TEXT

Numbers and Verses

Students may notice that the chapter break does not match the break in the two stories. The reason for this is that chapters and verses were only added very late in the history of the Bible, during the 1600s. Originally, each paragraph simply followed the previous one with no numbers and no headings.

People who studied the Bible before verses were numbered knew it from constant reading, but must have found it difficult to explain where they found a particular verse or idea. In the writings of early Christian theologians, Bible references were plentiful, but to find them, the reader had to know how to use a concordance or be familiar with the selection. The numbers and headings in today's Bible may not be "inspired text," but without them we'd have a much harder time studying it!

1. The theological function is the one which expresses the author's understanding of God. The "J" story sees God as similar to a human being, while the "P" story sees God as perfect and in total control.

2. Discuss the attitudes towards the environment that have been justified on the basis of the incorrect reading of the biblical stories.

3. The Sabbath rule is an example of the social function of myth. Students should recognize this because it concerns how society should be organized.

◆ The Fall

Development

What to Do

1. Ask the students to name things that are good in the world. List them on the board. Then, ask students to name one thing that is not right with the world. List these as well. Help the students to see that all lives have some wanted qualities and circumstances and some unwanted qualities and circumstances. Ask them why they think that is.

2. Have the students read the first two paragraphs of "The Fall." Discuss with them the fact that Israel also wanted to know what had caused this peculiar mix of beauty and ugliness in our life. Ask if students have ever wondered why life has to include so much unhappiness and disappointment.

3. Have all students read Genesis 3 and "Adam and Eve" in their text. When everyone is finished reading, form three groups. Assign the first theme in their text (awareness) to one group, the second (choice) to another, the third (consequences) to the last. The fourth (mercy) will be discussed by the whole class.

4. Have each group find in Genesis 3 the verses that illustrate its particular theme. Ask each group (or a chosen spokesperson) to explain the verses and their meaning to the rest of the class. Then have them look at Genesis 3:21. How does this express God's mercy?

5. Review the whole exercise by having the class read the "Themes

"P" finds significance in the seventh day, on which God rested. The Sabbath was very important for the Priestly writers. During the Exile, when the other leaders of the nation had been killed or scattered, priests were charged with preserving the religious traditions of Israel. One of the most important traditions was the Sabbath ("seventh day") rest. Work was not permitted on the Sabbath. By placing this tradition in the creation story, Yahweh is proclaimed the originator of the Sabbath and its rules.

Have You Considered?

1. How do you think the "J" and "P" stories differ on the theological function of myth? Which appeals to you more, and why?

2. Both the "J" and "P" stories suggest that humanity is "in charge" of creation. What kind of responsibility for the earth do you think this responsibility means we should have?

3. The "P" authors placed the Sabbath rule in their creation story, to make sure that people continued to obey the rule. Which function of myth was "P" using here? How do you know?

Perugino, *Expulsion from Paradise*. Fifteenth Century.

◆ The Fall

Just as all cultures have creation myths, they also have a story about what has "gone wrong" in human life; about how the perfection of creation has become messed up. And as their creation stories differ, so do their explanations about the cause of humanity's problems.

For example, the Babylonian epic, Gilgamesh, tells how human beings lost the chance to live forever. In this story, it is the failure to consume a life-giving substance that results in the loss of immortality. Notice the similarity with the "tree of life" in Genesis 2:9 and the "tree of the knowledge of good and evil" in Genesis 2:16.

Adam and Eve

Although there are similarities between Genesis and other mid-eastern fall myths, the Yahwist story of the fall is radically different from any other story.

- *Adam* ("man") and *Eve* ("mother of all living") are symbols of humankind.
- The garden of Eden is paradise, the perfect and free state where the relationship between God

Adam and Eve's expulsion from Paradise demonstrates the consequences of sin.

MORE ABOUT THE TEXT

The Sabbath Day

Because the Priestly writers wrote during the Exile, without any connection to the land or the Temple, they needed to emphasize the unique and precious Jewish customs to help them maintain their identity as a people. One of the traditions that became definitive for Judaism was the observance of the Sabbath day, celebrated with rest, worship, and joyful activities. The Sabbath has been observed in some form since the Covenant of Moses, but with the Exile, it now became crucial to Jewish identity. The Priestly writers emphasized the importance of the Sabbath at every opportunity. Here they assert that it was so important that it was part of the very creation itself.

and humans could be exactly as it was intended. What happens in the garden is symbolic of the events of human history.

- The responsibility for the fall belongs to man and woman together. They made the moral choice to disobey the rules of creation, so they bear responsibility for the fall and for the introduction of sin into the world.

Themes Presented

Genesis 3 develops four themes—awareness, choice, consequences, and mercy—and suggests that they are representative of the human condition.

1. **Awareness.** In their original state in the garden of Eden, Adam and Eve had no awareness of good and evil. It was only through disobedience that Adam and Eve gained this awareness

2. **Choice.** After choosing evil, Adam was afraid (*Genesis* 3:10). His act created a fear that he had never felt before. As a result, he did not want to bear responsibility for his own choice.

3. **Consequences.** The consequences of the wrong choice (*Genesis* 3:14–19) imposed by Yahweh meant that the necessary elements of life (childbirth, marital relationships, work) would from then on be mixtures of beauty and pain, desire and conflict.

4. **Mercy.** In Genesis 3:21, the Lord makes clothes for Adam and Eve. This act of mercy showed that though God is bound to respect the necessary consequences of human choice, God would not abandon humankind. Rather, Yahweh continued to care for them, even though they were no longer able to live in Eden and were barred from the "tree of life"—a symbol for immortality.

Social Function of the Fall

Remember that one of the functions of myth is to describe what society is like, and point out what it should be like. The story of the fall illustrates clearly this social function of myth.

In Genesis 3:16, Yahweh speaks to the woman, and says "Yet your urge shall be for your husband, and he shall be your master." This verse suggests that in a marriage, the husband will rule over the wife. The ancient Israelites lived in a society in which women were under the authority of men, so this verse was an accurate reflection of their social situation.

What people often fail to notice, however, is that Genesis 3:16 doesn't say this inequality is how life is supposed to be. Notice that Yahweh is speaking after

the fall. In other words, God is saying that the present relationship of men over women is a consequence of sin, not part of the divine plan. According to the story, therefore, inequality between men and women is sinful.

This observation illustrates an important lesson about reading the Bible: make sure to read verses in context, so you can make good decisions about what they mean.

The Pattern Repeats Itself

Three other stories—part of the Yahwist's creation narrative—repeat and emphasize the continuing pattern of sin in the world.

Cain And Abel (*Genesis* 4:1–16) Cain's sin of murdering his brother follows a pattern similar to his parents' sin. An awareness develops in Cain that he wants what God has refused him: a praise greater than was given to his brother Abel. Cain's choice—murder—is a violation of God's will. The consequences for his sin are even greater for Cain than they had been for Adam and Eve. He is driven from the community. Still, God's mercy abounds. Yahweh placed a mark—a sign of grace—on Cain so that he would not be killed in his wanderings.

The Tower of Babel is a symbol for us. When we try to reach God without God's help, our efforts end in failure.

Presented" section in their text. Have the students read "Social Function of the Fall." Ask them whether they agree with what their text says, since they have just read all of Genesis 3. Have students explain their opinions. Point out that the pattern of poor choice and unwelcome consequence can be found in the rest of the myths, as in all human life.

6. Have half of the class read Genesis 4:1–16, followed by the "Cain and Abel" subhead in the text. Ask them to identify by verse the pieces of the pattern that they recognize. Have the other half of the class do the same with Genesis 11:1–9 and the "Tower of Babel" subhead in their text. Let the groups share their findings.

7. Have the whole class read Genesis 6:5–9:17 and write the answers to the questions in the "Scripture Workshop," including the chapter and verse numbers where they found the answers.

8. Have everyone read "Insight for Today."

9. Lead a discussion of the questions in "Have You Considered."

Recall

Ask the students to write answers to "Chapter Review Q/A," Section Two, questions 1, 2, and 3.

Connect

What to Do

Homework Assignment: Ask the students to write a paragraph in response to this question: "How would you explain the presence of evil in our lives?"

What's Next?

What to Do

Say: "In the next class we look at the ancestral legends of the Israelites, as they are found in Genesis."

Have You Considered?

1. Student responses will vary. The teacher may wish to discuss how the concept of "original sin" has traditionally been connected with this story.

2. Point out to students that God created human beings with free will, so that they would be free to

choose disobedience. Such freedom is a necessary part of what being human means.

3. Students will have different ideas. Be sure to connect this statement with the creation stories and how God continued to build a relationship with humanity despite our disobedience and failures.

Bonus Focus for You ─────────

Reflect on Psalm 42:2–6. Although it may not at first seem connected to the lesson for today, notice that it, too, shows a mixture of experience.

Scripture Workshop

1. Genesis 6:5—God was grieved at the evidence of man's wickedness.

2. Genesis 6:9—Noah was spared because he was a good man and blameless.

3. Genesis 6:15—The ark would be 450 feet long, 75 feet wide, and 45 feet high.

4. Genesis 6:19–20—God tells Noah to bring one male and one female from all living creatures. Genesis 7:2–3—God says to take seven pairs of every clean animal and one pair of all other animals.

5. Genesis 7:12—The rain lasted for 40 days; Genesis 7:24—the waters maintained their crest for 150 days; Genesis 8:6—at the end of 40 days Noah opened the hatch; Genesis 8:10–12—Noah waited seven days and sent out a dove, and waited another seven. According to the days listed, the flood lasted 244 days. However, according to Genesis 8:13, the flood ended one year and ten days after it had begun.

6. Genesis 8:6–12—He released a raven, then two doves.

7. Genesis 8:20—Noah's first act was to build an altar to the Lord.

8. Genesis 9:11—God promised that never again shall all bodily creatures be destroyed by flood.

9. Genesis 9: 13—The rainbow symbolizes God's covenant.

The Flood (Genesis 6:5–9:17) The "P" and "J" versions of this story are woven together. Once again, it is "man's wickedness on earth" (6:5) that causes the ensuing destruction of the flood. God's mercy is experienced through Noah. In a binding, everlasting covenant, Yahweh promises "that never again shall all bodily creatures be destroyed by the waters of a flood; there shall not be another flood to devastate the earth" (9:11).

The Tower of Babel (Genesis 11:1–9) The story of humankind's desire to "build a city and tower with its top in the sky, and so make a name for ourselves" (11:4) is the last of the Creation narrative stories detailing the effects of humankind's fall. The decision to build a tower is seen to anger God, perhaps because of its arrogance and lack of humility.

Yahweh's decision to "scatter them all over the earth" (11:9) explains how the earth became populated with different races, nations, and languages.

Insight for Today

These stories of humanity's sin and fall from grace help to explain why life is such a mixed bag of beauty and pain, delight and struggle, goodness and evil. They communicate how the relationship between God and humans was meant to be good and close, but that somehow human beings misunderstood and disobeyed the only limit God made for them. This disobedience and its motive changed all of life.

Today, every person lives with the consequences that result from the first act of disobedience. Human nature was changed by it. Since every human has this nature, everyone lives in and with the same conditions. This common condition is what the Catholic Church calls "original sin."

Although the stories about the fall emphasize humanity's sinfulness and the consequences for that sin, they do not end there. The authors of Genesis were interested in showing God's saving action, not humanity's sinful behavior. If the tragic condition of the world was the author's concern, the Bible would end there. But it doesn't. By showing us the mess that humanity made of God's creation Genesis points out the simple truth that it is God who saves. The authors of Genesis, whether Yahwists or Priestly, leave no doubts that God has never abandoned us, even when we have made incredibly stupid decisions. God has never abandoned us! Think about it.

Scripture Workshop

Detailing the Flood

Read the story of the flood from Genesis 6:5–9:17. You will notice that events are repeated and that details do not agree. The evidence shows that two sets of traditional stories about the flood—Yahwist and Priestly—have been combined into one story.

As you read the story of the flood, find the answers to these questions:

1. Why did God flood the earth?
2. Why did God spare Noah?
3. A cubit is roughly 18 inches in length. In feet, how long was the ark? How wide? How high?
4. What directions does God give Noah in 6:19–20? How do these instructions differ from 7:2–3? What do you think explains these different instructions?
5. How long did the flood last? You can determine this by adding up the days mentioned in chapters 7 and 8.
6. How does Noah determine that the flood has subsided and that it's safe to leave the ark?
7. After the flood was over, what was Noah's first act on newly dried land?
8. What was God's promise to Noah after the flood?
9. What is God's sign of faithfulness after the flood?

Have You Considered?

1. In this section, Adam and Eve were described as "symbols" of humanity. Even if the story of Adam and Eve is not historically accurate, what truth does the myth of the fall communicate? How does it do so?
2. How does freedom play a part in each story of humanity's fall?
3. What are the implications in the statement that "God has never abandoned us"? How does that change how you think about God?

MORE ABOUT THE TEXT

Original Sin

One of the common misunderstandings of the notion of original sin may be expressed like this: "Why am I held guilty for something Adam and Eve did?" Many people, youth included, do feel guilty because of this teaching. Yet the Church does not teach "original guilt." We are not individually guilty for the human nature we have inherited from human ancestors. But we are still affected by that sin.

It may be explained in part like this: If a mother is a coke addict, should the baby, born addicted, be held responsible for its addiction? Of course not. However, the baby still has to suffer the consequences of its addiction and withdrawal even though he or she is innocent of any wrongdoing. While we are faced with the challenge of overcoming original sin, we need not feel guilty for the way we are.

◆ Legends of the Patriarchs

Beginning with Chapter 12, the stories in Genesis shift in focus. No longer concerned with the origins of the universe and humanity, these stories tell of the beginnings of a specific culture—the Hebrews, who in time were to become God's chosen people.

In telling the story, "J," "P," and "E" (The Yahwist, Priestly, and Elohist sources) focus on specific individuals: Abraham, Isaac, Jacob, and Joseph. These people are called the "patriarchs," or "ruling fathers."

The Book of Genesis describes Abraham as the father of Isaac, who is the father of Jacob, who in turn is father to twelve sons; these will become the 12 tribes of Israel. What are the implications of this story?

This arrangement was probably a device invented by the authors to include the traditions of several originally separate tribes. Recall that in the period of the Judges, many small clans joined the Covenant with Yahweh to become "the people of Israel." Each group brought their own traditions with them. Those traditions became part of Israel's accepted history. Because Israel later came to understand itself as one people, the biblical writers made these various traditions of Abraham, Isaac, and Jacob into one family story.

In these collected traditions, the Israelites felt themselves to be connected to the past. Israel found its deepest roots as Yahweh's Chosen People in these stories about their founders.

Abraham: Father of Faith

Abram was the first of the patriarchs to know Yahweh. As his story develops, his name will later be changed by God to Abraham. Like the other patriarchs, Abraham lived a *semi-nomadic* life, moving with his flocks and herds when the seasonal supply of pasture land and water demanded it, yet never venturing too far from the settled society.

Abraham's family originally came from Ur, which was south of Babylon along the Euphrates River (look again at the map on pg.58). The clan later moved to Haran along the northern part of the Euphrates.

Abraham's Call   The story of Abraham begins in Haran with a call from Yahweh:

Go forth from the land of your kinsfolk and from your father's house to a land that I will show you.

(Genesis 12:1)

Yahweh then promises Abraham that his descendants shall become the Chosen People. Yahweh says:

"Look up at the sky and count the stars, if you can. Just so . . . shall your descendants be."

(Genesis 15:5)

In a later story, Yahweh gives Abraham the sign of circumcision as a reminder of this covenant. In two separate accounts, God obliges Abraham to keep his promise to remain faithful. Abraham's role is to trust God and follow God's command.

God's Promises Fulfilled   For many years, Abraham had no idea at all about how God would fulfill the promises of "many descendants" made to him and Sarah since they had no children. He said:

What good will your gifts be, if I keep on being childless?

(Genesis 15:2)

In fact, Abraham and Sarah's frustration grew to the point that Sarah approved of Abraham having a child with her servant, Hagar. For a while, they thought Hagar's child, Ishmael, would be the child of the promise.

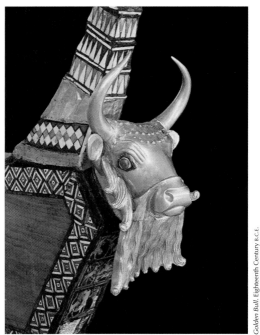

Golden Bull. Eighteenth Century B.C.E.

This Golden Bull, found in the city of Ur—Abraham's original city—represents the god of creation.

SECTION TWO

LESSON FOUR (pages 67–71)

◆ Legends of the Patriarchs

Welcome

Engage the students as a whole in conversation about how the class is going. What do they feel they are learning? Are they satisfied with their progress? Say: "I feel that we are growing closer together in our appreciation for each other through studying the Bible. Since the Bible touches our lives as much as we let it, we become a special kind of community when we are Bible students. How do you feel being a part of this Bible community?"

What to Do

Have everybody stand and form a circle, holding hands. Ask the students to close their eyes. Thank God for this circle of students and ask blessings on them. Now, ask the students to silently ask God to bless the person on their right (pause), and then on their left (pause). Then, offer the Our Father together.

Introducing the Lesson

Teaching Objectives

By the end of this lesson students should be able to:
• Begin to sense the scope of the patriarchal legends.
• Identify the basic stories of Abraham, Isaac, and Jacob.
• Enjoy and remember the story of Joseph.
• Regard these legends as part of our faith community's "family story."

◆ MORE ABOUT THE LESSON

The Journey

Tell the class that Abram (the original spelling of Abraham's name) did not make this journey all at once. He moved from Ur to Haran when his father was still alive. After Abram became head of the family, he followed God's call by moving again, this time into Palestine. Then, during the rest of his life, he traveled as a nomad throughout Palestine, across the Jordan River, and even into Egypt. Remind students that Abraham's journey into Palestine is usually dated between 1900 and 1750 B.C.E.

Development

What to Do

1. Have the students read the opening paragraphs of "Legends of the Patriarchs." Have the students turn back to page 58. Point out that although Jerusalem did not exist in Abraham's time, it would be a little north of Hebron. Ask the students to figure out the approximate distance of Abram's travels into Palestine (approximately 850 miles).

2. Tell or read the story of Abraham as given in Teacher's Resource 4B. Have the students read "Abraham: Father of Faith" and "Isaac." As the founder of Israelite culture, Abraham was the standard against which future leaders and policies had to be measured. Ask students to identify some of the key values and beliefs which are expressed in the stories about Abraham. Most notably, students should identify Abraham's total faith in Yahweh as a key value expressed in these stories.

3. Assign "Bible Activity" number 5 on page 72. When the exercise is complete, ask students if they feel what Abraham was asked to give up was "worth it" given the blessings he received in return. Ask students to give the reasons for their answers.

4. Tell or read the story of Jacob in Teacher's Resource 4C. Have the students read "Jacob" and "Twelve Tribes" in the text. In groups, ask students to debate the following

People of Note

Have the students read "People of Note" and look up the passages mentioned there. Include also Genesis 18:1–15 with 21:1–8 (about Sarah and the birth of Isaac). You may wish to discuss with students the meaning of the term "patriarch" (from two Greek words, "pater" meaning "father" and "arche" meaning "rule.") Given the important roles played by Sarah, Rebecca, and other women, does this word seem entirely correct to describe the founding figures of Israelite culture? Although the role of women in the Bible has long been ignored, many women today find tremendous inspiration in these stories.

68

People of Note

Sarah

Sarah is remembered as a wife to Abraham and a mother of Isaac. She is considered as the matriarch, or founding mother, of Israel.

Sarah probably came from an important family. Her original name, *Sarai,* means "princess," so she may have been from a noble family.

Researchers also suggest that Sarah was a priestess, with a religious authority of her own. Evidence of this includes when she is admitted to the harem in Egypt *(Genesis 12)* and when she is taken into custody by King Abimelech *(Genesis 26)*. In both stories, the rulers suffer serious difficulties because of her presence. If she had been a powerful priestess, such a reaction would have been expected.

Sarah also acted as a guardian of God's promise when she insisted that Hagar and Ishmael be sent away. Even God, though unhappy about it, tells Abraham to do as Sarah says *(Genesis 21:9–12)*. Although the verses make Sarah sound like a shrew, the tradition of Yahweh's approval suggests that Sarah was acting under divine authority more than out of simple jealousy.

Noticing Sarah's important role in the early days of God's people helps correct the mistaken, but too often assumed, idea that God works only through men. Women also have an important role in God's plan.

Then, God spoke to Abraham again, this time through three visitors. They predicted again that Sarah would have a child. Overhearing them, Sarah, who was at that time over ninety years old according to Genesis, laughed aloud. When God's promise was fulfilled and Sarah did have a son, they named him Isaac, a Hebrew word meaning "she laughed."

When Isaac was young, Sarah worried that he would have to share God's promise with Hagar's son, Ishmael. Because Ishmael was born first, he had the first claim to inherit the promise from Abraham. Sarah argued that Ishmael should be run off, which upset Abraham because he loved Ishmael. God intervened and said that Hagar and her son should leave; God promised Hagar that Ishmael, too, would have many descendants. The religion of Islam traces its roots back to Abraham through Ishmael.

The Test   Isaac would be the son of God's promise. But God was not through testing Abraham's faith. In an "E" story in Genesis 22, God commands that Abraham sacrifice Isaac as a burnt offering.

What a blow! After finally receiving the son that he had been promised so many years in the past, Abraham is once again asked to surrender his desires to God's wishes.

As difficult as it may have been for Abraham to honor God's request, his struggle is not mentioned in Genesis. His response to God is, "Ready" *(Genesis 22:1)*. Early the next morning he saddles up a donkey and heads off to Mount Moriah prepared to follow God's order. When Isaac is spared (an angel of God appears and tells Abraham to sacrifice a ram instead) God's promise is reinforced.

The stories of Abraham establish the model of faith for Israel; the faithful person is one who hears God's call and obeys. Yahweh was revealed as the master of history.

Isaac

Compared to the stories of the other patriarchs, there is relatively little information about the life of Isaac. The most famous of the Isaac traditions are his place in the near child sacrifice *(Genesis 22)*, and as an elderly victim of his son Jacob's deception *(Genesis 27)*.

However, the Priestly source considered Isaac's story an important one. He serves as the link in the family tree between Abraham and Jacob, and his story helps to give a better historical sense to the rest of Genesis. In fact, the entire grouping of Jacob stories is placed under the heading "This is the family history of Isaac, son of Abraham" *(Genesis 25:19)*.

Part of the reason more of Isaac's life is not detailed may be for lack of drama concerning his acceptance of God's promise. His father, Abraham, uprooted and moved an entire people at God's command; his son, Jacob, outwitted an older brother to gain God's blessing. Isaac simply accepted God's promises. That he did so is an essential, though undramatic, link in the story of the patriarchs and the Israelites.

Jacob Who Became Israel

If Isaac was a man strong of character, Jacob was another sort altogether. At the least, Jacob can be described as clever. At the worst, he might be called

---

MORE ABOUT THE TEXT

The Three Visitors

The Bible presents the three visitors to Abraham as angelic messengers, and (according to some translations of the Hebrew) a direct manifestation of the Lord God. It made little difference to Abraham which explanation was the most accurate. For him, it was a direct communication from God. (In Christian art the messengers' visit to Abraham became a symbolic way of painting the Trinity.)

Abraham is called the "father of faith," because of his consistent obedience to the often mysterious commands of the Lord. He obeyed because he trusted God. He believed in the Lord's promises and acted accordingly. Considering his response to God's test with Isaac, Abraham must have profoundly recognized that his life was totally given over to God and that God was fully in charge of bringing it to fulfillment.

a common thief. Nevertheless, his story shows the power of God to accomplish great things with less-than-perfect material. The story of Jacob reminded Israel that their election as God's People rests on God's free choice solely, and not on any individual's goodness or behavior.

The Inheritance   Jacob was the second son of Isaac; his brother, Esau, was the older twin. In what was the tradition of the time (in fact, still so in many countries of the world today), the first-born son would inherit the majority of the material goods or blessings from the father. This tradition meant that Esau was in line for the inheritance of Isaac. Jacob, meanwhile, looked for an opportunity to take it away from him.

Genesis 25:27–34 reports what happened. After a day of hunting, a famished Esau returned home. He asked Jacob for some of the lentil stew he was cooking. Jacob replied: "First give me your birthright in exchange for it."

"Look, I'm on the point of dying. What good will any birthright do me?" Esau said. The deal was quickly made; Jacob gave a starving Esau a bowl of stew, but only in exchange for his birthright.

The Final Blessing   Genesis leaves little doubt as to Jacob's true nature: he was a scoundrel. In Genesis 27:1–45, Jacob resorts to an outright lie to win his father's final and most powerful blessing.

- When Isaac is so old that he can no longer see, his wife, Rebekah, calls her son Jacob and advises him to trick his father.
- Jacob puts on Esau's clothes and enters Isaac's tent.
- Isaac is fooled, and grants Jacob his blessing.

In the ancient world, a father's final blessing was considered to be extremely valuable. Such attempts to steal a father's blessing (and, thus, a brother's inheritance) are condemned in other places in the Hebrew Scripture (see especially Hosea 12:4 and Jeremiah 9:3). Genesis, itself, leads the reader to sympathize with the innocent Esau. However, Jacob's behavior does serve a purpose. Through Jacob, Genesis shows how God uses even the weak and sinful to further the divine plan.

Jacob Marries   As you might expect, this last deception ends the relationship between the brothers. Jacob flees the area, and goes back to Haran (where Abraham had lived). There, he meets the shepherd, Laban. Jacob wishes to marry Laban's younger daughter Rachel, and agrees to work for seven years to win her hand.

Finally, the wedding night arrives, but Laban had planned a secret trick of his own. Older daughters were traditionally married before younger ones, so Laban substituted Rachel's older sister, Leah, for Jacob's beloved. Because brides were veiled and tents were dark, Jacob did not notice the deception until morning.

The victim of a devious scheme himself, Jacob now has to accept Leah as his wife and must labor another seven years to marry Rachel. Jacob does so. Later, he plans a return to Canaan where he will inevitably meet his brother again.

Jacob Wrestles with God   On the way home, Jacob encounters a messenger of God in a cave. The two wrestle until daybreak. Before the messenger departs, he asks: "What is your name?" After Jacob tells him, the man replies,

> You shall no longer be spoken of as Jacob, but as Israel, because you have contended with divine and human beings and have prevailed.
>
> (Genesis 32:29)

From that point on, the Genesis narrative no longer shows Jacob as the deceiver and thief, but rather as Israel, the important ancestor of Abraham and Isaac, and the father of the twelve tribes.

Notice how in both the Ishmael/Isaac story and the Esau/Jacob story, Genesis says that the divine promise passed to the younger brother. At this time, the standard practice among nations was that the oldest son inherited his father's place (for example, the oldest son of the king becomes king when the father dies). By showing that the promise passed to Isaac and Jacob, the authors of Genesis reinforced the idea that God's ways are often different from human expectations, and that God especially liked to use the weaker or lesser to accomplish splendid divine purposes.

Twelve Tribes

According to tradition, Jacob had twelve sons and one daughter.

- Six of the sons were born to Leah, his "unloved" wife (see Genesis 29:31–35). The names of those sons were Reuben, Simeon, Levi, Judah, Issachar, and Zebulun. Leah also had a daughter, Dinah.

question: "Given all of his misbehavior, should Jacob be regarded as a hero?" Point out that to ancient cultures, the kind of cunning Jacob exhibited was highly prized and celebrated, even if we might find it immoral.

5. Have the students look up Genesis 28:1–5, 10–22 and read about Jacob's famous dream. Ask, "What do you think this passage means?"

6. Direct students to read the final paragraph of "Jacob Who Became Israel." Ask them to name other instances we have encountered in which God's ways differ from human expectations.

7. Have the students dramatize the story of Joseph. List the characters on the board: Jacob (Israel); Joseph; his 11 brothers including specifically Reuben, Judah, and Benjamin; narrator (for some sections to be told instead of acted out); chief cup-bearer; chief baker; Pharaoh. Use Genesis 37, 39–45, 46:28–34; 47:1–12. Have everyone read it silently in the Bible and volunteer for character parts. Pass out photocopies for ease of reading. Jacob and the brothers get together and find and mark their parts in the beginning and end of the story. Other characters do the same. The students study their parts, plan their actions, and perform the story.

MORE ABOUT THE TEXT

A Change of Name

Abram had his name changed to Abraham. Sara's name became Sarah at the Lord's bidding. Jacob, after his experience of wrestling with the Lord became Israel. What do these changes in name signify?

A change of name, given by God or a great teacher, indicated a deep intimacy between the giver and receiver of the name. It was like a new "birth," or the beginning of a new life, based on that relationship. Abraham and Sarah were no longer the persons they had once been. Jacob, the trickster transformed into Israel, the father of the nation. When Jesus re-named Simon and called him Peter, the function of the new name was the same. It showed that once people came in contact with God, they left their old lives behind and became new men and women.

Practicing the Skills

What to Do

Form three small groups, one for the Abraham passages, one for Jacob and one for Joseph. Have them read these sections: Abraham (Genesis 12:1–9; 13:1–18; 15:1–18; 22:1–19). Jacob (Genesis 25:19–34; 27; 29:1–35; 30:25–43; 32:23–33). Joseph (Genesis 37, 39, 40, 41, 42, 44, 45:1–15). After planning, each group may tell its story.

Recall

Assign "Bible Activity" number 3 on page 72. Include this question: "Why would this remembrance have been included in a harvest ritual?" Have the students write their answers to the "Chapter Review Q/A," Section Two, numbers 4–8.

Connect

What to Do

Homework Assignment: Have the students write in their Spiritual Journals about their connection to each other in the class and to other members of their parish(es). Ask a few volunteers to share some of their reflections at the next session.

What's Next?

What to Do

Say: "The next lesson will return us to the story of Israel after the time of David. Remember the feeling of rootedness in the Israelite tradition and community, and your awareness of Israel's love of the patriarchs. Into this community, the Lord sent special people: the prophets. We will begin to learn about them next time."

- Through Leah's servant Zilpah, Jacob had the son, Gad.
- Like Sarah, Rachel was infertile, so she sent her servant Bilhah to Jacob. Bilhah had the sons Dan and Naphtali.
- Also like Sarah, Rachel had sons in her old age. They were named Joseph and Benjamin.

Over the centuries, as the final list of twelve tribes developed, the Israelites looked back to Jacob and credited him with fathering the first twelve tribes. The two sons of Joseph, Manasseh and Ephraim, split up his tribe, bringing the total to 12. (The tribe of Levi was not counted since they served as priests for all other tribes.) By tying all 12 tribes into a common family story, the authors of Genesis showed Israel that all her members shared a common bond. Despite the eventual split-up of Israel into northern and southern kingdoms, this family tree helped preserve an awareness of the unity of all Israelites.

Joseph

Jacob loved his sons by Rachel, especially Joseph. The story of Joseph in Genesis 37–50 is written as if it were a short novel, and shows evidence of both the "J" and "E" sources.

The story begins by establishing that Joseph is disliked by his older brothers because he is Jacob's favorite. Consider how you would feel toward a brother or sister whom you feel is your parents' favorite. Joseph is also disliked because he has the ability to interpret dreams. Unfortunately, every dream seems to elevate Joseph's stature, while downgrading that of his brothers. Joseph's brothers get even by selling him into slavery in Egypt.

In Egypt, however, Joseph's special abilities are soon noticed and he become a trusted assistant to the Pharaoh. Later there is a famine in the whole area of Canaan and Egypt. But Joseph, interpreting dreams, predicted the famine and organized a food

The saga of Joseph is preserved in the records of Egypt.

Egyptian, Fourteenth Century B.C.E.

MORE ABOUT THE TEXT

Jacob

The character of Jacob remains enigmatic, as are some of the issues raised by his relationship with the Lord. On the one hand, Jacob seems to have been destined from the beginning to be the more important twin (see *Genesis* 25:23). On the other hand, he resorted to deception to make this come about. As the second son, he would have otherwise had no legal right either to the inheritance of Isaac or to a special paternal blessing—these belonged to the eldest son alone. But through Esau's neglect and Jacob's deception (aided by Rebekah, his mother), Jacob became the stronger of the two. Although he was deceptive, Jacob was also blessed by the Lord with profound experiences of God's presence. His dreams, his awareness of the holiness of certain places, and his "wrestling match" with the angel all show Jacob's alertness to the Lord.

conservation program in Egypt. When Jacob's sons come to Egypt to buy food, they once again meet Joseph. Because of Joseph's success, the whole family moves to Egypt. Thus Joseph, by remaining true to God in spite of adversities, was able to save the family of Jacob/Israel, the traditional ancestor of the people of Israel.

This story forms a bridge between the patriarchs in Canaan and the nearly 500 years of history before the time when Moses would mold the people of Israel into God's Chosen People. Once again, it also shows us that God sometimes picks unlikely people to bear the promises of the covenant, as Joseph is the next to youngest of his brothers, and is sold into slavery as a youth.

It's possible that the story of Joseph was written by someone other than the "J," "P" or "E" sources. Joseph is the perfect example of the "wise man" whose life is totally successful because he behaves in a wise and good manner. This type of literature is typical of the "Wisdom school" which you will study in Chapter 9. In later times, beginning with Solomon, wisdom was a valued type of education. Some scholars think that Wisdom writers crafted the story of Joseph.

Have You Considered?

1. Genesis stresses again and again that God's promises are always kept, even if they are not immediately accomplished. Since the book was finalized during the Babylonian Exile, why would God's faithfulness be an important theme for the Israelites?
2. Why do you suppose that the authors of Genesis told negative stories such as those told about Jacob? What might they have been trying to say?
3. America is a place where many different cultures live side-by-side. How important do you think it is that we all share some common family story such as the one in Genesis? Would such a common story help us deal with the tensions that always exist between different groups?

Spiritual Reflection

Praying for our Ancestors

God said to Jacob/Israel:
"I am God Almighty;
be fruitful and multiply.
A nation, indeed an assembly of nations,
shall stem from you,
and kings shall issue from your loins.
The land I once gave to Abraham and Isaac
I now give you;
And to your descendants after you
will I give this land"

(Genesis 35:11–12)

As members of the Church, we pray for our ancestors in faith as they pray for us. Recite this prayer of blessing (from the final commendation and farewell of the Funeral rite), in memory of a friend or relative who has died:

Leader: Saints of God, come to their aid! Come to meet them, angels of the Lord!
Response: Receive their soul and present them to God the Most High.
Leader: May Christ, who called them, take them to Himself; may angels lead them to Abraham's side.
Response: Receive their soul and present them to God the Most High.
Leader: Give them eternal rest, O Lord, and may your light shine on them forever.
Response: Receive their soul and present them to God the Most High.

MORE ABOUT THE TEXT

Joseph

As a child, Joseph was precocious and conceited. It comes as no surprise that his brothers were wildly jealous of him. The special privileges granted Joseph by their father Jacob included what used to be translated as "a coat of many colors." Modern translations have changed this to a "long tunic with sleeves," but students may prefer the rainbow coat. In either case, the garment was a sign of Jacob's special favor for Joseph and it rankled in the hearts of his brothers.

The character of Joseph as an adult is almost too good to be believed. He was a person of integrity, who resisted the seductions of his boss's wife. Then, when he was in jail (falsely accused), he developed patience and faith. Clearly, he came to terms with his Egyptian life and trusted the Lord's ways. In the end, his integrity was the means of the Lord's salvation.

Q/A

Section One

1. A knowledge of one's roots provides a better foundation to live in the present, since it helps a person answer the question: Who am I?

2. A source is an original literary work used by the authors of the Bible in putting together their own book.

3. The Yahwist ("J") and Elohist ("E") authors bear those titles because those are the names used for God. The Priestly authors ("P") emphasized religious rituals. The "J" author wrote during the time of David and Solomon, the "E" author in the Northern kingdom, and the "P" authors in the Exile.

4. A myth is an imaginative story which embodies the beliefs and values of a group of people.

5. The theological function tells us what God is like and how God relates to us. The cosmic function tells us how the world works and it's purpose. The social functions tell us how society should be organized and who should be in charge. The ethical function tells us what values human beings should have and how we should behave.

6. The oral tradition is the process of preserving the memories of a culture through the telling and retelling of stories.

7. A legend is an unverifiable story about a famous person or an event from the past.

8. A saga is a story with elements of both legend and history which describes a famous person from the past.

Q/A

Section One

1. Why do all people and cultures cherish their family stories?
2. Define the term "source" as it is used in connection to the Bible.
3. Why are the three sources of Genesis known by the names Yahwist, Elohist, and Priestly? When did each of the three authors of Genesis ("J", "E", and "P") write?
4. What is a "myth"?
5. List and define the four functions of myth.
6. Define the "oral tradition."
7. What is a "legend"?
8. What is a "saga"?

Section Two

1. Name two differences and two similarities in comparing the "J" and "P" creation myths.
2. According to the Priestly author, what was the climax of creation?
3. How does the pattern of awareness, choice, conse-quences, and mercy repeat itself in the stories of Cain and Abel, the Flood, and the Tower of Babel?
4. Why were the stories of the patriarchs important to Israel?
5. What was the promise that Yahweh made to Abraham?
6. How is Isaac important to the story of the patriarchs?
7. What is learned from Yahweh's use of Jacob to further the divine plan?
8. How does the Joseph story show us that God sometimes works through unlikely people?

Legend has it that Noah's ark landed safely on Mount Ararat in modern Turkey. No physical evidence of the ark has ever been found.

BIBLE ACTIVITY

1. Psalm 104 is a hymn of praise to God the Creator. Select the verses that remind you of the Priestly story of creation.
2. Compare the waters of the Flood and the waters of Baptism. What are both waters intended to do?
3. Read Deuteronomy 26:5–10 and answer these questions: (a) Who is the "wandering Aramean"? (b) Who is "my father"? (3) What happened to the people in Egypt?
4. Write a story explaining how the patriarchs are your religious ancestors. If you don't feel that way about the patriarchs, pick people who you think are your religious ancestors, and write about them.
5. Divide a piece of paper into two columns. On the left side, list things that God asked Abraham to give up; on the right side list the blessings Abraham received from God. Use Genesis 12, 13, and 15 for reference.

BIBLE ACTIVITY

1. Student responses will vary. Ask students to justify their choices based on specific references to the "J" story.

2. The obvious similarity is that both waters are intended to wash away sins. Have students comment on other, less obvious points of contact. For example, baptism is generally done for infants, just as humanity was in its infancy at the time of the flood.

3. (a) The reference is to Abraham. (b) Abraham, the father of the Hebrew people. (c) The people were maltreated and reduced to slavery, but they were liberated by God.

4. Ask students to incorporate specific references to the stories about the patriarchs into their work. If they choose not to write about the patriarchs, ask them to include specific stories about the people they do choose.

GLOSSARY

- **Abraham:** The original patriarch and the first to receive God's promise.
- **Cosmic Function:** The function of myth which tells us what the world is like and what its purpose is.
- **Elohist:** The writer of some parts of Genesis and other books in the Pentateuch. The Elohist (or "E") is so named for calling God "Elohim."
- **Ethical Function:** The function of myth which tells us what values humans should have and how they should behave.
- **Legends:** Unverifiable stories about heroic people and significant events of the past; they include both fact and fiction.
- **Matriarch:** A woman who is the ancestor of a people, the "mother" of generations.
- **Myths:** Symbolic stories which express religious truths that cannot be proved by historical or scientific means.
- **Oral traditions:** Stories about events and people which are preserved by retelling; they are usually quite consistent. Oral traditions form the basis of much of the biblical writing.
- **Patriarch:** A man who is the "father" of many descendants, the ancestor of a people.
- **Priestly writers:** People during the Exile and post-Exile period who collected the sacred traditions of ancient Israel, preserved them, and interpreted them for future generations.
- **Saga:** A form of legend which concerns some important person of the past.
- **Scribe:** A professional writer and copyist who has responsibility for taking care of a culture's literature. Scribes often felt free to add to and/or rearrange the books they were given.
- **Social Function:** The function of myth which tells us how society should be organized and who should be in charge.
- **Theological Function:** The function of myth which tells people what the gods are like and how they relate with humans.
- **Yahwist:** Also known as the "J" author; the writer of some parts of Genesis, the rest of the Pentateuch, and other books; uses *Yahweh* as the name for God.

UNDERSTANDING MORE ABOUT:

Holy Places

You have already heard of the "Ark of the Covenant" in Chapter 3, when King David brought it to Jerusalem. The Ark was a symbol for the Israelites of their days as wanderers, as in the time of Abraham and the other patriarchs.

The Ark of the Covenant was a special container made of wood and covered with gold that housed the tablets with the written words of the Law and other sacred items. The word "ark" means "chest." When the Israelites traveled through the desert, the Ark led the way.

When the Israelites camped, the Ark was placed in the center of the *Meeting Tent,* also known as the *Dwelling* or *Tabernacle.* The priestly writers described the Dwelling as a tent with a long wooden frame which fit together and made a rectangular building 30 x 10 x 10 cubits (a cubit, remember, is a measure equivalent to about 1 1/2 feet).

The Dwelling was the center of the political and religious life of the Israelites. The Priestly writers acknowledged that God lived in heaven and not on earth. Thus, they did not say that God lived in the sanctuary, but rather that God "pitched His tent" there. The authors did not say that the Tent contained God, rather that God's name dwelt there.

Section Two

1. Two similarities: (1) God creates the world, (2) God creates humanity. Two differences: (1) In "P," everything goes as planned; in "J," God's plan goes awry; (2) in "P," creation happens over six full days; in "J," creation occurs in no fixed time.

2. The climax of the story is the creation of humanity, made in the divine image.

3. **Cain and Abel:** *Awareness*—Cain resents God's favoring of Abel, *Choice*—Cain chooses to kill Abel, *Consequences*—Cain becomes a restless wanderer on the earth, *Mercy*—God marks Cain so that he will not be killed.

   The Flood: *Awareness*—God realizes the extent of human wickedness, *Choice*—Humanity has chosen to disobey God, *Consequences*—God decides to wipe out humanity through a flood, *Mercy*—God spares Noah and make a covenant with him.

   Tower of Babel: *Awareness*—Humanity becomes aware of its own pride, *Choice*—Humanity chooses to build a tower into the sky, *Consequences*—God decides to confuse human speech by creating different languages, *Mercy*—God's purpose was to prevent humans from destroying themselves through arrogance.

4. The stories of the patriarchs served as examples of faith for the Israelites to model.

5. That his descendants would be as numerous as the stars, and would inhabit the land of Canaan.

6. Issac's story is important because it links Abraham and Jacob, and is an example of total faithfulness to God's promises.

7. Jacob's behavior is less than perfect, but God's choosing him shows that Israel's election rests solely on God's will, not on any individual's goodness.

8. Joseph is the youngest of his brothers, sold into slavery as a youth. Nevertheless, God chooses him to inherit the promise of the Covenant.

5. **Things given up:** Left his father's home, fled to Egypt to escape famine.

   Blessings: Promised to be the father of a great nation, his name will be great, all earth will find blessing in him, will be given the land of Canaan, will have descendants more numerous than the stars.

Chapter Overview

After the prosperity and victory of David's rule, the future seemed secure for the Israelite kingdom. However, in this chapter students will discover that such appearances can be deceiving. Through a combination of external (the rising military power of Assyria and Babylon) and internal (the greed of Israel's kings) factors, the Israelite kingdom weakened, split apart, and eventually was destroyed. Students will follow the story of the divided kingdoms, focusing especially on the word of those people who spoke for Yahweh without fear: the prophets.

Teaching Objectives

By the end of this chapter students will be able to:
• Explain the aspects of Solomon's rule which led to the divided kingdom.
• Understand how the two kingdoms violated the Covenant.
• Distinguish between the various kinds of prophets.
• Identify Elijah and Elisha.
• Make connections between the ancient prophets and their own roles as witnesses to God's word.

Welcome

What to Do

Greet the students, either as they arrive or as class begins, by pinning on each student's back a slip of paper on which is written the name of a biblical person you have studied.

The students are to mingle, asking each other questions about the identity of the person on their own slip that can be answered by "yes" or "no." Continue the game until almost everyone knows his or her identity.

This game requires students to recall (in order to form and answer questions) what they know of the biblical characters they have learned about in the previous lessons.

960	**960 B.C.E.** ● Solomon is king ● "E" document written in North
	926 ● Egypt invades Palestine and plunders Jerusalem **920** ● Rehoboam is king—Civil War
900	**900** ● India makes first steel ● First Etruscan towns in Italy
	876 ● Omri king in the North
850	**850** ● Ahab and Jezebel rule in the North **840** ● First Assyrian raid **830** ● King Jehu revolts in the North **825** ● Damascus gets stronger **813** ● Carthage founded
800	**800** ● Iliad and Odyssey written ● Assyria crushes Damascus ● Tribute paid to Assyria

Legend
● General History
● Biblical History
● Jewish History
● Books written

In the early 1960s, General Motors (GM), one of the largest corporations in the world, built a very popular, inexpensive sports car called the "Corvair." Over the course of a few years, however, evidence began to mount that the Corvair was more than an enjoyable car; because of design flaws, it was also a dangerous one. While many people knew about the Corvair's problems, few were willing to take on powerful GM to get the problems corrected.

Ralph Nader was not frightened away by GM's political or financial power. In his book, *Unsafe at Any Speed*, (1965), Nader argued that the American auto industry made cars that were dangerous to drive. Because of Nader's outspokenness and dedication to the truth, GM eventually decided to stop building the Corvair.

MORE ABOUT THE TEXT

Ralph Nader

Students may be curious about what Ralph Nader does today. Mr. Nader is still involved with the organization he founded, the Public Interest Research Group (PIRG), which has offices in Washington, D.C., and is active on a wide range of consumer and public-interest issues. Mr. Nader has never run for elective office or otherwise attempted to benefit from the celebrity status which the GM case won for him. He mobilized college students, nicknamed "Nader's Raiders," in study groups that investigated the activities of government regulatory agencies. The various Nader-affiliated groups research tax reform and health issues, monitor the activities of Congress and of corporations, lobby for new legislation, and finance legal action. In the 1980s Nader focused on insurance rate reduction as well as on a continuing crusade requiring air bags in all new automobiles.

Then, in 1966, the United States Congress passed legislation that set auto safety standards. Millions of people who have survived or even avoided auto accidents since 1966 owe their lives, in some degree, to the willingness of Ralph Nader to speak the truth without fear.

In 1940, Germany's war machine was wreaking havoc throughout the Western world. Its armies controlled all of Europe (except Great Britain and a few other countries) and Northern Africa, and was racing to Moscow in the Soviet Union. They seemed unbeatable. At home in Germany and in the territories they controlled, Adolph Hitler and his government were completing a plan that would be known as the "Final Solution:" the extermination of every Jew from the face of the earth.

While other citizens stood back and watched, the German police and groups of young thugs confiscated Jewish-owned properties, beat the Jewish people without mercy, and then stuffed them into cattle cars and shipped them by rail to concentration camps. Over 6 million Jews and a million others were murdered in these camps in what we now call the Holocaust.

Not all Germans stood quietly in the face of this evil. Some spoke out against the German government. Some, like Oskar Schindler—who rescued hundreds of Jewish prisoners from the death camps—did something quietly. Franz Jägerstätter simply told the truth. When drafted into the German Army, Franz refused to serve. He could have taken a status that would have allowed him to serve as a medical corpsman so that he personally would not have to fight, but he refused that as well.

Franz chose to denounce the evil that was all around him. He could not, as a person of integrity, ignore or be part of it. He was jailed for his statements and threatened with death. All that he would have to do was join the army and he would be saved. But Franz knew better, for he was a man of great faith. He was sure that God's teaching was against this war. Frans refused to join and was put to death for his stand.

Franz' death did not stop the war; it went on for several more years. But his death was not in vain either. Since the end of the war, Franz' story has spread throughout the world. He is honored as a hero in his country and serves as a solitary witness of strength for all people who take a stand against injustice. The book, *In Solitary Witness* by Gordon Zahn recounts Franz Jägerstätter's act of courage.

Have you ever met an inspiring person who was unafraid to speak the truth, even if it might embarrass someone very important? The Bible records the behavior and activities of a group of people who behaved in just this way. Today, these people might be called "loud mouths" or "troublemakers" for their seemingly rude or inconsiderate comments. The Bible, however, calls these people *"prophets."* In this chapter, you'll learn about these people who were unafraid to speak the truth.

MORE ABOUT THE TEXT

In Solitary Witness

In July, 1958, Gordon Zahn wrote an article for *America* magazine about Franz Jägerstätter with the title, "He Would Not Serve." In the article Zahn wrote, "St. Radegund is a village too small to have its own post office, too remote to be reached by normal transportation facilities. Yet in the tiny graveyard of its centuries-old church lie the ashes of a simple farmer who defied a tyrant who had brought all Europe to its knees. It is a quiet place; one feels, a holy place. It may someday be a place of pilgrimages." Zahn was himself something of a prophet: Jägerstätter has now been honored by Austria, and the Austrian bishops have petitioned Rome to declare Franz a saint for his willingness to sacrifice everything for the sake of his faith.

Introducing the Chapter

What to Do

The main concern of this chapter is the role of the prophets during the time of the divided kingdom. The prophets stood up to the powerful people in society, including the kings, and denounced the violations of the Covenant they saw around them. To introduce this concept, begin with how the students respond when they witness injustice.

• Begin the class with a prayer.

• Ask the students to talk about some instances of injustice or wrongdoing they have witnessed or experienced. The examples may come from school, family relationships, or social settings. Try to discourage historical or "current events" types of examples; encourage them instead to speak from personal experience.

• Once a number of examples have been mentioned, ask the students how they responded to these events. Did anyone speak up or take a stand? What difference did this action make?

• Explain to students that in this chapter, they will consider the lives of people who took a stand—the prophets. These people spoke God's words, despite the fact that it was often unpopular and, in many cases, personally very demanding.

Extend the Activity   Have the students read the opening spread in the text. Encourage the students to think of some other person, either in their own lives or in history, who has served as the role of a prophet.

Development

Using the Timeline

Direct students to the timeline. Begin by asking for a volunteer to explain the "E" document; they should remember this from the last chapter. Use the map from Chapter 6 (page 99 or from the Transparency Packet) to explain to students where Assyria and Damascus were located, and that these names will figure prominently in the next chapters.

Point out to students that in 900 B.C.E., after the glory days of David's rule and at the peak of Israel's power, Rome had not yet been founded! This observation may help students place these events in historical perspective.

◆ Politics

Teaching Objectives

By the end of this lesson students will be able to:

• Identify King Solomon.

• Explain why some of his policies led to the split between the Northern and Southern kingdoms.

Development

What to Do

1. Summarize (or have a student summarize) the section opening italicized paragraph and the learning objectives for the students.

2. Ask students to talk about the American Civil War (or any other civil war, including any that might now be occurring somewhere in the world). What were the causes of this civil strife? List the reasons on the board.

   Read the first four paragraphs in "Politics" and "Disunity Under Solomon." Explain to the students that the nation of Israel had probably never been fully unified. Remind them of the period of the judges, when certain tribes fought against one another, and rivalry between the northern and southern tribes seemed intense. While things were going well under King David, it was easy to ignore these divisions, but after David's death, they came to the surface once more.

3. Have the students read "Solomon Abuses His Power." Divide the class into two "political parties," "pro-Solomon" and "anti-Solomon." Have each group draft a "platform." How would the pro-Solomon group defend the king's behavior? How would the anti-Solomon group attack him? When the exercise is finished, bring the class back together and discuss whether or not these differences are serious enough to justify the civil war which followed.

4. Lead the class discussion of the questions in "Have You Considered?"

From David to the Divided Kingdom

Prophets were deeply involved with the political and social concerns of their society. They weren't just politicians, however; they viewed politics and society from the perspective of God's word and Israel's obligation under the Covenant. In fact, if their prophetic work had not been focused on God, it would have lost all meaning and the prophets would have been forgotten long ago. The messages of the prophets that we will consider in this chapter and Chapter 6 developed over a period of about 400 years.

Learning Objectives for Section One

By the end of this section, you will be able to:

• Explain how the policies of Solomon led to the split between North and South and violated the Covenant.

• Define "syncretism" and explain why it was a problem for the Israelites.

• Identify the nations of "Israel" and "Judah" after the Civil War.

◆ Politics

It is not unusual for countries to dissolve because of internal political disputes. Consider what happened when the former nation of Yugoslavia divided into the countries of Serbia, Croatia, Bosnia-Hercegovina, Montenegro, and Macedonia in the early 1990s.

Yugoslavia had been formed from many smaller ethnic territories in 1918. As long as strong political leadership existed, these unlikely partners stayed together as a nation. But with the fall of the Soviet Union, Yugoslavia quickly came apart. Feuds dating back to the Middle Ages, anger over supposed ethnic favoritism, and nationalistic desires erupted into brutal warfare, resulting in Hitler-like "ethnic cleansing" and the destruction of a once prosperous nation.

The nation of Israel experienced a similar division. You remember from Chapter 3 that when the tribal groups became the people of Israel, it was because of the Covenant with Yahweh, not because

they agreed on any particular political system. The Covenant was the reason the nation of Israel existed, and even then it took the genius of King David to form these vastly different tribes into what is called the *United Monarchy*. Although the Bible talks about the 12 Tribes of Israel as if they were a close-knit family, historical evidence—in the Bible and elsewhere—reveals an uneasy union.

Throughout Israel's history, both before and during the monarchy, ancient rivalries and disputes simmered, needing only a slight breeze from an inept leader to ignite the people into full-fledged rebellion. While it's true that Israel was also held together through the power of the Covenant, that power was limited. Ultimately, the people's commitment to the Covenant could not overcome problems of state.

Disunity Under Solomon

Solomon, the son of David and Bathsheba, inherited a strong empire. Israel's borders were broad and secure, its influence was widespread, and it had

---

MORE ABOUT THE TEXT

Solomon

Solomon is remembered by modern people in contradictory ways. 1 Kings regards Solomon with positive appreciation. He was a very fine king, a fine administrator according to the customs of the time. He brought great wealth into the United Kingdom of Israel. Israel was at peace under Solomon, because of his skill at international diplomacy. Solomon's famous wisdom, while not very well-explained in the Bible,

probably means that he was quite highly educated—unusual in a king, in fact, unusual for anyone. Education was a rare commodity. However, he certainly wasn't perfect. Consider his use of slave labor and his worship of gods other than Yahweh.

Today, it is easy for us to see how Solomon caused later problems for his people, but that is in hindsight. Despite these problems, students need to see that Solomon was a capable king.

been at peace with its neighbors for several decades. Yet, while the economy prospered, old hostilities festered like open wounds beneath the surface of outward tranquillity. As a result, the cracks of disunity widened in the kingdom during Solomon's reign.

Solomon's greatest strength, according to the Bible and Hebrew tradition, was a deep wisdom given to him by God. Solomon is said to have made excellent judgments and to have written thousands of proverbs. At the beginning of his reign, Solomon worshipped Yahweh and was humble before God.

Solomon may have been wise in important respects, but his policies contributed to the eventual division of Israel.

1. Even though the country was wealthy, the wealth was not equally distributed; the poor suffered while others became wealthy.
2. Solomon spent lavishly to build the Temple of the Lord, for which the Deuteronomic historian and all later biblical traditions honor him.
3. Solomon also built a large palace, including plenty of rooms for his huge harem.

Solomon spent Israel's wealth with little regard to stewardship for all his subjects.

Solomon Abuses His Power

Solomon's wealth was based on two factors: advantageous trade with other nations and the common use of forced labor. Both of these policies were disruptive to the life of Israel.

Scripture Workshop

Solomon's Wealth

- Read 1 Kings 10:14–29. If each shekel of gold was worth $10 in American money, and if each talent was worth fifteen hundred shekels, how much money did Solomon receive in gold every year? How much did he pay for horses and chariots? How much were each of his shields worth?
- Read 1 Kings 11:1–8. How many wives of princely rank did Solomon have? How did he show favor to them? (A "high place" is an altar or shrine to a foreign god, usually located on a hilltop.)
- Solomon built a large commercial shipping system. Read 1 Kings 9: 26–28. How much money in gold did these ships return from Ophir? In 1 Kings 10: 22–25, what did the ships bring Solomon?

Forced Labor   Forced labor meant that every able-bodied man was required to work directly for the king for a certain period every year. While he worked

Building the Temple is remembered as Solomon's greatest accomplishment.

Scripture Workshop

1 Kings 10:14–29—Solomon received 660 talents each year, for an equivalent total of $9,900,000 per year. His shields were each worth $6,000, and he paid $6,000 per chariot and $1,500 per horse.

1 Kings 11:1–8—He had 700 wives of princely rank. To honor them, he built high places to worship their gods.

1 Kings 9:26–28—The ships brought back the equivalent of $6,300,000 from Ophir.

1 Kings 10:22–25—The ships brought back gold, silver, ivory, apes, and monkeys.

Practicing the Skills

What to Do

Have the students find and read 1 Kings 1:4–15. Compare the picture of Solomon presented here to what else they have learned about him. How is it possible that all these things could be about the same person? For comparison's sake, ask students their opinions about a current political or social figure. When their opinions differ, discuss how the same person can give rise to widely varying impressions and traditions.

Recall

Have the students write the answers to "Chapter 5 Review Q/A," Section One, numbers 1–3, page 90.

Connect

What to Do

With the help of a librarian or another teacher, have the students find out about modern monarchies in the Near East or in Africa. Can they find common traits with Solomon? What differences do they find?

What's Next?

What to Do

Say: "Israel had much in common with other countries, as you are discovering. But Israel was also quite different, because of its relationship with Yahweh. Next time we will look at what that meant to them and what it can mean to us today."

MORE ABOUT THE TEXT

Forced Labor

Forced labor was the usual form of taxation among many ancient Near Eastern cultures. Seen from the usual social viewpoint, Solomon was doing nothing wrong here. Given the equality of people and clans before the Covenant (which the later writers and editors of the Bible understood better than those in Solomon's own time had understood it), however, this practice was wrong.

Help students to see that even though a custom may be legitimate in its own time, it can still be mistaken before God and therefore bring with it consequences that no one intended. Solomon was not a malicious tyrant, but a ruler whose understanding was appropriate for his time and place. The more serious issue for the Covenant people was the importing of foreign religions via the "summit marriages" of Solomon.

Share with the students the visit of the Queen of Sheba to Solomon, narrated in 1 Kings 10. Although it has sometimes been romanticized as an amorous encounter similar to Antony and Cleopatra, the evidence suggests that this was in fact a trading mission in which Solomon and the Queen exchanged goods. Nevertheless, the memory of this encounter as a testament to the wisdom of Solomon is very important in the Jewish tradition. Jesus refers to it in Matthew 12:42, where he recounts the story. Interestingly, he calls her the "Queen of the South," referring to the belief of the time that Sheba was located near Ethiopia, south of Egypt in Africa.

Have You Considered?

1. American slavery was clearly one of the causes of the American Civil War. Ask students to make comparisons between slavery in America and in ancient Israel. Note that in ancient Israel, as in most of the ancient world, slavery was not based on race, and was rarely a lifetime condition.

2. The first commandment of the Decalogue required the Israelites to worship Yahweh alone. The worship of the gods of Solomon's wives obviously violated this requirement.

3. Student responses will vary. Note events such as treaty signing ceremonies and cultural exchanges as symbols of agreements between nations.

Bonus Focus for You ────────

Reread Solomon's prayer at the dedication of the Temple, in 1 Kings 8:22–53. Hardly a verbatim report of Solomon's words, it was written centuries later, and reflects a later view. How does this later view relate to what is in the student text and the enrichment sections of this lesson? What is your personal assessment of Solomon?

for the king, his own job was neglected, he left his family behind, and he was not paid. It was his legal obligation to the king; he had no choice.

Many years before Solomon, when the people had begged for a king, Samuel had warned them that a king would use forced labor to generate wealth (1 *Samuel* 8:10–18).

Forced labor created discontent throughout Israel among the people and the leaders of the various tribes. This resentment was especially strong in the North, because most of the forced labor came from there, while most of the building took place in the South. The best example of a building project in the South is the famous Temple of Solomon.

Prosperous Trade   Israel also enjoyed prosperous trade relations made possible by Solomon's many alliances with other countries. Solomon secured Israel's alliances with these countries through the use of *"summit marriages."* Such a marriage occurs when a member of one royal family marries a member of another royal family. Once married, the two royal families (and therefore the nations) were considered allies for the duration of the marriage.

Kings were expected to have many wives for the benefit of the country. However, when Solomon's foreign wives also brought with them their own gods, religious practices, and priests, it was too much for the people of the Covenant to bear.

Note that neither forced labor nor summit marriages were considered wrong at this time. Solomon was doing only what all other kings had done for centuries. Today, in the democracy of the United States, we recognize that forced labor is an injustice. But in the ninth century B.C.E., in an economy not totally based on money, forced labor was simply a form of taxation. It was, as 1 Samuel 8:9,11 clearly says, the right of kings.

Have You Considered?

1. In what sense did forced labor help cause the Civil War in the United States? How similar was this situation to the one in the time of King Solomon?
2. Why would it bother the people of Israel for Solomon's wives to introduce the worship of their own gods? What part of the Law did this act violate?
3. Summit marriages were used to link countries together as allies. How are agreements sealed today?

Solomon's Mines

Solomon built a temple which was one of the wonders of the ancient world. The Temple was built with cedar and stone, but most of it was plated with gold, so that it reflected the sun and could be seen even at a great distance. Inside the Temple, the stonework was plated with gold and ivory. It must have been an awesome sight.

Solomon used so much gold in building the Temple that some people have speculated that he must have had a secret gold mine. 1 Kings 10:11 says that Solomon's fleet brought gold from a place called "Ophir." People have debated the location of Ophir for centuries, with some saying it was in Arabia, others in India, and still others in Africa.

A famous adventure story by H. Rider Haggard, *King Solomon's Mines*, placed Ophir in a fictional Central African country. In the nineteenth century, many people thought that the lost city of Zimbabwe in Africa contained the secret mine (a Roman coin was even found at the site).

Archaeologists have established, however, that Zimbabwe could not have been built before 500 C.E. Today, the most likely site for Ophir is thought to be a spot on the Red Sea in Saudi Arabia. This theory, however, has not stopped adventurers from seeking the "lost mine" in obscure places across the globe.

◆ Violations of Covenant Law

Israel was different from other countries because of the Covenant with Yahweh, which was the basic reason for the existence of the nation. Solomon's policies were seen by many Israelites, especially those in the northern part of the kingdom, as a violation of Covenant law.

The justice issue of forced labor was a major problem. The unequal distribution of the country's wealth was not only a source of individual discontent, but it was also a violation of the Covenant principle that all people were of equal worth before Yahweh, and therefore equal before the Law.

Solomon's foreign wives violated the Covenant. They brought with them into Israel religious allegiance to gods other than Yahweh. In order for the wives to practice their religion, shrines were built to idols. Furthermore, as Solomon grew older, he joined

---

◆ MORE ABOUT THE LESSON

Political Parties

Encourage students to exercise their creativity on this assignment. They might be directed to develop bumper stickers, signs, slogans, and even advertising campaigns. The value of the assignment is twofold:

• It deepens their understanding of the policies pursued by King Solomon.

• It helps them see the divisive potential of these policies.

If time permits, it would be helpful to have students consult a Bible encyclopedia or other resource to extend their knowledge of Solomon's reign.

his wives in the worship of these foreign gods (1 *Kings* 11:1–13). In doing so, Solomon was acting like any other king in the ancient world, who was expected to honor his wife's gods. What Solomon forgot, however, was the Covenant's demand that Israel be different than other nations.

The Importance of Religion

While living by their religious values is important for some Americans, for others today religion is largely separate from public life. Society is "secular," meaning non-religious. Our society does not assume that God is involved with politics, foreign policy, or military action. Many people who consider themselves religious think of religion only on Sunday or when tragedy occurs.

Even though we assume that this separation between religion and the rest of life is normal, it's not. Religion of some kind has influenced all previous cultures. Religion is the foundation of societies—their life-blood; the essence of their view of the world.

In the ancient Middle East, all of life was religious. A truly secular viewpoint was unimaginable. People believed that every event occurred because God wanted it to, so every event had religious importance. Religion included not only the individual, but the community and state as well. Government power was believed to come from their god, so foreign alliances were also religious alliances.

No doubt, an individual king might keep his private allegiance to his own god, as ordinary folks also did. In the Middle East, variety in religion was tolerated. Most people did not think it was a problem to mix religions, except for the Yahwists, whose God was known as the "Jealous One."

Why Worship Only One God?

Many people in Israel must have asked, "Why does Israel worship only Yahweh? If a lot of gods exist, why not respect and worship whichever ones can help us most?" This question was very practical, since ancient people assumed that different gods had different responsibilities: one god controlled the crops, another childbirth, another commerce, and so on. If this division of labor was true, didn't it simply make sense to honor all of those gods rather than just one?

People wanted very practical knowledge about the gods and wanted to know who was in charge. They wanted to know:

- Who can save us? Who can keep us from trouble and evil?
- Who is in charge of rain, storms and earthquakes?
- Who makes animals and plants reproduce? Who keeps the ground fertile? Who has power over this vast world?
- How does one get justice? Who is the real judge who keeps humans in line with justice? Who condemns and who sets free? What is the last court of appeal for people and for nations?
- Who answers prayer? Even if more than one god is "out there," who responds to my cry? How can I reach that one?
- Who determines which nation prospers and which languishes?
- Do human beings, especially the Israelites, have any control over their own lives? How?

These were living questions. The answers to them made a big difference in people's choices and behavior; the answers determined how people lived. Those answers also determined people's attitudes about how Israel should relate to other nations and their gods.

For strict Yahwists, the Covenant provided all the answers. Yahweh, the only God of the Israelites, was the force behind everything that happened to them. It took the Israelites centuries, however, to understand that Yahweh was the one real power in the universe.

Popular Religious Practice

Religions, in 850 B.C.E., were fully *syncretistic*. *Syncretism* means the attempt to blend differing religious systems into one belief, without distinguishing one from another.

Despite the demands of the Covenant, syncretism took place in Israel. Belief and worship of gods other than Yahweh gradually became part of Hebrew religious practices. This blending of beliefs came about quite gradually, so that most people would never have noticed the change. People could have mistakenly worshipped a foreign god when they thought that they were worshipping Yahweh as the Covenant demanded.

Ordinary people would probably have trouble explaining why they shouldn't mix religious practices. When the Israelites settled in Canaan among people who had been farmers for centuries, they had to learn how to be successful farmers themselves.

◆ MORE ABOUT THE LESSON

The Covenant

The important points about the Covenant here are that it defined Yahweh's relationship with the Israelites and that it promised lasting prosperity to the nation for keeping the Covenant, and problems if it did not. Although this understanding of the Covenant was fully developed only after the Exile (in order to explain why Judah and Israel had been destroyed), the witness and messages of the prophets to the dangers of ignoring the Covenant cannot be ignored. People were aware of the consequences of disobedience during the time of the divided kingdom, but continued to disregard them.

LESSON TWO (pages 78–82)

◆ Violations of Covenant Law

Welcome

What to Do

Set up a corner of the room with a Bible altar. Decorate a table (cloth, flowers, open Bible) and treat it as a place of honor.

With two or three volunteers, welcome the incoming students as you would welcome someone into your home. Ask the students to notice especially the "altar" that honors the Bible. Ask them to notice it each time they come in. Have the students gather, standing around the "altar" to pray together. Invite them to mention what they've learned so far. The group will respond "Thanks be to God" to each contribution.

Introducing the Lesson

Teaching Objectives

By the end of this lesson students will be able to:

- Explain the seriousness of Solomon's violations of the Covenant.
- Describe why worship of Yahweh alone was important to the Israelites.
- Define "syncretism."
- Describe the formation of Israel and Judah.
- Explain the effect civil war had on both kingdoms.

What to Do

Ask someone to review the meaning of "Covenant." Discuss with students why the demands of the Covenant were so important to the Israelites, and were so highly valued by the Deuteronomic historian, who wrote this account of Solomon's reign.

Development

What to Do

1. Have the students read "The Importance of Religion."

2. Challenge the students to use their imagination about what their life would be like if everything was believed to be connected to religion and to God. For example, invite them to consider possible divine explanations for

natural phenomena such as earthquakes and illnesses. Ask them to describe aspects of their own experience that might be different if this were so.

3. Have the students write in their Spiritual Journal their own opinions about this question: "How would my life be different if everything had a religious significance?"

4. Now review with students ancient Israel by having them read "Why Worship Only One God?" and "Popular Religious Practice."

5. Have the students discuss their reading, adding the input below in "More About the Text."

6. Review the provisions of the Covenant (the Ten Commandments in Exodus 20:1–17). Have them find the reference. Ask them whether or not today's society, church, and individuals live up to that Covenant foundation. Compare the reasons of the Israelites as given in their text with what they imagine are today's reasons.

7. Explain that the split between north and south occurred just after the death of Solomon, when his son Rehoboam took over. Remind students that like any conflict, the long-term issues which divided north and south required a "triggering event" to ignite the civil war. Rehoboam supplied such an event.

Practicing the Skills

What to Do

Have the students find and read 1 Kings 12:1–16. If they are interested in the immediate results of the secession, they can read the rest of Chapter 12 as well.

Have the students read "Understanding More About:" on page 91. Say: "This is only one of the difficulties faced by people in Solomon's kingdom." Have them look up and compare the references suggested in the feature: 1 Kings 17:2–24, 2 Kings 4:1–7, and Luke 7:11–17.

Have You Considered?

1. Encourage students to provide their own examples of a separation of religion from the rest of life. Note the tendency of modern people to "compartmentalize" religion as one aspect of their lives.

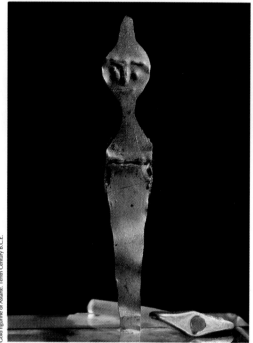

Gold figurine of Astarte. Tenth Century B.C.E.

The Canaanite people prayed to the goddess Astarte. The prophets complained that the Israelites also prayed to her.

- They needed to be sure of nature's cooperation: the right amount of rain and sun, and the natural reproductive cycles of their animals.
- They needed protection from natural disasters—drought, violent storm, earthquakes.

The Israelites saw the successful Canaanite farmers worshipping the gods of nature—the fertility god, *Baal*, and the fertility goddess, *Astarte*—whose sexual activity was believed to keep the earth and its inhabitants fertile.

Since it was the fertility gods' sexual activity that kept everything going in nature, worship of these gods involved sexual intercourse with "sacred prostitutes," women who dedicated themselves to the fertility god and gave their bodies to male worshippers for religious rites. Male "sacred prostitutes" performed similar homosexual rites. These rituals seemed logical to many Israelites, who thought they kept the earth fertile and the crops growing.

Even when fidelity to the Covenant was strong, many Israelites practiced fertility religion in addition to their worship of Yahweh. Isn't it logical that

in the Spotlight

Syncretism

Syncretism happens whenever different cultures come into contact and exchange religious ideas. As a result, almost all religions, past and present, have been affected by syncretism to some extent. Let's take two examples, one historical and one from the present, which illustrate how syncretism works.

Isis and Sarapis

Six centuries after Solomon, Alexander the Great conquered much of the world. He brought with him the culture of Greece, including Greek religious ideas. These ideas interacted with the religious concepts of the people Alexander conquered, often resulting in syncretism. An example of this are the Egyptian gods Isis and Sarapis.

Traditionally, the Egyptians thought of their gods in the form of animals. They worshipped the god Apis in the form of a bull, and Isis as a cow. Under the impact of Greek ideas, however, Apis was combined with the Greek god Zeus, and was pictured as a powerful male with a flowing beard. He was called Sarapis. Isis became the beautiful young female goddess Demeter. In this form, Isis and Sarapis became popular all over Europe and the Middle East. Like the Egyptian gods, they had power over immortality, but like the Greek gods, they had human forms and behaviors.

Santería

A contemporary example of syncretism is the religion called "Santería." Santeria has its roots in West African tribal religions focused on spirits and souls. When these religions were brought to islands such as Cuba and Haiti by African slaves, they interacted with the Roman Catholic faith of the European settlers. Santería, which blends elements of voodoo, tribal religion, and Catholicism, is a result of this interaction.

Santeros and Santeras (people who practice Santería) believe in many spirits (called orishas) who can bring good luck in business and love, and who can protect them from evil. Often, these spirits are depicted as Catholic saints, especially the Virgin Mary. Santeros sacrifice goats, chickens, pigs, roosters, and other animals to these spirits to win their favor. The U.S. Supreme Court ruled such sacrifices legal in 1993.

a farmer would want to worship the god that he believed had power over farming? And isn't it logical that a newcomer in a culture would learn from the natives in the area what it took to live successfully there?

◆ MORE ABOUT THE LESSON

A Religious Society

The imaginative discussion about a totally religious society may seem more like science fiction than anything else, but it is a good exercise to help the students try to "jump into the skin" of another kind of culture and experience. It may also help them to see areas where their faith could be relevant if they choose to make it so. You can stimulate their imagination with these questions and suggestions:

- How does faith affect how a person lives his or her life?
- How are ritual actions, like small sacrifices, signs of faith? (For example, in India a newly married couple is traditionally given a newly kindled fire, which will remain burning in their home all the rest of their lives, as a symbol of the silent witness of God to all that happens in that family.)

The Yahwists knew, however, that this logic was false. The people of the Covenant were committed to serve and worship one god only: Yahweh. Yahweh required total loyalty from Israel, and worship of other gods was a violation of the Covenant. Because of this violation of the Covenant, Yahweh sent prophets to call Israel back to faithfulness.

Have You Considered?

1. How do people today separate their religious life from their public or common life? What are the consequences of this behavior?
2. Israel was, for most of its history, a tiny nation against great empires. How do you think the prohibition against syncretism helped it maintain its identity in such a situation?
3. Exodus refers to Yahweh as "the Jealous One." Why would this understanding of the Covenant lead to inevitable conflict between those who strictly followed the Covenant and those who were willing to worship other gods?

Civil War is always brutal, whether in ninth century B.C.E. Israel or in twentieth century C.E. Bosnia.

◆ The Collapse of the Nation

The worship of foreign gods, the unequal distribution of wealth, and the injustice of forced labor were like small flames, waiting only for a wind to catch them and blow them into raging firestorms. This wind was to be Solomon's successor, his son, Rehoboam.

The elders of the northern tribes came to Rehoboam to find out what his policies were to be. Rehoboam, an egotistical brat, said to them, "If you think my father was difficult, wait until you see me." With that, the northern tribes rebelled. They expelled Rehoboam from the Covenant and seceded from the United Monarchy (1 *Kings* 12:1–16). It was civil war. The 12 tribes would never be united again.

Civil War

The kingdom put together by David and Solomon now split into two separate nations at war with each other: Israel to the north and Judah to the south. After this time, only the Northern kingdom is called "Israel."

Israel and Judah accused each other of violating the Covenant. The North objected to Solomon's policies. The South thought that rebellion against the House of David violated the Covenant. Further, because the northern king, Jeroboam, set up national shrines in Dan and Bethel so that his citizens would not be tempted to look to Jerusalem as their center of worship and government, Judah accused Israel of false worship.

By 850 B.C.E., sixty or seventy years of civil war had left the two nations greatly weakened. The borders of David's kingdom were now much smaller. Conditions in the countries were bad because so much of their resources went into the fight. Even when Israel and Judah were not actively at war, they were spying, intriguing and plotting against one another.

Fortunately for Israel's and Judah's continued existence, neither Egypt nor any of the Mesopotamian nations were aggressive during this time. Israel and Judah did struggle with the smaller countries around them—Moab, Edom, Syria, and Phoenicia. Since all of these countries were fairly evenly matched, none could really dominate. Power would ebb and flow between them.

2. The prohibition against syncretism helped protect Israelite religion from gradually blending in with other traditions.
3. Those who strictly followed the Covenant would see those who honored other gods as sinners who jeopardized the well-being of the nation. Conflict between the two groups was inevitable.

Bonus Focus for You ————

What do you include as important in your life that may not exactly go with your Christian understanding of God?

◆ The Collapse of the Nation

What to Do

Ask students if they have ever been part of a serious split between people or groups. Many students may have experienced the divorce of their parents, a split which has deep and long lasting consequences for all parties. If they can, ask them to discuss what this experience was like. In any event, encourage students to discuss the damage done by such break-ups. After a few minutes, make the transition to the split between Israel and Judah.

Development

What to Do

1. Have students read "Civil War." What might it be like to live through such an event?
2. Have students read "Conflicts between Rich and Poor." Ask: "Why would abuses of power become much more common in times of conflict, when legitimate authority breaks down? How do such abuses breed more conflict?
3. Ask the students to answer the questions in "Have You Considered?" as a group assignment.

Practicing the Skills

What to Do

Have the students do the exercise in "Learn from the Map." What did the division in the kingdom cost?

Recall

Ask students to mention the two or three most important points covered in this lesson. Remind them of

---

MORE ABOUT THE TEXT

Syncretism

The Covenant with Yahweh was actually a huge and challenging ideal presented by God to the Israelites. It required a lot of stretching for them even to consider it. From the earliest days of the Covenant, they had difficulty living up to this ideal, but Yahweh used their history to teach them.

If the students understand what they have read and can think a little bit like the Israelites, they may think that syncretism was a totally natural response to their situation—maybe not even so bad! Such an idea is thoughtful, but does not give the students the clear idea of how much better Yahweh's ideas and plans were. If the Israelites had been able to live out the Covenant, their history would have been very different and their life much more fruitful. We face the same dilemma as a Church. The Covenant Law is still not lived thoroughly.

the central points: the importance of the Covenant and the impact of the civil war on both kingdoms.

Connect

What to Do

Homework Assignment: Ask students to locate an article in an encyclopedia or other resource about life in the South after the American Civil War. Using this article as a point of departure, ask them to assume the identity of an Israelite who has just lived through the civil war, and is writing a letter to someone describing the experience, including specific names, dates, and locations.

What's Next?

What to Do

Review the stories in the opening spread of Chapter 5. Say: "Yahweh did not just abandon Israel for its Covenant violations. Instead, the Lord sent prophets to remind and teach them their obligation to the Covenant. The next two lessons are about these special messengers from God, especially one of the earliest and greatest."

Have You Considered?

1. Responses to this question will vary, but should include economic injustice and the use of forced labor.
2. Rehoboam demanded even more in taxes and labor from the people than did his father Solomon. He should have been more reasonable and listened to the legitimate needs of the north.
3. Obvious similarities include the split between north and south, cultural differences between the two groups, and the issue of slavery. Obvious differences include the outcome, the size and scope of the conflict.

Bonus Focus for You

Read 1 Kings 12 again, the description of Rehoboam and the split between north and south. How did Rehoboam fail as a leader in this situation? Apply whatever insights you gain to your own leadership role as teacher. How can you avoid the mistakes that Rehoboam made?

The poverty that most people lived in compared to the king's extravagance was a cause of Israel's civil war.

Conflicts between Rich and Poor

By 850, social conditions had also worsened. The poor were getting poorer, the rich richer. The weak had less and less power while the strong became more powerful. Royalty and the higher classes were now legally able to extort what they wanted from the lower class.

The two Israelite kingdoms were equally guilty of this behavior, although injustice seems to have been worse in the Northern kingdom than in the South. Such injustice was clearly a violation of the Covenant.

In the Covenant, Yahweh had established principles for people's relationship with each other based on *justice*. Yahweh's *Covenant law* was designed to ensure social harmony. The Covenant law treated all people equally: Just is just and crime is crime, no matter whether one is rich or poor, powerful or weak. Since the Covenant belonged to Yahweh, Yahweh was in charge of justice. But this aspect of Covenant Law was widely ignored by 850 B.C.E. Chief among those who were still loyal to the Covenant were the prophets.

Have You Considered?

1. What were the primary reasons the North broke away from the South? What were the secondary reasons?
2. Read 1 Kings 12:1–16. What major mistake did Rehoboam make with the people of Israel? What might he have done differently to preserve the nation?
3. Compare what you know about the American civil war with the fight between Israel and Judah. What do you think are the major similarities and differences?

LEARN FROM THE MAP

Ancient Israel

Although Saul was king of Israel, the country was surrounded by hostile neighbors. As king, David established Israel as a nation with borders respected by its neighbors. Under David's rule, Israel was able to expand its borders. Many of the small nations surrounding Israel were forced to pay tribute and to accept some degree of subordination to it.

After the death of Solomon, the ten northern tribes became the nation of Israel with its capitol and religious center in Samaria. The two southern tribes, Judah and Benjamin became the nation of Judah with its political and religious capitol in Jerusalem.

The two separate nations were never as strong as David's kingdom had been. They could not hold all of the territory that had been gained. The smaller nations that had paid David tribute reclaimed their independence and became military adversaries of Israel and Judah.

Compare David's empire with the kingdoms of Israel and Judah in 850 B.C.E. How do they differ? Explain the reasons for the differences.

©1994 Magellan Geographic™ Santa Barbara, CA.

Samaria

Your students may recognize Samaria from the Gospel parable about the "good Samaritan." Then, "Samaria" was the name of the capital of the Northern kingdom. Later, however, it became the name of the entire region above Judah and below Galilee. Hostility between the people of this region and those who lived in Judah dates as far back as the civil war. This hostility forms the backbone of Jesus' parable: It was the Samaritan, the enemy, who acted to help the injured Judahite, and not his countrymen.

The Role of the Prophets

Michelangelo, Sibyl, *The Prophetess of Cuma*, Sixteenth Century

The Hebrew word translated as "prophet" is nabi (<u>pronounced nah-bee</u>). Nabi can mean either "one who calls out, announces" or "one who is called."

The essential point about all the great prophets is that they were "possessed" by the spirit of Yahweh. Yahweh's spirit filled the personality of the individual, somewhat as it had changed the personalities of the judges years earlier and impelled the prophet to speak Yahweh's word and act out Yahweh's message. God used the prophets to affect the lives of people in both kingdoms.

Learning Objectives for Section Two

By the end of this section, you will be able to:

- Identify the different kinds of prophets.
- Understand the three elements of the prophetic word.
- Explain the significance of the prophets Elijah and Elisha to the history of Israel.
- Recognize the parallels between the prophets' situation and our own.

◆ Who Were the Prophets?

Different types of prophets are mentioned in the Old Testament. Some of them had official positions in society while others did not. Among the people who made their living as prophets were seers and official court prophets. "Unofficial" prophets served only when moved by the spirit of Yahweh and for them, prophecy was not a means of livelihood. Let's look at each of these types of prophets in turn.

Seers

From the time that Israel crossed the Jordan following the Exodus, there had been prophets loosely connected with shrines and places of worship around the country. There they offered answers to people who came to worship, to seek advice, or to ask a divine favor. These prophets were called "ecstatics" or "seers."

Seers seem to have depended on altered states of consciousness to receive their messages from Yahweh. They might listen to music to help them into these states, and sometimes they danced or sang as well. These ecstatic prophets saw visions, heard messages in dreams, and predicted the future. Their behavior suggested that they were not their usual selves, but were "possessed" by the spirit of Yahweh, and they acted accordingly.

Most prophets lived in groups. Today, we might call these groups *prophetic guilds*. Participation in a group often enhanced ecstatic states, for the condition seemed to be quite contagious when a person was susceptible (like Saul in 1 *Samuel* 10:10–13). Group life also helped, no doubt, with such necessities as food and shelter. Prophetic guilds lived on the edge of society and were sometimes summoned by the king or other officials to answer a question by the spirit of Yahweh (1 *Kings* 22, for example).

Samuel (mentioned in Chapter 3) is an example of a seer. He became a great leader of the Israelites, who revered his closeness to Yahweh.

MORE ABOUT THE TEXT

Seers

At the top of page 83 in the student text is Michelangelo's depiction of the Sibyl, the most popular seer in the ancient Roman world. A collection of works attributed to the Sibyl, called the "Sibylline Oracles," was kept in the Roman state archives and consulted on important decisions. This illustrates the cross-cultural nature of prophecy in the ancient world. All cultures had their prophets and seers who were believed to have special insight into the spiritual world. What made Israelite prophecy special was its insistence on righteousness and justice as prerequisites for gaining the favor of the gods.

LESSON THREE (pages 83–85)

◆ Who Were the Prophets?

Welcome

Greet the students as a group by sharing with them some of your interest and pleasure in being with them and learning together.

What to Do

Ask each student to say aloud one thing he or she likes best about the Bible. Write each item on the chalkboard. Ask your students to turn their appreciation into thanksgiving by writing a prayer. For example, "Thank you God for the story of Moses, which helps me to understand you better." Share these prayers aloud. The group can respond: "Thank you, God."

Introducing the Lesson

Teaching Objectives

By the end of this lesson students will be able to:

- Identify the three main kinds of prophets.
- Explain the type of message delivered by an unofficial prophet.
- Make connections between the functions of the prophets and their own lives.

What to Do

Say: "Today we will begin to learn about God's special messengers to Israel, the prophets. You may remember from Chapter 3 that Samuel was called a prophet, without explanation. What does it mean to be a prophet?"

Development

What to Do

1. Have the students look again at the timeline for Chapter 5, beginning with the year 876. Only the names of kings and countries are given there. Say: "The first of the so-called 'classical' prophets was Elijah, whom we will study tomorrow. He and his successor Elisha lived during the reign of Ahab and Jezebel in Israel. The work of the major prophets began with them. Locate this time on your timeline."

2. Have the students read "The Role of the Prophets" and the learning

objectives. Tell them that today's lesson focuses on the first two objectives. The next lesson focuses on the second two.

3. Ask a volunteer to describe the changes in the judges when they were filled with Yahweh's spirit, as they recall from Chapter 3.

4. Say: "Just as there were women judges, so also there were women who were prophets." Have the students open their Bibles, prepared to find passages. Have them read "People of Note" on page 84 and find each of the references given in the feature.

5. Now have everyone read "Court Prophets." Ask them to recall the story of David and Bathsheba. Have the students look up and read all the references mentioned in this section.

6. Discuss this question briefly with the class: "If Nathan was a typical court prophet, what would you think of court prophets and their work?"

7. Have the students read "Unofficial Prophets."

8. Have them look up and read Deuteronomy 18:15–22. Ask if they can find in Deuteronomy the three points listed in their text. What other points can they find?

9. Lead the class in a discussion of questions 1 and 2 of "Have You Considered?"

Practicing the Skills

Students learn to find and understand in the Bible the passages from which the text material is drawn.

What to Do

Point out the next three sections of their text: "Seers," "Court Prophets," and "Unofficial Prophets." Say: "These are the types of prophets in the Old Testament. Sometimes the 'types' overlapped, but no matter what type they were, what is important is the action of Yahweh through them."

Have everyone, with Bibles open, read "Seers." They are to find in the Bible the references given and describe what they read.

Recall

Ask the students to write out their answers to "Chapter 5 Review Q/A," Section Two, numbers 1–4, on

People of Note

Women Who Were Prophets

The Old Testament makes no distinction between male and female prophets. Even so, only a few women are called by that title. Female prophets include Miriam, Deborah, and Huldah.

- **Miriam** is the sister of Moses and Aaron and is often mentioned as one of the trio of leaders during the Exodus. The Lord spoke through her as well as Aaron and Moses, though Moses was clearly the greatest—as Miriam found out to her pain when she challenged him (Numbers 12:1–15). Miriam's death is recorded in Numbers 20:1, something the Old Testament does only for important people. Miriam is called a prophet in the Book of Exodus 15: 20–21.

- The prophet **Deborah** was a judge and a warrior in the period before Samuel. She held court under a palm tree, and people came to her to settle their disputes. She led Israel into battle and predicted its victory. The story of this battle is in Judges 4; it reads like a modern newspaper story. Judges 5 records a hymn of triumph attributed to Deborah herself.

- **Huldah** was also consulted by a king during a time of crisis. When he discovered a book in the Temple and wondered what to do, King Josiah (640–609 B.C.E.) ordered his priest and servants to "Go, consult the Lord for me." They went to Huldah, a prophet and the wife of the wardrobe keeper in the Jerusalem court. She gave them the word of the Lord. See 2 Kings 22:1–20.

Court Prophets

Other prophets, usually not of the ecstatic type, held official positions in the royal court. These prophets received messages from Yahweh through rolling dice or sometimes through a dream. They, too, were impelled by the spirit to speak and act out the words of Yahweh, no matter what the risk was to themselves.

Some court prophets had a function similar to public relations people today. Their job was to always predict great success and prosperity for the king, no matter what was going on. The king would usually keep a staff of such prophets to calm the public when things went wrong, and to dispute other prophets when they criticized the king. Nathan and later court prophets true to Yahweh were constantly arguing with these "P.R. prophets."

Although prophets were often treated with greater respect in Israel because the life of a prophet was considered sacred to Yahweh, their lives and income depended on the king. At this time, messengers who brought bad news to the king were often killed on the spot. A prophet who spoke the word of the Lord directly, no matter whom that word challenged—even the king—had to be courageous.

One such courageous prophet was Nathan. Nathan was the official court prophet for King David. He had personal access to the king and kept a history of events, which has been lost (see 1 Chronicles 29:29). David often sought Nathan's advice, such as when David wanted to build a temple for the Lord. Through Nathan, the Lord gave David information about his work and his dynasty (2 Samuel 7:1–17). We know little about Nathan except for his official prophetic work.

The word of Yahweh through Nathan was not always pleasant. As you recall from Chapter 3, God sent Nathan to challenge King David face to face, condemning David for taking Bathsheba and having her husband murdered. Review that story now by reading again 2 Samuel 12:1–25. Instead of concentrating on David, though, notice Nathan.

- What did Nathan do?
- Why did he do it?
- What does this story tell you about the role of a court prophet in Israel?

Nathan didn't always act solely on the word of Yahweh. He was also a shrewd political manipulator. Consider how he conspired with Bathsheba and the head of David's army to ensure Solomon's succession to the throne over his older brothers who had a better claim by birth (1 Kings 1:1–53).

Unofficial Prophets

Other prophets did not belong to a guild or hold a position at court or in the Temple. Most of the great prophets whose works appear in the Old Testament were unofficial prophets. Lack of a professional position, however, by no means kept the prophets from answering the spirit of Yahweh or from doing what that spirit requested of them. For them, prophecy was not a job—it was their whole life.

◆ MORE ABOUT THE LESSON

Court Prophets

This discussion is intended to help the students think about prophets without assuming that a prophet is somehow no longer human. Students' opinions of Nathan are less important than the process they go through to form that opinion.

When the spirit of Yahweh worked through a prophet, it did not do away with the prophet's personality. Prophets continued to live their lives and sometimes even did their work and perhaps never had another encounter with the spirit of the Lord after their work was done. We actually know very little about prophets' lives, even Nathan's.

The Bible describes a prophet in Deuteronomy 18:15–22. This description, probably written after the year 600 B.C.E., tells us what ancient Israel believed about Yahweh's prophets. It is a perfect description of the prophetic message.

1. **Clear and Direct.** The prophetic message did not come in the form of philosophical or theoretical explanations. Its words and acts were always about concrete situations and real-life issues. The prophets spoke and acted with power and persistence, sometimes with bitterness, sometimes with tenderness. Whatever the tone, their message was always directed to people's actual life situations, never to abstract principles.
2. **Addressed to Specific Audience.** The message might be directed to individuals, if they were socially important like the king or queen. Other messages were addressed to all the people of Israel or Judah.
3. **Immediate Action.** The message corresponded to issues happening right then in the society or the government. It was most often political—including Yahweh's word on foreign, military, or social policy. Yahweh sometimes inspired revolution and chose kings through the prophets, as he did through Elijah and Elisha (compare 1 *Kings* 19:15 with 2 *Kings* 8:7–15).

The prophetic word was never just information or advice. Yahweh's word was always a demand for action. People expected Yahweh to act in Israel's life; after all, that was how they had become a people under Moses.

Have You Considered?

1. Describe in your own words the difference between a court prophet, a seer, and an unofficial prophet.
2. Why would it take a great deal of courage to tell the king the truth, especially if the truth would be considered bad news? What might a less-than-brave prophet do in difficult situations?
3. If a prophet is someone who speaks the truth about politics and society on the basis of God's word, who are modern day prophets? What criteria would you use today to determine a modern prophet?

◆ Elijah

Elijah was an unofficial prophet. While he knew the prophetic guilds and sometimes associated with them, he generally acted alone. He was a faithful servant of Yahweh (1 *Kings* 18:36, 19:10), who followed the direction of the Lord. He was certainly not an ecstatic prophet. The description of the ecstatic Canaanite priests is in total contrast to the calm Elijah in 1 Kings 18.

Yet, Elijah was thoroughly possessed by Yahweh's powerful spirit. Through the Spirit, Elijah was a persistent and forceful advocate of Yahweh's Covenant with Israel.

The Challenge from King Ahab

By 850 B.C.E., the affairs of the Northern kingdom had reached a crisis stage. Ahab, the king of Israel, had married Jezebel, the daughter of the king of Tyre and Sidon (also called Phoenicia). The wedding of Ahab and Jezebel was a summit marriage designed to ratify an alliance between Israel and Phoenicia.

Jezebel brought with her to Israel a huge staff, including hundreds of priests of Baal-Melkart, a god of nature. She supported her staff from the public treasury. Ahab had a temple built for her to use. Although he himself probably was a Yahwist, he clearly saw no reason to be exclusive about his worship. Syncretism posed no problems for Ahab.

Ahab's father, Omri, had been a powerful ruler who built the city of Samaria for his capital. Samaria was so splendid that it remained the symbol of the Northern kingdom for centuries after its destruction. The "House of Omri" is mentioned in written records from surrounding countries, always with respect. The writer of the Book of Kings, however, did not approve of Omri's religious activities, so very little is said about him there (1 *Kings* 16:23–28).

Ahab continued to build in Samaria and in Jezreel, both important military and economic sites, because they were easy to defend and near trade routes. Ahab had a rich kingdom indeed, but it was based on the same policies that Solomon had used—and he was also dominated by his wife, who was aggressive in her worship of the foreign god, Baal.

An Unconventional Powerhouse of a Man

Under Ahab and Jezebel, the existing conflict in the kingdom of Israel worsened.

---

page 90. Add this question: By what criterion did the Israelites know whether a prophet was a "true" prophet or not?

Connect

Students will begin to think about and identify modern prophets.

What to Do

Discuss question 3 of "Have You Considered?" on page 85.

What's Next?

What to Do

Have the students read 1 Kings 18:36 and 19:10. Tell them that Elijah—a man you'd really want on your side in a conflict—will be the subject of the next class session.

Have You Considered?

1. A *court prophet* was one who worked in the king's court and generally delivered the message the king wanted to hear. A *seer* was a member of a prophetic guild who depended on altered states of consciousness to receive God's word. An *unofficial prophet* did not belong to a guild or group, but spoke God's word independent of the king or any other human authority.
2. The king might become enraged and punish the prophet. A prophet without great courage would be tempted to simply tell the king what he wanted to hear.
3. Allow students to develop criteria based on the profile of a prophet developed in this chapter. They might include someone who criticizes injustice, speaks God's word, or upholds the values of the Covenant. Students should be encouraged to provide several examples of modern prophets. Have students apply these criteria to the two stories presented on pages 74–75.

Bonus Focus for You

Read Psalm 25. Although attributed to David, it could just as well be on the lips of any of the prophets—or on your lips. Let this psalm be an insight into the heart that loves the Lord, and especially the one who is willing for the Lord to speak through his or her mouth as the prophets were.

◆ MORE ABOUT THE LESSON

Deuteronomy 18

In Deuteronomy 18:21, we find the criterion on which the Israelites decided whether a prophet spoke truly or not: the oracle had to be "fulfilled." This meant a prediction came to reality. These predictions were usually not something only a prophet could have known and were almost never aimed at a distant future. Often any astute observer of political and social trends could make a similar prediction, or at least it seems so to modern readers of the history. However, the word of the Lord in the prophet's mouth carried a strong power, and when a prediction did come true, it validated the rest of the prophet's message. The prophet's call to action and to change was always the central purpose of prophecy.

LESSON FIVE (pages 86–89)

◆ Elijah

Welcome

What to Do

Say: "Close your eyes and imagine. You live in Israel, on the outskirts of the capital, Samaria. It has not rained in Israel for over two years. Food is scarce. You hear that there is a prophet in the land who says the drought is divine punishment. It is said he can raise people from the dead and that he has caused this drought. You have a chance to meet him. Will you go?"

Introducing the Lesson

Teaching Objectives

By the end of this lesson students will be able to:
• Describe the situation that existed during Elijah's life.
• Explain the role of Elisha as Elijah's successor.
• Reflect on the importance of Elijah's message for our own culture.

What to Do

Have the students read the opening paragraphs of "Elijah," "The Challenge from King Ahab" and the first three paragraphs of "An Unconventional Powerhouse of a Man." Discuss with them what they think Elijah's major challenges will be.

Development

What to Do

1. Have the students read the rest of "Unconventional Powerhouse" and the first two paragraphs of "Elijah and Queen Jezebel."

2. Say: "The battle between Queen Jezebel and Elijah includes one of the most dramatic stories of the Bible. Read the rest of "Elijah and Queen Jezebel" aloud.

3. Assign "Bible Activity" number 2, on page 90.

4. In three small groups, have the students complete the Scripture Workshop in this way: the first group studies 1 Kings 18:1–15; the second group studies 1 Kings 18:16–39; the third group studies 1 Kings 18:41–46.

5. Each group dramatizes its part of the story for the other two groups.

A. Giovani, *Elijah and the Angel.* Fifteenth Century.

Elijah is considered the greatest prophet by the Jewish people.

• Violations of the Covenant were common.
• People worshipped whichever god seemed to have the most power for the matter at hand.
• Social conditions became more unequal.
• The king abused his royal power.
• The burdens of forced labor and taxation became far worse than they had been even under Solomon.
• International politics were more complicated and much more threatening than at any previous time in Israel's history.

The Northern kingdom may have looked reasonably prosperous to outsiders, but it was not at all a peaceful kingdom dedicated to the Covenant.

Into this chaos burst Elijah, perhaps the greatest of all the prophets. Even the gospels, nine centuries later, recognize him, telling us that Jesus' friends expected Elijah's return in their time (*Matthew* 17:9–13). Still today, Jewish tradition expects Elijah to return. At the Passover table, a place is set and wine is poured for Elijah—just in case he should return.

To have had such a powerful impact on people for more than twenty-five hundred years, Elijah must have been an extremely powerful person. The Bible suggests that he was ferocious and unpredictable. He wore animal skins, not cloth like other people. He lived alone in the desert, in caves and on mountains. He had a habit of appearing unexpectedly to challenge those in authority.

Elijah lived free of social restriction, coming and going as he wished, saying what he had to say. Elijah cared little about anything but Yahweh, to whom he was totally and fiercely devoted. At times, Yahweh's spirit and knowledge filled Elijah and drove him to action.

The Bible captures Elijah as a man of astounding power. He correctly predicted a long drought—some said he caused it! While other people suffered from thirst and hunger, Elijah ate and drank—first fed by ravens and then by a widow in Phoenicia. Elijah repaid her help by bringing her son back to life. Elijah is certainly best remembered, however, for his battles with Queen Jezebel.

Elijah and Queen Jezebel

Queen Jezebel worshipped Baal and Astarte, Canaanite gods. For unknown reasons, Jezebel set out to destroy the worship of Yahweh. Followers of fertility and nature gods usually were unconcerned with the worship of other gods, so Jezebel's hatred for the worshippers of Yahweh is unusual. Perhaps her dislike of Yahweh was politically motivated, since Jezebel was from Phoenicia.

Although prophets were considered sacred in Israel, this respect did not stop Jezebel from murdering the "prophets of the Lord" (1 *Kings* 18:3–4). When they opposed her plans to make Baal the god of Israel, she got rid of them. Jezebel was not an Israelite, and so was unconcerned about Yahweh's wrath. She

---

MORE ABOUT THE TEXT

International Politics

The student text says that international politics became more complicated and more threatening, during the period of the divided kingdom. Students may wonder what this means. In brief, the rise of two major military and political forces during this period posed a constant threat to the peace and prosperity of the Israelite kingdoms, Assyria and Babylon. As these empires competed with one another, and with Egypt, the two kingdoms were frequently caught in the middle. (At this point, you may wish to direct students to the map to illustrate what a precarious position the kingdoms occupied.) This led to a high stakes game of playing one power off against another, a juggling act that eventually brought down both kingdoms.

did not hesitate even to threaten Elijah's life when it suited her purposes.

Elijah Escapes   After Elijah's confrontation with the priests of Baal, Queen Jezebel was dishonored and bitterly angry. She put out a warrant for Elijah's death, forcing him to flee into the desert, frightened, near despair, and wanting to die. Yahweh, however, wasn't through with Elijah just yet; there was still work to be done.

An angel of the Lord fed Elijah and gave him orders: march to Mount Horeb (or Sinai), the mountain where Moses had received the Covenant for Israel. When Elijah arrived there, he was cared for by another angel, and reassured by a visit from the Lord (this part of the story is found in 1 *Kings* 19:1–18.) Back into the fray he went, even more faithful to Yahweh than before.

Elijah's Power   Elijah then entered politics. He stood up to Ahab when the king stole the vineyard

G. Bellini, *Transfiguration*, Fifteenth Century.

Elijah and Moses are seen with Jesus at the Transfiguration in Luke 9: 28–36.

Scripture Workshop

Elijah and the Priests of Baal

One of the most dramatic scenes in the Bible is Elijah's public challenge to Jezebel's Baalist priests, the staff of her shrine. Read 1 Kings 18:16–46. What was Elijah's main purpose in this contest?

In your own words, explain what happens at the following points:

1. The situation on Mount Carmel (*18:18–20*)
2. The challenge (*18:21–24*)
3. The test (*18:22–24*)
4. The Baalist efforts (*18:25–29*)
5. Elijah's efforts (*18:30–37*)
6. The result (*18:38–39*)

At the end of this confrontation, Elijah announced the end of the drought—and the rains came. Then Elijah, certainly no longer a young man, but filled with the spirit of Yahweh, ran ahead of the king's chariot from Mount Carmel to near Jezreel, a distance of 80 miles!

---

that had belonged to Naboth, an ordinary citizen, whom Jezebel had arranged to murder. This theft was an act particularly repulsive to Yahweh.

Later, Elijah condemned Ahab's son, Ahaziah, for seeking help from another god. Elijah also invoked the power of Yahweh to kill messengers sent by Ahaziah to request Elijah's help. Finally, Elijah climbed into a flaming chariot and was visibly lifted by a whirlwind into the skies. Elijah was seen no more, but hope for his return remained alive in the hearts of the Israelites.

Elijah's Successor, Elisha

Elijah, shortly before his death, was commanded by Yahweh to make Elisha his successor—the only time in the Scriptures that a prophet appoints a successor. Elijah's response to God's request is seen in 1 Kings 19:19–21.

In 2 Kings 2:1–18, we see Elijah passing on his spirit to Elisha, his disciple. Elisha picks up Elijah's fallen mantle or cloak and uses it with the same power with which Elijah had used it. In this way, the

---

6. When all parts of the story are complete, have the students read "Elijah Escapes" and "Elijah's Power."
7. Have the students read the story of Naboth's vineyard in 1 Kings 21:1–29. What do students think about it?
8. Lead the class in their discussion of questions 1 and 2 in "Have You Considered?"
9. Have the students read "Elijah's Successor, Elisha," then look up the references in the section. Discuss the comparisons and questions suggested there.

Practicing the Skills

What to Do

Have them look up and read 1 Kings 17, the beginning of the "Elijah cycle" of stories in 1 Kings. Ask them: "What is the main thing you learn about Elijah from this passage?" Allow for different responses, but be sure that answers are anchored in some specific aspect of this reading. Require students to justify their perceptions from a careful reading of the text.

Scripture Workshop

1. Elijah challenges Ahab to assemble all the prophets of Baal to meet him on Mt. Carmel.
2. Elijah tells the people they can't have it both ways; they are to follow Yahweh only, or worship Baal.
3. Elijah challenges the prophets of Baal to call on their god to start a fire. Elijah said that he will pray to Yahweh to do the same.
4. The prophets of Baal pray for hours, even slashing themselves with swords and spears, but nothing works.
5. Elijah builds an altar to the Lord, with 12 stones for each of the 12 tribes of Israel. He then prays to God to kindle the fire.
6. God's fire comes down and consumes the sacrifice. The people gather, then fall down and worship Yahweh.

◆ MORE ABOUT THE LESSON

Jezebel

Note that the references in the activity are 1 Kings 17, 18, 19, and 21 and 2 Kings 1 and 2:1–12. Students may work in groups in completing this assignment, and should be encouraged to be creative. Have them consider: Where would they film the video? Who would star in it? What would the musical score be? Students may wish to submit still images to show what the video might look like.

Have You Considered?

1. Have students discuss several possible motives for this action. The prohibition in the Decalogue against the worship of foreign gods should be part of this discussion.

2. Students should be encouraged to introduce several examples from their own experience.

3. The story calls to mind the episode of Moses parting the Red Sea. Have students discuss why the author might have wanted to draw this comparison. One motive might be to emphasize the consistency of God's saving actions.

◆ Importance for Today

What to Do

Ask students: "How much of what Elijah had to say do you think applies to us, today? What kind of impact do you think Elijah would have if he were around today?"

Development

What to Do

1. Have the students read "Importance for Today," stopping before "Raising Questions."

2. Using the questions in the text, lead a discussion of the issues that arise from the study of Elijah. Divide the class into four groups, and give each group one of the questions listed in the student text. Ask the group to do two things: first, suggest the answer Elijah would give to this question; and second, indicate what their own answer would be.

3. Read and discuss with students the first paragraph on page 89. Encourage students to share their reactions to people who display all the outer signs of a religious commitment, but whose lives don't match these symbols. Then ask students to reflect on their own faith "decisions."

4. Have the students read "Raising Questions." Divide the class into two groups for a debate. One group is to agree with the letter writer, the other group to disagree.

88 ◆ Unit One The Original Covenant

people of Israel learn that Elisha was a true disciple of Elijah and should be followed.

Elisha is remembered as a wonder-worker and a political activist, doing much that Elijah had done, including bringing a dead boy back to life (compare 1 *Kings* 17:1–24 with 2 *Kings* 4:1–37). He healed people (2 *Kings* 5), and found lost items (2 *Kings* 6). One of his miracles may remind you of an event in Jesus' life: compare 2 Kings 4:42–44 with John 6:1–13. Elisha also did a peculiar thing; read about Elisha and the children in 2 Kings 2:23–24. What do you think about Elisha's behavior?

Elisha was a central player in an important political drama. He inspired Jehu to revolt against Joram, Ahab's successor as king. Jehu's rebellion was successful, and Elijah's prophecy about the downfall of the house of Ahab came true.

When the king of Aram in Damascus, Ben-hadad, laid siege to Israel's capital, Samaria, Elisha was a key to Israel's survival:

> When told that the man of God had come there, the king said to Hazael, "Take a gift with you and go call on the man of God. Have him consult the Lord as to whether I shall recover from this sickness." On his arrival, he stood before the prophet and said, "Your son Ben-hadad, king of Aram, has sent me to ask you whether he will recover from his sickness." "Go and tell him," Elisha answered, "that he will surely recover. However, the Lord has showed me that he will in fact die.". . ."The Lord has showed you to me as king over Aram," replied Elisha. . . . And Hazael reigned in his stead.

(2 Kings 8:8–10, 13, 15).

Elisha was a worthy successor to Elijah, and his countrymen remembered him.

Have You Considered?

1. What do you think of Elijah's behavior after he defeated the prophets of Baal? Why do you suppose he put them to death?
2. Ahab called Elijah the "troubler of Israel," accusing him of causing problems by speaking the truth. Describe another situation in which someone was accused of being a troublemaker for trying to do the right thing. Do you think they were acting as a prophet? Why or why not?
3. Read 2 Kings 2: 6–8. What other biblical story does this episode remind you of? Why do you think the author included this story about Elijah?

◆ Importance for Today

In Elijah's time, just as today, people had divided opinions about the major questions of life. Elijah had only one answer to all the people's questions: Yahweh. Yahweh is the power over everything, Yahweh is the source of justice, and Yahweh directs national policies.

Elijah matters to us because he spoke the word of the Lord. That is the important thing about all the prophets. We have little personal information on most of them. Even Elijah is not well known to us. But in the Old Testament, a prophet is only as important as the message he carried from Yahweh to Israel.

Today, we know more about nature and the world than Elijah's people did. What difference, then, does it make to us what Elijah thought about Baal, Astarte, and Yahweh? Aren't our lives and problems so incredibly different from theirs that they just don't have anything to say to us?

We may not believe in Baal and Astarte, but are we really sure how God relates to our world? Are we sure of our place in it? Consider these questions:

1. **What do we know today about the environment and its importance to our lives?** If Elijah were alive now, what do you think he might say about ecology? What do you think God's word might be to us today from Elijah about how we treat the environment?
2. **Do you personally believe that God is in charge of nature?** What does God have to do with fire, storms, earthquakes, rain, sunrise and sunset, the orbits of planets, and the twirling of galaxies?
3. **Are our modern questions so different from ancient Israel's?** Don't we want to know about controlling nature? Our technology has given us a lot—but volcanoes and earthquakes and tidal waves and tornadoes still happen. How are they ordered? Why do they happen?
4. **How does reproduction happen at the cellular or atomic level in plants and animals?** Science describes it to a point, but the essence of life still eludes us. Who is in charge of life?

These are only modern versions of the same fundamental questions that Elijah's people asked. In response, Elijah insisted on seeing God's power behind all that happened, and demanded that people respond to God with faithfulness and courage.

MORE ABOUT THE TEXT

Elisha

Although he was the faithful disciple of Elijah, Elisha represented a definite contrast in style. Unlike Elijah, Elisha resided in the city and wore regular clothing. His beard and hair were trimmed, and he used a walking staff. What he is most remembered for, however, is his miraculous power. This power was not always used for ends that we might find appropriate or tasteful; 2 Kings 2 reports that Elisha once sent bears to devour children who had mocked his receding hairline. Nevertheless, Elisha was a powerful advocate for obedience to Yahweh, and he remained steadfast in the mission of the prophet to denounce violations of the Covenant when he saw them.

88

How do you respond to the prophet's answers? Do you know people today like the Israelites of Elijah's time, who cannot make a decision about God, who sit on the fence and try to have the advantages of life with God, as well as the indulgences of life without God? What do you think about people who can't decide? Elijah demanded decision. Have you decided for yourself? Are you thinking about it?

Raising Questions

If there had been newspapers in Elijah's time, someone might have written a letter to the editor like this:

Dear Editor,

Prophets like Elijah are a menace to the nation! The task of the prophet is to educate the people and to tell the word of the Lord. They are not supposed to interfere in the affairs of government and spoil the carefully laid plans of experienced leaders.

Prophets like Elijah, who go beyond religion and play politics, are a serious threat to the country, and the only way to remove this danger is to remove its source, as Queen Jezebel has tried to do.

Do you agree or disagree with the letter writer?

What about justice? Why is justice often so difficult to achieve in the courts of our land or in our relationships with other people? Look again at the story of Naboth's vineyard (1 Kings 21). How does Naboth's story remind you of what you see on TV or in a newspaper today? What do you think the word of God might say through a modern Elijah concerning justice? If asked who is ultimately in charge of justice, how would you answer? Can the oppressed ever find justice?

What about history? Whose decision is it that one nation is strongest, and how long its dominance lasts? What happens to superpowers? Just as these were Israel's questions, so, too, are they ours. How are Elijah's answers good for us today as well? Even if you can't totally accept his answers, how do they help you look at these issues in a new way?

Have You Considered?

1. Imagine the prophet Elijah appearing on a television talk show today. What questions might he be asked? How do you think he would respond?
2. Do you see a plan, a design, in the things that happen to you? Do you think what happens is just a product of chance? Why or why not? Could you ever prove or disprove an answer to this question?
3. Do you think religious people should keep their opinions out of politics? Or is religious belief a legitimate point of view in political debate?

Spiritual Reflection

In the Whisper of the Wind

One of Elijah's experiences may suggest how you can experience God for yourself. Read what happened on Mount Horeb (1 Kings 19:9–13).

Have you ever tried to be quiet enough to feel God's presence? Here is one way to seek God inside your heart.

- Go to a quiet place, where you can be alone, as you have before. Remember to take only your Bible and no other entertainment. Make yourself comfortable.
- When you're comfortably settled, wait a few moments. Relax. Allow yourself to become quiet. Take a few deep breaths.
- Open your Bible to 1 Kings 19:9, and read again

the story of Elijah in the cave. Read very slowly. Use your imagination. Imagine that you are beside Elijah, watching and listening with him. Take your time with this exercise. You too are waiting to experience the Lord. See if, with Elijah, you can be still enough to hear the "tiny whispering sound," inside yourself.
- Say something to the Lord in your heart. You may say anything, so long as it is honest. Prayer does not need to be special words or thoughts; it needs only to come from an honest heart.

When you are finished, thank God, get up, and go your way.

◆ MORE ABOUT THE LESSON

Interview

Students should write out the questions they want to ask their interviewee before the interview. They can either take notes on the answers or use a tape recorder during the conversation. Afterwards, students should write and turn in to you a paragraph describing their experience. You might give them several days or a week to complete this activity.

5. Lead a general discussion of the rest of the questions in "Raising Questions."
6. Have the students complete "Bible Activity" number 1, including the verse that gives them each answer.

Recall

Assign students to complete "Q/A" numbers 7 and 8 on page 90.

Connect

What to Do

Have the students think of a friend outside of class or an adult with whom they could discuss questions 2 and 3 of "Have You Considered?" on page 89. Have them plan a conversation or an interview, based on these two questions.

What's Next?

What to Do

Have the students look up the books of Isaiah and Jeremiah, noting that they are long writings. Say: "These two prophets are the subject of the next chapter."

Have You Considered?

1. Encourage students to probe areas in which modern society has fallen short of Covenant values, and ways in which Elijah might address these failures.
2. Emphasize that "proof" is impossible to achieve on this sort of question, and therefore it is a matter of individual faith.
3. Allow for discussion on this question. Students should be reminded that for the ancient Israelites, loyalty to the Covenant included a commitment to social justice, which often had influence on their political debates.

Bonus Focus for You

Read all of 1 Kings 19. Imagine yourself in Elijah's position: your life at stake, angry enough to die over what has happened to you, and yet willing to encounter the Lord more intimately—and after the experience, willing again to obey. What is the hardest situation in your own life right now? What does Elijah's learning in this chapter teach you?

Q/A

Section One

1. Solomon required Israelite males to pay taxes in the form of labor. Because the building projects constructed with this labor were in the south, many northerners resented the taxation.

2. The Covenant stipulated that all people were equal before Yahweh, and therefore forced labor was a violation of their rights.

3. A "summit marriage" is a marriage which seals an alliance between two nations.

4. Solomon's summit marriages violated the Covenant because they introduced the worship of his wives' foreign gods into Israel.

5. "Syncretism" is the blending of different cultural traditions into a new combination. An example is the modern religion of Santeria, blending native African religions with Catholicism.

6. Rehoboam was the son of Solomon, whose intolerance was the immediate cause of the split between north and south.

7. Israel refers to the Northern kingdom, Judah to the Southern.

8. Ancient societies perceived a direct link between religion and the cycle of nature. The nature worship of their Canaanite neighbors seemed logical to the Israelites.

CHAPTER 5 REVIEW

Q/A

Section One

1. Explain Solomon's policy of forced labor.
2. Why was forced labor a violation of the Covenant?
3. Explain what a "summit marriage" is.
4. Why were Solomon's summit marriages a violation of the Covenant?
5. Define "syncretism" and provide an example. How was syncretism a violation of the Covenant?
6. Identify: Rehoboam.
7. After Israel split into the Northern and Southern kingdoms, what do the terms "Israel" and "Judah" mean?
8. Why did fertility worship seem logical to the ancient Israelites?

Section Two

1. Define: seer, court prophet, unofficial prophet.
2. Identify: Samuel, Nathan.
3. Why did court prophets often say what the king wanted to hear?
4. What are the three elements of the prophetic message as described in Deuteronomy?
5. Describe the importance of Elijah in Jewish tradition.
6. What is Elisha best remembered for?
7. How do the questions Elijah raised relate to our own times?
8. How do Elijah's struggles for justice and the understanding of history relate to our own day?

BIBLE ACTIVITY

1. Read Sirach 47:23–25 and 48:1–12. These passages were written hundreds of years after the death of Elijah. (The unnamed person in Sirach 47:23 is probably Jeroboam, the first king of the Northern kingdom.) Answer the following: (a) What evils are meant in 47:24b–25? (b) What events are the basis for 48:1–3? (c) What future expectations are expressed in 48:10–12?

2. The stories of the battles between Elijah and Jezebel are detailed in 1 Kings 17–19, 21, and 2 Kings 1 and 2:1–12. Re-read them now. Imagine that you are making a video of these events. Let the scenes parade through your mind just as they are written. See the action, the colors. Imagine yourself in the middle of each event. Choose one of these stories and describe how you would make it come alive today if you were a video director.

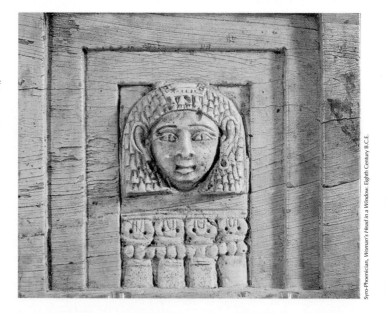

Syro-Phoenician, *Woman's Head in a Window*, Eighth Century B.C.E.

BIBLE ACTIVITY

1. (a) The evils are social injustice and the worship of foreign gods. (b) The reference is probably to the story about Elijah and the prophets of Baal in 1 Kings 18. (c) 1 Kings says that Elijah's life ended as he was carried into heaven by a whirlwind. This passage expresses the hope that Elijah will return and restore the 12 tribes of Israel to prominence.

2. Allow students to select the story they want to dramatize. Make sure that they describe in detail the specific points and the techniques they would use. The point of the exercise is to emphasize that these stories are *dramatic*. Students should emphasize the heated confrontation between God's spokespersons and those who fail to honor the Covenant.

GLOSSARY

- **Ahab:** King of Israel, the northern kingdom, during the mid-800's B.C.E.
- **Astarte and Baal:** Canaanite gods of nature, especially storms and fertility. Sometimes used to refer to someone other than the Canaanite god.
- **Court prophets:** Prophets who spoke Yahweh's word as officials of the royal court.
- **Deborah:** A prophet in the time of the Judges.
- **Elijah:** The great prophet who, by Yahweh's word, commanded nature to demonstrate Yahweh's power.
- **Elisha:** Elijah's successor as prophet.
- **Forced labor:** A policy pursued by Solomon and later kings, which required men to perform physical labor for the king during a certain portion of the year (or of their lifetimes) as a form of taxation.
- **Huldah:** A Jerusalem prophet of the Lord in the late 600s B.C.E. in the reign of King Josiah.
- **Jezebel:** The Phoenician princess who married Ahab, she brought foreign gods, especially Baal, with her to Israel.
- **Miriam:** The sister of Moses who is sometimes referred to as a prophet in the Biblical tradition.
- **Nabi:** The Hebrew word usually translated as "prophet."
- **Nathan:** A court prophet under King David who criticized the king for his affair with Bathsheba.
- **Prophet:** One who is filled by the spirit of Yahweh and is given a message to declare.
- **Rehoboam:** Solomon's son and successor.
- **Seer:** A type of prophet. They lived in groups and their messages appear to have been received through altered states of consciousness.
- **Summit marriage:** A marriage between one royal family and another, contracted in order to form an alliance between two nations.
- **Syncretism:** The attempt to blend differing religious ideas into one belief, without distinguishing one from the other.
- **Temple:** The structure built by Solomon for worship of Yahweh in Jerusalem.
- **Unofficial prophet:** A prophet who did not belong to a guild or hold a position at court.

UNDERSTANDING MORE ABOUT:

Caring for the Widow

A *widow* in the ancient Near East faced life-threatening circumstances. Because her husband was dead, she had no right to an inheritance and no other legal rights either. Women had very few opportunities to earn money on their own. While sometimes a second marriage took place with the dead husband's brother, this arrangement was rare. An adult son would take care of his widowed mother, but if she had no son, she could starve. What do you suppose might have happened to Naboth's widow after Jezebel killed him and Ahab took his property?

A widow was dependent on the good will of other people, including government officials, even for food. That is why Israel's laws include definite ways that widows are to be treated. Compare 1 Kings 17:7–24 with 2 Kings 4:1–7. If the prophet acts according to God's word, what do these stories tell us about God's attitude toward widows?

Widows still had the same problems in the time of Jesus and afterward. See Luke 7–11 for a story about Jesus and a widow. Notice especially the people's reactions.

Section Two

1. A court prophet was one who worked in the king's court and generally delivered the message the king wanted to hear. A seer was a member of a prophetic guild who depended on altered states of consciousness to receive God's word. An unofficial prophet did not belong to a guild or group, but spoke God's word independent of the king or any other human authority.

2. Samuel was the prophet and judge who anointed Saul and David. Nathan was David's court prophet, yet was unafraid to speak God's word even to the king.

3. Court prophets did not challenge the king's policies because they were afraid of the consequences.

4. The three elements found in Deuteronomy are: The message had to be (a) clear and direct, (b) addressed to a specific audience, (c) result in immediate action.

5. Elijah is remembered as a great prophet who spoke up for absolute fidelity to the Covenant.

6. Elisha is remembered as a wonder-worker and a political activist.

7. Several questions raised by Elijah relate to our own times, including: (a) the importance of the environment to our lives, (b) whether or not God is in charge of nature, (c) questions about why things happen, and (d) who is in charge of life.

8. Elijah stood up for justice and the idea that God was guiding the events of history. He lived in total confidence of the triumph of God's word. These beliefs remain vitally important for our own day.

Chapter Overview

This chapter looks at the historical events and issues of the time of the fall of Israel and Judah. Then, in Section Two, it focuses on the prophets who were active in Israel and in Judah.

Teaching Objectives

By the end of this chapter students will be able to:

Explain the circumstances leading up to the fall of both Israel and Judah.

• Describe the role of the prophets during this time period.

• Identify the important prophets from this era and explain their teachings: Amos, Hosea, Isaiah, and Jeremiah.

Welcome

Include in your greeting two or three things that you personally especially enjoy about the class.

What to Do

Ask the students to share one thing that they like, enjoy, or have learned so far in their Bible study.

Pray with your students. Ask students to express one thing for which they are grateful. At the end of each phrase, pause and ask the students to respond with "Thanks be to God."

Introducing the Chapter

What to Do

• Have the students read the story of Tom on the opening spread. What do they think of it. How have they experienced similar experiences of consequences when they broke an agreement?

Isaiah and Jeremiah

800

776 B.C.E.
● First Olympic Games in Greece

753
● Rome founded

750
● Amos

745–727
● Tiglath-pileser III, King of Assyria

742
● Hosea
Isaiah's call

721
● Fall of Israel

705–681
● Sennacherib, King of Assyria

700
● Isaiah 1–39

630
● Jeremiah's call

621
● Josiah's reforms
● Deuteronomy

605–562
● Nebuchadnezzar II, King of Babylon

600
● Phoenicians sail around Africa
● Jeremiah

587
● Fall of Jerusalem, Exile

563
● The Buddha born in India

550

Legend
● General History
● Biblical History
● Jewish History
● Books written

om loved the freedom he felt during his first year of college. He decided which classes he would take and what time he would take them. Especially, Tom liked living away from home in his own apartment; he cleaned his room when he felt like it, often kept late hours, and chose friends without worrying about whether or not his parents would approve of them.

When the second semester ended, Tom went home for the summer. He figured, "I am an adult now. There is no need for me to obey my parents' rules any longer."

Tom's parents had other ideas. They told him: "When you live in our home, you **will** follow our rules. That means keeping your room neat, letting us know when you won't be here for meals, and keeping a curfew at

---

◆ **MORE ABOUT THE LESSON**

Justice in Israel

In part, the Hebrew definition of justice matches ours: when someone gets justice, that person gets what he or she deserves, whether it is pleasant or unpleasant. However, the Hebrew word also entails the order of things in a society so constructed that every part functions in harmony with every other part. In such a sys-

tem, values would rule actions. Nothing would be decided without concern for its effect on the whole of society. Even though some might be richer than others, the relationships between people would be just and harmonious, not exploitative. This was the justice envisioned by the Covenant, the justice of God. The Israelites were not able to live this justice. Should we?

night." Tom listened to his parents' statement and agreed to abide by the rules. Then he ignored them and did what he pleased.

Late one night, about three hours after his parents' curfew, Tom came home and found the front light on and some of his clothes packed in a duffel bag on the porch. The note read simply,

You know the consequences of not obeying our family's rules. Please find another place to stay for as long as you continue to disregard them. We love you very much, Mom and Dad.

Shocked and surprised, Tom picked up his things and headed off to a friend's apartment. "How unfair," he mumbled to himself.

Responsibility

Were Tom's parents unfair? They were only holding Tom accountable for his actions. If you make a deal with someone and then that person doesn't hold up his or her end of the bargain, what would you do? We know what happens in the "real" world. If you borrow money for a car and then don't make the payments, the lender will take away the car. If you try out for a sport but don't go to practice, the coach will cut you from the team. Why should one's parents, or God for that matter, treat you any differently?

After Elisha, the prophets recognized that God would hold Israel accountable for its sins, and tried to warn the people of both the Northern and Southern kingdoms that they were headed for trouble. They had accepted the Covenant with Yahweh and expected God to protect them. But the Israelites ignored the rules of the Covenant. The worship of other gods, civil strife, and individual greed became increasingly prevalent.

In this chapter, you will read of the collapse of first the Northern, and then the Southern kingdom. You will learn how the prophets Isaiah and Jeremiah worked to save Judah during the last days. During this period of 160 years—from Isaiah's call to Jeremiah's death—the two nations would descend from the heights of prosperity to the depths of despair.

As Tom learned the hard way, every choice has a consequence, be it pleasant or unpleasant. The consequences for Israel were the result of many decades of ignoring the Covenant. Yet, the prophets' warnings did not end with the nation's destruction: Yahweh stood ready to welcome Israel back to the Covenant. The prophets preached a message of hope for those who could amend their lives and return to God's ways.

- Students may feel that someone who breaks the law should be punished. What should be the consequences if a member of a group commits a grievous offense? Should the whole group be punished or only the person who misbehaved?

- Use this as an opportunity to discuss your school's disciplinary system. How does it work? What behavior is penalized? What makes the system fair or unfair? What do students think about how justice is administered in the school? Be prepared for student indignation and strong opinion. Help them recognize that consequences are tied to people's behavior.

Extend the Activity   Have students evaluate the school's disciplinary code and suggest how it can be changed. Have the students present these changes to the school's administration for consideration.

Development

Using the Timeline

Call students' attention to the timeline. Notice that it covers 200 years—the two centuries that would change the history of God's chosen people forever.

Note other interesting events of this period: Olympic Games and the founding of Rome, the Phoenician accomplishment, and the birth of Buddha. Explain that some dates in Israel are not certain, but notice that Amos and Hosea are close together in the Northern kingdom, and Isaiah's work follows quickly in Jerusalem. Note that while the Book of Isaiah 1–39 was probably written around the same time as the Book of Jeremiah, the events that occurred in Isaiah happened several decades earlier.

MORE ABOUT THE TEXT

The Rise of the Assyrian Empire

The Assyrian empire rose to prominence in the latter half of the eighth century B.C.E. Historians consider this the first attempt by an empire to develop and organize its conquered territory. These territories were divided into provinces, and all paid tribute to the king. Many territories would maintain their old governments which had sworn loyalty to the Assyrian king.

Assyria used war chariots as well as heavy and light infantry. They developed siege engines to break down the massive walls of cities. The Assyrians deliberately encouraged stories of their ferocity in combat and bragged about the punishment they meted out to enemies. For a tiny nation like Israel to join a coalition against Assyria was suicidal. And that's what Isaiah told Israel!

◆ False Affluence

Teaching Objectives

By the end of this lesson students will be able to:

• Identify the reason Israel had a false sense of security prior to its destruction.

• Explain how these false perceptions kept them from listening to the prophets' warnings.

Development

What to Do

1. Ask the students to read the opening italicized paragraph and the learning objectives.

2. Have the students read "False Affluence," and all the subsections. Ask them to compare, point by point, the conditions in Israel and Judah with current conditions in the United States. What is the same? What is different?

3. Discuss: "Do you think God has anything to do with American prosperity?" Accept any opinions the students might have, but make sure that they can offer a reason for their answers. Assure the students that the Bible does not predict that America or any country will suffer the fate of Israel and Judah.

4. Ask students to consider the following questions: "Do you think our material comforts are a sign of God's favor? Is there anything more important to us today than affluent living? How are the country's problems related to our societal disinterest in religious faith and values?"

5. Have the students discuss questions 2 and 3 from "Have You Considered?" on page 95.

Practicing the Skills

What to Do

Have the students read 2 Kings 21 and 2 Chronicles 33. These chapters are about Manasseh (687–642) and Amon (642–640), kings of Judah between the times of Isaiah and Jeremiah. Then ask them to:

• Explain the meaning of all the things that Manasseh did, using a Bible dictionary as necessary.

◀◀ SECTION ONE 776 B.C.E.–500 B.C.E.

Israel and Judah Are Destroyed

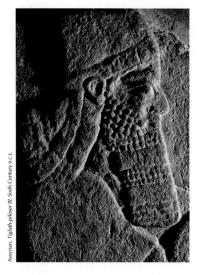

Assyrian, *Tiglath-pileser III.* Sixth Century B.C.E.

For almost two hundred years, the prophets warned the people of Israel and Judah of what would happen if they didn't obey the demands of the Covenant. From time to time the people would listen and repent, but they soon went back to living a lifestyle built on the worship of foreign gods and injustice. Israel, and then Judah, fell to their enemies. Yahweh allowed them to fall because of their disobedience. In this section, you'll follow the story of their destruction.

Learning Objectives for Section One

By the end of this section, you will be able to:

• Explain how the people violated the Covenant through the worship of foreign gods and injustice.

• Understand the warnings of the prophets.

• Explain the fall of the Northern kingdom.

• Explain the fall of the Southern kingdom.

◆ False Affluence

During the first fifty years of the eighth century B.C.E., both Israel and Judah were at the height of their material prosperity.

• They were strong, at peace with each other, and had considerable influence among their neighbors.

• Their populations increased and their industries flourished.

• Lucrative trade routes once again passed through Israel's territory as in the days of David and Solomon.

• More wealth was flowing into Israel and Judah than ever before—even Solomon's kingdom probably had not been as rich.

During this time of enormous confidence, it was easy for the people of Judah and Israel to believe that their prosperity would never end.

Growing Injustice

Wealth, however, was not a sign that Israel or Judah had found favor with God. Although they had become materially affluent, both societies had also become spiritually corrupt. Small farmers, for example, were constantly in debt to moneylenders. If one year's crop were to fail, the farmer could lose everything. The rich were getting richer and the poor were becoming poorer. Because the wealthy controlled the political system, the poor had little chance of justice.

Israel and Judah probably were no more unjust than any other country in either the ancient world or our own. But the People of God were supposed to be different—justice was one of the demands of the Covenant. When Israel and Judah put justice up for sale, they were not just acting like any other nation—they were violating the terms of their agreement with God.

MORE ABOUT THE TEXT

Material Prosperity

From 800–750 B.C.E., just before Isaiah began his work and before the Northern kingdom was destroyed, prosperity was evident everywhere. Archaeology has turned up luxurious homes, furnishings of ivory, and accounts of gold and silver traded for other precious and rare items. Israelites could afford to be concerned with the details of entertaining and the specialties of interior decorating, with new styles in military uniforms and chariots. They had much more than they needed—or if they lived at the poor end of the social continuum, they were hungry.

The socio-economic situation in Judah remained much the same from 800–680 B.C.E., highly prosperous, yet declining in the latter part of the period. The reason for decline was simple: Judah became increasingly dependent on Assyria and had to pay more and more tribute to maintain any kind of independence.

Israel was a very rich country prior to its destruction in 721 B.C.E. Archaeological finds indicate thriving industries in the production of cosmetics and fine cloth.

Worship of Foreign Gods

As discussed in Chapter 5, the Israelites' worship of Yahweh was influenced by the religious practices of other nations. After the death of Elisha,

- Shrines to fertility and nature gods once again flourished throughout the land.
- The sexual rites in honor of Baal and Asherah increased.

Evidence of these abuses is found throughout the writings of the prophets, whose constant references to the worship of Baal suggests that this was a dominant threat to the life of Israel.

Although not in keeping with what God had demanded at Sinai, the Israelites were unable to resist the temptation to honor the gods of nature and commerce popular among their neighbors. Despite the occasional attempt at religious reform, this problem simply got worse over time.

The Prophets Forecast Destruction

False perception can create real problems.

- The water in the pool may *seem* deep enough, but if you don't check before you dive in, you could end up with a broken neck.
- The meat may look cooked because it's brown on the outside, but, if eaten, it can cause sickness or death.

- The car may look in good condition, but if you don't have it checked out by an able mechanic you could end up buying a piece of junk.

During the period of the prophets, Israel and Judah were confronted with their misperceptions. While the affluence and success of both kingdoms made them unable (or unwilling) to see the problems that God saw, the prophets tried every means within their power to bring the people to see things as they really were. The prophets warned that destruction was coming if the people didn't obey the Covenant.

Unfortunately, the prophets' dire warnings were ignored. People chose to listen to the seduction of prosperity instead. In other words, they preferred their false perception to reality. This view of things, however, could only last so long.

Have You Considered?

1. Do you think today's American Christians have to be concerned with mixed religious observances? Why or why not?
2. What similarities do you see between the injustices in ancient Israel and Judah, and in our society today? What message do you suppose the prophets would have for us?
3. Describe a time when your perception of a situation was challenged by someone. How did you respond to that challenge? Why?

- Discuss how these horrors could be happening while the nation was prospering materially. Is there any contradiction in that?
- Make a list of the parallels between Manasseh's activity and today's American society.
- Discuss together question 1 from "Have You Considered?" page 95.

Recall

What to Do

Have the students write out their understanding of the first learning objective for Section One.

Connect

What to Do

Homework Assignment: Have the students write individual summaries of the relationships they see between Israel's experience then, and America's experience today.

What's Next?

What to Do

Remind students of the warnings of the prophets. Say: "These warnings came true. Ancient Israel could not survive the consequences of its choices. In the next lesson, we will see how God allowed the consequences to appear in history."

Have You Considered?

1. Allow students to express various opinions, but be sure the discussion centers around reasons why the Israelites were concerned about syncretism: the Covenant demand that they give honor to Yahweh alone and the threat to their cultural survival.
2. Students should mention exploitation of the poor, various forms of economic cheating and the increasing gap between the classes.
3. Direct students to the prophets' challenge of perception. Ask them to see things based on God's law, not in terms of material success.

Bonus Focus for You —————

Read Sirach 40:1–27. What items would you list as "good" and "better," as he does in verses 17–26?

LESSON TWO (pages 96–100)

◆ Israel Is Destroyed

Welcome

Students feel the sadness of today's lesson, since the greeting is so different from the usual welcome.

What to Do

Do not say hello to anyone. Have the room darkened as the students come in. Have a strip of black paper at each place, on which is written: "Israel is no more."

Ask the students how they might feel if the state whose borders are nearest to them had been taken over by a foreign power. Let them continue imagining for a few minutes.

Pray with your students. Include in your prayer a thanksgiving for the long history of military peace within the borders of the United States, and a plea that this peace be maintained through the increasing goodness of our peoples. Give the students a chance to add their own thoughts to this prayer. (After the prayer, turn the lights back on.)

Introducing the Lesson

Teaching Objectives

By the end of this lesson students will see the consequences both Israel and Judah experienced because of their actions.

What to Do

Recall the story of Tom from the chapter opening story. Say: "The people of Israel and Judah did not keep their agreement with Yahweh about the kind of religion and society they would have. The consequence for their behavior was that they ceased to exist as nations (not as individual people)."

Recall the timeline and have the students note the dates of the "Fall of Israel" and the "Fall of Jerusalem, Exile" (which is the fall of Judah).

Development

Students will understand the historical events which led to the destruction of both Israel and Judah, and see how these events can be interpreted from the viewpoint of the prophets.

Assyrian, *Assyrian Warriors*, Eighth Century B.C.E.

Assyrian warriors, like those shown in this relief from the Iraq Museum in Baghdad, captured Israel and scattered the Israelite people.

◆ Israel Is Destroyed

In time, neither Israel nor Judah could escape the consequences of their disobedience. Israel was the first to suffer, defeated by the Assyrians in 721 B.C.E. We have two records of the fall of the Northern kingdom. One is a historical interpretation of events put together by modern scholars. The other is the prophetic interpretation. According to the prophets, Israel's disobedient lifestyle was its most serious problem. To Israel's leaders, however, the threat of foreign invasion was the greater danger.

The Historical Interpretation

Historically, Assyria had been the major military threat to Israel's survival for over a century. But early in the eighth century Assyria declined, allowing Israel and Judah approximately 50 years to prosper without fear of war. Also, at this time both Israel and Judah

in the Spotlight

The Northern Tribes

Not everyone agrees that the ten tribes of the Northern kingdom were lost forever. Some people believe that they left Israel to look for a new home, and that their descendants still exist. One such group is the Church of Jesus Christ of Latter-Day Saints, popularly known in America as the "Mormons."

According to the *Book of Mormon*, a text they consider a third book of scripture, the ten tribes immigrated to America, where they built great civilizations. Ultimately, they all but destroyed themselves in a series of major wars. This is how they lost their historical memory and became the "Indians" encountered by European settlers. Mormons also believe that Jesus appeared in the New World to preach to the ten tribes after he disappeared from Palestine (when Christians believe he ascended into heaven).

◆ MORE ABOUT THE LESSON

The Debate

Each group can concentrate on the textual material for its side in the debate. More information can be found in a Bible atlas (for the historical side) and in readings from the prophets (for the prophets' side). Have students read those passages listed in the text, along with Amos 3:1–15; 4:6–12; 8:9–12; Hosea 4:1–3; 5:8–14; 8:1–14. Unfamiliar words can be found in a Bible dictionary.

The students may present their case in any way they wish: explanation, fist-shaking arguments, one-on-one discussion, or whatever they devise. Speakers should have a time limit and speak one at a time. If students come up with inventive means of presentation, encourage them to explore their ideas. When the allotted time for the debate is over, you and the two judges can determine who is the "winner."

The Bible in Context

Uncovering Other Records

Archaeologists have found many records left by the kings of other nations, including Assyria. Some of these records depict Israelite kings bringing tribute to Assyria's rulers. Others record the Assyrian takeover of Judah's cities, most notably, Lachish. One written record, called "The Annals of Sennacherib," was written in cuneiform on clay. It describes the result of Sennacherib's Palestinian campaign of 701:

> As for Hezekiah of Judah, he did not submit to my yoke and I laid siege to forty-six of his strong cities. . . . I made Hezekiah a prisoner in Jerusalem, like a bird in a cage. . . . Hezekiah was forced to send me 30 talents of gold, eight hundred talents of silver, precious stones, couches and chairs inlaid with ivory, elephant hides, ebony wood, box wood, and all kinds of valuable treasures.
>
> (Old Testament Parallels, by Victor H. Matthew and Don Benjamin. Paulist Press, 1991.)

had strong kings: Jeroboam in the North and Uzziah in the South. By 745 B.C.E., however, the situation was changing again.

After the deaths of Jeroboam and Uzziah, various kings ruled, many for only one to six months. These kings were murdered and then quickly replaced by others who wanted power. The civil battles in Israel provoked horrible atrocities. Because society was torn apart by the political chaos, the country was illprepared to face the renewed power of Assyria.

Israel's end was quick in coming:

- By the mid-700s, a new emperor, Tiglath-pileser, had Assyria prepared for conquest.
- Syria and Palestine with their natural resources and strategic locations were obvious targets for the Assyrians.
- Israel joined an alliance to resist the Assyrians.
- Tiglath-pileser invaded and demanded tribute from Israel.
- King Hoshea of Israel agreed to pay, but then held some of the tribute back.
- Sargon II became emperor of Assyria.
- In 721, Emperor Sargon II laid siege to Israel's capital, Samaria, which quickly fell.
- Israel became a province of the Assyrian Empire. Colonists from Babylonia and Hamath intermarried with the remaining Israelites.

In keeping with Assyrian policy, the defeated population of Israel was deported to discourage future rebellions. The ten northern tribes were removed, and resettled throughout the Assyrian Empire and Assyrian settlers entered Israelite territory. With that, the northern tribes depart from the pages of history.

How the Prophets Saw It

The prophets would not deny the historical facts covered above. They would say, however, that Assyria was not really the cause of Israel's problems: Israel was itself the cause. Without Israel's disobedience and neglect of the Covenant, the prophets would say, Yahweh would never have allowed Assyria to harm the Chosen People.

The prophets charged, among other things, that the unequal class structures and disregard for the poor by the rich caused the people of the North to be punished for their offenses. Consider:

- Merchants who tampered with scales to cheat customers out of their rightful purchase of food (Amos 8:5).
- Sexual abuses (Amos 2:7).
- Judges who accepted bribes to rule against the poor (Amos 5:12).
- A general mistreatment of the poor by those who were in power (Amos 2:6–13).

The prophets left no doubt that these atrocities, along with the mixing of religious practices, were the causes of Israel's destruction. As Amos said:

> I will turn your feasts into mourning and all your songs into lamentations. . . . Those who swear by the shameful idol of Samaria. . . . those shall fall, never to rise again.
>
> (Amos 8:10, 14)

Have You Considered?

1. Can the historical interpretation of the fall of Israel and the prophetic interpretation both be true? Why or why not?
2. Do you think it was fair of God to allow the destruction of Israel? Should God always allow people to suffer the consequences of their choices? Why or why not?
3. After the Assyrians deported them from Israel, the members of the ten northern tribes became refugees. Based on what you know about refugees today, what do you suppose life was like for them? What might this do to their faith in Yahweh?

What to Do

1. Have the students read "Israel Is Destroyed" and its subsections.
2. Prepare the class for a debate. Form two groups, one group to support the historical interpretation of events around the Fall of Israel and the other group to support the prophets' viewpoint. Have each group prepare its case with as much information as it can gather in a time frame you specify. Ask one student from each side to join you as "judges." Toss a coin to find which side is the first presenter.

   When the debate is over, have the students write individual lists of five things they learned from their study and argumentation, and turn them in to you.
3. For simple interest, have the students read "In the Spotlight."

Have You Considered?

1. Entertain various opinions. Point out to students that there are different senses of the word "truth." In terms of historical cause and effect, the historical interpretation is probably correct. But in terms of religious truth, or the truth about God which is behind history, the prophetic interpretation expresses the truth.
2. Expect students who have experienced loss or suffering to have strong opinions on this subject. Be sensitive to their feelings, but be sure to point out that human freedom would mean very little if God didn't allow people to accept the consequences of their choices.
3. Students might be encouraged to do some research on modern refugees and make comparisons between the situation facing these people and the ancient Israelites. Relevant similarities might include the loss of property, the experience of war, the sense of displacement, and the desire to "start over" somewhere else. One difference might be the global scale of today's refugee crisis.

MORE ABOUT THE TEXT

Ahaz

Ahaz was the king of Judah who actually drew Assyria's borders to meet Judah's borders, though he does not seem to have realized that would happen. Israel, in 735 or so, had joined forces with Damascus (Syria or Aram) in a coalition to try to throw off Assyrian domination. They wanted Judah to join them, so they would have an ally at their backs (to the south.) Ahaz, advised by Isaiah, was reluctant to join the coalition, so they threatened to attack Judah and force Ahaz' compliance. That frightened King Ahaz and he sent emissaries to Assyria, against Isaiah's advice, to ask the Empire for help. It came in the form of a thoroughly defeated coalition and the dispersing of Israel's population. Israel was no more and Judah's back door opened directly onto Assyrian territory. This is made clear in the map exercise.

Development

What to Do

1. Have the students read "Judah Is Destroyed" and its subsections. Point out that the same two interpretations hold in Judah's case as they just debated in Israel's case. Explain the situation created by Ahaz.

2. Have the students read "The Bible in Context" and compare Sennacherib's Annals with 2 Kings 18:13–16. King Hezekiah was the son and successor of King Ahaz.

3. Follow up with the story of the siege of Jerusalem (701 B.C.E.) and its mysterious ending; then have the students read 2 Kings 19:5–7 and 2 Kings 19:32–37. This is one of the rare moments in ancient Israel's history when a king obeyed a prophet on political matters. By doing so, he saved the capital and the country.

4. This event inspired a poem by Lord Byron. Read it to your students or have a student who is involved in drama prepare it and read it to the class. (See Teacher's Resource 6A: "The Destruction of Sennacherib.")

5. Say: "Hezekiah was an extraordinarily capable king, one of the few who tried to keep Judah's allegiance to Yahweh alive. He was forced to pay Assyrian tribute, but he maintained his own and his nation's relationship with the Lord. One of his great accomplishments was the bringing of a water supply inside Jerusalem's walls." Explain more about this. (See Teacher's Resource 6B.)

6. Say: "After Hezekiah died in 687, the situation in Judah became noticeably worse in every way. You have read about the atrocities of Manasseh, his successor. Then about 40 years later, King Josiah took the throne."

7. Lead a class discussion of the questions in "Have You Considered?"

Practicing the Skills

What to Do

• Say: "Look on your text map at the border between Israel and Judea, reaching east and west across Judah

◆ Judah Is Destroyed

When Israel had joined the rebellious coalition to try to resist Assyria, they had wanted to include King Ahaz of Judah. Ahaz refused, so the coalition threatened Judah with destruction. Ahaz, against the advice of the prophet Isaiah, then appealed to Assyria to save him. Ahaz apparently did not fully understand what could happen to him when he shared a border with Assyria.

When Israel then fell to Assyria in 721, Judah was little more than a province of the massive, aggressive empire. Now, Ahaz truly had reason to fear Assyria. To avoid trouble there, he repeatedly violated the Covenant by:

• Changing the altar in the Temple to conform to Assyrian patterns.
• Sacrificing his sons to a foreign god (according to 2 Chronicles 28) hoping for its protection.

In other words, Ahaz went against God in his attempt to save his kingdom. Needless to say, the consequences would come, but not in Ahaz's lifetime.

Ahaz's Successors

After Ahaz made his fateful appeal to Assyria, the end of Judah was assured. While the kings who followed him to the throne of Judah worked valiantly to undo the damage caused by Ahaz's folly, they were without success. Two kings in particular are singled out by the Bible for special attention: Hezekiah and Josiah.

Hezekiah   Ahaz's son, Hezekiah, tried to turn things around. He attempted to reform the religion of Judah by ending the worship of foreign gods. He also strengthened Judah militarily, and stopped paying tribute to Assyria. When the Assyrians invaded, they surrounded Hezekiah in Jerusalem and forced him to pay tribute, but stopped short of destroying the city. According to 2 Kings, God sent a plague upon the Assyrians, destroying the attacking army. Emperor Sennacherib was now forced to withdraw and end the siege.

Josiah   Like Hezekiah, King Josiah (641–610 B.C.E.) attempted religious reform in Judah. According to 2 Kings 22:8–23:7, the high priest Hilkiah found an ancient book of the Law in the Temple. When Josiah was given the book he was horrified by it because Judah had not been obeying these laws. He ordered that its rules should be immediately put in place.

This clay tablet records the military campaigns of the Assyrian King, Sennacherib (705–681 B.C.E.). Judah was threatened by the Assyrians (and paid tribute to them) but would not be destroyed by them. Judah remained independent until 587 B.C.E.

Assyrian, Naq Hammodi, Eighth Century B.C.E.

Most scholars agree that the book located by Hilkiah was the book of Deuteronomy, and for his devotion to it, the Deuteronomic historian honors Josiah as Judah's greatest king after David.

Judah Falls

Judah remained independent and at peace for some years after the fall of Israel. To some, it looked as if Judah might escape the verdict that had fallen upon Israel a hundred years earlier. This was not to be:

• Under Emperor Nebuchadnezzar, the Babylonians replaced the Assyrians as the major power in the Middle East.

Sennacherib's Siege of Jerusalem

After Hezekiah had paid tribute to Assyria, he must have tried once more to assert his independence from the Empire. This time Sennacherib, the Assyrian king, sent his armies to lay siege to Jerusalem. A brief period of serious threat followed, and Hezekiah, obeying Isaiah's word, appealed to the Lord. As a result, the Assyrian army vanished overnight.

It is unclear exactly what happened. 2 Kings 19:5–7 says that Isaiah predicted that a "report" would come which would cause the army to leave. 2 Kings 19:32–37 gives another version.

What is certain is that the Assyrian army abandoned the siege and Jerusalem was saved, the only city saved out of all the devastated countryside around her.

LEARN FROM THE MAP

Assyrian Domination

The map illustrates Assyria's borders in 750 B.C.E. Nineveh was the capital of Assyria. Note that the areas of Judah and Israel are highlighted in green. While in a dif-

ferent color, both nations must be considered under Assyria's control and domination. The coalition of Israel and Damascus fought the Assyrians in Syria. Why, then, was Judah's position important to both sides?

©1994 Magellan Geographix™ Santa Barbara, CA.

- Judah turned to Egypt for protection, and refused to pay tribute to Nebuchadnezzar.
- In 598, the Babylonians invaded Judah, took everything of value in the Temple, and sent the royal family into exile.
- After a brief uprising in Judah, the Babylonians again invaded in 587, and this time sent most of Judah's population into exile.
- The kingdom of Judah was now history, and the Israelites would not be independent again for another 400 years. Their darkest days were ahead, as they were forced out of the land of promise and into exile in Babylon.

The Prophetic Point of View

The prophets Isaiah and Jeremiah were active during the decline and fall of Judah. Like their coun-

terparts in the Northern kingdom, they denounced religious corruption and injustice, predicting that such behavior would not go unpunished for long.

Isaiah and Jeremiah also denounced what we might call the "foreign policy" of the kings of Judah. Both argued that faith in Yahweh, not alliances with foreign powers, was what would save the nation.

Isaiah denounced Ahaz for making a sacrifice to the Assyrians:

Unless your faith is firm, you will not be firm!

(Isaiah 7:9)

Isaiah also told Hezekiah to trust in God to save Judah and not fight back against the Assyrians. Hezekiah did what he was told and Judah survived. Jeremiah insisted that Judah not resist the Babylonians, and his warning also proved correct.

just a few miles north of Jerusalem. When Ahaz refused to join the coalition against Assyria, but instead asked the Assyrian empire for help, this line was the Israel-Judah border. When the Israel/Damascus coalition was defeated by Assyria, King Ahaz's throne stood less than five miles from the Assyrian Empire. Was that an advantageous situation for Judah? What do you think it contributed to Judah's life in the following century?"

- Ask students to compare the size of the Assyrian empire with that of Israel and Judah. What chance do students think either country had of withstanding the military onslaught of its much larger neighbor?

Recall

Have the students, orally as a whole class, complete "Bible Activity" number 1. Have the students write their answers to the Chapter Review Questions for Section One.

Connect

What to Do

- Say: "The prophets urged kings and people to depend on the Lord for all their needs, including national defense and foreign policy. On those few occasions when they obeyed, the nation was saved from danger. When they disobeyed, trouble and destruction came."
- Ask the students to discuss whether decisions should be based on trust in God or on rational calculation: personal decisions? parish decisions? municipal decisions? national decisions? Be sure students explain their opinions. Guide them to consider seriously the position of having complete trust in God.

What's Next?

What to Do

- Have the students mark the books of Amos, Hosea, and Isaiah. Explain that in the next session we will be reading from these prophets, whose names they have already heard in the previous lessons.
- Pray with your students. Recall briefly your class opening and the sadness of losing a national identity. Express sympathy for those countries today who have been taken over by others.

◆ MORE ABOUT THE LESSON

Trusting God

A quick glimpse at the map shows that neither Judah nor Israel could possibly have defeated the Assyrian Empire at this time; it was simply too strong. Once the Assyrians noticed a threat, their armies crushed it.

This may very well have been the wisdom behind the messages of Isaiah and Jeremiah. They

advised the kings to make their alliances with Yahweh and not the local strongman. They may have lost their independence and had to pay tribute to the king, but according to Assyrian custom, they would have kept their own self-rule and religion.

What messages might we read into this story about how we are to live God's will?

Have You Considered?

1. The basic mistake, pointed out to Ahaz by Isaiah, was relying on Assyria rather than Yahweh to deliver Judah to safety. Discuss whether faith in God and human efforts are necessarily mutually exclusive.

2. Discuss the American belief that dissent (or loyal opposition) is definitely a form of patriotism. Have students explain why dissent in good faith can be one of the highest forms of loyalty to a country, using the examples of Isaiah and Jeremiah.

3. Ask students to point to specific instances from the Bible story as part of this discussion.

Bonus Focus for you

Consider Psalm 107 in the light of events in Israel and Judah during this period of prophets, disobedience and obedience, and ultimately catastrophe. What is the turning point in each section of the psalm? How does this principle affect your life?

Scripture Workshop

1. When the book was read to him, Josiah tore his clothes and ordered his servants to consult prophets to find out what to do, since Judah had failed to obey the law prescribed in the book.

2. Huldah was a female prophet, who told Josiah that the Lord would bring destruction on Judah, but that the king himself would not live to see it.

3. Josiah promised the Lord that the people would obey the law fully. Josiah then led an effort to wipe out all the places of foreign worship in the land to restore proper worship of Yahweh.

4. According to the Deuteronomic historian, Josiah was the greatest king of Judah because of his faithfulness to the Covenant.

An altar to Baal was built in the Valley of Ben Hinom, near Jerusalem. According to Jeremiah 32:35, kings of Judah sacrificed their children here to the god, Molech, bringing destruction upon the nation.

In times of crisis, the advice of the prophets may often seem unrealistic or naive. The policies of the kings were surely more hardheaded and practical. But each was driven by different motives. The kings sought political survival while the prophets sought faithfulness to God.

Cold, rational decisions failed; Judah was conquered. The prophets, however, never abandoned their faith in God, and in the fall of Judah the people began to see that perhaps the prophets had been right all along.

Scripture Workshop

Josiah's Reforms

According to the Deuteronomic historian, Josiah was a great king because "He pleased the Lord and conducted himself unswervingly just as his ancestor David had done" (*2 Kings 22:2*). Josiah's greatest accomplishment was his religious reforms. Read about his reign in 2 Kings 22:1–23:30, and answer the following questions:

1. What did Josiah do and say when the book found in the Temple was read to him?
2. Who was Huldah? What message did she have for Josiah?
3. What promises did Josiah make to God? What did he do to carry out these promises?
4. How does Josiah rank among the kings of Judah, according to the Deuteronomic historian?

Have You Considered?

1. Assuming that Ahaz's motive was good—to save Judah—what was the mistake he made in trying to accomplish it?
2. There are some people who believe that anyone who criticizes his or her country is unpatriotic. Are there circumstances in which criticizing one's country can be a form of patriotism?
3. The kings of Judah felt that they had to set aside God's law to defend the nation. Do you think it's unrealistic to believe that a country can always behave morally? Why or why not?

MORE ABOUT THE TEXT

Molech and Child Sacrifice

Molech (also spelled Moloch) is the term used in the Bible to represent the practice of child sacrifice. There is some debate among scholars whether this term refers to a god that was worshipped, or if it referred to the practice itself. There is reason to believe that the word is formed from the Hebrew consonants for the word "king" and vowels for the word "shame." The term is often translated as a proper name.

The practice of child sacrifice was not unknown in Israel. It is mentioned in 1 Kings 11:1–8 as the "abomination of the Ammonites," Judges 11:24, Jeremiah 32:35, and 2 Kings 23:10. Judges 11:30–40 and 2 Kings 16:3; 17:17 mentions the practice of child sacrifice in Israel itself, but it was condemned by the Law (Leviticus 20:1–5) and the Prophets (Jeremiah 7:31 and Ezekial 16:20).

The Conscience of the People

You have already seen that during the period of the Northern and Southern kingdoms, prophets were powerful voices for God. They argued that the true threat to national security was neither Assyria nor Babylon, but disobedience to Yahweh. In their role as prophets they spoke with Yahweh's voice; they provided guidance and suggestions for moral living, and pronounced judgment on evil and unjust behavior. The prophets were the conscience of Israel and Judah.

In this section, you'll become more familiar with the lives and messages of these prophets.

Learning Objectives for Section Two

By the end of this section, you will be able to:

- Identify Amos' views on religious ritual.
- Explain Hosea's use of marriage as a metaphor.
- Describe the characteristics of Yahweh as revealed by Isaiah.
- Outline Jeremiah's career and message.

◆ The Prophets of the North: Amos and Hosea

Both Elijah and Elisha, studied in Chapter 5, were prophets who fought against the greed and foreign worship of the Northern kings. The same issues were later taken up by Amos and Hosea.

Amos

Amos was a herdsman, not a professional prophet. Although he addressed Israel, he was not from the North; he came from Tekoa in Judah around 750 B.C.E. After Yahweh commanded him to speak, Amos appeared one day at Israel's main shrine at Bethel and denounced the false worship taking place there. In uncompromising words, he proclaimed that their worship was useless because they lived unjustly.

Amos demanded to know why Israel seemed to have forgotten that Yahweh gave them the blessings of peace and prosperity. Why did Israel oppress the poor, trample the weak, and prostitute herself to fertility gods? Did they think that their religious rites were a substitute for just behavior?

Amos completely rejected the message of the court prophets, who said that God would smile on Israel as long as the correct religious rituals were observed by the priests. In rejecting this idea, Amos introduced a new emphasis in Covenant religion:

The person favored by God is not the one who performs the correct rituals, but the one who acts justly.

Amos says that public worship does no good for the person who "goes through the motions," but does not act in fairness to the disadvantaged and forgotten. These rituals, *by themselves*, mean nothing to God.

I hate, I spurn your feasts. I take no pleasure in your solemnities; Your cereal offerings I will not accept, nor consider your stall-fed offerings.

◆ MORE ABOUT THE LESSON

Take Your Time

When the Bible mentions "the gate" it is referring to the gate of the city, where marketing took place as people went in to their homes and out to their fields. Court cases were also held in this place, where there were benches for people to sit. (See Amos 5:15.)

In all of this lesson's readings, take care that the students understand what they are reading.

Do not hurry them. Usually, the meaning is understandable with attention, though the style may require a little extra effort. If needed, have them look up words in a Bible dictionary, or you may supply extra information from your own preparation of these readings.

LESSON THREE
(pages 101–105)

◆ The Prophets of the North: Amos and Hosea

Welcome

Have volunteer greeters "host" the incoming students and welcome them, either individually or with a prepared greeting.

What to Do

Ask: "Based on the last couple of lessons, what are your thoughts about whether or not God is in charge of historical events?" Suggest that they keep the question open until the end of this session.

Introducing the Lesson

Teaching Objectives

By the end of this lesson students will be able to:

- Explain the message of the prophets of the Northern kingdom.
- Describe how Amos connected acts of justice to worship.
- Compare Hosea's sense of betrayal with his wife to Yahweh's response to Israel.
- Articulate important aspects of Isaiah's message.

What to Do

- Have the students read the italicized opener and the learning objectives for Section Two.
- Say: "The only way to appreciate the prophets is to read their own words. At the end of the last lesson you marked the beginning of three books in the Bible. Open your Bibles now to Amos."
- Review the timeline with the students to make sure they have the times and order of events for Amos, Hosea and Isaiah of Jerusalem clear.

Development

What to Do

1. Pray with your students. Have volunteers (who have prepared ahead of time) to pray in their own words with and for the class.

2. Have the students read "Amos" in their text. Then have them read the following passages in Amos carefully: about Amos himself—Amos 1:1; 7:10–17; his message—Amos 5:7–17; 6:1–7; 9:1–6.

3. Using these passages, have the students write their own version of Amos's message.

4. When everyone is finished, assign these same readings to students who read easily and well. Ask them to read aloud, several verses each, as you have divided the passages.

5. Now have the students read the text on "Hosea." Say: "Hosea's message is based on his own real life experience, in the light of God's word." Then have the class read the passages pertaining to Hosea's life: Hosea 1 and 3. Point out the analogy between Hosea's marriage and the relationship of Yahweh (husband) and Israel (wife). Have the students read Hosea 2:4–15 and Hosea 7:1–16 and compare these sections with some part of Hosea's life.

6. Continuing with the marriage analogy, have the students read Hosea 6:1–10 and 14:2–8 and complete the "Bible Activity," number 2. Discuss these questions: "To what part of the story do these passages belong? Does Yahweh abandon his people even when they suffer consequences? What specific verses give you your answer?"

7. Lead the class in a discussion of "Have You Considered?"

Have You Considered?

1. Students should be encouraged to respond openly to this question, but without specifically naming anyone in the community. Adolescents are generally very sensitive to hypocrisy, and this question should allow them to explore those feelings.

2. Various opinions are possible. Direct students to consider Amos's point, which is not that ritual is unimportant, but rather that it cannot be substituted for justice.

3. Encourage students to share personal experiences honestly in response to this question. Refer students to Hosea, who transformed personal problems in his marriage into a way to talk about Israel's troubled relationship with God.

Away with your noisy songs! I will not listen to the melodies of your harps. But if you would offer me holocausts, then let justice surge like water, and righteousness like an ever-flowing stream.

(5:21–24)

Hosea

Shortly after Amos' ministry, Yahweh spoke through another prophet, Hosea. His work encompassed at least two decades, from 740 B.C.E. into the 720s. Hosea had a troubled marriage, and he turned this difficult personal experience into a powerful metaphor for the relationship between Yahweh and Israel.

Hosea's wife apparently deserted him and committed adultery, perhaps even in a fertility god's shrine. Hosea's agony stands as a symbol for Yahweh's suffering because of Israel's infidelity:

When Israel was a child I loved him, … The more I called them, the farther they went from me, sacrificing to the baals and burning incense to idols … I drew them with human cords, with bands of love; I fostered them like one who raised an infant to his cheeks; Yet, though I stooped to feed my child, they did not know that I was their healer.

(Hosea 11:1–2, 4)

Yahweh commanded Hosea to buy back his wife for the price of a slave, to discipline her, and reinstate her fully as his beloved wife. Just so, the prophet taught, will Yahweh do with Israel. Hosea named Assyria as the destroyer whom Yahweh would use to discipline Israel. As you already know, the Northern kingdom fell to Assyria in 721 B.C.E.

Have You Considered?

1. Do you know people who participate in religious rituals (such as going to church) but don't do anything to help others? What do you think of their behavior?

2. Amos said acting justly, not public worship, is the basis of religion. Does this mean someone can be "religious" without participating in ritual? Which is more important for a good relationship with God? Explain.

3. Describe a difficult personal experience you've had. How could you use this experience as a metaphor for our relationship with God? What can you learn from it?

4. Read the first chapter of Hosea. What is the significance of the names Hosea gives his children?

◆ Isaiah of Jerusalem

Isaiah of Jerusalem was the most influential prophet during the reigns of the Southern kings Jotham, Ahaz, and Hezekiah; a period of more than forty years.

The extent of Isaiah's influence is found in the Second Book of Kings, the Second Book of Chronicles, and from the book that bears his name. In actuality, not everything in the Book of Isaiah was written by the original prophet.

- Chapters 1–39 of the Book of Isaiah are the words of the prophet himself.
- Chapters 40–55, sometimes called "Second Isaiah," were written in Babylon after the fall of Judah. These chapters speak of a liberator who will free Israel.
- Chapters 56–66 are hopeful oracles written after the Babylonian Exile and are often known as "Third Isaiah."

You will study Second and Third Isaiah in a later chapter. The original prophet is called "Isaiah of Jerusalem" to distinguish him from these other two authors.

Isaiah's prophetic work extended far beyond his advice to the kings of Judah. Modern theologians credit Isaiah with understanding God and God's ways in a new light. Some of the major themes which appear in Isaiah's prophecy include:

- The holiness of Yahweh.
- The faithfulness of Yahweh.
- The justice of Yahweh.
- God's justice extends to all nations.

Let's look at each one of these in turn.

The Holiness of Yahweh

The story of Isaiah's call in Isaiah 6 reflects the holiness and reverence that Yahweh commanded. Isaiah encounters Yahweh at the Temple. Gazing through the Holy Place toward the Holy of Holies, Isaiah hears God's angels utter, "Holy, holy, holy is the Lord of hosts" (Isaiah 6:3).

Isaiah is frightened at the prospect of seeing God and responds:

Woe is me, I am doomed! For I am a man of unclean lips, living among a people of unclean lips, yet my eyes have seen the King, the Lord of hosts!

(Isaiah 6:5)

MORE ABOUT THE TEXT

Hosea

Although scholars do not always agree, most of them today reconstruct Hosea's experience as follows: He married a woman named Gomer, who bore three children. He gave them awful, symbolic names as part of his prophetic work.

At some time, Gomer deserted Hosea, most likely to become a "sacred prostitute" in one of the fertility shrines in the area. Later, the Lord commanded Hosea to go and buy her back for the price of a slave and reinstate her fully as his wife, after a period of disciplinary isolation. Because he followed the Lord, and because Hosea apparently always cherished his wife in spite of his agony, Hosea obeyed. It is unknown how things worked out, but if the analogy between Hosea's message and his life holds to the end, their marriage was fully restored.

The prophet Isaiah, portrayed in this eighteenth century C.E. fresco receiving divine
inspiration, called the nation of Judah to act justly and to trust in Yahweh.

In his vision, Isaiah saw Yahweh seated on a high
and lofty throne. Isaiah also saw Seraphim stationed
around Yahweh. The origin of the word *seraphim* suggests the "fiery one" or "burning one." In this passage,
the Seraphim are Yahweh's heavenly servants.

Isaiah also referred to smoke surrounding the
Holy One. While the smoke was physical smoke produced by the burning of incense in the Temple, it also
symbolized the mysterious presence of Yahweh—just
as the column of smoke had done during the Exodus.
All of these elements of Isaiah's vision emphasize the
supreme holiness of the God of Israel.

While Yahweh's holiness is seen here in the
Temple, it is found even more clearly in God's action
in the world beyond Israel. To understand more of
Isaiah's vision of Yahweh's all-encompassing holiness, read the following passages:

- Isaiah 1:4
- Isaiah 10:17, 20
- Isaiah 12:2–6
- Isaiah 29:18–19

How would you describe Isaiah's understanding
of Yahweh's holiness?

Because of Yahweh's holiness, any kind of
pride—whether national or personal—was, for Isaiah,
an insult. The holiness of God even ruled out pride
in the nation of Judah. This idea is reflected in Isaiah's
vision, in which the prophet says the Temple contained only the "train of God's robe." Yahweh is big-
ger, more holy, than even the great Temple. Isaiah,
therefore, warns Judah not to rely on the Temple for
protection, but rather, to do the will of God.

MORE ABOUT THE TEXT

The Holiness of Yahweh

Point out that Isaiah's experience was real.
His vision was a mixture of physical perception
and inner or spiritual perception. It must have
been quite an overwhelming experience for the
young man.

Notice, too, the words "Holy, holy, holy"
(which are repeated in every Mass). Hebrew had
no superlative form for adjectives (no good, better, best), so words were repeated several times
to demonstrate one's emphasis. Here, the repetition is equivalent to our calling God the most
holy one of all.

---

4. Hosea named his first child
Jezreel because God said, "In a little while I will punish the house
of Jehu for the bloodshed at
Jezreel" (Hosea 1:4). His daughter
was named Lo-ruhama because
God said, "I no longer feel pity for
the house of Israel" (Hosea 1:6).
The third child was named Lo-
ammi because God said, "You are
not My people, and I will not be
your God" (Hosea 1:8).

◆ Isaiah of Jerusalem

Development

What to Do

1. Have the students read Isaiah
40:1–2. Say: "Notice how different
the feeling and viewpoint are here
from the feelings expressed in
Hosea and Amos. As you will
soon see, they are equally different from the first 39 chapters of
Isaiah, written by the prophet in
Jerusalem. The break in the feeling here tipped scholars to the existence of a second book."

2. Have the students read "Isaiah of
Jerusalem" and discuss how Isaiah
is divided into three sections.

3. Read Isaiah 6:1–8, the call of
Isaiah to be a prophet and compare it with the text section, "The
Holiness of Yahweh," finding each
verse referred to in the text.

4. Remembering the result of
Hezekiah's obedience to Isaiah's
plea for quiet and trust, what do
the students now feel about waiting for God to act in their lives,
regarding the daily events and
decisions they face? Guide them
to consider talking everything
over with God and waiting for
God's guidance before taking
action.

5. Have the students read the passages listed under "The Justice of
Yahweh" and "Justice to All Nations," and answer the questions
which follow. Do this as a whole
class, with each passage read
aloud by a volunteer and followed
silently by the rest. Discussion
will follow and involve everyone.

6. Have the students find and read
the passage mentioned in "Hope
in a Faithful One" and list the requested qualities.

Recall

Have the students write out their answers to "Chapter 6 Review Q/A," Section Two, numbers 1–4.

Have them write a paragraph describing what they have learned that is most interesting to them and include it in their Spiritual Journal.

Connect

What to Do

Homework Assignment: Have the students take a single idea that they have learned so far from the prophets and bring it up with a family member or adult friend. They are to explain the idea carefully and ask the other person's opinion about the relevance of this idea for today's situation. They can report their conversation at the next class.

What's Next?

Tell the students that the next prophet is the one we have the most biographical information about. The story is also highly dramatic, so tell them that as they work through the lesson, they can be deciding whether they would like to spend extra time with the book of Jeremiah in order to dramatize the prophet's story and message.

The Faithfulness of Yahweh

If it was false pride that brought destruction, then it was faith, according to Isaiah, that brought life. The prophet describes his own faith in Isaiah 8:17:

> For I will trust in the Lord, who is hiding His face from the house of Jacob; yes, I will wait for him.

Here are two other passages that help to define the meaning of faith for Isaiah: Isaiah 7:4, 5, 9a and Isaiah 30:15. What do these passages urge about waiting quietly for the Lord to act in God's way and in God's time?

According to Isaiah, everyone—whether king or commoner—is called to become quiet, renounce all fear, and wait in patience for God to act. According to Isaiah, Yahweh's salvation depends on the king's and the people's total trust.

The Justice of Yahweh

Faith is never self-satisfied, however. Even as faith expresses itself through waiting for God to act, it also expresses itself in personal acts of justice. Justice demands that every element in society be judged according to how it contributes to a harmonious and sufficient life for all. Justice is a key element in the Covenant.

Isaiah preached against injustice ferociously. According to Isaiah, only when people live justly in all facets of society will the blessings of Yahweh be completely fulfilled.

- **Read Isaiah 1:15–16, 23–26 and Isaiah 3:13–15.** What is the main context of Isaiah's warnings to the people?

In Isaiah 5:1–7, Yahweh tells Isaiah how the beloved vineyard will be destroyed because the people disregarded the message to live justly:

> Yes, I will make it a ruin: it shall not be pruned or hoed, but overgrown with thorns and briers.
>
> (5:6)

In this passage, Judah is the vineyard, and the ruin refers to its coming destruction because of its disobedience.

- **Read Isaiah 5:8–25.** List the things in this passage that the people have done which the Lord so utterly rejects.

As Yahweh demands justice from the people, so will God act with justice in judgment. Isaiah says that Yahweh will see that Judah receives justice—and, unless its disobedient ways change, that's not good news. Although God's love for the people never changes, God's justice requires that the people suffer the consequences for their rejection of their Covenant promises.

Justice to All Nations

All of the prophets criticized the lack of justice within Israel and Judah, but Isaiah is the first to announce that Yahweh's justice extends to *all*

Vanni, *Heavenly Choirs. Fourteenth Century?*

Isaiah experienced the holiness of God in a vision of fiery Seraphim gathered around the throne of Yahweh.

The Justice of Yahweh

Answers to the in-text questions above.

Isaiah 1:15–16, 23–26, and 3:13–15: The main context of these warnings is the events that are taking place in the Southern kingdom of Judah, a short while before the Exile. The things the people have done which the Lord hates include:

- The wealthy joined house to house and field to field in order to grab control of the best land.

- The demand for strong drink and drunkeness.
- Justice was turned upside down; evil was called good and good was called evil.
- People thought themselves wise, and thus had no need for the wisdom of the prophet or of God.
- Justice was put up for sale; the wealthy could buy their way out of most any situation, especially when concerning the poor.

nations, and that Covenant commands apply to all people. For Isaiah, Yahweh commands all of the nations, not only Israel.

- **Read Isaiah 5:26–29.** What is the role of the "far-off" nation in this passage?
- **Read Isaiah 7:18–20.** How does this passage show that it is Yahweh who wields the real power?

According to Isaiah, nations are unknowingly used to accomplish God's purpose, but sometimes they go beyond God's wishes. When it destroyed much of Judah under Hezekiah, Assyria did not know that it was an instrument in the hands of Yahweh. When Assyria overstepped the task God had given it, Isaiah pronounced a message of doom on Assyria for its pride:

> *Therefore the Lord, the Lord of hosts, will send among His fat ones leanness, and instead of His glory there will be kindling like the kindling of fire.*
>
> (Isaiah 5:16)

The prophet foretold that after Assyria's destruction, Judah would be saved by Yahweh, but only through a small remnant of people. Read about the remnant in the following passages:

- Isaiah 8:3,16–20
- Isaiah 10:20–22
- Isaiah 14:32
- Isaiah 30:17

Hope in a Faithful One

Isaiah is not without hope for Israel in regard to its continuing relationship with Yahweh. Isaiah looks to the future and proclaims that a new king will arise, a king faithful to Yahweh and one specially appointed to do Yahweh's will. Isaiah tells us that this king is to be named "Immanuel," meaning "God is with us." He describes this new king and his kingdom in Isaiah 11:1–9. Read this passage and identify some of the qualities the expected king will have.

Even though this new king did not appear in Judah before the exile, Isaiah's prophecy kept hope alive for a king who would lead the people back to God.

Have You Considered?

1. Think about Isaiah's message concerning faith, destruction, social injustice, and hope for the future. What message would Isaiah give to our world and nation today? What should people do in response to that message?
2. Some people say that God's justice is too strict, that it was unfair of God to let Judah be destroyed. Do you agree? Why or why not? Could God allow people to have free choice, and yet not have to accept the consequences of their actions?
3. Isaiah said that Yahweh's holiness ruled out any false personal or national pride. How do you distinguish between pride that's legitimate, and pride that's false?

These seals from the thirteenth and twelfth centuries B.C.E. are marks of authenticity. Scribes, such as Baruch, would use these seals to guarantee that a document was genuine.

Justice to All Nations

The role of the faraway nation in Isaiah 5:26–29 is to defeat Israel and to punish it for its sins.

Isaiah 7:18–20 suggests that God will use nations such as the Assyrians as a razor to inflict suffering upon the sinful people.

Have You Considered?

1. Have students review Isaiah's message, especially his emphasis that proper worship and social justice are the proper responses to the majesty of God. For Isaiah, God was a living presence very close to him. Do students have a living sense of the holy in their lives? Do most people today have such a sense? Ask them to consider where such a sense comes from, and where they see it in today's world.
2. Give students other examples to focus on this question. For instance: Is it "unfair" to allow a drunk person to drive? Is it "unfair" to allow a student who is cheating to get caught and punished? Point out that free choice means nothing if the consequences aren't real.
3. Have students respond to this question on the basis of their own experience. When is pride a good thing, and when does it simply become "ego" and get in the way of accomplishing our goals? Refer students back to the story of Israel and Judah. Point out that in some ways, the pride of the rulers of these two nations led to their destruction, since they forgot about their reliance on Yahweh.

Bonus Focus for You ———

Read Isaiah 12:1–6. As in much of the prophetic work, this can be attached to a possible event (like Hezekiah's being saved from siege) or it can be interpreted inwardly and personally. Ponder whether there have been events in your own life when this meditation of praise would have been especially appropriate.

LESSON FOUR
(pages 106–109)

◆ Jeremiah

Welcome

What to Do

Ask the students: "What are the characteristics of a prophet?" List their answers on the board.

Pray with your students. Offer a prayer full of thanksgiving for your students and for the learning that they are demonstrating session by session. Praise them to the Lord.

Introducing the Lesson

Teaching Objectives

By the end of this lesson students will be able to name the themes found in the Book of Jeremiah.

What to Do

Retell or read the story of Jeremiah given in Teacher's Resource 6D. Ask the students to jot down the most interesting events of his life.

Development

What to Do

1. Treat this lesson as if it were a single, large scripture workshop. Have the students open their Bibles to Jeremiah and keep them ready to look at passages as they work through the text. They should also mark 2 Kings.

2. Begin by having the students read in their text the opening two paragraphs of "Jeremiah" and then immediately do the "Scripture Workshop" on page 107. They should start with Jeremiah 1:1–3 for background. For background to Jeremiah's story, have the students complete the "Bible Activity," numbers 3 and 4, on page 110 of their text, reading 2 Kings 21 and 22. (Chapters 18 and 19 belong to an earlier period, but are still valid reading.)

3. Form small groups of four or five students. Have the students read "Judah's Doom" and look up the biblical passages quoted. For better understanding, students should also read: Jeremiah 2:20–24, 3:6–10, 4:1–4. Each passage should be read aloud within the group. Each group is to write down its own answer to the question.

Michelangelo, *Prophet Jeremiah*. Sixteenth Century.

Michelangelo's painting of the prophet Jeremiah (from the Sistine Chapel in Saint Peter's Basilica in Rome) shows a troubled and brooding man. From your reading of the Book of Jeremiah, how would you describe the prophet?

◆ Jeremiah

Jeremiah was from a priestly family who lived two miles outside of Jerusalem in the small village of Anathoth. He never married or raised a family because he believed in the imminent destruction of Jerusalem. There is more information about the life of Jeremiah than about any other prophet. Jeremiah's prophecies were recorded by a secretary, Baruch. Jeremiah's career extended from the thirtieth year of King Josiah (627 B.C.E.) through the destruction of Jerusalem (587 B.C.E.).

As with all prophets, Jeremiah's message was addressed particularly to the times and conditions in which it was spoken. But its central themes have endured to warn, teach, and console many future generations as well. Many of Jeremiah's teachings are especially appropriate today.

Judah's Doom

According to Jeremiah, the kingdom of Israel had become as "a frenzied she-camel, coursing near and far" (Jeremiah 2:23). But Judah refused to learn from the experience of Israel:

> Then, even though her traitor sister Judah saw that for all the adulteries rebellious Israel had committed, I put her away and gave her a bill of divorce, nevertheless her traitor sister Judah was not frightened; she too went off and played the harlot.
>
> (Jeremiah 3:7–8)

The reforms instituted by King Josiah may have changed people's behavior somewhat, but to Jeremiah, they were simply a worthless, external show of devotion meaningless apart from any true internal conversion and repentance.

> For the sake of the Lord, be circumcised, remove the foreskins of your hearts, O men of Judah and citizens of Jerusalem.
>
> (Jeremiah 4:4)

◆ MORE ABOUT THE LESSON

Dramatization

Dramatizing Jeremiah's story is a wonderful opportunity for students to dig deeply into a prophet who experienced many feelings and situations that the students also might feel. Further, the story is itself intrinsically dramatic. There are two possible forms of dramatization which can be effective with Jeremiah: a spontaneous one, drawing only on the memories of the students when they have completed the lesson work; or a full dramatization, carefully planned and written (not every word, but the gist of the drama's events and dialogue). If the students choose a full dramatization, this is a wonderful project to share with other classes, with church groups or with a parent audience. You will see from the suggestions in Teacher's Resource 6D that the students will never forget Jeremiah if they choose a full dramatization!

Scripture Workshop

Jeremiah's Call

Jeremiah's personal agony began from the day he was called as a young man to be Yahweh's servant. Read Jeremiah 1:4–19. Answer the following questions:

- When did Jeremiah's call take place?
- How did Jeremiah respond? Who else in the Old Testament responded to God's call by worrying that he wouldn't know what to say?
- What was Yahweh's answer?
- What would be the purpose and character of Jeremiah's work?
- What was the main part of Jeremiah's message to be?
- What effect would the Lord's call have on Jeremiah's personality?

Read the following passages. Identify the reasons listed by Jeremiah for Judah's destruction:

- Jeremiah 2:1–13
- Jeremiah 5:26–31
- Jeremiah 9:1–5
- Jeremiah 23:13–17

What is a common thread in Jeremiah's warnings against Judah?

Jeremiah's Intense Views

Jeremiah preached of the coming disaster that would befall Judah. He was not, however, optimistic that Judah would listen to him and change its behavior. He felt that the hearts of the people were so hardened that their conversion was as unlikely as a leopard changing its spots (Jeremiah 13:23). According to Jeremiah, the day of reckoning was fast approaching:

> The Lord said to me: "Do not intercede for this people. If they fast, I will not listen to their supplication. If they offer holocausts or cereal offerings, I will not accept them. Rather, I will destroy them with the sword, famine, and pestilence."
>
> (Jeremiah 14:11)

How could the people of Judah be renewed? Read the following passages to find out.

- Jeremiah 4:1–4
- Jeremiah 5:1–9
- Jeremiah 13:20–25

Jeremiah's view of Judah is expressed in the story of the potter's flask in Jeremiah 18:1–12.

> I went down to the potter's house and there he was, working at the wheel. Whenever the object of clay which he was making turned out badly in his hand, he tried again, making of the clay another object of whatever sort he pleased. Then the word of the Lord came to me: "Can I not do to you, house of Israel, as this potter has done?" says the Lord. "Indeed, like clay in the hand of the potter, so are you in my hand, house of Israel."
>
> (Jeremiah 18:3–6)

The people of Judah refused to be shaped by the Covenant, just as the clay had not formed correctly in the potter's hands. If Judah could not be molded as God wished, then God would start over. To dramatize Judah's coming doom, Jeremiah smashed a clay pot to the ground and said:

> Thus says the Lord of hosts: I will smash this people and this city, as one smashes a clay pot so that it cannot be repaired.
>
> (Jeremiah 19:11)

Jeremiah's dramatic display of smashing the pot to illustrate God's unhappiness is called a "prophetic action." In the ancient world, prophetic action was a public gesture performed by a prophet for purposes of illustrating his or her message.

When Jeremiah smashed the clay pot in public, the priest, Pashur, had Jeremiah arrested and put in stocks for speaking out against the king's policies (Jeremiah 20:1–6).

Threats and Condemnations

To understand why Jeremiah's prophecies were so violently received, you need to remember a point made earlier: in the ancient world, there was no separation between religion and politics. Moreover, in Israel the spoken word was a vehicle of actual power, a real thing that could and did cause other things to happen. Therefore, when Jeremiah spoke against the king or the national policy, it amounted to an act of rebellion or near treason. Jeremiah's words were seen not only as predictions of the future, but also as causes of the results.

4. Have the students read "Jeremiah's Intense Views," then read the bulleted passages aloud and then answer the question of how the people of Judah could be renewed. They should list every possible behavior that might have been intended by Jeremiah. When the groups have finished, have them compare answers.
5. Read aloud the whole story of the pot: Jeremiah 18:1–12 and 19:1–11. Ask the students what they are thinking about these "words of the Lord" and the prophet's intensity.
6. Read Jeremiah 20:1–6 and "Jeremiah's Intense Views." (Note how fine a passage this is for possible dramatization.) Ask the students which would be more powerful in its impact today: prophetic action or prophetic words? Why?
7. Read "Threats and Condemnations," consider the passages that Jeremiah cited, and answer the questions raised.

Scripture Workshop

1. Jeremiah was called in the thirteenth year of the reign of King Josiah.
2. Jeremiah answered that he was too young and would not know what to say. This is similar to Moses' response to Yahweh, when Moses said that he would not know how to address the pharaoh.
3. Yahweh told Jeremiah that God would be with him as he spoke.
4. The purpose and character of Jeremiah's work was to destroy and to demolish nations, but also to build up and to plant.
5. Jeremiah is to announce the coming destruction of the people because of their infidelity to the Covenant.
6. Jeremiah is to withstand criticism and attacks from the whole land because of the message he has to deliver. He will be hated by his own people.

MORE ABOUT THE TEXT

Judah's Doom

Be sure to have the students read the context of the listed and quoted passages. The images and language of Jeremiah are very strong and surely would have caused intense reactions in their first hearers.

Today's students also will likely have strong reactions if they read enough—and those reactions can give rise to good discussion. Give them plenty of chance to react aloud. Do not worry if the students don't like what they are reading. Let them be "real" and spontaneous—the Bible can defend itself. Ask them to ponder whether Covenant goodness is so important to God that such awful consequences are necessary to teach people its value.

8. Ask: "Why would the people have hated Jeremiah even more than they had after his predictions came true?"

9. In their small groups, have the students read "The Confessions of Jeremiah," along with the bulleted passages, and answer the questions. Gather as a class to share their answers.

10. Complete "Bible Activity" number 6.

Extend the Activity To enhance their understanding of why Jeremiah became so discouraged sometimes, have the students read Jeremiah 37 and 38. Follow with "People of Note." The students will read Jeremiah 36 also, to get a full picture of Baruch's importance to Jeremiah.

Recall

Discuss the questions in "Have You Considered?" In addition, ask the students to write out the answers to "Chapter 6 Review Q/A," Section Two, numbers 5–8.

Connect

Homework Assignment: Have the students complete "Bible Activity" number 5, omitting the references in 2 Kings. They should also read "Hope for the Future" and write a half-page essay on the modern definition of "New Covenant."

What's Next?

Students are to decide whether or not to dramatize Jeremiah, and if so, how they want to do it.

What to Do

Ask for a student vote about the dramatization. If the vote is affirmative, follow the directions in Teacher's Resource 6D. If negative, say, "The next subject is the experience of the Jews in Exile. You can be thinking about how it would feel when all Jeremiah's predictions came true."

Give the students a few moments to collect their thoughts in quiet and ask them to express a prayer-thought related to what they have learned in Jeremiah. Close with a few words of your own and the Our Father, together.

108

People of Note

Baruch

Although Jeremiah comments on how he sometimes felt alone, we know that he had at least one companion: his friend, secretary, and assistant, Baruch.

In chapter 36, Jeremiah says that he is prevented from going to the Temple to announce the word of God. Therefore, he dictates a scroll which Baruch copies. Jeremiah then asks him to go to the Temple and to read it aloud to all who are there. Baruch follows his instructions, and afterwards he is called before the scribes of the king to repeat what he had said. He did so fearlessly, imitating the example of Jeremiah.

We also know that Baruch imitated Jeremiah in one other way: he, too, sometimes felt forgotten and depressed. In chapter 45, God speaks to Baruch through Jeremiah, warning him not to seek personal happiness while Judah is being destroyed. Nevertheless, Yahweh says that Baruch's life will be spared because of his services to Jeremiah.

Baruch was remembered by later generations of Jews, who used his name for the "Book of Baruch." This book was written two centuries after the Exile, to encourage Jews to remain faithful to the Law in the middle of Greek culture. Even then, Baruch was remembered as someone who had remained loyal to Yahweh despite the hardship it caused.

Baruch also offered a promise of hope:

"Fear not, Jerusalem! He who gave you your name is your encouragement."

(Baruch 4:30)

Because his predictions did not come true for many years, Jeremiah was long accused of false prophecy. But in the end, Judah was destroyed and Jerusalem was demolished. The people of Jerusalem then hated Jeremiah for his words even more!

Read the following passages. Try to determine what it was about these political messages that upset the people so much.

- Jeremiah 26:1–19. How did Jeremiah's supporters rescue him?
- Jeremiah 21:1–10. What statements sound like treason? Why do you think Jeremiah's fellow citizens would hate him for these words?
- Jeremiah 37–38. These chapters describe the same incident as in 21:1–10. Describe King Zedekiah's actions. What do you think about his decision in this case?

Even though punished, Jeremiah's voice was never stilled. He continued to offer counsel to all who would hear, especially to the king, Zedekiah, who kept seeking a way out of his nation's troubles and a deliverance from Yahweh that would never come.

The Confessions of Jeremiah

Despite Jeremiah's persistence, he experienced periods of self-doubt and depression. In several places, he expresses a sense of failure, bitterness towards his enemies, and resentment over how God has allowed him to be laughed at and persecuted.

Read what he has to say in these passages:

- Jeremiah 11:18–12:6. What does Jeremiah want God to do to the unrighteous?
- Jeremiah 15:10–21. Why does Jeremiah say he wishes he hadn't been born?
- Jeremiah 17:14–18. What line does Jeremiah say that his enemies use against him? What does he want God to do?
- Jeremiah 18:18–23. What does Jeremiah remind God of in this passage? Why?
- Jeremiah 20:7–18. Why does Jeremiah fear that he will end his days in shame?

Jeremiah is remarkably open about his feelings in these passages. Nowhere else do we get the opportunity to look so freely into the soul of a prophet.

These "confessions" help us get a sense of Jeremiah as a human being, a person who experienced sadness, hatred, and doubt, just as we all do. Despite his loneliness and frustration, however, Jeremiah experienced the continuing word of God so powerfully that he could not stop announcing it. Jeremiah pondered:

I say to myself, I will not mention him, I will speak in his name no more. But then it becomes like fire burning in my heart, imprisoned in my bones. I grow weary holding it in, I cannot endure it.

(Jeremiah 20:9)

So he continued to prophesy, in spite of trouble, rejection, suspicion, and oppression. And Yahweh sustained Jeremiah, as he had promised in the beginning, "Have no fear ... because I am with you to deliver you" (Jeremiah 1:8).

◆ MORE ABOUT THE LESSON

Answers to Judah's Doom

Reasons for Judah's destruction include: (a) they had forsaken authentic worship of Yahweh, (b) they had adopted the worship of foreign gods, (c) they had grown rich through treachery, (d) they had denied the claims of justice, (e) priests and prophets had spoken falsely and led the people astray, (f) the people had cheated and lied to one another, and (g) they had committed adultery.

One common thread is that Yahweh punishes the people for their disloyalty and disobedience.

Jeremiah's Call

Jeremiah must have been less than thirty, judging from the length of his prophetic work and the customary Hebrew view that a man was not mature until he was thirty. Jeremiah would have been expected to be mature before he could speak the word of the Lord.

Hope for the Future

Jeremiah offers hopeful words in chapters 30 to 33, sometimes called the "Book of Consolation." Many of Jeremiah's words of salvation recorded in these chapters were originally intended for the people of Israel after it fell to Assyria. Then, when Judah headed down the same path of destruction, the messages were extended to include it, too. Most of these writings were probably completed in the early part of Jeremiah's ministry.

Write on Their Hearts Unlike Isaiah's hopeful prophecies of a future king who would be the deliverer of the people, Jeremiah centers his message on why the people had not been able to keep the Covenant promises. He finally centers on the stubbornness and hardness of their hearts. Judah could only pray that Yahweh would form new hearts in them and bring about a total conversion of Judah.

> The days are coming, says the Lord, when I will make a new Covenant with the house of Israel and the house of Judah. . . . I will place my law within them, and write it upon their hearts; I will be their God, and they shall be My people.
>
> (Jeremiah 31:31, 33)

Jeremiah's Purchase Jeremiah's hope for Israel's restoration is real, so much so that he fulfills his family duty and purchases land from his cousin, even though the army of Babylon had already captured Jerusalem. This purchase symbolized the hope that someday he would be able to return and to farm the land. Jeremiah's purchase of the property was a sign that Judah would be restored and that the life of the people would continue:

> Thus says the Lord of hosts, the God of Israel: Take these deeds, both the sealed and the open deed of purchase, and put them in an earthen jar, so that they can be kept there a long time. For thus says the Lord of hosts, the God of Israel: Houses and fields and vineyards shall again be bought in this land.
>
> (Jeremiah 32:13–15)

While Jeremiah's words seemed to have few positive results at the time, they became a source of great comfort and hope during the time of exile. Through Jeremiah's guidance, the Israelites had reason to believe in God's goodness and looked for ways to revitalize the Covenant.

Have You Considered?

1. If Jeremiah was sure that Judah would not respond to his message, how do you think it made him feel to deliver that message anyway? Would you have delivered the message, if you were sure it wouldn't work?
2. Describe a modern example of a prophetic action.
3. Do you think that Jeremiah was right in believing that people's attitudes, rather than their leadership, would have to change if they were to follow God's law? Why or why not?

Spiritual Reflection

A New Covenant

Pray and reflect on Jeremiah's vision of a New Covenant between Yahweh and humankind, reading about it in Jeremiah 31:31–33. Do one of the following to express your images of the New Covenant in prayer:

- Reflect on the lyrics of a favorite song that includes a message of hope for the future. How can this song help inspire you to dedicate yourself to the vision of a New Covenant?

- Imagine a world where the New Covenant has taken effect. What would it look like? Draw this new world.
- Offer a sacrifice (a day of fast, a visit to someone who is lonely, etc.) in the name of the New Covenant.
- Compose a plan (either on your own or in a small group) of something you can undertake to help express the New Covenant.

Have You Considered?

1. Refer students back to the call of Jeremiah, in which God revealed that Jeremiah would withstand the criticism of the entire land. The purpose of this question is to encourage students to try to enter into Jeremiah's emotional condition as he spoke words he knew his people did not want to hear. Have students share an experience in which they had to tell people something they knew that they wouldn't like to hear. How did that feel? How does that help us understand what Jeremiah went through?

2. Ensure that students understand the definition of a prophetic action (a public gesture performed by a prophet to illustrate his or her message). Civil disobedience, such as that practiced in the civil rights movement, is an example.

3. Students should focus on what it means to follow God's law: Is it a matter of external observance, which could be mandated by the authorities, or of the heart, which requires a change in attitudes? Try to encourage students to recognize that obeying God is more than ritual (as Amos observed); it is, rather, a state of mind and heart.

Bonus Focus for You
Read and pray with Jeremiah 17:5–10. How do these words of Jeremiah, aimed at the individual, relate to your life and experience today? (Remember that in the Bible, "heart" is the deepest center of a human being.)

 Spiritual Reflection

Ask the students to choose any two of the four suggestions in "Spiritual Reflection" and write about their experience in their Spiritual Journal.

Q/A

Section One

1. Many examples of common injustices are possible: the debt of small farmers, the growing gap between rich and poor, the use of wealth to control the political system, and merchants tampering with scales to cheat customers are just a few.

2. The Assyrians deported conquered populations to reduce the threat of rebellions. When Israel was conquered, the 10 northern tribes were dislocated and disappear into history.

3. The prophets warned that destruction would occur because of the Israelites' failure to keep the Covenant.

4. Ahaz failed to trust in Yahweh, making an alliance with Tilgathpileser II instead.

5. Hezekiah was a king of the Southern kingdom when Sennacherib invaded in 701 B.C.E. Hezekiah was known for being a king loyal to Yahweh.

6. Josiah is honored as one who tried to restore pure worship of Yahweh to Judah.

7. Nebuchadnezzar was the emperor of Babylon when the Babylonians conquered Judah, taking the Jews into Exile.

8. Despite the efforts of Josiah, Judah, like Israel, disobeyed the Covenant and engaged in the worship of foreign gods and social injustice.

CHAPTER 6 REVIEW

Q/A

Section One

1. Give an example of the injustice common in the Northern and Southern kingdoms.
2. What was Assyria's policy on what to do with conquered populations? Because of this, what happened to the ten northern tribes?
3. How did the prophets explain the destruction of Israel?
4. How did Ahaz disobey Yahweh?
5. Identify: Hezekiah.
6. Why does the Deuteronomic historian honor King Josiah?
7. Identify: Nebuchadnezzar.
8. How did the prophets explain the destruction of Judah?

Section Two

1. What were Amos' views concerning public worship and justice?
2. What metaphor did Hosea use to describe the relationship between Yahweh and Israel?
3. Why is the prophet Isaiah called "Isaiah of Jerusalem"?
4. What is unique in what Isaiah says about God's attitude towards other nations?
5. To what did the story of the potter's flask refer?
6. Define: prophetic action.
7. Identify: Baruch.
8. What is the nature of the "New Covenant" that Jeremiah predicted?

BIBLE ACTIVITY

1. Read Sirach 48:15–25 and 49:1–6. These verses show how one of the later writers remembered the main characters at the time of the fall of the Northern and Southern kingdoms. Make a list of the information that is similar to what you learned in this chapter. Also, list any new information you discover and any information that Sirach left out.
2. Read Hosea 2:15–22 and 11:1–4. How do these passages express God's love for the people of Israel?
3. King Josiah's story is told in 2 Kings 22. Read the chapter to find out information on (1) the important object which was found, (2) the person to whom Josiah went for advice (3) the prophecy, and (4) the reward Josiah received for his sorrow.
4. Read 2 Kings 18–19 and 21. What was life like in Judah during a time of brief independence from around 630 B.C.E.?
5. Read Jeremiah 24:1–10. What was Jeremiah's message in this story of the two baskets of figs? Read 2 Kings 18–19 and 21.
6. Read Jeremiah 29:4–15 to find out (1) Yahweh's plan for the Judah and (2) the length of their captivity in Babylon.

BIBLE ACTIVITY

1. Information gained from these verses includes: (1) Destruction resulted from sin; (2) Sennacherib invaded during the time of Hezekiah; (3) God struck down the Assyrians with a plague; (4) Isaiah advised Hezekiah and interceded with God to add time to his life; (5) Isaiah foretold the restoration of Judah; (6) Josiah was loyal to Yahweh; (7) Jeremiah prophesied the destruction of Jerusalem. New information: Hezekiah dug a tunnel through rock with iron tools and had water brought into the city. Left out: the discovery of Deuteronomy by Josiah.

2. Allow students to express their own reactions to these verses. In Hosea 2:15–2, God speaks of the desire to return Israel to the desert and return her to pure worship of Yahweh. Hosea 11:1–4 speaks of God's loving care for the young nation.

3. The important object that was found was the book of the Law (probably Deuteronomy), the

GLOSSARY

- **Assyrians:** The powerful nation that overthrew the coalition of Israel and Damascus, and eventually destroyed the Northern kingdom.
- **Babylon:** The nation that conquered Judah and pillaged Jerusalem and its people.
- **Confessions of Jeremiah:** Passages in Jeremiah where the prophet reveals his inner feelings of anger, fear, and doubt.
- **False Pride:** An attitude denounced by Isaiah as inconsistent with the holiness of Yahweh, false pride values the self or nation too highly in comparison with God.
- **Holiness:** Yahweh's main characteristic according to Isaiah; it means separateness, majesty, and power.
- **Justice:** The harmonious order in society which requires all people to be treated fairly; in the Old Testament it is based on Covenant.
- **Lost Tribes:** A term for the ten northern tribes after they were deported by the Assyrians.
- **New Covenant:** The future situation predicted by Jeremiah when God will give humanity "new hearts" so people will be able to love and obey Yahweh completely.
- **Prophetic Action:** A dramatic public act performed by a prophet to illustrate his or her message.
- **Seraphim:** A fiery angel seen by Isaiah of Jerusalem during his vision of God, described in Chapter 6 of Isaiah.
- **Writing Prophets:** Prophets with books in the Old Testament that bear their names.

UNDERSTANDING MORE ABOUT:

Micah

Micah was active in Judah at the same time as Isaiah, and the two form an interesting pair: where Isaiah's words are polished, Micah's are blunt. Both men, however, attacked the greed and injustice which infected the nation. Micah's prophecies are recorded in the Old Testament book that bears his name.

Both Isaiah and Micah predict the future coming of a king who will save Israel and return it to faithfulness to Yahweh. Micah said that the future king would be born in Bethlehem, a small village a few miles south of Jerusalem where King David was born.

The most obvious similarity between Micah and Isaiah is that they share a vision of a future world governed by Yahweh. In this world, peace shall be the rule among nations. Isaiah 2:4 and Micah 4:3 use the identical words to describe this new world:

> They shall beat their swords into plowshares, and their spears into pruning hooks; One nation shall not raise the sword against another, nor shall they train for war again.

Today, their message is inscribed on a statue outside the United Nations, reminding the nations of the world of our common longing for peace.

Section Two

1. Amos felt that public worship was not pleasing to God unless the people also practiced social justice.
2. Hosea compared the relationship between the people and Yahweh to the unfaithfulness of his own wife.
3. He is known as Isaiah of Jerusalem because chapters 1–39 represent the teaching of the prophet who lived in Jerusalem during the time of the Southern kingdom. Later chapters of the Book of Isaiah were written at a later date by different authors.
4. Isaiah was the first to suggest that God controls the fate of other nations and, thus, the Covenant applies to all nations.
5. The potter's flask referred to the refusal of Judah to be shaped according to the Covenant, and God's decision to cast it aside and start over.
6. A prophetic action is a public gesture performed by a prophet to illustrate his or her message.
7. Baruch was Jeremiah's assistant and secretary, who recorded his prophecies.
8. The new covenant predicted by Jeremiah was to be formed in the hearts and minds of the people, rather than on stone, as the old one had been.

person Josiah turned to was Huldah the prophet, the prophecy was that Judah would be destroyed, and the king's reward was to be spared seeing the destruction.

4. Students will already be familiar with the events of Hezekiah's reign. Stress what occurred during the following reigns of Manasseh and Amon, who engaged extensively in foreign religious practices such as divination and soothsaying. 2 Kings even says that Manasseh followed the Canaanite custom of offering his firstborn son to Baal. Have

students discuss what the reaction in Judah must have been to these practices.

5. The vision means that Jeremiah expected no good to come from those who had been left behind in Judah; he held hope only for those who passed through the purification of Exile.

6. God instructed the Jews to settle in Babylon, to make homes there, and to support the cities in which they lived. The Exile, the Lord said, was destined to last 70 years.

Chapter Overview

This chapter explores how the Jewish religion was shaped by the Babylonian Exile. The important writings of this period come from Ezekiel, the Priestly Writers, and Second Isaiah.

Teaching Objectives

By the end of this chapter students will be able to:
• Describe the challenges the Jewish community faced when living in exile in order to preserve its culture and faith.
• Identify how Judaism became a codified religion built around the Law and synagogue worship under the influence of the Priestly Writers.
• Explain the importance of the prophets Ezekiel and Second Isaiah to the people in exile.

Welcome

What to Do

Before the students arrive, arrange their seats in rows along the walls, facing the walls. As the students arrive, tell them (in a voice that is neither threatening or inviting) to take any seat, but to remain quiet. Wait until all of the students are seated, then greet them very formally as a group, as if you were a stranger in authority over them. Be polite, but not especially warm. Speak to them from the center of the room. Adopt the attitude that you are a government official who must arrange the affairs of refugees.

CHAPTER

7

Exile: An Ending and a Beginning

France, Chartres Cathedral. Twelfth Century.

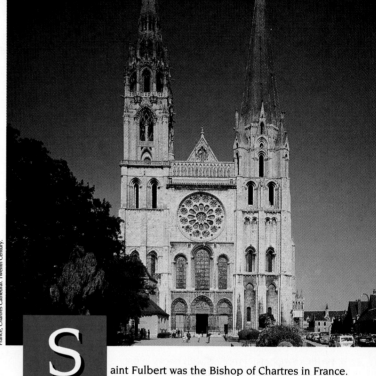

626 B.C.E.
● Babylon replaces Assyria as major power

600

597
● First deportation from Judah

592
● Ezekiel's call

587
● Destruction of Jerusalem; Exile

580
● Deuteronomic history

570
● Pentateuch, Jeremiah, Ezekiel

562
● Death of Nebuchadnezzar

550
● Pythagoras studies planets, the soul
● Priestly Writers
● Cyrus, King of Medes and Persians

540
● Second Isaiah
● Public libraries in Athens

539
● Babylon falls to Cyrus

538
● Edict of Cyrus; Return from Exile

509
500 ● Establishment of the Roman Republic

Legend

● General History
● Biblical History
● Jewish History
● Books written

S aint Fulbert was the Bishop of Chartres in France. Fulbert was a great scholar, a talented poet, and an inspired songwriter. He was also a gifted politician who knew most of the kings and diplomats in Europe. In 1020 C.E., he began a project that demanded the very best he could give in all of these areas: the building of the Chartres Cathedral.

Over the next 100 years, Christians from all over Europe donated time and money for the building of the finest cathedral ever raised in honor of the Virgin Mary. Fulbert began with the lowest part—the crypt. He then rapidly constructed the various chapels and the upper church. Finally, workers erected the towers, including the southern tower with its magnificent spire. In 1160, after Fulbert himself had died, "Fulbert's cathedral" was finished. It evoked awe in all who saw it. The people of

---

MORE ABOUT THE TEXT

Chartres Cathedral

Chartres Cathedral is considered one of the finest architectural structures in the world. While the building was built (and then rebuilt) with money from wealthy nobles and kings, it owes its existence to the enthusiasm and concern of the general population. Stories describe how people voluntarily harnessed themselves to carts in order to transport the stone used in its construction.

The building was never officially finished, since only two of its eight towers were ever completed with spires. It is still an amazing achievement. The western entrance is called the royal portal because of the statues of kings and queens above it. This entrance is flanked by the two towers and is dominated by four stained-glass windows that tell the Bible's story. Most notable of these windows is the "Jesse Tree." See Teacher's Resource 7A.

Chartres, exhausted from over 100 years of labor, thanked God for their success and rested.

Then, on July 10, 1194, the unthinkable happened: fire raged through the cathedral, destroying everything but the crypt and the towers. Fulbert's cathedral lay in ruins, and the people of Chartres were dazed. "How could God allow this to happen?" they wondered. Despite their sorrow and confusion, the people began the long process of rebuilding. Within only 25 years, the repairs were finished, and the people of Chartres could once again take pride in their beautiful cathedral.

How did they do it? A story told about the repairs gives us part of the answer. A European architect said that he had worked at construction sites for cathedrals all over Europe. At other places, he said, if you were to ask masons what they were doing, they would answer, "We're laying bricks," or if you asked the same question of carpenters, they would say, "We're cutting wood." But at Chartres, he said, even if you asked the most humble rock-hauler what he was doing, he would answer, "Why, I'm building a cathedral!"

The Importance of Attitude

This answer illustrates the importance of attitude in overcoming hardship. While the workers in other places knew their jobs, the people of Chartres had a sense of purpose—they were building a cathedral! Responding to the misfortune of the fire, the people showed courage and a positive attitude. These qualities enabled them to rebuild the cathedral that, even today, is acknowledged as one of the finest in the world.

When war destroys a country, and places its people under a new and unwelcome government, living with that, too, requires courage. After the fall of Jerusalem, the people of Judah faced the task of rediscovering what their faith and life meant during difficult times. What would be the attitude of the people? This chapter is about how they met their challenge.

Say: "Although you are strangers here, you are expected to live by our laws, which will soon be explained to you. You are expected to work hard and become model citizens. You will live in your own area of the city, which we expect you to maintain. You are not slaves or prisoners, but new members of the empire. You bring extra labor and more knowledge to our country, which we are glad to have. You will be instructed about food and water shortly, and will be assigned a place to stay. Until then, know that while you not prisoners, you will be watched very carefully until you learn our ways. Welcome to your new life."

Ask your students (with their backs still to you) to pray silently about this new situation. What will they say to God at this time? After a few minutes of silence, close by saying, "Amen."

Introducing the Chapter

What to Do

Have the students help you return the classroom to its normal arrangement. Then say: "Describe what your feelings were following the way class started: anger, fear, worry, pain? How did you react to this unwanted and new situation?" When a volunteer suggests a reaction, inquire how many others felt the same. Did anyone feel good, i.e. challenged but full of courage? How might the Jews in Exile have felt?

Using the Timeline

Review the timeline. Note especially the dates that pertain to the Jews: 597, 592, 587, 580, 570, 540, 539, and 538. Help the students to keep the sequence clear and note that the biblical books mentioned are "in progress," not completed at this time. They would not be completed until long after their return from exile.

◆ MORE ABOUT THE LESSON

Life in Exile

Students will probably consider life in exile to be a form of torture, possibly like being in prison. Help them to see that this was not the case. When Judah was captured and the first group was taken into exile, they were not taken as prisoners. Babylon was interested in expanding its political and economic base, not retribution or revenge. Babylon removed the ruling class and put a new Jewish government in place of the king with the hope that Judah would prosper.

The Babylonians hoped that people taken into exile would become productive citizens of the empire. Captured people—including Jews—were given a great deal of freedom with the intention that they would forget their cultural roots. They could work at almost any job in the empire, make money, and spend it freely, and even worship as they chose.

◆ Life during the Exile

Teaching Objectives

By the end of this lesson students will be able to:

• Identify the conditions of life for Jews during the Exile.

• Explain why the Exile threatened Jewish life.

• Describe the changes to Judaism that occurred during the Exile.

Development

What to Do

1. Have the students read the opening italics and the learning objectives. See if there are any questions.

2. Read the story about the building of the Chartres Cathedral. How important is one's attitude when it comes to accomplishing a goal or completing a task? How might the attitude of the people in exile have affected their behavior? Ask for a few examples when attitude made a noticeable difference to the outcome.

A Conquered People

Babylon, *Ishtar Gate. Sixth Century B.C.E.*

When Babylon conquered Judah in 587 B.C.E. and took most of its citizens into the Exile, it caused a great crisis of confidence among the people. For centuries, the people of Judah had believed that as God's chosen ones, they were protected against this sort of humiliation. "How could God abandon us like this?" they asked. "Has God forgotten about us?" These and other questions were asked by the people of Judah as they walked under guard to Babylon.

Learning Objectives for Section One

By the end of this section, you will be able to:

• Identify the conditions of life for Jews during the Exile.

• Discuss why Jews questioned the promises of Yahweh.

• Explain why the Exile was a threat to the existence of the Jewish community.

◆ Life During the Exile

Like Assyria, Babylon deported the population of territories it conquered. There were two reasons for this policy:

• The chances for rebellion in the conquered territory were greatly reduced if much of the population—especially anyone with leadership ability—was removed.

• The conquered people would be more likely to think of themselves as Babylonians if they were living in Babylon.

In keeping with these two goals, many Judahites were forced to move to Babylon after the defeat of Judah in 587 B.C.E.

Of course, it was impossible to move everyone.

1. If people wanted to hide in the wilderness, the Babylonians had neither the time nor the resources to track them down.

2. Somebody had to stay behind to raise the crops and care for the herds. Babylon wanted the lands of Judah to be productive and the Babylonian governors did not want to perform these tasks themselves.

Babylon, *Judah in Exile. Sixth Century B.C.E.*

This relief from a palace in Nineveh shows the people of Judah being driven into exile in 587 B.C.E.

◆ MORE ABOUT THE LESSON

Meaning of the Exile

As much as we might study the situation, it is difficult for us to know exactly what the Exile meant for the Jews. The writings that come down to us reflect a great longing to return to their native country. This could not have been true for them all, for many of them chose to stay in Babylon when they were given the chance to return to Jerusalem. Nevertheless, the Exile was a time of great personal upheaval, an equally intense search for a religious identity. This period is remembered and valued because of this religious re-evaluating. The people of Judah could have been swallowed up by the Babylonian culture just as happened to the ten northern tribes of Israel when they were defeated by the Assyrians. Instead, because of their quest for identity, the people of Judah survived the Exile as a people of faith.

LEARN FROM THE MAP

The Babylonian Empire

The Babylonian Empire lay at the head of the Persian Gulf in what is now Iraq. Often called "Mesopotamia," Greek for "the land between the rivers." Babylonia began in the fertile valley between the Tigris and Euphrates Rivers. Examine the Babylonian Empire in 586 B.C.E.

Compare it with the Assyrian Empire. Notice especially what has happened to Judah. Note the location of Babylon, the capital city. How far is it from Jerusalem to Babylon? Please note that while Judah is colored differently, it was definitely part of the Babylonian Empire.

©1994 Magellan Geographix™ Santa Barbara, CA.

Babylonian Empire

3. Preventing rebellion did not require that everybody be removed, just the scholars, priests, politicians, and community leaders. Many people stayed in Judah while their leaders went into Exile.

The Bible tends to focus only on those people who went to Babylon, because it is those people who produced the great literature of this period. The story of the Exile, however, also includes the fate of those who were left behind.

Unstable Government

After the Babylonian victory in 587, the immediate administration of Judah was left in the hands of a local governor, Gedaliah, a Judahite. He governed from the town of Mizpah, and supervised the Judahite farmers and herdsmen who had stayed.

Gedaliah's term in office was brief—only two years—before he was murdered by Ishmael, who wanted to be the governor himself. At a feast, Ishmael slaughtered Gedaliah and all of his followers, including some Babylonian soldiers. Two days later, he butchered seventy Judahites who had brought offerings to the site where the Temple lay in ruins.

Angered by this attack on its servant, Babylon deported all of the remaining Judahite leaders in 582 B.C.E. and divided the country into two parts. The northern half became part of an existing Babylonian province, while the southern part was annexed to Edom—a deep insult to the Judahites. Meanwhile,

---

3. Learn from the Map: Have the students examine the map and answer the questions in the caption. The scale of the map is .25" = 60 miles, the same as the maps in chapters 4 and 6. Point out that the distance from Jerusalem to Babylon in a straight line would not have been the distance the exiles were forced to walk. Their route was northwards from Judah to halfway between Damascus and Emesa, then eastward in a curve, then south again to Babylon. Their walk was approximately 540 miles from Jerusalem to Babylon.

3. Have the students read "The Bible in Context," and make sure they understand these three terms: Hebrew, Israelite, Jew.

4. Have the students review aloud everything they remember about the Deuteronomic historians/writers. Refer them back to pages 38 and 39 to help their recall. Discuss with them then why the work of these writers might have seemed so very important during the Exile. (Help them understand that while we know the end of their story, the people living during the Exile had no certainty that they would ever return to their homeland or have a temple.)

5. Ask the students to discuss what it might have been like to be young in the Exile: what did those youths look forward to? What could they plan for or expect? How could they build a life in Babylon? Lead the class discussion of the questions in "Have You Considered?" page 117.

◆ MORE ABOUT THE LESSON

The Importance of Culture

America was once known as the "melting pot"; many different races, religions, and cultures gathered together to form one people, one culture. If the United States was to grow together as a country, there had to be one dominant culture. The idea of the "melting pot" was that every culture would add something to the general stew, creating a new, unique blend. And, in many ways, this is what happened.

The "melting pot" image is not used much anymore. People have recognized that when they gave up their native culture to become American, they lost their own identity as a people with a distinct history and values. Over the last 40 years many people have attempted to find their cultural roots; what does it mean to be of Polish, Irish, African, Korean, or Turkish descent? What are the values and beliefs found in one's ancestral homeland?

Practicing the Skills

What to Do

Have the students read: Psalm 74:1–11, Psalm 79 and Psalm 137 and discuss the questions in "Bible Activity" number 1, page 128. Ask the students also to compare the feelings evoked by these psalms with the role-play just performed.

The Bible in Context

What Is a Jew?

Up to now, we have used the term "Hebrews," and then "Israelites," to refer to the people of the original Covenant. Now, it's time to introduce the last such term: "Jew." After the split between the two kingdoms, people living in Judah thought of themselves as "Judahites" rather than "Israelites" (remember that the Northern kingdom was called "Israel"). In Babylon, people from Judah were called "Yehudi" or Judeans. It was not long before "Judeans" was shortened to "Jews."

Today, the term "Jew" is used to refer to people who, either through birth or conversion, identify themselves with the religious and cultural traditions of ancient Israel. "Judaism" is the religion centered on obedience to the Law of Yahweh, kept alive by the Jews during the Exile.

the remaining associates of Gedaliah fled to Egypt for protection, taking Jeremiah with them. As a result, the people who were left in Judah felt even more abandoned.

The Ones Left Behind

The Second Book of Kings 24:14,16 says that more than 17,000 people were taken into exile in Babylon, while Jeremiah 52:28 gives the number of 4,600. Obviously, these numbers are not in agreement. In any case, they probably reflect only the number of free men sent into exile.

Whichever number is correct, historians estimate that after the first deportation in 597, perhaps as many as 125,000 people remained in Judah. Even after the murder of Gedaliah and the second deportation, over 100,000 Judahites were left. But by 530, barely 20,000 Judahites were to be found there.

Why did the population of Judah drop so dramatically in such a short time? Archaeological evidence shows that most of the cities in Judah had been destroyed in the war with Babylon prior to the Exile. With houses, trades, and crops destroyed, the land lay in ruin. The leaders were gone, and the promise of Judah as the "people of God" seemed forgotten. Those left behind after the second deportation were faced with the near-impossible task of surviving in a country without leadership or natural resources. As a result, many of them fled to places such as Egypt and Arabia. Over time, the number of those remaining in Judah dwindled to a handful.

From this time in history, the majority of Judahites would live outside the land of Judah. Even today, the majority of Jews live outside the nation of Israel. There are more Jews living in the United States, for example, than there are Jews living in Israel. This situation, in which the majority of the members of a nation live outside their traditional homeland, is called a "diaspora."

One spark of life remained in the land of Judah. People still made pilgrimages to the site of the Temple, although only shattered ruins remained. As the center of faith for over four hundred years, Jerusalem remained the focus of hope for many Jews. Even in exile, Jews would sometimes journey to the Temple ruins to pray and (perhaps) to offer sacrifice. Many certainly dreamed of a day when the Temple would be rebuilt. The base of Jewish life, however, was now firmly in Babylon.

Babylon, Babylonian Lion. Sixth Century B.C.E.

The growling lion was a symbol of Babylon's dominance. This wall painting was taken from Babylon and is now preserved in the Louvre Museum in Paris, France.

MORE ABOUT THE TEXT

The People of Judah

The feature "The Bible in Context" looks at the name given to the people of Judah during the Exile. The name is a cultural rather than a racial statement. The people who had lived in the country known as Judah were called "Judeans." The name Jew was probably no more pejorative than any other name given immigrants: Poles, Irish, Brits. This point is very important for your students to understand, especially when they begin to study the gospel accounts of the Passion. When the Gospel writers talk about the Jews, they are speaking about a religious or political group. Use of the word "Jew" in a pejorative sense should not be acceptable in your classroom.

Remind the students that the people who live in the Middle East are, for the most part, Semites. Today, Jews, Palestinians, Syrians, and Jordanians alike are almost all of the same race.

in the *Spotlight*

Other Forms of Worship

According to the Law, there could be no Temple or official worshipping cult outside of Jerusalem. For the Diaspora (Jews who did not live in Judah), however, visits to the Temple were impossible. Therefore, they had to find new ways to worship God.

- Jews living in upper Egypt, in a place called Elephantine, constructed and maintained their own temple. The worship there was an example of syncretism (the blending of various religious traditions). Influenced by Egyptian ideas, the Jews honored a female goddess as Yahweh's counterpart. The temple at Elephantine was destroyed by a rival religious group in 410 B.C.E.

- In Babylon, the exiles met in private homes for worship. These meeting places are the forerunners of the synagogue ("place of assembly"). Without altars for sacrifice, other modes of worship were used: prayers, the singing of psalms, oral readings, and the study of the Law. In these settings, Jewish children were trained in the faith and the community gathered. These meeting places were built facing the direction of the Temple in Jerusalem, and the worshippers faced Jerusalem when they prayed.

Conditions in Exile

For most Jews, what was happening in Judah no longer affected them directly. They now lived in Babylon, and it was the conditions in Babylon, not Judah, that determined the quality of their lives.

Actually, living conditions in Babylon for the Jews were not as horrible as one might think. The evidence we have shows that the Jews lived in communities of their own and that they enjoyed quite a bit of freedom. They could:

- meet together and listen to their leaders
- build houses
- farm
- engage in business
- work in the royal service

Work in Babylon   Archaeologists have found that banking was invented in Babylon a few decades before the Exile, and that soon after the deportations, some Jews became involved in that occupation. Others found positions in the court or worked for tradesmen who needed their particular skills. The Jews were allowed to keep their earnings, and some prospered. In fact, the material standard of living was so high for many Jews that they chose to remain in Babylon even after it was possible to return to Jerusalem.

Physically, then, conditions could have been much worse. Nevertheless, things were far from perfect.

- While not imprisoned, the Jews were forced to remain in Babylon.
- Though not tortured, they were watched and could not act with total freedom.
- Although allowed to participate in regular city life, the Jews were treated as lower class citizens.
- Most importantly, they were forbidden to live on their own land, the land promised to them long ago by Yahweh.

Guidance from Jeremiah   Between the first (597 B.C.E.) and second (587 B.C.E.) deportations, Jeremiah wrote a letter to those already in Babylon. In it, he proclaimed God's message, and advised the Jews to make a full life in the unwelcome country—to make homes and families for themselves and to do well. They are to "promote the welfare" of Babylon, because it was God's hand which had banished them there and because their welfare depended on the well-being of Babylon itself (*Jeremiah* 29:4–7). Despite the frustrations and imperfections of life in Babylon, in many ways the Jews followed Jeremiah's advice. They made a life for themselves in exile.

Have You Considered?

1. Describe a situation in your life in which you faced some difficulty. How did your attitude help or hurt you in dealing with this situation?
2. What do you think would be the hardest part of being forced to live in another culture: learning a new language? new customs? different religion? missing old friends? something else?
3. In Babylon, the Jews were offered the chance to prosper and lead a secure life, but they were forbidden to return to the land of Judah. Do you think people are sometimes willing to give up freedom for security? Describe the different attitudes towards Babylon you might find among the Jewish exiles living there.

Have You Considered?

1. Answers to this question will vary with the individual. Guide students to connect their own responses with the story of the Israelites in Exile, and the importance of attitude to their survival as a nation.
2. Again, answers will vary with the individual, but students should see their own experiences in the light of the Exile. What would be hardest for the Israelites, given their own unique customs and viewpoints?
3. Point out to students that the basis of civilization is the agreement to sacrifice a certain degree of freedom—the freedom to violate the rights of others—for the security of having our own rights protected. Given this fundamental human need for security, discuss why the relative safety of the Exile must have seemed very appealing to many Jews who found themselves there.

◆ MORE ABOUT THE LESSON

People Living in Exile

There are more political refugees today than there have ever been at any one time before. The United Nations High Commissioner on Refugees issued a study in 1994 reporting that more than seven million people had been forced from their homes and were living now in exile. As peace returned to their countries, refugees from Afghanistan, Cambodia, South Africa, and El Salvador were returning home. However, new refugees were fleeing for their lives in Rwanda and Haiti.

Have the students research the problem of refugees in the world today, identify the new refugee groups, and present a report on the conditions that forced them to flee from their homes. They should also include information on the conditions in refugee camps and what they can do to improve the lot of these people.

◆ Finding Meaning in Exile

Development

What to Do

1. Say: "What would you think if you called your best friend on the telephone and your friend's mother said, 'I'm sorry, but he (she) doesn't want to talk to you.'?" Students will probably share feelings of anger and hurt. Then ask: "How do you think the people of Judah felt when it appeared that God had forgotten and abandoned them?"

2. Have the students read "Finding Meaning in Exile." Have students explain what it might have been like for the people living in exile.

3. Pray with your students. Ask them to look up Psalm 124, read it over silently, and then pray it aloud together. Close with a few thankful words that apply the psalm to God's protection and help for individuals like your students.

Recall

What to Do

Have the students write out the answers to "Chapter 7 Review Q/A" for Section One, using their text as necessary.

Connect

What to Do

Have the students, working in small groups, complete "Scripture Workshop," reviewing Psalm 137 (which they have just read) and adding Lamentations 4. Have them make notes of their answers and share them with the whole group.

What's Next?

What to Do

Say: "Although the Jews probably felt abandoned by God while in Babylon, God had not forgotten them. The word of God was still being spoken by prophets. In our next lesson we will learn about one of the prophets who lived during the Exile: Ezekiel. We will also be learning more about the Priestly Writers."

◆ Finding Meaning in Exile

Although conditions in Judah itself may have been bleak, for the Jews living in Babylon the physical consequences of exile were not all that bad. There was a deeper disaster, however, which no amount of prosperity or material comfort could erase. This disaster was an inner one, because the Exile had shattered the Jews' understanding of Yahweh, of themselves, and of life. Questions and doubts were everywhere:

- Why had God permitted Judah to be destroyed?
- Did Yahweh no longer care about the Covenant with the Jews?
- Should Jews still obey the Law?
- What did all this change and suffering mean?

What the Jews faced, in other words, was a crisis of meaning.

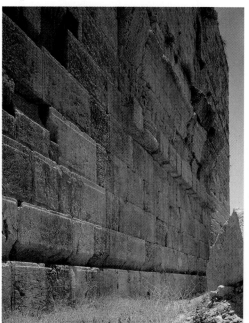

The "Western Wall" is all that remains of Herod's Temple, destroyed by the Romans in 70 C.E. It is a source of comfort for Jews even today. The ruins of the original Temple were also honored and served as a gathering place for prayer.

As you read now about this crisis, try to put yourself in the place of the Jewish exiles, for only by so doing can you understand what happened during this critical time.

The Promises of Yahweh

Recall that the faith of the ancient Israelites was founded on Yahweh's Covenant promises. The founding Covenant at Sinai promised the Hebrews land, prosperity, and a special relationship with the Lord. These promises had conditions. The conditions were listed in what we call "the Law." If the people obeyed these conditions, God's promises would also be kept.

When David was king, additional promises were made. Yahweh assured David that his descendants would always be on the throne in Jerusalem. As long as there was a king in Jerusalem, he had indeed descended from David. But the Jews believed that David's kingdom would last forever.

Over the years, the Jews forgot that the Covenant promises also included obligations. The people had come to believe that if they kept the required ritual of the Temple according to priestly interpretation, then Yahweh would always protect them and bring them prosperity. In spite of all the prophecies to the contrary, the Israelites were complacent.

With the destruction of Judah, Jerusalem, and the Temple, all such certainty was swept away. What were they now to believe about Yahweh?

God or Not? Their God or Not?

In one bitter decade, the people of Judah lost everything of value: families, friends, homes, and faith. Doubts about Yahweh were everywhere. Yahweh wasn't God at all, or if a god, Yahweh was at best only a very weak one. After all, the god of Babylon, Marduk, had defeated Yahweh's forces in battle. Even if Yahweh had been powerful once, now the conquering god must be stronger.

All the Jews needed to do to see which god was most powerful was look at the magnificence of Babylon. It was far more splendid than anything in Jerusalem, especially after the Temple had been stripped of its richest ornamentation to pay bribes to stronger nations. Even many Jews were materially better off in Babylon than they had been in Judah. It certainly looked as if Marduk was better able to provide for his people than Yahweh had been to provide for the Jews. Why should the Jews continue to worship Yahweh?

◆ MORE ABOUT THE LESSON

My God Can Beat Your God!

Have you ever seen two young children get in an argument and watched it escalate to the point of one-upping each other. "My big brother drives a bright new car." "Oh yeah? Well my sister gets straight A's." Often, the conversation reaches the "My-dad-can-whip-your-dad stage." This childish contest has similarities to the feelings of the Jews in exile. Remember that the worship of Yahweh by the Jews was still at this time a form of henotheism: Yahweh was the greatest God among many other gods and was their God. When first Israel and then Judah were destroyed by the forces of Assyria and Babylon, doubts would develop in the minds of the Jews.

Have students consider the taunts and ribbing that the Jews must have experienced from their Babylonian neighbors. You might have students actually participate in a verbal sparring match.

Scripture Workshop

Reactions to Exile

How did the Jews feel about their life in Babylon? Some poets of the Exile have left behind their reactions. Read Psalm 137 and Lamentations 5. To understand these two poems, you need to know that the word "Zion" means the same thing as Judah. Mount Zion was the hill in Jerusalem upon which the Temple was built, and, over time, came to refer to the entire country.

After you've read these two poems, answer the following questions:

1. What were the conditions in Jerusalem and Judah as described here?
2. What were the feelings of the people in Babylon?
3. How would you describe the tone of these passages?
4. In your own words, explain what these poems are about.

Who could blame the Jews if they started to wonder if Yahweh had come to hate them? Hadn't God abandoned them in their time of greatest need? Where was Yahweh when Babylon burned Jerusalem, or when they defiled and demolished the Temple, the house built especially for God? Perhaps God had not only abandoned the Jews, but had actually turned against them!

If these things were true, how could the Jews dare approach a god who either hated them, or couldn't do anything to help them? Why would one depend any longer on a god who had no power to protect or to save? Maybe they had deserved punishment for their national sins, but what good would punishment do if it destroyed the people forever?

For the Jews, Yahweh and their relationship with Yahweh were firmly connected to the land. It was centered in the Temple in Jerusalem, where Yahweh's glory dwelled. Even if Yahweh was still there, the Jews were not. Even if they repented of their sins, how could they reach God from Babylon to beg for mercy? However they interpreted the destruction of Judah, Jews found only despair.

The Threat to the Community

There were other problems facing the Jewish community as well. Since the Covenant was so closely connected to the land of Judah, faith in the Covenant was challenged when the people were scattered in the Diaspora. Think of the forces which threatened to pull their community apart:

- There was no central location where the people could gather for pilgrimage or festival.
- They were living far from the land and prevented even from visiting Jerusalem.
- They were dispersed over the vast ancient Middle East, far from other Jews.

How could such a non-community have any identity before the Lord? How could they be Yahweh's people if they were no people at all?

Furthermore, the wealth and power of Babylon and other Middle Eastern empires were a threat to the Jewish community. Many Jews were more comfortable in Babylon and Egypt than they had ever been in Judah. Their lives were secure, and they felt safe from danger. If the only reason to identify oneself as Jewish was because of the Covenant with Yahweh, and if Yahweh had failed to help the Jews, what was the point? Wouldn't it just be better to become Babylonians, or Egyptians, or members of another successful nation? Some Jews did exactly that; they stopped following the traditions of Judaism and *assimilated*.

These were the issues that faced the people of Judah during the Exile. In 721 B.C.E., the ten northern tribes had been scattered by the Assyrians, never to be heard from again. They were lost to Yahweh's community forever. Would history now repeat itself with the people of Judah? Would all of Israel disappear from the face of the earth?

Have You Considered?

1. What are living conditions like for refugees today? How does being a refugee affect a person's ability to earn a living? religious faith? family life? ways of thinking?
2. Describe a time when your self-image was challenged by a crisis. How did you respond?
3. Put yourself in the position of the exiled Jews. What reason would you have to continue to worship Yahweh? What would attract you to the gods of Babylon? Explain your answer.

MORE ABOUT THE TEXT

Marduk, the God of Babylon

Marduk began as a minimal city god of Babylon. As Babylon grew into a great empire, Marduk also increased in stature. The success of Babylonian armies were attributed to the greatness of Marduk.

According to Babylonian theology, Marduk was the son of the cosmic god, Enki (or Ea, god of the cosmic oceans). Marduk was given power over the heavens and the earth—literally the soil and plant life. Marduk was considered magically powerful, able to vanquish chaos and create man. (When you read the Creation stories in Genesis, note how Yahweh is the Lord who brought order to chaos and is the creator).

The Babylonian king's right to rule was drawn from Marduk's authority. Every year the king would assume the personality of Marduk in a cultic drama between the forces of good and evil to assure order in the world for the coming year.

◆ Ezekiel

Welcome

What to Do

1. As students enter the room, hand them each an unlined sheet of paper. Ask them to draw God. This is to be their own image and should not be copied from another student or taken from a classical work of art. You can add interest to this project by having available an assortment of colored pencils, marking pens, and crayons so that students can express themselves in color.

After five minutes, have students hang their work around the room. Ask for volunteers briefly to explain what they drew. Do not comment on these except to show that you welcome their sharing.

Call student attention to the picture on page 121 and ask them what they think of it. Does it look anything like how they have imagined God? How are their images like the vision of Ezekiel?

2. Pray with your students. Include a prayer of thanksgiving that the Lord never abandons people.

Introducing the Lesson

Teaching Objectives

By the end of this lesson students will be able to:

• Describe how Ezekiel adds important concepts to Judaism's understanding of God.

• Demonstrate the importance of symbolic action for communication.

• Explain how the Priestly Writers' emphasis on the Law shaped the Jewish religion.

What to Do

1. Have the students open their Bibles and have volunteers read the first chapter of Ezekiel aloud. Discuss with students the significance of Ezekiel's vision. What does it mean for them? Look again at the picture on page 121. How well did the artist Raphael capture Ezekiel's words?

Responding to the Crisis

Iran, *Torah Case*. Twentieth Century.

Despite appearances, Yahweh had neither abandoned Judah, nor was powerless. Yahweh's response was to act as God had always acted in times of national emergency: prophets were sent who spoke God's word. These prophets addressed the crisis of meaning experienced by the people and responded to their fears and doubts one by one. They brought the message that the relationship between Yahweh and the people was still intact. They helped the Jews maintain their community in the face of all the forces threatening to tear it apart. In this section, you'll hear the words that brought hope and consolation to the Jews in Exile.

Learning Objectives for Section Two

By the end of this section, you will be able to:

• Explain the important insights of Ezekiel.

• Describe the use of symbolism in Ezekiel.

• Discuss the importance of Law for the Priestly Writers.

• Explain Second Isaiah's message of hope.

◆ Ezekiel

Ezekiel was a priest and the first prophet of the Exile. He was respected by the people, and had been exiled with them in the first deportation in 597 B.C.E. His message helped the Jews respond to the various challenges facing them.

Ezekiel's Inner Experience

By modern standards, Ezekiel was quite strange. Even by Israel's standards—whose prophets had often behaved in an unusual manner—Ezekiel must have seemed weird. His personality was prone to profound spiritual experiences, dreams, and visions. These experiences were dramatic and unusual, even for prophets. Today they would perhaps be regarded as psychic, or even beyond that.

For example, Ezekiel described in detail his interior "trips" to Jerusalem, carried there in spirit by the power of the Lord. He had wild visions. He acted out his prophecies through symbolic gestures, like lying on his side for three months or digging his way under a wall. His emotions were tightly controlled by the Lord, so that he did not even mourn at the death of his wife, who was the "delight of his eyes."

So overpowering was Ezekiel's initial experience of Yahweh that for a week he sat among his people, overwhelmed, unable to tell them what he had seen. More experiences and visions followed, including explicit instructions for speech and symbolic actions. Throughout the Book of Ezekiel, one gets the sense that this was a man whose prayer life was alive with a powerful awareness of God's presence. These experiences helped make Ezekiel's message captivating for his audiences.

Symbolism in Ezekiel

Like Isaiah, Ezekiel was called through a vision. Ezekiel saw Yahweh's throne chariot approaching from a northern cloud, and surrounded by animals, birds, and human-like creatures supported on a

---

◆ MORE ABOUT THE LESSON

Bible Awareness

To help students develop a love and appreciation of the prophets, there is simply no substitute for encountering the images, words, and feelings of a prophet himself. Therefore, this lesson should be taught like one long scripture workshop.

• Work primarily with the Bible. Have students keep it open on their desks throughout the lesson.

• If you focus on the Bible itself, the text will become a secondary source. Use it that way. Summarize the questions and ideas presented within the text for the students instead of having them read the text itself. Or you can have volunteers read segments aloud.

• Let the students bring the work of the prophet to life. Have them role-play a prophesy or act out the vision. Encourage them to put meaning and image to the prophet's words.

moving wheel that was covered with eyes. Ezekiel describes his vision in great detail: strange forms and living winged creatures, brilliant colors and sheens, fire and more fire, interlocking wheels, and sound that was like the "din of an army." The splendor of his experience (like that of any true vision) was quite indescribable, so Ezekiel said, "such was the vision of the likeness of the glory of the Lord" (Ezekiel 1:28).

Through figures and symbols such as these, Ezekiel expressed that:

• The Lord is majestic and holy beyond imagination.
• Yahweh is totally mobile and can be anywhere in an instant.
• Yahweh can see everything at once, having eyes in every direction.
• Yahweh's power is awesome, and although it's held in check, it's ready at any instant to be unleashed.

Raphael, Ezekiel's Vision, Sixteenth Century.

The artist Raphael attempted to capture Ezekiel's vision on canvas. Read Chapter 1 of Ezekiel and compare Ezekiel's words to Raphael's depiction.

These were important realizations for Ezekiel and for the whole people. Ezekiel's visions responded to the concerns that the Exile raised about the nature of Yahweh. Throughout Ezekiel's career, he often communicated his understanding of God through such striking symbols and symbolic actions.

Before the Fall: Warnings of Destruction

Between the first deportation in 597 and the destruction of Jerusalem in 587, Ezekiel's responsibility to his people was just the same as Jeremiah's or Isaiah's had been: to call them to repentance before it was too late and Jerusalem destroyed. Like Jeremiah, Ezekiel sensed that his warning would be for nothing. Nevertheless, the Lord insisted that Ezekial give the people God's message.

Ezekiel told the Jews about the total devastation that was yet to come, even as some of the leaders were forced into Exile. Justice had to be fulfilled and, in Ezekiel's view, his people had much for which to suffer. According to Ezekiel, Israel had been untrue to the Lord from its first days in the desert, worshipping other gods and ignoring the Covenant. Yahweh's holiness, majesty, and justice demanded that now—finally, after centuries of disobedience and warning—discipline must be complete. The Lord would no longer hold back. These messages are found in the following verses of Ezekiel: 4; 5; 7:1–28; 20:1–17; 22:29–31.

Individual Responsibility

Among the crucial questions of the Exile, as you have read, was how the community could stay together now that the people were so scattered. This dispersion was a special problem for the Jews, who had always thought of themselves only as members of the group.

The Jews had a proverb to express this communal idea: "Fathers have eaten green grapes, thus their children's teeth are on edge." This proverb (which is also quoted in Jeremiah 31:29, so it must have been very common in ancient Israel) suggests that even though the parent disobeys the law, the children experience the bad results. That is, everyone is affected by the behavior of those who came before in community.

The proverb implied that the consequences of the sins of one generation were experienced by the next, or that the sins of a few in the nation would cause the whole nation to experience woes. This cultural assumption might be called "group solidar-

2. Return to the timeline on page 112. Note the date of Ezekiel's call and point out that we do not know how many years he prophesied, but that it is clear from what he wrote that he worked after 587, and thus during the Babylonian Captivity.

Development

What to Do

1. Have the students read the introductory paragraph and the learning objectives under "Responding to the Crisis." Ask whether they already have any ideas about these objectives. Remind them to look for these points in this lesson. Have them read the first paragraph of "Ezekiel" and the subsections "Ezekiel's Inner Experience" and "Symbolism in Ezekiel."

2. Ask them to find in Ezekiel 1 the symbols that communicate the bulleted points on page 121. Do the students think Ezekiel describes the Lord directly, that is, his physical appearance? (If they do, remind them of Ezekiel 1:28.) What do they think the symbols mean?

3. Review with students what they remember about the prophet Jeremiah. From what they know so far, how would they compare these two prophets? To refresh their memories, have them turn back to pages 106–109.

   Say: "Ezekiel not only had spectacular visions, but he also had a strong message. In some ways, Ezekiel's message was just as hard for people to grasp as was Jeremiah's. Ezekiel communicated the Lord's message as he was directed without concern for who it angered and what it cost. Like Jeremiah, proclaiming this message affected Ezekiel's personal life, too." Then have students read through page 122.

4. Form small groups (five if possible). Refer to "Before the Fall," then have each group read one of the following passages and explain it to the rest of the class: Ezekiel 4; Ezekiel 5; Ezekiel 7:1–28; Ezekiel 20:1–17; Ezekiel 22:23–31. (If there are not five groups, the passages can be distributed as you wish.)

MORE ABOUT THE TEXT

The Meaning of Symbols

Symbols, whether they originate in visions, in nature, or in day-to-day life, always have multiple, complementary meanings. They never stand for only one other thing. The symbols in Ezekiel are no exception.

When your students explore the symbols in Ezekiel's vision and the suggested meanings in "Symbolism in Ezekiel," allow them plenty of imagination and intuitive leeway. Often the untrained mind of the child is better at interpreting symbols than are the too-rational minds of adults. Children are especially apt at understanding symbols. Give them the freedom to do so.

5. Ask the students what they think of individual responsibility, as mentioned briefly in the discussion of Jeremiah. Do they think individuals receive the consequences of their own actions only, or do consequences also affect the innocent as well? What do they think of the situation when an innocent person experiences the consequences of others' choices, whether these consequences are pleasant or painful?

6. Have the students in each small group read Ezekiel 18:1–32 and then list the specific conditions of individual responsibility taught by Ezekiel. Ask them to name modern examples (from their own experience or that of others).

Have the spokesperson from each group share the results of this exercise with the whole class.

7. Have the students read Ezekiel 37:1–14, and decide what other interpretations might be found in the vision besides the meaning given in their text.

8. Play the spiritual, "Dry Bones," a musical version of this vision. (See Teacher's Resource 7B.)

9. Have the students read Ezekiel 36:23–28 and discuss what a "new heart" might mean, listing several possibilities in each small group. What sort of promise is the Lord making in these words?

Extend the Activity Lead the whole class in a discussion of the questions in "Have You Considered?"

Have You Considered?

1. Allow students to discuss their own experiences. Point out to students that such experiences, though powerful, are not a necessary condition of a healthy relationship with the Lord.

2. This message would reassure the Exiles because it meant that from now on, they would be judged on the basis of their own behavior, not the conduct of their leaders.

3. Ask students to discuss the religious symbols which mean something to them. Direct them to consider the sacraments, and ask whether they would be as effective in leading us to God if they were only words.

---

ity." Yet in the sixth century B.C.E., with Jews scattered so widely, such cohesion could not be maintained.

Ezekiel 18:1–32 announces the beginning of a new era, in which a person is responsible only for his or her own choices. With this new understanding, Jews were free to form community without the unrealistic expectation of total group solidarity. People could think of themselves as "Jews," even if there were no local Jewish community.

After the Fall: Ezekiel's Message of Hope

After the destruction of Jerusalem in 586, Ezekiel's message changed. The consequences of Israel's behavior had been terrible, but now that they were completed, it was time to begin again. Remember, the Lord always spoke to the immediate situation. For them, the Word of the Lord was always applicable to their moment in time. They did not speculate about philosophical principles that should last forever. The truths they proclaimed often turned out to be lasting, but the immediate intention of God's message was foremost. Now, in this time of tragedy and bitter agony, the people needed hope.

Dry Bones Will Rise Ezekiel's teaching includes the famous Valley of Dry Bones. In a vision, the prophet looked out over a valley filled with skeletons, and God tells him these bones will rise again. This vision means that God will restore the people of Judah to life. Further, Yahweh told Ezekiel that from this time on, the Lord would shepherd the people, since

the kings had so badly botched their responsibility. Read Ezekiel 34:7–16.

Yahweh's power, so evident to Ezekiel from his original vision, was about to be demonstrated again; this time not in terror, but in salvation and restoration. The actions of the Lord would begin in the heart, as Jeremiah, too, had understood. The land would be Israel's once again, but the center for God's people would be in their hearts (Ezekiel 36:23–28).

Vivid Visions Ezekiel's vision was vivid. The people themselves would become truly holy: a holy people for a holy God. Because of this expectation of holiness, the land too would become holy. At the center of the land would be a restored Temple, now with pure rites and true worship. Ezekiel predicts that all of this will come to pass so that people (the Jews and others, too) will know what Yahweh means by saying "I am the Lord." Yahweh wants people to understand who God is, and that all power lies in God. By both devastation and then by promise of a re-creation, Yahweh communicates this reality, this power. Israel will understand Yahweh as Lord of all.

Ezekiel's prophecy of a new nation directed by God wouldn't come true quickly. Until it did, many of the exiles rejected Ezekiel's word. Their tragedy was too deep for a rapid healing. Ezekiel's message was heard by some, but there is little evidence that it was believed. After all, Israel had long been in the habit of ignoring its prophets!

Still a few among the Exiles did heed Ezekiel. It is clear that Ezekiel influenced various priests and the elders who responded to his message of hope.

When Hurricane Andrew devastated South Florida in 1992, many people were left homeless. Some moved on rather than rebuilding. The same was true for the Jews after the destruction of Jerusalem.

Have You Considered?

1. Ezekiel's inner experience of the Lord was dramatic and powerful. Have you ever had an experience like his? Do you think such experiences are necessary for communicating with God?

2. Remember that the Deuteronomic historian and others said that the Jews had gone into exile because of the sins of their kings and other leaders. In this context, how would Ezekiel's message of individual responsibility be good news?

3. Ezekiel's message was filled with symbolism. Where do you find symbolism in your religious life? Do you think symbolism sometimes works better than normal speech for getting people's attention and putting them in touch with God? Why or why not?

MORE ABOUT THE TEXT

Bible Background

A study of the idea of God's holiness in the whole book of Ezekiel gives a more complete understanding than these visionary symbols alone. God's holiness means to Ezekiel that God is supremely free and supremely independent. God acts according to God's own nature, designs, and purposes. God plays no favorites, is just (lawful and harmonious) and is not influenced by "outside" forces. God is the center and source of all. God's will is strictly God's own. The holiness of God is made present in actual historical events, able to be seen by all. And the purpose of God's action is so that people will come to know that "I am the Lord," acknowledged and worshipped by all. This is what the Jews desperately needed to experience in the Exile.

◆ The Priestly Writers

Ezekiel was not the only person who tried to understand God in the face of ruin. The Lord also inspired the Jewish priests to re-examine the history of Yahweh, the people, and the Covenant. They had to understand better what God intended and what God was really like. Then they had to reinterpret their sacred traditions so that they and their children could understand them as well.

To this end, the priests collected the traditions that the Jews had brought with them into Exile, wrote them down, and then edited them. Now in Exile, the Priestly Writers looked back through the written and oral traditions of their people, searching for deeper understanding than they had known previously.

The Torah

The Priestly Writers came to understand that Yahweh always acted for a purpose. Looking over their past, the priests saw patterns of Yahweh's involvement in Israel's history. By studying these patterns, they found an explanation for the Exile. They then organized the Jewish traditions so that they resembled the order clearly seen in God's actions.

The Priestly Writers began with the act of creation—Genesis 1:1–2:3 is their composition. Creation was followed by the "fall" of humanity from God's grace, and then by the story of how civilization began. You traced all of these traditions in Chapter 4—remember the "P" source? These are the same writers.

Their creation story in Genesis was followed by the legends of the patriarchs and the Covenant with Abraham. Then came the story of Yahweh's deliverance of Israel from slavery in Egypt, and the Exodus. Finally, the Covenant of Sinai was recorded, and the Book of Deuteronomy was included. To these, the Priestly Writers added lists of peoples and nations, as well as genealogies, to emphasize that everything proceeded in an orderly fashion, according to the divine plan. The result of their labors is the Torah, the first five books of the Bible as we now have them.

This emphasis on the divine plan was the priests' answer to the question of whether Yahweh had abandoned them. The priests invited the Jews to look back over their history. Hadn't Yahweh always shaped events to achieve God's purposes? Hadn't Yahweh always brought order out of chaos? In the Exodus story, hadn't God brought the order of the Covenant out of the chaos of the wilderness? Surely, the priests suggested, Yahweh will also bring meaning out of the Exile. They suggested that this chaos, too, was part of the order of God.

In arguing that the Exile was part of the divine order, the priests constructed what is known as a *theodicy*, a "defense of God's goodness in the face of evil." The existence of evil is a problem that theologians and philosophers have wrestled with over the ages, but few have improved on the answer given by the Priestly Writers. They concluded that however difficult it might be to understand, God will bring meaning out of suffering.

Chasidic Jews, like these children who live in an Orthodox community in Galilee, base their entire lives on faithfully living the Law. The Law gives meaning to everything that they do.

MORE ABOUT THE TEXT

Individual Responsibility

When you discuss individual responsibility, help the students to see that life is a web, and while individuals do, indeed, experience their own consequences, we also affect each other profoundly for both great good and difficulties. The Israelites/Jews knew all about group consequences, but now the prophets continue to preach the message that Jeremiah began.

◆ The Priestly Writers

Development

1. Look at the "Priestly Writers" on page 123–124. Use these pages to reinforce students' understanding of how the Priestly Writers shaped the cultural heritage of the Jewish people.

2. For more examples of the work of the Priestly Writers, have the students read Leviticus 11 and 25. How do the students respond to these regulations?

Recall

Have students complete "Bible Activity" number 2 on page 128 as given, writing out their answers.

Connect

Homework Assignment: Have students write their answers to "Chapter 7 Review Q/A," Section Two, numbers 1–7.

What's Next?

What to Do

Say: "We will look at one of the most beautiful and best loved of all the prophetic works in the next lesson. It is the work of an unknown author written just prior to the end of the Exile. You will enjoy reading Second Isaiah and learning what he has to offer us today."

Have You Considered?

1. Student responses will vary, but encourage them to be open about their own experiences. Make sure the students see the connection between their own experience and the difficult times faced by the Israelites in the Exile.

2. Help students to think about their own families, clubs, or groups of friends. What unique traditions or customs do they share? Would the group be as strong without these traditions?

3. The rule of law is extremely important in modern society. Law establishes the basic ground rules around which society operates.

Bonus Focus for You ———

Read Ezekiel 36:22–24, 32. How would you answer Ezekiel's view here?

LESSON THREE
(pages 124–127)

◆ Second Isaiah

Welcome

What to Do

1. Greet each student with a flower (real or paper) or some other symbol of happiness, and welcome them to a "new prophecy of comfort, hope, and a glorious future."

2. Ask the students what qualities they most want in their lives, now and for the future. When they have suggested several, say: "During our study today, pay close attention to the qualities announced by Second Isaiah and see if you get any hints about how you might experience them for yourself. If you get such a tip, jot it down, because we'll be doing something with it at the end of this lesson." Students can make a "hints" column on their notes to remind themselves during the lesson.

3. Pray with your students. Thank God again that he did not abandon the Jews in their Exile, but continued to advise them through the prophets. Give thanks especially for the beauties of Second Isaiah and his hope-filled message of understanding. Invite the students to add their own thanks for some particular thing. Close with a "Glory Be to the Father."

Introducing the Lesson

Teaching Objectives

By the end of this lesson students will be able to:

• Identify the immediate sense of the change of prophetic direction that occurred in Second Isaiah.

• Explain the importance of Cyrus the Great to the history of Judaism.

What to Do

1. Have the students find and compare Isaiah 5:25 and 40:1–2. Do these passages sound like parts of the same prophet's message? Compare how they differ and how they are similar. Have the students leave a marker in Isaiah 40, for ease of looking up today's passages.

A Community Shaped by the Law

The Priestly Writers also considered the nature of the Jewish community. They recognized that as a scattered people, Jews could not rely on a nation to bind them with God. They would need to keep this bond alive in their own hearts and lives. But how?

They answered the question this way: people carry with them their traditional beliefs, customs and codes of behavior. From now on, these would be centered in the Law that unites the Jewish community with God. From this tradition, the Priestly Writers drew up the regulations governing thought and action that would hold the community together and keep it close to the Lord. The regulations they agreed upon emphasized

• Male circumcision as a sign of belonging to the Covenant.
• Keeping the Sabbath day holy.

These two acts, which could be done anywhere and under any circumstances, now became the chief expression of Jewish identity. In addition, the priests added many social and individual laws designed to promote justice and ritual purity. These laws are found in the Book of Leviticus. By keeping the Law, Jews would express their faith in God and their solidarity with one another.

The priests' answer to the Exiles' problem about community life would define for centuries what it meant to be Jewish: a Jew was one who kept the Law. This idea became the foundation of Judaism. The Law rooted the people in a community not bound by political borders.

Have You Considered?

1. In the middle of a tragedy, it is often difficult to see any purpose or order. Yet, people say they often learn most about themselves from difficult times. Describe a difficult time in your life. Looking back, can you see any purpose or order to the experience? Did you learn anything about yourself?
2. Describe a community to which you belong. How do your customs and traditions help unite the members of that community?
3. What is the importance of the rule of law in modern society? What are reasons people give for obeying or disregarding the law?

◆ "Second" Isaiah

When the Exile did finally approach its end, Yahweh sent a prophet to help the Jews understand what was happening. As Ezekiel had emphasized destruction and then hope and the Priestly Writers had collected the Law, this new prophet, known as Second Isaiah, proclaimed that Israel's time of punishment was at an end, and her future would hold unimagined glory.

In announcing this message, Second Isaiah expressed an understanding of God so profound and so moving, that many people feel that it has no equal anywhere. This writer (we don't even know his or her name) responded to the fears and despairs of the people living in Exile. This message was supported by events that the people themselves knew; Second Isaiah read the signs of the times and saw God's hands at work.

Why "Second" Isaiah?

This prophet of the Exile is called "Second" Isaiah because his or her words of comfort and expected greatness are found in chapters 40–55 of the Book of Isaiah. Second Isaiah was probably a later follower of Isaiah of Jerusalem, and the words of Second Isaiah were added to the works of the master after the Exile. There are many similarities in themes between the two, especially the common theme that God's kingdom would continue through a remnant of a people who have lived their lives in righteousness.

Nevertheless, there are easily recognizable differences of historical information, literary style, and theological interpretation that distinguish Isaiah of Jerusalem from Second Isaiah, who prophesied as the Exile was drawing to a close. Isaiah of Jerusalem's warnings of destruction are replaced by Second Isaiah's comforting promises of new life and restoration. Second Isaiah uses the words "comfort," "way," "servant," and "chosen" to call forth the hope of this new time.

Political Changes: Cyrus the Great

To understand Second Isaiah's message and the circumstances to which he or she spoke, we have to consider the changing players on the international scene. As Isaiah of Jerusalem had been the first to recognize, Yahweh's actions were not confined just to the people of Israel; foreign powers were used to accomplish God's purposes, too.

◆ MORE ABOUT THE LESSON

Bible Background

The logic of Isaiah's message about God's power was quite dramatic. Since there is no other god, all idols are illusions; they simply do not exist. Therefore, the Jews and all other peoples have to deal only with Yahweh.

If there is no other god, then the question of Yahweh being conquered by another god disappears. But this one God is also totally powerful and totally knowing. This God is, it turns out, the creator of all and therefore the real one in charge of nature and fertility. As the creator of all, God also knows the past, the present and the future planned for us.

In Second Isaiah, this glorious future is announced. With the ideas thoroughly understood, no Israelite could seriously worry about whether Yahweh was strong or cared about them: this understanding of one God finally answered all their conflicts.

- Following the death of the emperor, Nebuchadnezzar, in 562 B.C.E., Babylon was thrown into turmoil. Meanwhile, change was brewing in the East.
- The chief, or king, of the Persian tribes was a man named Cambyses, who was married to a daughter of the king of Media. Their son was named *Cyrus*.
- By 559, Cyrus had succeeded his father as king.
- Although Cyrus was greatly ambitious, he was not cruel, as most Assyrian and Babylonian kings before him had been.
- He was an exceptional leader of warriors, and equally talented at persuasion. If he could accomplish his goals by negotiation, he did so. His combined talents made him, by 550, king of all the Medes and the Persians.

Turning his attention to the west, Cyrus quickly captured Assyria, Asia Minor, and parts of Greece. Moving rapidly, he found little effective resistance anywhere. Without pause, Cyrus next turned his armies east of Media and conquered present-day Pakistan and Afghanistan.

Just before Cyrus turned his attention to Babylon, the prophet we call Second Isaiah began his work. Popular opinion of the day probably expected Cyrus to capture Babylon. Cyrus indeed took Babylon, and he then issued an edict which allowed the Jews to return to Judah and rebuild their lives there. For Second Isaiah to see this event happening is not remarkable. The beauty and power of this prophet is in the significance he or she sees in these events.

No Other God

Second Isaiah begins with an announcement of the core of the Lord's message. Isaiah 40:1 says, "Give comfort to my people, says your God," which Second Isaiah did. The ideas expressed were not totally new, yet were expressed with great power and beauty. Second Isaiah responded with words powerful enough to calm the terror people still felt about their separation from Yahweh.

Second Isaiah answered their fears about the power of Yahweh by recognizing that:

- Yahweh was all-powerful—Yahweh was the creator of everything.
- Yahweh was the *only* God.

For Second Isaiah it was clear that Yahweh could not have been conquered by other gods, because there were no other gods. The statues of other gods were just that, statues, and nothing more.

Scripture Workshop

Second Isaiah's Promise of Glory

As you know, the basic message of Second Isaiah is to show that God was only correcting Judah because of its sin, just as a parent must correct a wayward child. However, God has never stopped loving Judah and is now preparing a new stage of Covenant living for the Jews.

Read the following passages from Second Isaiah and answer the corresponding questions about God's plan.

- **Read Isaiah 48:6b-8a and Isaiah 43:18–21.** What are the elements of Yahweh's new act so far?
- **Read Isaiah 48:14–21.** What must the people do (especially in verse 20) to receive the new action of God?
- **Read Isaiah 44:1–5.** What will the quality of their life be in the future?
- **Read Isaiah 49:8–32.** What will their trip homeward be like?

In saying this, Second Isaiah brought the growing monotheism of the Jews to completion. Previously, they had usually declared that Yahweh was the only god for them, but they had not denied the existence of other gods. Now, however, Second Isaiah tells the people that there are no other gods. Yahweh's power is unrivaled in the universe, because God is all-powerful, all-holy, and one. Faced with terrible alternatives, the Jews finally understood this to be the truth.

Just knowing that Yahweh was the Creator and God of all was not enough, however. The people in exile also felt abandoned by God. Second Isaiah responded to this fear as well. He asserted that Yahweh continued to care for Israel, just as God had cared for them from the beginning, and that God had brought about everything that had happened. Their present punishment was required by their sins, but their future glory would truly show the greatness of God.

A Glorious Future

One of the unique elements of Second Isaiah's message is the idea that God has great things in store for the nation of Israel. According to Second Isaiah,

MORE ABOUT THE TEXT

Monotheism

The Jewish religion is strictly monotheistic. This means that Jews believe that there is only one God, Yahweh, and that there cannot be any other gods. As has been stated throughout this text numerous times, this belief in the oneness of God developed over time. It is not until this period after the Exile that we have the prophet Second Isaiah stating clearly that God is one.

This great leap of belief marks a turning point for the Jewish faith. While it is not possible to say how much Second Isaiah was influenced in his beliefs by the Priestly Writers (or they in their belief by him), we can say that the entire codification of Jewish faith starts from this newly found premise that no matter how many gods people may worship, there is only one God.

2. Refer back to the timeline on page 112. Notice the date of Second Isaiah in relationship to the dates pertaining to Cyrus and Babylon.

Development

What to Do

1. Have the students read the opening paragraphs under "Second Isaiah" and the subsections "Why 'Second' Isaiah?" "Political Changes: Cyrus the Great," and "People of Note" (on page 126). Read aloud Isaiah 44:28 and 45:1–4, to see how clearly Second Isaiah's prophecy referred to Cyrus and the Lord's purposes with Cyrus.
2. Say: "We have learned of some of the fears and temptations among the Exiles—to think that Yahweh was conquered or powerless, or that he hated them or had abandoned them. Second Isaiah combats those fears, as described in your text."
3. Have the students read "No Other God." Have students read Isaiah 45:5–25 and 46:1–10. Ask them to find out how many times the prophet says there is no other God but the Lord, and give the verse numbers for each one. Ask them to list the images or ideas (with verse numbers) they find here that show God's mighty power still intact. Discuss their discoveries.
4. Complete the "Bible Activity" number 3 on page 128.
5. Have the students read "A Glorious Future."

Scripture Workshop

1. Yahweh is preparing a place in the desert for the chosen people to live.
2. The people must hearken to God's commandments.
3. Their offspring will be blessed, and they shall spring up and identify themselves as children of Jacob.
4. Their return home will be safe and pleasant, and their guides shall be kings and princes, who will honor them as they go.

6. Discuss these questions: "Why is it hard to believe in God when times are tough? Why is it hard to believe in the love of your parents when they are disciplining you? Suppose you have a dog on a leash and you have to yank hard on the leash to drag him out of the way of an approaching car: does the dog understand your loving intention? Are we, perhaps, like dogs in that way? Do we know what God's consequences are really for?" This was part of the learning the Jews had to acquire in the Exile. Second Isaiah tried to make this message clear to them.

7. Have the students read Isaiah 54:4–8 and ask them to relate it to the discussion you have just had. Form four small groups. Have each group do one of the passages and questions in the "Scripture Workshop." Then each group can choose a way of sharing their findings with the rest of the class: by simple reporting, by dramatizing, or however they like.

8. Have the students read "The Suffering Servant" and then read Isaiah 42:1–9 and 52:13–53:12 (two of the "servant songs"). What are the qualities of the servant which they find in these passages?

9. Lead the class in discussion of the questions in "Have You Considered?"

Recall

Have the students answer "Chapter 7 Review Q/A," question number 8 in Section Two.

Connect

What to Do

Ask the students to share any tips they have gotten for experiencing the qualities they want in their lives and futures. Make a list of all the tips. Then, one by one, ask volunteers to apply the tip to their immediate life: what could they do right now to begin to follow these hints?

Homework Assignment: Students are to pray the "Spiritual Reflection" and write their experiences in their Spiritual Journals.

People of Note

Cyrus the Great

Part of King Cyrus's character was a remarkable tolerance for people of other nations and cultures, certainly a rare characteristic for rulers of his day. Cyrus learned that he was able to govern conquered peoples better if he honored, rather than insulted, their religious beliefs.

He was also a brilliant general, whose military success put him in command of the largest empire the world had ever known. By 540 B.C.E., it was obvious to Second Isaiah that Cyrus would defeat the Babylonians. This prediction came true in 539 when the city of Babylon welcomed Cyrus as conqueror.

One way in which Cyrus respected the beliefs of his subject was by allowing all of the exiles to return to their homelands and rebuild their fallen shrines. In fact, according to Ezra 6:4, Cyrus even donated funds for rebuilding the Temple. No wonder, then, that Second Isaiah and other Jews saw the hand of God in Cyrus' victories.

Mount Zion will be the seat of God's rule over all the universe, and other nations will come streaming to Jerusalem to humble themselves before the throne of Yahweh.

You have seen that Second Isaiah stresses how all nations are part of God's saving plan. The consequence of this observation is that Yahweh is the real king of the world, and Second Isaiah announces that God's rule will now be made known to all. Second Isaiah does not speak of the return of a Davidic king to Judah. Rather, God will establish a covenant directly with the whole people, and will rule over them and all nations from Zion. All the peoples of the earth will come to Jerusalem to pay tribute, and to learn from Israel the power and goodness of the Lord.

These images of future glory brought tremendous excitement and comfort to the exiles. Perhaps, they began to sense that their suffering had not been in vain.

Why Had They Suffered?   Even if the people began to comprehend that destruction was over and a wonderful future lay ahead of them, many must have still wondered why they had suffered. Yes, the nation had been sinful, that was clear enough. But now Yahweh was going to change it all around. Why? What was God's purpose in all this?

Second Isaiah said there were three reasons for God's action:

- It was necessary that Israel feel the consequences of its wrongs. That was merely justice.
- The destruction was to purify them.
- Yahweh did it for the sake of the holy name.

This last point was one that Ezekiel also had made: Yahweh doesn't act out of any particular desire to benefit people, but for the sake of the divine name.

The Holy Name   What did it mean that Yahweh acted for the sake of the holy name? To help you understand, remember what "name" meant in Israel. One's name is one's essence, one's true being, one's own nature and source of one's power. So Yahweh's action here is not for the sake of a reputation, but because it is in God's nature to act in these ways.

When the nation was prosperous but rebellious and forgetful of the Covenant, it was Yahweh's nature and justice to discipline and purify Israel. When they were living in devastation, but willing finally to hear God's word to them, it was Yahweh's justice and holiness to act on their behalf.

In all actions, then, no matter how they may appear to human beings, Second Isaiah announces that it is the nature of God to act in majesty and holiness. That profound quality is often beyond human understanding, but holiness and integrity are Yahweh's essential nature. So of course they are expressed in all of God's actions.

The Suffering Servant

Second Isaiah includes a few passages of a special character. These passages have been called the "Servant Songs," because they speak of a particular servant of Yahweh who has a special calling from the Lord.

It's not exactly clear, however, who this servant is. Sometimes the songs seem to speak of an individual, and sometimes they seem to mean the whole people of Israel. At least once, Israel is mentioned by name, but most scholars think that this verse may have been added by a later editor. Even if we can't name the servant, however, it is still quite possible to see the servant's purpose.

◆ MORE ABOUT THE LESSON

The Suffering Servant

Did Second Isaiah have any particular person in mind when he wrote about the Suffering Servant? Sometimes it sounds like Isaiah is talking about an individual; sometimes it seems as if he were talking about the entire people of Judah. The roles and qualities of the servant, however, are clear enough and discoverable by close examination of the Servant Songs. In addition to the two used in this lesson plan, the others are Isaiah 49:1–7 and 50:4–11.

The "Servant Song" passages have been applied to Jesus from the earliest days of Christianity. Did Isaiah himself know about Jesus? Most unlikely. But then, as we have seen before, it was not always necessary for a prophet to understand every word he was called upon by God to deliver.

• This servant fulfills a prophet's role. The servant is sent by Yahweh to speak God's message in word and in action to the people. That word will bring justice and mercy. The outstanding quality of the Servant's work is seen in its gentleness and patience. By fulfilling his purpose, the Servant will actually make people righteous before the Lord.

• The servant will be an intercessor between the people and the Lord, as Moses and other prophets were. In this role, the prophet prayed and argued with the Lord, trying to call forth divine mercy and forgiveness. This servant will do more than that: he will suffer the penalties of the people's sins, so that justice is satisfied and the people can enjoy a new relationship with God. The suffering of the servant will restore the people of Israel to God.

• The servant will be victorious over suffering through confidence in God. The servant will actually be glorified by God, not only in the sight of Israel, but in the sight of the whole world. Consistently, the servant's mission is not only to Israel, but is universal. People from all over the world will benefit from his suffering and will acknowledge him.

Thus the "Servant Songs" of Second Isaiah expand the meaning of Israel's Exile far beyond the exiled people themselves. They know now that other nations are being used as agents of Yahweh, for Yahweh is God of the whole world and creator of all. There is only one God. Although some of the prophets believed that, none before Second Isaiah announced it with such unmistakable power and clarity. The "Servant Songs" reveal that God plans to act to restore and redeem the whole world, not only the people of Israel.

Have You Considered?

1. Second Isaiah saw the hand of God in the political events of the time. Do you believe God is involved in political events today? Why or why not?
2. Second Isaiah said that God would make Israel glorious in the sight of all other nations. How would this promise help reassure the Jews that they were still a chosen people?
3. In the "Servant Songs," Second Isaiah said that Israel would be glorified through her suffering. Why is it that sometimes the greatest victories are won not through force, but through accepting suffering? Consider the examples of Gandhi and Martin Luther King Jr. in your answer.

Spiritual Reflection

Second Isaiah

Probably no experience in American history comes as close to the exile in Babylon as the enslavement of Africans before the Civil War. Like the Judahites, these people were forced into exile and made to labor for a foreign master. When they arrived in America, many of these Africans were baptized as Christians and became familiar with the Bible. They found comfort in the Bible and hope in the words of Second Isaiah. Of all the passages in the Bible, the most popular for sermons in slave churches may have been this one from Isaiah 40:

Comfort, comfort my people;—it is the voice of your God; speak tenderly to Jerusalem and tell her this, that she has fulfilled her term of bondage, that her penalty is paid.

(40:1–2)

These words remind us of the suffering of oppressed people, as well as the power of God to liberate them. For your prayer experience, do the following:

• Reread the passage above from Second Isaiah.
• Meditate upon the words.
• Think of someone you know who is suffering. This might be a group of people, or a personal friend or relative.
• Pray that God may see their suffering, and send consolation to them, as Second Isaiah brought comfort to Israel.
• Thank God for hearing you, and go your way!

What's Next?

What to Do

Have the students read Isaiah 40:3–5. Say: "This describes in poetic language the quality of experience Isaiah expected when he predicted that the people would return to Jerusalem and the Exile would be over. What do you think the people did about that prediction? We will find out in the next lesson."

Have You Considered?

1. This question calls for subjective responses from the students. Ask them to give specific reasons for whichever response they choose.
2. The promise of glory in the sight of other nations would reassure the Israelites they were still God's chosen nation among all the others on earth.
3. With Martin Luther King Jr. and Ghandi, they were able to win victories not through force, but by the moral conviction they inspired in others because of their courage and righteousness. Point out to students that violence can force people to do things, but only moral persuasion can change attitudes.

Bonus Focus for You

Isaiah 55 is one of the most beautiful passages in this prophet's work. Use it for your personal meditation and write in your journal what it means to you.

◆ MORE ABOUT THE LESSON

Further Questions for Review
• Who was Cyrus and what did Second Isaiah think of him?
• List the main ideas of Second Isaiah which responded to the Exiles' fears and temptations.
• What is the meaning of the term "Suffering Servant"?

• To whom do the Suffering Servant songs refer? How does Isaiah identify this person?
• What is the significance of the emphasis on God's holy name? How was this emphasis made significant in Judaism?

Q/A

Section One

1. Two reasons why Babylon deported conquered people are: (a) the conquered peoples would be more likely to think of themselves as Babylonians, and (b) the chances for rebellion were reduced.

2. Two reasons that people stayed behind in Judah are: (a) someone had to stay behind to care for the crops and herds, and (b) reducing the risk of rebellion only required that the leaders of the people be removed.

3. The Diaspora is the scattering of the Jews in the Exile. Gedeliah was the Jewish governor left behind to govern the Jews who remained in Judah after the first deportation. Jew is what the Judahites were called beginning in the Exile.

4. In exile the Jews could meet together and listen to their leaders, build houses, farm, engage in business, and work in the royal service.

5. Not all Jews in the Exile suffered poverty. Some prospered in business and government careers.

6. The Jews faced several critical questions in exile: Why had God allowed Judah to be destroyed? Did Yahweh no longer care about the Covenant? What did all the change and suffering mean?

7. Three threats to the Jewish community were: (a) there was no central place to meet for pilgrimage or festival, (b) they were living far from the land and prevented from visiting Jerusalem, (c) they were dispersed far and wide.

CHAPTER 7 REVIEW

Q/A

Section One

1. List two reasons why the Babylonians deported conquered people.
2. List two reasons why some people stayed behind in Judah.
3. Define: diaspora, Gedaliah, Jew.
4. What freedoms did the people enjoy in the Exile?
5. Were all Jews in the Exile poor?
6. Describe the crisis of meaning experienced by the people during the Exile.
7. List three threats to the Jewish community in the Exile.

Section Two

1. What was the first message of Ezekiel?
2. What did the symbolism of his visions teach Ezekiel about God?
3. What did Ezekiel's "Valley of Dry Bones" vision mean?
4. What did the Priestly Writers do with the traditions brought by the Jews into exile?
5. How did the Priestly Writers answer the question of whether God had abandoned the people of Judah?
6. How did the priests decide to unify the Jewish community?
7. What two actions were the center of the priestly Law?
8. Why is the last prophet of the Exile called "Second" Isaiah?

BIBLE ACTIVITY

1. Read the following passages from the Book of Psalms: Psalm 74:1–11, Psalm 79, Psalm 126 and Psalm 147. What relationships can you describe between these psalms and the events described in this chapter? When do you think these psalms might have been written?

2. Read Ezekiel 1:10–28 and 3:1–15, and then answer the following: (a) Where was Ezekiel when he received his call? (b) Describe the four living creatures he saw. (c) What did God command Ezekiel to eat? (d) Name the place where Ezekiel stayed for seven days.

3. Ezekiel and Second Isaiah both describe the restoration of Israel using the imagery of a shepherd and a flock. Read Ezekiel 34 and Isaiah 40:10–11. Write a comparison of the two passages.

BIBLE ACTIVITY

1. Psalm 74 describes the destruction of Jerusalem by the Babylonians. It was probably written in the Exile. Psalm 79 also describes the destruction and asks God how long the suffering will endure. It, too, was probably written in the Exile. Psalm 126 describes the people's happiness upon their return from exile. Psalm 147 is a song of gratitude for the successful rebuilding of Jerusalem accomplished after the return from exile.

2. (a) Ezekiel was in exile by the river Chebar when he was called by God. (b) The creatures he saw had a human form, but each had four faces and four legs. The faces were of a man, an ox, a lion, and an eagle. Their faces looked out on all four sides, so they did not turn as they moved. They each had two sets of two wings, and each glowed like fire. (c) God commanded Ezekiel to eat a scroll. (d) Ezekiel stayed for seven days among the exiles by the river Chebar.

GLOSSARY

- **Assimilation:** The process through which Jews abandoned their traditions and became members of other cultures.
- **Circumcision:** Jewish rite performed on male infants as a sign of membership in the community; made a central aspect of the Law by the Priestly Writers.
- **Cyrus:** King of the Medes and the Persians; conqueror of Babylon; freed Jews from Exile.
- **Diaspora:** Scattering of the Jews into many lands and nations after the Babylonian Exile.
- **Exile:** The period of time from 587 B.C.E. to 538 B.C.E. when the people of Judah were forced to live in Babylon.
- **Ezekiel:** Prophet of hope during the Exile.
- **Holy Name:** Phrase used by Second Isaiah to refer to the "essence" or "nature" of God.
- **Jew:** Short for "Yehudi" ("Judean"). Used for the Judahites beginning with the Exile.
- **Marduk:** The god of Babylon when Judah was exiled and when Cyrus took over the Babylonian Empire.
- **Nebuchadnezzar:** Babylon's most powerful king, responsible for the Exile.
- **Sabbath:** Rule that Jews must not work from sundown Friday to sundown Saturday; made a central observance by the Priestly writers.
- **Second Isaiah:** The author of Isaiah 40–55; prophet of the Exile who announced the end of suffering and the promise of future glory.
- **Suffering Servant:** Figure in "Servant Songs" in Second Isaiah who will announce God's words, intercede between God and the people, and glorify Israel through suffering.
- **Synagogue:** Term meaning "gathering place," referring to houses of worship built for Jews who could no longer go to the Temple.
- **Theodicy:** A defense of God's goodness in the face of evil.
- **Zion:** The hill in Jerusalem upon which Solomon's temple was constructed; usually refers to Judah.

UNDERSTANDING MORE ABOUT:

Isaiah 40–55

These chapters were written, as you know, by a much later disciple of Isaiah of Jerusalem. Nothing personal is known about the author, so this anonymous prophet is called simply, Second (or "Deutero," which means second), Isaiah. The reasons for separating chapters 40–55 from the earlier part of the book are historical as well as literary and content-oriented:

- **Historical,** because it is obvious that a different period in history is known and discussed.
- **Literary,** because the styles of the two sections are widely different in form and in vocabulary.
- **Contextually,** because chapters 1–39 speak primarily of future doom, while Second Isaiah speaks only of the restoration in the near future and the destruction in the recent past.

This work can be dated fairly precisely (540 or 539 B.C.E.) because of the prophet's knowledge of King Cyrus. The chapters of Second Isaiah are as complete a unit as there is in the Bible. Few scholars see much evidence of editorial work in these chapters.

Section Two

1. Ezekiel first warned the people that total destruction was coming because of their disobedience.
2. The symbolism of his visions taught Ezekiel that Yahweh is majestic, that Yahweh is everywhere, that Yahweh can see all at once, and that Yahweh's power is awesome.
3. The Valley of Dry Bones image meant that if God could raise people from dry bones, God could rebuild the people from their present devastation.
4. The Priestly Writers adapted those traditions to the need to reform the people along religious and cultural lines, and then produced the final version of the Pentateuch.
5. The Priestly Writers stressed that God had not abandoned the people, and that God's plan always included bringing order out of chaos. This message reassured the people that God was still in control of events and would restore their fortunes.
6. The priests decided to unify the community as a religious people shaped by obedience to the law.
7. Two actions central to the law are male circumcision and keeping the Sabbath day holy. These actions could be done anywhere and under any circumstances.
8. The last prophet of the Exile is called "second" Isaiah because his work follows closely that of Isaiah of Jerusalem, the prophet whose teachings are present in chapters 1–39 of the book of Isaiah.

3. Isaiah describes how God cares for us like a shepherd cares for his flock. Ezekiel discusses the poor shepherds, the kings, who had been caring for the people but doing a poor job. In comparison, he says, God will now care for the people directly, treating them with care as a good shepherd should, seeing that they are comfortable and safe from danger. However, Ezekiel also says that God will judge the sheep, a warning to the leaders who violated the Covenant and ruined the lives of the people.

Return and Rebuilding

Chapter Overview

The return to Jerusalem after the Exile was not easy. The Jews who returned faced many challenges, including rebuilding the city and resettling the land. They were led in this endeavor by Ezra and Nehemiah. This chapter will examine the history of Judaism following the Exile, including how the emphasis on the Law became the key aspect of Jewish faith.

With the conquests of Alexander the Great, Judaism went through another troublesome period. It was once again affected by outside influences. Judaism was once again in jeopardy of being assimilated into another culture. The heroes of this period were the Maccabees. This chapter will explore how Greek culture (Hellenism) affected the Jewish religion and how the Maccabees responded to this threat.

Teaching Objectives

By the end of this chapter students will be able to:
- Discuss the problems faced by those who returned to Jerusalem.
- Explain the importance of the religious reforms of Ezra.
- Demonstrate how Greek culture shaped Jewish belief.

Welcome

What to Do

Ask the students to close their eyes and use their imaginations. Say: "Pretend that you, at your present age, were living in Babylon, where you had been born. Your parents also were born here, but your grandparents had lived in Jerusalem, long ago. You love and have faith in the God of your ancestors and have sometimes wondered what life in Jerusalem was like. Yesterday you heard a man, who many in the community consider a prophet, urging people to return to Jerusalem. He promised that God would be with the travelers in a special way, making everything turn out well for them. What would be your feelings

---

Return and Rebuilding

550

537 B.C.E.
● First Return from Exile

522
● Haggai and Zechariah

515
● Temple dedicated

500
● King Darius I of Persia

465
● King Artaxerxes I
● Golden Age of Athens in Greece

445–400
● Nehemiah and Ezra in Jerusalem

427
● Plato born

400
● 1 and 2 Chronicles, Ezra, Nehemiah

336
● Alexander the Great defeats the Persians

230
● Hannibal fights the Romans

214
● Great Wall of China begun
● Rome wins First Macedonian War

200
● Daniel, Esther, Tobit, Jonah

164
● Temple rededicated

157
● Judah ruled by the Maccabees

54
● Temple plundered by Romans

20
● Temple rebuilt by Herod the Great

10

Legend
● General History
● Biblical History
● Jewish History
● Books written

Radovan, *Rebuilding the Temple*. Twentieth Century.

Alexandra remembered the time she lived in California as the best of her life. Her family lived in a small town near the ocean. Their house sat on a quiet street, and Alex had the front bedroom with a big bay window. In the backyard, her grandfather had built her a wooden clubhouse with a swing and a slide.

Alex's favorite memory of California was of her best friend, Maria. As little girls, Alex and Maria would drag their doll collections up to the clubhouse. Then, Alex's mom would bring them lunch, which they would pretend to share with their dolls.

When she was in third grade, Alex's father was transferred to a new job in Ohio. Life wasn't all bad there for Alex, as she enjoyed her new school and made new friends. Still, she missed her old house, old school, and especially Maria. For a while, the two girls wrote letters to each other.

◆ MORE ABOUT THE LESSON

Fulfilling the Promise

When it comes to the effectiveness of the prophets we witness an amazing phenomenon: when they predicted doom and terror, few believed them and few acted on their words; yet when Second Isaiah predicted a wonderful end to the Exile, few believed or acted on his message either. The invitation of the Lord to return to Jerusalem was, on the surface, the answer to the prayers of a generation or more of exiles.

Yet, when looking at the realities of God's invitation, the Jews living in exile seemed to prefer the comfort and certainty of staying in Babylon to the adventure of obeying the Lord. Very few took the journey to Jerusalem.

What amount of courage was necessary for people to overcome their fear in order to return to Jerusalem? What must they have thought when they arrived back in Jerusalem to find nothing but ruin?

Then, the letters stopped. Things had changed since Alex and Maria were little girls; in the fall, both would be entering high school.

Just after junior high graduation, Alex's dad had another surprise: the family was moving back to California! They had never sold their old house. As their tenant's lease was expiring, they could move back right away. Alex was the most excited of all. She couldn't wait to see her old bedroom again, the clubhouse, and, of course, Maria.

The move back was difficult for Alex. Nothing was as she remembered it; her old room was decorated with football players, and the clubhouse was tiny and falling apart. Alex looked forward to seeing Maria and getting back to the way things used to be.

As she approached Maria's house, Alex was relieved to see Maria's father working in the yard. "Maria is inside with her boyfriend," he said. "Go right in, she'll be surprised to see you." The girls hugged and laughed. After a few minutes, Maria said that they were heading for the beach. Alex listened for an invitation to join them, but it never came.

Alex walked back home, feeling depressed. "This place isn't the way I remember it at all," she told her father angrily.

Unrealistic Expectations

Like Alex, the people of Judah went home expecting to pick up where they had left off. They remembered the promises of Second Isaiah:

- All of the people of Israel would return to their own land.
- The Temple would be rebuilt and Yahweh would once again dwell in Jerusalem.
- Judah would be the center of God's rule over the world.

They, too, were disappointed when life turned out different from what they had expected. Those who accepted King Cyrus's offer to return to Jerusalem found that fulfilling the prophet's predictions would not be easy. Building a city and reestablishing themselves as a people would be a major challenge.

◆ MORE ABOUT THE LESSON

Rebuilding the Covenant

Even with the emphasis on the Law, Judaism is primarily about the Hebrew people's covenant relationship with God. The destruction of Jerusalem and the Exile seriously damaged Judah's trust in the Covenant.

During the Exile, the Jews had come to a more complete understanding of their relationship with God.

The predictions of glory, comfort, beauty and ease offered through Second Isaiah were not immediately apparent. People had to struggle to understand Second Isaiah as they struggled to survive. How would the conditions in Palestine have changed for the better if most of the people had returned from exile instead of just a small number? How were the hardships experienced the consequence of this?

---

if your parents decided to go? On what would your reaction depend? What if your friends' families did not choose to go back?"

Pray with your students. Have the students locate Psalm 126 and read it together aloud, remembering the difficult decision to return to Jerusalem.

Introducing the Chapter

What to Do

1. Ask students how they would feel if the following event happened to them.

    "A person you barely know calls and asks if you would like to go to a concert on Saturday. Since you have wanted to get to know this person anyway, you accept the invitation gladly. Saturday comes and you are all excited. Then your date arrives elegantly dressed, while you are in your concert clothes: jeans, torn t-shirt, and gym shoes. Your friend had invited you to the symphony orchestra playing Vivaldi, but you had expected Pearl Jam. What do you feel when you expect one thing and something else happens?" Discuss with students times when they have been disappointed when their expectations have not been met.

2. Have the students read Alexandra's story on the opening spread. Why was she so disappointed on her return to her old home? Do students feel that her disappointment was unrealistic?

3. Discuss with students what they think the Jews might have felt when they returned to Jerusalem after 50 years in exile.

Extend the Activity   Have students write or discuss what they think will happen next for Alexandra.

Development

Using the Timeline

While this lesson deals only with the first item on the timeline, review it with the students to help them place this period in history. Recall that the prophet Second Isaiah prophesied just prior to this period, around 540 or 539.

LESSON ONE (pages 132–136)

◆ Going Home: Promises and Perils

Teaching Objectives

By the end of this lesson students will be able to:

- Identify the problems the returning Jews had in reestablishing Jerusalem.
- Explain the role of the prophets Haggai and Zechariah in the return from the Exile.
- Discuss the importance of Nehemiah and Ezra to the continued life of Judaism.

Development

What to Do

1. Have the students read "Why Go Back?" and compare the information there with Isaiah 49:8–13. How do they think the difference in feeling expressed here might be explained?

2. Have the students read "The First Group." Divide the class in half. One group is to imagine itself Samaritans, the other returnees. They are to converse with each other from that viewpoint. Have them use "Bible Activity" number 4 (page 146) as part of their conversation.

3. The students have discussed the idea that Jewish beliefs were constantly being influenced by the religious beliefs of neighboring religious groups many times. Use this opportunity to review how this would happen and to name the consequences that would result from this violation of the Covenant.

4. Lead the class discussion of the questions in "Have You Considered?"

Judah after the Exile

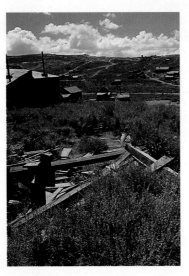

When the first group of Jews returned to Judah, they faced many challenges. Living conditions were terrible, and to survive they had to defend themselves from other groups. They also had to renew themselves as a community. All this had to be done while living under foreign rule, a special challenge for the people commanded to be "unlike other nations." What must it have been like to be one of the first returnees to Judah? Where would one start in rebuilding the nation? What unexpected surprises lay in store for the weary returnee?

Learning Objectives for Section One

By the end of this section, you will be able to:

- List several problems experienced by the Jews on their return to Judah.
- Discuss the importance of the work of Haggai, Zechariah, and Nehemiah.
- Explain the religious reforms of Ezra.
- Define "Hellenization" and describe its impact on Judah.

◆ Going Home: Promises and Perils

Second Isaiah had promised that greatness and glory would await the people when they returned to Judah. Those Jews who made the trip back went with high hopes. However, making Second Isaiah's promise come true would be a very difficult task.

Why Go Back?

King Cyrus had made it possible for the Jews to return to Judah, but many people simply did not want to go. Why should they? By 538 B.C.E., the date of Cyrus' edict, only a few of the oldest Judahites would have had any personal memory of their homeland. Everyone else would have been born and raised in exile, where they had become established. Babylon was now their home. For them to return to Jerusalem, would be a major uprooting.

There were other issues to consider about a possible move back to Judah:

- Since Jerusalem had been pillaged, it would have to be rebuilt.
- The journey from Babylon to Jerusalem was at least a 1,000 mile trip through a desolate desert, and most of the travelers would have to walk.
- Other people had settled in and around Judah, replacing the Jews. Tensions between those who were already there and those who would come could lead to conflict.

Second Isaiah had said to the people,

Go forth from Babylon, flee from Chaldea! I, the Lord, your God, teach you what is for your good, and lead you on the way you should go.

(Isaiah 48:20, 17)

Given all the obstacles listed above, it would take a special kind of person to take up Second Isaiah's challenge and make the trip.

MORE ABOUT THE TEXT

Scholars Say

Actually very little is known about the period after the Exile. The information here is pieced together from fairly confused sources—Ezra's and Nehemiah's activities are not actually as clear as they appear to be in the student text. Yet the main thrust of the experience is clear: the returnees struggled in great faith and courage, and they were given success by the Lord who watched over them. If that success did not feel quite like the glorious predictions of Second Isaiah, nevertheless the people must have experienced a profound victory over their difficulties.

The dedication of the rebuilt Temple and the rejoicing over a walled city must have been a wonderful experience. Over time, as the resettlement progressed, more Jews returned to Palestine from Babylon.

The First Group

Only a tiny group, at first, returned to Judah. From the start, they experienced difficulty. The harvest was meager, so food supplies were short. Much of the economic aid that had been promised by King Cyrus never arrived. Survival itself became a challenge. It was painfully obvious that the resettlement demanded great vision and endurance. To make matters worse, the Jews experienced hostility from the people who had claimed their land during the Exile.

Imagine that your parents had bought an abandoned house 50 years ago. They had worked hard over the years, fixing the place up and making it their home. You were born there, and that's where your parents lived until they died. When they died, you inherited the house. One day, a stranger knocks on your door and says that her grandfather had owned the house many years before and had been forced to leave it by the government.

- How would you feel if she claimed that this house—the one that your parents had worked so hard for and that you thought was yours—really belonged to her?
- How would you react to her statement? What would you do?

You now have some idea of a problem the Jews faced when they returned from Babylon. After the Jews were forcibly removed, other people claimed their land. These people were not very happy 50 years later

A Samaritan community continues to live in the Middle East and to worship Yahweh as they have for nearly 2700 years. This picture shows the slaughter of the lamb in preparation for Passover

when the Jews returned, wanting their property back and claiming a slice of the already-scarce economic pie. Among the many groups who resisted the Jews' return, the biggest challenge probably came from the Samaritans.

The Samaritans   Over time, the citizens of the Northern kingdom who had been left behind by the Assyrians intermarried with members of the Canaanite, Assyrian, and other local nations. They became a new cultural group called "Samaritans" after the capital city of the area, Samaria. Tensions between these Samaritans and the returning Jews flared up when the Samaritans realized that the Jews intended to rebuild the Temple in Jerusalem. This project would make Judah a strong political and economic rival to Samaria.

The rivalry between the Samaritans and the Jews was further complicated by religion. The Samaritans—descendants of the nation of Israel who worshipped Yahweh—practiced their own form of religion, which was centered in the temple they had built on Mount Gerizim. The Samaritans believed that they were living faithful to the Covenant. Relations between the Jews and the Samaritans worsened, until, eventually, their hatred for one another became legendary.

Foreign Religions   The final peril faced by those who returned to Judah was spiritual. Jewish beliefs continued to be influenced by foreign religious ideas. Some of the returnees brought with them spouses from other religions and cultures whom they had married while in Babylon. These marriages resulted in a mixing of religion and worship—actions prohibited by Jewish law. Keeping the worship of Yahweh pure was the chief goal of the next generation of Jewish leaders.

Purity of worship was important to the Jews, because the memory of the Exile was fresh in their minds. They believed that this disaster had resulted from the nation's infidelity to the Covenant.

Have You Considered?

1. Do you think the rivalry between the returnees and the Samaritans would have been as intense if the Samaritans had not also claimed God's Covenant? Why or why not?
2. Have you ever been part of a situation in which a person from one religion wanted to marry a person from another? Why do you think families often don't want their children to marry outside of their religion?

until each student has someone else's. Now they are to imagine they are the friends in Babylon to whom these letters are addressed. Have them respond back to these letters.

6. Have the students work in small groups to do the "Scripture Workshop."

7. Pray with your students. Include in your prayer a thanksgiving for the willingness of the Jews under Ezra to make such great sacrifices, for without them, the Jewish people might not have survived. Ask the Lord to keep us aware of our debt to them and of the wonderful interconnections among us all.

Scripture Workshop

1. 1 Chronicles 29:1–20 presents David as collecting items for worship and praying for the construction of the Temple. 16:8–36 is a collection of references to several of the Psalms, which refer to God's "holy place." Both reflect the Chronicler's theme that the Temple was part of God's plan from the very beginning, blessed and supported also by King David.

2. 2 Samuel 11:2–29 is the story of David and Bathsheba. The Chronicler, who regarded David as the perfect embodiment of obedience to the Covenant, was embarrassed by this episode, and so left it out of the history. This deletion also reflects the changed circumstances after the return from Exile, where membership in the community was defined by personal piety, rather than national citizenship.

◆ A New Generation of Jewish Leaders

In the face of these obstacles, the people remained busy rebuilding their own homes and workshops. Judah began to take shape once more as a result of their efforts. Rivalries with neighbors and frequent economic problems seemed to be the biggest challenges facing the people. Yet, as these external troubles continued, Yahweh sent two prophets to remind them that their spiritual obligation came first.

Haggai and Zechariah: Rebuilding the Temple

Faced with the difficulty of physical survival, the people felt that they just didn't have the resources to rebuild the Temple right away. The prophet, Haggai, felt differently. He announced that the problems people were having were caused by their neglect of God. They had rebuilt their own homes first while neglecting God's house, the Temple. Haggai's message to them was,

> Now has the time come to rebuild the house of the Lord. Is it time for you to dwell in your own paneled houses, while this house lies in ruin?
>
> (Haggai 1:3)

Shamed by Haggai's message, the people began to rebuild the Temple.

The prophet, Zechariah, told of the "new prince" who was to rule Judah: Zerubbabel, a descendant of King David. In about 520 B.C.E., Zerubbabel did come to Judah, bringing with him the promised money from the imperial treasury. With the influx of additional workers and money, the new Temple was completed by 515 B.C.E. Although the new Temple was much smaller and less elaborate than Solomon's had been, it nevertheless represented a spiritual victory for the Jewish people. Their life as the People of God could begin anew.

Nehemiah: Rebuilding the City

Over the next 70 years, two other important leaders emerged. The first, Nehemiah, who was himself a Jew, served as an official in the Persian court. Nehemiah convinced King Artaxerxes to make Judah an independent province and to make him its first governor.

Scripture Workshop

The Chronicler

Working at the same time as Ezra, another Jewish leader put together a work which reviewed the history of the nation. We call this person "the Chronicler" because the two books he or she produced are 1 and 2 Chronicles. Like Ezra, this author emphasized the importance of the Temple and personal piety.

By comparing Chronicles to the Deuteronomic history, we can get a sense of the special interests of the Chronicler. Try it for yourself—read 1 Chronicles 29:1–20 and 16:8–36, both of which are episodes not in the Deuteronomic history. Then read 2 Samuel 11:2–29, a part not in Chronicles. Now answer these questions:

- How is the Chronicler's interest in the Temple evident in the passages added to the history?
- How is the Chronicler's interest in personal piety obvious in the passages left out of the history?

During this time, as new returnees continued to arrive, the population of Judah doubled. While their new energy and money helped to improve civic life, the increased numbers of residents also intensified the conflicts with the neighboring peoples who felt threatened by Judah's growth. Faced with these new threats of attack, Nehemiah's first task was to rebuild the city walls of Jerusalem. According to the Book of Nehemiah, the people's reply to Nehemiah's request was, "Let us be up and building!" (*Nehemiah* 2:18). The walls were rebuilt in only 52 days, a task that normally would have taken many months. Nehemiah must have been a great motivator and a super organizer!

Now that the walls had been rebuilt and Jerusalem could be defended, Nehemiah arranged for volunteers to move from their outlying farmland and villages into the ruined capital. Jerusalem needed a population to care for it and to gradually rebuild it, surrounding the new Temple with the beginnings of a city. Rebuilding the city, however, was still only a first step: the Jews also had to rebuild themselves as a people.

MORE ABOUT THE TEXT

The Books of the Chronicler

The two books of Chronicles, along with the books of Ezra and Nehemiah, were originally combined into one historical work, similar in style and basic ideas.

The Greek title for this work, *paraleipomena*, means "things that were ignored or omitted." Thus, this one book was considered material that was important but not included in the books of Samuel and Kings. Though never named, some scholars think that Ezra may have been the Chronicler.

Written near the end of the fifth century B.C.E. (c. 400), the Chronicler realized that Judah's days as a political power were over. Judah would exist as a people under God, or it would not exist. If Judaism was to survive, then the people would have to devoutly serve Yahweh and participate freely in Temple worship.

Ezra: Renewing the Law

The second important leader after the Exile was Ezra, a priest and a "scribe well-versed in the law of Moses" (Ezra 7:6). Ezra was sent by the king to check on the religious conditions in Judah, to organize its funding, and to install judges to rule using the Jewish law. Since he was appointed by the king, he had legal as well as religious authority. Because of this combination, he was able to do more than Nehemiah in regard to the regulation and reform of Jewish life.

Reading the Law   At the time of the ancient Feast of Booths, Ezra called the Jewish community together in Jerusalem. Then he stood on a platform and read to them the scroll of the Law which he had brought from Babylon. Some scholars think this was the Torah, the first five books of the Bible, recently compiled by the priests. Ezra read for hours in Hebrew as the Levite priests stood nearby to translate the words into Aramaic, the language of the common people.

Unknown, Ezra, Seventh Century?

When the Jews returned to Jerulsalem from Exile they survived because of the leadership of Nehemiah and Ezra (shown here).

The Bible in Context

The Feast of the Booths

The Feast of the Booths, also known as the Festival of Tabernacles, was originally a Canaanite celebration of the end of the harvest. The people would live in booths to symbolize the small huts that farmers stayed in during the harvesting season. Later, the Jews applied a new religious meaning to the festival, viewing it as a reminder of their wanderings in the wilderness.

Recalling Ezra's reading of the Law, the Festival of Booths requires that the Torah be read to the entire community. Throughout the year, the reading of the Torah is arranged so that it is completed during this festival. As soon as it is finished, however, the cycle of readings begins again. This shows that the Torah has no beginning or end. This part of the festival is called Simhat Torah, which means "Rejoicing of the Torah."

When Ezra finished, the people began to weep. They had no idea their lives were so far from God's Law! Ezra urged them not to be sad, but to rejoice because it was a holy day to the Lord. Yahweh was offering a gift to the people—the gift of a renewed awareness of the Law.

> *"And, now, but a short time ago, mercy came to us from the Lord our God, who left us a remnant and gave us a stake in his holy place; thus our God has brightened our eyes and given us relief in our servitude. . . . O Lord, God of Israel, you are just; yet we have been spared, the remnant we are today. Here we are before you in our sins. Because of all this, we can no longer stand in your presence."*
>
> (Ezra 9:8,15)

Sacrificing for the Law   Two months after the reading of the Torah, the people assembled again before the Temple, this time in a driving rainstorm. Ezra said that God required them to separate from their non-Jewish wives. As a result of Ezra's words, Jews divorced their spouses who were not Jewish and forced them to leave the land.

What else did the Law require? The Jewish community agreed that they would:

- Keep holy the Sabbath and the holy days of the year.
- Support one another in the form of tithes and offerings.
- Help to maintain the Temple with an annual tax.

MORE ABOUT THE TEXT

According to the Law

Many students will react against the notion that marriages had to be changed to accommodate the provisions of the Law. Our feelings about personal decisions make us uneasy with Ezra's command.

One way of thinking about the issue is this: What in life might be more important than any individual preference? Would the survival of the United States as a nation be important enough

for some people to give up everything else? What about in time of war or terrible governmental wrongs (like the Nazi period in Germany, for example)?

Ezra's community believed the group was more important than any individual, but more immediately, they felt that their willingness to live strictly by the Law would determine their fate. Personal interests simply were less important than the people's survival and well-being.

The Bible in Context

Have the students read Psalm 147, silently. Then, to share in the ancient rejoicing, have the students read the psalm aloud, in two choirs, alternating verses.

Recall

Have the students answer orally "Chapter 8 Review Q/A," Section One, questions 1–4.

Connect

What to Do

Have the students answer "Bible Activity" number 1. Discuss students' sacrifices in the large group.

What's Next?

What to Do

Homework Assignment: Ask the students to write a paragraph describing what life might be like if they were forced to live under the rule of an invading country. (If some of your students have had this experience, have them write about their own memories.)

Have You Considered?

1. The Temple's reconstruction symbolized the return of Yahweh's presence to the land of Israel.
2. Encourage students to discuss their own experiences of religious and cultural diversity. Explore some of the factors that create tension in such situations: mistrust, fear, scapegoating. Then direct students to apply these factors to the situation of the Jews returning from exile.
3. Encourage students to focus on shared traditions: holiday meals, favorite pastimes, and devotions.

Bonus Focus for You ———

Ponder the sacrifices made by the people of this period, for the sake of God's Law and God's people. What is so important to you personally that you would sacrifice as intensely for its sake?

LESSON TWO (pages 136–138)

◆ Living under Foreign Rule

Welcome

What to Do

Share with the students something that has happened or is happening in class that gives you particular delight in them. Praise them for all they do to make class a pleasure for everyone.

Pray with your students. Close by reading Psalm 150 aloud. Use a choral reading style to encourage everyone's participation.

Ask the students to share the homework paragraphs they wrote about living under foreign rule. If some of these paragraphs are actual memories, be sure they are heard with great respect.

Introducing the Lesson

Teaching Objectives

By the end of this lesson students will be able to:
- Explain the effect Alexander the Great had on Jewish religion and culture.
- Describe the reasons for and the results of the Maccabean revolt.
- Identify the Book of Esther as a work of fiction written to show the importance of personal heroism in a time of struggle.

What to Do

Referring to the timeline on page 130, have students notice the Palestinian events and biblical books mentioned between 400 and 157 B.C.E.

Looking together at the map, note that the Persian Empire was very extensive. Notice how much larger Alexander's empire became, extending into India.

Remind the students that during post-Exilic centuries, most of the Jews did not live in Judea, but were scattered between these two widespread empires. They usually lived in communities close to each other, but they were never isolated from the cultures where they lived.

LEARN FROM THE MAP

Alexander's Conquests

The map outlines the course of Alexander the Great's conquests. Note that Alexander's route of conquest did not travel through Jerusalem. According to legend, Alexander was so impressed by a procession of priests from the Temple that he did not destroy the city.

Empire of Alexander the Great in the late Fourth Century

Alexander's Empire
Former Persian Empire

©1994 Magellan Geographix℠ Santa Barbara, CA.

Ezra's return marked a turning point for the Jews. In the first stages of the return to Judah, their struggle was to make the new nation survive. Ezra reminded them, however, that their first loyalty was to the Covenant, not the nation, and therefore their chief goal must be to keep the Law. Ever after, Judaism would be centered on the Law.

Have You Considered?

1. Why do you suppose Haggai insisted that rebuilding the Temple should be such a priority for the Jews? What did the Temple symbolize that would help them meet the challenges they faced?
2. Why is it often difficult for people of different religious and cultural backgrounds to live together in peace? Apply your answer to the conflicts faced by those who returned to Judah.
3. Are you part of a group that's scattered in more than one location? How does your group stay together despite the distance?

◆ Living Under Foreign Rule

Although the Jews were able to return to Judah from Babylon, they were not to have political freedom. They were continually under the control of foreign powers, a situation their Israelite ancestors had never tolerated, and one that the Jews also considered unacceptable. The Jews' desire to be ruled by God and through God's Law made them different from other cultures. This lack of political freedom was to be an ongoing source of conflict for Judah and its neighbors.

The Persians

Very little is known of Jewish history during the final century of Persian rule after the reforms of Nehemiah and Ezra. Judah was an isolated nation during this time and still a part of the larger Persian empire. One result of Persian rule was the widespread

◆ MORE ABOUT THE LESSON

A Matter of Sequence

The sequence of the lessons for Chapter 8 can be confusing. The first two lessons (Section One) deal mostly with the historical events. Section Two deals with religious and social issues which arose among the Jews during both Persian and Greek periods. Be sure to explain this to your students, because the bulk of the material in Lessons Three and Four relates more to the Persian period than to the Greeks. Unless the students understand this movement back and forth through time, they may become confused.

Take a few minutes as you begin this lesson to clarify this point. You will want to remind students of this movement again as you begin the next lesson.

use of the Aramaic language among Jews. Aramaic was the official language for the Persians, and Jews had to learn it to do business in the empire.

Alexander the Great: The Rise of Greek Influence

In 336 B.C.E., Alexander the Great defeated the Persians. For the next 272 years the Middle East, including Judah, would be dominated by the Greeks. Under their rule, Greek political, social, and religious customs became common practice, even for many Jews. Greek became the language of educated people everywhere.

Hellenization

Contact between Greek and Jewish cultures produced incredible changes within Jewish life.

• Because Greek commercial life often required sacrifices to gods of commerce such as Hermes, Jewish businessmen were often forced to participate in Greek religious rituals.
• Greek education emphasized physical fitness, Greek philosophy, and respect for the gods. All citizens who wished to prosper under Greek rule had to participate in this educational system.
• The Old Testament was translated into Greek, a translation called the "Septuagint" (Greek for "seventy"). According to legend, 70 translators, working independently, each achieved exactly the same translation from the Hebrew text.

All of these changes added up to a process known as "Hellenization," which means "becoming like the Greeks." Conservative Jews saw this behavior as a betrayal of the Law and were opposed to it.

The Maccabees' Revolt

After Alexander's death, his empire was split into several kingdoms, including the *Ptolemies* in Egypt and the *Seleucids* in Syria. It was the Ptolemies that originally ruled Judah after Alexander's death. There was to be no peace, however. The Ptolemies and Seleucids were to fight for control of the Middle East—including Judah—for close to 150 years, before the Seleucids emerged victorious.

Like the Ptolemies before them, the Seleucids originally chose to leave the Jews to their own internal affairs. This policy was to change radically under King Antiochus IV. When Antiochus needed money, he raided the Temple. Antiochus's greater crime, though, was the desecration of the Temple.

As an emphatic proponent of Greek religion, Antiochus decreed that a statue of Zeus was to be worshipped in the Temple. He also ordered that pigs be sacrificed there. These decrees were meant to humiliate the Jews. Putting a statue of Zeus in the Temple not only violated the Commandment against false God, but placing the statue in the Temple was terribly offensive. The sacrifice of pigs violated the Jewish prohibition against unclean animals and called into question all Jewish sacrifices. By this decree, Antiochus mocked the Jews and, in effect, slapped them in the face.

Outraged by what had happened, the Jewish people rebelled. In 167 B.C.E., Mattathias, the leader of a strong Jewish family, did not remain quiet.

> When he [Mattathias] saw the sacrileges that were being committed in Judah and in Jerusalem, he said: "Woe is me! Why was I born to see the ruin of my people and the ruin of the holy city, and to sit idle while it is given into the hands of enemies, and the sanctuary into the hands of strangers?"
>
> (1 Maccabees 2:6–7)

He refused to offer the repulsive sacrifice and took a group of soldiers into the Judean hills. After Mattathias' death, his son Judas—nicknamed Maccabeus ("the Hammer")—took over as the leader of some 3,000 troops.

Using guerrilla style warfare, Judas and his men were successful in battle against Antiochus IV's army. They also waged war on any Jew who sided with the Greeks. The Maccabee fighters were zealots determined to defend the faith of their ancestors and cleanse Judah of its oppressors.

After three years of bloody struggle, the revolt succeeded. The Temple was cleansed and the Jews gathered in joy to celebrate its rededication. The Feast of Hanukkah ("dedication") commemorates that event, when the lamps of dedication miraculously burned for eight days, even though the Maccabees had only enough oil to last one day.

The rebellion of the Maccabees continued in an effort to gain full political independence for the Jewish nation. And, for a brief period of time, the Jews gained independence. But this freedom did not last. In 63 B.C.E., the Roman general Pompey came to Jerusalem, imprisoned the Jewish high priest, and appointed his own puppet high priest, Hyrcanus. Once again, the Jews served a foreign master, this time the mighty Republic of Rome.

Development

What to Do

1. Say: "The Persian Empire was a highly developed and valuable civilization. The Persians gave the Jews the time and resources they needed to re-shape their lives following the Exile. The period following the return from exile was in many ways similar to the years spent in the desert following the Exodus."
2. Have the students read "Living under Foreign Rule." Say: "During the four centuries after the Exile, several biblical books appeared. Among them are the books of Esther, Tobit, Judith, and Maccabees."
3. Have the students do the "Scripture Workshop" on page 141 of their text.
4. Pray with your students.

Practicing the Skills

What to Do

Have the students divide in three groups. They are to summarize the stories of Esther, Judith, and the Maccabees for presentation to the class. They may give an oral presentation, read aloud from the books themselves, develop a skit that shares the story, or produce their own video if they'd like.

When all three stories have been told, have a celebration of the victories.

Recall

Have the students write their answers to "Chapter Review Q/A" Section One, questions 5–8, and then share them with the class.

Connect

What to Do

Lead a discussion of the questions in "Have You Considered?" Add this one: "Esther and Judith handled their problems quite differently. Which woman do you admire more and why?"

What's Next?

What to Do

Remind the students that the next two lessons are about the religious and social effects of living closely with Persian, then with Greek, values and assumptions.

Homework Assignment:
Ask students to write two paragraphs on these questions: "How might living under foreign domination change your ideas about life? Would you adopt new ideas or strengthen those you already believe in? Why? What do other family members think about this issue? If you don't know, then ask them."

Have You Considered?

1. Foreign rulers usually encouraged conquered people to change to the religion of the victorious culture. Such pressure would contradict Jewish emphasis on the worship of Yahweh alone. Also, the Jewish belief that they were especially chosen from among the nations was difficult to sustain in the face of conquest and foreign rule.

2. Different answers are possible, but require students to justify their responses with specific references to Jewish beliefs and practices. Historically, the pressure to engage in Greek religion in order to prosper economically and politically was perhaps the most controversial effect of Hellenization, not only because it violated the Covenant and alienated pious Jews, but also because it accelerated the division between economic classes in Jewish life.

3. Allow students to form their own opinions on this question. Perhaps it would help to compare this situation to that of the policy of many countries of executing traitors (Julius and Ethel Rosenberg, who were put to death during the Cold War, are examples that could be used from American history).

Bonus Focus for You
Read Nehemiah 9:32–37. Does this summary of Israelite history agree with your own view? Do you think it is analogous to modern individual (or group) experience of history and of God? What would be your own response to God, if you felt this were true about your own life?

Have You Considered?

1. No nation enjoys being ruled by another, but given their identity as the Chosen People and their law against worshipping false gods, why do you think it was especially hard for Jews to be ruled by other nations?

2. Read through the list above of the ways in which Greek culture influenced Judaism. Which of these acts do you think would be most offensive to traditional Jews? Explain your answer.

3. The Maccabees killed many Jews who supported Hellenization to insure the existence of the Jewish community. Explain why this behavior can or cannot be justified.

in the Spotlight
The Book of Esther
The Book of Esther was written near the close of the fourth century B.C.E. to explain the winter feast of *Purim*. Purim celebrates the Jews' deliverance from Persian oppression during the reign of King Xerxes (485–465 B.C.E.). In the Book of Esther, Xerxes is known as Ahaseurus.

Esther is a fictional account of how a Jewish princess, Esther, and her cousin, Mordecai, were successful in stopping a Persian plot led by the evil official, Haman, to massacre the Jews. Being fictional doesn't make the story any less important, however. Today in Jewish synagogues, the scroll of the Book of Esther, called the Megillah, is read in its entirety twice on the Feast of Purim. This story is a remarkable sign of God's love for the Jews.

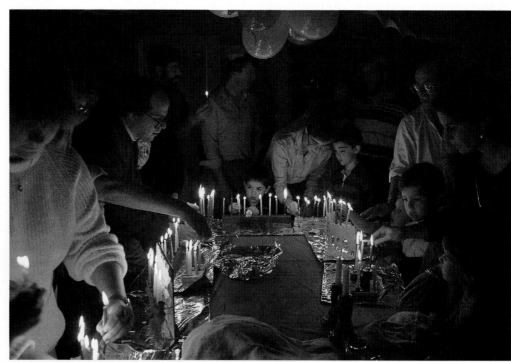

The Jewish feast of Hanukkah celebrates the rededication of the Temple after the Maccabean revolt.

MORE ABOUT THE TEXT

Alexander the Great
Alexander was a phenomenal commander, loved and followed by his soldiers. His ten years (aged 23 to 33) of expeditions gained for the Greeks the whole Persian Empire and more besides. It was Alexander's dream that the whole world should be governed by Greek cultural and philosophical ideals (he had been a student of Aristotle). He very nearly made it happen. But he died too soon. After his death, his empire was divided and the struggle for power quickly became more important than his visionary dream. Nevertheless, Greek culture was firmly implanted in all parts of the Mediterranean, to be the predominant influence there even through the Roman period.

For the Jews, the Greek period was a great threat to their survival as a people of faith. The Greeks tried to force everyone to be like them. Conflict with the Jews was inevitable.

God's People in Changing Times

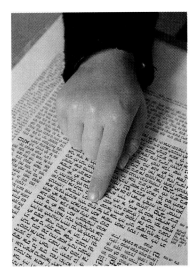

You have already learned that the term "salvation history," means that God directs the events of history to bring us to salvation. God's plan unfolds over time, and throughout history Yahweh has shaped our traditions and beliefs to help us better understand God's will. In this section, you'll see how God used changing historical circumstances after the Exile to reshape Judaism and to bring the people to a new level of spiritual awareness.

Learning Objectives for Section Two

By the end of this section, you will be able to:

- Discuss the purpose of Ezra's rule on intermarriage.
- Describe the roles of the synagogue and the priesthood in Judah.
- Explain God's use of foreign nations to broaden Israel's religious understanding.
- Explain the process of discernment.

◆ A New Identity for the Diaspora

You read in Chapter 7 how, because of the Diaspora, the Priestly Writers tried to unify the Jews through their common traditions rather than through a national government. Ezra confirmed that decision and put it into practice. God had scattered the Jews throughout the world, and Ezra recognized that the Law would have to be adapted so that it would hold the Jews together as a people wherever they might live. Ezra's first responsibility, however, was to boost the morale of the returnees in Judah and to make sure that they remained loyal to the Covenant.

Ezra and the People of Judah

The Jews had hoped that when the Temple was rebuilt, all their people would come streaming back to Judah, and they would live in perfect obedience to the demands of the Covenant. These hopes, however, were soon disappointed. The presence of the rebuilt Temple failed to attract many Jews to return to Jerusalem. In fact, as reported in Malachi, the general lack of support for the Temple resulted in unpaid taxes and unholy sacrifices:

> Oh, that one among you would shut the Temple gates to keep you from kindling fire on my altar in vain! I have no pleasure in you, says the Lord of hosts; neither will I accept any sacrifice from your hands.
> (Malachi 1:10)

Breaking the Law   The most basic commands of the Law were neglected. The law forbidding work on the Sabbath was broken as peasants cut grain and merchants set up tables at the Temple on the Sabbath as if it were just another day. Levites, members of the priestly family who were supposed to be cared for by the community, now had to take jobs in the fields. The increasing number of marriages between Jews and *Gentiles* (non-Jews) also proved a most serious problem.

◆ MORE ABOUT THE LESSON

Alternative Lessons

Use the following lesson in place of a field trip or guest speaker.

- Welcome students by having them share their homework paragraphs with the class.
- Write on the board the following words, "Law," "Synagogue," "Torah," and "Priests."
- Read aloud the material from page 139 to "Have You Considered?" on page 142. As students come across information about any of

these four words, write that information on the board under its proper heading. Answer any questions students might have about any of these terms. Use Teacher's Resource 8A for a fuller understanding of these terms. Note that the priestly office does not exist today; there is no temple in which to offer sacrifice.

- Work with students on the features "Malachi" and "Scripture Workshop." Answer the questions in "Have You Considered?"

SECTION TWO

LESSON THREE

(pages 139–142)

◆ A New Identity for the Diaspora

Special Instructions

As presented here, this lesson will require two days to complete. The first day, the students will work with the material in the text and formulate questions they would like to ask to a local rabbi. The second day presumes that you will have a local rabbi speak to your class, or that as a class you will take a field trip to visit a local synagogue to speak with a rabbi. If neither of these options are possible, use the lesson found in "More about the Lesson" on page 139.

Welcome

What to Do

Ask volunteers to read their homework paragraphs aloud. Discuss as needed.

Say: "Today we are going to make plans for a field trip and/or a conversation with a rabbi of the local synagogue. Our trip will give us new experiences and new ideas."

Pray with your students. Ask the Lord for blessings on the planning and on the events of the visit to the synagogue and the students' meeting with the rabbi and/or other Jews in the group.

Introducing the Lesson

Teaching Objectives

By the end of this lesson students will be able to:
- Explain the importance of the Law to Jewish life.
- Explain the importance of the synagogue to Jewish worship.

What to Do

Have the students read silently the whole of "A New Identity for the Diaspora." Ask them to pause at the end of each subsection (except the one on the "Priestly Office" which no longer exists) and write down a question they might like to ask a rabbi today about that section's content.

Development

What to Do

1. Compile a list on the board of all of the students' questions. Together, search through them and decide which ones can be answered in class and which would have the most relationship to today's synagogue practices.

2. Ask the students if they have other questions they might like to ask the rabbi.

3. When all the questions are listed on the board, let the students decide which are the most important to ask. Divide the questions into three categories: "most important," "medium important," "less important." Some questions can also be eliminated.

4. Make a plan with your students for conducting the conversation with the Jewish rabbi.

5. Have a rabbi or a representative from a local Jewish synagogue discuss with students the importance of the Law and the synagogue in Jewish life today. Students' questions from the prepared list should be used.

6. Close this lesson with a prayer. Invite the rabbi to lead the class in a traditional Jewish prayer.

Recall

Review this experience using the questions developed by the students. What answers to these questions do they remember?

Connect

What to Do

Ask the students what they thought of Jewish religious customs and ideas before the trip. Ask them to write in their Spiritual Journal what they most value in their learning from this trip.

What's Next?

What to Do

Say: "You have experienced some changes in your ideas of Jewish people and Jewish religion because of your contact with them. So did the ancient Jews experience changes because of their contacts with Persians and Greeks. Our next lesson will show us a few of these changes and their importance for us today.

140

People of Note

"Malachi"

The Book of Malachi was written during the period between the prophecy of Haggai and the arrival of Nehemiah in Judah (approximately in 445 B.C.E.). It is the last book of the Old Testament in the Christian arrangement of the Bible.

Early translators thought that the word, "malachi"—an unusual Hebrew word—was the name of the prophet who wrote this book. The word is, in fact, merely a title meaning, "My Messenger." It is used twice, in Malachi 1:1 and 3:1, to refer to the book's author, indicating the author's desire to remain anonymous. The title is a good choice for a name, though, because in a sense all of the prophets were "malachi:" messengers from God.

The Book of Malachi is the source of the Jewish belief that the prophet Elijah will return to earth (*Malachi* 3:23–24). Barely three chapters in length, the Book of Malachi can be read quickly.

Ezra's Motives   Ezra's motives in forbidding marriages between Jews and Gentiles were not based on hatred of a particular race of people. Rather, Ezra understood that the very survival of the Jewish people depended on their preserving their religious culture. Marriages between Jews and Gentiles had always meant a mixing of the two religious cultures. Ezra's demand served to purify the Jewish religion from the influences of other religions to insure its survival.

Given this motive, Ezra's command can be viewed as a necessary measure taken to save Jewish culture. Still, it may seem to have been a harsh reaction, especially unfair to those non-Jews whom Ezra forced out of Judah.

The Center of Jewish Life

Ezra's rule against intermarriage helped the new nation of Judah survive. The future of Judaism, however, would no longer depend on the nation of Judah. Following the Exile, the majority of the Jewish people would now live elsewhere than Judah. Although many Jews dreamed of a ruler (a *messiah*) who would be anointed by God to restore the people to Israel, for now the focus would be on religious and cultural solidarity rather than on political unity.

Ezra responded to this new situation by making the Law the center of Jewish life, and for this achievement he is know as the "Father of Judaism." From his time onward, the Jewish people would be known as the people of the Law, or the "people of the book." Ezra looked to the Torah, or Pentateuch, as the unifying basis for all of Jewish life.

There was a danger in Ezra's method, however. Many have accused him of being a legalist who placed a far greater emphasis on the letter of the law than he should have. By raising the importance of law to

Orthodox Jews continue to follow Ezra's law concerning intermarriage. The ceremony binds the couple together as part of the Covenant.

◆ MORE ABOUT THE LESSON

Visiting a Synagogue

You will have to plan well ahead for this trip. The nearest rabbi should be contacted. Tell him or her about your studies and that the subject of this particular lesson is the origin of the synagogue and the importance of the Law. Ask if your students might meet with him and others, perhaps even Jewish youth, to discuss what they are learning. If the synagogue has a youth study program similar to yours, perhaps you could visit their classes, too. Ask also if your class could experience a Sabbath service as part of this visit.

The plan for the conversation should include decisions like: Who will start the discussion after you introduce yourselves and your interests to the rabbi and others? In what order and by whom will the questions be asked? Will any of the students take notes for later recall? About how long should the conversation last?

such a high standard, a false emphasis could be placed on obeying laws simply for the sake of obedience. All law is designed to protect and enhance people's lives, but no law is complete, and there are times when the purpose of a law conflicts with its literal meaning.

Ezra's positive influence cannot be overestimated. Without his efforts, there would have been no focal point for Jewish identity—especially among the people living in the Diaspora. Without the focus on the Law, it is doubtful that Judaism could have survived the influence of Greek culture.

Ezra and the Canon of the Bible

The *Talmud*—the Jewish book that interprets the Law and Tradition—calls Ezra the "second Moses," and says that the Torah would have been given to Israel through Ezra, had not Moses lived first. The Talmud also recognizes Ezra as the person who established the canon of the Tanakh. It was Ezra's Hebrew canon, or list of accepted books, that would later be adopted by the rabbis, and, much later, by the Protestant churches. You will remember that the Catholic Church accepts the Greek canon of the Septuagint. Several books and parts of books included in the Septuagint are not found in Ezra's collection. These books, which are part of the Bible for Catholics but not for Jews and Protestants, are often called *apocrypha*. They include Judith, Tobit, Baruch, 1 and 2 Maccabees, Sirach, and Wisdom, along with parts of Esther and Daniel.

The Synagogue

The Exile in Babylon, through God's guidance, gave Ezra a model for reorganizing Jewish worship, the synagogue, based on Jewish community gatherings in Babylon. Ezra began this reform during his first meeting with the people.

> Now when the seventh month came, the whole people gathered as one man before the Water Gate, and they called upon Ezra the scribe to bring forth the book of the Law of Moses which the Lord prescribed for Israel.
> (Nehemiah 8:2–3)

Synagogue Origins   The origins of the synagogue came from the need to have a meeting area where the Torah could be studied and taught. Jews living in the Diaspora needed a place to worship. Over the next several centuries, synagogues were built in villages in Judah and throughout the Roman empire.

Synagogue Architecture   The architecture of the synagogue was based on the Jerusalem Temple. There was a gathering place open to men, women, and children and a central chamber for prayer and the reading of the Law. The Torah and other scriptural scrolls were contained in a special area. There was no table for sacrifices, because the Temple was the only place where sacrifices could be made. For the same reason, there were no priests in the synagogue. A rabbi, or "teacher," was elected to supervise the worship, teaching, and maintenance of the synagogue.

Synagogue Worship   The Sabbath prayer was the main worship service. The Sabbath started at sundown on Friday. The worship service was quite simple. As it began, everyone would turn toward Jerusalem and then recite a prayer. The prayer was followed by a reading from the Torah according to the particular season of the year. The reader would then offer a comment on what was read. This change enabled Judaism to survive the final destruction of the Temple in 70 C.E., and continues even today.

Scripture Workshop

Hanukkah

A mark of modern Jewish identity is the Jewish celebration of the Feast of Light, or *Hanukkah,* which lasts for eight days in December. The feast commemorates the Maccabees' victory over the Seleucid king, Antiochus IV, the purification of the Temple, and the people's rededication to God and the Law.

The story of this ceremony is found in 1 Maccabees 4:26–59. Read it and then answer these questions:

1. Describe the Temple as the Maccabees found it after their victory.
2. What do you suppose the "Abomination" mentioned was?
3. What did the Maccabees do with the altar that had been desecrated?
4. How long is the festival?
5. When is the festival supposed to occur?

MORE ABOUT THE TEXT

Celebrating Hanukkah

Hanukkah celebrates the rededication of the Temple by Judas Maccabee on the twenty-fifth day of Chislev (December) in 164 B.C.E., following its desecration by Antiochus Epiphanes three years earlier.

The feast has been celebrated since that time. Since the tabernacle was destroyed in 70 C.E., the feast has focused on the ritual of lights. On the first night of the eight-day feast, a lamp is lit before each house, and on each of the following nights of the feast, another lamp is lit until the last night of the celebration. The historian Josephus called it the "Feast of Lights." He said that the lights symbolized the freedom that shone unexpectedly upon the Jews. Other writers have suggested that the lamps (or candles) are lit as a symbol of the importance of the Law.

Have You Considered?

1. Allow for a variety of opinions. Both points of view can be defended.
2. Encourage students to respond to this question on the basis of their own personal experience. Make sure the discussion returns to the policies of Ezra and Nehemiah.
3. An example of a country in which the religious and political leaders are the same would be the Islamic Republic of Iran. The difficulty with such a system is that political leaders abuse their spiritual authority to force their policies onto people.

Bonus Focus for You

Review Nehemiah 8:9–12 again. Does such a celebration reflect your own attitude toward the laws of God? Do you consider them a gift or find them a burden? Is your attitude one you cherish and would like to keep? Or would you rather change it? Why? Write your reflections in your journal.

Scripture Workshop

1. After the Maccabees' victory they found the sanctuary desolate, the altar desecrated, the gates burned, weeds growing in the courts as in a forest, and the priests' chambers demolished.
2. The Abomination was a pagan religious statue which the Seleucids had erected in the Temple.
3. The Maccabees tore down the desecrated altar, storing the stones on the Temple hill until a prophet could decide what to do with them. Then, they built a new altar.
4. The festival of Hanukkah lasts for eight days.
5. The festival begins early in the morning on the twenty-fifth day of the ninth month, named *Chislev.*

◆ New Religious Ideas

Welcome

Greet the students in a way new for you: shake their hands, or bow to them, or speak very kindly in a foreign language—whatever you want to do is fine. Be as elaborate (a Japanese Tea Party, possibly) or as silly as you like.

What to Do

Ask the students for their reaction to your new style of greeting. After a few responses, say: "It is so easy to get used to things being done in a certain way, isn't it? Sometimes we tend to think that the way things are done today is the way they have always been and the way they will always be. But that is not true. Perhaps the Jews, after the Exile, thought that every possible new thing had happened to them. But there were still new ideas to be met and assimilated into their thinking. Life for them and for us does not go forever on automatic."

Pray with your students. Include a prayer of thanksgiving for the variety of newness in life and ask for the blessings of openness and interest in new ideas, new ways of doing daily things.

Introducing the Lesson

Teaching Objectives

By the end of this lesson the students will be able to:
• Explain how the concepts of angelic and demonic beings entered Jewish belief.
• Discuss how Jewish belief was changed by outside influences concerning the qualities of God, the afterlife and judgment, and the intercessory power of prayer.
• Recognize and explain the purpose of Apocalyptic literature.

Functions of the Priestly Office

The end of the exile gave Ezra an opportunity to restore the the priests to their proper function in Temple ritual. Prior to the Exile, the king would commonly offer the sacrifice. After the Exile, Nehemiah and Ezra told the people that this practice was wrong, and that only the priests were to offer sacrifice.

After the Exile, the head of the clergy became designated as the high priest. When Joshua, the high priest, assumed the position of leadership in 537 B.C.E., the office took on a new dual role. The high priest became the political leader as well as the religious leader. Following the Maccabee's revolt in the second century B.C.E., the high priest also adopted the title of "king." Although it sounds as if making the priest and the king the same person might be a good idea it didn't actually work out well. The holders of the office quickly became corrupt, using it for their own personal power.

On the positive side, the restored priestly office was of great religious benefit to the Jews. The high priests encouraged the study of the Law and Jewish traditions. Through their efforts, people in all walks of life became familiar with the Torah.

The reformation efforts of Nehemiah and Ezra helped the people not only to recall their past, but to look with hope to the future as well—a future in which their identity would be based on allegiance to God's Law, as found in the written word. The Jewish identity of this period was one of restored spirit and hope that Yahweh was still their God and that they were still God's people.

Have You Considered?

1. What do you think of Ezra's rule against intermarriage? Do you think it was justified by the need for survival, or was it unfair to the foreign wives? Could it be both? Explain your answer.
2. Describe a situation in which someone followed the letter of the law rather than its spirit. How would you have handled the situation differently?
3. What do you think the dangers would be in having religious leaders serve as political leaders as well? Do you think it would be more difficult for people to challenge their decisions? Why or why not? Are there situations today where the political and religious leader of a country are the same person?

◆ New Religious Ideas

The prophets recognized that Yahweh sometimes used foreign nations to teach Israel lessons. For example, Isaiah said that Assyria had been Yahweh's "rod in anger" and "staff in wrath," with which the Northern kingdom was punished for its disobedience (Isaiah 10:5). After the Exile, the people also realized that foreign nations could also be God's instruments for positive change.

Following the return to Judah, the Jews were dominated by a series of foreign powers. As was mentioned earlier, the Jews did not willingly submit to the influences of these nations. There were, though, ideas and beliefs expressed by these other religious traditions that expanded Judah's understanding of God. Because of the demands of the Covenant, however, the Jews never merely "borrowed" these new ideas and beliefs. Instead, they used them as gifts from God. They studied them deeply and eventually made them a part of their religion, faithful to their unique tradition.

The Persian Influence: Angels and Demons

While Cyrus allowed the Jews to return to Judah and rebuild the Temple, Judah was not given its political freedom. It remained a Persian province. During their 200 year rule, Persian beliefs gradually found their way into Jewish beliefs and practices.

The Persian religion was founded by Zoroaster, who lived around 600 B.C.E. He was a monotheist, who gave the name *Ahura Mazda* ("God of Heaven") to the one God he worshipped. In the Book of Ezra, this same title is used for Yahweh nine times, showing just how much Jewish religious practice was influenced by Persian religious thought.

Zoroaster taught that God created everything in existence, and was ultimately just and totally powerful. According to Zoroaster, the universe was also filled with other spirits.

• The two most powerful of these lesser spirits or "angels," were a chief good spirit and a chief evil spirit.
• Each one had its own creation within the creation of the one God, and there was a constant battle between the forces of good and the forces of evil.
• Below these two chief spirits, there were numerous lesser good and evil spirits.

MORE ABOUT THE TEXT

Demonic Influences

At this time in history people thought physical diseases and emotional illnesses were caused by demons inhabiting the sick person. We no longer believe demons cause disease, because we look for the physical causes. Yet throughout Christian history, the presence of demons has been mentioned as an experience that sometimes comes to people. Today, once again, there is considerable talk about it.

This lesson is a good opportunity to help students to understand that God is always stronger than any evil influences that might exist. Persian thought mistakenly assumed that good and evil powers were equal. Judaism recognized—and we need to remember—that the powerful love of God is stronger than any form of demonic activity. Christians depend upon God, who is always present to help when asked.

Signorelli, Angels at the Last Judgement. Sixteenth Century.

The Persian beliefs of angels and devils influenced Jewish thought. The Jews did not simply adopt these teachings, however. Angels were seen solely as messengers of God and never as gods themselves.

We know from Acts 23:8 in the New Testament that some Jewish groups, especially the Pharisees, accepted the existence of angels and demons as fact. Although the Jews adopted the idea of angels from the Persians, they developed it in light of their own experience of Yahweh.

- Where Zoroaster had thought that the good and evil spirits had separate creations, Jewish tradition emphasized that there is only one created world, and it is good.
- Where the Persians saw angels and spirits as separate powers, apart from God, the Jews recognized God's supreme power over all that existed.

In this way, the Jews acknowledged the role of spiritual beings, without forgetting that all real power flowed from Yahweh.

The Qualities of God

After the Persians, the Jews were ruled over by a series of Hellenistic kingdoms. The Greeks had very definite ideas about God. Although Greek mythology was full of bloodthirsty, petty behavior among their gods, these images were not taken literally by most educated people. Their understanding of God came from philosophy, which thought of God as eternal, unchanging, all-powerful, and completely perfect in every respect.

Although Jews had always known of Yahweh's power, they were also accustomed to thinking of Yahweh as capable of love and hate, anger and compassion, and as someone who acted in human history. From the Greeks, the Jews learned to express God's complete perfection in precise philosophical terms. However, they never lost their sense of Yahweh as active and passionate for them. Again, therefore, they adapted these ideas to their tradition, and in so doing arrived at a deeper understanding of God.

The Second Book of Maccabees shows the influence of this process, in which the Jewish and Greek understandings of God are fused. In it, God's power is described by the qualities of justice, kindness, and providence. God is active in the lives of the people and has chosen them specially. The Jewish priest Jonathan prayed:

> Lord God, creator of all things, awesome and strong, just and merciful, the only king and benefactor, who alone are gracious, just, almighty, and eternal, Israel's savior from all evil, who chose our forefathers and sanctified them.
>
> (2 Maccabees 1:24–25)

Afterlife and Judgment

The ideas of an "afterlife" and of "eternal judgment" did not appear in the Old Testament prior to the Exile. The Jewish people, on the whole, had not believed in an afterlife. When you died, you were simply dead, period. Their name for the place where the spirits of the dead went is *sheol*. The spirits in sheol, however, lost their individual personality, and simply existed in a vague "holding pattern."

Persian religion preached the reality of an afterlife; it was viewed as a time when the dead would be resurrected and judged, and then sent to heaven or hell according to their earthly deeds. After the time of Alexander, the Greeks also developed the idea of an afterlife. They stressed that some gods loved human beings enough to make sure that they had a happy fate after death, and these gods could be approached through secret rituals called "mystery cults." On the other hand, the unrighteous would be punished in the afterlife by physical torment.

◆ MORE ABOUT THE LESSON

God's Qualities

The students' discussion of the qualities of God is not meant to yield correct answers, but to stimulate their thinking and to exercise their young, growing powers of discrimination. Their understanding will change with the years, if they can be involved in pondering the questions now. Help them see that the Bible never makes a final statement of how God is. The writers of the Bible recognized that our understanding of God continues to grow and will continue to grow. This does not mean that God changes. Rather, God is so much beyond our limited human capacity that any words we attempt to use to explain God cannot come close to actually describing God.

Help students understand that just because an idea was incorporated from another culture doesn't make the idea wrong. Judaism accepted ideas from other cultures as God's gifts.

What to Do

Form small groups. Say: "Some of the religious ideas that we take for granted were not originally part of ancient Israel's religious tradition, but were introduced to the faith during the period of Persian and Greek domination." Ask students to discuss each of these questions briefly: "What do you think of demons and angels? Do you believe in an afterlife (heaven and hell)? What do you imagine the afterlife will be like? Do you pray to saints or other people that have died? Why or why not?"

Development

What to Do

1. Still in small groups, have the students read "New Religious Ideas," (not including "Apocalyptic Literature"). Ask the students to review in their minds what they know about God. Have them list the qualities of God that they believe to be true, and any other qualities God seems to have in the Bible which they do not believe to be true. Suggest that they be ready to explain their answers.

2. A spokesperson from each group reads its list to the whole class. Invite the listening groups to challenge the lists of the others with questions like "Why do you believe that?" "Why do you reject that?"

3. Have the students read "Apocalyptic Literature" and "Understanding More About" in the text. Remind them that Ezekiel wrote to describe the symbols which he had seen in his visions. So Ezekiel's work was symbolic, but not apocalyptic, because it did not refer to events expected at the end of an age. Daniel is quite different in that regard.

4. Have the students read Daniel 2:31–44 as an example of symbolic language (and an interpretation) to express ideas. Have them read Daniel 7:1–14 as an example of apocalyptic symbolism. What difference do the students see between these two readings?

5. Have the students do "Bible Activity" number 2. When they have drawn pictures as suggested (and they don't need to show them to anyone!), ask if these pictures are symbols for them. Do they evoke the ideas expressed in words in the Bible verses?

6. Lead the class discussion of the questions in "Have You Considered?" Add this question to the first item: "Could you consider your personal pictures of angels and demons as symbolic language? Why or why not?"

7. Say: "Jonah is a piece of inspired fiction in the Bible. It is a funny story as well as a teaching story, and it includes some symbols. Please turn to 'Bible Activity' number 5 and complete it now."

8. Pray with your students. Offer a simple thanksgiving for the students' participation in this lesson and blessings on the rest of their day.

Practicing the Skills

What to Do

Have the students read 2 Maccabees 2:1–42 and 15:12–16, looking for all the ideas mentioned in "New Religious Ideas." Have them write down the verse numbers for each idea. Have volunteers read aloud the verses that express each idea. Ask how many of the students have known and loved someone who has died—a friend or family member. Have they ever thought of asking that person to pray to God for them? Have them write a "letter" or prayer to that person in their Spiritual Journal, expressing what they would like them to ask God for, on their behalf.

Recall

Have the students write their answers to the "Chapter 8 Review Q/A," Section Two. Ask them to answer this question also: "What was the single most vivid memory you have from our field trip to the synagogue?"

The vivid imagery of the afterlife, which came from the Persian and Greek traditions, definitely influenced Jewish authors. As Jews grew in their understanding of the afterlife, they came to believe in a final judgment and the resurrection of the dead.

As had happened with other foreign religious ideas, however, these concepts were enhanced as they passed into Jewish tradition. The Jews did not understand resurrection simply as a return to life as it had been; they believed that Yahweh would create new lives for them in a new world. In this way they associated their belief in judgment and resurrection with the prophets' prediction of a coming "Day of the Lord" which would mark the end of the present order of existence.

The story found in 2 Maccabees 7:1–42 presents the themes of afterlife and judgment. This is the story of a woman and her seven sons who are *martyred* (when someone is killed for his or her faith) because they will not give up the Jewish Law. This story expresses the belief that the just are rewarded for their goodness and the wicked are punished for their crimes. The story also expresses the belief in the resurrection of the dead:

- God will raise the just to new life with their bodies fully restored.
- The sins of the wicked, however, merit punishment; they will suffer and not share in the resurrection.

As the first brother pointed out to Antiochus:

You are depriving us of this life, but the King of the world will raise us up to live again forever. It is for His laws that we are dying.

(2 Maccabees 7:8)

Intercession

Both the Greeks and the Romans believed it was possible to call upon their dead ancestors to intercede for them with the gods. This idea is called "intercession," and it is first expressed in the Second Book of Maccabees.

From 2 Maccabees we learn of the value of intercessory prayer in which both the living and dead can help their brothers and sisters attain full salvation. Second Maccabees 15:12–16 tells how, prior to battle, Judas Maccabeus related a vision to his soldiers in which he saw Onias, a former high priest, praying with outstretched arms for the entire Jewish community. This revelation introduced the belief that the dead pray for us before God; a whole new concept in bibilical faith.

From the Greeks and the Romans the Jews learned to call upon their ancestors for support in prayer. Unlike the Greeks and Romans, however, the Jews never developed a "cult of the dead" in which they worshipped their ancestors. The Jews realized that only Yahweh deserved worship. Instead, they came to understand that the dead, preserved through the love of God, could still help the living through prayer.

Apocalyptic Literature

The term "apocalyptic" refers to the visions and warnings given by the prophets, such as those made by Isaiah and Jeremiah, announcing what will happen at the end of the present age. In the Persian and Greek periods, apocalyptic warnings became more frequent, and they developed into a style of literature all their own.

Daniel The best example of apocalyptic literature in the Old Testament is the Book of Daniel.

Pinturicchio, *Resurrection*, Fifteenth Century.

The idea of an afterlife and resurrection entered Jewish thought through Persian influences.

◆ MORE ABOUT THE LESSON

The Book of Jonah

Written in the period after the Exile, the Book of Jonah is a humorous story with an important theological message. In many ways, Jonah is the Bible's response to an extreme interpretation of the teaching of Ezra. Ezra's insistence on the purity of cultic practices, when taken to the extreme, would exclude all other races and faiths from God's grace. The writer of Jonah did not agree, so Jonah's story is told as irony.

Jonah, a true believer, refuses to carry out God's message to preach repentance to the hated Assyrians. Each time Jonah balks, God refuses to take "No" for an answer. When Jonah finally does as God commands, the Assyrians repent immediately, something the Jews never did. Jonah cannot accept God's graciousness to the Assyrians; God's concern should be for the Jews only. The writer says that God works as God wishes, not according to our prejudices.

Daniel 2:32–35 illustrates this well. This book is set during the Babylonian Exile, but it was clearly written during the reign of Antiochus IV, most likely between 167 and 164 B.C.E. after the Temple had been desecrated but before the Maccabees' revolt.

Chapters 7–12 are the main apocalyptic section of the book. They recount visions and symbols which purport to predict the future. They tell of the end of captivity for those Jews living in Babylon during the Exile, and of the end of persecution for those Jews oppressed by the Greeks centuries later. The effect on the hearers of these visions was to assure them that God had known all along about the modern persecutions, and that God was very much in control of their history.

Symbolic Language   Apocalyptic literature is filled with symbolic language. It tries to communicate what the experience of seeing God is like.

You probably use symbolic language regularly. Symbolic language helps us to express our feelings and experiences most vividly. If the day is very hot you might say, "It's as hot as a furnace outside." Is that statement literally true? Of course not. Furnaces reach temperatures well over 300°F. The temperature outside is merely 98° in the shade. But, 98° does not communicate the idea of oppressive heat nearly as well as the word "furnace."

Symbolism, then, evokes feelings as well as facts, enriching the ideas. As you remember, the prophets Isaiah and Jeremiah used symbolic images to express their visions of God.

Symbolic language also very easy to misunderstand or misinterpret. Unfortunately, symbolic language is sometimes taken literally by those who misunderstand its purpose. In Daniel 7:1–14, Daniel has a vision in which he sees a beast devouring the entire earth. He says that this beast will have its way for "a year, two years, and a half-year" before it is destroyed by God. On this basis, various groups have tried to calculate when God will end the present age.

Apocalyptic literature is not designed to be read literally. Its purpose is, through the use of symbols and warnings, to assure people that God knows their struggles, and that God's help is on the way. Again, the events of history are used to bring people to a new understanding of God's design.

Have You Considered?

1. Describe your own understanding of angels and demons. How do you picture their appearance? What do you think their functions are?
2. Apocalyptic literature is usually popular among groups who feel that they are oppressed. Why do you suppose this is? How does apocalyptic literature offer them hope?

Spiritual Reflection

Rededication Ceremony

During part of the modern Hanukkah ceremony, Jews place lighted wicks in dishes of olive oil and read a prayer of dedication. You can rededicate yourself to God through a similar ceremony.

What would you like to change in your life? How can you live more in touch with God's love? Decide what you need to do and how you need to change your life in order to rededicate it to God. Then, light a candle and speak this psalm prayer aloud.

Let my cry come before you, O Lord; in keeping with your word, give me discernment. My lips pour forth your praise, because you teach me your statutes. May my tongue sing of your promise, for all your commands are just. Let your hand be ready to help me, for I have chosen your precepts. I long for your salvation, O Lord, and your law is my delight. Let my soul live to praise you.

(Psalm 119:169, 171–175a)

Connect

What to Do

Say: "When we look at new ideas, we often find that our lives change. Sometimes a new idea shows us something that we would like to be different, sometimes a new idea simply makes something possible that we didn't know was possible before. Now is a good time to remember that the Jews were open to new ideas and changes, and to ask ourselves if we are open in a similar way. To help us do that, we are going to do the "Spiritual Reflection" as a group ceremony."

What's Next?

What to Do

Have the students turn the page, so they see the scene from "The Karate Kid." Ask them what they think that movie might have to do with the Bible. Don't answer the question—let it hang for the next lesson.

Have You Considered?

1. Allow students to express their own understandings of these concepts. Point out to students that most of their visual images of angels and demons comes out of centuries of western art, and the religious poetry of authors such as Dante, rather than the Bible. The idea than angels have wings and demons have tridents are artistic embellishments, not articles of faith.
2. Apocalyptic literature reassures readers that God is in charge of events, and a divine plan is at work in the present events of history. It also tells readers that God has planned a future deliverance which will end their suffering and punish the wicked. All these messages are of tremendous comfort to groups that are oppressed and that question why God allows such things to happen to them.

Bonus Focus for You ——————

Consider Jonah. What feelings did he have that you also have experienced? Did you need something as dramatic as Jonah did to teach you? How does God generally teach you your next step in trust and obedient growth? Write your reflections in your journal.

Q/A

Section One

1. Jews living in Babylon would not want to return to Jerusalem because in many ways their lives were comfortable there: they were economically prosperous and militarily secure. Also, the return posed other difficult challenges.

2. Relations were tense because the Samaritans feared the rebuilding of the Temple would make the Jews a national and economic rival. Also, both the Jews and the Samaritans called themselves people of the Covenant.

3. Haggai said that rebuilding the Temple was their priority.

4. Nehemiah successfully rebuilt the city of Jerusalem.

5. Examples of Hellenization include: Jewish businessmen engaging in Greek religious practices to solidify trading relationships, Jewish youth participating in Greek education, and the translation of the Old Testament into Greek.

6. Many Jews opposed Hellenization because they saw it as a threat to the Covenant and a betrayal of the Law, since the Jews were supposed to be unlike other nations.

7. The Ptolemies were the Hellenistic successors of Alexander who ruled Egypt; the Seleucids were Hellenistic kings who ruled Syria. Both groups fought for control of Palestine.

8. The Maccabees were Jewish rebels who defeated the Seleucids and rededicated the Temple in Jerusalem in 164 B.C.E. The victory of the Maccabees marked the last period of Jewish political independence until the creation of the modern state of Israel in 1948.

CHAPTER 8 REVIEW

Q/A

Section One

1. Why would Jews living in Babylon not want to return to Judah?
2. Why were relations between the Samaritans and the returning Jews tense?
3. What did Haggai tell the people?
4. What was Nehemiah's major accomplishment?
5. Provide two examples of the process called "Hellenization."
6. Why did many Jews oppose Hellenization?
7. Identify: Ptolemies, Seleucids
8. Who were the Maccabees?

Section Two

1. How did God use foreign nations for the betterment of Judah?
2. Why is Ezra called "the father of Judaism"?
3. What was the danger in Ezra's emphasis on the Law?
4. What is a synagogue?
5. Define: rabbi, high priest
6. Cite two differences between the Persian and the Israelite views of angels and demons.
7. How did the Jews adapt Greek ideas about God?
8. What is the purpose of symbolism in apocalyptic literature?

BIBLE ACTIVITY

1. Nehemiah 11:1–2 describes the willingness of some of the Jews to make a sacrifice for God by moving into Jerusalem's ruins for the benefit of the whole community. What is one sacrifice that you have made? How did your sacrifice benefit another?
2. Read the selection of the hymn of the three young men in Daniel 3:52–90. Illustrate your favorite verses.
3. Read Nehemiah 8:1–12. Imagine that you were in the crowd listening to Ezra. Write your reactions to Ezra's words.
4. Read Ezra 4:1–5. Write additional details explaining to the crowd of Samaritans why they should not be permitted to help with the rebuilding of the Temple.
5. Read the entire Book of Jonah. Retell the incident of the vine (chapter four) and explain its symbolism.

Athens, Greece, Acropolis, Fifth Century B.C.E.

BIBLE ACTIVITY

1. Responses will vary with the individual. Ask students to compare their experiences with the situation faced by those who decided to move into Jerusalem.

2. Ask students to explain why they chose to illustrate these verses in their particular way. Use the better illustrations to help teach the verses to the class.

3. Ask students to imagine the emotional state of Jews who had recently returned from the Exile out of faith and a commitment to live the Covenant. How would hearing the law recited in Jerusalem have made them feel?

4. Expect student responses to vary, but ensure that students give reasons which are legitimate in light of their knowledge of ancient Judaism and the relationship with the Samaritans. Other reasons might include: the

GLOSSARY

- **Ahura Mazda:** The chief Persian god, referred to as "God of Heaven"; this phrase is used of Yahweh in Ezra.
- **Apocalyptic literature:** A stylized and symbolic literature that spoke about immediate problems and their solutions as if they had happened in the past.
- **Apocrypha:** Term for the books and parts of books included in the Septuagint, but not in Ezra's canon of the Old Testament.
- **Feast of Booths:** Originally an agricultural festival during which the people would live in outdoor huts, this festival also became a celebration of the Torah in the time of Ezra.
- **Hanukkah:** Eight-day celebration which commemorates the victory of the Maccabees over the Seleucids.
- **Hellenization:** To "hellenize" means to imitate Greek culture.
- **High Priest:** Title invented under Ezra; the term referring to the chief priest.
- **Intercessory prayer:** Prayers of the living or dead that have benefit for the salvation of all in the human race.
- **Maccabees:** Family of conservative Jews, led by Judas Maccabeus, who revolted against the Seleucids.
- **Martyr:** From the Greek word for "witness;" a person who dies for his or her faith.
- **Rabbi:** The "teacher" of the Law.
- **Samaritans:** Cultural group made up of descendants of the northern tribes who intermarried with Canaanites and Assyrians.
- **Seleucids:** Kings after Alexander the Great who ruled Syria.
- **Septuagint:** The Greek translation of the Hebrew Scriptures.
- **Sheol:** Place where Jews believed the "shades" of the dead were kept.
- **Synagogue:** The meeting place of the Jews for study and worship.

UNDERSTANDING MORE ABOUT:

Apocalyptic Literature

Between the Maccabees and the time of Jesus (usually called the "Intertestamental Period"), apocalyptic literature was abundant. Several apocalyptic books were written during this period, among them 1 and 2 Enoch, Jubilees, and the Testaments of the Patriarchs.

These books typically are even more mystical and symbolic than the apocalyptic parts of the Bible. The chief difference between these books and those in the Bible, however, is that intertestamental texts are much more pronounced in their opposition to the Romans. Jews resented the presence of Roman troops as occupiers, and they hated the taxes and forced labor that Rome demanded. Jews dreamed of a day when God would send a messiah, an anointed king, to overthrow the Romans and reestablish the throne of David. Apocalyptic authors used symbols and visions to describe the coming of the messiah and the punishment that he would inflict on the unrighteous, especially the Romans.

These books were not included in the Bible, but they show us the hopes and fears of many Jews at an important time. Their popularity is reflected in the fact that the New Testament Book of Jude quotes the apocalyptic Book of Enoch.

Chapter 8 Review ◆ 147

Section Two

1. Through contact with foreign nations, the Jews deepened their own religious understanding. For example, contact with the Persians led the Jews to expand their understanding of angels and demons.

2. Ezra is called the "father of Judaism" because he organized the people into a religious body, giving them institutions such as the synagogue and the canon of the Jewish Bible, and he made the Law the center of Jewish life.

3. The danger of Ezra emphasis on Law is that such emphasis can become one-sided and legalistic, harming the very people it was intended to serve.

4. A synagogue is a gathering place for worship, which allowed those Jews in the Diaspora who could not visit the Temple to continue their worship of Yahweh.

5. A rabbi is a teacher, one who presides in the synagogue. The high priest was the head of the clergy who served both as the religious and political leader. This office was developed by Ezra to respond to the need for new forms of leadership after the Exile. The office of priest no longer exists in Judaism because there is no Temple in which to offer sacrifice.

6. Two important differences are:
   1) Jews believed that there is only the created world, and it is good;
   2) Jews acknowledged God's supreme power over all that exists, including angels and demons.

7. The Jews took Greek ideas about God's permanence and perfection, and about intercessory prayer, and adapted to their own unique belief in Yahweh, a personal God who responded to their needs.

8. Symbolism aims to explain a difficult concept by use of more familiar words and images.

self-interested motives of the Samaritans, the religious differences between the two peoples, and the desire of the people to create a symbol of their return to the land.

5. The author is clearly pointing out Jonah's selfishness, since he appears to be more concerned over this plant which brought him shade than over the fate of the people of Nineveh. The vine may also be a symbol for the fate of Israel; it was God who built it up, and then God who tore it down. If so, what right had the people to complain about God's action? Instead, they must trust in God to make things turn out as they should.

Wisdom

Chapter Overview

This chapter looks at the biblical books known collectively as the "Wisdom literature." Students will study how Wisdom literature was present in all Middle Eastern cultures, examine each of the Wisdom books, and recognize the importance of wisdom for living a good life.

Teaching Objectives

By the end of this chapter students will be able to:
- Define wisdom.
- Demonstrate an understanding of the importance of the Wisdom tradition in Judaism.
- Explain the methods by which wisdom was learned and taught.
- Identify the qualities of a wise person and explain the importance of those qualities for daily living.

Welcome

What to Do

Meet the students at the door with a basket or hat full of sayings from the Wisdom literature.

Have the students read their "slip of wisdom," and reflect for a moment on whether it has any relationship to their life. Ask a few volunteers to share their reflections.

Pray with your students. Include thanksgiving for the efforts made by people in the past to discover the best way to live, and for their willingness to communicate their discoveries. Ask blessings on your students' interest in learning a wise approach to living.

CHAPTER

9

Wisdom

1200	**1200 B.C.E.** ● Amen-em-ope's wisdom teaching in Egypt
1000	**1000** ● First written collections of wisdom traditions under David ● First collection of Proverbs
	700 ● Wisdom of Ahiqar in Egypt ● Poetic section of Job?
	587 ● Increased interest in wisdom in Exile ● Prose section of Job? ● Final collection of Proverbs, Psalms
500	**510** ● Confucius's wisdom teaching in China
	460 ● Socrates's wisdom teaching in Greece
	400 ● Song of Songs
	300 ● Impact of Greek wisdom traditions ● Ecclesiastes
	200 ● Writing of the Bhagavad-Gita in India
100	**150** ● Sirach, Wisdom

Legend
- ● General History
- ● Biblical History
- ● Jewish History
- ● Books written

I t was 6 am and Daniel was not in the mood to read the note he found posted on Mr. Miyagi's door: "Gone fishing. Paint the house. Remember: up-down, up-down."

Daniel ripped the note. He kicked the paint cans. He threw the paint brush. What was going on here? Miyagi had promised to teach him karate, and all Daniel had done so far was polish Miyagi's cars, sand his deck, and paint his fence.

"I haven't learned a thing," Daniel yelled on Miyagi's return. "Things are not as they seem," Miyagi reminded Daniel.

If you've seen the movie *The Karate Kid*, you know the story. Daniel, a new student in high school, is threatened by a group of bullies. He finds comfort in the workroom of the building's manager, an older man from Japan who shapes bonsai trees. Daniel appreciates the man's kindness,

◆ MORE ABOUT THE LESSON

Preparation

Prepare these slips of wisdom ahead of time: one verse on a slip, then folded in half. Teacher's Resource 9A provides a list of sayings that you can quickly prepare for the students. If you wish to prepare your own materials, consider the following:

Sirach 2:12–13—"Take care of your father when he is old; grieve him not as long as he live. Even if his mind fail, be considerate with him."

Sirach 4:1–3—"My son, rob not the poor man of his livelihood; force not the eyes of the needy to turn away. A hungry man grieve not, a needy man anger not; do not exasperate the downtrodden; delay not to give to the needy."

Sirach 9:10—"Discard not an old friend, for the new one cannot equal him. A new friend is like new wine which you drink with pleasure only when it has aged."

and listens carefully to his words. As Daniel begins to trim his own tree, Miyagi tells him: "Close your eyes and trust. Make a picture. Nothing else exists in the whole world except the tree. Trust the picture."

Eventually Miyagi agrees to be Daniel's karate master. "I promise to teach you karate. I say, you do. That's your part." What follows is a series of unusual orders given by Miyagi.

"Wash my cars, then wax them. Wax on with right hand. Wax off with left hand."

Daniel obeys, but resents being treated like a servant. After he blows up over Miyagi's note, the karate master shows Daniel how each of the movements he has perfected by waxing, sanding, and painting are used in karate.

Daniel learned more than karate from Mr. Miyagi; he was given a new view of life. He was able to understand more about how all the pieces of his life fit into the whole. He really was able to see things in a new way, much as Miyagi had promised him: "Things are not as they seem."

For centuries, the people of Israel sought out masters for answers to life's big questions in much the same way that Daniel attached himself to Miyagi. These wise teachers, called *sages*, searched for the best quality of life. They wanted to be in tune with universal wisdom. They sought it by observation and practice, then passed it along to their students.

The oral teachings of the sages were eventually developed into the Wisdom literature of the Bible. Wisdom literature was designed to teach people how to live well and wisely. In this chapter, you will explore Wisdom literature. You'll look at some of the questions these books pose and the answers they provide about the real meaning of life.

The movie "The Karate Kid" offers an example of how students learn a skill through a master's teaching. Students of biblical wisdom also learn through the patient teaching found in the Wisdom literature.

Introducing the Chapter

Students are to learn what it means for a person to be wise and recognize how this wisdom can be gained.

What to Do

• Have the students read the story of Daniel on the opening spread. Ask the students to share their first reaction to this story and/or their response to the movie, if they have seen it. How has Daniel learned wisdom from Mr. Miyagi? What kind of wisdom would students expect to find in the Bible?

• Introduce the word "sage." Ask students to define the word for you. (A "sage" is a wise person who is able and willing to hand down his or her wisdom to a disciple or student.) Do they think of Mr. Miyagi as a sage?

Using the Timeline

Have the students read down the timeline, noticing how many centuries the Israelite Wisdom tradition was developing in written form. Notice the other Wisdom traditions mentioned there as well: Egyptian, Chinese, Greek, and Indian. What do students make of the many different Wisdom traditions?

MORE ABOUT THE TEXT

The Wisdom Tradition

• Wisdom in Egypt can be traced back at least to around the year 4000 B.C.E. It is one of the oldest Wisdom traditions—certainly the oldest in the Middle East.

• Confucius (from China) was one of the greatest teachers ever known. Although he was not interested in religion as such, he was profoundly wise about living a balanced life in tune with all of nature.

• Socrates was a Greek philosopher, whose method of teaching was asking students to answer questions, thus gradually leading their thought to the desired conclusion.

• The "Bhagavad Gita" is a long poem of a conversation between a warrior and his charioteer, who is really the Lord Krishna. The Gita sets forth the essence of many centuries of Indian wisdom and understanding.

◆ The Wisdom Tradition: Beginnings

Teaching Objectives

By the end of this lesson students will be able to:

• Define wisdom and identify the elements that make up the Wisdom tradition.

• Demonstrate an understanding of the relationship between the Israelite Wisdom tradition and Wisdom traditions from other cultures.

Development

What to Do

1. Have the students read all of "The Wisdom Tradition: Beginnings."

2. Ask the students to write in their Spiritual Journal their present answers to the four bulleted questions on page 150. Tell them that these should reflect their understanding now, and they'll have a second pass at the same questions toward the end of this chapter.

3. Have the students read Psalms 29 and 68. Ask them to guess what makes these two psalms seem close to the Canaanite approach to wisdom.

4. Have the students complete the "Scripture Workshop." Lead a discussion on their findings, guiding them away from a misunderstanding of "fear of the Lord" as abject fright. When meanings are clear, ask them if they have experienced fear of the Lord in the biblical sense and what it means.

5. Lead the class in a discussion of the questions in "Have You Considered?"

6. Pray with your students. Include in your prayer both the students' interest in Israelite Wisdom literature and their individual need for living wisely.

The Development of Israelite Wisdom

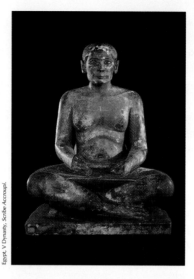

Egypt, V Dynasty, *Scribe Accroupi*.

Israel searched for wisdom from the very beginning. Several wisdom books in the Bible have teachings that have been passed down for thousands of years from Israel's sages, from the time before Israel became a nation after the Exodus from Egypt. The Wisdom tradition developed gradually over many centuries. Growth came as new ideas were developed in response to Israel's neighbors, and as Israel came to new understandings of its tradition in light of changing historical circumstances.

Learning Objectives for Section One

By the end of this section, you will be able to:

• Define wisdom.

• Demonstrate an understanding of the relationship between Israelite wisdom and other ancient Middle Eastern wisdom traditions.

• List and discuss several of the Wisdom books.

◆ The Wisdom Tradition: Beginnings

Every ancient Middle Eastern culture, including Israel, was involved in the search for wisdom. Israel's own Wisdom tradition grew up in the context of this wider Middle Eastern interest. For the Israelites, the search for wisdom was especially important, because it helped them to better live out their relationship with Yahweh. The Israelites studied the Wisdom teachings of other Middle Eastern cultures for any insights they could offer. Before we can focus on this tradition, however, we first have to define the concept of wisdom.

What Is Wisdom?

If you look up the word "wisdom" in a dictionary, you will find a definition that speaks of knowledge or intelligence. Although these words can sometimes be used interchangeably, the Wisdom tradition used them quite differently. To the sage, someone can be wise but have very little knowledge, or someone can be extremely intelligent and yet not be wise. What, then, does the Wisdom tradition mean by wisdom?

"To have wisdom" means to have an understanding of what life is all about and how to live well. The Wisdom tradition is concerned with difficult questions:

• "What is the purpose of life?"
• "What can I do to gain lifelong happiness?"
• "How should I treat other people?"
• "How can I know right from wrong?"

Wisdom also includes the ability to make responsible moral decisions.

You can see from the following example how wisdom differs from knowledge or intelligence. During the Second World War, medical doctors in Nazi concentration camps performed cruel experiments on prisoners, such as plunging them into ice-cold water and observing their reactions. These doctors were not insane. They were well-trained scientists who made

---

MORE ABOUT THE TEXT

Simplicity or Depth?

Each Wisdom tradition is different from every other tradition. However, one experience seems to be common in each: The Wisdom sayings are so simple and straight forward that it is easy to find them, and the ideas they express, too obvious and possibly banal, especially when they are about behavior. This is a sentiment expressed by many modern students of the Israelite Wisdom tradition.

To help students get beyond this apparent banality, ask them to explain what inner, personal capacities are necessary in order to behave in a certain way. For example, in order to be an effective user of karate, one must be confident and calm. One must have a solid grasp of the moves, be well practiced, and always in control. The behaviors labeled "wise" in the Bible also require these same qualities, which a few minutes of reflection can reveal to the students.

careful notes and observations. However, they treated people in a heartless way. Despite their scientific intelligence, these doctors could not see that what they were doing was wrong.

For the ancient Israelites, a wise man was one who knew how to live a moral life of self-discipline, moderation, and justice. Such wisdom depended upon a long period of study and thought, and nowhere was the devotion to wisdom pursued with more dedication than in the ancient Middle East.

Wisdom in the Ancient Middle East

One form of Middle Eastern Wisdom teaching originated in the courts of kings. In Egypt, sages working in the court of the pharaoh developed sayings and stories with which they instructed their young students. They stressed self-control and eloquence as trademarks of the wise person, two qualities someone living at court surely needed. In ancient Egypt, this ideal was called *ma'at*. Other cultures developed similar ideals.

Other sages were not attached to the king's court. These teachers were interested in discovering what a wise life meant for ordinary people. Their instruction emphasized obedience and respect for elders. Later, after the development of cities and trade, wisdom sayings stressed the qualities of honesty and hard work important to merchants.

Israel's Wisdom teachings reflect these common Middle Eastern concerns. Because Wisdom teaching

Raphael, School of Athens, Sixteenth Century.

The study of wisdom has been important throughout human history. This painting by Raphael attempts to capture the great Greek philosophers and scientists at work.

Scripture Workshop

The Fear of the Lord

To find out what "fear of the Lord" is, read:

- Proverbs 2:5, 10:27, 14:25–27, 22:4
- Sirach 1:11–25, 40:27

Now answer the following questions:

1. What does "fear of the Lord" mean?
2. What are the benefits of fearing the Lord?
3. How does "fear of the Lord" develop?

addressed questions about the nature of life and how to live it, it was international. This universality encouraged the sharing of traditions, which is evident in the Wisdom literature of the Old Testament.

- Psalms 29 and 68, for example, seem related to Canaanite wisdom texts.
- Much of the Book of Proverbs is similar, either in form or content, to wisdom sayings drawn from Egyptian culture.

The Israelites were open to these new ideas, but they were always adapted to Israel's unique religious beliefs, especially their faith in Yahweh as the Creator and source of all wisdom.

Faith in Yahweh made the Wisdom tradition of Israel different from those of her Middle Eastern neighbors. In other countries, the search for "wisdom" was not an especially religious act. Most ancient peoples believed that wise living could be learned by observation of nature and society. In Egypt and Babylon, for example, sages did not refer to the gods, nor did they say that a wise person should pray or make sacrifice. Because Israel regarded Yahweh as the creator of both nature and society, however, Israelite wisdom from the beginning emphasized respect for God. This concept was often expressed as "fear" of Yahweh, a word which meant respect and admiration rather than actual fright. This idea is expressed in Proverbs 9:10, "The beginning of wisdom is the fear of the Lord."

Practicing the Skills

What to Do

Have the students read Proverbs 8:1–36, 9:1–6, and 13–18 as examples of the personification of wisdom. Have them locate the verses in these two chapters that express the ideas in each of the paragraphs in "The Personification of Wisdom."

Recall

Have the students write the answers to "Chapter 9 Review Q/A," for Section One, numbers 1–5.

Connect

What to Do

Homework Assignment: Students are to write a description of any one person whom they think is wise. They are to tell why they think this person is wise and name the characteristics of wisdom that person has. How might they learn from that person?

What's Next?

What to Do

Tell the students that in the next two lessons, they will be considering each of the Wisdom Books.

Scripture Workshop

1. Fear of the Lord prolongs life (*Proverbs* 10:27, 14:27); it is a defense for children (*Proverbs* 14:26); it bestows riches, honor and life (*Proverbs* 22:4); it ensures a happy end (*Sirach* 1:11); it gives one peace, and perfect health (*Sirach* 1:16); it awards prudence (*Sirach* 1:22).

2. Fear of the Lord is formed with the faithful in the womb (*Sirach* 1:12), and for those who wish to pursue it, they should obey the commandments and it will come (*Sirach* 1:23).

3. Fear of the Lord means knowledge of God (*Proverbs* 2:5), as well as wisdom and culture, and loyal humility before the Lord (*Sirach* 1:24). In this sense, "fear" might perhaps be better translated as "respect" or even "awe."

MORE ABOUT THE TEXT

Psalm 29 and Psalm 68

Psalm 29 offers a personification of the Lord with a voice so strong that it "breaks the cedars": the Lord controls nature. Psalm 68 is a song of power. Once again, God is seen as the one who controls nature: "The earth quaked; it rained from heaven at the presence of God … a bountiful rain you showered down, O God, upon your inheritance; you restored the land when it languished."

Remember that the Canaanites were very interested in nature and its powers. It's not uncommon to see a certain personification of these powers. One can see commonalties with these psalms. Note that Psalm 68 had brought nature themes and the Exodus themes together; have the students notice that Exodus is uniquely Israelite, while nature themes abound in all the ancient Middle Eastern religions.

1. Any number of examples are possible here. An example of a character who was deeply wise without necessarily being "intelligent" was Morgan Freeman's character in the film "Driving Miss Daisy." Without being able to read, he knew more about life and how to treat others than most people. For an example of someone who is intelligent without being wise, consider Richard Attenborough's character from "Jurassic Park." He was able to develop a method to clone dinosaurs, but not wise enough to ask whether or not he should.

2. The ancient Israelite tradition held that "the beginning of wisdom is fear of the Lord." For them, a humble respect for God was a necessary element of being wise. Students should consider what the consequences can be when human wisdom is substituted for the truth which comes from God. For example, students might consider how wisdom which begins with God's law and human wisdom might differ on issues such as abortion and euthanasia.

3. If God is the author of nature, then in some sense a study of nature should give us insight into the character of God. Allow students to discuss how the experience of a waterfall, or a beautiful sunset, might be a means of revelation for them. Of course, this cannot be carried to extremes—not everything that happens in nature is necessarily the will of God (for example, disease). We live in a fallen world, and that has consequences in nature as well. Students should realize that it is not as simple as saying "it is natural, therefore it is right."

Bonus Focus for You

Read Wisdom 8:22–30, one of the most beautiful descriptions of the qualities of wisdom. What changes might you experience in your life if you developed a devotion to this Lady Wisdom and allowed her to penetrate your own being?

Wisdom Schools

In Israel, as well as elsewhere in the Middle East, sages often banded into groups we call "Wisdom schools." Generally, these were groups of students who studied the wisdom of a master, and developed it into new sayings and stories. In Israel the various Wisdom schools kept alive the sayings, poems, and essays which make up the Wisdom literature of the Bible.

These Wisdom schools developed alongside the historical and prophetic books. Some of the Wisdom literature (many of the Proverbs, for example) are very old, perhaps the oldest material to be found in the Bible. Much of the Wisdom literature was not written until after the Exile, and some books are among the Bible's most recent writings. As the search for the good life continued throughout Israel's history, so did the search for wisdom.

The problems Wisdom literature deals with are universal human themes:

- love
- honor
- honesty
- justice
- the goodness of God

Such themes make the Wisdom literature "timeless." Works such as the Psalms and Book of Job are extremely popular today because people continue to find meaning in their words.

The Personification of Wisdom

In Israel, where goodness was directly connected to the Jewish people's special relationship with Yahweh, wisdom was especially important. This search for wisdom became so intense that Israelite authors began to depict it as an entity who called to people, asked for their obedience, and offered them comfort.

This personification of wisdom comes across most clearly in the Book of Proverbs. There, Wisdom speaks in the same manner as one of the prophets.

She demands obedience to her instructions, and says that her enemies are doomed to destruction. Those who listen to her and follow her voice, however, will find rest and peace. The author contrasts Wisdom to a woman named Folly. Wisdom invites her guests to a great banquet. Folly, a word meaning "error," invites people to a meal of stolen bread and water, which leads to Sheol (something like a land of ghosts). The point of the contrast is that wisdom leads to life, while ignorance brings death.

Wisdom says that she has always existed, and that she assisted God in the act of creation. Wisdom is depicted as measuring the heavens and laying plans for the earth. These images express the Israelite belief that the world exhibits the wisdom of God, and that creation is one way God is revealed to humanity. Studying nature can put us in touch with God's plans and intentions for our lives.

As time went on, a new facet was added to the traditional characterization of Wisdom: not only did she come to reveal truth, but it was her fate to be rejected by her people, to suffer under them, and to return to God. In the period between the Old and New Testaments, Wisdom schools in Israel were very interested in the idea of a "suffering revealer."

The personification of wisdom in the Bible shows that the Wisdom tradition was alive and growing throughout Israel's history. This is because Wisdom teaching answers a very basic human need, the need to know how to live correctly and happily.

Have You Considered?

1. Describe a person, such as a historical figure or a TV character, who was intelligent without being wise, or wise without being intelligent.
2. Ancient Israel's Wisdom tradition differed from those of her neighbors by concentrating on God. Do you think it's possible for a person to be wise without considering God? Why or why not?
3. Do you agree that we can learn about God from studying nature? Provide an example with your answer.

MORE ABOUT THE TEXT

Wisdom Schools

Scholars debate about Wisdom schools and their purpose. Opinions vary, and are represented in the student text by speaking of differing "branches" or types of wisdom.

One possibility not always considered thoroughly is an exact analogy to the story of Daniel and Mr. Miyagi: the master who gives a pupil (or several pupils) semi-secret knowledge that enables the young person to live a life of extraordinary quality and perspective.

By the time of the later Wisdom writings (Sirach, for example), any secret element was probably gone, but in earlier centuries it may have been quite strong. Sayings likes those in Proverbs could have been used as practice for the skill of writing, so the pupil learned the ideas at the same time he learned to write.

◆ The Bible's Wisdom Books

Wisdom writings in the Bible offer an incredible degree of diversity in style, content, and point of view. These books reveal the thoughts of authors who struggled to understand God, the meaning of life, and the moral dimension of human behavior.

Job

The Book of Job is one of the most challenging portions of the Old Testament. Its main subject is the problem of righteous suffering, but it also studies the questions of goodness, evil, justice, and how they relate to human life.

The Book of Job is divided into two major sections. The first, written as prose sometime during the Exile (after 587 B.C.E.), frames the book (chapters 1–2 includes everything in between. The poetic section, believed to have been written during the eighth century B.C.E., contains the complaints of Job, a man who was faithful to Yahweh and yet experienced all sorts of troubles. This section of the book begins by asking the question, "Why do innocent people suffer?" and ends with the admission that only God knows the answer to that question, and God's not telling! Although the prose section reveals that God was only testing Job's faith, scholars believe that this explanation for Job's suffering were not part of the original. They were added to take some of the sting from Job's suffering.

The poetic section of the Book of Job challenges a common opinion found in Wisdom literature, that suffering results from sin. People commonly believed that those who suffered were being punished for evil they had done. The Book of Job rejects this view. Job suffers in spite of his righteous life. When Job is visited by three "friends" who try to convince him that he must have done something wrong, Job strongly disagrees with them. Job knows the truth—he has not sinned—and so continues to affirm his innocence.

Job endures losses, physical pain, and obnoxious visitors. Eventually, after a long period of suffering, Job takes his appeal directly to God and demands a response. When God finally responds to Job (see Chapter 38)—it is not with words, but with an experience deep within Job's heart. Job is satisfied by his experience of God. Job says, "I had heard of You by word of mouth, but now my eye has seen You" (42:5). Now Job's heart understands what his mind cannot comprehend or explain.

Bartolomeo, *The Prophet Job*. Sixteenth Century.

The Book of Job is one of the most unusual stories found in the Bible. A work of fiction, the book considers why evil things happen to good people.

The Book of Sirach

Sirach was written in the late second century or early first century B.C.E. when conflicts between the Jewish tradition and the Hellenistic way of life were at their height. The writer, Ben Sira, was a scribe and a teacher. He had his own academy where he instructed Jewish youth in the true values of life as set forth in the ancient holy writings of Israel. Also, he was an expert in the Prophets, the Law, and the Writings: the entire Tanakh.

The Book of Sirach (also called *Liber Ecclesiasticus* or "Church book") was used by the early Christians to teach the basic principles of good living. The book is written mostly in the form of proverbs. Beginning with Chapter 44, it praises the heroes of Israel and the traditions of the Jewish people, saying that wisdom comes through the Law. Sirach therefore underlines

SECTION TWO

LESSON TWO (pages 153–155)

◆ The Bible's Wisdom Books

Welcome

What to Do

Remind the students that today they will learn about the books of Job, Sirach, Wisdom, and some of the psalms.

Pray with your students. Have the volunteer greeters also lead the prayer today.

Introducing the Lesson

Teaching Objectives

By the end of this lesson students will be able to:

- Discuss the Book of Job as a fictional response to the question, "Why does evil happen to good people?'
- Demonstrate how the Book of Sirach is a guide to good living.
- Explain the Wisdom content of the Book of Psalms.

What to Do

- Introduce students to the story of Clara.

"During her first year of high school Clara excelled. She was well liked by her classmates. There was never a dull moment when Clara was around. Clara was always one of the group, always willing to help. Clara was also a promising athlete. She made the junior varsity basketball team and looked like she would play varsity as a sophomore.

Clara never saw her sophomore year. While at a summer training camp, Clara had a brain hemorrhage and died immediately. On their return to school that fall, her classmates kept asking each other why Clara had to die."

- Have students discuss Clara's story. Ask: "Why did Clara have to die? How can someone so young and talented be taken away so quickly?" What questions do students have about why evil happens to good people?
- Explain that this question of "why evil happens to good people" seems always to have been a source of mystery for humanity. Much of what is written in the Wisdom literature focuses on just this question.

◆ MORE ABOUT THE LESSON

The Book of Job

Job is written in the form of a drama. In the poetic sections, three of Job's friends—Eliphaz, Bildad, and Zophar—speak with him about the horrors he is suffering. Each of these friends in turn discusses Job's situation from standard wisdom. They feel that since Job is suffering, he must have done something wrong. The way for Job to get out from under the suffering is to admit his sin, throw himself on God's mercy, and receive God's pardon and healing. (With friends like these, who needs enemies?)

Job is not having any of this and repeatedly refutes each speaker in turn. Job brings his case before God, but not as a penitent. Rather, he demands legal redress for the injustices that have been done to him. Job's final comfort is not an explanation, but a direct result of his experience of the majesty of God. Compared to such an experience, Job's suffering seems almost irrelevant.

Development

What to Do

1. Have the students read their text about Job, Sirach, and Wisdom.

2. Have the students read "in the Spotlight." Tell the students about Job. Have them glance quickly at the beginning of chapters 3, 4, 6, 8, 9, and 11 to have them find other things to add to your telling of the story.

3. Have the students read Job 38:1–15, then Job 42:1–6. Have students explain Job's experience of God in their own words.

4. Have the students turn to Sirach and read the introduction and the foreword. Then have the students open Sirach at random. Ask for several volunteers to each read a few verses they found randomly. Chapters 44 to 50 have a different quality from the rest because they focus on praising the ancestors of the Jews instead of offering guidance for wise living.

5. Have the students compare Job with Sirach. Have the students notice the headings, then read Chapters 7–9, which purport to be by Solomon.

6. Have the students write down three ideas or images they found in Wisdom 7–9, and reflect on their meaning in their Spiritual Journal.

7. Have the students read "The Book of Psalms" and choose one example of each type of psalm to read silently. Then ask them to describe the differences in the four types, and illustrate their comments with specific verses.

8. Lead a class discussion of the questions in "Have You Considered?"

9. Pray with your students.

Practicing the Skills

What to Do

Have the students discuss what kind of material is found in the Book of Sirach. Is it practical, theoretical, or useful for today?

154

the unique Israelite perspective: Wisdom comes from one's relationship with Yahweh. There is no wisdom without that relationship.

The Book of Wisdom

Bible scholars offer many differing opinions about the Book of Wisdom—especially concerning its authorship and original language. The Book of Wisdom is assumed to have been written around the time of 100 B.C.E. when many Greek ideas were being adapted to Jewish thought. Written in the name of King Solomon, its author is, nevertheless, anonymous.

Besides considering the age-old question about why good people suffer, the Book of Wisdom also examines the belief in life after death. The Book of Wisdom recounts the story of the Exodus to help strengthen the faith of the people. The author exhorts the Jews to seek wisdom, for even though there are many things people do not understand, if they have wisdom they can see their way through

---

The Bible in Context

Parallelism in the Psalms

Psalms is the best example we have of religious poetry from ancient Israel. Developing from song and dance, Israel's poetry appealed to the ear through rhythm rather than rhyme. Rhythm was created by a structure called "parallelism," in which the second line expresses the basic idea of the first in slightly different words.

There are three different kinds of parallelism, that differ by the way the second line expands the thought of the first. The three kinds are:

- **Similar.** The idea in the first line is repeated in the second, with only minor word changes. Psalm 19:1 is an example: "The heavens declare the glory of God, and the firmament proclaims his handiwork."
- **Opposite.** The first line expresses an idea, and the second line states its opposite. Psalm 27:10 illustrates this type: "Though my mother and father forsake me, yet the Lord will receive me."
- **Completed.** The second line adds to the thought expressed in the first, bringing it to completion. Psalm 28:7 provides an example: "In him my heart trust, and I find help; then my heart exults, and with my song I give him thanks."

---

in the *Spotlight*
Conflict in the Wisdom Tradition

The early Israelite sages said that God would reward the wise with happiness. Of course, they recognized that this wasn't always so, but they were passing on "tried and true" advice that usually worked. Some people misunderstood the advice, and came to believe that God's justice would ensure that the good always prosper and the bad always suffer.

After the Exile, the Wisdom literature shows a dissatisfaction with such neat, logical positions. Instead, Wisdom writing points out that, indeed, evil people **did** sometimes prosper, and the good **did** sometimes suffer. Disasters could happen without any obvious reason or purpose. The Book of Job considers this final point of view.

Job criticizes those sages who claimed to be able to see the logic of God behind certain events. "How agreeable are honest words; yet how unconvincing is your argument!" *(Job 6:25)*. The Book of Job argues forcefully that the workings of the universe are often beyond human understanding. The Book of Job's author knew nothing about black holes, quarks, or any of the modern discoveries of physics, yet his or her conclusions remain true. Even in our scientific world, much about the universe continues to be beyond human understanding. Although we trust in faith that there are reasons for everything, Job's story reminds us that we cannot fully understand God's plan.

The Book of Psalms

The Book of Psalms is a collection of 150 songs that were written at various times by the people of Israel. Although not generally considered one of the books of wisdom, the poetry of Psalms responds to many of the themes considered in Wisdom literature. Most of the psalms were written to be used in public worship, although some are designed for individual, ritual use in the Temple.

There are a number of types of psalms. Some were composed for specific occasions or needs, while others are quite general. Among these are:

- **Laments,** or prayers of deliverance from a terrible need or danger. Examples: Psalms 9, 30, 118, and 124.

◆ MORE ABOUT THE LESSON

Bible Aids

In most modern editions of the Bible, every book has an introduction written by scholars for the help of modern readers. The introduction to the Book of Sirach is such an aid. Sirach also has a feature found in no other Old Testament book; it has a foreword. This foreword to Sirach was written by the supposed author of Sirach, but is not considered inspired text by modern scholars. The "Jesus" mentioned is clearly not the Christian Jesus. Jesus was a common name in the ancient Middle East.

Written by Solomon?

Needless to say, chapters 7–9 of the Book of Wisdom were not written by Solomon, but this section does include beautiful reflections on living with wisdom. The ideas expressed here could be adopted by anyone and turned into prayer for a deeper, more effective life.

LEARN FROM THE MAP

Greece and Israel

Find Greece and Israel on this map. Notice how close they are to one another. Because Alexander the Great opened new possibilities for trade, increased boat travel across the Mediterranean contributed to the spread of Greek ideas to Israel.

Early Greek Culture
Alexander's Influence

- **Hymns of praise** set as accolades to God. Usually the reasons for praise are given in the psalm itself. Examples: Psalms 29, 103, and 148.
- **Royal psalms** related to the king in some way. They may have been written for his personal worship or enthronement ceremonies. Examples: Psalms 2, 18, 45, and 132.
- **Wisdom psalms** including proverbs, a teacher's address to a student, or general advice about living. The writing style of the wisdom psalms is similar to other Wisdom literature. Examples: Psalms 1, 37, and 112.

Have You Considered?

1. The Book of Job was probably finished during the Exile. Why do you suppose Job's point of view would have been popular to people living then?
2. Summarize in a few sentences the explanation given by the Deuteronomic historian for why the Exile happened. Would Job agree or disagree with this explanation? Explain your answer.
3. Sirach was written at a time when the Jewish community was worried about losing its identity to foreign beliefs. How would Sirach's claim that wisdom was contained in the Law help the community maintain its identity?

MORE ABOUT THE TEXT

Background on the Psalms

Strictly speaking, most of the psalms belong to the liturgical tradition of the Temple, and not to the Wisdom tradition. The laments, hymns of praise, and royal psalms, all part of liturgical literature, were used by individuals in the Temple, as well as by groups in festival liturgies.

The Book of Psalms is often included in listings of Wisdom literature mostly because it doesn't fit any better in any other category.

◆ MORE ABOUT THE LESSON

Choral Readings

Choral reading is quite simple to do. Go through each verse of a psalm and label it either "A," "B," or "C." Repeat that category for the entire psalm. Form the class into three groups named "A," "B," or "C." Each group is to then read the psalm verse marked with its letter. For help in directing the choral readings, see Teacher's Resource 9B.

Recall

Have the students write their answers to "Chapter 9 Review Q/A," Section One, numbers 6–8.

Connect

What to Do

Have the students complete "Bible Activity" number 2. Have them make at least ten cards. Keep the work light-hearted—this can be a fun exercise.

What's Next?

What to Do

Say: "In the next lesson, we will continue our look at Wisdom literature, looking at three very different books which relate directly to our spiritual growth in unexpected ways."

Have You Considered?

1. No doubt, many of the people who went into Exile had done their best to live righteous lives according to Wisdom teaching. They had expected long lives, happiness, peace, and all the other promised blessings of wisdom. Suddenly, all that was denied to them, and they suffered instead. Job's message that the purposes of God are not always clear to the human intellect would be very reassuring in such a setting.
2. The Deuteronomic historian said that the Exile was God's punishment upon Judah for the sins of her leaders and people. Job, no doubt, would reject this explanation, arguing that it is impossible for a human being to understand God's motives.
3. Since Ezra, the unifying principle in the Jewish community had been its obedience to the Law. Sirach reminded the people that their unity as a nation, and their special relationship with God, was centered upon the Law.

Bonus Focus for You

Go "treasure troving" in Wisdom and Sirach, and choose half a dozen or so of your own favorite passages. Write them in your journal and make them a regular part of your prayer life for several days.

◆ Wisdom and Spiritual Life

Welcome

What to Do

Greet the students when they are all seated. Keep it brief and to the point.

Read to them Proverbs 2:1–6, 13–18. (Many teachers will feel comfortable adjusting the language as necessary to include both boys and girls in these sayings. Some, however, will not. You may want to use this as an opportunity to explore the language in which the Bible was written. Although the translation uses the generic "man," the message of the proverbs are addressed equally to both genders.)

Pray with your students.

Introducing the Lesson

Teaching Objectives

By the end of this lesson students will be able to:
• Demonstrate an understanding of the Book of Proverbs.
• Explain the central message of the Book of Ecclesiastes.
• Explain why the Song of Songs uses romantic imagery.

What to Do

• Have the students read the opening italics of Section Two, and the learning objectives.
• Review with students that while Proverbs, Ecclesiastes, and Song of Songs are each Wisdom books, they are all three written using a different literary style. Have students page through the three books and offer suggestions as to how these styles are different.

Learning from the Wisdom Tradition

Egypt, Ptolemaic Cameo, Third Century B.C.E.

You have seen how the sages, or wisdom teachers, devoted themselves to the "big questions" of human life. Looking for answers to these questions, the sages developed a method of finding clues to the big picture in nature and daily events. In the end, they identified the qualities which a wise person should possess. In this section, you'll investigate these qualities. First, however, you'll study the insight contained in the three most famous wisdom texts of all.

Learning Objectives for Section Two

By the end of this section, you will be able to:

• Explain the methods taught by the sages for seeking wisdom.
• List and explain the qualities of the wise person.
• List several ways wisdom helps people to live well.
• Identify the qualities of a wise person and explain how those qualities can be recognized in daily living.

◆ Wisdom and the Spiritual Life

Saint Gregory of Nyssa (332–395 C.E.) was a theologian and biblical scholar who was especially interested in the Wisdom literature. Saint Gregory commented that the Book of Proverbs was the best book for beginners to use in order to develop a spiritual life; that Ecclesiastes was better suited to those a bit more advanced in wisdom; and that the Song of Songs was a book for those who had mastered the spiritual experience.

In a sense, Gregory suggested that these three books provided a school for the spiritual life. Much as a person learning the martial arts moves up by a belt color each time he or she has mastered the earlier level, or a scout moves up in rank after completing a particular challenge, so to, according to Gregory, should people progress through these books.

Proverbs

The Book of Proverbs is not a collection of works by one author. Israelite tradition credited Solomon with many of the proverbs as it credited the Torah to Moses and the Psalms to David, but Solomon is not the author of the book as it now stands. Perhaps some of the proverbs originated in Solomon's court. Scholars generally agree that the majority of the proverbs were written before the Exile. The introduction (chapters 1–9) was probably completed in the fourth century B.C.E.

The Book of Proverbs is divided into two parts:

1. Instructions about how to live.
2. Sayings, in couplet form, which are actual proverbs.

The Book of Proverbs also uses a literary style called the *mashal*—short sayings based on practical experience and application. The Hebrew proverb is a short, simple saying meant to be retained through the generations. They suggest that the way to true

---

MORE ABOUT THE TEXT

A Beginner's Book

Proverbs is called the beginner's book in spiritual growth because it is mostly about behavior; it emphasizes the external issues of living, which is where all people must begin. But the process of learning how to behave wisely helps create inner growth, just as the "Karate Kid" learned some of the movements of karate by doing familiar things. To live wholly according to Proverbs would require considerable strength and determination, as well as a pure heart. What motivates a search for wisdom? Wanting to be happy, longing for goodness, wanting an effective and successful life, wanting to know God— all these draw people into learning today, just as they did in ancient times.

People of Note

Gregory of Nyssa

Gregory wrote his own exposition of the Catholic faith, the Catechetical Discourse. In his studies, he concentrated on the spiritual and mystical meaning of the Bible. Throughout his life, Gregory had a special interest in how people could grow spiritually through appreciation of the Bible's symbolism and insight. Gregory died in 395 C.E., and his feast day is March 9.

On Perfection

"Therefore, let no one be grieved if he sees in his nature a penchant for change… For this is truly perfection: never to stop growing towards what is better and never placing any limit on perfection."

happiness is through the common virtues of hard work, careful speech, good manners, and discipline. Though the Book of Proverbs has a distinctly religious dimension too, these themes of universal wisdom provide an opportune starting place for the beginner, as Gregory of Nyssa suggested.

Gregory of Nyssa is a Father of the Church. Gregory's entire family, including his brother, Basil the Great, have been named saints by the Church.

On the surface, the book offers little more than the wisdom of the world. In the introduction, chapters 1–9, the collection represents the earliest stage of Israel's understanding of wisdom. Men and women both are warned to avoid drunkenness, poor manners, and laziness. They are encouraged to seek out wisdom through study, training, instruction, and discipline. The purpose of the proverbs is described in the introduction:

> That men may appreciate wisdom and discipline, may understand words of intelligence; may receive training in wise conduct, in what is right, just, and honest; that resourcefulness may be imparted to the simple, to the young man knowledge and discretion. A wise man by hearing them will advance in learning, an intelligent man will gain sound guidance, that he may comprehend proverb and parable, the words of the wise and their riddles.

(Proverbs 1:2–7)

In some places, the wisdom of Proverbs comes out of the actual experience of the sages themselves. Read the following passages and imagine the dialogue taking place between an instructor and a student concerning the content of these readings:

- Proverbs 1–9
- Proverbs 22:17–24:22
- Proverbs 31:1–9

Yet, from a wider view, the wisdom of Proverbs particularly emphasizes Israel's religion. Much of the moral code of Israel is found in the second part of the Book of Proverbs, especially that part of the code which speaks of the love and service of one person for another.

All of the principles of the Ten Commandments as well as the Sabbath regulations are included in the Book of Proverbs. Familiar themes covered by the prophets are mentioned as well. See if you can find

---

◆ MORE ABOUT THE LESSON

Proverbs

Some students may find reading large sections of Proverbs boring, because the collection seems only to repeat what they already know. Have them refer to the topical list they made for the first bulleted passages, and ask them: "How would you go about doing this (behaving in this way) yourself?" Guide them to reflect on behavior and its connections with inner attitudes.

Turn, Turn, Turn

The song "Turn, Turn, Turn" was written by Pete Seeger and was made popular in the folk-rock version by "The Byrds" during the 1960s. This song can be found on both "The Byrds' Greatest Hits" and "Twenty Essential Tracks" by The "Byrds." The recording is also found on several of the collected works of Pete Seeger.

Development

What to Do

1. Have the students read the opening paragraphs of "Wisdom and the Spiritual Life," "People of Note," and the section on "Proverbs."

2. Have the students find in their Bibles three bulleted references mentioned in the text on page 157. Have volunteers read these passages aloud.

3. Have the students find the second set of bulleted passages (Proverbs), listed in their text on page 158. Once again, have volunteers read these passages aloud. Ask students to name the verses where the mentioned themes occur.

4. Ask students what they think about the Book of Proverbs. What value do they think these sayings might have in their own lives?

5. Have the students read "Ecclesiastes." Next, have them read Ecclesiastes 2:1–17. Discuss with them what this passage suggests about the materialist, consumer values of Western society.

6. Play for them the song, "Turn, Turn, Turn." Then have them read Ecclesiastes 3:1–8. Let them hear the song again, following along in the Bible text.

7. Have the students find the bulleted passages listed on page 158 related to Ecclesiastes and find the themes mentioned in their text.

8. Have the students read "Song of Songs." Introduce the biblical book by saying: "Most of the Bible's books can be interpreted in many ways. They have several levels of meaning. That principle is especially clear with Song of Songs. On the surface, it is very romantic love-poetry. A deeper, symbolic look opens to us the deep wisdom of an intimate relationship with God."

9. Have the students come to an agreement about the answers to the questions in "Scripture Workshop."

10. Have the groups read Song of Songs 2 and 4. Ask them to choose favorite poetic images. How would these sound today

on valentines? What might these images suggest about love between God and people?

11. Pray with your students.

Answers to Page 158

1. Proverbs 15:27 and 17:15—The theme of injustice is in the first passage, as well as the second.

2. Proverbs 22:22ff—This passage reflects the theme of mistreatment of the poor (justice).

3. Proverbs 11:17, 14:22, 16:6, 24:10—11:17, 14:22, and 16:6 discuss kindness, 24:10 deals with compassion.

Practicing the Skills

What to Do

Have the students read Ecclesiastes 11:7–12:8. Ask them to name the main theme and to explain the meaning of the symbols there.

Recall

Have the students write the answers to the "Chapter 9 Review Q/A," Section Two, numbers 1–8.

Connect

What to Do

Lead the class discussion of the questions in "Have You Considered?"

What's Next?

What to Do

Say: "How do you suppose the Wisdom teachers got their wisdom?"

the themes of injustice, mistreatment of the poor, compassion, and kindness in the following passages:

- Proverbs 15:27 and 17:15
- Proverbs 22:22ff
- Proverbs 11:17, 14:22, 16:6, and 24:10

Proverbs represents the traditional ideas about wisdom which were inherited by later writers such as the authors of Job and Ecclesiastes. As such, they set the tone for all of Israel's later seekers of wisdom.

Ecclesiastes

A man serving a life sentence in prison was asked if he had a favorite book in the Bible. "As a matter of fact I do," he said. "My favorite book is Ecclesiastes because it tells the truth about life." Similarly, a dying woman in a nursing home also named Ecclesiastes as her favorite book. Why? "It makes me feel part of the great stream of life. It keeps me from feeling all alone." What is it about Ecclesiastes that inspires people in such difficult conditions? What is the secret of its appeal to so many people, so different from each other?

Ecclesiastes challenges the reader to look more deeply at life and its issues than does Proverbs. The book takes the form of a series of personal reflections by the author, known as Qoheleth, from the Hebrew word for "one who assembles a congregation." The grammatical form of Qoheleth is feminine, so it is possible that this author/sage was a woman. The Book of Ecclesiastes is generally thought to have been written in the second century B.C.E.

In Ecclesiastes, Qoheleth shares new and unconventional views on a wide range of topics. The author's aim is to see life with total clarity, without bias caused by beliefs, desires, or culture. According to the author, such clarity is important if one is to develop a true relationship with God, because only a person who wants to know the truth can really know God.

Basically, the message of Ecclesiastes is a simple one: the pleasures of this world are not able to satisfy the desires of human beings. There is nothing secure about earthly happiness. Even if someone gained every imaginable pleasure and desire, he or she would not be perfectly happy. True happiness is the major theme of the Book of Ecclesiastes. It is also a natural "second course" in discovering the meaning of true wisdom.

The form of the book is a series of personal reflections, expressed through the popular sayings of

the day and through longer poems. The book begins and ends with the same words: "Vanity of vanities! All things are vanity" (*Ecclesiastes* 1:2 *and* 12:8). To Qoheleth, finding true happiness and pleasure in the world is not possible because this ideal truth cannot be found there. For example:

- A just person is outlived by his wicked neighbor (see *Ecclesiastes* 7:15).
- Gaining material riches does not guarantee happiness (see *Ecclesiastes* 5:10–17).
- Ultimately, death claims all human beings just as it does any "beast." (see *Ecclesiastes* 3:19–21).

Ecclesiastes shows with total clarity that only God never changes. That is why reflection on the Book of Ecclesiastes is useful for the person who is moving forward in spiritual growth. It teaches and reminds the disciple of what must be fully realized in daily attitudes and daily choices. Only God is permanent; the person who clings to anything less than God will suffer much pain in life.

When everything has been completely considered, Qoheleth finally decides that the best thing to do—since nothing in life is guaranteed—is to enjoy what you have in the present moment and not to reach for what is too far beyond your grasp. For example, if you have a family, work, and food, enjoy them! Whatever comes your way, do it wholeheartedly, so that some joy might be yours in the doing. Nevertheless, do not expect too much from life.

Perhaps the greatest contribution of Ecclesiastes is its skepticism and its accompanying message that humankind would do well to reject all the simple solutions to the mysteries of life. This is a quality of the Book of Ecclesiastes that continues to attract people to its message.

Song of Songs

The Song of Songs is a poem about love. It describes ideal human love, as well as the great depth of love between God and people. The author of Song of Songs presents Israel as the intimate lover of the Lord, united to God in perfect love. Saint Gregory considered this book to be important for the "advanced" students of wisdom. Those who had reached this point are able to find true knowledge of God in love.

The Song of Songs translates from the Hebrew as "The Greatest Song." It was originally written as a long, intense, and beautiful poem about love. With this interpretation, the Song of Songs is often quoted in love notes and even in wedding ceremonies. The

---

◆ MORE ABOUT THE LESSON

Poem on Old Age

The poem found in Ecclesiastes recommends that the young learn to enjoy the present moment, because in old age, their experience will be very different. The symbols refer to conditions that many experience in old age: lessening clarity of vision, weakness in muscles, loss of teeth, loss of hearing, fears of loss of balance,

gray hair, loss of appetite and finally death. If the students have difficulty with some of these, ask them to check the footnotes at the end of Ecclesiastes. Ask the students if all older people today still have these experiences. Would Ecclesiastes still say the same things today, looking at people in their sixties and seventies?

presence of such love poetry in the Scripture suggests that married love has a sacred dimension, merging at some mysterious point with divine love.

But as you know, biblical writings are not limited to one meaning only, and the celebration of love in Song of Songs can be understood on several levels. For example, Jewish tradition understands Song of Songs as a parable that describes the delights of the love between God and Israel.

On another level, Song of Songs conveys the ecstasies of love that flow between God and humanity. This power and wonder can never be simply described in words. Rather, images must be used to communicate what the experience is like. The author uses the beauty of mountains and sunsets as symbols of the beauty one experiences in union with God. Song of Songs sums up Israel's Wisdom tradition, helping the

Have You Considered?

1. Proverbs says that hard work and good moral behavior lead to success in life. Do you think this is true?
2. Describe a time when someone tried to give you a simplistic explanation. How did it make you feel? Do you agree with Ecclesiastes that it's important to reject simplistic answers?
3. Do you agree with Song of Songs that what two people feel for each other when they're in love is a symbol for the love between God and humanity? Why or why not?

reader to understand the love of Yahweh.

◆ The Methods of the Sage

The task of the sage was to help people to reach their fullest potential. To do this, they corrected, approved, praised, and condemned their students. While their subject matter was concerned with the entirety of human behavior, the importance of God was never overshadowed in their message.

The sages taught their students two primary principles or methods of uncovering wisdom:

1. **Observation**
2. **Reflection**

Let's look at these two methods in more detail.

Observation

The sages were great observers. They noticed everything that happened around them. They observed nature, its cycles, the growth and decay of plants, the sky, the earth, and the sea. They paid special attention to human behavior. They taught their students how to observe the changes in human circumstances and their interconnections. Wisdom students learned how to observe human choices and their results. The examples used in Wisdom literature resulted from these precise observations.

Most people see well enough to get by in life, but very few people are actually careful observers who closely examine themselves, their lives, and the people around them. Few people truly consider circumstances before acting. People who observe carefully, learn to take a more detached attitude towards life, much as witnesses to a crime must do in court. They "step back" and pay attention to what happens, not just what they think is happening.

Skillful observation increases only through practice. As people master this skill of external observation, they can then begin to observe more internal things. For example, the sages were very skilled at observing their own emotions and how the body was affected by them. For example:

Anxiety in a man's heart depresses it, but a kindly word makes it glad!

(Proverbs 12:25)

A tranquil mind gives life to the body, but jealousy rots the bones.

(Proverbs 14:30)

Introducing the Lesson

Teaching Objectives

By the end of this lesson students will be able to:
- Identify the methods used by sages to reach their understanding of wisdom.
- Apply the four aspects of wisdom to life situations.

What to Do

Discuss with students the value of what they have learned from the previous three lessons. How do they think a person would benefit from being a wise person? How might someone come to wisdom? Put their answers on the board, for later use.

Development

Students learn that one can come to wisdom by observing life and reflecting on it.

What to Do

1. Say: "How do you suppose people get to be wise?"
2. Have the students read "The Methods of the Sage."
3. Students now are to open the Book of Proverbs at random and pick out two or three proverbs that come from observation.
4. Form small groups. Each small group is to name half a dozen things that they have observed in their own experience.
5. Explain that half the value of observing well is being able to express what has been seen so that others can see it as well. Have the students write their own proverbs, based on their observations, and share their proverbs with the class.
6. Have the class as a whole state some observations about nature, then reflect on them as suggested in their text.
7. Have each student write two proverbs that come from this reflection on nature. Ask volunteers to share their proverbs. You may wish to gather all the proverbs and make a collection to be photocopied for everyone's use. Students might also enjoy doing this as a special project.
8. Lead the class discussion of the questions in "Have You Considered?"

Reflection

The second method for finding wisdom is reflection. Once you've made careful observations about nature and other people, you have to sort out what you've seen, and decide which behaviors and attitudes seem most wise. This is the act of reflection.

Reflecting on your observation of nature, which attitudes feel most appropriate? Does respect for the natural world seem like a better, more fitting response than carelessness? Watching other people, who seem the most content and at peace with themselves? What makes them that way? Thinking about such questions leads one to a wise, mature understanding of life.

The sages asked many of these same questions. They took the time to observe their own and other's experiences more closely. In reflecting on these observations, they came to a clearer understanding of the meaning of wisdom.

Have You Considered?

1. How do you think the study of nature can help teach us wisdom? Write down one lesson you think human beings should learn from the natural world.
2. Describe a time when an event changed your life in some way. Do you think it's true that everything that happens to you has some meaning or purpose? Why or why not?

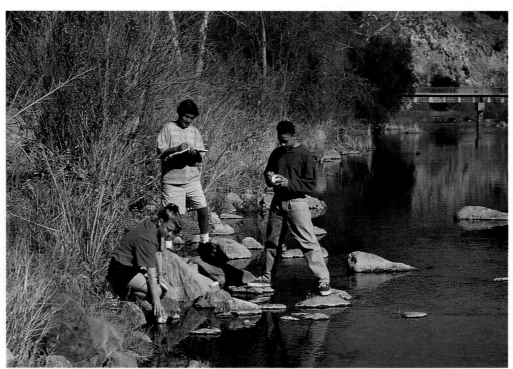

The sages came to their wisdom often through the study of nature. What can you learn about how to live your life from studying the way the world is?

◆ MORE ABOUT THE LESSON

Treats

There are many types of treats you can give to students. The quickest way is to take a few small pieces of candy, along with a proverb, and wrap it in aluminum foil. Students then simply unwrap their treat. You can also bake (or have someone bake) cookies or cupcakes with proverbs in them. Each proverb is written or typed on a piece of paper, which is then folded to a tiny size and enclosed in foil. These are then placed in the center of the batter just before baking. This is usually a lot of fun for everyone—decidedly worth the trouble! (A few students might enjoy preparing these cupcakes.)

◆ The Advantages of Wisdom

Have you ever tried to juggle three or more balls in the air? Unless you are a rare exception, your first attempts at juggling left balls scattered everywhere. Juggling requires excellent hand/eye coordination. Until you develop that skill, you simply can't keep more than two balls in the air at the same time. Once you can juggle three balls, however, you can proceed to more difficult juggling skills.

Learning to be wise is very similar to learning how to juggle. There are skills that must be learned at the basic level before moving on to the more difficult ones. It takes time to develop new skills. The difficulty in becoming wise is not that the answers themselves are very difficult—concepts such as respect for others, honesty, love of God, and care of oneself are not exactly new. The hard part is developing a character based on these ideals. Doing so takes time, effort, and moral courage.

The Qualities of a Wise Person

There are four main characteristics of being wise, and they will benefit anyone who pursues them. They are **balance, certainty, integrity,** and a **listening heart**.

Balance   A balanced person is able to respond with true wisdom of heart and mind to anything that happens, just as an excellent tennis player is balanced and ready to return the ball no matter to what area of the court it is hit.

A balanced person knows how to enjoy life, but is not thrown around by extremes. For a balanced person, every setback is not a crisis, and every step forward is not a major triumph. He or she responds calmly, thoughtfully, and confidently to situations, feeling his or her emotions, but also controlling them.

Certainty   A person of certainty is one who has a strong sense of security and is able to live without anxiety in most situations. Inner certainty means knowing who you are and what your life is about; it means being strong enough that you can be yourself, without worrying about what everybody else will think.

Such certainty requires a willingness to accept responsibility for one's own choices and their consequences. Everyone makes many choices about actions and attitudes, but some mistakenly think that these choices are without consequence. The wise person knows that every choice brings with it a result or consequence, takes that information into account, and then accepts full responsibility for his or her personal choice. This requires conviction and security.

Integrity   A person of integrity is honest about his or her experiences, observations, and perceptions. The wise person does not buy into every new or faddish idea that comes along, especially when it conflicts with his or her own experience.

People of integrity are humble. They recognize that they do not know everything. People of integrity accept criticism and corrections willingly; it's just a part of the learning experience. Wise people are humble; they want to know and to improve themselves. Learning is more important than defending themselves or proving that they are right.

Sometimes people speak as if they are on automatic pilot. They gossip about others and their words

The four main characteristics of a wise person — balance, certainty, integrity, and a listening heart — take time to develop. This is why most wise people are older. However, not all older people are wise and not all younger people are foolish.

◆ MORE ABOUT THE LESSON

Proverbs

The topics of proverbs do not need to be religious or even profound. The point is the observation. One such modern proverb would be: "The mistake of a person is easily corrected, but the error of a computer goes on and on."

The custom of most writers of proverbs was to use a couplet form, and these followed the same conventions as you learned for the psalms (see page 154, "The Bible in Context"). Have the students review these forms and use them to write their proverbs. The ancient rules of observation and formulation were quite definite; it is enjoyable to try to imitate them.

Practicing the Skills

What to Do

Form three or four small groups. Assign each of the groups several of the sentences in bold print (page 163). Each group is to look through the books of Proverbs, Sirach, and Wisdom to find at least two examples for each topic. Share the results with all.

Have the students write a paragraph in their Spiritual Journal about the benefit of wisdom they would most like to acquire, including how they think they might go about it and why they want it.

Recall

Have the students write their answers to "Chapter 9 Review Q/A," Section Two, numbers 7–8.

Connect

What to Do

Have the students do the Spiritual Reflection as a homework assignment and write the results of their reflection in their Spiritual Journal.

What's Next?

What to Do

Have the students turn to the Unit One Review in their text. Note with them that there are both questions and activities to complete. Tell them that the next lesson will focus on their review of Unit One.

162

are thoughtless. The wise person speaks with care and speaks only what is well-said and true. Oftentimes, this means that the wise person speaks hardly at all. "As you hedge round your vineyard with thorns, set barred doors over your mouth" (*Sirach* 28:24).

Integrity also means that the wise person practices a virtuous life. Did you know that the word "virtue" means strength? What do you think it means to have virtue?

There are also inner virtues which wisdom says matter more than external actions: honesty, humility, kindliness, generosity, justice, love, and purity of intention.

A Listening Heart   Like the other qualities embraced by wisdom, a listening heart is the product of long practice.

In the Bible, the heart is the center of the person, from which all thoughts, feelings, and actions come. Listening with one's entire being is different from listening only with one's ears or mind. One "takes it to heart," contemplates what is heard, and seriously applies its lessons to life. A "listening heart" requires that we stop thinking of ourselves as having all the answers or that others have nothing to teach us. Everyone has a story to tell, and a person with a listening heart will learn from other's experiences.

Most of all, those with such wisdom realize that they are not the center of creation, but simply and deeply **belong to** creation. They acknowledge that they, along with all other people, are subject to the Creator as a participant in God's gifts. For them, every experience is an occasion for thanksgiving, even those

Chagall, *Ahasver, The Wandering Jew*, Twentieth Century.

The Bible's Wisdom tradition recognizes that wisdom was not something to be had, but a journey to be traveled. The wise person continues to grow wiser each day. The legendary Jewish figure, Ahasver, wanders eternally seeking true Wisdom.

MORE ABOUT THE TEXT

The Wandering Jew

The legend of the Wandering Jew is an ancient tale that relates the fate of a man who scolded Jesus and urged him to walk faster up the hill to Calvary. According to the legend Jesus said, "I am indeed going, but you will wait until I return." The man who spoke so thoughtlessly is thus condemned to walk the earth looking for wisdom until Jesus returns (the Second Coming).

The first written record of this legend is found in the *Flores historiarum* (1235) of Roger of Wendover, who casts Pilate's doorkeeper as the wanderer.

The story became popular after the publication in 1602 of a German pamphlet which linked the legend with a Jewish shoemaker named Ahasver (or Ahasuerus). In the German version, Ahasver represents the persecuted Jewish people, dispersed over the earth.

that at first seem unpleasant. All that happens in creation happens in relationship to God—this is something that the sages never forgot.

How Wisdom Helps

The sages communicated to their audiences the numerous advantages of gaining wisdom. In no particular order of importance, here are some of the results of having wisdom. Find others as you read from the Wisdom literature.

• **Wisdom is a protector and guard.** It keeps a person away from dangerous situations. It gives one security and freedom from fear.
• **Wisdom helps a person to live a long time.**
• **Wisdom keeps life peaceful and pleasant.** Being happy and content helps a person to prosper.
• **Wisdom is like a light in the darkness.** It enables a person to live without confusion or ignorance.
• **Wisdom keeps you from making a fool of yourself in public.** The wise person knows when to act and when to do nothing.
• **Wisdom makes you thankful and keeps you from depression.**
• **Wisdom keeps you away from quarrels.**
• **The wise spread healing and joy.**
• **Wisdom draws the favor of authorities.**

• **The wise one does not have to hurry.** He or she understands the importance of good timing and knows how to use it.
• **Wisdom brings self-respect and the respect of others.**
• **Wisdom brings wonderful, loyal friends.**
• **Wisdom never fails, even when everything seems lost.**

How can wisdom benefit you? Wisdom allows you to interpret all of human experience and determine the most intelligent and practical way of living. As you uncover more of the depth of Wisdom literature, consider how it can be of service to your own life and the lives of those around you.

Have You Considered?

1. Pick one of the four characteristics of the wise person discussed above. Do you think you have this quality? If so, how did you get it? If not, how do you think having it would help you?
2. Describe a situation in which you learned a valuable lesson from an unexpected source. How does this help show you the value of a listening heart?
3. Pick one of the benefits of wisdom listed above. How could this help you? Be specific.

Spiritual Reflection

Psalm 29

Psalm 29 is an ancient hymn of praise to God. Scholars believe that it was composed for worship in the Temple. This hymn of praise to God has been used in prayer for nearly 3000 years.

The psalm uses symbolic language throughout.

Open your Bible to Psalm 29. Read each verse to yourself slowly. Picture the image that is being painted for you by the psalmist. See the mighty deeds of the Lord, feel the Lord's mighty words. See how many symbols you can find.

What do you think the following symbols might mean?

• The voice of the Lord breaks the cedars.

• He makes Lebanon leap like a calf and Sirion like a young bull.
• The voice of the Lord strikes fiery flames; the voice of the Lord shakes the desert, the Lord shakes the wilderness of Kadesh.
• The voice of the Lord twists the oaks and strips the forests.

When you finish reading the entire psalm, select one phrase that you like. Keep that phrase clearly in mind while you meditate on some problem you're facing, then ask God to see you through it. Pray quietly for a few moments, letting the phrase you picked run through your mind. Try to feel God's concern and love for you as you meditate on this phrase.

◆ MORE ABOUT THE LESSON

Practicing the Skills

"Looking through" large sections of biblical material will have many good side effects; the students will find interesting things besides the ones that they are looking for. If they find other benefits to being wise, they can add them to the list in the text. If any group has great difficulty finding their assigned ideas, they can use a concordance: think of a key word, look it up in the concordance, check under the listings for the wisdom books (by name) until they find a verse that fills the requirement.

Q/A

Section One

1. "Wisdom" means an understanding of what life is about and how to live it well, including the ability to make responsible moral decisions.

2. Wisdom is not the same as knowledge because one can be very knowledgeable without being wise, and vice-versa.

3. In Israel, wisdom was always connected to the religious beliefs and traditions of the people while in other countries wisdom did not have to have a religious tradition.

4. A Wisdom school is a group of people, usually scribes, who develop and pass along a collection of Wisdom teachings.

5. In the period between the Old and New Testaments, Wisdom schools were interested in the idea of a "suffering revealer."

6. Job challenges the idea that wisdom will always lead to external success, and evil will always lead to bad fortune.

7. Sirach's unique insight is that wisdom comes from one's relationship with Yahweh.

8. Four kinds of Psalms are: (A) Lament—prayers of deliverance from a terrible need or danger; (B) Hymns of praise—Accolades to God; (C) Royal Psalms—Prayers related to the king in some way; (D) Wisdom Psalms—Proverbs, a teacher's address to a student, or general advice about living.

Q/A

Section One

1. Define what the term "wisdom" means in Wisdom literature.
2. Explain why wisdom is not the same thing as knowledge or intelligence.
3. What is one quality that distinguishes wisdom in ancient Israel from other Middle Eastern wisdom traditions?
4. What is a Wisdom school?
5. What aspect of Wisdom interested Wisdom schools in the period between the Old and New Testaments?
6. How does Job challenge the earlier Wisdom tradition?
7. What unique insight does Sirach have?
8. List and describe four kinds of Psalms.

Section Two

1. Who was Gregory of Nyssa?
2. Define "mashal."
3. Who is Qoheleth? What is unusual about this name?
4. What is the basic message of Ecclesiastes? How can it be interpreted positively?
5. What kind of love was originally described in the Song of Songs?
6. How does the Song of Songs sum up the Wisdom tradition?
7. Describe the two methods of learning wisdom developed by the sages.
8. List and define four qualities of a wise person.

BIBLE ACTIVITY

1. Go back to Section One and review the "The Bible in Context" feature on parallelism. Write three couplets in your own words, one for each of the types of parallelism.
2. Choose one of the following books: Proverbs, Ecclesiastes, Song of Songs, and Sirach 1–43. Look for verses that apply to you or to people you know. Copy them on index cards. Give them as gifts or keep them as personal, inspirational reminders.
3. Read Proverbs 12:19. Share a story about gossiping and about how you have found this proverb to be truthful.
4. Write a story detailing the importance of friends in your life. In your story, quote these passages from the Book of Sirach: 6:5–17, 13:5–7, and 22:19–22.

BIBLE ACTIVITY

1. Ensure that student responses here follow the format for similar, opposite, and completed parallelism. Remind students that Hebrew poetry achieved its effect not through rhyme, but through repetition and subtle variation. Point out also that most of the psalms were not originally intended to be read, but to be sung in public worship. In that sense, it's like studying the lyrics to songs without the music.

2. Ask students, either on the cards themselves or in a separate place, to give their reasons for choosing these particular verses. Ask them to consider their reasons in light of the discussion of wisdom in this chapter.

3. Proverbs 12:19 reads, "Truthful lips endure forever, the lying tongue, for only a moment." Encourage students to focus on how lying usually works its way back and does harm to the person who told the lie. Students should recognize that this insight is a good example

CHAPTER 9 REVIEW

GLOSSARY

- **Balance:** One of the qualities of a wise person; a state of calmness and the ability to use good judgment.
- **Certainty:** One of the qualities of a wise person; refers to inner confidence in one's identity.
- **Fear of the Lord:** Respect and humility before God; not the same thing as actual fright.
- **Integrity:** One of the qualities of a wise person; means honesty about one's observations, perceptions and experiences.
- **Listening heart:** One of the qualities of a wise person; having a willingness to hear what others have to say and learn from what is heard.
- **Ma'at:** Egyptian concept of wisdom as self-control and eloquence.
- **Mashal:** A short saying based on practical experience that is universal in its application.
- **Parallelism:** Structure of Hebrew poetry in which rhythm is produced by pairs of lines, in which the second repeats the idea of the first in slightly different words; types include similar, opposite, and completed.
- **Proverb:** A saying which expresses something true in an artful and easy-to-remember way.
- **Qoheleth:** The Hebrew word for teacher or preacher, feminine in grammatical form. It is another name for Ecclesiastes.
- **Sages:** Wise people who are venerated and respected for their wisdom, experience, and judgment; the term is often used to describe the writers of Old Testament Wisdom literature.
- **Secular:** Relating to worldly things rather than things of religion.
- **Wisdom:** A sense of what life is all about and how to live it well; insight into God, human nature, and ethical behavior.
- **Wisdom School:** A group of students organized around the teaching of a certain sage.

UNDERSTANDING MORE ABOUT:

The Divine Office

Every day, at fixed times established by centuries-old tradition, Catholics around the world pray something called the "divine office." It is a liturgy for individual or small group use. It is also called "the Liturgy of the Hours," because different prayers are used at particular times of the day. The Church considers it her duty to say these daily prayers—indeed, the divine office is considered to contain some of the most important prayers of the Church.

The heart of the divine office consists of psalms. The Church believes that these psalms should be recited every day, because they so perfectly express God's glory and majesty and because they profoundly reflect every human heart. Since the psalms also formed part of the daily Temple liturgy in ancient Israel, this means that for nearly 3,000 years, these songs have been lifted up every day in praise of Yahweh.

of wisdom, observed in personal experience and the behavior of others. Also point out to the students that this verse is a perfect example of opposite parallelism.

4. These passages deal with the value of true friendship. Ask students to show their understanding of the verses in the way they construct their story.

Section Two

1. Gregory of Nyssa (332–395 C.E.) was a theologian and biblical scholar interested in the Wisdom literature.
2. Mashal refers to short sayings, such as those found in the Book of Proverbs.
3. Qoheleth is the name of the speaker in the Book of Ecclesiastes. The unusual thing about the name is that grammatically, it is feminine.
4. Ecclesiastes says that earthly happiness is insecure and ultimately unsatisfying. Positively, this message can be interpreted as meaning that only God can bring true happiness, and therefore our energies should be turned to the Lord.
5. Originally, Song of Songs described the wonders of married love.
6. Song of Songs sums up the Wisdom tradition by reminding the reader that wisdom ultimately is a way of describing the love that binds Yahweh to humanity.
7. The sages used observation and reflection to gain wisdom. Observation refers to the careful study of things around us: nature, other people, ourselves. Reflection is the process of sorting out our observations and deciding which behaviors and attitudes seem most wise.
8. Four qualities of a wise person are: (A) Balance—the ability to respond calmly and with confidence at any time; (B) Certainty—Knowing who you are and what your life is about, including the willingness to accept responsibility for your own choices; (C) Integrity—Being honest about your experiences and observations, including the qualities of humility and an ability to control your speech; (D) A Listening Heart—The ability to genuinely hear the insights which come from experience and other people, and taking those insights to heart.

Bible Literacy

1. A covenant is an unbreakable agreement between God and humanity, which binds them in a special, loving relationship.

2. Moses led the Hebrews out of slavery in Egypt, and then received the law on Mount Sinai.

3. During their time in the wilderness, the Hebrews were dependent upon God's leadership.

4. The Decalogue refers to the 10 Commandments.

5. The Deuteronomic history includes the biblical books of Joshua, Judges, 1 and 2 Samuel, and 1 and 2 Kings.

6. Ancient historians wanted to relay the meaning of the past. Modern historians want to record "what actually happened."

7. The main theological idea in Judges is that when Israel sins, it suffers, but when it is loyal to Yahweh, prosperity follows.

8. God's covenant with David promised that descendants of David would always sit on his throne and rule over Israel.

9. A "source" is a written document used by one or more biblical authors in putting together their own work.

10. Myths are imaginative stories which use narrative to express abstract ideas, such as a culture's values and identity.

11. The "J" and "P" stories acknowledge God as the creator of the universe, and emphasize God's loving concern for humanity. They differ in their images of God.

12. Yahweh promised Abraham that his descendants would be numerous, and that they would live in the land of Canaan.

13. Solomon violated the Covenant by committing acts of injustice, and by worshipping foreign gods.

14. Syncretism is the blending of different cultural traditions into something new.

15. Elijah was a prophet in the Northern kingdom.

166

Looking Back

The Old Testament is the story of the people of Israel and the Covenant which unites them with God. The books of the Old Testament are an important part of the family story of the Christian faith community. These books teach us, inspire us, and fill us with a sense that God's loving concern for us never ends, despite all the changes that happen over the course of our lives.

Bible Literacy

1. Define the term "covenant."
2. Why is Moses such an important figure in Israel's history?
3. How did the Hebrews' time in the wilderness form them as a people of faith?
4. What is the decalogue?
5. What is meant by the phrase "the Deuteronomic history"?
6. Discuss the differences in approach between ancient and modern historians.
7. What is the main theological idea in the Book of Judges?
8. Describe God's covenant with David.
9. In biblical studies, what is meant by the word "source"?
10. In what sense are the creation stories in Genesis myths?
11. How are the "J" and "P" creation stories similar? How are they different?
12. What was Yahweh's promise to Abraham?
13. How did King Solomon violate the Covenant?
14. What is syncretism, and why is it a violation of the Covenant?
15. Summarize the important events in the career of Elijah.
16. In what ways was the social situation during Elijah's life similar to our own?
17. How were the Northern and Southern kingdoms unjust?
18. How did the prophets explain the fall of the Northern kingdom?
19. How are the messages of Isaiah and Jeremiah different? How are they similar?
20. Why did some Jews stay behind in Babylon after the Exile?
21. What is the diaspora?
22. List three important messages of the prophet Ezekiel.
23. How did Second Isaiah encourage the people of the Exile?
24. What was Nehemiah's major accomplishment?
25. How did Alexander the Great change life for the Jews?
26. How did God teach Israel with foreign nations after the Exile?
27. In what way is life a conversation with God?
28. Define Wisdom literature
29. How are the Israelite wisdom books similar to and different from non-Israelite wisdom?
30. Explain the qualities of a wise person.

Bible Activities

Laws of Exodus

1. No, he is not right. The Law states that a slave must go free in the seventh year, without cost. The only exception is a slave who does not wish to leave his wife or children, who then will remain a slave forever. But this slave has not married, and therefore the law requires that he be set free. (21:1–6)

2. No, there is no obligation to pay the owner. The Law states that if the caretaker swears before God that he did not lay hands on his neighbor's property, the neighbor must accept the oath. If the caretaker is guilty of the injury, he must make restitution. (22:9–11)

3. The Law requires the Israelites never to molest or oppress aliens, for the Israelites were once aliens in Egypt. Therefore, the brother is obligated to repay the Hittite for the money the brother stole from him. (22:20–23)

The Judges

1. Deborah—Judges 4–5; Samson—13–16; Ehud—3; and Gideon—6–8. Ehud first,

Review

Bible Activities

The Laws of Exodus

Many of the laws given to Moses on Mount Sinai are found in Exodus 20-23. Imagine that you are an Israelite lawyer in 303 B.C.E., and people ask you the following legal questions. Look up the law that applies to their case, and then write a response.

1. "I have served my master as a slave for five years, and have never married. Now he says I have to work five more years for him before I can go free. Is he right?"
2. "My neighbor asked me to take care of his ox while he was away on business. While he was gone, the ox died, even though I took good care of it. No one witnessed what happened, and now my neighbor is demanding that I pay him for the ox. Do I have to?"
3. "My brother stole some money from a Hittite. I told him he'd better pay it back, but he said that since the Hittite is an alien, he doesn't have to pay him. What should I tell him?"

The Judges

Open your Bible to Judges. Find the stories of the following four judges: Deborah, Samson, Ehud, and Gideon, and then answer the following questions.

1. In what order do these stories appear?
2. Which tribe does each judge represent?
3. Check the map in Chapter 3 on page 42. What pattern do you notice when you compare the order of the stories to the judge's tribe? What importance do you find in this pattern?

Solomon's Temple

How big was Solomon's Temple *(see 1 Kings 6)*? Knowing that a cubit equals 18 inches, in yards:

1. What were the dimensions of the Temple?
2. How wide were the three stories of the annex?
3. What was the area of the sanctuary for the Ark of the Covenant?

Ezekiel's Symbols

Drawing on your knowledge of the circumstances surrounding the Exile, explain the meaning of the following symbols.

1. The Lord tells Ezekiel to take two sticks, labeled Judah and Israel, and to put them together in his hand. He is then to show the united stick to the people.
2. Another time, the Lord tells Ezekiel to pack his luggage as if he is about to move. He is to take his bags out in public and leave them there. Later, he's to move from where he lives to another place, covering his eyes so he can no longer see his home.

Now look up the description of these symbols in Ezekiel and see whether your interpretation agrees with his. The symbol of the sticks in Ezekiel 37:15-22; the symbolic trip is in 12:1-6.

Praying with the Bible

The most important concept in the Old Testament is the Covenant which binds Israel to God. In Chapter 2, you learned that the Covenant was accepted by the people through a special ritual, based on the elements of an ancient Middle Eastern vassal treaty. As a class, you can also pledge yourself to honoring the Covenant through your own ceremony.
Description of the Greatness of God Read aloud the description of God's majesty and special love for Israel in Deuteronomy 10:12-22.
Rules and Stipulations Take turns reading aloud the list of the Ten Commandments found in Deuteronomy 5:6-21. After each, pause a moment to let everyone think about what God is asking.
Witnesses Another reader announces the witnesses to the Covenant proclaimed by God in Deuteronomy 30:19-20.
Blessing and Curses As Moses and the ancient Israelites did, you will finish your ceremony by pronouncing the curses for breaking the Covenant and the blessings for keeping it as found in Deuteronomy 27-28. One person acts as the leader, and the rest of the class will be the community. After each curse or blessing is read, everyone should respond, "Amen."

16. In Elijah's time, the rich took advantage of the poor, the political leaders acted for personal gain.
17. These two kingdoms failed to care adequately for the poor, the widows, the aliens, and the orphans.
18. The prophets explained the fall of the Northern kingdom as the inevitable result of its sinfulness.
19. Both Isaiah and Jeremiah agreed that Judah was courting disaster because of its unwillingness to follow God's law. They differed, however, as to what each hoped.
20. Jews stayed in Babylon because life there was comfortable, secure, and prosperous.
21. The Diaspora is the scattering of Jews throughout the world because of the Exile.
22. Three messages of Ezekiel include: (A) Yahweh is holy, majestic, and powerful; (B) A new period of individual responsibility has begun; (C) A time will come when God will restore the people and rebuild the nation.
23. Second Isaiah spoke in glowing terms of the return from Exile.
24. Nehemiah's major accomplishment was the rebuilding of the city of Jerusalem.
25. Alexander changed life for the Jews because he stimulated the spread of Greek culture around the ancient world.
26. God taught Israel with foreign nations by exposing Israel to the religious ideas of these nations.
27. Life is a conversation with God who speaks to us through Scripture, the Church, other people, and our own experiences.
28. Wisdom literature is the third major division of the Old Testament; it includes books which deal with universal human questions, such as the meaning of suffering.
29. The various wisdom books are similar because the pursuit of wisdom was an international interest. They are different because unlike most other nations, Israel never separated the pursuit of wisdom from its religious beliefs and traditions.
30. Wise people are balanced, they have certainty, they have integrity, and they have a listening heart.

Deborah second, Gideon third, and Samson fourth.
2. Ehud—Benjamin, Deborah—Ephraim, Gideon—Manasseh, and Samson—Dan.
3. The judges stories move south to north.

Solomon's Temple
1. The Temple was 30 yards x 10 yards x 12.5 yards.
2. The first story was 2.5 yards wide, the middle was 3 yards, and the top was 3.5 yards.
3. The area of the sanctuary would be 100 yards.

Ezekiel's Symbols
1. The two sticks refers to the hope that God would return the Jews to the land of Israel and allow them once again to live as a united nation.
2. This luggage refers to the Exile; it occurred early in Ezekiel's ministry, when his function was still to warn the Jews of the destruction which was coming.

Unit Overview

This unit looks at the books of the New Testament.

• In chapters 10 and 11, Jesus' teaching is explored along with an overview of the formation of the four gospels.

• Chapter 12 presents the Acts of the Apostles and the role of the Spirit in the formation of the Church.

• Chapter 13 explores the teaching of Saint Paul and his importance to the formation of the Church. Paul's letters to the Thessalonians, Galatians, Corinthians, and Romans are presented.

• Chapter 14 considers the further development of the early Church and the importance of the Catholic Letters in this regard. Hebrews, James, the letters of Peter, and Revelation are specifically addressed.

• Chapter 15 invites students to look back at their study of the Bible. What are the specific skills that they have learned through this course of study? How can these skills be of value to them throughout their lives?

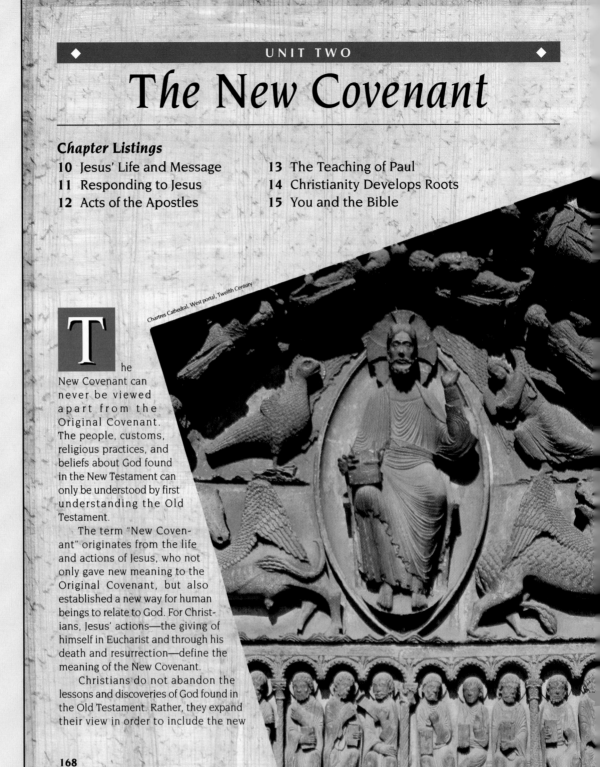

◆ UNIT TWO ◆

The New Covenant

Chapter Listings

10 Jesus' Life and Message
11 Responding to Jesus
12 Acts of the Apostles

13 The Teaching of Paul
14 Christianity Develops Roots
15 You and the Bible

Chartres Cathedral, West portal, Twelfth Century

The New Covenant can never be viewed apart from the Original Covenant. The people, customs, religious practices, and beliefs about God found in the New Testament can only be understood by first understanding the Old Testament.

The term "New Covenant" originates from the life and actions of Jesus, who not only gave new meaning to the Original Covenant, but also established a new way for human beings to relate to God. For Christians, Jesus' actions—the giving of himself in Eucharist and through his death and resurrection—define the meaning of the New Covenant.

Christians do not abandon the lessons and discoveries of God found in the Old Testament. Rather, they expand their view in order to include the new

168

◆ MORE ABOUT THE LESSON

Finding Books Quickly

There are hints that you can give to the students to help them find the books of the New Testament quickly.

First, note that the page numbers of the Bible start over again with the Old Testament. The Gospel According to Saint Matthew will always begin on page 1.

Second, the Old Testament takes up most of the Bible's pages. Once they have found the page number a book starts on, the students can simply turn to the back of the Bible and start looking for the proper page.

Third, there is a memory aid to help them keep the letters in order: Ro-Co-Co (Romans, 1 & 2 Corinthians), Gal-E-Ph (Galatians, Ephesians, Philippians), Co-5T, Ph-He (Colossians, 1 & 2 Thessalonians, 1 & 2 Timothy, Titus, Philemon, Hebrews), J-2P, 4-J, R (James, 1 and 2 Peter, 1, 2, 3 John, Jude, and Revelation).

understandings of God offered by Jesus through his teaching and by his example.

Books of the New Testament

The collection of writings that forms the New Covenant includes

- **Four Gospel Accounts.** *Mark, Matthew, Luke,* and *John.* These books provide us a look into Jesus' life. They tell us some of what Jesus said and did while he was alive. These four books were each written for different audiences and so emphasize different aspects of Jesus' life and teaching. Although similar in style to a biography, the gospel accounts are a new type of literature.
- **The Acts of the Apostles.** This book describes how Christianity grew in a world officially hostile to Jews and their descendants. The stories of the missionary work of the early followers, especially Peter and Paul, are preserved here. The "main character," however, is the Holy Spirit.
- **Letters.** There are 21 documents that take the form of letters. Paul is associated with thirteen of these letters.

  Captivity Letters—*Philippians, Philemon, Colossians,* and *Ephesians* are known as "captivity letters" because they were written by Paul to Christian communities while he was in prison.

  Pastoral Letters—*Other letters attributed to Paul are known as "pastoral letters" because they pay special attention to the organization of Church structures and to the moral issues facing the early Christians.*

  Catholic Letters—*Seven letters are traditionally known as "catholic letters" because they were addressed to the entire universal Church. These letters are attributed to Paul, James, Peter, John, and Jude.*
- **The Revelation to John,** or the *Apocalypse,* speaks in a symbolic way of the Church that is to come. It is written in an apocalyptic style.

These books of the New Testament were written by a number of authors over a period of fifty years or more. The earliest writing in the New Testament canon is a letter attributed to Paul written around 50 C.E. The latest may be the Second Letter of Peter, which reached its final form possibly as late as 125 C.E.

Living the Good News

Whereas there are four specific gospel accounts, there is only one Gospel, or "Good News," present in all of the Christian Scriptures. This Good News describes the great victory over death won by Jesus for all who believe. This use of the term "gospel" is the original one. Paul refers to his message about the death and resurrection of Jesus as his "gospel"—his "Good News."

In Unit 2, you will read of the Good News of the New Covenant as it was arranged in Christian Scriptures. The *synoptic* accounts ("seeing together with the same eye")—Mark, Matthew, and Luke—emphasize similar words and events from Jesus' life from different perspectives. *John* reflects the Christian community's growing understanding of Jesus as Lord and Savior.

These books of the New Covenant are important to Christians because they describe the life of Jesus and the faith of his early followers, the Church.

The Second Vatican Council taught that the gospel accounts

> faithfully hand on what Jesus, the Son of God, while he lived among men, really did and taught for their eternal Salvation, until the day when he was taken up. For, after the ascension of the Lord, the apostles handed on to their hearers what he had said and done, but with that fuller understanding which they, instructed by the glorious events of Christ and enlightened by the Spirit of truth, now enjoyed. The sacred authors, in writing the four Gospels, selected certain of the many elements which had been handed on, either orally or already in written form, others synthesized or explained with an eye to the situation of the churches, the while sustaining the form of preaching, but always in such a fashion that they have told us the honest truth about Jesus. Whether they relied on their own memory and recollections or on the testimony of those who "from the beginning were eyewitnesses and ministers of the Word," their purpose in writing was that we might know the "truth" concerning the things of which we have been informed.
>
> (Dei Verbum, V, 19).

Intimately tied with the Original Covenant, the New Covenant ushers in a new age in which all people are invited to share in God's kingdom. It is this invitation and this story that is told in the pages of the Christian Scriptures.

169

What to Do

1. Have the students read "The New Covenant" two-page spread (up to "Living the Good News") to themselves.
2. Have the students open their Bibles to the table of contents for the New Testament and find the names of the books listed in "Books of the New Testament" and then locate each of its books.
3. Note the general order: the Gospels first, then Acts; then Paul's letters in order of their length (longest first); then the Pastoral and Catholic letters, concluded by Revelation.
4. Have students read "Living the Good News." Ask them to describe how Jesus' victory over death is good news for them.
5. Ask the students to explain the meaning of the quotation from *Dei Verbum*.
6. Ask students to define what is meant by the Original Covenant. Ask how the New Covenant differs from the original one.

Extending the Lesson Have students make tabs to mark the beginning of various books of the New Testament. These can be made with cardboard and tape, and marked with a felt marker.

Chapter Overview

This chapter explores the life of Jesus and places it in historical context. After an overview of the four gospel accounts, students will be introduced to Jesus' teaching about the kingdom and to the signs and miracles he worked.

Teaching Objectives

By the end of this chapter students will be able to:
• Distinguish between the Jesus of history and the Christ of faith.
• Describe the historical context of Jesus' life.
• Explain the origins of the four gospel accounts.
• Discuss the importance of the kingdom in Jesus' teaching.

Welcome

Students need to be aware that they are moving into a new area of study. Vary your routine so that students sense something different is about to occur. You may want to have music playing when they arrive; enlist several students to serve as greeters at the door; or have a video of Jesus' life playing when students arrive.

What to Do

When everyone has gathered, say: "Today we enter a world quite different from the one we have been studying. It is a new time, a new approach, and offers a chance for many new understandings. You will find, however, that its roots are deep in the Israelite world. Today we begin the study of the New Testament, the New Covenant."

CHAPTER 10

Jesus' Life and Message

70

63 B.C.E.
● Pompey annexes Palestine for Rome

37
● Herod the Great becomes King of Judea

4 B.C.E.–6 C.E.
● Birth of Jesus

6
6
● Rome begins to rule Judea directly

19
● Jews banished from Rome

26–36
● Pontius Pilate Procurator of Judea

27
● Augustus becomes the first Emperor

ca. 30
● Beginning of Jesus' public mission

ca. 33
● Crucifixion of Jesus

40
● Missionary efforts of the early Church

50
50
● First letter of Paul (Thessalonians)

66–70
● Gospel of Mark

70
● Vespasian becomes Emperor
● First Jewish Revolt against Rome

83–87
● Gospel of Matthew
● Gospel of Luke

ca. 91
● Christians persecuted under Emperor Domitian

95–99
● Gospel of John, Catholic epistles

100

Legend

● General History
● Biblical History
● Jewish History
● Books written

M ichael was the kind of guy nobody really liked. He was rude, and always saying mean things to people. His appearance and personal habits didn't win him many friends either. If people paid any attention to him at all, it was either to laugh at or to pity him. The only people at school who ever talked to him were the counselors, who constantly called him in to talk about his poor behavior.

One day a new student, Joshua, arrived at school. People liked him right away. Josh seemed to have a different take on life. He was self-confident, but he didn't need to put people down to make his point. He became popular enough that he could have his pick of friends.

Not long after Joshua arrived, he spotted Michael sitting by himself in the cafeteria. He went over and sat down. After a few minutes, Michael

---

MORE ABOUT THE TEXT

Changing Rulers

Remember that Judah was never to gain its independence as a nation after its defeat at the hands of the Babylonians in 587 B.C.E. For the next five hundred years or so it would be controlled first by the Persians (Cyrus the Great) and then by the Greeks (Alexander the Great). After the Maccabean revolt in the second century B.C.E., Judah regained a little of its autonomy while remaining a subject nation.

Jerusalem came under Roman rule in 63 B.C.E. at a time when the Empire was experiencing great change. Only seven years before, Pompey and Crassus had used their troops to gain the counselship of Rome. Three years later, Julius Caesar entered into the Roman government. For the next fourteen years, these three co-rulers were to fight each other until Julius Caesar emerged the victor in 44 B.C.E. During this time of conflict, Judah was mostly ignored.

got up, screamed "Leave me alone!" and stomped away. The other students in the cafeteria laughed loudly at Michael's response. They were sure that Joshua would realize his mistake and forget about Michael. Joshua was not so easily discouraged. He sought out Michael each day, and gradually Michael let his guard down. As Michael accepted Joshua's persistent attention, he began to trust him. Within a few weeks, Michael looked forward to seeing Joshua and talked with him about many things. Eventually, Joshua and Michael became friends, and with such a good friend, Michael's outlook on life improved. The counselor called this change in Michael a "miracle."

The rest of the student body was very much aware of Joshua's affect on Michael. They asked a lot of questions: "Why did Joshua spend so much time with Michael? Why did he care so much?" "What was it about Joshua that enabled him to get through to Michael when everyone else had failed?" "How could one person have so much impact on another?" "Is it possible for other people to be like Joshua?"

An Amazing Man

Jesus had a similar impact on the people he met. People living in the first century of the common era asked many similiar questions after Jesus' life, death, and resurrection. Like Joshua, Jesus came on the scene unexpectedly and attracted large crowds of people. Yet, he didn't seek out the company of only the elite; he also spent a great amount of time with social outcasts and the poor. During his short life, he, too, accomplished what people called miracles. After he was gone, people wondered "Who was this man and what do his life and teachings mean?" In the New Testament, we read the answers to these questions as given by a variety of early Christian authors.

Introducing the Chapter

What to Do

Pray with your students. Include thanksgiving for the knowledge and understanding the students have gained of the Original Covenant and of the People of God. Ask blessings on them and yourself for the new studies now opening before you. Speak especially to Jesus, since he is the main topic of the New Covenant.

Have the students read the opening story for Chapter 10. Ask: "What is so special about Joshua? Why was Joshua able to reach Michael when everyone else failed? How is Joshua very much like Jesus?" (He listens, cares for the outcast, pays attention, doesn't quit.) Note for students that "Joshua" is Hebrew for "Jesus."

Development

Students will see that Jesus lived and died during a particular time in a particular place. He was born and raised in Judea under Roman rule.

Using the Timeline

Have the students examine the timeline for Chapter 10. Look especially for the items pertaining to Judean history.

Point out to the students that Jesus' birth date remains unknown, and the dates of his public life are uncertain.

MORE ABOUT THE TEXT

The Destruction of the Second Temple

Solomon's Temple had been destroyed by the Babylonians in 587 B.C.E. The Temple was rebuilt by Nehemiah after the Jews returned from Exile and was rededicated in 515 B.C.E. After the period of the Abomination, the Temple was purified and rededicated in 164 B.C.E.

In 54 B.C.E., the Roman counsel Crassus was fighting with the other two counsels, Caesar and Pompey, over who would rule Rome. Crassus's forces were losing the battle and Crassus needed money fast. To get it, Crassus plundered the Temple in Jerusalem. Once again the people of Judah were deprived of temple sacrifice. The Temple would not be rebuilt for twenty-four years until construction was begun on the final Temple by Herod the Great.

◆ The Historical Jesus

Teaching Objectives

By the end of this lesson students will be able to:
- Explain the difference between the Jesus of history and the Christ of faith.
- Place Jesus' life in its historical context.
- Tell why the gospel accounts are not considered historical sources.

Development

- The students will see that while the Gospel tells us much about Jesus, they were not written as histories. They are, rather, statements of faith about Jesus.
- The students will recognize the three layers of information present in the formation of the gospel accounts.
- The students will understand that Jesus was a real person who lived during a specific time in history.

What to Do

1. Have the students read the italicized paragraphs and learning objectives for Section One. Ask questions of them, seeking to clarify their understanding. What do the students think they know of Jesus?

2. Make two columns on the board. Have students tell you what they already know about Jesus and write their answers in the first column. Then, have the students tell you what they would like to know about Jesus' life and personality. List their questions in the second column.

3. Ask for volunteers to take turns reading "The Historical Jesus" aloud. Then, look at the list on the board and ask the students which of their questions about Jesus might be answered in the Gospel? They can keep these in mind as they study about Jesus.

Who Was Jesus?

Ravenna, *Christ as Warrior, Second Century?*

Imagine that you are asked, "Who was Jesus?" What would you say? You might think of him as God, or as a great teacher, or as a healer. Depending on the teaching you have received, you might know some theological ideas about Jesus, like those in the Creed we say at Mass. You might call him savior or redeemer, too. But theology about Jesus is not everything we want to know about him.

In this section, you'll learn what we can know about the life and times of Jesus. You'll also discover the limits to a truly historical investigation of Jesus' life, and why our faith in Jesus goes beyond what can be proven about him.

Learning Objectives for Section One

By the end of this section, you will be able to:

- Define: "Christ of faith," "Jesus of history."
- Discuss the problem of knowing the historical Jesus.
- Understand the various Jewish sects at the time of Jesus.
- Explain the origins of the four gospel accounts.

◆ The Historical Jesus

Bible scholars often distinguish between the "Christ of faith," the Jesus who we believe is Lord and Savior through the tradition of the Church, and the "Jesus of History," the flesh-and-blood person, Jesus of Nazareth. You probably already know a lot about the Christ of faith. But what do you know about the historical Jesus? What was his life like, and what did he do and say that caused people to see him as special and even divine?

Gospel Accounts: Historical Sources?

The basic sources of evidence we have about the life of Jesus are the four gospel accounts in the New Testament. Each gospel account is full of information about the details of Jesus' life, and much of this information is accurate and reliable. The gospel accounts are not, however, historical works. Their primary purpose was to preach about the risen Jesus, and to convince others to recognize him as the Lord, **not** to record historically accurate information. Remember what you learned in Chapter 1: what is important is that the meaning is presented correctly.

Throughout the years, the gospel accounts have presented Jesus' life and teaching to millions of believers. As statements of faith they have been wildly successful. As statements of fact, however, they often frustrate our historical curiosity.

If you were to write a biography of Jesus, what material would you include?

- Where and when he was born?
- Did he have a happy childhood?
- Who were his best friends?
- Where did he go to school and who were his important teachers?

Wouldn't you want to include as much background on his childhood and adolescence as you could find?

MORE ABOUT THE TEXT

Prayer of Imagination

While the gospel accounts give us little real description of Jesus and his daily experience, it has been Christian practice for centuries to reflect on Jesus' life. Reflection on Jesus and what he was like is speculation from a factual viewpoint that can help Christians to grow in their appreciation of Jesus and in their sense of closeness to him. Invite the students to approach the historical Jesus with a little imagination.

Introduce your students to the *Prayer of Imagination*. They place themselves at the scene of various stories about Jesus from the gospel accounts, imagining what it would have been like to be: Jesus when his parents found him in the Temple in Jerusalem, one of the servants who sees Jesus change water into wine, Peter when he realizes that he has denied knowing Jesus, or Mary Magdalene when she hears the risen Christ call her by name.

Oddly enough, except for one story in Luke (see *Luke* 2:41–52), the writers of the gospel accounts show no interest in Jesus' childhood, adolescence, and young adulthood. They move directly from Jesus' infancy to his life at about the age of 30, when he began his public career.

Once again consider what you would include in your biography of Jesus, but this time concentrate on his years of ministry. You most definitely would want to know how he got started, when he made his first major speech, as well as the important people with whom he dealt. You would think that for a man of such importance, writers would want to follow his career carefully, documenting everything to make sure that nothing was left out.

The writers of the Gospel didn't think of history in these terms. They actually tell us very little about what physically happened during Jesus' ministry. Most of the events they record could have taken place over a period of a few weeks. How did Jesus spend the rest of his time? What else did he do? We don't learn about it from the gospel accounts. The Gospel writers are interested only in enough details from Jesus' life to show his significance; those that will help us see him as the Son of God and teacher about God's kingdom.

Layers within the Gospels

"Okay," you may be saying, "the gospel accounts are not historical records, but I can at least be sure about the details they do include, can't I?" Well, the gospels do include a wealth of historically accurate information, but sometimes details are confused or altered to bring them into line with the overall purpose of the particular gospel account.

The Catholic Church (see *The Catechism of the Catholic Church*, #126) recognizes three layers of information in the gospel accounts:

1. Sayings and events which go back to the historical Jesus.
2. Material which comes from the teaching of the apostles.
3. Material which comes from the teaching of the gospel writer.

The gospels do not distinguish these layers for us, so in some cases we're not sure if we're reading about the historical Jesus, or if it comes from the later teaching of the apostles, or if it was created by the writer directly. Therefore, even though the Gospel tells us a great deal about the historical Jesus, it leaves out information we would like to have.

Development of the Four Gospel Accounts

Historical Jesus

Apostolic Tradition: Community Memories Christian Experience

Writers of the Gospel Accounts

Have You Considered?

1. How important do you think it is to know about the historical Jesus? What do you think we need to know?
2. Think about a favorite relative or friend. If you were to write a biography of this person, how might your memories be influenced by how you felt about this person?
3. Can a life-story of someone be wrong about some of the minor details, and yet still be "true" in its overall picture? Explain your answer.

3. Have the students read "The Context of Jesus' Life" silently. Those who finish quickly can go on to read "Understanding More About" on page 187. Given this information, ask the students to discuss what they think the ordinary person in Judea might have experienced during the first 30 years of the first century.

Recall

Allow students to form small groups to answer questions 1–6 of the "Chapter 10 Review Q/A" for Section One on page 186.

Connect

What to Do

Homework assignment: "Find out what your family members know about the historical Jesus, or about what life was like for Jews living under Roman rule." Ask them also what they can tell you about the sources of the stories in the four gospel accounts. Have them write a few paragraphs about what they learn from their family."

What's Next?

What to Do

Have the students mark the first page of each of the four gospel accounts in their Bibles with small slips of paper. Ask them to compare the first two verses of each Gospel. Are they surprised? How might they explain these differences? Make sure students leave the markers in place; they will be using them again for the next lesson.

Ask the students to tell you some of the things about Jesus they are thankful for. Gather these into a prayer and close by praying the "Our Father" together.

in the Spotlight

Ask one student to read "in the Spotlight" aloud and point out that the picture on page 172 is an early representation of Jesus. The book he holds reads, "Ego sum Via Veritas et Vita," or "I am the Way, the Truth and the Life," a Latin quotation from the Gospel of John.

◆ The Context of Jesus' Life: Roman Palestine

One way to know more about the historical Jesus is to investigate the time and place in which he lived. Jesus' work took place in Palestine in the first century C.E., during the time Palestine was part of the Roman empire. To understand Jesus, we need to know how Roman occupation changed life for his Jewish community.

Life under the Romans

In 63 B.C.E., the Roman General Pompey conquered Jerusalem and annexed Palestine. From then on, Palestine was under the control of Rome.

- The Roman territory of "Judea"—basically the same as that of ancient Judah—was ruled by a king, "Herod the Great" from 37 to 4 B.C.E.
- After Herod's death, Judea was ruled by his brother Archelaus. He was such an ineffective king that Caesar Augustus banished him and made Judea a province.
- Provinces were governed by Roman governors called prefects or procurators such as Pontius Pilate, whose rule in Judea began in 26 C.E.
- Pilate was hated in Judea, because he had no respect for the Jewish religion. In Jerusalem, he put up images of the emperor for the Roman soldiers to worship. Only the threat of widespread armed rebellion convinced Pilate to remove these idols. Even so, the adversarial relationship with the Jewish leadership was firmly established.

The Romans continued the process of Hellenization begun in the early fourth century B.C.E. Some Jews embraced Roman rule and adopted a Hellenized lifestyle, often becoming wealthy in the process. For most Jews, however, the Roman period was a time of increasing poverty and hardship.

- They lived under the heavy taxation of the Romans.
- Land was increasingly concentrated in the hands of a few wealthy property owners.
- Small farmers were forced off their farms and into the city, where they generally did not find work.
- Economic and social unrest was common. This was not a peaceful time.

Many people blamed these conditions on the Romans and their governors. For these reasons, the threat of outright rebellion was never far away. When Jesus preached the kingdom of God, therefore, many people wanted to hear in his words a promise of action against the Romans, leading to Jewish independence. As we will see, however, this was not Jesus' message.

Jewish Sects at the Time of Jesus

One of the important aspects of Jewish life in Jesus' lifetime was the existence of groups of Jews organized around certain ideas. We sometimes call these groups "sects," although they may have been only interest groups similar in some ways to political parties.

in the Spotlight
A Portrait of Jesus?

If you were asked to describe Jesus' physical appearance, what would you say? A man with long hair, a beard, and perhaps wearing a robe? That's certainly the way Jesus has been pictured in Western art for centuries. However, that's not the way the earliest artists depicted Jesus.

The oldest picture of Jesus is a wall painting in the Greek Chapel, found among the "catacombs," or early Christian burial chambers, in Rome. In this painting, dated to around 150 C.E., Jesus is shown as a beardless young adult with short hair. A third century house in Syria also shows Jesus as beardless. Other early pictures show Jesus with long, curly hair, but still no beard. The beard doesn't appear until the fourth century.

The picture of Jesus with long hair and a beard may be closer to the truth than the earlier examples. The earliest painting of Jesus is clearly idealized. They show him much as an upperclass, Roman Christian, with short hair and a clean face. This portrait would be very acceptable and non-threatening to Roman citizens. However, Jewish males in Palestine during Jesus' day were very likely to have long hair, both because of observance of the laws regulating shaving, and as a way of protesting Israel's occupation by the short-haired Romans.

The Bible tells us nothing about what Jesus looked like. But since Jesus was from the Middle East, he almost certainly would have had dark hair and skin.

MORE ABOUT THE TEXT

Roman Rule

Daily life under Roman rule was not necessarily terrible for the Jews. They had their own businesses (like Peter's fishing fleet) and ran their own lives. Judean government was often a compromise between Roman and Jewish law—at the insistence of the Jews. Rome, while not favoring the Jews (who puzzled them enormously), allowed the practice of Jewish religious customs and often deferred to Jewish preferences in social and some governmental matters. Still, the law of the land was Roman, and Judea was occupied territory.

The likelihood of armed outbreak was always present in Judea, where people agitated for independence. More Roman legionnaries per capita of native population were stationed in Judea than anywhere else in the Empire. Every town had local representatives of the hated Roman military.

The Sadducees   The *Sadducees* came from wealthy, aristocratic families who controlled the Temple and supported Roman rule. Some had priestly ancestors. A few seem to have been high priests in the Temple. They emphasized the Torah, and rejected religious ideas such as angels, demons, and resurrection. Opposed to Jesus, their leadership was too cozy with the Roman ruler to be popular.

The Pharisees   The *Pharisees* were closely associated with another group called the "scribes." The Pharisees stressed the Law, but they believed that it should be interpreted differently under different circumstances. They avoided contact with Gentiles and with Jews who did not keep the Law, whom they called "sinners." The Pharisees and the Sadducees often opposed each another. The Pharisees believed in the idea of a resurrection (an afterlife). They were highly regarded by the Jewish people. Rabbis (teachers) usually came from this group.

The Essenes   Originally the *Essenes* and the Pharisees were part of a larger group of Jews opposed to Hellenization. Unlike the Pharisees, however, the Essenes decided that to keep the Law it was necessary to flee the cities and live in the wilderness. They

The Bible in Context

The Dead Sea Scrolls

In 1945, a shepherd boy discovered a few old jars in a cave near the Dead Sea. Inside these jars were pieces of leather covered with ancient writing. Soon many more documents were found in the desert caves. These documents, usually written on animals skins called "parchment," are known as the "Dead Sea Scrolls."

The scrolls were hidden in the caves sometime before the fall of Jerusalem in 70 C.E., but most of them were written more than a hundred years earlier by unknown writers. Some scrolls are copies of individual books from the Old Testament, and they represent the oldest Bible manuscripts in existence.

The rest of the manuscripts are original writings that show us the concerns and ideas which were current among Jews at this time. One such original writing is the "War Scroll," an apocalyptic book which predicts the overthrow of the Romans and the purification of the Temple.

Early Christian writers such as John may have been influenced by this or another such writing which contrasts "light" and "darkness." Another scroll uses the phrase "Son of God" to refer to the coming Messiah, showing that some Jews expected such a figure during this period.

The Dead Sea Scrolls were found in these and other similar caves in the hills surrounding the Dead Sea.

built communities in the desert for their members. Despite this isolation, many of their religious ideas were well-known. Some early Christians were influenced by them, although they are not mentioned in the New Testament.

Have You Considered?

1. How does the culture and time period in which someone is raised affect his or her ideas and values? Provide an example with your answer.
2. Describe any parallels you see between Roman Palestine and the world today. Which area of the world today most resembles the conditions of Roman Palestine? Why?

LESSON TWO (pages 176–178)

◆ The Gospel Accounts

Welcome

What to Do

Greet the students as they enter and find their seats. When everyone has arrived, ask the students to name the qualities they appreciate most in their friends.

Offer a prayer giving thanks for the qualities your students mention; then, ask the students to close their eyes and pray silently for the person to their left and to their right. Finish your prayer by asking for God's blessing on yourself and your students.

Introducing the Lesson

Teaching Objectives

By the end of this lesson students will be able to:
• Identify the three synoptic gospels and explain how they are related.
• Describe when, where, and for whom the four gospel accounts were written.
• Explain some of the differences and similarities in the four gospel accounts and how these differences affect our knowledge of the historical Jesus.

What to Do

Remind the students of the last exercise of the previous session, and the differences they found in the first verses of each account. Ask the students to compare the last paragraphs of each account as well. Call on various students who will tell you what they have found. Which are most similar? Is there one that seems particularly different?

Draw the students' attention to the timeline on page 170. Tell them that one possible reason for the differences in the four accounts is that they were written at different times. Ask the students to find out when each of the four accounts was written. What difference do they think it might make that Mark's account was written only thirty years after Jesus' crucifixion, while John's was written nearly seventy years later?

◆ The Gospel Accounts

The four gospel accounts are the basic sources we have for the life and teaching of Jesus. The common message shared by these four writings is called the "Gospel," from a Greek word meaning "good news." Although all the gospel accounts feature Jesus as their central character, each tells the story in a unique way, based on the circumstances in which it was written and the viewpoint of its writer. Despite these differences, Mark, Luke, and Matthew have much in common. They're often called the "synoptic" gospels, meaning "seeing together." John offers a distinctive account of the Gospel. Let's take a look at these four different ways of telling the "good news" about Jesus.

Mark

Mark was written in the 60s C.E., and like all the gospel accounts, it was originally written in Greek. Mark repeatedly explains Aramaic words and Jewish customs, he seldom makes reference to the Old Testament, and he seems confused about the geography of Palestine, so it seems likely that Mark's readers were Gentiles who lived outside of Palestine, probably in Rome.

Mark's account is rather stark. For Mark, the suffering of Jesus is the main point of a *Passion Story*, a story about the suffering and crucifixion of Jesus. Mark also presents the least flattering pictures of Jesus' disciples—they are often afraid of Jesus, unable to understand his message, and they fail miserably at Jesus' death.

Luke

The Gospel according to Luke and the Acts of the Apostles were written by the same person, whom we call "Luke." Luke's Gospel account interprets the Greek Old Testament (Septuagint) from a Gentile viewpoint, for a Gentile community. Because Luke's account is aware of the destruction of the Temple in 70 C.E., but does not treat this as an immediate crisis, its writing is usually dated to 80–85 C.E.

Wm. Blake, *Christ Appearing to the Apostles after the Resurrection.* Eighteenth Century.

Each of the gospel accounts describe Jesus' appearing to the Apostles following the Resurrection, but each report is different. Read the last chapter of each account to see how they differ.

◆ MORE ABOUT THE LESSON

The Whole Picture

When discussing the differences among the gospel accounts, a good analogy to use is the four-color printing process. In order to print full color pictures in books or magazines, printers used to take photographs of the original picture in each of four different colors (red, blue, yellow and black). Then they would print them, one on top of the other, to get the final full-color picture. This is similar to what happens when we read the four accounts of the Gospel: although reading any one of them gives us a good picture of Jesus' life, when we put them all together we come to a fuller, more accurate understanding.

Scripture Workshop

Q

Bible scholars believe that Mark was the first gospel account to be written, and that Matthew and Luke copied much from Mark. There are passages that Matthew and Luke have in common, however, that did not come from Mark. Because it's clear that Matthew and Luke did not copy from each other, scholars believe they must have used another source, which is called "Q" (from the German word *Quelle*, meaning "source"). You can examine this theory for yourself. Look up the following pairs of verses from Matthew and Luke:

(1) Luke 7:6–9, Matthew 8:8–10
(2) Luke 10:13–15, Matthew 11:21–23
(3) Luke 11:24–26, Matthew 12:43–45
(4) Luke 13:34–35, Matthew 23:37–39

In your Bible, underline once all the words that are exactly the same in the two passages. Then underline twice the words that are basically the same as those in the other passage. Answer these questions:

1. Are these similarities strong enough to support the theory of a common source? Why or why not?
2. What do these four pairs of passages have in common?

Nowhere in the accounts are we given even a hint about where Luke lived. Some have thought he was from either Asia Minor or Syria, but no one can know for sure. Luke shows greater interest in women, in the poor, and in those who have no social status. He also develops the theory of salvation history, dividing time into the three periods of Israel, Jesus, and the Church.

Matthew

The author of the Gospel according to Matthew could not have been the same person as the apostle

Matthew found in Acts of the Apostles 1:13. Because this gospel account is aware of arguments between Christians and Jewish leaders, which became intense after the destruction of the Temple, the writing is usually dated to 85–90. Matthew's text is full of allusions to the Old Testament. Judging from the interests expressed in the book itself, Matthew wrote for a community that included mostly Christians who were Jewish in background, but also Christians who were Gentiles. Matthew is interested in the ongoing relationship between the Old Testament (Law and Prophets) and Jesus and his followers. This account relies heavily on the Old Testament, in order to show what is in the new Covenant and how the new "fulfills" the old.

John

John did not rely on the traditions used in the synoptic gospels. Instead, John formed the traditions of early Christianity into a unique vision. Because of John's view of Jesus, his nature and his mission, many scholars think John was written later than the other accounts, perhaps in the 90s C.E. It's possible that a community of students, founded by John, was involved in putting together the account that bears his name.

John's gospel account features speeches by Jesus. While Jesus usually begins the speech, the writer's reflections blend it into a consistent teaching. John uses symbols more than the other gospels do. John's irony is famous: he puts truth into the words of Jesus' opponents, for example, or has a person totally misunderstand what is happening so that Jesus can discuss the truth. Finally, John's story of the passion of Jesus portrays a Jesus quite different from the one seen in the Synoptic accounts.

Have You Considered?

1. As discussed, each gospel account has its own point of view. How is it that two people can write about exactly the same subject, and yet end up with very different stories?
2. None of the gospel accounts is likely to have been written by actual followers of Jesus. What does that mean, in terms of their value as historical sources about the life of Jesus?
3. All of the gospel accounts were written in Greek. What can we learn from this observation?

Development

What to Do

1. Give the students a few moments to read "The Gospel Accounts." When they have finished you may want to share with them the analogy of the four-color printing process suggested in the "More about the Lesson" on page 176.
2. Read Mark 2:1–12 to your students without telling them which account you are reading. Ask if there is anything in the passage that leads them to believe it is characteristic of one particular author. Then point out the argument that arises between Jesus and the scribes.
3. Complete the activities in the "Scripture Workshop."

Have You Considered?

1. Any two witnesses to the same event will give different accounts, influenced by where they were, what they saw, and their own preconceptions.
2. The gospel accounts are witnesses to the faith convictions of the early Church.
3. The Gospels are translations from the original language.

Scripture Workshop

1. The verbal similarities (in many cases, the words are identical) strongly suggest reliance on a written, rather than merely oral, common source.
2. The four passages are all sayings of Jesus. "Q" is sometimes called the "sayings source."

MORE ABOUT THE TEXT

Luke

Luke's writings—both his gospel account and the Acts of Apostles—show clearly his interest in salvation history. Scholars note the following divisions in his work: the first four chapters of Luke emphasize God's promises to the chosen people; the rest of Luke belongs to the period of Jesus; and, finally the Acts of the Apostles portrays the age of the Holy Spirit, the beginning of the life of the Church.

John

The difference between John's account of the Passion and the Synoptic accounts is one of emphasis and perspective. For the Synoptics, Jesus is victim and sacrifice; he remains mostly silent and allows events to happen to him. In John's account, however, Jesus is totally in charge of the Passion; active and vocal, he orchestrates everything that occurs.

◆ The Quest for the Historical Jesus

Development

What to Do

1. "Learn from the Map." Direct the students' attention to the map on page 178.
2. Have students read "The Quest for the Historical Jesus."

LEARN FROM THE MAP

1. A distance of approximately 80 miles, about a four-day trip.
2. The closest Phoenician city would be Tyre, approximately 32 miles from Capernaum (a two day walk).
3. Answers should be in the range of 160 miles, a nine-day trip.

Practicing the Skills

What to Do

Instruct the students to use a concordance to locate at least one Gospel reference for each of the towns and areas mentioned in "Learn from the Map."

Recall

Ask for volunteers to answer questions 7–11 in Section One of the "Chapter 10 Review, Q/A."

Connect

What to Do

Ask the students what they learned from looking up all the Gospel references in this lesson.

What's Next?

What to Do

Homework Assignment: "Ask someone in your family what was the main point of Jesus' teaching."

Have You Considered?

1. None of the historical theories about Jesus can be proved based on the available evidence.
2. Faith and proof are essentially incompatible.
3. Jesus was fully human. Although he never sinned, he was tempted.

Bonus Focus for You ————
Read John 15:1–17. Write your reflection in your journal.

178

LEARN FROM THE MAP

Roman Palestine

To follow Jesus' story more closely, use this map and locate the following places: the district of Galilee, the Sea of Galilee, Judea, the Jordan River, the Dead Sea, Samaria, Nazareth, Bethlehem, Jerusalem, Cana, Capernaum, Bethany, and Jericho. Using the distances from the map legend, answer these questions:

1. Determine how far Jesus might have walked from Capernaum to Jerusalem. How many days might that have taken if he went directly?
2. The Gospel says that Jesus made at least one trip to Phoenicia, looking (unsuccessfully) for solitude. If he left from Capernaum, how far did he walk?
3. Apparently from Phoenicia Jesus went further north, then around to Decapolis, healing and teaching among the Gentile cities there. How long a trip might that have been?

©1994 Magellan Geographix℠ Santa Barbara, CA.

◆ The Quest for the Historical Jesus

On the cover of *Time* magazine on August 13, 1988, were the three words "Who Was Jesus?" The accompanying article covered the various theories scholars have proposed over the years in answer to this question, using the gospel accounts and information from Roman Palestine as their sources. This debate among scholars about who Jesus of Nazareth was, and what he stood for, is called the "quest for the historical Jesus."

Although each of the theories is interesting, none is provable because of the limits of the historical evidence. So what's the value of the historical approach, if it can't give us certainty about who Jesus was?

For one thing, what can be established about the historical Jesus is important. The historical evidence shows us a Jesus who valued all people equally, whether they were poor or rich. Jesus looked into the heart of each person with compassion and offered healing and goodness to all. The importance of the historical approach is that it emphasizes that Jesus was fully human, subject to the demands, temptations, and frustrations we all feel. By itself, this insight justifies the search for the Jesus of history.

Ultimately, however, our faith in Jesus does not rest on the historical evidence. As Catholic Christians, our faith includes the testimony of Church tradition, that Jesus is the Lord of humanity, the Son of God, who existed from the beginning of time, became human, died for our sins, and rose again. These points cannot be proved historically, but are verified in the experience of Christians who open their hearts to Jesus' healing presence.

Have You Considered?

1. Why can't our faith in Jesus be based only on historical evidence?
2. Can you believe something in faith if it can also be proven? Or does "faith" require the absence of proof? Explain your answer.
3. What does it mean to say that Jesus was subject to the same problems and concerns that you face?

◆ MORE ABOUT THE LESSON

Other Sources

There are historical documents that cover the same time period as the four gospel accounts that mention the activities of Jesus, or of his followers, such as those by Tacitus, Pliny the Younger, and Josephus. There are, indeed, other gospels, such as the Gospel According to Thomas, that tell the Christian story. These documents, while not part of the Christian canon, have helped scholars in their quest to understand more of the political and social atmosphere both during Jesus' life and during the early days of the Christian Church. You may want to consider assigning a research project that requires students to compare the information in these other sources with what they find in the gospel accounts.

The Kingdom of God

Unknown, St. John the Evangelist, Second Century?

One point on which historians do agree is that the center of Jesus' preaching and teaching was a reality he called the "kingdom of God" (some Bibles translate this as the "kingdom of Heaven" or as the "reign of God"). In fact, many Bible scholars have suggested that everything Jesus said and did illustrates the nature of the kingdom. Many people thought Jesus meant royalty, political authority, and military power. In this section, we'll explore the kingdom of God as Jesus understood it.

Learning Objectives for Section Two

By the end of the section, you will be able to:

- Explain the two dimensions of the kingdom of God.
- Demonstrate the special aspects of parables.
- Explain how Jesus' healing power paints a picture of what the kingdom is like.
- Describe how the kingdom applies to everyday life.

◆ The Nature of the Kingdom

We call the period in Jesus' life from approximately age 30 to 33, his *public ministry*. During this time, Jesus traveled from place to place, teaching people, healing the sick, and proclaiming the kingdom. Jesus built his ministry around the message he brought concerning this kingdom, and it was this message that changed peoples' lives and the course of history. Despite the tremendous importance Jesus attached to the phrase, "kingdom of God," it was often misunderstood. People formed many different expectations of what a "kingdom of God" could be.

Has this ever happened to you: a friend invites you to a party, but doesn't tell you what type of party it is? When you arrive, you find that you're dressed inappropriately because your idea of a party differs from that of the party's giver? That is exactly the experience of the people who heard Jesus' message.

They accepted Jesus' invitation to the kingdom but had the wrong idea as to what that kingdom was to be.

Misconceptions about the Kingdom

Jesus' message that the kingdom was at hand was frequently misunderstood by his first listeners, who doubtlessly understood this teaching through their own long-held expectations: they expected God to re-create an independent Jewish nation, ruled directly by a messiah (anointed king). As God had ruled the Israelites in their earliest days, so many Jews thought God would one day rule again. Included in this belief was the expected defeat of the oppressive Romans. It's not surprising, then, that many of the first people who heard Jesus, understood a political message about an earthly, Jewish kingdom.

After Jesus' death and resurrection, however, people came to understand that he had not been talking about an earthly kingdom at all. They remembered that he had said things like "the kingdom of God is

---

◆ MORE ABOUT THE LESSON

Understanding the Kingdom

The chances are that many of your students will think of the kingdom of God as heaven or life with God after death. This is a common notion among adults as well. Sometimes today it is also suggested that the "kingdom of God on earth" means a kingdom of political and social justice. Some people think of themselves as

"building the kingdom" in this sense. These two conceptions are a little different from the Gospel understanding, however. You may wish to point out that misconceptions of the nature of the kingdom have persisted through the centuries, though current misunderstandings or mis-emphasis are different from the earliest ones.

SECTION TWO

LESSON THREE
(pages 179–181)

◆ The Nature of the Kingdom

Welcome

What to Do

Greet the students personally as they enter. When they are all together, remind them of their homework assignment. Find out what their family members said about Jesus' main teaching and what the students added. Ask them to keep those ideas in mind as they work through today's lesson.

Pray with your students. Make this a prayer of thanksgiving for Jesus and for all that he taught us by his word and his example. Try to mention specifically some of the teachings brought out in your discussion of the students' homework. Ask for awareness of his presence during today's class.

Introducing the Lesson

Teaching Objectives

By the end of this lesson students will be able to:
- Understand what "the kingdom" meant in Jesus' teaching.
- Recognize some early misconceptions about the kingdom which Jesus struggled against during his ministry.
- Identify the two dimensions of the kingdom of God as Christians understand them today.

What to Do

Have the students read the opening paragraph (in italics) and the Learning Objectives for Section Two. Ask your class if they think this answers the question about the main topic of Jesus' teaching. Be sure they give reasons to support their answers and provide an opportunity for disagreement.

Development

What to Do

1. Before beginning the lesson, ask the students what they think is meant by the phrase, "kingdom of God." Then have the students read the opening two paragraphs of "The Nature of the Kingdom" plus "Misconceptions about the

Kingdom" and "Two Dimensions of the Kingdom." There is additional information with which you can supplement the student text in "More about the Text" on page 180.

2. Allow the students to form small groups to complete "Bible Activity" 1 on page 186 and write their shared responses.

3. Ask for three volunteers to read the last three subsections of "The Nature of the Kingdom" aloud. Then, still in their small groups, tell the students to list any new ideas that they have found in these three subsections.

4. Ask them to find and read the Gospel references given in "Entering the Kingdom." Give them some time to list several ways teenagers might begin to seek life in the kingdom, and the kingdom in life, and then ask each group to share its list with the whole class.

5. There is a Gospel passage cited in "New Attitudes" that focuses on Jesus' call for forgiveness. Have the students read Matthew 18:21–35, which includes that cited passage. Then, lead a discussion about the meaning of forgiveness. There are suggestions in More about the Lesson on page 181, that will give you help with this.

Practicing the Skills

What to Do

Have the students look up the following passages, identify which dimension of the kingdom they address, and explain what they say about life in the kingdom: Matthew 4:23; John 14:22–23; Mark 8:27–30; Matthew 4:17; Matthew 25:34; Luke 12:32; John 18:36; Luke 6:20, 10:9, 17:21; Acts 1:6–7. For more practice, students can also read the following references: Matthew 6:31–34; 18:2–4; Mark 10:15; Luke 6:27–35.

Recall

Ask each student to name one image of the kingdom and to explain what that image tells them about the kingdom.

Balling, *Ulysses S. Grant. Nineteenth Century.*

Many people heard Jesus' message of the kingdom and expected a great military leader to come forward to defeat the Romans, much as General Grant was able to defeat General Lee in the American Civil War.

at hand" or "the kingdom of God is within you" or "the reign of God is in your midst," and he referred to the parables he told as "the mysteries of the kingdom." What, then, did Jesus have in mind?

Two Dimensions of the Kingdom

The early Christians gradually realized that the kingdom of God Jesus proclaimed had two dimensions:

1. Jesus would return at the end of time when everything that he had promised would be fulfilled.
2. Jesus was inviting his followers to adopt a new style and quality of life.

The Second Coming Following Jesus' ascension into heaven, Christians expected him to return to earth during their lifetimes to establish the kingdom. This return is known as the *Second Coming*, or the *parousia*. The early Christians, in keeping with the traditional Jewish idea, expected Jesus to rule over the world and to destroy all the existing sources of power and authority when he returned. Saint Paul even had

to write a letter (Second Thessalonians) urging Christians not to quit their jobs and leave their families in expectation of the parousia!

The Kingdom Is Now! As they studied Jesus' ministry, Christians discovered the second dimension of his teaching about the kingdom: a spiritual, interior quality of life in relation to God that is available now, here, in this life on earth. This kingdom of God occurs in an individual who recognizes God as a real king and experiences himself or herself as a child in that kingdom. In this kingdom, people experience God as their common ruler, and treat others as fellow subjects of their heavenly king.

Living in the kingdom means living a life centered on:

• Love of God
• Love of others.

This was what Jesus said when asked about the commandments:

"You shall love the Lord your God with all your heart, with all your soul, with all your mind, and with all your strength...You shall love your neighbor as yourself. There is no other commandment greater than these."

(Mark 12:30–31)

Living in the kingdom, therefore, means loving God and serving others in loving ways.

The Kingdom Gives Rest

This kingdom is good news for everyone, because the qualities of life in Jesus' kingdom are the qualities everybody wants: a life that is deeply serene and confident; a life that is full of joy and enthusiasm and energy; a life that is happy because it is lived in love. This kind of life takes effort, but it doesn't feel like a constant test of the will. Instead, living in the kingdom feels like a giant weight has been lifted from your shoulders:

"Come to me," Jesus said, "all you who labor and are burdened, and I will give you rest.... For my yoke is easy, and my burden light."

(Matthew 11:28–30)

Why does living in the kingdom feel so restful and satisfying? It's because life in the kingdom is the only true path to happiness. When we're focused on ourselves, happiness always seems to be just out of our reach. Just when we feel that we've found happiness, it quickly fades away. But when we focus on something larger than ourselves—on God and others,

---

MORE ABOUT THE TEXT

Jewish Expectations of the Messiah

The people of Jesus' time naturally did not understand at first what Jesus meant by the kingdom. Ever since the Exile, the Jews had wished for the restoration of a permanent kingdom like the one they had long before under King David. For at least three centuries, the Jews had hoped for, prayed for, and believed in an "anointed one" (Messiah) who would return them to political independence.

For many Jews the expectation of a Messiah was almost an article of faith: the Lord would one day send them a strong ruler who would make their national aspirations come true. Justice would then reign and they could live directly under God with no hindrances from other peoples and governments. Many believed this was part of the Covenant with Yahweh, the promise to David, and God's assurance forever.

perhaps—and concentrate on service, we find that our own happiness results. Happiness comes from seeking the beauty of God and the good of other people, not from seeking personal satisfaction. This simple truth is the real secret of the kingdom of God.

Entering the Kingdom

While Jesus insisted that the life of the kingdom is waiting for all who wish to enter it, we can't become people of the kingdom all at once. Learning to live in the kingdom takes time and effort. The hardest part is simply getting started.

In reality, the only thing that must be given up is selfishness. Instead of putting ourselves at the center of the universe and measuring everything by how it affects us, we can put the kingdom of God at the center and measure everything else by its effect on our experience of God and other people. In fact, that's what Jesus said eventually would happen in the daily living of anyone who desires this kingdom.

Jesus said the kingdom begins for most people in small ways, then grows little by little until it embraces everything. Its growth is like the growth of a plant. Read Luke 13:18–19 and Matthew 13:31–32 to see how Jesus compares this small beginning to a mustard seed, which is very tiny, but grows into a large plant. In actuality, a mustard plant does not get big enough for birds to roost in it, but Jesus is exaggerating to show the tremendous fruitfulness—beyond all expectation—of the kingdom in a person's life.

Your tiny beginning might be anything—a single choice made with God in mind, or a small act of generosity for the sake of the Lord, or a change in your thinking. You only have to decide that you want kingdom-quality life and begin to cooperate with God's action to help it happen inside you.

New Attitudes

Jesus says the kingdom is always available to anyone who will accept it. But what does that mean? People who accept the kingdom also choose a new way of living and a new attitude about life.

One important area in which our attitudes need to change concerns material things. How much of your personal happiness is connected to items you may own: stereo system, designer clothes, $100 shoes? Western culture tends to judge happiness in terms of what we own, which promotes greed. When a person is greedy, who or what is the focus of attention? Is it God? Is it Jesus? Is it oneself? Is it the physical object that is desired?

Jesus taught people to have a new attitude toward God. The Sermon on the Mount taught people to be concerned for others as a way to fulfill the Law.

When a person is focused on himself or herself, the kingdom is treated as just another object to own, worth no more than anything else. Jesus said,

"No one can serve two masters. He will either hate one and love the other, or be devoted to one and despise the other. You cannot serve God and mammon [money]."
(Matthew 6:24)

Jesus urges people to forgive. In Matthew 18:21–22, Peter asks Jesus how often a person is to forgive wrongs. Jesus says, "seventy-seven times." In symbolic language this number means "every time." Think of it in mathematical terms as "infinity X infinity."

Have You Considered?

1. What do you think the world would be like if everyone lived the kingdom of God as Jesus described it?
2. Give an example of a situation in which someone's desire to accumulate material things interfered with his or her happiness.
3. What do you suppose it means to "let go of anger"? How can we train ourselves to do this?

Connect

What to Do

Homework Assignment: Have the students complete the "Spiritual Reflection" on page 185 at home and write about their experience in their Spiritual Journal.

What's Next?

What to Do

Have students name as many parables as they can think of, listing them on the board. Let them know that you will be discussing Jesus' use of parables in the next lesson.

Have You Considered?

1. Ask students to be as specific as possible: which aspects of life today would change, and in which ways, if people lived in the kingdom?
2. The classic example from Greek mythology is King Midas. Everything he touched would turn to gold. But quickly he found that he could not feed himself, get himself a drink of water, or enjoy any other simple pleasure, because everything became gold at his touch. Discuss the truth embodied in this myth.
3. Letting go of anger means that we refuse to let our lives be governed by anger, that destructive feelings are replaced by feelings of calm and acceptance. Letting go of anger is not only appropriate when we're in the wrong, but also where we're "right."

Bonus Focus for You

Read Luke 7:36–50. What relationship do you see here between forgiveness and love? How can you apply this to your own life? Which character in the story can you most easily identify with?

◆ MORE ABOUT THE LESSON

Forgiveness

The forgiveness of sins is an essential element of Christian understanding. Jesus came so that sins could be freely forgiven: God could forgive human sin and people could forgive each other's wrongs. Jesus even said that if we do not forgive each other, God will not forgive us (*Matthew* 6:14–15).

Forgiveness is an aspect of love. Forgiveness affirms that a loving relationship is more important than any harm that has been done by one to the other. But forgiveness is seldom easy, especially when the hurt is deep.

In his Parable of the Unforgiving Servant (*Matthew* 18:21-35), Jesus mentions "the torturers." Who are they? They are parts of ourselves. If we choose to hold a grudge (the opposite of forgiving), then we are always angry and tense about the other person. We destroy our own peace of mind by holding on to anger.

◆ Jesus Uses Parables to Illustrate the Kingdom

Welcome

What to Do

Ask the students to think of a short story that is important to them. Ask a couple of students to tell their story briefly and explain what they learned from it or why they remember it.

Pray with your students.

Introducing the Lesson

Teaching Objectives

By the end of this lesson students will be able to:

• Explain how Jesus made use of parables.

• Explain the structure of parables and be familiar with some of the parables Jesus used.

• Discuss how Jesus used his powers of healing.

• Provide examples of the four types of healing Jesus performed and explain the significance of each.

Scripture Workshop

1. Surprise Ending—*Wily Manager*: the rich man is not angry with the manager, but rather gives him credit for being enterprising. *Laborers in the Vineyard*: The master gives the same wage to all the laborers.

2. Why is this surprising? *Wily Manager*: the audience expects the rich man to punish the manager. *Laborers in the Vineyard*: Normally, laborers are paid for the amount for work they do or the amount of time they work

3. *Wily Manager*: In the kingdom, one does not seek revenge for wrongs done. *Laborers in the Vineyard*: People's merit (time served) does not earn them a place in the kingdom; it happens through God's grace.

182

◆ Jesus Uses Parables to Illustrate the Kingdom

In Jesus' teaching about the kingdom, he employed many forms of speech, such as wisdom sayings and stories. The most distinctive kind of speech Jesus used, however, is called a *parable*. From two Greek words meaning "to throw alongside," a parable is a figure of speech in which two things are thrown together for purposes of comparison. Jesus used these comparisons to help people understand life in the kingdom.

What Is a Parable?

A parable is a specific type of comparison, in which something familiar is used to explain something unfamiliar. For example, someone might explain the concept of justice by telling a story about a little boy who stole an apple from a neighbor's tree, and got caught. The everyday, familiar example of the boy's behavior helps people understand the more abstract concept.

Parables were a common form of speech in the ancient world. Jesus, however, used them in a special way. His parables upset the familiar by featuring surprise endings and unexpected behavior. Through these "twists," Jesus shows us how the kingdom is different from the world. The key to Jesus' parables lies in the element of surprise.

The Good Samaritan

Probably the most famous of all Jesus' parables is about the Good Samaritan. It reads as follows:

> "A man fell victim to robbers as he went down from Jerusalem to Jericho. They stripped and beat him, and went off leaving him half-dead. A priest happened to be going down that road, but when he saw him, he passed by on the opposite side. Likewise a Levite came to the place, and when he saw him he passed by on the opposite side."
>
> (Luke 10:30–32)

So far, the parable is drawing on experiences and images which would have been extremely familiar to Jesus' audience. Travel in the ancient world was very dangerous, and there was a constant risk of being robbed. This danger was especially real in first-

---

Scripture Workshop

Interpreting the Parables

A key to understanding the parables of Jesus is to study the "surprise endings" which reverse traditional images and expectations. Read the following parables:

• The Wily Manager *(Luke 16:1–8)*
• The Laborers in the Vineyard *(Matthew 20:1–16)*
• The Invitation to the Banquet *(Matthew 22:1–14)*

After you have thought about these parables, answer the following questions:

1. What is the "surprise ending" in each parable?
2. Why would this surprise Jesus' audience?
3. What does the surprise ending in each parable tell you about the kingdom?
4. What lesson do you take away from reading these parables?

---

century Palestine under Roman occupation. Further, the lack of concern shown by the priest and Levite would also have been familiar to the common people, who often accused their leaders of indifference to their suffering. The refusal of the priest and the Levite to help the injured man would also have made sense to Jesus' audience, who knew about the ritual purity laws in Leviticus—Jews who had touched blood could not offer sacrifice in the Temple without first being "purified."

Jesus' teaching about the kingdom does not lie in these familiar ideas, however; it's found in the element of surprise which comes next:

> "But a Samaritan traveler who came upon him was moved to compassion at the sight. He approached the victim, poured oil and wine over his wounds, and bandaged them. He then lifted him up on his own animal, took him to an inn, and cared for him. The next day he took out two silver coins and gave them to the innkeeper with the instruction: 'Take care of him. If you spend more than what I have given you, I shall repay you on the way back.'"
>
> (Luke 10:33–35)

◆ MORE ABOUT THE LESSON

Multiple Meanings

Like symbols, most parables have several layers of meaning. It is impossible to tie them to just one interpretation. Jesus' parables have been interpreted in many different ways by various modern and ancient scholars. To give you an idea of how widely varied parable interpretation has been, here is the framework of an interpretation of the Good Samaritan parable from about the fourth century C.E.:

The Jericho road was the road of human life. The man fallen among thieves was an archetype of humanity. The priest and Levite represented the Original Covenant. The Good Samaritan was Jesus. The inn was the Christian Church and the innkeeper was St. Paul.

Your students might enjoy hearing this different interpretation after they have had the chance to practice interpretation on their own today.

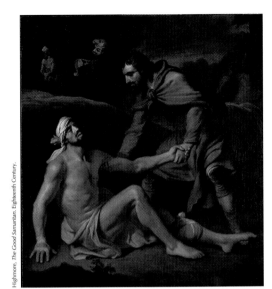

Highmore, *The Good Samaritan*, Eighteenth Century.

From what you know about the Good Samaritan story, why would Jesus' listeners have been troubled by it?

A Samaritan! This development would have struck Jesus' hearers as a major surprise. Remember what you read about relations between Jews and Samaritans in Chapter 8; the two groups were legendary for their hatred of each other. The dislike was so intense that Jews traveling from Galilee to Jerusalem would cross the Jordan River and go dozens of miles out of their way to avoid crossing Samaritan territory. By suggesting that the Samaritan did the right thing where Jewish leaders had failed, Jesus turns this traditional hatred upside down.

Jesus ends the parable by saying "Go and do likewise." A person living in the kingdom will, like the Samaritan, put the expression of love above law, custom, tradition, or individual preferences.

Have You Considered?

1. Explain why Jesus' understanding of the kingdom is best revealed in surprising, rather than in everyday, images.
2. One lesson of the parable of the good Samaritan is to see people as individuals, rather than as members of groups. Do you think this lesson is important for us today? Why or why not?

◆ Jesus' Healing Illustrates the Kingdom

Jesus didn't rely just on his parables or other sayings to share his vision. His actions also were designed to illustrate what life in the kingdom was like. Saint Augustine recognized this when he said that Jesus' actions are "for us, words, too." What Jesus *did* can teach us as much as what Jesus *said*. Probably the best example of how Jesus' actions reveal the kingdom is the healing stories. By healing people, Jesus showed the love for others, and the power to renew life that comes from living in the kingdom.

Types of Healing

Jesus performed several kinds of healing. In each case, the healing reflects the compassion that always moved Jesus to reach out to others. The healings can be broken down into four categories: physical healing, spiritual healing, resurrection, and moral healing.

Physical Healing   Jesus healed people who suffered from physical illnesses, such as blindness, uncontrollable bleeding, and leprosy. He made a special effort to reach out to lepers, people often neglected and scorned in his society. Two physical healings that you can read are the healing of a deaf person who could not speak well in Mark 7:31–35, and the healing of a leper in Luke 5:12–13. We call such healings *miracles*, exceptions to the normal course of ordinary events. Through these healings, Jesus demonstrated enormous power over nature and illness. The point of the healings was never, however, simply to display Jesus' power. Instead, they expressed the compassion and concern for others which is part of kingdom life. Later, Jesus' disciples also healed sick people in his name. Even today, some people have been given the capacity to heal in Jesus' name.

Spiritual Healing   At several points in the Gospel, Jesus heals people who are described as possessed by an "unclean spirit." Because the ancient world had no concept of psychology as we understand it, some behaviors which we would see as the result of mental illness were ascribed to demon possession.

Jesus showed amazing powers to heal such illnesses. One of the best known is the healing of the man from Gerasa. This man had been living naked

What to Do

Remind students of the list they made at the end of the previous lesson. Give them an opportunity to add to the list now. Call their attention to any parables on the list that will be covered in today's lesson. Then have the students read "Jesus Uses Parables to Illustrate the Kingdom."

Development

What to Do

1. Have the students complete "Bible Activity" number 2.
2. Draw the students' attention to the Parable of the Good Samaritan in their text. Help them to determine the main point of the parable.
3. Ask the students to express what they have learned about working with parables and finding their meaning.
4. In small groups, complete the "Scripture Workshop," reading the parables and discussing the questions. Ask them to consider whether or not the ending is surprising in the context of our society today.

Have You Considered?

1. Life in the kingdom is quite different from the way life is generally lived today.
2. Encourage them to discuss their own experience, not examples which come from media or classwork.

◆ Jesus' Healing Illustrates the Kingdom

Development

What to Do

1. Give the students a few minutes to read "Jesus' Healing Illustrates the Kingdom," marking the biblical references as they occur.
2. Have the students read Mark 7:31–35 and Luke 5:12–13, mentioned in "Physical Healing." These stories will have more impact if you can find two or three reliable students to dramatize them for the class.

◆ MORE ABOUT THE LESSON

Interpreting Parables

Many people find that they interpret parables almost intuitively, because of their recognition of analogies and comparisons. Still, several mental processes must occur to interpret parables well. Here are some of them:

• learning as much as possible about the cultural or natural facts related to the story;
• noticing analogies to life experience;

• making analogies with modern experience;
• noticing the "surprise endings" or exaggerations or symbols that are in the parable;
• asking how the meanings, as you unfold them, are congruent with the rest of Jesus' teaching, as far as you know. (If there are flat contradictions, you are probably misunderstanding something.)

3. Read aloud Luke 8:26–35, mentioned in "Spiritual Healing," then discuss these questions: "What do they think about possession by spirits? What do they know about psychosis? Would it have made any difference to Jesus which one it really was for the Gerasene man?"

4. Have the students read Luke 19:1–10, mentioned in "Moral Healing." Ask: "How might Zacchaeus have justified his thievery before Jesus met him? Why did the Gospel writer include information about Zacchaeus's height in the story? What quality in Jesus made everything seem different to Zacchaeus?"

Practicing the Skills

What to Do

In small groups, ask the students to complete "Bible Activity" 3. They should collaborate on a modern version of the parable. Then have each group's spokesperson read its story to the whole class. Ask the rest of the students to listen carefully to see if the main point of the parable has been kept in each new story. Let the class choose the best story, and make plans to dramatize it. See the notes in "More about the Lesson" for suggestions about the performance.

Recall

Have the students write their answers to "Chapter 10 Review Q/A," Section Two, questions 1–11. This will cover information from the last two lessons.

Connect

What to Do

Homework Assignment: Have the students do a spiritual reflection, similar to the one they did after the last lesson, based on Matthew 13:1–9. Give them the following questions for reflection:
• I am the ground on which the seed of God's sowing has fallen. What kind of ground have I been lately?
• What kind of ground would I like to be?
• How might I begin to become what I want to be?
They can write their reflections in their Spiritual Journals.

184

People of Note

The Blind Bartimaeus

Bible scholars have observed that the healing stories in the gospel accounts sometimes serve literary purposes as well. A good example of this is Mark 10:46–52, the healing of a blind man named Bartimaeus. Mark says that as Jesus left Jericho, Bartimaeus called out to him, referring to him as the "Son of David." Jesus approached him and asked him what he wanted. Bartimaeus, calling Jesus "Master," asked to see. Jesus told him, "Go your way; your faith has saved you." Immediately Bartimaeus recovered his sight.

This story comes at the end of a section in which Mark talks about how Jesus' message was misunderstood. The literary message of the story is that while a blind man could "see" the truth about Jesus because of his faith, those with good eyes who lacked faith could not.

The Bible tell us neither what happened to Bartimaeus after he recovered his sight nor how he felt about this remarkable gesture. Finish his story. Describe Bartimaeus's feelings once he could finally see. Would this gift turn out to be a blessing or a problem? How does Bartimaeus witness to the power of the kingdom?

---

out in the cemetery and was so strong that no chain could hold him. He sometimes attacked other people without cause. Today, he might be called psychotic. Was he possessed or was he mentally disturbed? All we know is that Jesus healed him. This frightening man calmly sat at Jesus' feet "clothed and in his right mind" (Luke 8:26–35). As with the physical healing, Jesus' use of power demonstrates a sign of the kingdom, where people are healed in mind and body.

Resurrection Jesus, like the great prophet, Elijah, brought people who had died back to life. Consider the story of Lazarus in John 11:17–44.

Jesus was some distance away when he heard that his friend, Lazarus, was ill. When he finally arrived, Lazarus had already been in his tomb for four days. In fact, when Jesus said the tomb should be opened, Lazarus' sister Martha—a very practical woman—objected because the corpse would surely be corrupt. But Jesus insisted that the stone cover be removed. Then he prayed to his beloved Father and cried out, "Lazarus, come out!" Lazarus came, still wrapped in the burial clothes. This episode shows us that the kingdom has the ultimate power, the power of life.

Moral Healing Finally, Jesus healed people in a way that did not involve their bodies directly. It might be called a healing of character or a moral healing. Luke tells the story of Zacchaeus, a tax collector who had gotten rich off his job—an achievement easily possible if the collector was a crook. Zacchaeus was also a very short man.

When Jesus came to his town, Zacchaeus tried to see him, but couldn't see over the crowd, so he climbed a sycamore tree alongside the road. Jesus spotted Zacchaeus in the tree and invited himself to Zacchaeus' house for dinner.

The story does not say exactly what happened, but at dinner Zacchaeus promised Jesus he would give half of his possessions to the poor and repay anyone he had injured four times over! Jesus rejoiced that "salvation has come to this house" (Luke 19:1–10). The story indicates that the kingdom has the power to change our lives, if we accept it.

Healings Reveal the Kingdom

The healings performed by Jesus illustrate the nature of the kingdom of God in several important ways:

• The kingdom has tremendous power to heal our bodies, minds, and souls.
• Living in the kingdom means having compassion for the suffering of others. We cannot ignore physical, mental or spiritual pain, wherever we find it.
• In the kingdom, the focus is always on God, and then on others. By living close to God, kingdom people *want* to respond to the needs of other people. In doing so, they find their own mental and spiritual peace.

When Jesus healed, he acted from a profound compassion for people. He also wanted people to wake up to the power of the kingdom in their midst. If Jesus is our example, we, too, are called to learn compassion—to feel deeply for all other living beings. Then, following Jesus, we are invited to act out our compassion.

◆ MORE ABOUT THE LESSON

Modern Samaritan Story/drama

Dramatizations of a modern version of this parable make wonderful pieces for your class to share with other groups: at gatherings of other students or parents, as a special program for younger children, or even as a homily at a school Mass. Begin with an impromptu dramatization, then have them polish their presentation. Making arrangements for the students to perform their pieces for at least one other group will encourage them to put their best efforts into the project and will raise their confidence in their ability to understand and communicate the message of the kingdom effectively.

What can you do in your daily living that will reveal God's kingdom to others?

- We can pray for others.
- We can take actions that relieve suffering.
- We can express understanding for the pain of others.

In doing so, we will discover a joy that belongs to the kingdom of God and cannot be taken away from us.

Have You Considered?

1. How does the behavior of people tell you more about them than what they say? Explain your answer.
2. Most of us do not have the power to heal physical illness immediately as Jesus did. What can you do to ease physical suffering?
3. Describe two or three examples from your own experience where you see people in mental or spiritual pain. What could you do to bring them relief? Be as specific as possible.

Spiritual Reflection

Praying the Parables

Read Jesus' parable of the Rich Fool in Luke 12:16–21. Quietly put yourself in God's presence. Now, think about these questions:

- What are my goals, as far as I know them right now? What long term or short term dreams or hopes do I have? Do they involve money or other material things?
- What do you think would be a good attitude to cultivate about goals and material things, judging from this parable?

- One of the best ways to handle material things well is to consider that they are "on loan" from God and that you are responsible for them. Try thinking about the "Rich Fool" in this way: if he had thought that the material possessions were on loan from God, what might he have done differently? Explain your answer.

Use your answers to these questions as an occasion for prayer. Ask God to guide you in forming goals that will bring you lasting happiness. Also ask God to help you encourage the hopes and dreams of others as well as your own. After you're finished, thank God for this time.

MORE ABOUT THE TEXT

The Gerasene

This man's symptoms suggest strongly that he was psychotic; strength like his sometimes appears in psychotic rages. Possession is also a genuine possibility, although most disturbances which Jesus' contemporaries attributed to spirits were probably troubles which we would name differently. They often appear to us as psychosis or epilepsy, for example. What you want your students to understand is that Jesus was a Jew of the first century; he would have shared the "diagnosis" of his time. But his capacity to heal did not depend on the diagnosis. Whatever a disturbance was called, however it was understood, Jesus' power reached beyond reason to the essence of the problem and made the person whole and well. In so doing, he opened up the kingdom of God.

What's Next?

What to Do

Ask students to name as many followers of Jesus as they can. If they seem to be naming only biblical figures such as the twelve disciples, Paul, or Mary Magdalene, remind them of more current followers such as Dorothy Day, Archbishop Oscar Romero, or Martin Luther King, Jr. They may also name family members or friends who are examples to them of what it means to follow Jesus, perhaps their godparents or Confirmation sponsors, a teacher, priest, parent, or family friend. You may want to ask them how they know these people are disciples of Jesus. Let them know that discipleship will be the theme of the next chapter and invite them to begin to consider what they know already about being a disciple.

Have You Considered?

1. Behavior is important because it is easy to deceive others through speech, but our actions will reveal how we are and what we value.
2. Allow students to generate a number of suggestions as to how they can help ease physical suffering. Possibilities include: praying for others, sharing time with them, caring for them as much as possible, and working for political and social conditions in which suffering is minimized.
3. Ask students to be specific in the responses they give, both as to the situations they describe and the steps they believe they could take to ease people's mental or spiritual pain.

Bonus Focus for You

Read Luke 15:11–32, the Parable of the Prodigal Son. Sometimes people think this story refers only to the truly dissolute, but it points to us all whenever we are separated from God. Put yourself in the position of the lost son, and prayerfully imagine yourself moving through the whole parable. Write your experience in your journal.

Q/A

Section One

1. "Christ of Faith" refers to the Jesus who we believe is Lord and Savior. "Jesus of History" refers to the flesh-and-blood person, Jesus of Nazareth, based on the historical evidence.

2. The primary purpose of the Gospel was to preach the risen Jesus, not to record history.

3. The three levels in the Gospel are: (A) the words and deeds of the historical Jesus; (B) the oral teaching of the apostles; (C) the contributions of the individual evangelists.

4. Several factors contributed to this hardship: (A) The Jews lived under a double tax burden, from both the Temple and the Romans; (B) Land was concentrated in the hands of a few, wealthy property-owners; (C) Small farmers were forced into the cities, where they often could not find work.

5. Four important Jewish groups were: (A) Sadducees; (B) Pharisees; (C) Essenes; (D) Scribes.

6. The Dead Sea Scrolls open a window into first century B.C.E. Jewish thought and culture.

7. Because the Gospel of Mark features several mistaken references to Palestinian geography, it is clear that Mark was unfamiliar with the area.

8. Luke has a special interest in women, the poor, and those without social status.

9. "Q" is a sayings source used by Matthew and Luke in the construction of their gospel accounts.

10. Two advantages of the historical approach are: (A) It shows us that Jesus opposed the wealthy and powerful on behalf of the poor and those despised by society; (B) It emphasizes the humanity of Jesus.

11. The historical evidence is not strong enough to support the beliefs which we hold in faith about the significance of Jesus.

Q/A

Section One

1. Define: "Christ of Faith," "Jesus of History."
2. What is the primary purpose of the gospel accounts?
3. List three layers of material in the gospel accounts.
4. Why did Roman occupation mean economic hardship for most Jews?
5. Name and describe four important Jewish groups at the time of Jesus.
6. What is the significance of the Dead Sea Scrolls?
7. How do we know that Mark's community was outside Palestine?
8. What are Luke's special interests?
9. Define "Q"
10. What are two reasons why the historical approach is valuable?
11. Why does our faith not rest on the historical approach?

Section Two

1. Why did many Jews misunderstand Jesus' message about the kingdom?
2. What does living in the kingdom mean?
3. Why does life in the kingdom feel restful and satisfying?
4. Explain two areas in which the kingdom requires a new attitude.
5. Define: "parable"
6. What is the key to understanding Jesus' parables?
7. What is the surprise in the parable of the Good Samaritan?
8. Explain the four kinds of healing performed by Jesus.
9. Why did Jesus work miracles?
10. List three ways in which the healing revealed the kingdom.
11. In kingdom living, is it enough to feel compassion for others? Why or why not?

BIBLE ACTIVITY

1. Life in the kingdom means, above all else, a life centered on loving God. One of the most important ways this happens is through prayer. Read what Jesus had to say about prayer in two passages from Matthew: 6:5–8, and 7:7–11. Based on these two passages, describe what you think is the attitude towards prayer of someone living in the kingdom.

2. Read Jesus' parable of the hidden treasure in Matthew 13:44–46. What's the element of surprise in this parable? How does this parable illustrate the kingdom? Make a list of what you'd be willing to "sell" to acquire life in the kingdom.

3. Go back over the parable of the good Samaritan in Luke 10:29–37. Now rewrite the parable, bringing it up to date. Include characters and events that reflect modern times, but be sure that the message of the parable remains the same.

4. Read the healing story in Matthew 12:22–28. What do the Pharisees accuse Jesus of doing? How does Jesus respond? Why do you think Matthew includes this story?

The Good News of Jesus calls us to find our rest in him.

BIBLE ACTIVITY

1. Important ideas about prayer included in these two passages include: the proper attitude in prayer is humility; one should pray privately, rather than making a public performance out of it; one should ask things of God, confident of a positive response; one can be confident in prayer because of God's great love for us.

2. The element of surprise is the man's willingness to give up all that he had to acquire this hidden treasure. The insight about the kingdom in this parable is that people must be willing to detach themselves from all their possessions and conceits in order to be able to enter kingdom life.

3. Encourage student creativity on this assignment. Students may be asked to perform the more creative responses in the form of a skit or dramatic reading for the class.

GLOSSARY

- **Christ of Faith:** Jesus as he is known through the faith tradition of the Church.
- **Dead Sea Scrolls:** Writings which reflect opinions within Judaism shortly before the time of Jesus.
- **Gospel:** The "good news" of Jesus contained in the four gospel accounts and other Christian literature.
- **Gospel Accounts:** The four New Testament books which provide evidence of Jesus' life and importance.
- **Jesus of History:** The flesh-and-blood person, Jesus of Nazareth.
- **Kingdom of God:** The main theme of Jesus' preaching and teaching; a life centered on love of God and love of others.
- **Miracle:** An exception to the normal flow of ordinary events.
- **Moral Healing:** Healing of someone's values and character.
- **Parables:** Comparison of something familiar to something unfamiliar, used by Jesus to teach about the kingdom.
- **Parousia:** When Jesus will return in power to establish the kingdom in its fullness; "Second Coming."
- **Pharisees:** Jewish group which stressed the Law, but interpreted it to fit new situations.
- **Physical Healing:** Healing a bodily illness, such as leprosy.
- **Procurator:** Head of Roman government in Judea.
- **Province:** An area of the empire under direct Roman control.
- **Public Ministry:** Jesus' career from age 30 to 33.
- **Q:** Hypothetical sayings source used by Matthew and Luke; the letter comes from the German word, "Quelle," meaning "source."
- **Sadducees:** Wealthy aristocrats who were religious conservatives, held the power in the Temple.
- **Second Coming:** The event at the end of time when Jesus will return in power to establish the kingdom in its fullness; also called "Parousia."
- **Spiritual healing:** Healing of a mental illness, often thought of by ancient people as casting out a demon.
- **Synoptics:** Matthew, Mark, and Luke.

UNDERSTANDING MORE ABOUT:

The Zealots

In Luke 6:15, we hear of a follower of Jesus known as "Simon the Zealot." Many people associate Simon with the Jewish political party called "the Zealots." This party was violently opposed to Roman rule of Israel, and its members were ready to rise up in armed revolt. The party is not mentioned in other historical sources until the 60s C.E., however, and so the word "zealot" in Simon's case may have its more normal meaning of someone who was determined to uphold Jewish traditions in any circumstances.

There is another disciple of Jesus, however, who may have been connected to armed opposition to Rome: Judas Iscariot. Before the Zealots came together as a party, individual Jews tried to undercut the Romans by assassinating their officials, as well as any Jews who went along with them. Because they used short daggers known as "sicae," they were called the "sicarii." Some Bible scholars think that "Iscariot" may be related to the term "sicarii."

Section Two

1. Many Jews hoped for a military victory over their enemies and the restoration of the nation. In contrast, Jesus talked about the kingdom as a state of mind and soul.

2. Living in the kingdom means living a life centered on love of God and love of others.

3. Life in the kingdom feels restful and satisfying because it is the only true path.

4. Two areas for new attitudes are: (A) the desire for material things; (B) the need to forgive others.

5. A parable is a figure of speech in which two things are put together for purposes of comparison.

6. The key to understanding the parable lies in the surprise endings which reverse traditional values and provide insight into kingdom life.

7. The surprise in this parable is that the one who exhibits kingdom living is not an Israelite, but a Samaritan, someone whom the Jews considered an enemy.

8. Four kinds of healing are: (A) Physical; (B) Resurrection; (C) Spiritual; (D) Moral.

9. The miracles were signs of the kingdom revealing God's power to end physical and mental suffering.

10. Healings reveal the kingdom in these ways: (A) The kingdom has power to heal mind, body and soul; (B) Living in the kingdom means having compassion for suffering; (C) By focusing on the suffering of others, we find ways to end our own.

11. Feeling compassion is not enough; we must also act to do whatever we can to end the suffering of others.

4. The Pharisees accuse Jesus of casting out demons with the help of Satan, the prince of demons. Jesus responds that it is not logical to think that Satan was helping him to undo Satan's own work. Therefore, the healings he performs must be from God. Historically, Matthew probably included this story be-cause one of the charges made by Pharisees was that Jesus had power over demons be-cause he was demonic himself. Theologically, Matthew wishes to stress the superior wisdom of Jesus, who cannot be verbally or intellectually trapped by his opponents.

Responding to Jesus

Chapter Overview

This chapter focuses on the concept of discipleship, introducing students to various followers of Jesus, exploring the effect of the Passion and Resurrection on Jesus' followers, and presenting the different emphases the four Gospel writers placed on being a disciple.

Teaching Objectives

By the end of this chapter students will be able to:
• Recognize and appreciate many different ways of following Jesus.
• Begin to consider the kind of discipleship to which they feel called.

Welcome

Let the students know you have been praying for them, and that you have prayed that they will have a close relationship with Jesus.

What to Do

Play a short game of "Simon Says" or "Follow the Leader" with your class. Then use the game to discuss the behavior and responsibilities of followers. Point out the repercussions for those who can't follow, and for the group if everyone tries to lead.

Introducing the Chapter

What to Do

The central theme in Chapter 11 is discipleship. Take a few moments to explore ways your students already experience discipleship in their lives:

• Begin the lesson with prayer. Use the "Our Father" to close your prayer, making a point of the fact that it was the prayer Jesus taught his disciples when they asked for his guidance.
• Mention some of the current models for discipleship that your students will recognize: new doctors who must do two years of residency before they can practice medicine independently; athletes who put themselves into the care of their coach; students of music working

---

CHAPTER 11

Responding to Jesus

30	**27 B.C.E.–14 C.E.** ● Reign of Emperor Augustus
	4 B.C.E.–6 C.E. ● Archelaus rules Judea
	4 B.C.E.–34 C.E. ● Philip rules the Greek cities
	4 B.C.E.–39 C.E. ● Herod Antipas rules Galilee
1	
	14–37 C.E. ● Reign of Emperor Tiberius
	ca. 30 ● Jesus' public ministry begins
	ca. 33 ● Jesus' death and resurrection
	66–70 ● Gospel according to Mark
	83–87 ● Gospel according to Luke ● Gospel according to Matthew
	95–99 ● Gospel according to John, Catholic Epistles
100	

Legend

● General History
● Biblical History
● Regional History
● Books of the Bible

uisa couldn't believe it. She'd always looked forward to Mass on Sunday mornings—she liked the singing, and the family breakfast afterwards was always fun. But she had *never* experienced anything like this.

This Sunday, Father Reuben announced to the parish that a visiting priest, Father Gabriel, from Zaire, Africa, would be giving the homily. Luisa hadn't even realized that there were Catholics in Africa. Father Gabriel looked to be about her parents' age, and walked with a slight limp. He was truly an African, too, which surprised Luisa even more. She had never considered that dark skinned people could be priests. All of the priests that she had ever seen had been white. As soon as Father Gabriel began to speak, however, Luisa forgot about everything else; she sat spellbound, listening carefully to what he said.

MORE ABOUT THE TEXT

Counter-Cultural

Patriotic or nationalistic pride is very prominent in many cultures. People bend over backwards to claim some hero or important scientist as a resident of their nation. The same is true about Jesus and his teaching. Many (if not most) cultures want to claim faithfulness to Jesus, to the point where religion and nationality go together. For three hundred years, and more, following the Reformation, Christians

fought each other, justifying their actions with the claim that "Jesus is on our side!"

Much of the problem that Father Gabriel experienced in the story is tied to cultural pride. Even though Christianity is a worldwide religion, many people feel that the way that they live the faith is the right way, while every other way is wrong. Cultural behavior is taken as a divine truth and not a variable.

Father Gabriel started slowly, talking about his experience of bringing the Gospel to poor families in rural Africa. As he went on, he talked more loudly about God's love and kingdom. By the time he finished his talk, Father Gabriel was almost shouting, crying out about how the Holy Spirit fills us with love for God and one another. Some members of the parish were clapping and shouting in response, and Luisa found herself joining them. No homily had ever made her feel this way before.

For the rest of the Mass, Luisa felt a new enthusiasm. She joined in the singing, prayed deeply, and went to Communion eagerly. Father Gabriel was right; she could feel the Spirit filling her with love. As she looked around at the other members of her family, she could tell they felt the same way.

After Mass, Luisa hurried to get into the line to meet Father Gabriel. She wanted to thank him for making this Mass so memorable. Luisa knew that her faith was now more important to her than ever before.

As she neared Father Gabriel, she could tell something was wrong. "What was that all about?" she heard someone snap angrily. "Church is no place for shouting and carrying on!" Another parishioner yelled, "You're a disgrace!"

"I'm sorry you feel that way," Father Gabriel said. "But it's important for people to know that God's love is real, and that God is reaching out to them, right now." Not satisfied with his words, several people walked away, complaining that he behaved more like a rock star than a priest.

Luisa couldn't believe people were reacting like this. Couldn't they tell that Father Gabriel was special, someone who really made God's love come alive? What was it about him that bothered them? Why couldn't they hear what she had heard?

Hearing the Message

People also reacted in many different ways to Jesus' words and actions. Some were touched by him, and gave up everything to follow him. Others liked what they heard, but stayed at a distance. Some felt threatened by Jesus, violently opposed him, and eventually had him killed. The story did not end there, however, for Jesus rose from the grave, met with his followers, and then returned to God. In this chapter, you will study the different ways people reacted to Jesus during his lifetime. You'll also take a closer look at how the writers of the four gospel accounts found in the Bible responded to Jesus and his message. In so doing, you'll discover that Jesus called people to him, and that we also are invited to answer Jesus in our own way.

under the tutelage of a trained musician. Ask your students to think of some additional models. Begin to consider the relationships between the disciples and their teachers.

• Explain that Jesus was an unusual teacher who invited and continues to invite people to follow him in a special way. Not everyone appreciated his leadership then; even among his followers there were differences in the ways people responded. This is also true of people today: everyone's relationship with Jesus is unique.

Development

What to Do

1. Have the students read and briefly discuss the opening spread (pages 188–189). Focus your discussion on the different responses people had to Father Gabriel and his sermon. Let your students consider how they might respond to a controversial or out-of-the-ordinary speaker. Remind them that Jesus was a very unusual teacher in his time, saying and doing much that was unexpected and controversial. Help them to consider what their first response would likely have been to Jesus' actions.

2. Discuss with students what it takes for them to be tolerant of other people's opinions, cultures, and attitudes. Note that tolerance was an important part of Jesus' teaching and an important virtue for those who want to follow Jesus.

3. Have students look at the timeline and compare it with the timeline from Chapter 10 on page 170. The timeline for Chapter 11 has many fewer dates to show the three-decade gap between Jesus' death and when the first account of the Gospel was written. Have students consider the implications of such a gap between the event and when the books were written.

◆ MORE ABOUT THE LESSON

Teaching Tolerance

The story about Luisa and Father Gabriel presents the teacher with an ideal opportunity to teach students to tolerate people who think and act differently than they do.

Toleration is very important in the world today. People who are tolerant know that no one culture or nationality has all of the answers, yet all of the diverse cultures together can teach us aspects about life that we never would have known without the knowledge and help of other people.

Ask students for ways that they can show tolerance. In addition, ask students to identify the biggest challenge they face in their efforts to be tolerant on a daily basis.

◆ The Disciples

Teaching Objectives

By the end of this lesson students will be able:
• To explain the significance of Jesus' personal invitations to follow him, and of his relationships with outsiders, women, and "sinners."
• To identify three different types of disciples who supported Jesus.
• To identify the groups that opposed Jesus and explain the reasons behind their opposition.

Development

What to Do

1. Give the students time to read the opening italics and Learning Objectives, plus "The Disciples." When they are finished, ask if the students can think of another word that looks like or is related to "disciple" (discipline). How does that word shed light on who is a disciple? See "More about the Lesson" on page 190.

2. Have the students read the following Gospel references, which add depth to the information in the text:
• Personal Invitations: Luke 5:1–11; John 1:35-49
• Unlikely Candidates: Luke 19:1–9; Luke 8:1–3; John 19:38–39.
• The Twelve: See "Understanding More About" on page 209 of the text. Add to their information from "More about the Text" on page 191.
• A Wider Circle: Luke 10:1–9; Matthew 27:55–56; for a reverse example, recall the story of the Gerasene in Luke and re-read Luke 8:38–39.

3. Lead a class discussion about what students have learned from these references, being sure to answer any questions they might have. Help the students to consider these questions: "Why do you think so many people were ready to spend so much time with Jesus? Do you think Jesus invited Peter and the others the very first time they saw him? Why or why not?"

190

A Sign That Will Be Opposed

Schottenmeister, *The Presentation of Jesus in the Temple.* Fifteenth Century.

Luke's gospel account tells how Joseph and Mary brought the infant Jesus to the Temple for a blessing (Luke 2:25–35). Simeon, the old man who blessed the child, told Mary that Jesus would be "a sign that will be opposed." For some people, Jesus was a sign who pointed the way to the kingdom of God. For others, Jesus was a threat who had to be dealt with once and for all.

In this section, you will study about those who followed Jesus, those who opposed him, how Jesus died, and how he was glorified in the Resurrection.

Learning Objectives for Section One

By the end of this section, you will be able to:
• Identify the different kinds of disciples who followed Jesus.
• Identify the various groups which opposed Jesus and explain why they did so.
• Describe the events of Jesus' passion.
• Understand how the Resurrection affected Jesus' followers.

◆ The Disciples

The word "disciple" is Latin for "student." We use this word for followers of Jesus because they study and try to live out his teachings. Just as today there are many kinds of people who follow Jesus, there were different groups of followers in Jesus' lifetime. Some traveled with Jesus. Others were called to leadership roles. Still others supported him without leaving their homes or jobs. Christians continue to respond to Jesus in a variety of ways.

Literal Followers

One group of disciples literally followed Jesus. They moved about Judea with him wherever he went. Some of these disciples left their friends, their family, and their jobs to be close to Jesus. Members of this group studied Jesus' message, shared part of his ministry, and helped him meet his needs. For example, these disciples arranged for Jesus' important meals, such as the Passover supper (Mark 14:12–16).

In the ancient world, it wasn't unusual for a teacher to have disciples who followed him to receive his teaching. Two things, however, make the relationship between Jesus and his disciples noteworthy for us:

1. Jesus offered personal invitations. Jesus called these disciples by name, asking that they leave their past lives behind to follow him. In Mark's gospel account we read how Jesus saw Simon and Andrew fishing on the shores of the Sea of Galilee. He offered them this invitation, "Come after me, and I will make you fishers of men" (Mark 1:17). Simon and Andrew dropped everything and followed Jesus. This story illustrates an important point about discipleship. Following Jesus isn't only something we choose; it's also an answer to an invitation, another response in our on-going conversation with God.

2. Jesus called unlikely candidates. Jesus didn't always call the type of disciples that people expected. For one thing, Jesus invited many women to follow him. He was willing to teach them and treat them as partners. In a society that assumed women

---

◆ MORE ABOUT THE LESSON

Disciples

If you ask them, your students will probably suggest "discipline" as a word closely related to "disciple." Students who follow a master in any field practice definite disciplines—that is, they train body, mind, or spirit to become like the master. A disciplined person is well-trained and has a high degree of self-control. These are all qualities of discipleship to Jesus.

should be "seen and not heard," this was quite radical. Jesus also called "sinners," people who were not considered pure according to a strict interpretation of Jewish law. The disciple, Levi, a tax collector who worked for the Romans, was scorned by many Jews. Jesus invited him to become one of his disciples, showing that all people can follow Jesus.

The Twelve

Within the larger number of his disciples, Jesus formed a special group called "the Twelve." To these twelve people Jesus entrusted leadership responsibilities. After the death of Jesus, "the Twelve" became the leaders of the early Church. Although each gospel account names the Twelve slightly differently, five stand out as important members: Peter, Andrew, James, John, and Judas Iscariot.

Remember that ancient Israel was organized into 12 tribes. By choosing twelve members to lead his disciples, Jesus showed symbolically that all Israel was called to live life in the kingdom. The Twelve also shared in Jesus' mission. In Mark 6:7–13, the disciples are sent out by Jesus to bring the message of the kingdom to Israel. The Twelve are usually called *apostles*, a Greek word which means "messengers."

A Wider Circle of Friends

Jesus touched many people with his words and deeds, but not all of them left their families and jobs to follow him. These people became supporters of Jesus. While they remained in their communities, doing their regular jobs, they experienced life differently because of their commitment to Jesus.

The most familiar members of this wider circle of followers were Martha and Mary, sisters who lived in

Jesus' first followers were fishermen from Gallilee. Growing up in Nazareth, Jesus would have felt very comfortable around fishermen.

The Bible in Context

Jesus and Women

Jesus stood out from other important teachers of his day in many ways. One was his attitude towards women. Many ancient cultures considered women "impure," meaning that they were unfit to offer proper worship. Women were often viewed as inferior to men, sometimes even as property. Despite these prejudices, Jesus respected women and treated them equally as individuals. He demonstrates this attitude in the story of the woman with a hemorrhage.

In Mark 5:25–34, a woman who is suffering from a hemorrhage (a flow of blood) approaches Jesus, hoping to be cured. As a woman, and especially one who is bleeding, she knows that under Jewish law she is considered impure. A man who touched her, even if only accidentally, would immediately become impure, and thus unable to worship God in the Temple. Thus women during menstruation and at other time when they bled vaginally (such as after childbirth) avoided all contact with men.

Nonetheless, this woman tries to touch Jesus without being noticed, hoping to be healed by his power. Jesus, realizing immediately that someone in need of healing has touched him, searches for the person. The woman, caught in her act of desperation, falls down before Jesus in fear. Instead of reprimanding her, however, Jesus commends her faith and sends her home in peace.

By such public gestures as this, Jesus showed that he was not controlled by public attitudes or tradition.

Bethany with their brother, Lazarus. Luke 10:38–42 describes the hospitality they extended to Jesus. He stopped at their home on the way to Jerusalem to rest and prepare for the remainder of his journey. Jesus had supporters like Martha and Mary located throughout Israel. Many such supporters lived in Jerusalem, which is one reason why the early Church developed there after Jesus' death.

Have You Considered?

1. Do you think Jesus still calls disciples today? If so, how? If not, why not?
2. Why do you suppose Jesus didn't ask all of his disciples to become literal followers?
3. As disciples of Jesus, what lesson do you think we should learn from his call of people who were looked down upon by the rest of society?

MORE ABOUT THE TEXT

The Twelve

Twelve was an important symbolic number in the ancient Middle East referring to completion or fullness. As you know from the Old Testament, the "12 tribes" were not always twelve, but were remembered in this way for symbolic reasons. So also with Jesus' twelve: original manuscripts show that the lists of individuals differ (more than some New Testament versions show).

In Acts 1:15–26, the disciples find it necessary to replace Judas Iscariot in order to keep the number whole. Those to be considered had to be "men who had accompanied us the whole time the Lord Jesus came and went among us," so there were clearly more than the official twelve in Jesus' inner circle.

◆ Jesus' Opposition

What to Do

1. Have the students read "Jesus' Opposition." For an example of a much stronger denunciation of the legalists and hypocrites among the Pharisees and leaders, have the students read Matthew 23. What were Jesus' main concerns here? Let the students discuss their reaction to this chapter.

2. Have the students do "Bible Activity" number 2 individually or in small groups. In addition to answering the questions in their text, have the students find anything in the infancy stories that shows either appreciation for Jesus or opposition to Jesus. The students should see that the infancy stories foreshadow much of what comes up later in the Gospel. For example, Mary's Magnificat (*Luke* 1:46–55) introduces the concern for the poor that is prevalent throughout Luke's Gospel.

3. Direct the students' attention to the "Scripture Workshop." To explain the concept of a "leading question" more fully, have the students consider this question: "Are you still cheating on all your math tests?" If they answer "yes" they admit to cheating in the past; if they say "no" then it sounds as though they are regular cheaters. Jesus' enemies often present questions that seem to have only two possible answers, either one of which will somehow be damaging, yet Jesus seems to find a new approach to the question that gives him a third answer.

Scripture Workshop

1. Specific place and time: "on that day," (place given in *Matthew* 22:23)

2. Attempt to trap Jesus with a leading question: "Now at the resurrection, of the seven, whose wife will she be?" (*Matthew* 22:28)

3. Short, powerful statement: "At the resurrection, they neither marry nor are given in marriage but are like the angels in heaven." (*Matthew* 22:30)

◆ Jesus' Opposition

Jesus attracted followers because he announced that the kingdom of God was here, and that Israel was being renewed. Many people greeted this as a hoped-for message of joy. Others, however, who benefited from the injustice of the way things were, or who had a different vision of Israel's future, were threatened by what Jesus said. Those groups responded to Jesus by opposing him, and eventually they killed him. Why would anyone oppose Jesus? Because what Jesus had to say challenged people not willing to accept the kingdom.

Conflicts over the Law

One source of tension between Jesus and other Jewish leaders was the Law. Since the time of Ezra, Jews had regarded the Law as the single most important way they expressed their relationship to God. Observance of the Law was the way they maintained their part of that relationship. God would give well-being according to the ancient Covenant. Over time, the Law became an end in itself, and obedience was a demand rather than an expression of love for God. Jesus challenged this view, arguing that the Law existed to serve people, and there were times when the Law had to be ignored to meet people's needs.

Mark 3:1–6 tells of a man with a withered hand. Jesus was in the synagogue in Capernaum on the Sabbath, a day on which no one was supposed to work (healing was considered work). When he spotted the man whose hand was shriveled, Jesus asked him to stand up. Jesus then asked the crowd whether it was better to do a good deed on the Sabbath by healing the man, or an evil one by allowing him to suffer. Jesus then healed the man in violation of the Sabbath law. This act angered those Pharisees and Sadducees who were present. Mark goes on to say that from this point forward, these groups plotted to kill Jesus.

Jesus was not alone in reminding people that the original purpose of the Law was to help others. In the first century B.C.E., Rabbi Hillel was asked to summarize his religion "standing on one foot" (meaning "briefly"). Hillel responded, "What is hateful to you, don't do to your neighbor. The rest is commentary—now go and study." Jesus says much the same thing in Matthew 7:12. It is important to remember that even when Jesus criticized the attitudes and practices of some of his fellow Jews, he did so as someone speaking from inside the Jewish tradition.

Scripture Workshop

Controversy Stories

The conflict between Jesus and other Jewish groups is often expressed through a literary form called a "controversy story." This type of story has three elements:

1. a specific place and time
2. an attempt by Jesus' enemies to trap him with a leading question (a question in which either way he answers, he says something that can be held against him)
3. a short, powerful statement by Jesus which avoids the trap

Matthew 22:23–33 contains a controversy story in which the Sadducees ridicule Jesus' belief in resurrection. Read this story, outlining it using the three story elements listed above.

Jesus Denounces Hypocrisy

Opposition to Jesus didn't arise only because he reminded people of the real purpose of the Law. He went further, criticizing the hypocrisy and self-interest which many leaders disguised as religion. He called on people to reject this kind of behavior. His words in Mark must have sounded like a direct challenge to those he addressed:

"Beware of the scribes, who like to go around in long robes and accept greetings in the marketplaces, seats of honor in synagogues, and places of honor at banquets. They devour the houses of widows and, as a pretext, recite lengthy prayers. They will receive a very severe condemnation."

(Mark 12:38–40)

In Jesus' day, some professional scribes used their positions selfishly. As Jesus said, they enriched themselves on the contributions of widows and other poor people. Of course, not all Jewish leaders behaved this way, but some gave in to the temptation that comes with positions of power. By publicly criticizing these wealthy and powerful men, Jesus knew he was inviting dangerous opposition. Despite the

---

The Other Disciples

The student text almost suggests that "disciple" refers only to the famous "twelve." In part, this reflects Scripture, which gives us very little information about any of Jesus' other followers; but Jesus had many loyal disciples whose names we do not know, and who weren't members of the Twelve. The Scripture references in this lesson highlight this fact.

Other Apostles

The word "apostle" does not apply only to the Twelve. In the New Testament, Paul, Barnabas, and others are also called apostles. A little later in the church, special commemorations of apostles were developed, called feasts. A feast for Mary Magdalene, called the "Apostle to the Apostles" because she was the first to see and announce the resurrection of Jesus (John 20), was celebrated until the tenth century.

danger, Jesus had to denounce behavior that so obviously contradicted the message of the kingdom.

The Powerful Feel Threatened

As Jesus spread the message of the kingdom, he attracted a large number of followers. His popularity made the official leaders, the Jewish high priests and the Romans, nervous. Although the Romans ruled Israel, they allowed the native officials to run things, as long as there was no trouble. A popular figure such as Jesus, by denouncing injustice, threatened the control of the local leaders, and possibly, the Romans themselves, was a danger to everyone in authority.

Added to this general concern was a very specific issue: Jesus' teaching of the kingdom. Although Jesus did not present himself as an earthly king to rival the Romans, he did say that life in the kingdom was very different from the way things were. He criticized how the Temple was used, saying that it was for financial gain rather than for honoring God. The Temple was the center of political as well as religious authority. When Jesus denounced its leaders, the priests and Romans heard this as a direct challenge to their authority.

Have You Considered?

1. Along with other Jewish teachers, Jesus said that it was wrong to obey the Law when it contradicted the goal of helping people. Give an example of how obeying rules might get in the way of helping people.
2. Jesus denounced powerful people who used religion to disguise their own greed. Do you think this still happens today? Why or why not?
3. Jesus had a lot to say to those in authority. What do you think the qualities of a good leader are, from Jesus' point of view?

The Temple in Jerusalem was the center of religious power in Judea. This model of the Temple can be found in modern Israel.

Recall

Have the students discuss and then write about "Chapter 11 Review Q/A," Section One, questions 1–9. Be sure they include what they have learned from your explanations, their biblical work, and the text.

Connect

What to Do

With the students, invent several questions about today's lesson that they can use to find out what their families and others think or feel about Jesus' disciples and about the Pharisees and Sadducees of Jesus' time. Help them to look for people's feelings or attitudes more than for factual information. Include a question about who they see as Pharisees or Sadducees today. Have the students copy the questions and take them home to guide them when they interview family members.

What's Next?

What to Do

Say: "The next lesson will take us into the most dramatic days of Jesus' life and the lives of his followers. Be ready to recall what you already know, and to add to it."

Have You Considered?

1. Point out that such instances do not invalidate the need for rules, but rather demonstrate that rules should be made to help people.
2. This is another question which draws upon the instinctive adolescent aversion to hypocrisy. Explore with the students why using religion to camouflage greed is so offensive: because it is a perversion of the very ideals which the religious person claims to follow.
3. Students will have a variety of responses. The unifying point should be that a good leader is sensitive to the unique needs and circumstances of people—and that people are more important than rules and power.

Bonus Focus for You ——————

Read Matthew 22:1–14. Reflect on its meaning in relation to the varied reactions of people to Jesus in his own time. Are these truths still relevant for today? Write your reflections in your journal.

MORE ABOUT THE TEXT

The Law

By the time of Jesus, "the Law" did not mean only the Ten Commandments or even the Torah itself. These do not make exaggerated demands. But in the centuries after the Exile, the Law multiplied through interpretations to include a legal statement on almost every aspect of life: how to prepare and eat food, how to handle almost everything (some things couldn't be touched), when particular activities were appropriate or forbidden, the details of weddings, burials, and other celebrations. Examples of some of the most legalistic might include that it was forbidden to carry anything heavier than a fig or to walk more than a very short distance (about 50 feet) on the Sabbath.

Jesus was not against the "weighty" parts of the ancient Law, but saw clearly that the little rules were so many and so picky that they prevented people from the joy of loving God.

LESSON TWO (pages 194–197)

◆ Jesus' Death and Resurrection

Welcome

What to Do

• As they gather, give students palm fronds or reeds—real ones if you can get them, but paper ones will do—and ask each to mark Psalm 24 in his or her Bible.

• When they are ready, ask them to stand and hold their palms. Read Matthew 21:8–11 and invite your students to picture the scene in their minds.

• Then say: "The last events of Jesus' life have become central for Christians and are recalled in the annual celebrations of Holy Week. Of course, it is not just what happened, but what it meant and means that matters today. Psalm 24, which is used in the Mass on Palm Sunday, tells us something about the meaning of Jesus' Passion and Resurrection. Please read it with me." Pause for a moment and then begin reading. Close with a simple thanksgiving for Jesus, his teaching and his sacrifice.

Introducing the Lesson

Teaching Objectives

By the end of this lesson students will be able to:

• Describe the events leading up to and including Jesus' Passion and Resurrection.

• Understand the effects of these events on Jesus' followers.

• Appreciate the significance of these events for themselves and for all people.

Using the Timeline

In order to understand the events of Jesus' trial and execution, the students will need to be aware of the religious and political authorities in control of Jerusalem and Palestine at that time.

What to Do

Direct the students' attention to the timeline on page 188. Ask them to determine which of the rulers were in power at the time of Jesus' death. When they have identified the Roman rulers, remind them that the Jewish people

---

◆ Jesus' Death and Resurrection

The opponents of Jesus wanted to publicly humiliate him. They wanted to show that Jesus was nothing special. By killing him, Jesus' opponents thought that they had solved their problems. Little did they know of the power of God!

When Jesus rose from the grave and appeared to his disciples on Easter Sunday, he wrecked the plans of his opponents. Instead of being silenced, Jesus was now able to spread his message to a much larger group than ever before. He commissioned his disciples to spread the word of what had happened to the whole world, making disciples as they went.

The Church recalls these events during Holy Week, the days leading up to Easter Sunday, and on Easter itself. These are the holiest days of the Church year, because they celebrate the central event in salvation history: Christians believe that all of Israel's past led up to this moment, and all of Church history

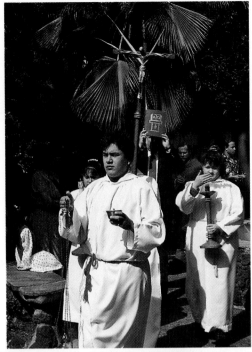

Every year on Palm Sunday, the Lord's joyous entrance into Jerusalem is celebrated with a procession and a blessing of palm branches.

Angelico, *The Women at the Tomb. Fifteenth Century.*

On Easter Sunday, Christians celebrate Jesus' Resurrection from the dead. Mark 16:1–8 tells of the women who came to the tomb to anoint Jesus.

flows out of it. Let's look at how the gospel accounts record this story.

The Entry into Jerusalem

In Jesus' day, Jews who could afford the trip traveled to Jerusalem for the spring festival of Passover. The final week in Jesus' life began with his arrival in Jerusalem to prepare for the holy day. All four gospel accounts agree that Jesus entered Jerusalem in a very public way. He rode into the city on the back of a donkey, in fulfillment of prophecy:

Rejoice heartily, O daughter Zion, shout for joy, O daughter Jerusalem! See, your king shall come to you; a just savior is he, meek, and riding on an ass, on a colt, the foal of an ass.

(Zechariah 9:9)

Bible scholars generally agree that Jesus focused on his message of the kingdom, rather than on himself as the messenger. This gesture, therefore, was probably not intended to proclaim himself as king or

---

MORE ABOUT THE TEXT

Jesus in the Temple

The business that was taking place in the Temple was totally legitimate. Jews came from all parts of the Roman Empire to celebrate pilgrimage festivals in Jerusalem and to offer sacrifices in the Temple. Travel wasn't easy and they could hardly bring their sacrificial animals with them. When they got to Jerusalem, the Temple provided animals that could be purchased for sacrifice. The Temple had its own coinage; common Roman coinage with its images of the emperor would defile the Temple. Roman money had to be exchanged for Temple coinage before the animals could be bought and offered to God. Although the situation was open to corruption (as most situations are), the practice itself was a convenience for pilgrims. In objecting to it, Jesus pointed to something more important than the business: a revaluation of the purpose of the Temple.

LEARN FROM THE MAP

Events of Holy Week

The four gospel accounts vary as to Jesus' actions during Holy Week. Tradition holds that Jesus entered Jerusalem on Sunday, celebrated the Passover meal on Thursday, and was convicted and crucified on Friday.

The locations of Jesus' activities during his last week are not known with great certainty, but even so, it will help you visualize them if you find them on the map. Locate the following places:

• Kidron Valley • Garden of Gethsemane • High priest's neighborhood • Golgotha • Herod Antipas' vacation palace

Trace on your map the route Jesus and his friends might have taken.

Holy Week sites
— Holy Thursday and Good Friday journey

▪ Building   ＝ Stairs   — Wall

messiah, although it would be seen this way by later Christians. Instead, the act was intended to announce to the Jews gathered in the city that the kingdom which Jesus preached had arrived.

This public act excited the crowds gathered for the festival. What Jesus did next also got people's attention: he marched onto the Temple grounds and threw out the merchants and money-changers doing business there! He shouted that they did not belong in the house of God. In taking this step, Jesus claimed the authority to decide what was appropriate in the Temple, a privilege claimed by the priestly families. Jesus' action directly challenged how the priests oversaw their office. This was the last straw; Jesus had to be stopped.

The Last Supper

Over the next few days, opposition to Jesus grew stronger. By Thursday of that week, it was clear to Jesus that they intended to arrest him. Jesus gathered his closest disciples together for what he knew might be their final meal together. This is the meal we know as the "Last Supper."

The synoptic accounts say that the Last Supper was the Passover meal itself, while John indicated that the meal took place the night before Passover. Many scholars today tend to follow John, and place the meal the night before the Passover. No one knows for sure when the Last Supper occurred.

However, we do know that during this meal, Jesus performed three actions of great importance:

1.   **Jesus washed the feet of his disciples.** In the ancient world, when most travel was by foot, servants would wash the feet of their masters when they arrived home. It was the work required of the lowest household servants. Peter, knowing this, protested that Jesus should never wash *his* feet. But Jesus explains that acceptance of the master's service is part of the relationship between the disciple and the Lord. Moreover, Jesus tells them to follow his example and do this for one another. For the kingdom of God, service is more important than a desire for power or glory.

2.   **Jesus asked his disciples to go out and continue his mission.** In John's gospel account, Jesus recites a long prayer for the disciples, asking God to guide them as they proclaim the kingdom to the world.

were also under the authority of their religious leaders, the high priests. They will need to recognize the name Caiaphas, who was high priest from 18–36 C.E. Herod Antipas who was the ruler of Galilee also had authority over Jesus because Jesus was from Nazareth in Galilee. His political power was backed by the Romans, as was Pilate's, the governor appointed by Caesar to rule in Jerusalem. Students will encounter all of these figures in today's lesson.

Development

What to Do

1. Have the students read "Jesus' Death and Resurrection." Then have them read and compare Matthew 21:1–17 and John 12:12–19. Note the differences they find on the blackboard, then have them look at John 3:13–22. What reasons can they imagine for the different order of events in John's gospel account?

2. Have the students examine the map of Jerusalem on page 195. (Bethany, which is a town outside of Jerusalem to the southeast, can be found on the map on page 178). Have the students locate the rest of the places mentioned and follow the possible route of Jesus given in red.

3. Ask the students to review the subsection, "Trial and Execution." Then, have the students do a detailed comparison of the passion stories in Luke and John. The students should go through both Gospel accounts very carefully to find those events which are reported differently and those which are the same.

4. Have the students read John 20:24–28, and review the subsection, "Resurrection!" with them.

5. After forming small groups, have the students complete "Bible Activity" number 1. In addition to the questions in their text, ask the students to identify their favorite accounts and to explain their choices. Which account of the Gospel do they think provides the most convincing, moving, or powerful account of the Resurrection? The groups should share their answers with the whole class.

◆ MORE ABOUT THE LESSON

Comparing the Passions

Distribute photocopies of Luke 22–23 and John 18–19. Enlarge the text, if possible, before photocopying. Make paper, scissors and paste, or tape available. First, have the students cut the columns apart, so they can lay a single column of Luke alongside a single column of John. Have them read both carefully, comparing as they go. Ask these questions:

• What scenes are only in Luke? only in John?

• What does Jesus do and say in each account?

• In scenes that are similar, what items are the same? what are different?

• Do events happen in the same order?

• What points indicate that Jesus is more victimized in Luke? more in charge in John?

Ask your students to ponder what the differences might mean and to explain which story they prefer.

LEARN FROM THE MAP

The path traced by students should have the following sequence: (A) Entry into Jerusalem from Bethany, (B) Exit Jerusalem following the Cleaning of the Temple, (C) Return from Bethany into Jerusalem via Kedron Valley to site of the Last Supper, (D) Last Supper to Gethsemane, (e) Gethsemane to House of Caiaphas, (F) Caiaphas to Pilate, (G) Pilate to Antipas and back, (H) Golgatha, (I) Joseph's tomb.

Practicing the Skills

What to Do

Remind the students that their text provides a combination and summary of the four accounts of the Last Supper. Point out, for example, that only John has the story of the feet-washing. Invite the students to look at some passages that describe the events mentioned in their text:
- *Footwashing*: John 13:1–15 (notice especially verses 3–4).
- *Continuation of Jesus' work*: John 17:1–26 (the prayer mentioned in the text); Mark 16:14–18 (notice that this is placed after the resurrection); Matthew 28:18–20 (also after the resurrection).
- *The Eucharist*: Luke 22:14–20; Mark 14:22–26; Matthew 26:26–30 (for the earliest written record of the Eucharist, see 1 Corinthians 11:23–26, where Paul is explaining it to the Christians in Corinth, ca. 57 C.E.).

Be sure the students notice what all the references have in common and what is different among them. Then compare the Bible stories with the information in their text.

Recall

Ask the students to write a list of six main points they have learned that they think are especially important or interesting. Have as many students as possible read their lists to the class, so that all can be helped to recall as much as possible of today's lesson.

End your review with a prayer based on Matthew 28:5–10. Read it aloud slowly, reflectively, and let them follow along silently as you pray. Say a simple thanks to close.

3. **Jesus gave the gift of the Eucharist to his disciples.** At the Last Supper, Jesus took bread and wine and pronounced the traditional Jewish blessing over them. He then added that in consuming the bread and wine, the disciples were eating his own flesh and blood. He said that the disciples were to repeat this ritual in memory of him. Every day, when Christians receive Communion, they are carrying out these instructions of Jesus. The word *Eucharist* means "thanksgiving," and when we repeat these actions of Jesus, we thank him for his gift of himself.

Trial and Execution

After the Last Supper, Jesus and a few of his disciples went to the garden of Gethsemane on the Mount of Olives. There, Jesus prayed intensely about God's will, for he knew what was coming.

Soon, a party of guards sent by the high priest arrived with Judas, the disciple who betrayed Jesus. When Judas identified Jesus, the guards arrested him and took him to the priests. Although the gospel accounts give slightly differing versions of what happened next, they generally agree that the Jewish officials charged Jesus with blasphemy—probably for his remarks about the Temple. The Jewish officials then took him to Pilate, the Roman procurator of Judea, seeking the death penalty.

Pilate didn't care much about the religious differences between Jesus and the Jewish leaders, but he was known as a ruthless governor who would execute anyone who might threaten his control of Judea. Jesus was not unknown to Pilate. Jesus' popular following, and his preaching about the kingdom, worried the governor. Brought to him as a criminal, Pilate had Jesus beaten, in an attempt to force Jesus to admit that Caesar was the only king. When this tactic failed, Pilate ordered Jesus put to death. Although the gospel

in the Spotlight
What Did the Last Supper Look Like?

Many people have a copy of Leonardo Da Vinci's famous painting "The Last Supper" somewhere in their homes. This masterpiece shows Jesus in the center of a long bench with disciples on either side. Jesus is seated behind the table.

Da Vinci visualized the Last Supper in the same way that Italian peasants of the sixteenth century ate their meals. Jesus and his disciples, however, lived in a Hellenistic world. They would have eaten the Last Supper laying on their sides on couches surrounding a small table called a *triforium*.

The most important suggestion for this idea comes in John 13:23, which says that the disciples "reclined" at the table. This verb generally means "to lie down." Da Vinci's painting shows us, therefore, that sometimes our imagination of Biblical events has been colored by influences far removed from the Bible itself.

da Vinci, *The Last Supper*, Fifteenth Century.

Leonardo da Vinci's painting of the Last Supper portrays the Apostles as they are identified by the gospel accounts. From this painting, what would you say about the Apostles?

MORE ABOUT THE TEXT

Who's on Trial?

As is usual in his most important passages, highly symbolic events occur in John's account of the Passion. One is of particular interest to students here, though they may not be able to see it in their translation (some versions have tried to smooth it out).

In John 19:13, Pilate brings Jesus before the crowd for the last time. Someone sits on the judge's bench. Normally this would have been Pilate, because he is about to deliver his judgment of Jesus' case. But the Greek verb can equally well indicate that Pilate had Jesus sit on the judge's bench. If that is the case, who is really on trial? The crowd, of course! This is a typical kind of twist for John and leaves modern readers with both frustrating historical ambiguities and rich symbolic possibilities.

Johnson, *Mount Calvary*, Twentieth Century.

The Romans used crucifixion as a means of capital punishment, especially against those people found guilty of rebellion against the state. Which Gospel passages are illustrated in this painting?

accounts present Pilate sympathetically, it was the Roman government through Pilate, and not the Jewish leaders, who ultimately had Jesus put to death.

Jesus was forced to carry his own cross up Mount Golgotha, where he was crucified. The sign above him on the cross listed Jesus' offense: "Jesus of Nazareth, King of the Jews." Although death by crucifixion could sometimes take days, by that afternoon Jesus cried out—quoting Psalm 22—and then died.

He was surrounded at his death by only a handful of women, his male disciples apparently having deserted him in fear. The synoptic gospel accounts indicate that they either watched "from a distance" or make no mention of them. The exception is in John 19:26–27, where the "beloved disciple" remained at the cross. Later, Jesus' body was taken down and placed in a tomb. For a while, it appeared as if the opposition had succeeded in silencing Jesus' message.

Resurrection!

The story did not end there. Each gospel account tells what happened next differently, but they all agree on certain points.

- The women who followed Jesus went to the tomb on Sunday to anoint the body and prepare it for final burial.
- When they arrived, they found the tomb empty.
- A messenger (sometimes described as an angel) told them that Jesus was risen from the grave, and that they should tell the other disciples.

- Later, Jesus himself appeared, first to Mary Magdalene and then to his other disciples.

The risen Jesus was not some kind of ghost; John says that Jesus invited Thomas to feel his wounds in order to convince Thomas that Jesus was real (John 20:26–28). In Luke we learn that the risen Jesus ate with his disciples even though his body had been glorified.

> While they were still speaking about this, he stood in their midst and said to them, "Peace be with you." But they were startled and terrified and thought that they were seeing a ghost. Then he said to them, "Why are you troubled? And why do questions arise in your hearts? Look at my hands and my feet, that it is I myself. Touch me and see, because a ghost does not have flesh and bones as you can see I have." And as he said this, he showed them his hands and his feet. While they were still incredulous for joy and were amazed, he asked them, "Have you anything here to eat?" They gave a piece of baked fish; he took it and ate it in front of them.
>
> (Luke 24:36–43)

He had the ability to pass through locked doors (John 20:19). Through experiences such as these, the disciples became convinced that Jesus had risen from the dead.

Jesus commissioned his disciples to continue his work. They were to become "apostles," or messengers, carrying the news that Jesus had risen and the kingdom had begun. After a period described as lasting 40 days, Jesus gathered his disciples for a final time, promised that the Spirit would guide them, and then ascended into Heaven. He left behind the memory of his victory over death, and the promise of life in the kingdom for those who would hear his words. Preserving these memories and promises was the mission of the early Church.

Have You Considered?

1. Why do you think Jesus objected to finding merchants and money changers in the Temple?
2. By washing his disciples' feet, Jesus said that leadership must be built on serving others. Give an example of leadership built on service from your own experience.
3. Put yourself in the position of one of Jesus' disciples. What would it have taken to convince you that Jesus was risen from the grave? Do you think Thomas was wrong to want proof?

MORE ABOUT THE TEXT

Doubting Thomas

The traditional nickname "Doubter" for Thomas may not be as appropriate as we think. For one thing, in John 11:16, we learn that when Jesus decided to go to Lazarus, his disciples were certain that his life was at risk. Thomas was the first who was willing to go with him.

In the "Doubting Thomas" story, Thomas is only asking for what the rest of the disciples

have already had: a firsthand experience of the risen Jesus. They didn't have to accept it on anyone's word, why should Thomas? In fact, according to Mark and Luke, all the disciples refused to believe the testimony of Mary Magdalene and the other women until Jesus appeared to them as well.

Connect

Homework Assignment: In the "Chapter 11 Review Q/A," have the students write answers to questions 10–12 of Section One. Also, have them explain their understanding of the last two learning objectives on page 190 in a few short paragraphs.

What's Next?

What to Do

Ask the students to write in their journals a personal one-sentence definition of Christian discipleship for use in the next lesson.

Have You Considered?

1. Make sure students understand that whatever his motives, Jesus' action would certainly have been understood as more than a religious complaint—it was also an attack on the political and economic system under which the people lived, and would have been seen as such by the Jewish authorities.
2. Have students think about the most effective leaders they know. Generally, these will be people who lead by example.
3. Students will generally be sympathetic to Thomas and his desire for evidence. Recall for students Jesus' words: "Blessed are you who believe and have not seen." To have faith means that we believe in the truth of the Resurrection in the absence of conclusive proof.

Bonus Focus for You

Read John 21, which tells the story of the breakfast Jesus ate with his disciples. Imagine yourself as one of the people eating with the other disciples, fed by Jesus after having been out fishing all night. Write your reflections in your journal.

in the Spotlight

Have the students read "in the Spotlight." If you have any other pictures of the Last Supper, show them to the students.

LESSON THREE
(pages 198–204)

◆ Discipleship in the Gospels

Welcome

1. **Greeting:** As the students gather, greet them using "brother" or "sister" before their names. When everyone has come in, explain that in many Christian denominations and Catholic religious orders, people call one another "sister" and "brother" to express their awareness that they are closely related in Christ. Welcome your students as fellow disciples, your younger sisters and brothers in Christ.

2. Invite them to greet their classmates using "brother" or "sister" before their names. It may sound awkward at first and, because this address is common in African-American communities, you will want to watch for racial overtones in their conversations. Address this issue if it comes up so that your students learn to accept and respect cultural differences. But the experience will help bring home to your students that they are all united in Christ and part of God's family.

3. Finally, ask your students to join hands and pray the "Our Father" together. Stress that since we all have one father, who is also the father of Jesus, we are all family, all brothers and sisters of Jesus, all children of God.

Introducing the Lesson

Teaching Objectives

By the end of this lesson students will be able to:
• Identify, in detail, the unique emphasis of each writer of the Gospel in telling the Christian story.
• Explain the different aspects of discipleship expressed in the four accounts of the Gospel.

What to Do

Have the students read the opening italics, learning objectives, and the first three paragraphs of "Discipleship in the Gospels."

What Does It Mean to Be a Disciple?

The "good news" of Jesus' resurrection from the dead spread quickly. Many people who heard this message responded to Jesus in faith and became Christians. Joining the Church, however, was only the first step in a long journey. These early Christians then had to figure out what it meant to be a disciple of Jesus. The gospel accounts helped early Christians discover the meaning of discipleship. They can help us do the same. In this section, you'll look at the four gospel accounts, paying special attention to how each interprets discipleship. Then, you'll consider what being a disciple means today. In this way, you'll think about the consequences of responding to Jesus by becoming his follower.

Learning Objectives for Section Two:

By the end of this section, you will be able to:

• Discuss the unique perspectives of the gospel writers.

• Explain how each gospel writer understands the meaning of discipleship.

• Describe what it means to be a disciple.

◆ Discipleship in the Gospels

Jesus' disciples quickly took his message far and wide. While they weren't successful everywhere they went, Christian communities soon developed around the Mid-East. Before long, these newly formed communities were asking for guidance in how to "follow Jesus." The gospel accounts were written, in part, to answer the needs of these Christians.

The authors of the gospel accounts organized their stories and sayings about Jesus with several goals in mind. One key aim of each writer was to help Christians in the community grow in discipleship. Each writer shares a common faith in Jesus, but expresses the meaning of that faith differently. Taken together, these four accounts provide us with a well-rounded picture of what discipleship means.

Saint Irenaeus, an early Church Father of the third century, said that the four gospel accounts are like the four points of the compass: without each of the four, we wouldn't be able to find our way.

Mark

Mark is the shortest of the gospel accounts, and the first to be written (probably around 66–70 C.E.). In Mark, Jesus is presented as the Son of God who possessed great authority: in fact, all of his words and deeds reflect his divine power. Often, Mark presents demons as recognizing Jesus and bowing to his authority, suggesting that they knew him as the Son of God. For example, a demon cries out upon seeing Jesus: "I know who you are—the holy One of God!" (*Mark* 1:24,). Mark also points out that not everyone accepted Jesus' authority; Jesus was killed by those who rejected it. The Resurrection, however, showed that Jesus had the greater power.

Despite this emphasis on his authority, Mark shows Jesus as more than a powerful, divine figure. Mark also stresses that suffering was part of Jesus' mission. Throughout Mark, Jesus reminds his follow-

---

◆ MORE ABOUT THE LESSON

Different Gospels?

While it is useful to consider the qualities of discipleship expressed in each account of the Gospel, it is important to recognize that the differences are variations in emphasis, not in subject. Mark, for example, is not about suffering as such. The Gospel is about Jesus, his significance, and the importance of trusting one's life to him. Any careful comparative work shows that the commonalties among the four accounts are much stronger and more numerous than their variations. In fact, the variations are subtle enough that other writers might suggest that very different aspects of discipleship are central to each account's primary understanding.

In your discussions you will want to remind your students that the four accounts are more alike than they are different; proclaiming the good news is an important part of being a disciple.

ers that he must suffer and die before his mission is complete. Mark presents the disciples as often misunderstanding this point. Peter, for example, argues that as the Messiah, Jesus should not allow himself to suffer. Jesus responds intensely:

> "Get behind me, Satan! You are thinking not as God does but as human beings do."
>
> (Mark 8:33)

In other words, Jesus tells Peter that his glory will come only by accepting suffering, not by avoiding it.

One of the unique themes in Mark's account is the "messianic secret." This modern term refers to the fact that in Mark, Jesus demands that his identity as the Messiah be kept secret until after his suffering and death. At one point Jesus asks his disciples who they think he is:

> Now Jesus and his disciples set out for the villages around Caesarea Philippi. Along the way he asked his disciples: "Who do people say that I am?" They said, "John the Baptist, others, Elijah, still others, one of the prophets." And he asked them, "But who do you say that I am?" Peter said to him, "You are the Messiah!" Then he warned them not to tell anyone about him.
>
> (Mark 8:27–30)

Here Mark shows Jesus accepting Peter's recognition of him as the Messiah. Why then would Jesus order them not to tell anyone what they believed? Probably because Mark wants to drive home the point mentioned above: that no one can understand Jesus' mission until they know that he had to suffer and die to do God's will. In other words, Mark says that what it means for Jesus to be the messiah can only be understood after his passion. One can understand Jesus only in light of the end of his life, especially his death on the cross.

For Mark, discipleship is revealed through emphasis on the suffering of Jesus. The true disciple, according to Mark, is one who suffers along with Jesus. Jesus says:

> "Whoever wishes to come after me must deny himself, take up his cross, and follow me. For whoever will preserve his life would lose it, but whoever loses his life for my sake and that of the gospel will save it."
>
> (Mark 8:34–35)

Mark's purpose here is very clear. Mark wrote for a community of Christians who faced the danger of persecution by the Romans, and he reminded them that this was part of the plan. "Don't worry," Mark seemed to say. "We must suffer just as Jesus suffered.

Mantegna, *Crucifixion*, Fifteenth Century.

While all four gospel accounts have the soldiers throwing dice for Jesus' garments, which ones mention: the disciple that Jesus loved? the faithful women? the thieves? the centurion?

MORE ABOUT THE TEXT

Christian Suffering

The mystery of human suffering is one that people have struggled to understand for centuries. Why, if our God loves us, are there so many tragedies in our lives? Why do bad things happen to good people? Does God send suffering to punish or test us? Your students will likely ask questions like these during your discussions in this lesson. Make sure they understand that saying we can learn from our suffering, or we can be united to Jesus in our suffering, is *not* the same as saying God sends us suffering to "teach us a lesson," to "punish us for our sins," or to "test our faith." Our God is a loving God who wants what is good for us, who wants only the best for us. God will help us to survive painful situations, will surely be with us when we suffer, and may even bring some good out of our suffering, but God does not cause or want our suffering.

Development

What to Do

1. Have the students read "Mark." Ask the students what they think of suffering. Let them share personal experiences if they wish. Then ask if they learned anything from their suffering, if anyone else was helped by their pain, or if it was something they just wanted to be rid of as quickly as possible. See "More about the Lesson" on page 199 for help with this discussion.

2. Have the students read Mark 10:17–31 and explore its message about discipleship. They should identify ideas like total focus, full loyalty, disinterest in wealth, and the willingness to do without whatever is necessary in order to be with Jesus. In other words, they should put Jesus first.

3. Have the students read "Matthew" and briefly discuss with them the three points made in the text. Give the students a few moments to skim through Matthew 5, 6, and 7, noting some of the examples and images Jesus used in his teaching as they go. Remind them that this address is a highly condensed collection of sayings remembered by Jesus' followers and not a single speech.

4. Then, ask the students to look closely at Matthew 6:33–34 and 7:21–23 and consider what they teach about being a disciple.

5. Ask the students to read "Luke" and discuss the material briefly with them, clarifying any questions they may have. Ask for a volunteer to read Luke 16:19–31, as an illustration of the relationship between the rich and the poor. Luke 17:7–10 and Luke 22:24–27 will give the students some insight into the attitude Luke expects of true disciples. After the students have read it they should be able to identify the following aspects of discipleship: hard work, humility, willingness to do whatever is commanded, duty, and the reversal of common expectations.

6. Have the students read "John," finding and reading the scripture references mentioned as they go. (They can skim through the longer sections such as John 14–17.) Spend a few moments discussing

the four elements of discipleship identified in the text. Then look closely at a few passages in John 14–17 with the students; be sure they notice the references Jesus makes to closeness and oneness with Jesus and the Father (John 14:20–23), to joy (John 15:11; 16:21–24; 17:13), to peace (John 14:27); and to answers to prayer (John 14:14; 15:7). These balance and deepen the statements about suffering and persecution.

7. Share some quotations from mystical saints who have experienced unity with Jesus, along with a short biography of each saint, with your students (see Teacher's Resource 11B). Read them aloud, asking the students to follow along. Let the students explore them and consider the possibilities they offer to the culmination of discipleship as John expresses it.

Practicing the Skills

What to Do

Plan a service project with the students, using John 13:1–14 and Luke 22:24–27 to help them understand the spirit of Christian service before they begin. Should it be easy? Should it be comfortable? Should it contribute something to the community? Should it be a proud gift or a humble response to real needs? There are some ideas in "More about the Lesson," on page 200 which may help you.

Recall

Ask the students to take out a piece of paper, fold it in quarters, and label each quarter with the names of the four accounts. Then ask them to draw a symbol that captures an aspect of discipleship that is important to each Gospel writer. Give as many students as possible a chance to show and explain their symbols to the class.

But just as Jesus was glorified through his suffering, glory awaits us, too." For Mark, the true disciple is one who follows Jesus even if it leads to suffering or death.

Matthew

Matthew, like Mark, stresses the authority of Jesus. He uses the title "Son of God" to refer to Jesus. Matthew also shows Jesus speaking and healing with authority.

Jesus the Teacher Matthew is most interested, however, in Jesus as a teacher. Matthew organizes the sayings of Jesus into five major speeches, the most famous being the Sermon on the Mount, which is found in Matthew 5–7. By collecting these sayings into five units, and giving each such promi-

nence, Matthew identifies them as the basic teachings of the Church. If you want to understand what Jesus stood for, Matthew suggests that you turn to these speeches.

Some Bible scholars think the Sermon on the Mount was structured as a parallel to the Torah, the first five books of the Old Testament, called "the books of Moses" by Jews. Matthew is clearly comparing Jesus, the new lawgiver and teacher, to Moses, the original lawgiver and teacher. In addition, Matthew also compares Jesus to Moses in the infancy story which opens the gospel account. Matthew's purpose in making the comparison between Jesus and Moses is to show that Jesus has also created a community centered around the Covenant, in this case, the early Church.

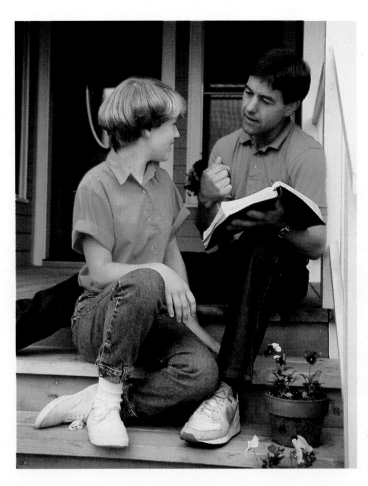

The Gospel according to Matthew presents Jesus as the great teacher. The challenge of discipleship is to follow the master and live out what he taught.

Matthew's special interest in the teaching of Jesus comes across in the two main themes that he finds in that teaching: justice and the Law. Matthew's Jesus stresses that obedience to the Father requires us to act in just ways toward others. Matthew shares with Luke the saying of Jesus known as the *golden rule*: "Do to others whatever you would have them do to you" (*Matthew* 7:12.)

As mentioned earlier, Jesus also shared this idea with other Jewish teachers such as Rabbi Hillel. When Matthew adds, "this sums up the Law and the prophets," it suggests that just behavior is required as an obligation to God. In Matthew, Jesus also points out that it was not his intention to overturn the Law. In fact, he came to confirm it:

> "Do not think that I have come to abolish the Law or the prophets. I have come not to abolish but to fulfill. Amen, I say to you, until heaven and earth pass away, not the smallest letter or the smallest part of a letter will pass from the Law until all things have taken place."
>
> (Matthew 5:17–18)

Matthew does not mean that Jesus viewed the Law as absolute; like Mark, Matthew points out that Jesus would sometimes disobey the Law in order to help people in need. Rather, Matthew says, Jesus came to "fulfill" the Law, to accomplish its purposes. The original purpose of the Law was to guide people in moral behavior towards God and each other, and Jesus says that the Law must continue to perform this function.

Jesus and the Old Testament   Matthew also stresses the connections between Jesus and the Old Testament. Matthew uses *formula citations*—quotes from the Old Testament—that show Jesus fulfilling prophecies. Consider one of Matthew's infancy stories: Jesus' family fled to Egypt to escape King Herod's order that all male infants should be killed.

> He stayed there until the death of Herod, that what the Lord had said through the prophet might be fulfilled: "Out of Egypt I called my son."
>
> (Matthew 2:15)

Taken from the prophet Hosea, this line referred to Israel's deliverance from Egypt. Matthew uses the quotation to show God's protection of Jesus.

By emphasizing the Law and the traditions of Israel, Matthew grounds his community firmly in the ancient ways. He shows that Jesus did not destroy those foundations, but built upon them. Note how Matthew's community resolved problems: They looked to the Jewish traditions and also to the teach-

Scripture Workshop

The Beatitudes

Read Matthew 5:1–12 and Luke 6:20–26, then do the following:

- List all the differences between the two versions.
- Describe how these differences illustrate Luke's concern for the poor.
- Tell what values are present in Matthew's Sermon on the Mount?
- Describe how Matthew challenges Christians to live as a community of faith.
- Explain from the differences, Matthew's special concern.

ings of Jesus as they remembered them for guidance. Some of these procedures are reflected in Chapter 18, the third in a series of chapters related to discipleship and community. There, Jesus establishes procedures for settling disputes among Church members and for making decisions affecting the whole community. Jesus also indicates that the community has the power to forgive sins. In Chapter 16, Jesus designates Peter to head the Church. These passages in Matthew reflect early applications of Jesus' teaching in the Christian community.

Jesus and the Community   As Matthew well knows, true discipleship does not take place in isolation. Sharing life and faith with others is important for keeping discipleship strong. The teachings of Jesus are not always easy to follow, though they always result in a much richer life.

Christians help each other by participating in a community of faith. Just as the very first disciples became a community of friends because of their shared love for Jesus, so today Christians can become a community because of the same shared love and faith. The community helps the individual disciple and the disciple in return nourishes the other members of the

Scripture Workshop

1. Differences: (A) Matthew says "poor in spirit" (v.3); Luke has "poor" (v.20). (B) Matthew says "hunger and thirst for holiness (v.6); Luke says "hunger" (v.20). (C) On persecution beatitude, Luke adds "Thus it was that their fathers treated the prophets." (v.23). (D) Matthew adds beatitudes for the lowly, those who show mercy, the single-hearted, and the peacemakers. (E) Luke adds "woe" statements for the rich, the full, and those laughing, as well as Christians when all speak well of them.
2. While Matthew speaks of the poor "in spirit" and those who hunger "for holiness," Luke is talking about the materially hungry and poor.
3. Matthew clearly values interpersonal qualities of humility, loyalty, and a capacity to forgive.
4. Matthew challenges Christians to remain members of the community despite persecution and rejection by the world. Matthew also encourages Christians to posses interpersonal qualities which will help keep the community together.
5. Matthew's special concern for the community is evident in his additions to the beatitudes.

◆ MORE ABOUT THE LESSON

Service Projects

Service projects require planning with the students and usually with the recipients as well. You may wish to join projects existing in your area (for example, helping Habitat for Humanity, building a house, or volunteering at a soup kitchen). Students can also visit a nursing home, do yard or house work for ill or elderly people, or spruce up church property. The possibilities are endless. Let the students decide what they'd like to do, as well as when, and how to get it done. Let them explore what it means to give genuinely, without expecting credit or money or any kind of reward in return.

Connect

Students continue to apply principles of discipleship to their own experience.

What to Do

Homework Assignment: Ask the students to reflect on the emphasis for discipleship expressed in the gospel accounts and write a few paragraphs telling which emphasis they express most often in their lives, and which they find most difficult to put into practice. Ask them to identify one thing they can do to live out each aspect of discipleship more fully. They will need to bring these lists to the next lesson.

What's Next?

What to Do

Have the students review the sentence on discipleship they wrote at the end of Lesson Two in this chapter. Ask them to revise it according to their present understanding. Explain that they will learn even more about being a disciple in the next lesson, so they should keep both their first sentence and today's revision.

community. In this way, the church continues to grow in knowledge of the Lord and in Christian action in the community and the world.

For Matthew, discipleship means being part of a believing community. In that community, the Church applies Jesus' words about justice and the Law to daily life. Discipleship means studying the teachings of Jesus, especially those contained in the five speeches that detail the obligations of those who accept the Covenant with God established through Jesus. The role of the disciple is to study and live out these teachings as a member of the wider Church community. A disciple participates in the community and includes the community in decision making.

Luke

Luke addresses his gospel account to an audience that is primarily Gentile (non-Jewish). They are mostly Greek-speaking people who have converted to Christianity.

Life is very difficult for these Christians. They are trying to live out their faith in an empire hostile towards Judaism. The Romans originally considered Christianity as just another Jewish political party.

The Christians to whom Luke writes have recently experienced the destruction of Jerusalem. They are worried about their own fate. If God allowed Jerusalem to be wrecked and the Temple to be demolished, how can they believe that God will be faithful to them?

Luke's answer to this question is that God has been faithful to Israel, but in an unexpected way. Through Jesus, God has created a "new Israel" which includes Gentiles, people considered to be "sinners" such as tax collectors, and all those at the margins of society: the poor, the elderly, and the forgotten. Luke identifies this new Israel with the Christian Church, and says that it has inherited the promises made by God in the Old Testament.

In this new Israel, membership is no longer determined by birth, or by obedience to the Law. Everyone is eligible to share in God's promise of the eternal Covenant. The only requirement for sharing in God's gift is to have a heart open to love. The story of the penitent woman makes this point:

> Now there was a sinful woman in the city who learned that he was at table in the house of the Pharisee. Bringing an alabaster flask of ointment, she stood behind him at his feet weeping and began to bathe his feet with her tears. Then she wiped them with her hair, kissed them, and anointed them with ointment.

> When the Pharisee who had invited him saw this he said to himself, "If this man were a prophet, he would know who and what sort of woman this is who is touching him, that she is a sinner." . . . [Jesus said] "So I tell you, her many sins have been forgiven; hence, she has shown great love. But the one to whom little is forgiven, loves little."

(Luke 7:37–39,47)

Luke's gospel account is sometimes called the "social gospel" because it emphasizes a concern for the poor and those neglected by society. For example, in Luke 14:13, Jesus says that when we have a reception, we should invite beggars, the crippled, the lame, and the blind, rather than our relatives and wealthy neighbors. In this way, Jesus says, we will be rewarded in the resurrection.

Luke's concern for the poor also comes across in his version of the "Beatitudes" or the Sermon on the Plains. This list of blessings which Jesus offers is given in both Matthew and Luke. The lists are not the same, however. Whereas in Matthew Jesus says, "Blessed are the poor in spirit," (*Matthew* 5:3) Luke quotes Jesus as saying, "Blessed are the poor." (*Luke* 6:20) Like sinners and gentiles, the poor are welcome in the new Israel which Jesus has founded.

What, then, is required of the members of this new Israel? Luke emphasizes that being a disciple means spreading the good news about Jesus. He says that God will give his messengers special powers to accomplish this task. In both Matthew and Luke, Jesus sends out disciples to spread his teachings. Only in Luke, however, do they report the powers they were given:

> The seventy-two returned in jubilation saying, "Master, even the demons are subject to us in your name." [Jesus] said in reply: "I watched Satan fall from the sky like lightning. See what I have done; I have given you the power to tread on snakes and scorpions and all the forces of the enemy, and nothing shall ever injure you. Nevertheless, do not rejoice so much in the fact that the devils are subject to you as that your names are inscribed in heaven."

(Luke 10:17–20)

Here, Jesus indicates that God will provide the abilities necessary to ensure that Jesus' messengers succeed. Luke stresses many times that God will respond when the disciples present their needs in prayer.

Such gifts from God, however, mean that the disciples have a special responsibility to do God's will. Luke quotes Jesus as saying,

---

◆ MORE ABOUT THE LESSON

More about Service Projects

What happens after a service project can just be as important for helping your students understand Christian service as what happens during the project. Close your service project with a time of sharing about the experience (what happened, what they liked and didn't like, what they learned, what it meant to them). You may want to include some form of symbolic offering such as a few sentences of paper that can be burned in offering or made into a boat to be set afloat down a stream. Ask a student to read Psalm 41:2–4 and then read Psalm 138 as a closing prayer.

When much has been given a man, much will be required of him. More will be asked of a man to whom more has been entrusted.

(Luke 12:48)

A disciple, therefore, is under an obligation to use God's gifts positively. In Chapter 17, Luke also reminds his readers not to expect tremendous honors or riches for their efforts; spreading God's word is simply their duty.

For Luke, therefore, a disciple is one who does the work of God, especially spreading the good news about Jesus, believing in faith that God will provide the gifts needed to succeed. Luke reminds his readers that anyone, regardless of social status or past mistakes, may be a disciple of Jesus. All that is needed is a loving heart and confidence in God's protection.

John

John's account is very different from the other three. Unlike the synoptics, which follow basically the same story line, and include much of the same material, John's account uses very different stories and sayings. Probably the most unusual feature in John is his tendency to quote Jesus as giving long speeches, called "discourses." In fact, the majority of the gospel account consists not of stories about Jesus, but of these discourses. In most cases, biblical scholars believe that these discourses are not Jesus' own words. Instead, they represent ideas which came from Jesus that were shaped by John to teach his own Christian community.

Most Bible scholars think that John's account of the Gospel was written later than the other three, and that the members of his community were already familiar with the accounts written by the synoptics. John's account was then written to deepen their faith and to guide them in becoming better disciples of Jesus.

John's gospel account presents a very exalted view of Jesus. Jesus is the "logos," or "Word," that has existed with God from the beginning of time. It was by the Word, in fact, that the universe was created. Later, John says, the Word became flesh in Jesus. Although the synoptic gospels referred to Jesus as the Son of God, and thought of him as divine, John emphasizes that in Jesus, God took on human form. We call this theological point the *Incarnation*.

John recognizes Jesus as the divine Son of God. In John, Jesus repeatedly makes "I am" statements. You remember that for the Jews, the name of God is "Yahweh," a word which means "I am." When Jesus refers to himself as "I am," John's Jewish audience would clearly understand Jesus to mean that he was God. Such a saying is found in John 8:24.

This saying highlights another important aspect of John's thought. John believes that faith in Jesus is necessary for his readers to be saved. John defines "faith" as believing in the special relationship which connects Jesus and the Father and trusting totally in Jesus for everything related to eternal life. Jesus speaks of this relationship in many places within the gospel:

"Whoever has seen me has seen the Father. How can you say, 'Show us the Father?' Do you not believe that I am in the Father and the Father is in me?"

(John 14:9b–10a)

John stresses that to know Jesus is to know the Father (*John* 8:19). By reflecting on Jesus' words and actions, therefore, John's readers come to a deeper understanding of God.

More than with any other gospel account, John is written with the specific needs of a particular community of believers in mind. Therefore, it is not surprising that John provides guidelines for discipleship. In chapters 13–17, John presents Jesus as delivering his last discourse before his arrest. In it, Jesus tells his followers what being his disciple means.

1. Service. Jesus washes the feet of his disciples, telling them that even though he is the master and they are the servants, it is necessary for him to humble himself and serve them. In the same way, it is necessary for disciples to humble themselves and serve others.

2. Doing his works. This involves teaching, healing, and revealing the Father to other people. Jesus promises his followers that whatever they ask, if they ask in his name, the Father will provide it to them. Like Luke, John stresses that God will provide the disciples with what they need to do Jesus' work. In John, Jesus promises the disciples that he will send a Paraclete to them. In Greek law, a "paraclete" was like a defense attorney: someone who defends you and speaks for you. Jesus refers here to the Holy Spirit, who will come to the disciples and guide them in following Jesus.

MORE ABOUT THE TEXT

Closing Reflection

The following reflection may help your students to connect this lesson with their own lives and experiences. Have them clear their desks of paper, books, or other distractions; lower the lights; provide quiet instrumental music as a background if you can. Explain that you will pause occasionally so that they can think about the prayer. Then read slowly, pausing for silence where the ellipses appear:

Lord Jesus, discipleship looks both wonderful and scary to me … I find these things beautiful about you and about discipleship … I'd like to follow you, but so many other things in my life are attractive, too … I don't know what will happen about these things in my life if I choose to follow you … Please guide me to know what I really want … Thank you for always loving me, no matter what. Amen.

Have You Considered?

1. Students should recognize that the passion story is an essential component of Jesus' story. Jesus' willingness to suffer for others perfectly illustrates the character of the kingdom.

2. Point out to students that most cultures have a variation on this idea. The saying was common among Jewish teachers before Jesus, and appears in Confucian literature as well. In most cases, it is a basic expression of the principle of justice: we cannot expect fair treatment from others if we do not offer it ourselves.

3. Have students answer this question from their own experience before moving on to the "global" issue. Christianity at large has a mixed track record on this question. On the one hand, the various Christian churches probably represent the largest collection of charitable organizations in the world. Every day, millions of people are fed, housed, and cared for who otherwise would not be because of the generosity and self-giving of Christians. On the other hand, some Christian churches have grown quite wealthy, and many question whether or not those resources could be used to help the poor. Also, Christian leaders have sometimes supported political and social systems which perpetuate poverty.

4. "I am" is from the name of God, Yahweh, as revealed in Exodus. From this, we can conclude that John and his audience had a Jewish religious background. Such a claim would be scandalous to Jews, since merely pronouncing the name of God was offensive to pious Jews, let alone the claim that a certain human being was God.

Bonus Focus for You

Read John 10:10–11. What does "abundant life" mean to you? How is it related to discipleship? Write your reflections in your journal.

◆ Being a Disciple

Welcome

What to Do

Write the word "disciple" on the board in capital letters, vertically. Have the students call out as many qualities or ideas for each letter as they can think of pertaining to Jesus and to following Jesus. (A few possibilities are given in "More about the Lesson" on page 204. The students may think much more creatively than this!)

Introducing the Lesson

Teaching Objectives

By the end of this lesson students will be able to:
• Demonstrate how the lessons of the Gospel can be applied to modern life.
• Apply the lessons about discipleship expressed in the Gospel to their own lives and experiences.
• Translate the early Christians' experiences into situations common in life today.

What to Do

Have the students read the first paragraph under "Being a Disciple." Before they read any further, ask them to look over their homework assignment from the last lesson. Ask for volunteers to share from their list of things they could do to live out their discipleship more fully.

Development

What to Do

1. Have the students read "Suffering with Jesus." After a brief discussion, ask them to evaluate the three positive outcomes of suffering listed in the text. Which do they think is most true of their own reactions to suffering? Which will be most helpful to think about the next time they experience disappointment or pain in their lives or see it in the lives of their friends or family?

2. Have the students read "Belonging to the Community." Note that while many communities of

3. Living out the commandments he has given. The most important of these commands, he says, is to love one another, even to the point of accepting death:

> "This is my commandment: love one another as I love you. No one has greater love than this, to lay down one's life for one's friends. You are my friends if you do what I command you.
>
> (John 15:12–14)

The true test of discipleship is love. If we love one another, then we are obeying Jesus' commands and living as his disciple.

4. Seeking unity with Jesus. The foundation and goal of everything else in John is the possibility of becoming one with Jesus. This glorious hope is the basis of John 14–17. There, Jesus speaks again and again of how he wants his disciples to be one with him and with the Father, just as he himself is one with the Father. He says he and the Father will dwell in the heart of the disciple who keeps his words and loves his commandments. Without this goal, the other actions are incomplete. With this hope, everything else is seen to be as full and rich as Christ himself.

John warns his readers that following Jesus will not be easy. "The world will not support you," he says, "in fact, people will persecute you." John tells his community to accept that they are not "of the world," and to endure in being disciples no matter what comes. If they do this, he says, God will not abandon them in need. "Your fruit must endure," Jesus says,

> "It was not you who chose me, but I who chose you and appointed you to go and bear fruit that will remain, so that whatever you ask the Father in my name he may give you"
>
> (John 15:16).

Have You Considered?

1. Mark says that one cannot understand Jesus without knowing about his suffering. Do you agree? Why or why not?
2. Matthew and Luke both contain Jesus' golden rule: "Treat others as you would have them treat you." Explain what this statement means.
3. Luke says that Christianity must reach out to the poor and neglected people in society. Do you think Christianity today does this? Why or why not?
4. In John, Jesus refers to himself as "I am." What can we learn from this about the religious background of John's audience? How might they have reacted to Jesus calling himself by this name?

◆ Being a Disciple

The four gospel accounts give us four complementary images of discipleship. Discipleship is:

1. For Mark, suffering with Jesus.
2. For Matthew, following Jesus' teaching in a believing community.
3. For Luke, proclaiming the kingdom to all.
4. For John, loving others and seeking unity with Jesus.

In thinking about what being a disciple might mean for you today, let's consider each image in turn.

Suffering with Jesus

In the early Church, when persecution by the Romans was a constant threat, Mark's theme of suffering with Jesus was understood very literally. Even today, there are places where Christians suffer and die for their faith. In 1980, Archbishop Oscar Romero was shot and killed while saying Mass in El Salvador. Romero was murdered because he demanded justice for the poor. A disciple of Jesus must be willing to suffer for Jesus.

Since most of us will, hopefully, never experience any suffering this dramatic, how can we "take up the cross" and suffer with Jesus? Although we may not always have to endure physical pain, all of us have our share of suffering. All of us have disappointments and frustrations with which we have to deal. Maybe it's a job we hoped for over the summer that fell through; maybe it's a relationship that grew apart. Whatever it is, we know what it feels like to be sad and hurt. Suffering with Jesus means accepting these trials as part of God's plan. Being a disciple means finding meaning and value in the disappointments that come our way.

What value can there possibly be in suffering? According to Mark, it can be found in at least three ways:

1. **Suffering can help us in our prayer lives.** Suffering can help us to understand and appreciate the sacrifice Jesus made on our behalf. We can offer up our own pain to Jesus, putting it in his hands and reminding ourselves of his suffering on the cross.
2. **Suffering can help us feel the pain of others.** It can make us more sympathetic and sensitive when we see others having trouble. We are better able to help others when we've dealt with pain ourselves.

◆ MORE ABOUT THE LESSON

Welcoming Activity

Here are some ideas the students might come up with as part of the creative welcoming activity:

D — discipline
I — "I AM"
S — service, suffering
C — compassion
I — interest, integrity
P — prayer, peace, persecution
L — love
E — eternal life

People
of Note

Have the students read "People of Note." Ask them, "What feelings or thoughts would make a person willing to die for another person or a belief?"

People of Note

Saint Perpetua

In the first three centuries C.E., the Church often faced persecution. Hundreds of Christians shared the suffering of Jesus in the most literal way, by dying for the faith. Among the most famous of these early martyrs is Saint Perpetua. Although the story of her death has been exaggerated, as many legends about the saints have been, it served to convince its early hearers of the love of God and the holiness of martyrdom.

Perpetua was arrested in North Africa (in modern Tunisia). As part of their public festivals, Romans sometimes executed prisoners by putting them in a pit with wild beasts. Perpetua had to walk through two lines of men striking her with whips before she was thrown into the pit. The beasts attacked her, but she was not injured. Next, a Roman soldier was sent to kill her with a sword. He struck her, but again God preserved her from harm. Finally, Perpetua guided the soldier in putting the sword to her throat. She died from this wound, a model of a disciple who embraced suffering in faith.

3. **Suffering can help us appreciate God's blessings when they come.** We can put all the good things about our lives into better perspective when we've experienced a few disappointments.

By finding value in our pain, and using our bad experiences to become better people, we grow in maturity and become close disciples of Jesus.

Belonging to the Community

As you have read, the Gospel according to Matthew has a special interest in community life. That's understandable, for Matthew was written, many scholars think, to provide direction to the early Christian communities. Remember, these communities did not have the gospel accounts, letters of Paul, or, for that matter, the church structure that we know.

For Matthew, discipleship means being one with the community of faith. Read Matthew 16:13–20 for an explanation of this photo. What does this say about being a disciple?

Perugino, Christ Delivering the Keys to St. Peter. Fifteenth Century.

Matthew's time may have had access to some of the letters of Paul, the collection, as we know it, did not exist, and some communities would not have read any of the letters.

3. Discuss these questions with the students: What difference does it make with whom you associate in life? What kinds of friends do you choose? Why? In the groups you belong to, do the members influence you more than you influence them, or vice versa?

4. Invite the students to reflect on whether the groups they belong to agree with the following:

• The company we keep can make it harder or easier to be a disciple of Jesus.

• Sharing sports, social gatherings, study, and other activities with other disciples of Jesus will be more fun for everyone.

• Being disciples of Jesus gives people the opportunity to reach out or offer help to others in a more effective way.

They can write their reflections in their Spiritual Journal. It is most important that they consider whether their group of friends really makes it easier or harder for them to follow Jesus.

5. Have the students read "Proclaiming the Kingdom." Ask the students to recall the story of Joshua and Michael at the beginning of Chapter 10. Ask for a volunteer to recap the story for the class. Then discuss the following questions: Was Joshua acting as a disciple? Who might have been influenced by his behavior? Did he proclaim the kingdom?

6. Discuss the differences between proclaiming the kingdom by talking about one's faith, and by living out kingdom values in one's life. Can we do one without doing the other? Ask the students to list some examples of

MORE ABOUT THE TEXT

Suffering

Many people, in response to suffering in their own lives, are motivated to try to find ways to relieve or prevent similar suffering in others, or at least to provide support for other who suffer in ways similar to the way they have. Mothers and Students Against Drunk Driving (MADD and SADD), for example, were founded by people who lost loved ones in alcohol-related accidents and who are determined to reduce drunk driving in their communities so that others won't suffer similar losses. In addition to the work these groups do to prevent human suffering, they also serve as support groups for those people who are in pain.

Giving your students examples like these may help them to understand how many people can benefit from the suffering of a few, as well as how we can be empowered to help others when we have experienced pain ourselves.

kingdom values they can live out in their lives; encourage them to make positive and specific statements (e.g., "I will forgive my sister when she 'borrows' my things without asking") rather than negative or vague ones (e.g., "I won't fight with people").

7. Remind the students that peace is one of the gifts that results from living in the kingdom. Ask them to remember a time when they felt really peaceful. Then ask: "Did you realize that what you experienced was God's gift of peace to you?" Have them write in their Spiritual Journal their answer to this question: How could I have brought that feeling of peace into something that has happened to me in the last week?

8. Have the students read "Loving One Another." It is important that they be able to distinguish between the emotional response we associate with the word "love" and the kind of love, *agape*, expressed in John's account.

9. Have the students read John 21:15–17 in small groups. Point out that Jesus is speaking not only to Peter, but to all of us, and ask the groups to consider these questions: If we love Jesus, do we need to feed his sheep? What does it mean to "feed my sheep?" Who are the sheep? How are they fed? How could you feed another student? a teacher? your family members? a priest? Have each group write at least five suggestions for each person they might "feed," and share their lists with the class.

10. End your lesson with a prayer based on this last activity. Ask students to volunteer some of the ideas they had for "feeding Jesus' sheep" as subjects for prayer.

Recall

Have the students find the definitions of discipleship that they have written for each of the last two lessons. Ask them to write down their present understanding, including all that they have learned in this lesson. Volunteers can share their new sentences. Encourage them to see the growth in their understanding, and praise them for the efforts they have made.

206

They were pioneers, figuring out as they went how to bring Jesus' teaching to life.

In those early days, community life had its ups and downs, just like shared life anywhere always has. Even though Christians were focused on Jesus, they did not always agree or do the right thing. They were growing into their faith through participation in the community. It's understandable that tensions developed.

Matthew's approach to these tensions was to urge Christians to have a forgiving and loving heart out of love for Jesus. Today, these principles are just as true as they were then.

Matthew's emphasis on the disciple's life in community can be applied to your life. You can make any situation better by putting your Christian faith into action.

What does it mean for you to be a disciple? What can you do to live as a student of the Lord Jesus and proclaim the Gospel with your life?

Proclaiming the Kingdom

Luke's account emphasizes that a disciple spreads the Good News about Jesus regardless of the dangers or difficulties involved, confident that God will help. For the early Church, the danger of spreading the Gospel was much more immediate. Christians risked arrest, torture and death. Today, that risk still exists in some places. In the People's Republic of China, for instance, it is illegal to belong to the Roman Catholic Church. Anyone caught distributing its literature or speaking on its behalf risks persecution.

Most of us will never face this kind of organized opposition. In fact, we live in a country that, at least statistically, is overwhelmingly Christian. What does "proclaiming the kingdom" mean for us now?

First, it means being willing to talk openly about our faith. Many people find it difficult to talk about their spiritual lives with others. Often this reluctance comes from humility, which is, in itself, a good thing. Sometimes, however, people don't get the encouragement they need to grow in their relationship with God. People, especially teenagers, need support from their peers to feel good about what they're doing. Being a disciple means reaching out and sharing God's love when it is possible to do so in a quiet, supportive way.

Second, proclaiming the kingdom means living out its values as an example for others. Our challenge is to provide people with living examples of what the kingdom has to offer: peace, contentment, and moral conduct. As the saying goes, "Actions speak louder than words." The best way to proclaim the kingdom is to live lovingly. By doing so, we'll serve as role models for others and be effective disciples.

Loving One Another

Finally, John said that a disciple is one who follows the commandment of Jesus to love one another as the core of their unity with Jesus. This command, however, is very general. Practically, what does it mean to say a disciple is one who loves others?

The Greek word used here for love, "agape," is not primarily an emotional attitude. It has little to do with how you *feel*. Agape means "to value" or "to prize." In other words, "loving one another" means valuing other people, treating them with great respect and caring for them as people with dignity. The word con-

---

MORE ABOUT THE TEXT

Screwtape Letters

C.S. Lewis wrote about the effects of discipleship in his tongue-in-cheek work, "The Screwtape Letters." In these letters, Screwtape, a middle-level devil writes to his nephew, a young imp, some of the devilish temptations hell was offering to humans to lead them astray from the teachings of Jesus. What makes the letters most interesting is that they present these teachings in reverse: Jesus' teachings are evil and the devil's teachings good. You may wish to read some of these letters with your students and have them identify the truly positive benefits of living a life of discipleship.

cerns your attitudes and how you *act*. Agape has to do with the way you interact with the people in your life. "Loving one another" means valuing the well-being of others. We can express agape on two levels.

1. **"Large-scale agape"** refers to the value we attach to the well-being of groups of people. As disciples, Jesus calls us to be aware of the world in which we live. Where we see poverty and injustice, conditions in which people don't enjoy the dignity they deserve, it's our duty to act. This may mean volunteering to help the homeless, supporting a candidate for office, or giving money to a charitable organization. Whatever our contribution may be, as disciples, Jesus asks us to help make the world a place that values the worth of all people.

2. **"Small-scale agape"** is the way we treat the individuals in our own lives. It means taking the time to do something around the house without being asked. It means behaving with respect in the classroom. It means standing up for somebody in school who needs your help. Whatever

the situation, as disciples we have to show our love to the people we meet on a daily basis. Actually, practicing small-scale agape can be much more difficult than large-scale agape. It's easy to make a small gesture for someone you've never even met. It can be very difficult to act generously towards someone who irritates you. Nevertheless, Jesus calls us as disciples to show love towards all.

Have You Considered?

1. Describe a disappointment you've experienced. How can you find value in this experience?
2. Which communities do you belong to? How can you be a good member of these communities?
3. Do you think it's more effective to proclaim the kingdom by example rather than through words? Are both necessary? Explain your answer.

Spiritual Reflection

On Being a Disciple

The New Testament provides us with many examples of discipleship. Luke 10:25–37 offers one of the most intriguing parables in the Gospel. You've probably heard the story of the good Samaritan many times; now, take the time to pray with the story and see what it tells you about discipleship.

Read the parable slowly and carefully, making sure that you understand everything. When you're finished, take a moment to become quiet inside. Then, think about the various characters that are presented in the story:

- Why does the scholar come to Jesus? How should a disciple come to Jesus?
- Although you would expect the Levite and priest to be good neighbors, they would be violating the Law if they helped the wounded man. What does this tell you about being a disciple?
- What do you know about the relationship between Jews and Samaritans? Think about your worst enemy,

the person you dislike most in the whole world. That person is the Samaritan in this story. How can this person remain an enemy? What is the responsibility of discipleship?

- Try to picture the scene in which Jesus says to the scholar, "Which of these three, in your opinion, was neighbor to the robbers' victim?" Imagine that Jesus is talking to you. Hear Jesus' tell you to go and show mercy to those you meet. How do you respond?
- Pray that God may strengthen you to be a good disciple, and give you the ability to forgive those who have injured you and to show mercy to those most in need of it.
- Decide on one thing that you can do differently in your life, immediately, in order to be a better disciple of Jesus; then act on your decision.

When you've finished, take another moment to be quiet inside, and then thank God for this time.

◆ MORE ABOUT THE LESSON

John 21 and *Agape*

This is a very rich passage for those who explore it carefully. Greek scholars tell us that the first two times Jesus asks Peter if he loves him, he uses the verb meaning "agape" love. The third time he uses a different verb meaning intense friendship. The two are not contradictory and both are part of the Gospel's understanding of the relationship between Jesus and his disciples. "Agape" is specifically the kind of love

that God and Jesus have for us. So Jesus here is asking the disciple to learn to love with the most intense friendship, but also to stretch for a divine quality of love. Serving others is both a way to learn about divine love and, at the same time, an expression of it. Help your students to stretch for these concepts, so that they really understand that loving feelings, or "warm fuzzies" have little to do with the love of a disciple for Jesus or for other people.

Connect

What to Do

Quiet the room, dim the lights, remove any distractions. Then ask the students to work through the Spiritual Reflection on their own. They can write their responses in their Spiritual Journal.

What's Next?

What to Do

Show the students the map of the Mediterranean on page 217. Point out Jerusalem, where the events discussed in this chapter occurred, and then point out some of the places that will be important in the next chapter: Rome, Antioch, Corinth, Ephesus, Philippi. Ask them to consider how difficult it might be to try to spread an important, but forbidden message from Jerusalem to Rome.

Have You Considered?

1. Discuss with students how disappointments often teach us more about ourselves than successes do. By living through disappointments, we discover inner strengths as well as blind spots we hadn't previously realized.

2. Encourage students to notice that what makes them a good member of one community makes them a good member of all.

3. Students will probably show a preference for actions over words, a typical American response. Point out that in some ways, both are necessary. The words of Jesus give us the "theory" we need to understand what the kingdom is all about. Jesus' actions then show us how to put that theory into practice.

Bonus Focus for You ———

Read Luke 14:25–33. Ponder whether or not you have calculated the conditions of discipleship thoroughly enough to know if you really want to be one. What more might you need to reflect upon? How might you understand discipleship better? What could you do to help yourself? What kind of help can you ask of the Lord? Write your reflections in your journal.

Q/A

Section One

1. A "disciple" literally is a student, or more generally, a follower of Jesus.

2. Literal followers abandoned their homes, families and occupations, and traveled from place to place receiving Jesus' teaching and assisting in his ministry.

3. Two things that make the literal followers noteworthy are that Jesus issued personal invitations and called unlikely candidates.

4. Jesus respected women and treated them as equals.

5. The Twelve had special leadership responsibilities, especially after the death of Jesus in the early Church.

6. The Twelve symbolized the twelve tribes of Israel.

7. Jesus objected to the attitude that made the Law more important than the needs of the people it was designed to serve.

8. Jesus criticized hypocrisy because it contradicted the values of the kingdom which Jesus came to proclaim.

9. The Romans feared a popular uprising against their rule, and felt that Jesus' popularity threatened their control.

10. The two actions Jesus performed were the entry into Jerusalem and the cleansing of the Temple.

11. The three important actions at the Last Supper are washing the feet of the disciples, asking them to continue his mission, and giving them the Eucharist.

12. The charge against Jesus was blasphemy.

Q/A

Section One

1. What does the word "disciple" mean?
2. What did it mean to literally follow Jesus?
3. List two things that made the literal followers of Jesus noteworthy.
4. What was unusual in Jesus' attitude towards women?
5. What was the purpose of the group known as "the Twelve?"
6. What did the Twelve symbolize?
7. To what attitude about the Law did Jesus object?
8. Why did Jesus criticize the hypocrisy of some religious leaders?
9. Why did Jesus' popularity among the common people of Judea threaten the Romans?
10. What two actions did Jesus perform when he arrived in Jerusalem for Passover?
11. What three important actions did Jesus perform at the Last Supper?
12. What was the charge against Jesus by the Jewish leaders?

Section Two

1. How is Jesus presented in Mark?
2. What do the disciples in Mark misunderstand about Jesus?
3. What is the "messianic secret?"
4. How does Mark understand discipleship?
5. How does Matthew compare Jesus to Moses?
6. In Matthew, what are the two most important themes of Jesus' teaching?
7. For Matthew, in what sense does Jesus fulfill the Law?
8. How does Matthew understand discipleship?
9. In what way is Luke the "social gospel?"
10. How does Luke understand discipleship?
11. What does the term "logos" mean in John?
12. What does the term "incarnation" mean?
13. What is significant about Jesus saying "I am?"
14. What is John's understanding of discipleship?
15. Define "agape."

BIBLE ACTIVITIES

1. Each of the four gospel accounts contains a different story about the resurrection of Jesus. Read these stories in Mark 16:9–20, Matthew 28, Luke 24, and John 20–21. For each story, answer the following questions:
   - To whom did Jesus appear?
   - Where did the appearances occur?
   - What did Jesus say?
   What do all four stories have in common? How do you explain the differences between them?

2. Both Matthew and Luke begin their accounts with stories of Jesus' infancy. These stories are very different from one another. Read both stories in Matthew 1–2 and Luke 1–2. List all the elements the two stories have in common. On what do both stories agree concerning Jesus' infancy?

3. Matthew's account shows a special interest in Church discipline. Read Chapter 18:1–14, 21–35 in Matthew, and then answer the following question: according to Matthew, what should I do if a fellow Christian wrongs me in some way?

BIBLE ACTIVITIES

1. Resurrection Stories
- To whom did Jesus appear? *Matthew:* Mary Magdalene and the other Mary; then the eleven disciples; *Mark:* Mary Magdalene; then two others; then the eleven; *Luke:* two on the road to Emmaus; then the eleven; *John:* Mary Magdalene; then the eleven; then to seven of the disciples.
- Where did the appearances take place? *Matthew:* in Jerusalem, then Galilee; *Mark:* not clear; *Luke:* on the road to Emmaus, then in Jerusalem; *John:* Jerusalem, then Galilee.
- What did Jesus say? *Matthew:* the Great Commission; *Mark:* Commissions disciples to make converts, promises them special powers; *Luke:* Speaks with the disciples on the road, interpreting Scripture; tells disciples to remain in Jerusalem; *John:* Gave disciples the power of the Holy Spirit to loose and to bind; asked Peter if Peter loved him; spoke to the beloved disciple.

GLOSSARY

- **Agape**: Greek word for "love"; it refers to valuing others for who they are.
- **Beatitude**: Important teachings of Jesus which begin "Blessed are."
- **Controversy Story**: Story in which Jesus' enemies try to trap him in a dilemma, but from which he escapes.
- **Disciple**: Term meaning "student"; one who learns from Jesus and follows him.
- **Discipleship**: The process of trying to live like Jesus.
- **Discourse**: Long speeches given by Jesus in John; Jesus' own words blended with the understanding of the gospel writer and his community.
- **Easter**: The day on which Jesus rose from the grave.
- **Eucharist**: The word means "thanksgiving"; the sacrament of receiving bread and wine as the body and blood of Christ.
- **Formula Citation**: A device used in Matthew to show that Jesus fulfilled Old Testament prophecy.
- **Incarnation**: The Christian belief that God took on human flesh in Jesus.
- **Last Supper**: The final meal shared by Jesus and his disciples.
- **Literal Followers**: People who gave up their families and jobs to travel with Jesus and receive his teaching.
- **Logos**: Greek term for "word"; in John, Jesus is identified as the Word of God which has existed from the beginning and assisted in creation.
- **Messianic Secret**: In Mark, the idea that Jesus kept secret his identity as the messiah until he had suffered and died.
- **Passion**: The suffering and death of Jesus.
- **Sinner**: Under a strict interpretation of Jewish law anyone who was "impure," such as people holding certain jobs (for example, tax collector).
- **The Twelve**: The inner group of Jesus' disciples entrusted with leadership responsibilities; the "apostles."

UNDERSTANDING MORE ABOUT:

The Twelve

You learned in this chapter that the Twelve were sometimes called apostles. The word "apostle" literally means "one who is sent." This word was later used for other disciples besides the Twelve, including Paul and Barnabas. You also learned that the various gospel accounts differ slightly in their lists of the Twelve. Compare the lists below. How do they differ?

Matthew 10:1–4
"Then he summoned his twelve disciples and gave them authority over unclean spirits to drive them out and to cure every disease and every illness. The names of the twelve apostles are these: first, Simon called Peter, and his brother Andrew; James, the son of Zebedee, and his brother John; Philip and Bartholomew, Thomas and Matthew the tax collector; James, the son of Alphaeus, and Thaddeus; Simon the Cananean, and Judas Iscariot who betrayed him."

Mark 3:13–19
"He went up the mountain and summoned those whom he wanted and they came to him. He appointed twelve [whom he named apostles] that they might be with him and he might send them forth to preach and to have authority to drive out demons: [he appointed the twelve:] Simon, whom he named Peter; James, son of Zebedee, and John the brother of James, who he named Boanerges, that is sons of thunder; Andrew, Philip, Bartholomew, Matthew, Thomas, James the son of Alphaeus; Thaddeus, Simon the Cananean, and Judas Iscariot who betrayed him."

Luke 6:12–16
"In those days he departed to the mountain to pray, and he spent the night in prayer to God. When day came, he called his disciples to himself, and from them he chose Twelve, whom he also named apostles: Simon, whom he named Peter, and his brother Andrew, James, John, Philip, Bartholomew, Matthew, Thomas, James the son of Alphaeus, Simon who was called a Zealot, and Judas the son of James, and Judas Iscariot, who became a traitor."

Section Two

1. Mark presents Jesus as the Son of God who had great authority.
2. The disciples do not understand that suffering is part of what it means for Jesus to be the Messiah.
3. The messianic secret is the theme in Mark that Jesus kept the fact that he was the Messiah a secret until the truth about his suffering was revealed.
4. Mark understands discipleship as sharing in the suffering of Jesus.
5. By composing an infancy narrative parallel to that of Moses, and by organizing the teaching of Jesus into five great "books" similar to the five books of the Law, Jesus is compared to Moses.
6. The two main themes in Matthew are justice and the Law.
7. Matthew means that Jesus came to accomplish the purposes of the Law.
8. For Matthew, a disciple is a good member of the faith community.
9. Luke shows a special interest in the condition of women, the poor, and the oppressed.
10. For Luke, being a disciple means spreading the good news about Jesus.
11. The "logos" is the Word of God, Jesus.
12. Incarnation refers to the idea that in Jesus, God took on human flesh (from two Latin words, in + carnem = "into flesh").
13. "I am" was the name of God as revealed on Mt. Sinai. By using this name to refer to himself, Jesus makes the claim that he is divine.
14. A disciple for John is one who loves others and seeks unity with Jesus.
15. Agape means valuing other people, treating them with great respect, and caring for them as people with dignity.

- The stories have in common an appearance to the eleven. Also, Mary Magdalene figures in all four stories.
- Differences include whether to stay in Jerusalem (Luke) or go out to all the nations (Matthew) and where the appearance to the eleven took place (Matthew in Galilee; Luke in Jerusalem; John in both).

2. The two infancy stories have in common that messages come from angels, the birth of Jesus is marked by extraordinary events, and the coming of Jesus is the fulfillment of scriptural hopes. Jesus was marked even as a baby as one who would do God's will.

3. If a fellow Christian wrongs me I should privately point out the wrong. If he (or she) does not listen, I should summon another as a witness. I should then refer it to the Church. If he or she ignores the Church, then I should treat him or her as an outcast. *Matthew 18:15–18.*

Chapter Overview

More than any other book of the New Testament, the Acts of the Apostles traces the development of the early Church. Luke wrote as he did to show the many ways the Holy Spirit guided the work of the Apostles to shape the Church. This chapter introduces students to Luke's thinking and explores the key concepts introduced in Acts.

Teaching Objectives

By the end of this chapter students will be able to:
• Define salvation history and explain its meaning in Acts.
• Demonstrate an understanding of the ministry of Peter and Paul.
• Explain the Holy Spirit's role in the formation of the Church.
• Discuss how the gifts of the Spirit can be lived today.

Welcome

What to Do

Ask students what they know about the early Church after Jesus departed. What do they know about the roles of Peter, Paul, James, Philip, or Barnabas? What are the significant events in the life of the early Church? List all student answers on the board.

Pray with your students. Give thanks that the Ascension was not the end of the story, that the Spirit continued to work in the lives of the early Christians, and that the same Spirit is with us today. Ask blessings on yourself and your students.

CHAPTER

12 Acts of the Apostles

30	**33 C.E.** ● Pentecost
	36 ● Conversion of Saul ● Pilate recalled to Rome
	37–41 ● Caligula Emperor of Rome
	41–54 ● Claudius Emperor of Rome
50	**49** ● Council of Jerusalem
	52 ● Paul charged before Gallio ● Felix, Procurator of Judea
	54–68 ● Nero Emperor of Rome
	60 ● Festus, Procurator of Judea
	63 ● Peter and Paul killed in Rome
100	**80–85** ● Acts of the Apostles

Legend

● General History
● Biblical History
● Regional History
● Books written

LaTina hated summer camp. Every year, she went to the same hot, dusty place for two weeks. She had to go without TV, shopping with her friends, and all the other things that made summer great. Mostly, though, she had to put up with a roomful of other girls she'd never met and wouldn't like. All in all, LaTina thought camp was a miserable experience.

This year threatened to be the worst yet. Since she was starting high school next year, LaTina thought her parents might let her stay home this year. No such luck; not only was she going, but her parents had signed her up for the overnight canoe trip down the river as well. LaTina was horrified. At least this would be her last year there.

When her parents dropped LaTina off at camp, she headed for her assigned bunkhouse. Slowly, the other girls arrived. They didn't seem to

---

MORE ABOUT THE TEXT

Acts

The Acts of the Apostles is the second of Luke's two presentations of biblical history describing how the salvation promised to Israel and won by Jesus has been extended to the Gentiles through the efforts of the Holy Spirit. Luke's emphasis is on the working of the Spirit, and so he ignores the work of most of the Apostles, other than that of Peter and Paul. For Luke, the Spirit works through the Christian communities.

Luke traces the development of the Church from its emergence in Jerusalem to its becoming an important world religion. Through the Church's early struggles, Luke recognizes God acting to bring salvation to the world. For Luke, this is an inclusive world, both Gentile and Jew.

be any happier to be there than LaTina. They unpacked their bags in relative silence, not saying much at all. Before long it was dinner time, and they went to the mess hall.

Over dinner, the girls began to talk, since there was nothing else to do. They started by making fun of the baked beans.

"Gross," Millie said. "Do they really expect us to eat this stuff?"

Then somebody dropped a roll on the table. "Thunk!" The roll didn't bounce or roll at all. It simply stopped where it had landed.

"I think these are the same rolls that we had at last year's closing dinner. They weren't any softer then either." Soon everyone was laughing and having a good time.

They talked about school, their friends back home, and even how much they hated coming to camp. Their laughter could be heard all over the mess hall. LaTina found herself actually enjoying their company. "This is amazing," she thought.

Over the next two weeks, the girls from LaTina's bunkhouse grew very close. Working as a team, they won most of their competitions: archery, tug-of-war, even arts and crafts. What worried LaTina was the canoe trip; she was the only one in the bunk house scheduled to go. She told one of the girls about her concern. Before she knew it, the entire group went to the counselor's office and added their names to the list. With her new friends along, the canoe trip was a great success, and LaTina had the best time of her life.

When her parents came to pick her up, her Mom hugged LaTina and said, "Well, you don't have to go through that again. How do you feel?" When LaTina said that she had a delightful time and wanted to come back next year as a counselor, her mother was shocked.

"Something different happened this time," LaTina explained. "It really felt good, like we were a family. I don't know what it was, but there was a different spirit with these girls."

The Guiding Spirit

LaTina's Mom smiled and said a silent prayer of thanks to the Holy Spirit. LaTina's mother, like generations of Christians, had faith that the Holy Spirit was active in her daughter's life. She believed that the Spirit shaped and guided the lives of every believer, just as the Spirit guided the members of the early Christian communities.

Much of what we know about the Spirit's role in the Christian community comes from the Acts of the Apostles. In Acts, we see how the Church grew under the Spirit's guidance and how Christians overcame hardship and persecution with the Spirit's protection.

◆ MORE ABOUT THE LESSON

Building Communities

Some of the elements students might expect to find in community include:
- friendship
- understanding
- trust
- respect
- support
- encouragement
- guidance
- responsibility

All of these elements could be expected in a Christian community, along with an emphasis on faith in Jesus, personal integrity, moral living, justice, charity, and hope.

Introducing the Chapter

What to Do

- Ask students to discuss what it means to be a member of a community. To how many communities do they presently belong? What are some of the obligations that go along with being a member of a community?
- Have the students read the story on the opening spread about LaTina and summer camp. What similar experiences have students had when a situation they dreaded was changed by the presence of other people whom they liked. From this story, what would they add about the importance of forming communities?
- Return to students' comments about community. Ask them to describe how a Christian community might be different from another kind of community.
- Explain that the Acts of the Apostles looks at the formation of the early Christian communities. These communities that formed around the message of the Gospel, were the beginning of the Church.
- Review with students the intention of biblical authors. They were not interested in merely leaving an account of the events that happened. They also wanted to explain why things happened as they did. Acts is no exception. Luke, writing at least 40 years after the events presented, is interested in showing how the Church was formed through the heroic actions of the Apostles who were guided by the Holy Spirit. That being said, the record provided by Luke remains the best guide we have for understanding early Christianity.

Using the Timeline

Have the students read the timeline and answer the following questions.
- Who was Roman emperor when the Council of Jerusalem was held?
- How long after Jesus' death was Paul converted?
- Who was emperor when Peter and Paul were killed?

◆ Acts: The Book of the Spirit

Teaching Objectives

By the end of this lesson students will be able to:

- Explain the idea of salvation history.
- Describe the importance of the Church opening itself up to Gentiles.
- Discuss the role of the Spirit in guiding the Church.
- Name the key leaders of early Christianity.

Development

What to Do

1. Have the students read the opening italics and the Learning Objectives.

2. Have the students open their Bibles and mark the beginning of Acts. Then have them find and mark the following:

   - Acts 1:6—A story of Jesus' ascension into heaven
   - Acts 2:1—The beginning of the story of Pentecost
   - Acts 2:42–47 A description of the earliest Christian community
   - Acts 6:8–7:60—The story of Stephen, deacon and first martyr
   - Acts 9:1—The beginning of a story of Paul's conversion
   - Acts 10—The beginning of Peter's work with Gentiles
   - Acts 13—The beginning of Paul's missionary work
   - Acts 15—The Council of Jerusalem
   - Acts 21:27—Paul is arrested
   - Acts 27—Paul travels to Rome

3. Have the students read "Acts: The Book of the Spirit."

4. Explain the problem of Gentiles becoming Christian. See "More about the Text" on page 212.

5. Have the students read and discuss "The Bible in Context."

6. Form small groups and have the students complete the "Scripture Workshop." Have them list all the similarities they find, with the verses numbered. Then the lists can be pooled for sharing.

Acts and Salvation History

The book known as the Acts of the Apostles was written by Luke, the author of the gospel account which bears the same name. Acts tells the story of the early Christian Church, and pays extra attention to the two apostles, Peter and Paul, who were its most important leaders. Originally, Luke's gospel account and Acts went together as a two-volume set. In them, Luke shows that all of the events in the salvation story—from the birth of Jesus to the spread of Christianity to Rome—were directed by the Holy Spirit in fulfillment of God's will. In this section, you'll look at the unfolding of salvation history in Acts.

Learning Objectives for Section One

By the end of this section, you will be able to:

- Explain Luke's idea of salvation history.
- Discuss how Luke understood the relationship between Christianity and the Greek and Roman religions.
- List important aspects of Peter's ministry.
- Describe the highlights of Paul's ministry.

◆ Acts: The Book of the Spirit

In Acts, we read about the growing number of people in the first century who changed their lives based on the Gospel of Jesus. At first, these people were simply called members of the "Way"; only later, first in Antioch, were they known as "Christians." Although Acts contains the stories of many memorable Christian leaders such as Peter, Paul, Stephen, Philip, and Barnabas, the most important character in the story is really the Holy Spirit.

From the very beginning, Luke tells us that the spread of the Christian faith was the work of the Spirit. Acts emphasized that the growth of Christianity was part of God's plan to bring salvation to the world. With the guidance of the Spirit, the early Christian apostles spread the good news about Jesus throughout the Roman Empire.

Why the Gentiles?

When the Gospel according to Luke and the Acts of the Apostles were written, the Church consisted of small communities found in cities throughout the Mediterranean Sea area. The missionaries who started these communities often were persecuted because of their message. In many places they were simply ignored or received with indifference. It took many years of witnessing to Jesus' message for even the smallest community of believers to start.

Most Jews rejected the message that Jesus was the promised messiah, and many were hostile to any claim that Jesus might be God's son. There was only one God, Yahweh. Any claim that Jesus was divine called that belief into question.

The missionaries had better luck converting Gentiles to the new faith, although the total number of believers was still very small. Luke wrote Acts, therefore, to point out the direction the Spirit was leading the Church.

MORE ABOUT THE TEXT

Early Christians

Virtually all the first Christians were Jews. They were not yet even called Christians, but considered themselves Jews who believed in Jesus and followed "The Way," that is, Jesus' way of life. They continued to live as the good and dutiful Jews they had always been.

As time went on, it became apparent that the Holy Spirit intended to include Gentiles in the communities also. This created difficulties. First,

Gentiles had never kept Jewish laws and customs. Did they have to follow Jewish Law and custom (i.e., circumcision and the Sabbath requirements) to become Christians?

Second, many Gentiles, if they had been religious at all, had not considered religious belief connected with the way one lived. That had been taken for granted by Jews forever, but now the Gentiles had to learn it. It was not easy for them, and their struggles were hard.

Before Luke could convince his readers that Christianity was destined to reach the ends of the earth, he first had to deal with the doubts held by many people. Such doubts can be expressed in two basic questions:

- Why do so many Jews reject the Gospel?
- How can Gentiles claim salvation from the fulfillment of a promise made to Jews?

These were important questions. Remember, Jesus was a Jew, and Christianity was rooted in the traditions and beliefs of Judaism. Yet, while Gentiles were responding to Jesus' message, the Jews rejected it. Luke's answer to these questions was the same: God's plan for salvation had always included the Gentiles.

According to Luke, God's salvation is first made known through the people of Israel and then through the message and ministry of Jesus. Following Jesus' death and resurrection, salvation is offered to the

Michelangelo, *Conversion of St. Paul*, Sixteenth Century.

Saul was a pious Jew before his conversion. He persecuted those Jews who became Christians. After his conversion, Paul became a missionary who spread the Good News of Jesus.

Scripture Workshop

Peter and Paul

In Acts, Peter and Paul are presented as heroes of the faith whose lives are modeled on the experiences of Jesus. Luke deliberately parallels Peter and Paul to show that the Spirit guided both of them in similar ways. Read the following pairs of passages from Acts and, for each, determine the similarity between Peter and Paul which appears in that pair:

1. 8:9–24 and 13:6–12
2. 10:25–26 and 14:13–15
3. 9:36–43 and 20:9–12
4. 12:6–11 and 16:24–26
5. 8:14–17 and 19:1–6

whole world through the Church. For Luke, each of these stages represents a particular part of God's plan. It is clear in Acts that after Jesus died, the teachings of the Old Testament, all the promises of the Covenant, and the hope of salvation were offered to Jews and non-Jews alike.

From Luke's time onwards, Christianity became less a group within Judaism and more a new religious movement of Gentiles. Luke shows that this change was neither an accident nor a clever strategy: it was the result of the Spirit working to fulfill God's plan for salvation history.

The Guidance of the Spirit

Throughout Acts, Luke sees the influence of the Spirit in the Church. He announces this theme at the very beginning of the book, when Jesus says to the disciples:

"But you will receive power when the Holy Spirit comes upon you, and you will be my witnesses in Jerusalem, throughout Judea and Samaria, and even to the ends of the earth."

(Acts 1:8)

7. Say: "The real main character in Acts is the Holy Spirit. Everything that happens in Acts happens because of the Spirit. Have the students look in a concordance for the word "spirit" and find the references belonging to Acts.

8. Give each group a piece a paper with the name of an early Church hero written on it. Say: "There are also other heroes in Acts besides Peter and Paul. Each group is to use the concordance to find out what it can about these heroes in the Book of Acts."

9. Lead the class discussion of the questions in "Have You Considered?"

10. Pray with your students. Include thanksgiving for the inclusion of Gentiles in Christianity and those Jewish Christians who were open to the Spirit. Close with the "Come Holy Spirit:"

Come Holy Spirit and fill the hearts of your faithful;

Enkindle in them the fire of your love;

Send forth your Spirit and all shall be created

And You shall renew the face of the earth.

Scripture Workshop

1. Acts 8:9–24 and 13:6–12—In both stories Peter and Paul confront magicians: Peter, Simon Magus, and Paul, Elymas.

2. Acts 10: 25–26 and 14: 13–15—In both cases, people treat Peter and Paul as if they were divine, and Peter and Paul have to remind them they are only human.

3. Acts 9:36–43 and 20:9–12—Peter raises Dorcas from the dead, while Paul restores life to Eutychus.

4. Acts 12:6–11 and 16:24–26 In both cases, Peter and Paul are miraculously delivered from imprisonment.

5. Acts 8:14–17 and 19:1–6 Both Peter and Paul lay their hands on people and give the Holy Spirit to them.

MORE ABOUT THE TEXT

Legal Status

Opening up Christianity to Gentiles as well as Jews raised legal problems as well as religious ones.

Judaism was protected by the Roman Empire. It became one of the many religions allowed to flourish. As long as followers of Jesus were considered Jews, Rome was unconcerned. But when Gentiles in some numbers became Christians, Rome looked at the religion differently. By the time Acts was written, a Jewish revolt had been crushed and the Temple destroyed (70 C.E.), which made it necessary for Jews once again to define themselves.

When they excluded Christians from Jewish life, they excluded them from the legal status enjoyed by Jews. Christians became officially illegal. This may explain Luke's interest in demonstrating that Christianity was no threat to Rome.

Practicing the Skills

What to Do

Preaching the Gospel was not always successful. Have the students read Acts 17:16–34. Who are the two converts named there? This remembrance is their only "claim to fame;" neither is mentioned anywhere else in the Scripture.

Recall

Have the students write their answers to "Chapter 12 Review Q/A," Section One, questions 1–5.

Connect

Have the students discuss this question: "If you converted from Christianity to another religion, how do you think your parents would feel?"

What's Next?

What to Do

Remind the students that Peter and Paul are the most discussed characters in the Acts of the Apostles. Tell them that the next lesson is about their activities as Christian leaders.

Have You Considered?

1. Christians believed that Jesus came in fulfillment of promises made in the Jewish scriptures. Therefore, it troubled them that so many Jews apparently did not recognize Jesus as the messiah anticipated in Jewish traditions.
2. Students should speak from their own personal experience.
3. Students will have different responses. Many Catholic theologians have talked about the possibility of "anonymous Christians."

Bonus Focus for You

Read Acts 11:26. Put yourself in the place of one of the characters or unnamed people in this story. What was it like to be an early convert to Jesus? Write your reflections in your journal.

The Bible in Context

Greek and Roman Religion

The Greeks and Romans were "polytheists," meaning that they worshipped many gods. During the first century C.E., the Greeks and Romans adopted many new gods, sometimes borrowing them from Eastern religions. Afraid that they might miss an important god, the Romans built a temple in Rome called the "Pantheon," or "Temple of All the Gods." In this way every god would be worshipped, even if not directly by name.

Paul responds to this desire for true worship by pointing out that behind every image of divinity lies the one God who raised Jesus from the dead. This message appealed to many Gentiles, who became Christian and helped to spread the Gospel of Jesus.

The spread of Christianity throughout Palestine and into the rest of the Empire, therefore, happened through the guidance of the Spirit. The power Jesus had promised became real on the Jewish feast of Pentecost, when the Holy Spirit filled the gathered community members with its presence, and inspired them to preach the faith courageously (*see Acts 1:13–14, and 2:1ff*).

The first Christian mission started when Greek-speaking Jewish Christians were thrown out of Jerusalem because of their belief. They left Jerusalem and made converts in Samaria and the surrounding areas of Syria as they traveled.

The Heroes of the Faith

Besides the Holy Spirit, the leading characters in Acts are the apostles, Peter and Paul. Peter is seen as the leader of the early Christian Church who begins the mission to the Gentiles. Paul is the apostle called by Jesus to take over this mission and to bring it to completion. Luke sees Peter and Paul as the most important leaders of the Church, after Jesus himself.

Peter and Paul both begin to preach under the influence of the Spirit, both heal and teach, both have visions related to their missions, and both are imprisoned for their beliefs. Finally they both are put to death in Rome because of the message they

proclaimed. These major parallels are supported by many smaller similarities.

The pattern Luke sees in the lives of Peter and Paul comes from the life of Jesus. In their experience of preaching, healing, suffering, rejection, and imprisonment, Peter and Paul follow the path walked by Jesus. In this way, Luke shows that the same Spirit of Jesus also guided Peter and Paul.

Hope of the Gentiles

Luke believes that just as Christianity fulfills the promises of the Old Testament, it also fulfills the religious hopes of the Gentiles. Consider the speech Paul makes in Athens:

> "You Athenians, I see that in every respect you are very religious. For as I walked around looking carefully at your shrines, I even discovered an altar inscribed 'To an unknown God.' What therefore you unknowingly worship, I proclaim to you. The God who made the world and all that is in it, the Lord of heaven and earth, does not dwell in sanctuaries made by human hands, nor is he served by human hands because he needs anything. Rather, it is he who gives to everyone life and breath and everything."
>
> (Acts 17:22–25,31)

Paul here says that the Greeks and Romans have been worshipping the Christian God, ignorant of God's true name. The Spirit has been at work in their religious longings, preparing them to recognize Jesus as Lord. Even though Paul did not make many converts in Athens, Luke considers the trip a success: the Gospel has been proclaimed to the Gentiles.

Have You Considered?

1. Why do you suppose it worried Christians that many Jews seemed to reject the Gospel of Jesus?
2. Luke says that the Holy Spirit can use misfortune to bring about God's plan. Can you think of a time in your life when a misfortune led to a positive outcome?
3. Luke says that the Greeks and Romans worshipped the God of Christians without knowing it. Do you think it is possible for people to worship God today without knowing it? Why or why not?

◆ MORE ABOUT THE LESSON

Other Heroes

Here are the names of other people in Acts for your students to investigate (omitted from this list are Cornelius and Philip because they appear in later lessons in some detail):

- Stephen
- Barnabas
- Tabitha (also called Dorcas)
- Mark or John Mark
- Silas
- Timothy
- Priscilla (or Prisca) and Aquila
- James

◆ Peter, the Leader of the Apostles

In the Acts of the Apostles we see Peter acting with authority as the leader of the early Church. We also see him beginning the mission to the Gentiles, and spreading this new era in salvation history.

Peter's Authority

Peter is the leader of the early Christian community according to Acts.

- When the apostles chose a replacement for Judas Iscariot, Peter is the one who decided how it would be done (Acts 1:15–26).
- The Holy Spirit filled Peter and inspired him to preach the Gospel without fear. (Acts 2:14–41).
- Peter was given the power to heal, and he used it to convince people of the truth of the Gospel. (Acts 3:1–10).
- Peter is arrested as the leader of Jesus' followers and is tried, but because of the power of his preaching, he is set free (Acts 3:11–4:22).
- People would carry their sick into the streets hoping that Peter's shadow would fall upon them and heal them (Acts 5:12–16).
- Peter welcomed the first Gentile believers in Jesus into the Christian community (Acts 10:1–48).
- Peter sides with Paul at the Council of Jerusalem on accepting Gentiles into the faith (Acts 15:1–12).

Ribera, St. Peter, Sixteenth Century.

Saint Peter is usually shown holding keys and a book. The keys stand for his authority in the Church (see Matthew 16:13–20) and the book, his proclamation of the Gospel of Jesus Christ.

Peter and the Gentiles

Luke shows that the mission to the Gentiles began with Peter, so that Christian missionaries who made Gentile converts could point to Peter's example as the authority for their work.

Peter's first Gentile convert was Cornelius, a Roman officer. At first, Peter did not want to convert him, but several visions inspired by the Holy Spirit led Peter to understand that this was God's will (Acts 10). Peter baptized Cornelius and made him a member of the Christian community. This act set the stage for Paul, the man who would become known as the "apostle to the Gentiles," to take Christianity to most of the Roman Empire.

Have You Considered?

1. What is the significance of Peter using his authority to open the Gospel up to the Gentiles? How did this decision change the life of the Church?
2. How are the signs of Peter's authority as presented in Acts similar to stories about Jesus?

in the Spotlight

God-Fearers

Luke calls Cornelius, the first Gentile convert, a "God-fearer." This term had a technical meaning during the first century C.E. It referred to Gentiles who attended the Jewish synagogue because they admired Judaism, but who were not willing to accept circumcision and the other demands of the Law of Moses. Many Gentiles were attracted to Judaism because of its monotheism and moral code. Because they weren't members of the people of Israel, however, they couldn't participate fully in the worship or practice of the faith. The Gospel appealed to these people very much. Paul often addressed this group in the synagogue, as he does in Acts 13:16.

◆ MORE ABOUT THE LESSON

Peter

Although other apostles have some of Peter's gifts (like healing and preaching), the community of the 80s remembered Peter as the primary leader. This is not to say that he never made mistakes and was never opposed. Some of Peter's fear of other people's opinions apparently remained after the Resurrection.

Nevertheless, his strong belief in the Holy Spirit and the honor of the community were firmly his and he was remembered with great affection.

Tradition tells us that Peter was put to death in Rome under Nero, crucified (upside-down, by his own request, feeling unworthy to die as his Lord had died) in the terrors of that emperor's reign.

SECTION ONE

LESSON TWO (pages 215–217)

◆ Peter, the Leader of the Apostles

Welcome

What to Do

Ask: "What is the role of a missionary? What does a missionary do?" Explain that today we are studying the two most famous missionaries in the early church: Peter and Paul.

Pray with your students.

Introducing the Lesson

Teaching Objectives

By the end of this lesson students will be able to:
- Explain Peter's authority as the leader of the Apostles.
- Describe Peter's role in opening Christianity to Gentiles.
- Demonstrate the importance of Paul's missionary journeys to the spreading of Christianity.

What to Do

Ask students to tell you what they know about Saint Peter. List their comments on the board. If their memories need jogging, have them read Luke 5:1–11; Mark 8:27–33; Luke 22:54–62; and John 21:1–19.

Ask students to tell you what they know about Saint Paul and again list their comments on the board. Explain that they will learn more about Paul shortly.

Development

What to Do

1. Have the students read "Peter, the Leader of the Apostles" and "in the Spotlight."
2. Form small groups. Have each group read two or three of the bulleted references on page 215. Ask each group to retell its stories to the rest of the class.
3. Lead a discussion of what they have learned about Peter's role in the Church.
4. Have the students read "Understanding More About" on page 227 and read the whole story of this incident in Acts 8.
5. Lead the class discussion of the questions in "Have You Considered?"

1. By using his authority to open Christianity to Gentiles, Peter changed the life of the Church forever.

2. The stories about Peter in Acts are similar to the Jesus traditions in many ways. Peter preaches, heals, suffers, is arrested, and rejected, just as Jesus was. The story of Peter and Cornelius is similar in some ways to the story of Jesus and the Roman centurion.

◆ Paul: the Apostle to the Gentiles

Development

1. Have the students read "Paul, the Apostle to the Gentiles."

2. Examine the map on page 217 and have the students answer the questions mentioned there.

3. Complete "Bible Activity" number 2, using Acts 17:1–9. Supplement their study from "More about the Lesson" on page 217.

4. Assign as a project "Bible Activity" number 3.

5. Read the dramatic story of Paul's arrest in Acts 21:27–40, 22:22–29. You may wish to have students dramatize this reading. See Teacher's Resource 12A for suggestions.

6. Discuss the questions in "Have You Considered?"

7. Pray with your students.

Recall

Have the students write their answers to "Chapter 12 Review Q/A," Section One questions 6–8.

Connect

What to Do

Ask the students to imagine they are helping to hire a new youth minister for their parish. Read the application in Teacher's Resource 12B and ask for their responses. Would they hire this applicant?

What do they learn from this exercise? Help them to recognize that God can do great things with all kinds of human material and that things are not always as they seem. Draw the connection back to other unlikely biblical heroes: Jacob, David the shepherd, and Moses.

◆ Paul, the Apostle to the Gentiles

Paul is an even more important character in Acts than Peter. While Peter figures in eleven chapters in Acts, Paul dominates 20. As you will see, Paul's most important gift to the early Church were the many letters he wrote. Luke, however, is not interested in Paul's letters, and he never mentions them. (Luke may not have even known of Paul's letters; remember, there were no printing presses or national bookstore chains in the first century C.E.) Paul is the ideal missionary, empowered by the Holy Spirit to spread the Gospel to all people.

Corinth was a major center of commerce in the first century C.E. Ships from all over the Roman Empire traded there. Christianity took root quickly in this city through Paul's preaching.

The Early Years

Luke tells us that Paul (earlier known as Saul) was from Tarsus, an important Hellenistic city (now part of modern Turkey). Paul was born a Roman citizen. Growing up, he was educated in Greek literature and culture, as well as in the traditions of his Jewish ancestors. Paul studied in Jerusalem with the highly influential rabbi, Gamaliel. Paul was a very strict Jew and considered himself a Pharisee. He took it upon himself to enforce the Law. As the apostles proclaimed Jesus' Resurrection, Paul took offense. He persecuted followers of the Way, whom he considered violators of the Law.

Paul's Missionary Career

While traveling to Damascus, in Syria, to persecute Christians, Paul experienced a vision of Jesus. Paul's life was radically changed by this vision. After several years of prayer and preparation, Paul became a missionary for the very Way which he had once opposed. Paul's home at this time was Antioch, whose Christian community supported his missionary efforts. Today, some scholars divide Paul's travels into three great "missionary journeys."

The First Journey (46–49 C.E.) This journey saw Paul in the company of Barnabas and John-Mark. They traveled across many islands in the Mediterranean Sea, and then landed in South Galatia (modern Turkey). Each place they went, Paul preached in the synagogue, where he often met with resistance and even with violence. Rejected by the Jews, Paul began preaching to Gentiles.

The Second Journey (50–52 C.E.) His second trip took Paul into Europe for the first time. Paul founded Christian communities (which he called churches) in Philippi, Thessalonica, and Corinth in Greece, and at Ephesus in Asia Minor. Paul practiced his trade while preaching the Gospel. (Luke calls Paul a "tent-maker.")

Because of his lengthy stay there, Paul's church in Corinth grew rapidly and became one of the most important communities in the early Church. Towards the end of his stay there, some Jews complained about Paul to the Roman governor, Gallio. Gallio investigated the complaint but found no cause to charge Paul with a crime. Paul left Corinth shortly thereafter, stopping in Jerusalem before returning to his home in Antioch.

The Third Journey (54–58 C.E.) Paul stayed for three years in Ephesus. On leaving Ephesus, Paul

---

◆ MORE ABOUT THE LESSON

Paul

Here are some additional points of interest about Paul's life:

• Paul did not simply set out to destroy Christians on his own. He acted as an agent of Temple officials, aiming to bring violators of Jewish laws to "justice."

• Paul's trade of "tentmaker" probably implies that he was a leather worker. If so, he would have been able to (and did, according to his letters) find work in any town he visited. He remained self-supporting while traveling and preaching.

• For centuries people have thought that Paul's unmarried state at the time of his letters meant that he never married. Some modern scholars, however, think that Paul was widowed.

• Paul was a Roman citizen with certain rights, among them the right to appeal a legal case to Caesar.

LEARN FROM THE MAP

Paul's Missionary Journeys

Using the scale of 1/4″ = 60 miles, figure out how many miles Paul traveled on each of his three missionary journeys. Use the key to determine which arrow goes with which journey. Then, find each of the places below on the map. On which journey did Paul visit each city?

Antioch, Salamis, Lystra, Thessalonica, Corinth, Ephesus

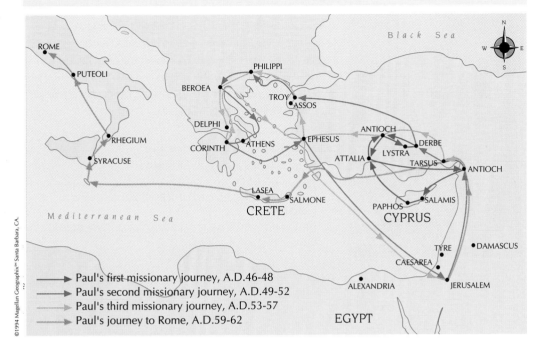

©1994 Magellan Geographix℠ Santa Barbara, CA.

Key:
⟶ Paul's first missionary journey, A.D.46-48
⟶ Paul's second missionary journey, A.D.49-52
⟶ Paul's third missionary journey, A.D.53-57
⟶ Paul's journey to Rome, A.D.59-62

traveled through Macedonia on his way to Corinth and then sailed for Jerusalem.

Paul's Arrest

Paul was a very successful apostle to the Gentiles, but some people resented the growing number of Gentiles who were becoming Christian. This resentment exploded on Paul's return to Jerusalem. Paul escaped death only because he asserted his Roman citizenship. He was taken into protective custody by the soldiers.

The Romans usually ignored local religious feuds as long as they did not cause public uprisings. As a citizen of Rome, however, Paul had a right to have the argument heard by the procurator, Felix. Although he was once again found innocent, Paul was kept in prison this time for two years. Felix, it seems, thought Paul an important person and expected a bribe for Paul's release.

Felix was replaced as procurator by Festus, who sent Paul to Rome with a guard. Despite experiencing many obstacles on the trip, Paul safely arrived in Rome, where he was kept under house arrest for two years. Acts ends there, with Paul in Rome receiving people who wanted to hear the Gospel of Jesus.

Have You Considered?

1. As a young man, Paul was such a loyal Jew that he persecuted others who didn't observe the Law. Why do you suppose people sometimes strike out at those who don't agree with them?
2. How do you suppose Christians would have reacted to seeing Paul, who had once persecuted them, now preaching the Gospel?

MORE ABOUT THE TEXT

Paul in the Synagogue

In Paul's own letters, he expressed his deep love and concern for his own people, the Jews. It was only natural then that he would go to the synagogue. Synagogue custom allowed visitors to speak to the assembly, to share news and information about other Jewish communities. Paul took advantage of this custom to talk about Jesus. Only when the Jews in a town rejected his preaching did he turn to the Gentiles there.

Source of Information

The biographical material mentioned in this lesson is taken from Acts. Any further study of these stories can be done by following the chapters in Acts.

What's Next?

What to Do

Say: "Four very dramatic events occured in Acts that changed the development of early Christianity. The Holy Spirit was behind them all. We will explore them in the next lesson."

LEARN FROM THE MAP

Note that the city of Thessalonica is missing on the map. It would be about 50 miles southwest of Philippi.

1. The approximate distance of the four journeys are:
- Trip 1: approximately 600 miles
- Trip 2: approximately 2,100 miles
- Trip 3: approximately 1,850 miles
- Trip 4: approximately 1900 miles
2. Paul visited Antioch on each of the three journeys, Salamis and Lystra on the first journey only, and Thessalonica, Corinth, and Ephesus on journeys two and three.

Have You Considered?

1. Let students speak from their own experience on this question. Psychologically, there is probably an element of insecurity in such behavior. People who need to force others to adopt their own beliefs, at some level, are probably not so sure about those beliefs themselves.
2. Clearly there would be a period of doubt and hard feelings at seeing Paul as a member of the faith. Ask students to consider similar examples: How would they feel, for example, if someone who had always treated them poorly suddenly began acting like their best friend?

Bonus Focus for You

Read Romans 9:1–5, where Paul writes of his love for his fellow Jews. He makes an extreme statement there. Is there anyone you care about that much? What is the most important aspect of your life? Reflect in your journal.

LESSON THREE
(pages 218–222)

◆ Pentecost

Welcome

What to Do

Give students a piece of paper, cut out to look like a flame, as they enter the room. The first students to arrive can help pass them out.

Ask the students: "Why do you think we've handed out flames today?" (If they don't guess the answer, leave it hanging—they'll get it soon enough!)

Pray with your students. Read aloud Psalm 51:11–14,17 as your prayer today.

Introducing the Lesson

Teaching Objectives

By the end of this lesson students will be able to:

• Discuss the events of Pentecost in relation to their influence on Christianity.

• Explain the importance of the conversion of Cornelius and Paul, as well as the Council of Jerusalem.

What to Do

Have the students read the opening italics and the learning objectives. Ask them what they already know about Pentecost. List their comments on the board.

Development

Students will see by the use of dramatic stories some of the Holy Spirit's action in the early Christian community.

What to Do

1. Have the students read "Pentecost" up to the "Conversion of Cornelius."

2. Have the students read Acts 2. Say: "The Holy Spirit gave the earliest Christians the inner power they needed to spread the good news of Jesus. The speeches in Acts show the basic content of early preaching. From them we can learn what the first Christians taught. What would you say are the main points of Peter's speech here?" List the main points on the board. Include the following if they are not mentioned by the students:

The Spirit Leads the Way

El Greco, Pentecost. Sixteenth Century.

*You have seen how Luke believed that the growth of Christianity among the Gentiles was the work of the Holy Spirit, through the apostles Peter and Paul. In this section, you'll look more closely at four critical points in this growth: (1) **Pentecost**, when the Spirit first came upon the disciples. (2) **The baptism of Cornelius**, when Peter began the Gentile mission. (3) **Paul's vision of Jesus and his call** to become a Christian missionary. (4) **The Council of Jerusalem**, when the Church approved the conversion of Gentiles without first making them Jews.*

Learning Objectives for Section Two

By the end of this section, you will be able to:

• Explain how the Spirit guided the apostles at Pentecost, the baptism of Cornelius, the call of Paul, and the Council of Jerusalem.

• Discuss the gifts the Holy Spirit offers to us today and how those gifts shape our lives.

◆ Pentecost

The Book of Acts opens with the ascension of Jesus to heaven. After Jesus' resurrection, the apostles had retreated to a locked room in Jerusalem, where they were joined by Mary, Jesus' mother, some members of his family, and some of the women who had followed Jesus. There, they prayed and waited for the Spirit that Jesus had promised.

On the festival of Pentecost, 50 days after Passover, the Holy Spirit came upon the gathered disciples and filled them with God's gifts, especially the ability and courage to preach the Good News boldly.

When the time for Pentecost was fulfilled, they were all in one place together. And suddenly there came from the sky a noise like a strong driving wind, and it filled the entire house in which they were. Then there appeared to them tongues as of fire, which parted and came to rest on each one of them. And they were all filled with the Holy Spirit and began to speak in different tongues, as the Spirit enabled them to proclaim.
(Acts 2:1–4)

Luke says that people from all of Israel were in Jerusalem for the festival. Just as Jesus came to announce the kingdom to all of Israel, the apostles preached to all. For Jews, Pentecost was a celebration of God's gifts of the land of Israel and the Law. To that celebration God has added the gifts of the Holy Spirit. With the Spirit, they will preach the Good News, heal in Jesus' name, and lead people to God's kingdom.

After being filled with the Spirit, Peter rose and delivered a sermon to the assembly of Jews. His words were *inspired*—filled with the Spirit. Quoting the prophet Joel, Peter said:

"It will come to pass in the last days, God says, that I will pour out a portion of my spirit on all flesh. Your sons and daughters shall prophesy, your young men shall see visions, your old men shall dream dreams."
(Acts 2:17; Joel 3:1)

◆ MORE ABOUT THE LESSON

Guest Speaker

Invite someone from a local parish who can share his or her personal experience of the Spirit. A likely place to inquire about a speaker is among parish charismatic or prayer groups. Choose someone who is articulate about his or her personal experience, but neither fundamentalistic nor inclined to push his or her opinion on others. Neither should this guest be a person who "knows" about the Spirit, but has not had a personal experience.

Topics that could be included are: sharing the good news, the power of healing, speaking in tongues, and the changes in everyday life after the "baptism of the Spirit."

Peter told the crowd about Jesus, who worked signs among them, who had risen from the dead, and now was at the right hand of God. Jesus' spirit had filled the disciples.

Many in the crowd were amazed at the force of Peter's words. They asked, "What should we do?" Peter responded by telling them that they must reform their lives and be baptized. This passage is the first to identify baptism as the sacrament of initiation into the Christian community. As Luke tells us later in Acts, when a person is baptized, he or she receives the Holy Spirit. Acts says 3,000 people were moved by Peter's sermon and accepted baptism on Pentecost.

Here, Luke underlines the central point of the Book of Acts: Christianity originated in the inspiration of God, not in human activity. The spread of the Gospel is the work of the Spirit, Luke says. Today, Pentecost is the feast day on which Catholics celebrate the gift of the Holy Spirit.

The Conversion of Cornelius

Acts 10:1–11:18 describes Peter's conversion of Cornelius, a Roman officer and a Gentile. The story opens with a messenger from God speaking to Cornelius in a vision. The messenger tells Cornelius that God has seen his prayer and good works. He instructs Cornelius to send for Peter and to await his arrival. Cornelius agrees, and immediately sends two men to find Peter.

Before they arrive, Peter also has a vision.

- He sees all the animals of the earth on top of a large canvas.
- A voice tells him to slaughter and eat what he sees.
- Peter, being a good Jew, refuses, insisting that he has never eaten anything impure in his life. The voice, however, says, "What God has purified, you are not to call impure" (Acts 10:15).
- The Holy Spirit then speaks to Peter, telling him that he should receive Cornelius' messengers.

These two visions emphasize that Peter's encounter with Cornelius is not something that either man planned. Instead, God is bringing Peter to Cornelius, and what follows is God's will.

When Peter arrives at Cornelius' home, he goes inside and greets Cornelius' household. He says that as a Jew, he would never associate with impure Gentiles, but God has shown him that no one should call another person impure. Peter then delivers a sermon, saying that all who fear God are acceptable to Him. He relays the good news that Jesus is risen. As he is talking, the Holy Spirit descends on everyone present, and they begin to "speak in tongues."

This ability to "speak in tongues" is known as *glossolalia*. It enables a person to speak without intentionally doing so. Sometimes this means speaking in a foreign language (as with the disciples on

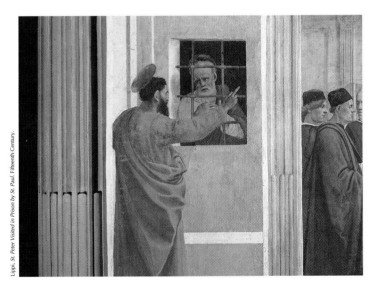

The Acts of the Apostles tells of the spread of Christianity. Peter and Paul, through the guidance of the Holy Spirit, are the central characters of the book. This painting shows Peter, imprisoned in Rome, being visited by Paul.

Lippi. *St. Peter Visited in Prison by St. Paul.* Fifteenth Century.

- The Apostles are not drunk, but have received the Spirit.
- The prophecy of Joel has been fulfilled.
- Jesus, a Jew who worked wonders and was then killed by the Jews, has been raised by God. Jesus has been exalted by God and has sent the Spirit.
- Jesus is the Messiah.

3. Discuss with students the signs of the Spirit in the early Church: people spoke and understood different languages; they were moved to live in community with others, sharing freely of what they had; some people were given the power to heal.

4. Ask: "What are signs of the Spirit active in the world today? Who are some people whom you think are touched by the Spirit of God?" Discuss these signs of the Spirit. How would students determine whether someone was operating under the guidance of the Spirit?

Extend the Lesson   Note: This will extend the lesson over two days. Invite a guest speaker to discuss the actions of the Holy Spirit in his or her life. Introduce the person you have invited to the class. Say: "Modern Christians have also had wonderful experiences of the Holy Spirit in their lives. The Spirit has given many gifts. We'll be studying some of them in the next lesson. Today, I have invited (name) to share with you about the experience of the Spirit in the lives of Christians today. She (he) will speak for a short while, and then we will have a chance to ask questions. Let's give a big welcome to (name)."

Guide the discussion between guest and students, keeping it close to the students' interests and referring to the Scripture when possible.

5. Have the students read "The Conversion of Cornelius." Discuss with students what would have happened to Christianity if the message had not been offered to Gentiles. What is the significance of Cornelius's conversion?

6. Form small groups. Have the students read "The Conversion of Paul." How does this material change their understanding

MORE ABOUT THE TEXT

Bible Background: Paul

Luke's tradition about Paul's conversion experience was a vivid part of early Christian memory. Its drama has captured the imagination of countless artists and retellers over the centuries. Details (like a horse) have been added or changed by many of them. The main point, however, remains: Jesus revealed himself directly to Saul the Pharisee, in an experience that changed his life's direction totally. What Paul did after Ananias healed his eyes is not clear, because Acts and Paul's words in Galatians do not completely agree. However, it does seem that Paul lived very quietly, probably in Arabia, for a number of years before he resurfaced as a preacher of the Gospel. It is important to take seriously his own statements in Galatians that he received no instruction from Apostles, but learned the Gospel from the risen Christ.

of Paul's conversion. This is a good story to have students dramatize.

7. Have the students complete the "Scripture Workshop" and share their results with the whole class.

8. Ask for volunteers to dramatize the story in Acts 8:26–40. Then have the students complete "Bible Activity" number 1. Add Acts 8:1–8 as an introduction.

9. Have the students read "The Council of Jerusalem." Discuss the Council with them. Note that the council is important not only because it established the religious practice of Gentiles, but it also established the form of governance that is used in the Church even today—bishops meeting in council.

10. Guide the student discussion of the questions in "Have You Considered?"

11. Pray with your students. Have the students join hands and pray the "Come Holy Spirit" prayer together.

Scripture Workshop

1. In 22:3–21, Luke includes a speech by Ananias, who in Chapter 9 of Acts cured Paul of his blindness, telling Paul that God has designated him to look on Jesus. Further, God planned from the beginning of time for Paul to spread Jesus' word. Later in the Temple, Paul sees a vision of Jesus, in which Jesus tells Paul that he is to preach to the Gentiles.

2. In this speech (Acts 26: 2–23), Luke presents Paul as emphasizing the ferocity of his earlier campaigns to persecute Christians. Later, when Paul tells the story of his conversion, he relates a speech from Jesus commissioning Paul an apostle.

   In both cases, we see Luke emphasizing that God called Paul to be the apostle to the Gentiles, and that the inclusion of Gentiles into Christianity was part of God's plan from the very beginning.

Pentecost), and sometimes it means uttering mysterious, unknown words. In this case, Luke tells us that the Gentiles "glorified God," so those around them were able to understand what they said. Peter, along with the other Jews who had traveled with him, is amazed that the Holy Spirit should come upon Gentiles in this way.

Peter declares that since the Gentiles have received the Holy Spirit, there is no reason they should not be baptized. He then baptizes them, making them part of the Christian community.

Afterwards, when he returns to Jerusalem, some Jewish-Christians object to Peter's conversion of Gentiles. Peter describes how God led him through signs and visions to take this step. Those present realize that what has happened is God's will:

> When they heard this, they stopped objecting and glorified God saying: "God has then granted life-giving repentance to the Gentiles too."
>
> (Acts 11:18)

The Conversion of Paul

Luke considers the story of Paul's conversion so important that he repeats it. The original form of the story is in Acts 9:1–19, and then Luke quotes Paul as giving two different versions of the story in 22:3–21 and 26:2–23. In each case, there are differences in minor details. Could those who were with Paul hear the voice which spoke to him? Were the others standing or kneeling when the voice spoke? Although the answers to these questions vary, the point of the story is always the same: Saul, who had persecuted Christians out of zeal for the Law, becomes a Christian.

You already know that Saul was a very religious and obedient Jew. He was willing to force Jews to follow the Law's commands. At the time of his conversion, Luke says that Saul was on his way to Damascus to arrest Christians. He had been given power to do so by the high priest. Although usually this power was reserved by the Roman procurator, this event probably occurred in the period between the administrations of Pilate and Marcellus (approximately 36 C.E.). If so, the local Jewish leaders may have temporarily assumed the authority that normally belonged to the Roman governor.

While Saul is on the road, a light from the sky flashes above him and knocks him to the ground. A voice calls out "Saul, Saul, why do you persecute me?" Saul asks who is speaking, and the voice replies that it is Jesus, the one whom Saul is persecuting. Notice

Scripture Workshop

Paul in Acts

Bible scholars generally agree that Luke had a source about Paul's conversion which he edited for use in the Book of Acts. Because the speeches in Acts show much evidence of Luke's editing, the version of Paul's conversion in Acts 9 is generally regarded as the closest to the original.

In the two retellings of the conversion contained in Paul's speeches, at 22:3–21 and 26:2–23, we see Luke's point of view. To understand Luke's point, do the following:

- Read each of the three versions of Paul's conversion.
- Make a list of the things Luke adds in the last two versions of the event.
- Based on these additions, tell what Luke believes is most important about Paul's conversion.
- Compare these versions with Paul's description in Galatians 1:11–18.

Luke's idea about discipleship in this passage: Jesus is with the disciples, and when Saul persecutes them, he persecutes Jesus himself.

After this event, Saul is referred to by a new name: Paul. (Remember similar stories from the Old Testament—Abram becomes Abraham, Jacob becomes Israel.) The name change symbolizes that Saul has been touched by God. Next, the voice tells Paul to go into the city and wait for God's call. Paul has been blinded by the flash of light, so his companions lead him to Damascus. There, Paul refuses food or water for three days, waiting to see what the Lord has in store.

As Paul waits, the Lord comes in a vision to Ananias, a disciple of Jesus. God instructs Ananias to go to Paul, to pray for him, and to cure his blindness. Ananias protests, reminding the Lord that Paul has persecuted Christians and presently has the power to arrest Christians on sight.

The Lord insists that Ananias carry out these instructions. God then announces that Paul has been chosen to be the person who brings the Gospel to the Gentiles:

◆ MORE ABOUT THE LESSON

Other Disciples

Remind the students that although Acts gives us the most information about Peter and Paul, there were other apostles and many other heroic disciples in the first 50 years after Jesus. When Stephen died, many disciples left Jerusalem, preaching the Good News as they went; thus, the Gospel began to spread.

Philip is one of those who traveled and preached. His dramatic encounter with an Ethiopian Jew returning home after a big festival is a wonderful story. Invite the students to notice how definitely the Spirit guided Philip and how immediate was Philip's obedience. What do they think of the apparent disappearance of Philip and his sudden "arrival" in Azotus, a number of miles distant?

"Go, for this man is a chosen instrument of mine to carry my name before the Gentiles, kings and Israelites, and I will show him what he will have to suffer for my name."

(Acts 9:15–16)

With a disciple's true courage, Ananias went to Paul, placed his hands on him, and prayed for him. Paul recovered his sight and was filled with the Holy Spirit at Ananias's touch. For the rest of his life, Paul preached the Gospel of the risen Jesus, beginning in Damascus.

As you already know, Paul is the hero of the rest of Acts. His success in converting Gentiles, however, was not celebrated by everyone. Some Christians saw

Saint James, one of the Apostles, was the leader of the church in Jerusalem. He headed the council there in 49 C.E. that validated Paul's preaching the Good News to Gentiles.

his mission as a betrayal of Judaism, and the result was a controversy that could only be settled by a meeting of all the leaders of the Church.

The Council of Jerusalem

In Acts 15, Luke tells the story of this meeting in Jerusalem in 49 C.E. Biblical scholars say that in this chapter, Luke has combined two separate events. One was a meeting of the apostles to discuss the question of the mission to the Gentiles. The other was a later controversy over whether Gentile converts should have to follow the Jewish dietary laws. Luke puts these two events together because they both involve the Spirit's guidance of the community towards accepting Gentiles as Christians.

James, described as a "brother of the Lord," heads this meeting in Jerusalem. Whatever his exact relationship to Jesus, James was a member of Jesus' family, and in the ancient world this meant that he had a claim to inherit his relative's authority. (This idea remained so strong that several decades later, the Emperor Vespasian arrested two distant cousins of Jesus, afraid that they might challenge his authority.) Because of James' relationship with Jesus, he became the head of the Christian community in Jerusalem.

Luke's story begins with Paul in Antioch, after the first missionary journey. Some Pharisees who had converted to Christianity traveled to Antioch, where they saw Gentiles worshipping with Jewish-Christians. The Pharisees demanded that the Gentiles should be circumcised in keeping with the Law of Moses. Paul refused, arguing that it was not necessary for the Gentiles to become Jews before entering the Christian community. They were members because of their faith in Jesus, not because they obeyed the Law. The Pharisees were not satisfied with Paul's response, so they demanded a hearing in Jerusalem.

When Paul and Barnabas arrived in Jerusalem, the apostles and other assembled leaders listened to their case. Next, some believing Pharisees stated their objections. The council considered the matter for a while, and then Peter rose to speak. He reminded them that the Spirit had called him to make the first Gentile convert. Then, he asked why the Gentiles should be required to obey the Law, since neither the apostles nor their ancestors had been able to do so:

"And God, who knows the heart, bore witness by granting them the Holy Spirit just as he did us. He made no distinction between us and them, for by faith he purified their hearts. Why, then, are you now

Practicing the Skills

What to Do
Have the students read Acts 10 and 11:1–18, the story of Cornelius and Peter. Ask them to list the main points of the Acts story. Ask: "What is the most significant reason for including it in the Bible?" When they have reached a decision, ask them to compare it with the text.

Recall

What to Do
Have the students search out and write the answers to "Chapter 12 Review Q/A," Section Two, questions 1–9.

Connect
Students will think about the Holy Spirit in relation to themselves.

What to Do
Homework Assignment: Have the students reflect on the following questions and write their responses in their Spiritual Journal. Suggest that they pray about their answers before (and after) they write:
• Is the Holy Spirit active in my life?
• What experiences of the Holy Spirit have I had?
• What qualities showed up in the early Christians that I would like to have?
• Would I like for the Holy Spirit to be more alive inside me?

What's Next?

What to Do
Say: "Your homework reflection will lead you into the next lesson's topic. The lesson will tell us about the qualities in the life of a person whose heart is filled with the Holy Spirit. They are very attractive qualities, so it will be interesting to learn about them."

MORE ABOUT THE TEXT

The First Council
Students may have difficulty at first appreciating the enormity of the policy set at the Council of Jerusalem. Without it, Gentiles would never have been able to follow Jesus and remain connected to Jesus' first apostles. Christianity might have died altogether if it had been confined to the Jewish community, because by 90 C.E. (at the latest), Jews who believed in Jesus were not allowed to participate in synagogue life. The Jewish decision, of course, was largely necessitated by the Christian policy established in Jerusalem, to admit Gentiles to full fellowship with Jewish Christians.

After the Council, Christianity was seen as a threat to Judaism. But for Christians, the Council's decision meant that Gentiles and Jews could share meals, celebrate social occasions, and worship together.

Have You Considered?

1. Society provides several examples of this. Often, people regard the homeless and poor as impure, wishing to avoid contact with them. Another good example is people infected with HIV—again, there is often a tendency to treat these individuals as if they were impure. Students should also share personal experiences, perhaps about individuals in school or elsewhere who received this kind of treatment.

2. As a extension question, once students have given examples of changing their minds, you may wish to ask them if they see the hand of God at work in their "conversion," in a way similar to Paul's experience.

3. Jews who follow the dietary laws are unable to dine with people who don't. At this time, the main gathering of the day in the Christian community was a shared meal. For this reason, if Christians wanted to be able to maintain their table unity with one another, it would be necessary for all to follow the basic laws of kosher. James was concerned about keeping the Christian community intact.

Bonus Focus for You

Read Acts 4:32–35. How does the situation of this first community strike you? How close do people have to feel to each other to share all their material possessions in this way? Can such closeness of life be experienced in the Christian community today, even without economic commonalty? Is it possible for us to see that "there is no needy one" among us, even though we all have our own possessions? Write your reflections in your journal.

putting God to the test by placing on the shoulders of these disciples a yoke that neither our ancestors nor we have been able to bear? On the contrary, we believe that we are saved through the grace of the Lord Jesus, in the same way as they."

(Acts 15:8–11)

This speech was probably the original end of the discussion. As a result of Peter's words, the leaders of the community decided to accept Gentile converts without insisting that they first become Jews or obey Jewish laws. Because it was the Spirit which led Peter to convert Cornelius, they agreed that it was also the Spirit which led them to this decision.

Luke also includes here a speech given by James about the question of whether Gentile Christians need to obey the dietary rules in the Law of Moses. James says that they do not have to obey the entire law, but they should observe three basic rules:

- Do not eat the meat of animals sacrificed to idols.
- Do not eat the meat of strangled animals.
- Do not drink blood.

James also adds that Gentiles should also observe the basic rules of sexual morality and thus avoid scandal.

We have looked at four crucial events:

- Pentecost
- The conversion of Cornelius
- Paul's conversion
- The Council of Jerusalem

In describing these events, Luke expresses his belief that at every critical moment, the Holy Spirit led the early Christian community. Through the working of the Spirit, God's plan for salvation opened its third and final stage, the period of the Church.

Have You Considered?

1. Peter said that no one should call another person impure. Do you think some people still regard others as "impure"? Explain your answer.
2. Paul went from persecuting Christians to preaching Christ. Has your mind ever been changed completely like this? Describe your experience.
3. Why do you suppose James thought it would be a problem for Jewish-Christians and Gentile-Christians to live together if the Gentiles didn't follow the dietary rules?

◆ The Gifts of the Spirit

Catholics believe that the Holy Spirit continues to be with Christians today. In fact, Pope John XXIII, who called the Second Vatican Council (1962–65) because of a sudden prompting from the Spirit, called our age "a new Pentecost." He said that our times should be called "the age of the Holy Spirit," because the Spirit calls us today in a special way to reform and renewal.

The Holy Spirit is at work today in the life of every believer, helping us to become better, more holy people. In Catholic tradition, the help the Spirit can give to each of us has been described as seven "gifts." The original list is found in Isaiah 11:1–2, but we can also see the basis of these seven gifts in Acts.

Wisdom The first gift of the Spirit is wisdom, a quality you've already studied in Chapter 9. The wisdom given by the Spirit is different, however, from the insights that can be achieved solely through human effort. The Spirit gives us the wisdom to "see through God's eyes," to evaluate things as God sees them. This is the challenge God gave to Ananias, when he was afraid to go to Paul. The Lord said that Ananias must see Paul in God's terms, not his own fear. This kind of wisdom is shaped by love, so that we judge everything from a loving perspective.

To see as God sees might mean looking past external appearance or behavior to see the good-hearted, loving person inside. It might mean judging a social situation not by the fun you might have, but by whether others are being excluded or hurt by it. The wisdom of the Spirit helps us to set aside our own self-interest and perceive a situation honestly, so that we can make decisions based on love.

Understanding Understanding is the ability to grasp revealed truths easily and deeply. A "revealed" truth is one which has been given to us by God through Jesus and the teaching of the Church. For example, we believe that God the Father, God the Son, and God the Holy Spirit are three really distinct Persons relative to each other in the one and only God. This truth can't be "proven" by human reason, but we believe it still. Paul didn't come to the conclusion that Jesus was the Lord by reason. Through the Spirit, he simply "saw" that it was true. The Spirit gives us the ability to see the truth of revealed teachings without struggle or doubt.

Understanding is an important gift, because we all face doubts at different points in our lives. For example, when a close friend or family member is ill,

---

MORE ABOUT THE TEXT

The Brother of the Lord

Some student is bound to ask about James, the "brother of the Lord." In Aramaic, the language spoken by Jesus, the word for "brother" can equally well mean "cousin" or "relative." Families were very close. In Greek, the language of Acts and the rest of the New Testament, this doesn't work. Brother means brother.

As the Christian community developed a growing devotion to Mary, the mother of Jesus,

Christians came to believe that not only had Mary been a virgin when Jesus was born (which was believed very early on), but that she remained a virgin forever. This belief seems to conflict with several places in the New Testament where brothers and sisters of Jesus are mentioned. The evidence is inconclusive. The doctrine of the Catholic Church is that Mary was ever-virgin and never had other children.

it's difficult to understand how God can be loving and yet allow such things to happen. Sometimes we know Catholics who are mean-spirited or dishonest, and we have trouble believing in the Church. Understanding helps us overcome such doubts by seeing the truth of God's love and the inspiration of the Church, even when we can't prove them by facts or logic.

Knowledge   The knowledge given by the Spirit has been called the "science of the saints." It enables us to recognize the true value of created things. We appreciate them as gifts of God, but we recognize that they have no meaning in themselves. Only our salvation has true value; other things may bring us pleasure, but they can never be at the top of our priority list. Cornelius, the Roman centurion, had this gift. Although he was a powerful military leader, he saw that without salvation, all his worldly success meant nothing. This realization led him to call for Peter's help.

Knowledge helps us cope with the conflicts over material things that always come up in our lives.

Sometimes we want something so much that we're tempted to behave badly to get it. Knowledge helps us see that no created thing is worth sacrificing our morality or our relationship with God and other people. Knowledge helps us to see the true worth of things, and to see that only love has lasting value.

Counsel   Wisdom, understanding, and knowledge are gifts which help us understand things properly. Counsel helps us apply that understanding to the practical situations that we face every day. As Saint Augustine said, it is not external teachers who show us the truth, but the "Truth that presides within."

Through counsel, we are able to make wise moral judgments even in complicated circumstances. Counsel also helps us to give good advice to others, always guided by the principles of forgiveness and generosity.

When the other apostles turned to Peter on the question of whether or not to accept Gentiles, he spoke with counsel. He applied his own experience with Cornelius to the larger issue of Gentile

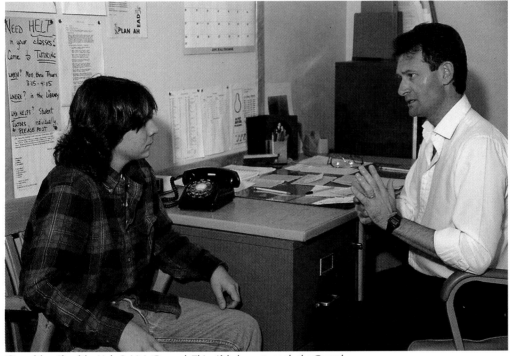

One of the gifts of the Holy Spirit is Counsel. This gift helps us to apply the Gospel to practical situations we face everyday.

MORE ABOUT THE TEXT

Eisegesis

In this lesson, we are doing what scholars call "eisegesis." It means taking what we already know or believe and trying to find it in the Scripture, that is "reading into" the Scripture what we already think. That is different from "exegesis" or trying to find out what the Scripture says on its own terms, which has been the aim of the rest of course. The "Seven Gifts" of the Spirit are part of Church tradition, not really part

of the Scripture as such. The subject is highly important, so that students have a grasp of the possible practical effect of the Spirit in their lives. But it should be explained to them that these "gifts" are not drawn directly from Scripture, but from the Church's understanding of a virtuous and holy life, which can be affirmed by some aspects of the Bible, as this lesson does.

LESSON FOUR
(pages 223–225)

◆ The Gifts of the Spirit

Welcome

Students are reminded of the role of the Holy Spirit in Christian life.

What to Do

Welcome the students "in the name of the Holy Spirit who binds us together in love."

Ask the students to share some of their reflections from the homework assignment. What do they think and feel about the Holy Spirit now?

Pray with your students. Ask for the blessings of the Lord on today's session and pray together the "Come Holy Spirit" prayer.

Introducing the Lesson

Students will understand that not only dramatic experience, but daily help, is available from the Holy Spirit.

Teaching Objectives

By the end of this lesson students will be able to:
• Identify the gifts of the Holy Spirit as seen in Acts.
• Determine how the gifts of the Spirit can be used today.

What to Do

Say: "The Holy Spirit helps us in many ways. The Spirit brings us the experience of the Lord and it gives us abilities and strengths that we would not have on our own. For those who love the Spirit and ask for the Spirit's help, the Spirit becomes a constant companion in life—supporting, guiding, protecting, and loving them. Today we will learn about the qualities given by the Spirit which are traditionally recognized and honored in the Church."

Development

Students will know more clearly what specific qualities to expect from the help of the Holy Spirit.

What to Do

1. Have the students read "The Gifts of the Spirit."

2. Discuss each of the subsections with the students. Use these Scripture passages for the matching subject to enrich and challenge their understanding:

- *Introduction*: Isaiah 11:2
- *Wisdom*: Isaiah 55:8–9; Matthew 16:21–23; Romans 12:9–21
- *Understanding*: John 16:13–14; John 8:32; 1 John 5:1–5 (This is a letter the students haven't opened yet; they can look it up in the table of contents.)
- *Knowledge*: Luke 16:19–31; Matthew 6:25–34; Ecclesiastes 3:12–14
- *Counsel*: Acts 6:1–6; Galatians 5:19–23; Matthew 25:31–45
- *Piety*: Matthew 5:43–48; Amos 5:21–24 (Remember that feasts, solemnities, cereal offerings, holocausts are all acts of worship in Israel.); Sirach 41:18–24
- *Fortitude*: Romans 8:38–39; Luke 9:62; Hebrews 12:7; 1 Peter 2:19–20
- *Fear of the Lord*: Proverbs 1:7; 1 John 4:13–21; John 15:9–10

3. Lead the class discussion of the questions in "Have You Considered?"

4. Pray with your students. Ask a student to lead the class in prayer. End with the "Come Holy Spirit" prayer.

Recall

Have the students write their answer to "Chapter 12 Review Q/A," Section Two, question 10.

Connect

What to Do

Have the students complete the Spiritual Reflection and write about their experience in their Spiritual Journal.

What's Next

What to Do

Say: "Remember that Paul was a teacher or coach for Christian life in all the communities he founded.

224

People of Note

Barnabas

As you know, Barnabas traveled with Paul on his first missionary journey. In fact, Barnabas was a prominent leader in the early Church, and Paul was probably originally his assistant. Paul, however, quickly became a leader in his own right.

Barnabas and Paul separated at the beginning of the second journey, and like Paul, Barnabas continued to travel widely. He founded the Christian Church on the island of Cyprus, and the Church Father, Tertullian (along with some biblical scholars today) credited him with writing the *Letter to the Hebrews*. Barnabas' success as a missionary, and as the person who launched Paul's career, again shows the active role played by the Holy Spirit in the life of the early Church.

Christians, and steered the Church in the proper direction. We all have to deal with difficult moral decisions. Counsel helps us make the best possible one.

Piety   The gift of piety helps us worship God in the proper way. Piety means much more, however, than simply praying sincerely. Piety means that we show reverence for God and all of God's creatures. A pious person honors God with his or her work. A pious person also sees other people as brothers and sisters rather than competitors or enemies. This kind of piety led Paul to defend the right of Gentiles to become full members of the Christian Church.

A cliché says that we should love people and use things, not the other way around. When we are pious, we treat other people with dignity and respect, because they are images of God. They are members of our family, with God as our Father. With the gift of piety, we also honor God by thinking and acting in ways of which we can be proud. Piety helps us regard ourselves, other people, and the whole world as deserving of our love and care.

Fortitude   The word fortitude means "courage." This gift helps us to be brave. There are two different kinds of fortitude which the Spirit gives:

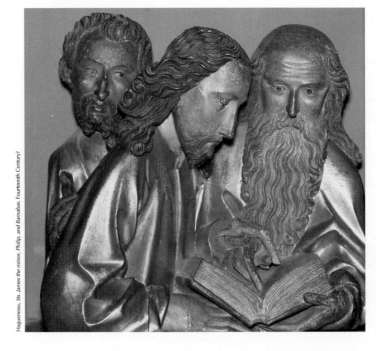

Hagueneau, *Sts. James the minor, Philip, and Barnabas. Fourteenth Century?*

Although Paul is the best known missionary of the early Church, Saint Barnabas also played an important role in spreading the Gospel. Barnabas is shown in this woodcut with Saint James the minor and Saint Philip.

MORE ABOUT THE TEXT

Barnabas

Barnabas is the surname given to Joseph the Levite from Cyprus. Barnabas was an early convert to Christianity. He was a man much respected in the Christian community, as seen by the responsibility that he was given: he was responsible for Paul. Barnabas brought Paul to Antioch, and they preached together in Cyprus and Asia Minor. The Church of Jerusalem called Barnabas an apostle to the Gentiles (see Galatians 2). After leaving Paul, Barnabas is thought to have returned to Cyprus where he was martyred.

1. The courage to undertake difficult tasks.
2. The courage to persist in our commitments.

The first kind of courage helps us not to be afraid when something seems impossible. We can face the challenge bravely, knowing the Spirit will provide the strength we need. The second kind of courage helps us to keep going, even when we're tired and the road ahead seems long. The Spirit is there to help us on the way.

Both kinds of courage are necessary. On Pentecost, the apostles faced a large, hostile crowd and still preached the Gospel. Later, Paul's mission took many years and required thousands of miles of traveling. In overcoming such hardships, he showed great courage. Both kinds of courage are necessary to live the Gospel, and the Spirit offers both through the gift of fortitude.

Fear of the Lord   Fear of the Lord was also discussed in Chapter 9. In the Israelite wisdom tradition, fear of the Lord meant awe and respect for God and commitment to the Covenant. These ideas are included in this gift, but the Spirit moves us beyond them to also feel an intense love for God. This kind of love is similar to what you feel for a parent, or for your favorite teacher or priest. You don't want to let them down in anything that you do. The "fear" you feel is not the fear of punishment, but the fear of causing disappointment.

Sin sometimes involves an injury to someone else, but it always injures our relationship with God. When we are motivated by fear of the Lord, we feel shame for sin most of all because we've strayed from the love and trust God offers us. We want forgiveness not because we fear God's anger, but because we want to repair our relationship. The Spirit gives us this intense love, and helps us to keep our love for God central to every decision we make.

Have You Considered?

1. Give an example of how "seeing things through God's eyes" is different from the way the world normally looks at things.
2. Have you ever had an experience where you simply "saw" that something had to be true? If so, describe it. If not, describe what you think such an experience might be like.
3. Describe an example you have personally witnessed of each of the two different kinds of fortitude.

Spiritual Reflection

Prayer to the Holy Spirit

Many great poets have expressed their love for the Holy Spirit. One of the most famous hymns to the Spirit is that of Brother Adam, who lived in the Abbey of Saint Victor near Paris in the twelfth century C.E. Adam was famous for his knowledge of Scripture and his use of it in his poems.

Use his "Hymn for the Feast of Pentecost" below as the basis for your prayer. Become quiet and ask the Spirit to enter you. Reflect on the gifts of the Spirit, thinking about how each could help you face the challenges in your life. When you feel ready, quietly pray the words of Brother Adam's poem:

You who come from the Father and the Son,
Equally from both, the Paraclete!
Give us eloquent speech,

And make our souls on fire for you
Through the flames you send.
The loved one of the Father and the Son,
Equal of both, companion and exact likeness of each:
Inspiring all, loving all,
Guiding the stars and moving the heavens,
Always the same.
Clear light, dear light,
Chase away the mists of my inner darkness.
The world and everything in it comes from you.
May you do away with sin,
And the stain sin leaves behind.

When you're finished, silently ask the Spirit's blessing.

In the next chapter we begin to study Paul's teaching and learn more about his life."

Have You Considered?

1. Seeing through God's eyes involves a complete reversal of perspective and values. Someone who seems quite successful from the world's point of view may be quite the reverse when God sees that person. Students should be encouraged to give specific examples of how things seem different when one tries to adopt God's perspective.

2. The most likely area for such experiences is students' emotions. For example, students may have had the experience of "seeing" that they cared for someone, even if they couldn't really provide the reasons for this response. Another possible area is interpersonal relationships: sometimes we simply "see" when someone is being less than truthful with us, or when they are being honest, even if we can't provide a completely rational basis for these instincts. Also discuss with students how such instincts are not always completely reliable, because they can be clouded by emotions.

3. The first kind of courage is that of undertaking difficult tasks. If you're stuck for an example, consider the heroism of people who sacrifice themselves to help others in tragedies, such as fires and earthquakes. Encourage students to discuss examples of this that they personally have witnessed. The other kind of courage is more long-term, the courage to stick with one's commitments. Ask students to consider examples such as married couples who have made their relationships work, or athletes who stick it out despite injuries.

Bonus Focus for You
In the light of today's lesson, take a look at your own life. Which of these gifts of the Spirit would you like to have more of? Why? Ponder this and write your reflections in your journal.

◆ MORE ABOUT THE LESSON

Additional Prayers

On Pentecost the Church traditionally prays the Sequence:

Come, thou Holy Spirit, come! And from thy celestial home Shed a ray of light divine! Come, thou Father of the poor! Come, thou source of all our store! Come, within our bosoms shine!

Thou, of comforters the best; Thou, the soul's most welcome guest; Sweet refreshment here below; In our labor, rest most sweet; Grateful coolness in the heat; Solace in the midst of woe.

Heal our wounds, our strength renew; on our dryness pour thy dew; Wash the stains of guilt away . . .

Give them virtue's sure reward; Give them thy salvation, Lord; Give them joys that never end. Amen. Alleluia.

(The entire hymn can be found in the TRB.)

Q/A

Section One

1. Luke wrote the Book of Acts.

2. The most important character in Acts is the Holy Spirit.

3. Luke addresses why Jews reject the Gospel, and how Gentiles can claim salvation from a promise made to Jews.

4. The conversion of Gentiles was controversial because Christians believed Jesus to be the Jewish Messiah, and that his mission was to Jews.

5. Three ways in which the stories of Peter and Paul are parallel include: (A) both confront magicians, (B) both convert Gentiles, and (C) both were arrested for their message.

6. A god-fearer was a Gentile who honored the traditions of Judaism, prayed to the Jewish God and attended the synagogue, but who did not convert to Judaism.

7. Paul was a Pharisee well-trained in the Law, but he also received an extensive education in Greek literature and philosophy.

8. On the first journey, Paul went to the Mediterranean islands and then to south Galatia. Rejected by Jews, Paul began converting Gentiles. On the second journey, Paul founded Christian communities in Greece. During this time, he worked as a leather-worker in Ephesus. On the third journey, Paul lived in Ephesus for three years, making many Gentile converts. He then went to Corinth and returned to Jerusalem, taking up a collection for the poor.

Q/A

Section One

1. Who wrote the Book of Acts?
2. Who is the most important character in the Book of Acts?
3. What two doubts about early Christianity does Luke address?
4. Why was the conversion of Gentiles controversial?
5. List three ways in which the stories about Peter and Paul parallel each other.
6. Define: "god-fearer"
7. Describe Paul's early education and religious formation.
8. Describe Paul's three missionary journeys.

Section Two

1. When was the feast of Pentecost held?
2. What did Peter say in his sermon on Pentecost?
3. What is the central message of Acts?
4. What does Peter's vision in the Cornelius story mean?
5. What leads Peter to baptize the Gentiles?
6. Explain why it is historically possible for Paul to have had authority to arrest Christians as Luke says.
7. How does Paul's conversion show Luke's idea of discipleship?
8. What was the issue addressed by the Council of Jerusalem? What position does Peter take in this controversy?
9. Who is James? What does James say regarding Gentiles and the dietary laws?
10. List and describe the seven gifts of the Holy Spirit.

BIBLE ACTIVITIES

1. In Acts 8:26–40, Luke tells the story of the encounter between Philip and the Ethiopian. Read this story. Use the footnotes in your Bible to figure out where the scripture passage Philip quotes originated. Then, write an essay on how you would explain this passage to the Ethiopian.

2. Luke says that Paul always began in a new city by preaching to the Jews, but in almost every case they opposed him. Read the story of what happened to Paul in Thessalonica *(Acts 17:1–9)*. Then answer these questions: (a) What charge do the Jews bring against Paul? (b) Why would this charge be likely to get the attention of the Roman governor? (c) Is this charge true? Why or why not?

3. Paul gives several speeches in his own defense in the Book of Acts. Read the speech he gives to the Miletus elders in 20:17–35. Based on this speech, make a list of the charges against Paul which were known to Luke. Write an essay taking the position of a Jewish-Christian opposed to Paul, and include these charges.

BIBLE ACTIVITY

1. The quote comes from the book of Isaiah, 53:7f. In their essays, require students to refer back to material covered in Chapter 7 on Second Isaiah, the author of this passage. Then have students discuss how the hopes of this author, in Christian belief, were realized in the person of Jesus.

2. The story of Paul in Thessalonica appears in Acts 17:1–9. (A) The Jews charge Paul with creating a disturbance. (B) The function of the Roman governor, first and foremost, was to keep the peace and prevent popular uprisings. (C) It is true that Paul's teaching sparked controversy, but this uprising was manufactured to discredit Paul.

3. Possible charges against Paul include: (A) Paul was arrogant. (B) Paul taught only in private, hiding his words. (C) Paul was greedy, envying the wealth and fancy clothes of others. (D) Paul lived off the work of others. Encourage students to put themselves in

GLOSSARY

- **Cornelius**: The first Gentile convert to Christianity, baptized by Peter.
- **Council of Jerusalem**: Meeting of the early Church in 49 C.E.; approval of the mission to the Gentiles.
- **Counsel**: Gift of the Holy Spirit; the ability to apply other gifts to practical situations.
- **Fear of the Lord**: Gift of the Holy Spirit; a love of God so intense that we are motivated to please God.
- **Fortitude**: Gift of the Holy Spirit; the courage to undertake difficult tasks and to persist in our commitments.
- **Glossolalia**: Ability, given by the Holy Spirit, to speak (or understand) in foreign languages or in mysterious tongues.
- **God-fearer**: A Gentile who respected the religious ideas and traditions of Judaism but who did not accept circumcision or other Jewish laws.
- **Inspire**: Literally means to fill with the Spirit.
- **Knowledge**: Gift of the Holy Spirit; helps us realize the true value of created things.
- **Pentecost**: The day on which the Spirit descended on the disciples and they began their mission of spreading the Gospel.
- **Piety**: Gift of the Holy Spirit; reverence for God and for one another.
- **Understanding**: Gift of the Holy Spirit; helps us accept revealed truths easily and deeply.
- **Wisdom**: Gift of the Holy Spirit; the ability to "see through God's eyes," to evaluate things as God sees them.

UNDERSTANDING MORE ABOUT:

Simon Magus

Chapter 8 of Acts describes a magician named Simon, whose abilities to perform tricks impressed the Samaritans. Although he had been baptized by Philip, Simon's desire was to acquire more power, not to reform his life.

When Peter and John blessed people after their baptism, they received the Holy Spirit. Simon, who had not received the Spirit following his baptism, offered the apostles money if they would give him this amazing power as well. Peter refused, saying that the Spirit was not for sale.

The word "simony" comes from this passage in Acts. Simony is the sin of buying or selling an office in the Church. According to tradition, Simon Magus, angered by the apostles' rejection, became a most difficult opponent for them. The *Acts of Peter*, a non-canonical Christian book, tells of a clash of powers between Simon and Peter at the Roman Forum, in which Peter triumphed.

the position of Paul's' opponents, and try to reconstruct the charges brought against him. Ask students to find other passages in Acts where they might find support for their complaints.

Section Two

1. The feast of Pentecost is held 50 days after the conclusion of Passover.

2. In his sermon, Peter told the story of Jesus, relating it to the scriptural promises which Jesus fulfilled.

3. The central message in Acts is that Christianity originated in the inspiration of God, not in human activity.

4. Peter's vision means that Christians are not bound to follow the purity rules of the Jewish law; thus, Peter may convert the Gentile, Cornelius.

5. Peter baptizes the Gentiles when he sees that they have received the Holy Spirit just as the Jews did.

6. Paul could arrest Christians because during the time after the removal of Pilate, there was no direct Roman administration in Judea, and Jewish officials assumed authority.

7. Paul's conversion fulfills Luke's understanding of a disciple as one who spreads the good news.

8. The Council of Jerusalem considered whether Gentile converts had to obey the Jewish law. Peter argues that they do not have to do so.

9. James is the brother of the Lord who was in charge of the church in Jerusalem. James says that Gentiles should obey the four basic dietary rules, but other than that, they should not be burdened.

10. The gifts of the Spirit are: wisdom—the ability to see through God's eyes; understanding—the ability to grasp revealed truths easily and deeply; knowledge—the ability to recognize the true value of created things; counsel—the ability to make prudent decisions in our everyday lives; piety—the ability to worship God in the proper way; fortitude—the ability to undertake difficult tasks, and to persist in our commitments; fear of the Lord—an intense love for God.

The Teaching of Paul

Chapter Overview

Paul was not only an untiring missionary. He also cared deeply for the communities he founded. His concern for them is seen in the many letters he wrote. These letters, the oldest existing written records from the early Church are the subject of this lesson. As Paul responded to the needs and concerns of his communities, he established the foundations on which the Church's theology was to grow. You will also explore the theology developed in Paul's letters.

Teaching Objectives

By the end of this chapter students will be able to:
• Explain the factors that led to Paul's missionary success.
• Discuss the format of Paul's letters and explain how they came to be written.
• Demonstrate an understanding of Paul's principle teachings.

Welcome

What to Do

Hand each student a note (two or three sentences in length) expressing your appreciation of one of his or her qualities.

Call attention to the "letter-like" quality of your greeting. Chat with the students about whether, and on what occasions, they write letters. Do they like to get letters? How does a written note (like the one they have just received) compare to the same message spoken face to face?

Pray with your students. Give thanks for all the wonderful qualities in your students and for all the wonderful qualities you've learned about in the early Christians. Ask for God's blessing on this lesson.

Introducing the Chapter

The art of letter writing is little practiced in this day of instant communication. Yet, letters serve an important purpose. They allow us to

---

The Teaching of Paul

41	**41–54 C.E.** ●Claudius Emperor of Rome
	49 ●Council of Jerusalem
	50 ●Famine in the Eastern Empire
	51 ●1 Thessalonians
	51–52 ●Gallio Proconsul in Achaia
	54 ●Galatians
	54–57 ●1 and 2 Corinthians
	54–68 ●Nero Emperor of Rome
	56–58 ●Philippians
	57–58 ●Romans
	58 ●Paul arrested at the Temple
	60 ●Paul in Rome ●Philemon
64	**64** ●Great Fire in Rome; Christians Persecuted

Legend

●General History
●Regional History
●Christian History
●Books written

J avier was devastated when his father died. He remembered things they had done together: the fishing trips, baseball games, going for doughnuts on Saturday morning. When he first heard that his father had cancer, he didn't believe it. As things got worse, Javier slowly realized that his father wasn't going to get better. Nothing could prepare him for the shock he felt at the news of his father's death. Javier didn't know that it was possible to feel so much pain.

As time passed, Javier learned to live with the fact that his father was gone, but he didn't miss him any less. To live with his loss, Javier drove himself to make his father proud. A freshman in high school when his father died, Javier threw himself into his studies. He went on to excel in college and then in business school. After graduation, Javier quickly found

---

MORE ABOUT THE TEXT

The Letters of Paul

There is some discussion among scholars as to which letters can be attributed to Paul. Although the Letter to the Hebrews is sometimes listed as being Paul's, most scholars today would not agree. The letter itself does not claim to have been written by Paul. The generally accepted belief is that Hebrews was credited to Paul to make sure that it was included in the canon.

There is also some doubt as to whether Paul or some of his disciples actually wrote Ephesians, Colossians, 2 Thessalonians, and 1 Timothy. Regardless of who actually wrote them, these four letters express Paul's beliefs and are written in Paul's name.

Finally, it is quite possible that Paul wrote other letters that didn't survive to become part of Scripture. In addition, some of the letters we do have appear to have once been two letters.

an exciting job. Before long, he had a family of his own. He loved taking his children to visit their grandmother, who still lived in the house where Javier grew up.

On one such trip, after the children had gone to bed, Javier sat down to talk to his mother.

The other day, Helena asked why she had three grandparents and other kids in second grade had four. So I sat down with her and Enrique and started telling them about Papa.

Then, Helena wanted to know where he was born, and I didn't know, except in Mexico somewhere. I realized that after all these years of missing Papa, I still really don't know that much about him. What was he like as a young man? How did he build his business? Who were his friends? There are so many things I wonder.

His mother smiled, took him by the hand, and led him into the old study. "After your father died," she said, "I collected copies of everything I could find. It's all here in this storage box. These records will tell you much about him." With that, she handed Javier a stack of correspondence, and left the room.

Javier sat down at his father's desk and began to read. Some of the letter were written to his mother, some were for business, and others were to friends. There were even several "Letters to the Editor."

Javier learned that his father arrived in America from Jalisco, Mexico, where he had been born. His father didn't speak any English when he arrived in America, and went to night school to learn it. His father got a job working at a garage sweeping floors, working his way up to Head Mechanic, then built a thriving auto-parts business.

Javier also discovered that his father loved poetry, and had written several poems home to his wife during the Vietnam War. Javier had had no idea! His father also had strong political convictions, and had written to the local newspaper to protest city regulations frequently.

From these letters, Javier discovered much about who his father was. They confirmed the impression he had formed as a child of his father as being a strong, caring man. Now, it was Javier's turn to be proud. The next morning, Javier thanked his mother for showing him the letters. "Now I know who Papa was," he said, "and I feel closer to him than ever."

A Lasting Impression

Just as his father left a strong impression on Javier, the apostle Paul left a lasting impression on the early Church. To get to know Paul, we have to turn to his letters. In them, the personality and the ideas of the apostle are revealed in passionate, forceful language. In this chapter, you'll learn about the letters of Paul.

◆ MORE ABOUT THE LESSON

Media Awareness

You can also tie a media awareness lesson in the letter writing experience. Students are major consumers of the broadcast media's product, whether in the form of radio, television, CDs and tapes, video cassettes, or movies. Few students take the opportunity to shape the decisions that are made concerning what they watch or hear. They are passive receivers only.

They can use this letter writing skill to take a more active voice. If the class has a concern about a particular media event (concert, movie, television program), have them write and express their concern. The addresses for the major television networks are included in Teacher's Resource 13A.

---

collect our thoughts over a period of time, shape them so that we actually say what we mean, and leave a legacy that can be reviewed whenever we wish. The introduction to this chapter should focus on the value of all letters, not just those of Paul.

What to Do

Have the students read the story about Javier on pages 228–229. How did Javier benefit from reading his father's letters?

Review the format of a letter with students. All letters start by identifying the letter's intended recipient, along with a *greeting*. The greeting can be either formal or informal. The letter then continues in the *body*. Here the message of the letter is contained. Letters end with a closing message of endearment, followed by a signature. Have students practice writing a letter until they become comfortable with its format.

Ask: "What is the importance of letters today? Why and how is that different than the importance of letters 100 or 2,000 years ago? Discuss that letters are one of our most important ways of documenting history. While most people in the past would never consider writing a biography or history, many of them did write letters setting out the details that occurred during a historical event. Because of these letters, we can now know what happened then. Without these letters, we would not know.

Extending the Lesson   The intent of this activity is so that students learn the power of the letter. Have students write actual letters. The letters can be addressed to the school's principal expressing students' comments about the school, they can be addressed to your local government expressing students' concerns on a local issue, or they can be addressed to a national figure (president, senator, or congressional representative) expressing concern about a world event. Actually mail the letters.

Using the Timeline

Have the students read through the timeline, noticing especially the dates the books were written—they are all Paul's letters.

◆ **Paul's Success
as a Missionary**

Development

What to Do

1. Have the students read the opening italics and Learning Objectives.

2. Have the students read all of "Paul's Success as a Missionary."

3. The scale for the map on page 231 is 250 miles per .25 inch. Using this scale, have the students complete the map exercises. Ask: "Why do you suppose the Romans called the Mediterranean 'our lake'?"

4. Have the students read "The Bible in Context" and "in the Spotlight."

5. Discuss with the students the three characteristics of the Roman Empire which helped Paul's mission be so successful: a common language, safe travel, and the presence of Jewish communities all over the Empire. Ask: "What do you think Paul's task of spreading the Gospel would have been like without any one of these? What do you think a missionary task is like today in Africa or Asia? Do they have these same advantages?"

6. Have the students consider Paul's character. What kind of person do they think he was?

7. Have the students look up "Lord" in a concordance and count the number of times Paul used that word. Say: "Paul thought about Christ all the time. What do you think it would be like to have such a close relationship with Jesus Christ? What would it take to form such a close relationship with Christ?"

8. Say: "We have already considered part of Paul's method in approaching a new city to spread the Gospel. In 'Paul's Communities' the rest of his approach is described."

9. Divide the students into two groups. Have one group imagine that they are Jewish youth in the synagogue when Paul comes to

❮❮ SECTION ONE 40 C.E.–65 C.E.

Letter-Writing and Paul's Mission

Monreale, *St. Paul Preaches in the Synagogue.* Twelfth Century.

You already know from Chapter 12 that Paul was a great missionary. As the "apostle to the Gentiles," Paul founded Christian churches throughout the Roman Empire. In this section, you'll study the external circumstances and Paul's own inner qualities that accounted for his success. This section also introduces you to the format used in these letters, and how Paul used letters as part of his mission.

Learning Objectives for Section One:

By the end of this section, you will be able to:

• Explain how the organization of the Roman Empire contributed to Paul's success.

• Describe Paul's gifts as a missionary.

• Discuss the format of Paul's letters.

• Understand the character of Paul's letters as part of his mission.

◆ Paul's Success as a Missionary

In the Acts of the Apostles, Luke tells us of Paul's success as a missionary. Luke emphasizes that the Holy Spirit was the driving force behind Paul's progress. An important factor in Paul's success, however, was Paul's willingness to carry out the Spirit's task.

Throughout the empire, Paul founded Christian communities who responded to the gospel message he carried. Through his letters, Paul continued to guide and inspire these communities even after he had moved on to another city. These communities prospered under Paul's leadership. Paul's letters continue to give direction to the Church even today.

The Roman World

When Paul began his missionary career, the Roman Empire was in many ways the ideal place for him to work. Paul's travels took him to locations in what are now the modern countries of Syria, Turkey, Macedonia, and Greece. On his second trip, he traveled approximately 1,800 miles, a distance more than one-half the width of North America. Paul made this journey several times in almost 20 years.

Paul was able to speak to people in a language they would understand. Wherever he traveled, he was initially accepted as a friend because he was Jewish. All of these factors contributed to Paul's success.

A Common Language In Paul's day, almost everyone spoke Greek. The form spoken by most people was called *koine*, or "common" Greek. In cities, Greek was always used on the job and in politics. When Paul entered a city, he could preach in Greek and assume that he would be understood; this was an enormous advantage for a missionary who didn't have time to learn local languages.

Safe Travel Conditions were perfect for Paul's mission. Before the Roman Empire, anyone who ventured onto the sea was in danger of being kidnapped by pirates, and travelers over the roads had to worry about thieves. The Roman army and navy did away

---

MORE ABOUT THE TEXT

An Intense Relationship

Paul is recognized as a wonderful thinker and preacher. He was also a profoundly involved pastor, caring intensely about the quality of his converts' relationship with Christ, just as he cared intensely about Christ himself.

Paul's relationship with Christ is never described directly. Yet everything we know about this relationship shows that Paul was in constant inner contact with the Lord, that he sought the Lord's guidance about everything, and obeyed everything he heard without reserve. All of his innate abilities were focused on this central relationship of Paul's life.

LEARN FROM THE MAP

The Roman Empire

Transportation around and across the Mediterranean Sea was generally easy and safe under Roman administration. The Romans called the Mediterranean "mare nostrum," or "our lake." Using the route marked on the map, trace the course Paul probably followed from Philippi to Thessalonica.

- What was the name of the route he used?
- Approximately how far would the trip have been? (scale: 1/3" = 100 miles)

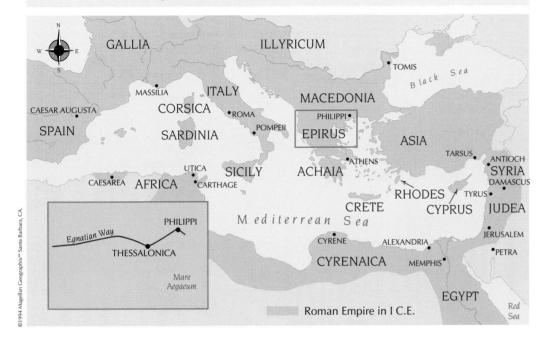

©1994 Magellan Geographix℠ Santa Barbara, CA.

Roman Empire in I C.E.

with most of these problems, making travel safe. This period of peace is known as the *Pax Romana*, or "Roman peace."

Under the Emperor Augustus, travelers did not need special papers to pass from one area to another. Certain tolls might be charged, but they had been significantly lowered under Augustus. A regular schedule of boat travel had been established across the Mediterranean. Paul also did not have to worry about encountering different laws as he moved about, since Roman law applied everywhere.

The Jewish Community   A third factor which contributed to Paul's success was the presence of Jewish communities in every large city. Paul knew that he could find lodging and work through them. He would also be allowed to preach in the synagogue. Even though most of the Jews would reject his mes-

sage, he always made a handful of converts. These people, then, helped him reach out to the Gentiles in that city.

All of these conditions helped Paul's ministry succeed. However, it was Paul's unique personality that allowed him to use these conditions to spread the gospel "to the ends of the earth."

Paul's Character

Sometimes people think that when God calls someone to do a job, he or she has to change completely to carry it out. Although this may sometimes be true, it was not the case with Paul. Rarely has anyone been more perfectly suited to a vocation than Paul was to his missionary calling.

- Paul was raised a Jew and spoke Hebrew. He had instant access to Jewish communities.

visit. Have the other group imagine that they are Gentile youths who hear Paul preaching in a city square. Each student is to write a letter to a friend, describing his or her experience of this preacher of Jesus Christ, including his or her own personal reaction to Paul as a person and to his message.

Ask for volunteers to read their letters aloud. After each reading, compliment the student, then ask for a letter that is quite different.

10. Lead the class discussion of the questions in "Have You Considered?"

11. Pray with your students. Have the students read aloud Colossians 4:12–17. Ask God to give you and your students the necessary interest and strength to experience the Lord as described here.

LEARN FROM THE MAP

1. The name of the route is the Via Egnatia, or Ignatian Way.
2. The trip would have been approximately 50 miles long.

Practicing the Skills

What to Do

Have the students read 2 Corinthians 12:2–7, as well as 1 Corinthians 7:25, where Paul answers a question. Note that this approach indicates that Paul talks everything over with the Lord.

Recall

Have the students answer "Chapter 13 Review Q/A," Section One questions 1–6.

Connect

What to Do

Show the students a video of one of today's mission projects. Have the students discuss the video, especially comparing today's missionary work with what they know about Paul.

What's Next?

What to Do

Have the students look at the table of contents in their Bibles for the New Testament. Using the list on page 234, have them note (or mark) which of the New Testament letters were written by Paul.

Say: "In our next lesson, we will begin to get acquainted with the letters Paul wrote to his friends. Some of them have come down to us in the New Testament."

Have You Considered?

1. Some important similarities between Paul's time and ours might include the general prosperity of the United States and the ease of travel in the modern world, with the social mobility that it makes possible. An important difference is the lack of a common language (although English is very widely-spoken). Another important difference is how we have access to various forms of mass communication today, which did not exist in the ancient world. Encourage students to consider whether, if Paul were alive today, he would be more or less successful.

2. Various responses are possible. Historically, his ability to be equally at home in Jewish and Graeco-Roman settings, including his fluent bilinguals, has been considered his greatest asset.

3. Paul was asking Jews to embrace Jesus as the Messiah. Many Jews, including most of the Jewish leaders, did not see Jesus this way. Therefore, they objected to Paul's attempts to convert their congregations, and generally ended up by driving him away.

Bonus Focus for You

Read 1 Corinthians 1:4–9, taking it very personally, as addressed specifically to you. Reflect on your life in light of this passage. Write your reflections in your journal.

- Paul knew Greek literature and spoke Greek fluently, so he was equally at home with Gentiles.
- Paul tailored his preaching specifically to each audience, guiding them in their growth.
- He was able to make his complex message understandable. He looked for practical solutions to immediate problems.
- Paul was a driven, energetic man. After his vision of Jesus, he devoted his life to helping people believe and live the Gospel.

Paul could speak with authority about the risen Christ, because Jesus had personally made him an apostle.

Paul's prayer life, might today be called mystical. He describes a few of his prayer experiences in 2 Corinthians 12:2–7. This profound spiritual experience gave him energy and a never-ending commitment to his mission. Paul's dedication—he never quit no matter what he encountered—can be attrib-

Unknown, Augustus Caesar, First Century B.C.E.

During the reign of Augustus Caesar, trade and travel flourished in the Roman Empire. This time of prosperity, the Pax Romana, made Paul's missionary journeys possible.

The Bible in Context

Roman Roads

One of the longest lasting physical remnants of the Roman Empire are its durable roads. In Paul's day, travel along these roads was safe, and, in some places, much more efficient than it is today. Some people, usually wealthy citizens or high government officials, traveled in carriages pulled by oxen, horses, or mules. Other travelers would ride on horseback. To travel by foot was a sign of poverty, or a commitment to a simple life. Paul may have made longer trips on horseback and shorter ones on foot. On the road, he would encounter travelers of all types: politicians, soldiers, traders, lawyers, and even tourists.

uted to his strong commitment to prayer, the heart of his relationship with Jesus.

Although his supporters often helped him, Paul did not take advantage of others. Because he had learned his family's leather goods trade (remember Luke calls Paul a tent-maker) as a young man, Paul earned a living while he did his missionary work.

Though other apostles traveled and founded Christian communities, none could match Paul's intellectual abilities or his success with the Gentiles. In Paul, God found the perfect tool to ensure the spread of the Christian faith.

Paul's Communities

When Paul arrived in a new city:

1. **He would head for the local synagogue.** There, Jewish tradition held that a visiting male should be invited to address the assembly. Paul used this opportunity to announce the Good News about Jesus. Reactions to Paul's message were usually mixed. Some immediately rejected it, while others wanted to hear more. A few even accepted faith in Jesus.
2. **The Jewish leadership would drive Paul out of the synagogue.**
3. **Paul would then take his message to the Gentiles.** He would preach outside the Gentile temples, in the marketplace, even in private homes.
4. **Paul would begin a local church.** Usually, this group of believers met in a private home. To have a house big enough to accommodate everyone, that person had to be fairly wealthy. This person generally became one of the leaders of the local church.

◆ MORE ABOUT THE LESSON

Missionary Efforts

Videos of modern missionary efforts are often available from your diocesan office of religious education, office of justice and peace, or vocations office. This resource can sometimes also be acquired from a missionary religious order, like the Maryknoll order. If you have a "live" missionary (who has worked in a foreign mission) in your area, invite that person to your classroom as a guest speaker. Your parish priest should be able to help you locate a missionary.

in the *Spotlight*

Paul's Jewish Background

Despite his Greek education, Paul was a faithful Jew. It's important to keep this in mind when reading his letters. For example, in Romans 12:20 Paul says:

If your enemy is hungry, feed him; if he is thirsty, give him something to drink; by doing this you will heap burning coals on his head.

What? Be nice to somebody so you can burn them? Actually, Paul is quoting from Proverbs 25:21–22 here. Putting ashes on oneself as a sign of repentance was a traditional Jewish custom (Job does it; see Job 2:12, 42:16). Paul means that by treating your enemies with love, you will move them to repent. To catch this point, you have to respect Paul's Jewish heritage.

5. Paul would stay with the local group for a while before moving on. He stayed for varying amounts of time; he was in Corinth for over two years, but in other places he stayed only a few days.

When Paul was ready to go, he left "elders" in charge of the local community. These new leaders inherited a challenging situation. For one thing, their community was made up of Jews and Gentiles, who often did not get along. Also, if the community was located in a major city, new ideas and philosophies were common. These new ideas were often made part of the communities' belief in Jesus whether they were compatible with that faith or not. Finally, problems would occur that Paul had never discussed. Because Paul was no longer around to immediately resolve these matters, arguments developed that threatened to split the community apart.

When such problems arose, the elders appealed to Paul for directions. Paul responded to these requests by letter. His letters reveal his missionary and leadership abilities.

Have You Considered?

1. How similar were the conditions in the Roman Empire in Paul's time to conditions in America today? What are some important differences?
2. Which part of Paul's character do you think helped him most as a missionary? Why?
3. Why do you suppose the local Jewish leaders usually drove Paul out of the synagogue?

◆ Paul's Letters

Paul's success in making converts didn't mean that things always went smoothly in his new churches. To deal with problems as they came up, and to remind these Christians of the practical side of their faith, Paul wrote letters. Several of these letters were passed from church to church, and they eventually became part of the New Testament.

Generations of people have studied Paul's letters because of their rich personal advice to Christians, as well as their importance in Church history. In their studies, scholars have made important observations about their structure and content. These observations can help us better understand Paul's message.

The Letter Formula

Paul's education shows in his letters. He wrote in the proper Greek letter form, but adjusted this format to his own unique purpose. Paul's letters usually follow the following format:

1. Opening
- Paul identifies himself as the author, and indicates to whom the letter is addressed.
- Co-senders, usually fellow missionaries with Paul, are mentioned.
- Paul greets people, usually wishing them "grace and peace." This element is a combination of the customary Greek greeting ("grace") and the Jewish one ("peace").

2. Thanksgiving Here, Paul expresses his gratitude for the goodness shown to him in the past by the people to whom he is writing. He may also talk about how the community has made him proud by their growth in Christian living. When Paul is angry, he skips this stage entirely.

3. Message The bulk of the letter comes in this section. Usually, Paul divides what he has to say in two sections. The first is the doctrinal section, containing his ideas about the Father, Jesus, and the Church. The second section is instructional; Paul tells this community how it should live.

4. Conclusion At the end of his letter, Paul sometimes passes on personal news or advice for specific people. Sometimes he indicates that he has signed the letter in his own hand, to guarantee its legitimacy.

5. Final blessing Usually, Paul ends his letters with the blessing "May the grace of our Lord Jesus Christ be with you." Grace is one of the most important themes in Paul's thought.

SECTION ONE

LESSON TWO (pages 233–236)

◆ Paul's Letters

Welcome

What to Do

Greet the students warmly.

Have the students think of some problem they know about (not too big). They are to write a short proposal offering a solution to the problem. What do they think about this exercise? What is it like to solve other people's problems?

Pray with your students.

Introducing the Lesson

Teaching Objectives

By the end of this lesson students will be able to:
- Describe the structure found in Paul's letters.
- Name which letters were definitely written by Paul, which were probably by Paul, and which are questionably by Paul.
- Explain the nature of Paul's letters: why they were written, to whom, and what they present to the reader.

What to Do

Have the students read "Paul's Letters" to themselves. They are to make notes of each part that they think is valuable.

Development

What to Do

1. Ask the students to review the letter formula again carefully. How is this formula similar to the letters they wrote in an earlier lesson? Have students describe in their own words Paul's letter formula. Have students open their Bibles to Galatians and name the chapter and verse where each part of the formula begins. (*Opening*—Galatians 1:1–2; *Thanksgiving*—1:3–5; *Message*—1:6–6:10; *Conclusion*—6:11–17; *Final Blessing*—6:18.)

2. Have the students read "Understanding More About" on page 247. How does this letter fit into students' understanding of Paul's letters?

3. Have the students look quickly again at "The Genuine Letters of Paul," noting especially which letters are definitely Paul's. Have

them read the references to the Corinthian correspondence to verify their text.

4. Assign "Bible Activity" number 2 and discuss the question there.

5. Lead the students' discussion of the questions in "Have You Considered?"

Extend the Lesson Complete the "Scripture Workshop" on page 234.

Practicing the Skills

What to Do

Have the students read the Letter to Philemon. Ask: "What are the reasons behind this letter?" Have them offer opinions as to the background of this letter.

When they have put together the correct answer, encourage them by saying: "You have now done real biblical scholarship. Understanding an historical situation from the material presented in the Bible is called 'reconstruction.' A great deal of scholarly knowledge is acquired in this way."

Have You Considered?

1. In most cases, Paul is writing to communities which include both Jewish and Gentile members. A greeting with both Hebrew and Greek elements symbolizes the union of Jews and Greeks in the Christian church.

2. That Paul may not have written all of the books attributed to him should not be surprising. In the ancient world, it was common for books which were written "in the spirit" of a famous person to be regarded as "written" by that person.

Scripture Workshop

1. *Opening*: (*Philippians* 1:1–2)

2. *Thanksgiving*: (*Philippians* 1:3–26)

3. *Message*: (A) Doctrinal Section—(*Philippians* 2:1–3:17); (B) Instructional Section—(*Philippians* 4:1–19)

4. *Conclusion*: (*Philippians* 4:21–22)

5. *Final blessing*: (*Philippians* 4:23)

The Genuine Letters of Paul

Paul's letters were so well received by the churches that they were shared between cities. Other authors imitated Paul's style or attributed letters to Paul so that their letters would be accepted by the churches as well. Although these letters were not written by Paul, they did represent his ideas. Over the course of time, however, some of these letters became identified as Paul's. Today, there is some confusion as to which of the "letters of Paul" in the New Testament were actually written by the apostle.

Catholic Bible scholars usually divide the letters into three categories:

- **Definitely written by Paul**: 1–2 Thessalonians, Galatians, Philemon, Philippians, 1–2 Corinthians, and Romans.

What do you say when you answer the telephone? Do you use a standard greeting? Paul, in his letters to the various communities he founded, usually began by wishing them grace and peace.

- **Probably written by Paul**: Colossians and Ephesians.
- **Probably not written by Paul**: 1–2 Timothy, Titus, and Hebrews.

In addition to the genuine letters of Paul in the New Testament, we know that Paul wrote other letters. 1 Corinthians 5:9 refers to an earlier letter he had written to Corinth. 2 Corinthians 2:3–4 talks about a "letter of tears" which was written after 1 Corinthians but before 2 Corinthians. Further, some of the letters of Paul may combine two or more originally separate letters. For example, Chapter 16 of Romans may originally have been a separate letter to the church in Ephesus. Corinthians may include parts of several other letters as well.

By knowing which New Testament letters best represent Paul's own thoughts, we can be sure we're hearing his voice when we read them. By knowing Paul's style, we can notice when he makes certain points to a particular community. Such careful study helps us to understand Paul's meaning.

Have You Considered?

1. Why do you suppose Paul included Greek and Jewish elements in his greeting?
2. Based on what you know about how books were written in the ancient world, is it surprising that some letters not written by Paul were attributed to him? Why or why not?

MORE ABOUT THE TEXT

Philemon

Paul's letter to Philemon is actually addressed to three specific individuals: Philemon, Apphia, and Archippus. The letter concerns the slave Onesimus who had run away from his master, possibly guilty of theft. Onesimus comes into Paul's care and is baptized. Paul sends Onesimus back to his master, asking that Onesimus be treated no longer as a slave but as a brother in Christ.

Paul does not attack the institution of slavery directly. Thinking that the Lord will return shortly, Paul may not feel it important to question the social condition of slavery. However, Paul does introduce the idea that all are equal in the Lord.

◆ The Nature of Paul's Letters

Some people who read Paul's letters expect them to be like a careful philosophical essay, where all ideas are explained, all terms defined, and everything develops in a logical manner. Although this style might be boring, it would make everything easy to understand. Paul's letters, however, are never boring. They are usually written in response to a crisis in the local community, and they show all the signs of being hasty, spur-of-the-moment compositions. Even though his letters represent his best thinking about Christianity and the Church, Paul just didn't have time to pursue every argument or define every term. Knowing this about the letters makes a big difference in how we read them.

Addressed to Specific Situations

Paul's letters are "slices of life," reflecting his relationship with various churches. Paul speaks from his own experience and his knowledge of the Gospel, addressing issues faced by his communities. His words are meant to be immediately applied to people's problems, mistakes, and doubts. Paul's letters are never formal or abstract; they are concrete and immediate.

The letters are part of an ongoing conversation between Paul and his communities. Sometimes this creates problems for us, because Paul refers to ideas

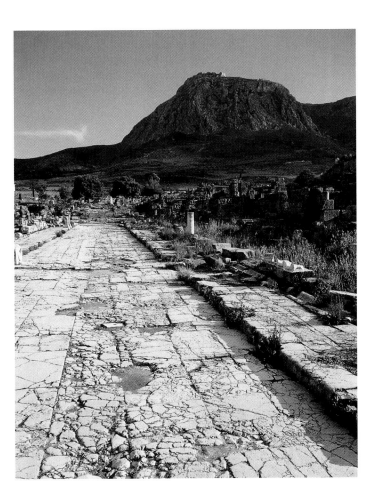

Paul did most of his travel using the famous Roman roads. Paul most likely traveled on foot, although he could have traveled on horseback, by donkey, or in a carriage.

◆ The Nature of Paul's Letters

Development

What to Do

1. Have the students read "The Nature of Paul's Letters." Ask: "Would you say that Paul's letter to Philemon is a 'slice' of life or an abstract discussion?" Have students offer reasons for their answers.

2. Explain to the students how Paul probably wrote his letters. (See "More about the Lesson" on page 235.)

3. Remind the students, "All through our study we have been trying to 'jump out of our skin' and into a world we do not understand. Paul may sound more familiar than one of the prophets, Jeremiah perhaps, but he, too, was a man of his time, not ours. We need to keep that in mind when we read his letters, as with the example given in your text." (See "More about the Text" page 236.)

4. Lead the class discussion of the questions in "Have You Considered?"

5. Pray with your students. Suggest that the students pray silently today and give them a couple minutes of total quiet. You may close the time with a quiet "Amen."

Recall

Have the students write their answers to "Chapter 13 Review Q/A," Section One questions 7–11.

Connect

What to Do

Homework Assignment: Say: "Listen closely at Mass this Sunday and find out which letter is read. Was the letter introduced as being written by Paul? Was the letter actually written by Paul?"

◆ MORE ABOUT THE LESSON

On Paul's Writing

The customs of the time, and all indications in the New Testament, suggest that Paul rarely wrote anything himself. He could write (see Galatians 6:1), but everybody who had to write much employed a scribe. Paul probably dictated his letters. The scribe settled himself to write what was spoken, sometimes improving its style as he wrote.

Imagine the scene: two men seated near one another, one talking and the other writing. For the writing of Galatians, imagine Paul pacing furiously, gesticulating and shouting while the scribe tries to write down what is being said.

What's Next?

What to Do

Have the students locate the letters to the Thessalonians and the Galatians, leaving markers at the beginning of each. Say, "These are the two letters we are going to examine in detail during the next class."

Have You *Considered*?

1. If you heard only one side of the conversation, you would have to guess at the questions the other party asked and the statements he or she made. Although it is generally possible to follow the main points of a conversation when you hear only one side, many of the finer points will be missed or confused.

2. Allow students to share their experiences. One problem with this material is that many students do not write letters, or do so only when forced; if several students are stuck for this reason, allow them to substitute an important phone call. Ask students to include how their knowledge of the person to whom they were writing or calling, influenced the way they phrased their letter or phone call.

3. Many applications are possible. One that students might find interesting is how they dress for the Eucharist. They might feel comfortable attending in tattered clothes. However, if they followed Paul's directive in 1 Corinthians 11:4–6, they would dress nicely so as not to offend anyone.

Bonus Focus for You ——————

Consider this description of Paul from the apocryphal book, *Acts of Paul*: "Small of stature, balding, bow legs, large eyes, eyebrows meeting, nose slightly hooked … His appearance was full of grace: sometimes he looked more like an angel than a man." What do you imagine Paul to have looked like? Does it matter?

or events familiar to his community but not to us. For example, 2 Thessalonians reminds the reader of Paul's teaching about a "man of lawlessness." Unfortunately, we don't know what he taught, so it's hard to know what Paul meant.

A more frequent difficulty is with Paul's writing style. Paul wrote (or dictated) spontaneously and with great passion. These qualities make his letters seem alive even today, but they can sometimes be frustrating to read. Paul doesn't always follow a line of thought carefully, and sometimes he'll mix up one argument with something entirely different. His language can be difficult to understand, because he sometimes uses unfamiliar terms, and other times he gives terms his own unique meanings without fully explaining what they are.

Moreover, in his letters, Paul often defends himself or his message from attacks. We don't know what these attacks were, since all we have is Paul's response to them. However, Paul isn't impossible to understand; in most cases, Paul speaks clearly and directly. We simply have to pay careful attention to make sure we understand what Paul is saying.

The Letters Give General Principles

It will help our understanding if we remember that Paul wrote in a different time and place, with different cultural rules and assumptions. This creates problems when people attempt to apply what Paul says to our own time. We have to look for the general principle in what Paul says rather than his specific instructions.

For example, Paul says in 1 Corinthians 11:4–6 that at church meetings, a man must always pray with his head uncovered, while a woman must have her head covered. This rule actually has nothing to do with the value of prayer. Instead, it reflects the culture of Paul's day. People considered it immodest and provocative for a woman's head to be uncovered in public. Paul's point was not that it is necessary for a woman to cover her head to be heard by God. Rather, he means that Christians should not upset their neighbors by behaving in ways that will offend them. Today, Western society no longer finds it offensive for women's hair to be visible (although many Islamic cultures still follow this practice), so it's not important whether it's covered in church or not.

The principle found in this passage is that Christians should respect other's feelings. This principle is timeless and applies equally well in any cultural situation. The concrete instruction Paul derives from this principle, however, does not. We need to look for these general principles in Paul and not be distracted by specific rules that no longer make sense in our own culture.

Written under the inspiration of the same Holy Spirit that guided the growth of the early Church, Paul's letters are relevant to Christians of every generation. Through careful study, we can hear in these letters the voice of the apostle, sharing the Gospel and inviting us to join him on a journey of faith. Paul's letters can also help us in very practical ways to become better Christians and better people. When we read these letters, we recapture the excitement and sense of discovery of the early Christians, and in so doing, renew our own faith and our commitment to living a life centered on the Gospel.

Have You *Considered*?

1. Imagine hearing only one side of a telephone conversation. What would the problems be in understanding what was said?
2. Describe a time when you had to write an important letter to someone. What was the situation? How did things turn out?
3. The general principle we found in the passage from 1 Corinthians is that Christians should behave in ways that don't offend their neighbors. What would be a specific application of that principle be today?

MORE ABOUT THE TEXT

Paul's Time and Culture

Paul's primary concern in his letters was with the truth of Jesus Christ, which, in its essence, is beyond cultural differences. But faith is always expressed in terms of the time and culture of the believer. When a true principle is acted out, the form of the action will be different from culture to culture. This is especially true for many questions about behavior and what various choices reflect about Christian principles.

Some of Paul's answers today might look quite different if he were writing in Africa or Japan. (And we would still have trouble understanding them in the United States.) So it is important when reading Paul to distinguish between timeless truths and behavioral notions related to social standards of the day. (All of Paul's statements about women and marriage need to be considered with these distinctions in mind.)

Paul's Timeless Themes

Paul's letters were addressed to communities experiencing very concrete struggles. To answer those specific situations, Paul offered basic themes on (a) how Christians should live, (b) the need for unity among Christians, (c) freedom from the Law and from sin, and (d) the grace given through Jesus' death.

These themes run through all of Paul's writings, and they are as important for us today as they were for his missionary communities almost 2,000 years ago. In this section, you'll study these themes as they appear in Paul's letters to four churches: Thessalonians, Galatians, Corinthians, and Romans.

Learning Objectives for Section Two

By the end of this section, you will be able to:

- Explain Paul's views on Christian living.
- Discuss Paul's teaching on the Law.
- Explain what Paul says about right relations with God.
- Understand the relevance of Paul's themes to Christian living.

◆ The Thessalonian Letters

Paul's earliest letter is 1 Thessalonians, probably written in 51 C.E. Both 1 and 2 Thessalonians reflect the situation in the Thessalonian church, and give us a glimpse of Paul's relationship with this community. In these letters, we see Paul's first important theme: the need for Christians to live moral lives.

The Church in Thessalonica

Thessalonica was a seaport in the north of Greece and the capital of the province of Macedonia. Geographically, it was important because it was situated on the *Via Egnatia*, the main road connecting the eastern portion of the empire to the west. Paul's visit there probably lasted several months.

Paul shows great affection for the community at Thessalonica. He says:

For what is our hope or joy or crown to boast of in the presence of our Lord Jesus at his coming if not you yourselves? For you are our glory and joy.
(1 Thessalonians 2:19–20)

In this spirit of mutual love, Paul reminds the Thessalonians that his assistant Timothy has just brought news to him of their faith and love. Paul tells the Thessalonians that he longs to see them.

The Parousia

This does not mean that things were perfect among the new Christians in Thessalonica. Disputes had come up, and Paul was needed to settle them. One important controversy was over the second coming of Jesus, a doctrine called the *parousia* (a Greek word which means "presence").

Early Christians believed that Jesus would come again soon to judge people and to establish the kingdom of God in all its fullness. This idea was an important part of early Christian preaching. New Christians looked forward to the parousia with

---

MORE ABOUT THE TEXT

Coming to Thessalonica

The first letter to the Thessalonians marks a change in Paul's missionary career. As Paul began his second journey, Barnabas left to return to Cyprus (Acts 15:36–41). Paul was now the head of the missionary team (so to speak). He chose Silvanus (Silas) and Timothy (Acts 16:1–3) to travel with him.

Paul arrived in Greece, and around 50 C.E. began his preaching in Philippi. He succeeded in making converts there and soon expanded his mission to nearby Thessalonica. Because of his success, Paul was persecuted by Jews and Gentiles alike. He was forced to flee to Athens after one particularly vicious attack, but sent Silvanus and Timothy back to strengthen the community. Timothy's report to Paul is the reason for the first letter.

LESSON THREE
(pages 237–240)

◆ The Thessalonian Letters

Welcome

What to Do

Say: "From all you have learned so far, what kinds of problems do you think Paul's communities might have had? Use your imagination. Make some educated guesses." List their comments on the board.

Pray with your students.

Introducing the Lesson

In the letters to the Thessalonians and Galatians, Paul offers these communities answers to some of the problems that they were experiencing. As students read Paul's letters they need to realize that they are responding to particular concerns, and are not making attempts to work out a full theological treatment of Christian belief.

Teaching Objectives

By the end of this lesson students will be able to:
- Explain the importance of understanding the context of Paul's letters in understanding their content.
- Describe the key points presented in the Letters to the Thessalonians.
- Explain the significance of the Letter to the Galatians.

What to Do

Hold a one-way phone conversation. See Teacher's Resource 13C for an example.

Ask students to identify what took place in this conversation. Who was the second person in the conversation? What questions were asked or statements were made to elicit the responses you gave? You could have been speaking to anyone. You decide. How does changing the audience change the meaning of the conversation?

Have the students read the opening italics and the Learning Objectives.

Development

What to Do

1. Have the students find Thessalonica on the map on page 256. Have them then look at the map

on page 217 and find out which ones of Paul's journeys might have included Thessalonica and the approximate dates of those journeys.

2. Have the students read the opening paragraph in "The Thessalonian Letters" and the subsection "The Church in Thessalonica."

3. Read 1 Thessalonians 1:1–5. Ask: "How would you describe the relationship between Paul and the Thessalonians?

4. Have the students read "The Parousia." Read 1 Thessalonians 4:13–18 and 5:1–11, to get the full flavor of Paul's comments about the Parousia.

5. Distribute Teacher's Resource 13B and have everyone read it. What do students think about the Second Coming and the resurrection of the dead?

6. Have the students read "Moral Living."

7. Form small groups. Have each group choose several of Paul's instructions and apply them to appropriate situations.

8. Lead a class discussion of the questions in "Have You Considered?"

Practicing the Skills

What to Do
Have the students read 1 Thessalonians 4:9–12 and 5:12–22. What do students think about Paul's approach?

Have You Considered?

1. When students are finished offering their answers, dissect the images presented. How many of the images come from scripture or the teaching tradition of the Church, and how many from western art and the media?

2. Steer students away from "because we have to" kinds of answers.

eagerness and excitement. They hoped for the end of this age, when they were a small, persecuted minority. More importantly, they looked forward to meeting Jesus. Soon, the idea of the second coming began to dominate the Thessalonian Church. Questions and disagreements about it, however, began to divide the church. Paul addressed this conflict.

What About the Dead?   The Thessalonians worried about what would happen to the members of their community who had already died. Would they be included in the kingdom? Paul assured them that both the living and the dead will join Jesus on the great day to come.

> For the Lord himself, with a word of command, with the voice of an archangel and with the trumpet of God, will come down from heaven, and the dead in Christ will rise first. Then we who are alive, who are left, will be caught up together with them in the clouds to meet the Lord in the air. Thus we shall always be with the Lord. Therefore, console one another with these words.
>
> (1 Thessalonians 4:16–17)

Through these vivid images, Paul reassured the community that all its members, living and dead, share in the love of Christ. In fact, death makes no difference at all; once joined to Christ, a person belongs to him forever.

When Will Jesus Return?   Excited by Paul's description of the coming day, many Thessalonians wanted to know when to expect Jesus' return. Paul told them that no one knows the precise date, but

Unknown, *Bacchus*, Second Century B.C.E.?

Moral conduct was not a part of the Greek or Roman religions. The Romans, in fact, worshipped the god Bacchus by drinking great amounts of wine and overeating.

that God's purposes are certain. The important thing is knowing that it will happen. Not satisfied, some Thessalonians concluded that the parousia was coming any day, and quit their jobs to wait. The second letter has to lay down the law: "if anyone was unwilling to work, neither should that one eat." (2 *Thessalonians* 3:10).

Moral Living

Paul said that the proper way to prepare for the parousia is to live a life worthy of approval by Christ. To do that, Christians should always live moral, loving lives. Our energies should go into preparing for Jesus, rather than worrying about when he will come.

Many Gentiles found this to be an unfamiliar message, since Greek and Roman religion generally did not make any connection between one's religious belief and moral behavior. Paul stressed repeatedly that being Christian meant living a life centered on the Gospel.

> This is the will of God, your holiness: that you refrain from immorality, that each of you know how to acquire a wife for himself in holiness and honor, not in lustful passion as do the Gentiles who do not know God; not to take advantage of or exploit a brother in this matter, for the Lord is an avenger in all these things, as we told you before and solemnly affirmed. For God did not call us to impurity but to holiness. Therefore, whoever disregards this, disregards not a human being but God, who [also] gives his holy Spirit to you.
>
> (1 Thessalonians 4:3–8)

Paul urged the Thessalonians to do good, because God wills it and in preparation for Jesus' return. This message is as important for us today as it was for the Thessalonians. Paul reminds us that being Christian is not just a matter of going to Church. It also means living responsible moral lives, centered first on love of God and next on love of others.

Have You Considered?

1. Using your imagination, what do you think the parousia will be like? How do you envision judgment taking place?

2. Suppose you met someone who had just become a Christian, and she asked you what Paul meant by saying that Christians must lead moral lives. What would you say?

MORE ABOUT THE TEXT

To the Galatians
Many of Paul's letters were written to Christian communities that he founded in cities. While we know much about the cities of Ephesus, Phillipi, Thessalonica, and Corinth, the location of the Christian community in Galatia is not so well understood.

Galatia is a general geographic area in Asia, not a city. To complicate matters, southern Galatia was a Roman province, while northern Galatia was held by various rulers. Paul had founded communities in both provinces; the letter could be addressed to either. If Paul was writing to the northern communities, scholars date the letter in 54 or 55 C.E. If he was writing to the southern communities, the letter was written as early as 49–50 C.E.

◆ The Letter to the Galatians

In Galatians, we see a very different side of Paul's personality. In the Thessalonian letters, Paul was like a proud father gently urging his children to make further progress. In Galatians, Paul is clearly angry, and his words are blistering. He is responding to charges made against him after he left the community, and he can't understand how the Galatians could question him or his message so soon after his departure. In Paul's most forceful letter, the apostle firmly restates his message to refute his critics and remove any doubt the Galatians might have.

The Churches in Galatia

Unlike Thessalonians, the Letter to the Galatians is probably not directed to a single community. Instead, it is written for a group of churches in the area of Asia Minor called "Galatia." You may remember from Chapter 12 that on each of his missionary journeys, Paul passed through this area, so the communities here probably saw more of Paul than any others. This fact may account for part of Paul's anger.

The people of Galatia were actually not Greeks at all, even though they spoke the language. They were "Gauls," Germanic tribes from the north who had been accepted into the empire. They were known for their courage and enthusiasm. They also seemed to have had trouble making a lasting commitment, explaining, in part, Paul's frustration with them.

Unknown, *Sacrifice to the Gods*, First Century C.E.

The Gentiles and the Law

After Paul had left the Galatian churches, some other Christian missionaries arrived in the area. These missionaries were apparently Jewish-Christians, perhaps members of the Pharisee party. They insisted that the Gentile Galatian converts be circumcised and obey the other laws of Moses as part of their conversion to Christianity. While some Galatians were persuaded by these arguments, Paul angrily rejected them.

Paul reminded the Galatians of what had happened in 49 C.E., when he and Barnabas went to Jerusalem to meet with the other apostles. He tells them that the apostles approved making Gentiles full members of the Christian community without forcing them to obey the Jewish law (See Acts 15:1–21).

Paul then tells of another incident not recorded in Acts. Paul says that after the Council, Peter went to Antioch and ate with the Gentile Christians there. When Jewish-Christians from Jerusalem arrived and complained about the practice, Peter pulled back. Paul then rebuked Peter:

> If you who are a Jew are living according to Gentile ways rather than Jewish, by what logic do you force the Gentiles to adopt Jewish ways?
>
> (Galatians 2:14)

Paul asserts throughout Galatians that both Jews and Gentiles have salvation because of Jesus' death on the cross, not because of the Law. For that reason, Paul asserts, it is unnecessary for Gentiles to become Jewish. Jews may follow the Law, because it is their custom, but they have no right to force it on the Gentiles.

In Roman worship, animals sacrificed to the gods were then eaten by the worshippers. Whether or not Christians could eat food sacrificed to the gods was a question addressed by Paul in 1 Corinthians 8.

MORE ABOUT THE TEXT

Writing Letters

Remind students that Paul most probably dictated his letters and did not write them on paper himself. Language scholars tell us that the Greek used in Galatians is very rough and difficult to translate. Apparently, Paul was so angry that his words tumbled over one another too fast and too furiously for the scribe to improve or clarify.

Paul's anger is the result of his intense caring for the people of Galatia, somewhat like the anger a parent may feel when a child has endangered his or her life and barely escaped. Encourage the students to feel the force of Paul's caring as well as his fury.

◆ The Letter to the Galatians

Development

What to Do

1. Have the students read the introductory paragraph to "The Letter to the Galatians" and "The Churches in Galatia." Then have a strong reader proclaim the blistering language of Galatians 3:1–5. How are these comments different from those to the Thessalonians? Have the students complete the "Scripture Workshop" on page 240.

2. Have the students locate Asia on the map on page 231. What does that tell them about the location of Galatia? (Near the Black Sea.) Have them find on the map on page 217 how many of Paul's missionary journeys seem to have passed through Galatia. (Paul's second and third journeys went through Galatia.)

3. Form small groups. Have the students complete "Bible Activity" number 3, reading Galatians 1—2:1–14.

4. Have the students read "The Gentiles and the Law" and "Abraham, the Father of the Gentiles." Does this concur with their own reading of Galatians 1 and 2? Is anything different? Have the students look at Galatians 3:6–14 for the piece about Abraham.

5. Read both "Slaves No Longer" and Galatians 5:13–26. Discuss what it means to be free to love. Have them write a paragraph in their Spiritual Journal describing their ability to love and then imagine what Paul might say to them.

6. Lead a class discussion of the questions in "Have You Considered?"

7. Pray with your students using ideas from 1 Thessalonians 9–12. That is, they pray for these things.

Recall

Have the students look at their list of possible problems in Paul's communities (on the board) and add what they have learned in this lesson, and remove anything that is contradictory to today's learning.

Have the students write their answers to "Chapter 13 Review Q/A," Section Two questions 1–8.

Connect

What to Do

Ask: "What is the single most interesting idea you have learned today? Write it down in a sentence or two." Have them take this idea home and explain it to someone in the family, finding out what they think of it and, if it fits, sharing parts of Paul's letters with that family member.

What's Next?

What to Do

Have the students locate and mark the beginning of 1 and 2 Corinthians and Romans in their Bibles. Say: "These are our topics for tomorrow."

Have You *Considered*?

1. Jewish-Christians might argue that Jesus was the Jewish Messiah, and that he fulfilled the Jewish scriptures; therefore, converts to Christianity should likewise first become Jews and obey the Jewish Law. Paul responds that Jews and Gentiles are both saved by Jesus' death on the cross, not through the Law.

2. Before Jesus, the Gentiles were just as incapable as the Jews of living fully moral lives and earning salvation. In this sense, they were slaves to sin.

Bonus Focus for You ———

Read Galatians 6:1–5 and reflect on its significance for your teaching and your relationship with your students. Write your reflections in your journal.

Scripture *Workshop*

1. The Thanksgiving element of the format is missing.

2. Paul replaces the thanksgiving with an attack on the foolishness of the Galatians for deserting the message he had given them.

3. Paul is angry, and does not want to hide his feelings.

Scripture Workshop

The Letter to the Galatians

Review the format for Paul's letters covered earlier in this chapter. Then, read Galatians 1. Answer the following questions:

- Which element of the format is missing?
- With what does Paul replace it?
- What does this tell you about the tone of the letter?

Abraham, the Father of the Gentiles

Paul uses the example of Abraham to make his case that the Gentiles are justified before God, apart from the Law. His Jewish-Christian opponents would of course have to admit that Abraham, the father of the Hebrew people, was someone who was acceptable to God. Paul then posed the question, Was Abraham justified through the Law? Obviously, the answer had to be "No," since Abraham lived hundreds of years before Moses and the gift of the Law on Mount Sinai. Paul says that if Abraham could enter a relationship with God apart from the Law, then so can the Gentiles.

Paul further asserts that the Old Testament predicted that Abraham would become the father of the Gentiles who are justified through faith.

> *Scripture, which saw in advance that God would justify the Gentiles by faith, foretold the good news to Abraham, saying "Through you shall all nations be blessed." Consequently, those who have faith are blessed along with Abraham, who had faith.*
>
> (Galatians 3:7–9)

Through all of this, Paul does not mean that the Law is not good, or that Jews are wrong to obey it. He simply insists that adhering to the Law is not necessary to be a good Christian, and therefore the Galatians are wrong to insist that the Gentiles accept it.

Slaves No Longer

Paul compares the function of the Law to that of a household slave whose responsibility was to educate and discipline children. Paul says that Christians no longer need the Law in this way, because they have been freed from it by Christ. Similarly, the Gentiles were slaves to the power of sin, but they, too, have been freed. From this point forward, Paul says, both Jew and Gentile should live as free people, no longer as slaves.

Called to a Higher Standard Living as a free person does not mean living without rules. Paul emphasizes, as he did in Thessalonians, that Christians are called to a high standard of action. Christian freedom is the freedom to live as brothers and sisters, knowing that all are united with Jesus in faith.

> *For all of you who were baptized into Christ have clothed yourselves with Christ. There is neither Jew nor Greek, there is neither slave nor free person, there is not male and female; for you are all one in Christ Jesus.*
>
> (Galatians 3:27–28)

Meaning of Freedom Christian freedom is another of Paul's great themes. Because of Jesus, Christians live in a new world, one in which sin no longer separates them from the full love of God. Christians are no longer under the power of sin, and can love one another fully and honestly.

What is Christian freedom? It is both a freedom **from** sin and a freedom **to** love. Most importantly, freedom is possible. For Paul, before Christ, human beings could not live as God asks, because the power of sin was too strong. Jesus delivered us from this power, and we now are free to love God. Despite all the forces and influences the world throws our way, Christian freedom allows us to act as children of God.

Have You Considered?

1. Put yourself in the position of Paul's Jewish-Christian opponents in Galatia. What arguments might you make to support your position that Gentile converts had to be circumcised? How does Paul, in his letter, respond to these arguments?

2. What do you suppose Paul meant when he said that before Jesus, the Gentiles had been "slaves to sin"?

◆ MORE ABOUT THE LESSON

Charges against Paul

Several charges may be involved here in Galatians: "currying favor" with the elite of society; false apostleship or false Gospel teaching; violating Jewish law without permission.

Paul replies that his apostleship and teaching is from Christ and has been approved by the first and chief Apostles (Peter [or Kephas], James, and John), that the Jewish law of circumcision need not be observed, and that the Galatians have been seduced away from the true understanding of Christianity that he preached to them. The controversies addressed here must have been hot topics in Galatia for Paul to respond as he did.

◆ The Letters to Corinth

Although there are two letters to the Corinthians in the New Testament, Paul probably wrote more than that to them. Paul spent two years among the Corinthians, and the community there had a special place in his heart. The first letter is Paul's response to unhappy news about what was going on in Corinth. The love and concern he felt for the Christians there is readily apparent.

The Corinthian community faced special challenges, many stemming from the city in which they lived. Corinth was one of the largest and most important cities in the Roman Empire. It was a major center for trade, so people were constantly moving. New philosophies and religious beliefs repeatedly swept through the city. Further, Corinthian citizens had a reputation for immoral behavior. The Greek verb "to corinthize" means to engage in sexual immorality. The city had more brothels and taverns than any other city in the empire. Given these forces competing for the people's attention, it's not surprising that several problems came up.

Competing Factions

There were quarreling factions within the Corinthian church. One cause of the fights seems to have been that people were claiming intense alle-

giance to different Christian leaders, such as Paul or another disciple named Apollos. It would be as if today some Christians claimed to follow Mother Theresa, while others followed Oscar Romero.

Paul does not object to the Corinthians admiring good leaders, but apparently they were saying things like "I'm better because I belong to Paul," or "I'm better because Apollos baptized me." Paul frowned on such childish rivalry. If loyalty to a particular teacher distracts you from your first loyalty to Christ, your allegiance is likewise misplaced.

Claims to Wisdom

Some individuals in the community acted with superiority, claiming to have received a higher knowledge. In Greek, the term for this special knowledge is *gnosis*. "Gnostics," people who claimed to have secret knowledge about the heavens, were common in the Roman Empire. Some Corinthians had combined gnostic ideas with their faith in Jesus.

Paul didn't directly say that the gnostics were wrong. Instead, he pointed out the difference between human wisdom and the wisdom that comes from God. Paul showed that worldly wisdom is not the same as God's wisdom. He used the case of the crucifixion of Christ to make this point.

Logically, how could a crucified man do anything for anyone? According to conventional wisdom, Jesus was powerless to help anybody. Nevertheless, the Corinthians had experienced changes in their lives because of their faith in Jesus. Since Jesus was cruci-

Paul stayed with the community in Corinth for over two years. His letters back to the community addressed issues of jealousy, Gnostic beliefs, morality, the importance of the Eucharist, and the need for the community to be one.

MORE ABOUT THE TEXT

The Church in Corinth

Paul established the Christian community in Corinth on his second journey, about 51 C.E. Corinth was a commercial center for the eastern part of the Roman Empire and was marked by the diversity of nationalities and faiths gathered there. As has been the case with seaports throughout history, Corinth was a city where any and all vices could be fulfilled.

Acts 18:1–8 suggests that Paul was at first well received by the Jewish community in Corinth, only to have them later turn against him. Paul next began to preach to the Gentiles where he found much greater success, especially among the poor and underprivileged. (From this you can better understand Paul's anger with the divisiveness at the Eucharist between rich and poor.)

SECTION TWO

LESSON FOUR
(pages 241–245)

◆ The Letters to Corinth

Welcome

What to Do

Greet students using 1 Corinthians 1:3–5.

Have the students look again at the list of possible problems in Paul's communities, which they made during the previous lesson. Ask: "How did Paul answer some of these problems?" Refer to the list as you work through today's session.

Pray with your students. Read Ephesians 3:14–21 as your class prayer.

Introducing the Lesson

Teaching Objectives

By the end of this lesson students will be able to:
• Demonstrate the understanding of the key issues presented in the letters to the Corinthians.
• Explain Paul's response in the Letter to the Romans to the important issues faced by that community.

What to Do

Using the map on page 217, have the students locate Corinth and determine which missionary journeys Paul took there and their dates; have them check the timeline, page 228, for the approximate dates of writing for Corinthians. Note that the letters were probably written between the two journeys.

Development

Students will develop a feel for Paul's concern for the community in Corinth.

What to Do

1. Have the students read the first two paragraphs of "The Letters to Corinth" and 1 Corinthians 1:1–9 and 3:1–3. Ask: "What was Paul's basic attitude toward the Christians in Corinth?"

2. Say: "The community in Corinth faced a number of difficult problems which Paul attempts to resolve in these letters. Paul's response here is not a well-ordered list, however. You can sense some of Paul's anxiety

about these Christians in the chaotic nature of these letters." Have the students read "Competing Factions" and "Claims to Wisdom" and discuss why these issues would have been problematic.

3. Have the students read "Immorality" and 1 Corinthians 5:9–11; 6:12–20. Ask the students to apply what they find here to today's questions and problems. Begin by having students name the key elements of what they read, writing their findings on the board. Then ask them to find a current issue to which Paul's comments can be applied. If Paul's themes are applied, how does the current problem change?

4. Have the students read "The Eucharist" and "Christian Unity." Compare 1 Corinthians 11:17–34 with the words of Consecration of the bread and wine in each of the four Eucharistic prayers (see Teacher's Resource 13D). Ask, "Which of the words have been considered most important by the Church? How do you know?"

5. Ask a volunteer to proclaim 1 Corinthians 12 for the class. Encourage the students to savor its beauty as well as understanding its ideas.

6. In small groups, have the students complete "Bible Activity" number 1, then share their findings with the class.

7. Lead the class discussion of the questions in "Have You Considered?"

Practicing the Skills

Students will be asked to stretch their minds to understand a difficult passage, even if they can't quite "get it" the first time.

What to Do

Form small groups. Have the students read 1 Corinthians 1:17 2:16. Each group is to write a paragraph explaining what they learn from these verses. Then read subsection "Claims to Wisdom," and ask students to compare their understanding with their text.

Some of the Christians in Corinth behaved at the Eucharist as if it were a common party. In his response to this problem, Paul retells the story of the Last Supper.

fied according to the wisdom of God, Paul says that "God's folly is wiser than men" (1 *Corinthians* 1:25), and therefore arguments over which Christians are the wisest make no sense. Paul concludes:

> God chose the foolish of the world to shame the wise, and God chose the weak of the world to shame the strong, and God chose the lowly and despised of the world, those who count for nothing, to reduce to nothing those who are something, so that no human being might boast before God. . . . "Whoever boasts should boast in the Lord."
>
> (1 Corinthians 1:26–28,31)

Immorality

In view of the general situation in Corinth, it's not surprising that Paul should have to reaffirm his views on moral living. For one thing, incest of varying degrees was practiced by certain Corinthian Christians, along with many other kinds of immoral behavior, including:

- Robbery
- Drunkenness
- Adultery
- Idolatry

Paul not only rejects such behavior, but says the community should be responsible for the behavior of its members. Christians should be helped by love and correction, but if they persist in wrongdoing, Paul says they should be expelled from the community.

The Eucharist

Early Christians often met together for a common meal before they celebrated the formal Eucharist. This common meal was often called the "agape," or "love feast." In Corinth, some Christians treated the agape like a common party, drinking wine until they were drunk. As a result, they could not celebrate the Eucharist properly. Then, as now, the Eucharist was intended to honor Christ, but these people were fighting, rushing to their food, and causing chaos.

In response, Paul wrote the earliest record we have of Jesus' words at the Last Supper (probably around 55 C.E.). This passage is found in 1 Corinthians 11:17–34. Given the special character of the Eucharist as a time to remember and honor Jesus, Paul demands that the Corinthians behave appropriately.

Christian Unity

Underlying all these other problems, Paul saw one major challenge: the need for Christian unity. Quarreling, boasting, immorality and poor behavior at the Eucharist were all signs that the Corinthians weren't living as a true community, working for the good of all. Paul says that Christ is present in the whole community, all the Christians together. Splitting the unity of the membership, Paul says, is a sin against Christ.

To make his point about the importance of unity, Paul uses the famous analogy of the body. The Christian community, Paul says, is the body of Christ. If the toe were gone, the whole body would be in trouble. Conversely, the toe has no life apart from the body. Therefore, the community needs each member, and each member needs the community. God gives different gifts to different people, Paul says, but all these gifts are of equal value in keeping the community whole.

Unity is the third great theme in Paul's letters. Paul says that all members of the community should make unity their highest goal:

> If [one] part suffers, all the parts suffer with it; if one part is honored, all the parts share its joy.
>
> (1 Corinthians 12:26)

Have You Considered?

1. Do you think there are factions in the Church today, as in ancient Corinth? Why or why not?
2. Do you agree with Paul that unity is the answer to all the other problems of the community? Do you think that many of the world's problems would be lessened if we all lived as a community? Why or why not?

◆ **MORE ABOUT THE LESSON**

The Eucharist

Corinthians 11:23–26—"Jesus, on the night he was handed over, took bread, and after he had given thanks, broke it and said, 'This is my body that is for you. Do this in remembrance of me.' In the same way, also the cup, after supper, saying, 'This cup is the new covenant in my blood. Do this, as often as you drink it, in remembrance of me.'"

Eucharistic Prayer II—"(H)e took bread and gave you thanks. He broke the bread, gave it to his disciples, and said: 'Take this, all of you, and eat it: this is my body which will be given up for you.' When supper was ended, he took the cup. Again he gave you thanks and praise, gave the cup to his disciples, and said: 'Take this, all of you, and drink from it: this is the cup of my blood, the blood of the new and everlasting covenant.'"

◆ The Letter to the Romans

When Paul wrote to Rome, he was writing to a community he had neither founded nor visited, although he did know some people there. In Romans 16, he greets a number of people by name, including Prisca and Aquila. Even so, this is not his community. Instead, he is expressing his joy at being able to visit them for the first time.

Since Romans is a letter of introduction rather than a response to a specific crisis, it is Paul's most carefully developed writing. He wants to explain his message to the Romans before he arrives.

Romans is a very complex letter. In it, Paul expresses his understanding of Jesus and the Christian message. Sometimes his reasoning is not easy to follow. You may have difficulty understanding it as you read it for the first time. You will want to return to Romans repeatedly in your life to gain a deeper understanding of its message.

Conflict between Gentiles and Jews

You already know about the tensions between Jewish-Christians and Gentile-Christians. Jewish-Christians in Rome continued to insist that Gentiles must obey the Law of Moses and all of its interpretations. Paul responds to this by concentrating on how a person enters into a right relationship with God. Paul used the words "righteousness," "justification," and "justice" to express this relationship.

For Jews, the answer to the question, What makes us acceptable to God? was fulfilling the demands of the Law. Paul pointed out that there are simply too many commands, and no human can keep them all perfectly.

If the Law can't make us acceptable to God, then, what can? Paul's answer is simple: God makes us acceptable through "grace" which we receive through faith in Christ.

The Grace of God

According to Paul, "All have sinned and are deprived of the glory of God" (*Romans* 3:23). For imperfect human beings, it is impossible to **earn** a right relationship with God. God must give it to us. God's gift depends, not on our behavior, but on our faith. God offers us the gift of faith, and when we accept it, we are "justified." Then we may enjoy a proper relationship with God. This justification comes to us as a free gift, and has nothing to do with whether we "deserve" it on the basis of our behavior.

This gift springs from God's unconditional love for all people. Paul saw it most clearly in Jesus who freely gave of his life. Paul called God's free gift,

Shrines and statues to all of the gods could be found in the Pantheon in Rome. It was in a similar pantheon in Athens that Paul claimed the "unnamed god" as the God which he proclaimed.

MORE ABOUT THE TEXT

Systematic Thought

Romans has long been considered Paul's most important and consequential letter. It is by far the longest and most systematic presentation of his thought. This letter was not written to a familiar community, or written in response to some crisis or other. Romans is different. In Romans, Paul presents a much more fully developed theological presentation of the Christian faith.

This letter speaks of salvation and justification through faith in Christ. Paul states that just as God's wrath is against all wickedness and sin, whether committed by a Jew or a Gentile, God's power to save all people is experienced through Jesus. Paul expresses the hope that some day, all Israel will be saved through God's mercy.

---

4. Have the students write the answers to "Bible Activity" number 4. Ask volunteers to share their answers and give the verses which support their ideas.

5. Read Romans 5:1–11 to fill out the details already presented in the text.

6. Have them read Romans 8:14–17 and 8:28–39. Ask: "What do you understand from these passages?" Point out especially 8:28 and 8:38–39. Ask for your students' responses to Paul's intense assurance. Would it be a good basis for security in their lives? Ask: "Do you think Paul knew these assurances were true?" Then have them read 2 Corinthians 11:22–29. Ask: "How do you think a person can go through all that pain and still believe what you just read in Romans? How does it make you feel about your own future?"

7. Lead the class discussion of the questions in "Have You Considered?"

Recall

Have the students look again at the list of possible problems faced in the Christian communities and Paul's responses to them. Add to the list as necessary and delete what no longer fits. Then ask them to indicate Paul's responses to the newly mentioned problems.

Have the students write their answers to "Chapter 13 Review Q/A," Section Two questions 9–14.

Connect

What to Do

Have the students write a paragraph taking one of Paul's big ideas (of their choice) and telling how it applies to their own life.

Ask the students to complete the "Spiritual Reflection" at home and write their responses in their Spiritual Journal. Encourage them to take their time and be comfortable with it.

People of Note

Prisca and Aquila

Among the people Paul sends greetings to in his letter to the Romans are those who meet in the house church of Prisca and Aquila. This couple is mentioned six times in the New Testament. They worked alongside Paul in the leather trade in Corinth before moving to Rome.

Prisca and Aquila may have been slaves of a Roman family who managed to buy their own freedom. As the leaders of a house church in Rome, their worldly status had risen greatly. Under Roman law, however, freed slaves still owed loyalty to their masters, and Prisca and Aquila risked angering them by openly practicing Christianity.

Interestingly, Paul always mentions the female name, Prisca, first, suggesting that her importance in the Church surpassed that of her husband, a degree of equality unusual for that time.

"grace," meaning that it happens without cost to us. A right relationship with God is the most profound and beautiful gift possible. Paul sums up his argument this way:

> Therefore, since we have been justified by faith, we have peace with God through our Lord Jesus Christ, through whom we have gained access [by faith] to this grace in which we stand, and we boast in hope for the glory of God. . . . How much more then, since we are now justified by his blood, will we be saved through him from the wrath. Indeed, if while we were enemies, we were reconciled to God through the death of his Son, how much more once reconciled, will we be saved by his life.

(Romans 5:1–2,9–10)

Living in Grace

Paul says our behavior has nothing to do with our justification; there's nothing we can do to deserve it. Because God has chosen to freely give us justification, when we accept this gift we should respond by honoring God in the way we live. After Christians have received justification, they still grow actively in living the Gospel. The basic challenge to that growth is sin, and the way we overcome it is grace.

Sin, Paul said, came into the world through one person's disobedience (Adam), and this act brought death. Through the obedience of Christ, grace has now entered the world, bringing life. Because we now live in grace, Paul says, our actions take on a special importance. We want to strive to love God and one another totally, because God's grace offers total love to us. In fact, we are the adopted children of God, and

This plastic reconstruction of ancient Rome can be found in the Rome Museum of Civilization. Paul's missionary journeys ended in Rome where he was martyred during the persecutions of Nero in 65 C.E.

MORE ABOUT THE TEXT

A Little Help from His Friends

Paul's ministry was very successful; the two thousand-year history of the Church proves it. But while Paul deserves a great deal of credit for his work and thought, it is important that students recognize that Paul did not work alone. Paul was able to proclaim the Gospel as effectively as he did because he had help. Not just Barnabas or Timothy, but also many other special "ordinary" people like Prisca and Aquila.

Prisca (or as she is called in Acts 18:2, Priscilla) and Aquila worked with Paul in Corinth. It is quite likely that they were influential in bringing Paul to Rome. When the Emperor Claudius ordered the expulsion of the Jews from Rome in 49 C.E. because of a fight over the messiahship of Jesus, it is very probable that Prisca and Aquila were forced to leave as well, taking refuge in Corinth. They later were to befriend Paul there and help him find work.

we inherit everything Christ was and has. Whatever troubles Christians may have to go through are nothing compared with the wonders they will experience when they are perfected in Christ's glory. Through the grace given by the Holy Spirit, Christians can live in total confidence that God will be with them always. Grace is Paul's fourth major theme. Paul's concept of grace sums up his understanding of God as merciful, patient, and most of all, completely loving.

We have looked at four major themes in Paul's teaching:

- The importance of moral living
- Freedom from the Law and from sin
- Christian unity
- The grace of God

Taken together, these four themes point the way to proper Christian living, and give us confidence that we can meet its demands. Paul's letters have inspired generations of Christians to deepen their faith and to grow in love of God and each other. If we read them with patience and prayer, they can do the same for us.

Have You Considered?

1. Do you agree with Paul that it is impossible for anyone to keep the Law absolutely perfectly? Why or why not?
2. Where have you heard the word "grace" before? What does it mean to you? How close is your understanding to the way Paul used the word?
3. Assume you have a friend who worries about whether she'll be saved by God. Using the idea of grace as expressed in Romans, how would you reassure her?

Spiritual Reflection

The Love of God

Paul spoke often of the love God offers us through Christ. In 1 Corinthians, Paul described what the love of God is like. For your spiritual reflection in this chapter, pray that God's love may enter you and guide you, using this passage as the focus for your prayer.

Go to a quiet place, and take a few moments to ask God to share his love with you. Then, read the following passages from 1 Corinthians.

> Love is patient, love is kind. It is not jealous, [love] is not pompous, it is not inflated, it is not rude, it does not seek its own interests, it is not quick-tempered, it does not brood over injury, it does not rejoice over wrongdoing but rejoices with the truth. It bears all things, believes all things, hopes all things, endures all things.
>
> (1 Corinthians 13:4–7)

Consider each phrase of the passage. Evaluate your own behavior using Paul's words. How can your life be changed by love?

When you are finished praying this passage, move on to the next part of 1 Corinthians.

> Love never fails. If there are prophecies, they will be brought to nothing, if tongues, they will cease, if knowledge, it will be brought to nothing. For we know partially and we prophesy partially, but when the perfect comes, the partial will pass away. When I was a child, I used to talk as a child, think as a child, reason as a child; when I became a man, I put aside childish things. At present we see indistinctly, as in a mirror, but then face to face. At present I know partially; then I shall know fully as I am fully known. So faith, hope, love remain, these three; but the greatest of these is love.
>
> (1 Corinthians 13:8–13)

As you pray this passage, ask God to reveal to you how you need to grow in love. Reflect on each verse, stopping when you feel the need. When you're finished, thank God for this time together, and then go on with your day.

What's Next?

What to Do

Read Ephesians 4:1–7; have the students rewrite the ideas as a prayer. Give them a few moments of quiet, then read the prayer together. Close with an "Amen."

Have You Considered?

1. Students should recognize that however hard we try, none of us is morally perfect, and therefore no one can keep the Law perfectly. For this reason, Paul's message that God has acted to save us despite our weakness and imperfection should come as a tremendous relief.

2. In modern English, "grace" has come to mean simply "elegance" or "charm." Students may be familiar with this use of the term. Students who have studied Romance languages will also know that "gracias" in Spanish and "grati" in Italian, both meaning "thank you," are forms of the same word. All of these uses are related to Paul's sense of what grace is: God's free gift of a right relationship to humanity. God's loving kindness is elegant, and the proper acknowledgment of this action is to say "thank you."

3. The friend should be assured that anxiety over our salvation is no longer necessary: God has saved us, completely apart from whether or not we deserve it. All we have to do is to accept God's free gift.

Bonus Focus for You ———

Read Philippians 2:12–14. Ponder long over each phrase, emphasizing those that strike your heart the most forcefully. Write your experience in your journal.

MORE ABOUT THE TEXT

Saved by Faith

Romans presents one doctrine that will be an unceasing source of consternation, the doctrine of justification by faith. Paul's argument (later picked up by Martin Luther and leading to the Protestant Reformation) is that salvation comes from Jesus' death and resurrection. There is no way that we can win salvation on our own; we must accept it simply as gift. Paul is here developing the argument he has repeatedly presented against those Jewish-Christians who demanded that Gentiles obey the Mosaic Law. Paul's point is that faithfulness to the Law (or good works) means nothing if there has not also been an internal conversion, a change of heart. Good works will be an automatic event after changing one's life and saying yes to Jesus. Paul is saying that good works are an effect, not a cause.

Q/A

Section One

1. Koine Greek was the universal language of the eastern Roman empire.

2. Most people were bilingual, speaking Greek and their local language; well-educated people would also be able to speak Latin.

3. Paul was equally at home with Jews and Gentiles because he spoke fluent Hebrew, was fluent in Greek, and was well educated.

4. Paul spoke with authority because Jesus had personally made him an Apostle.

5. Paul was a worker in leather goods.

6. Paul visited the local synagogue and spoke to the Jews gathered there when he entered a city.

7. The format of Paul's letters had five elements: (A) Opening, (B) Thanksgiving, (C) Message, (D) Conclusion, and (E) Final Blessing.

8. Disciples of Paul wrote books expanding his teaching and applying it to other situations, and some of these books came to regarded as "by" Paul.

9. With the possible exception of Romans, these are not carefully written literary works, but quick letters drafted to respond to specific problems in Paul's communities.

10. We are not quite sure in many cases what question is being addressed or what problem Paul is responding to, because we only see one side of the conversation.

11. We should look for general principles in Paul's letters, since the specific instructions will vary with the context.

Q/A

Section One

1. What was the universal language in the eastern Roman Empire?
2. How many languages were spoken by most people in the eastern empire?
3. Why was Paul equally at home with Jews and Gentiles?
4. How could Paul speak with authority about the risen Jesus?
5. What was Paul's trade?
6. What did Paul do first when he entered a new city?
7. Describe the format of Paul's letters.
8. How did books not written by Paul come to be ascribed to him?
9. Are Paul's letters careful literary works? Explain.
10. Why is it a problem for us that Paul's letters represent one side of a conversation?
11. In reading Paul's letters, should we look for general principles or specific instructions? Why?

Section Two

1. Which letter was Paul's earliest?
2. What questions did Paul answer about the parousia?
3. What is the connection between the parousia and Christian living?
4. Who were the Galatians?
5. What problems does Paul's letter to the Galatians address?
6. Describe Paul's confrontation with Peter in Antioch.
7. Explain Paul's argument about the Gentiles and Abraham.
8. What does Paul mean by "Christian freedom."
9. What were the special challenges faced by the church in Corinth?
10. What was Paul's teaching about true wisdom?
11. Explain Paul's analogy of the body.
12. What was Paul's reason for writing the letter to the Romans?
13. Define "grace."
14. According to Paul, can someone earn a right relationship with God? Why or why not?

BIBLE ACTIVITIES

1. In 1 Corinthians 14:20–33, Paul addresses an issue that has occurred in Corinth. The problem concerns glossolalia, the gift of speaking in tongues. Read this passage and answer the following questions:

- What is the problem Paul is concerned with?
- What does Paul say is the purpose of speaking in tongues?
- What concerns Paul about the Corinthians' behavior?
- How does Paul say speaking in tongues should be handled?

2. Some scholars have suggested that Chapter 16 of Romans was originally separate from the rest of the letter. Read chapters 15 and 16 of Romans together, referring to Paul's letter format as discussed in Section One of this chapter. Why might people think that Chapter 16 was a separate letter?

3. In Galatia, Paul not only had to respond to the arguments of the Jewish-Christian missionaries about Gentiles and the Law, he also had to defend himself against their charges. One such charge appears in Galatians 1:6–10. What is the charge in this passage? Based on what you know about Paul's teachings on Gentiles and the Law, why do you think this particular charge was made against him?

4. In Romans 7, Paul explains his view about the purpose of the Law. Read that passage and answer the following questions:

- Does Paul think the Law is good or bad?
- What negative consequences did the Law bring?
- How did the Law bring these consequences?
- What happened to the Law because of Christ?

BIBLE ACTIVITIES

1. Glossolalia
   a. Apparently, Christian congregations in Corinth were falling into chaos as everyone was trying to speak in tongues at once, and no one could understand what was going on.
   b. Paul says that tongues are a sign to the unbeliever.
   c. Paul is worried that unbelievers will walk into Christian services and believe that they are out of their minds.
   d. Paul says speaking in tongues is fine, but it should be done in an orderly fashion, with someone on hand to interpret.

2. Romans 15:30–33 is a conclusion and final blessing. Romans 16:1–16 is in the form of an opening, while 16:21–27 appears to be another closing and final blessing. This leads scholars to suspect that Chapter 16 was originally separate.

3. The charge in Galatians 1:6-10 is that Paul is simply trying to win approval from his

GLOSSARY

- **Elders**: Local leaders left in charge of a church community after Paul left.
- **Final Blessing:** Last element in Paul's letter format.
- **Freedom:** Christian freedom is both a freedom from sin and a freedom to give oneself totally in love.
- **Gnosis:** Greek word for "knowledge."
- **Grace:** God's free gift.
- **Greeting:** First element of Paul's letter format.
- **House Church:** Meeting place for early Christians, usually the home of a wealthy members.
- **Justification:** Right relationship with God, made possible by the death of Jesus.
- **Koine:** "Common" Greek spoken by most citizens of the eastern portion of the Roman empire.
- **Pax Romana:** "Roman peace."
- **Righteousness:** A term for a right relationship with God.
- **Thanksgiving:** Element in Paul's letter format in which Paul expresses his pride and gratitude to his community.

UNDERSTANDING MORE ABOUT:

Paul and Happiness

Early Christians loved Jesus because believing in him and living his way brought them great joy—so much joy, in fact, that sometimes they went to their deaths singing. Paul's letter to the Philippians resounds with great happiness.

This letter is a thank you note that Paul wrote to his friends in Philippi *(Philippians 4:10–14)*. Paul was in jail for preaching, and the Christians in Philippi had sent him gifts. He writes to them with obvious affection. He delights in them. Then in Philippians 4:4–9, Paul encourages them to be happy, to be joyful. He reminds them not to be nervous about life, but to ask God gratefully for everything they need. Then he tells them how to think, so, that peace and happiness will be theirs:

> *Whatever is true . . . honorable . . . just . . . pure . . . lovely . . . gracious; if there is any excellence . . . anything worthy of praise, think about these things. . . . Then the God of peace will be with you.*
> (Philippians 4:8–9)

This is Paul's prescription for joy: love Christ, rejoice in the Christian life, and think about wonderful things. Happiness will be yours then, in every circumstance.

Chapter 13 Review ◆ 247

Section Two

1. 1 Thessalonians is Paul's earliest letter, written in 51 C.E.
2. The term "Parousia" refers to the second coming of Jesus. Paul responded to questions about when it was coming and whether or not it had already happened.
3. Paul said Christians should live moral lives as the proper way to prepare for Jesus' return.
4. The Galatians were members of a variety of churches in the southern part of Asia Minor.
5. Paul is addressing the charges made by Jewish-Christian opponents, who argued that it was necessary for Gentile converts to follow the law of Moses.
6. Peter had been eating with Gentiles until some Jewish-Christians arrived and complained about his behavior. Paul rebuked Peter for backtracking on his commitment to the Gentiles.
7. Paul argued that since Abraham had been justified by faith before the giving of the Law, Gentiles could be justified by faith as well.
8. Christian freedom is brought about by the grace of Jesus.
9. Corinth was a city with a reputation for immoral behavior. Further, most of Paul's converts were Gentiles, who brought a Graeco-Roman background to Christianity.
10. Paul taught that true wisdom comes through God's revelation.
11. Paul said that just as the human body has various parts with different functions, all of which work together, the Church has members with different gifts, but they all must work together for the good of the body (the Church).
12. Paul was traveling to Rome to make his case before the Emperor, and he wrote Romans to introduce himself to the Christian community there.
13. Grace is God's free gift to humanity.
14. No one can earn salvation, because no human can live a perfect life.

audience, rather than speaking the word of God. Since Paul said that Gentiles did not have to obey the Law, it is possible to see why Jewish-Christians might make this charge against him. They might contend that Paul was simply trying to make it easy for the Gentiles to become Christians, rather than speaking what God's law truly commanded.

4. Romans 7
a. Paul says the Law is good; 7:12, "Yet the law is holy and the commandment is holy and just and good."

b. The Law brought about the knowledge of sin; by telling people what not to do, it created in them temptation.
c. Sin used the Law to bring about evil, by creating in humanity an evil impulse to sin.
d. Christians died to the Law through Christ, and so live in the power of the Spirit serving the risen Jesus. The Law has no power over them.

Chapter Overview

The New Testament grew out of the faith experience of the early Christian communities much as the Old Testament developed out of the faith of the Hebrew people. This is seen nowhere more clearly than in the letters presented in this chapter. While the letters can be studied on their own, this chapter presents them in the context of how they shaped Church practice and doctrine.

Teaching Objectives

By the end of this chapter students will be able to:

• Explain how the development of various Church offices can be traced through the Bible.

• Discuss how many of the letters in the New Testament were shaped by persecution.

• Demonstrate an understanding of the teaching presented in Hebrews, James, Peter, and Revelation.

Welcome

What to Do

Greet as many students as possible as they arrive. Mention to each something good you've recently heard about him or her.

Change the Bible prayer table before class. Point out to the students that a change has been made. Ask if they know what the symbolic items on it are called, what they symbolize, and why they are there with the Bible. If they don't, explain them. (See "More about the Lesson" on page 249.)

Pray with your students. Give thanks that they are part of the Church and students of the Bible, for their growth in faith, and for the Church's treasuring its tradition and keeping the Bible over the centuries so we can learn from it today.

CHAPTER

14

Christianity
Develops Roots

50

54–68 C.E.
● Emperor Nero

64
● Nero's Fire in Rome
● Persecution of Christians in Rome

65
● James
● 1 Peter

66–70
● Jewish revolt

69–79
● Emperor Vespasian

70
● Destruction of the Temple in Jerusalem

79–81
● Emperor Titus

79
● Eruption of Mount Vesuvius

80
● Construction of the Coliseum in Rome
● Hebrews

81–96
● Emperor Domitian

100   100
● 1 and 2 Timothy

125
● 2 Peter

Robert LaFollette. 1855–1925.

Legend
● World History
● Regional History
● Biblical History
● Books written

R obert LaFollette was a brilliant speaker; it was said that he could enter a room full of people completely opposed to everything he stood for, and before he left they'd be cheering for him at the top of their lungs. He was first a member of the United States House of Representatives, and then the Governor of Wisconsin. Later, he served as a United States Senator, and, in 1924, ran for President.

But LaFollette is best remembered for his ideas. He championed the interests of the common people—the farmers and the industrial laborers. As Governor, LaFollette based his administration on what he called the "Wisconsin Idea," a program for ensuring decent wages and protecting the rights of workers. Later, as a Senator and a presidential candidate, LaFollette argued that these policies should apply to the

MORE ABOUT THE TEXT

Robert LaFollette

Robert Marion LaFollette was born in 1855. He served as both governor of Wisconsin and United States senator. He was, for the first half of his life, a conservative Republican before becoming a progressive. After failing twice to win the governorship, LaFollette was finally elected in 1900, and reelected in 1902 and 1904. LaFollette's tenure in office led to vast changes in Wisconsin law in support of workers. The power of railroads was reduced, progressive tax laws were instituted, and a civil service system was introduced.

LaFollette sought the Republican nomination for President in 1912, but lost it when he had a temporary breakdown. He was invited by a conference for progressive political action to run for President in 1924 and garnered nearly 5 million votes.

entire country. To accomplish this, LaFollette said the government should regulate private wealth and use it for the public good.

Millions of Americans supported LaFollette. When he found that the Republican Party did not share his ideas, LaFollette and others formed the Progressive Party. For a while, it looked as if this third political party would stand on its own and compete with the Republicans and Democrats. With LaFollette at its head, they couldn't miss! Then, unexpectedly, LaFollette died in 1925. With him, the Progressive Party died as well. An attempt was made to revive the party in 1948, but its presidential candidate got fewer than a million votes, and it faded quietly into history.

What happened? Why did the Progressive Party come to such a quick end? The problem wasn't with its ideas, because much of LaFollette's program became law under President Franklin D. Roosevelt in the 1930s. So why did the party die? Most historians think it died because the Progressives grew so rapidly, and were successful so quickly that they never took time to build an organization. They went from campaign to campaign without preparing for the future. They didn't establish any local chapters or local leaders. The entire movement depended upon LaFollette personally. The party fell apart when he died. The Progressives had assumed that LaFollette's charisma would be enough. It wasn't.

The Early Church

Like the Progressive Party, many movements fade away after early triumphs because they never prepared for the future. The movement is unprepared for difficult times and, unable to respond to the challenge, breaks apart. Movements that last recognize when it's time to organize their ideas and structure its chain-of-command in order to address any problems that occur.

At the end of the first century, Christianity faced the need to establish roots. Christian missionaries, especially Paul, had achieved spectacular successes, and Christian communities thrived everywhere in the Roman Empire. However, these communities were young and unsure of the future. There were many internal arguments about who was in charge now that the apostles had died. Arguments erupted about how to interpret the teachings they had been given. These early communities also were being persecuted by the Roman government.

For Christianity to survive, it required new leadership after the death of the apostles, and a clarification of its basic teachings. Christians facing persecution also needed hope and consolation. The last several books in the New Testament, from Hebrews to Revelation, responded to these challenges.

Introducing the Lesson

The earliest Christian communities were loosely organized under the direction of a follower of one of the Apostles. These loose organizations soon developed into more formal structures. This is understandable. Although guided by the Holy Spirit, the Church is still a human institution. And human institutions succeed only through a structured operation. Help students recognize the natural growth that took place in the Church as witnessed in the letters being studied in this chapter.

What to Do
• Have the students read the opening spread. Discuss with students the implications of the story. What happened to the Progressive Party at the death of Robert LaFollette? Why did it collapse? What could have been done to prevent it from collapsing?
• Ask students to think about what they know with regard to the early Church. How was the Church then similar to the Progressive Party? What could have happened to the Church when its leaders died? What could the Church do to insure its continuation?

Using the Timeline
Have the students read the timeline, noting especially the dates the various books mentioned were written. Point out to students that all of the books that they will study in this chapter were written after the death of the two great leaders of the early Church, Peter and Paul (63 C.E.) and during the time when Christianity faced great persecution, both from the Romans and from the Jews.

◆ MORE ABOUT THE LESSON

Decorating the Bible Table
You will need to borrow or make a drawing or some other artistic presentation of the following items. On the Bible table you will want a stole, a miter or zuchetto (pink skullcap), and a veil. You can also place there pictures of saints and modern day deacons, bishops, priests, and widows.

The stole is the primary symbol of the priesthood; the miter and zuchetto are worn only by a bishop; and the "veil" is part of a Sister's habit (often the only part still worn by them today). They are on the Bible table to show that these offices in the Church have their roots in Scripture and that the Scripture is the book of the Church.

SECTION ONE

LESSON ONE (pages 248–252)

◆ Church Offices

Teaching Objectives

By the end of this lesson students will be able to:

• Discuss the development in the early Church of the offices of priest, deacon, and bishop.

• Explain the Office of Widow and its significance.

Development

What to Do

1. Have the students read the opening italics and Learning Objectives.

2. Ask: "Who are your student body officers? What are the purposes of their offices? How does someone get to be a student body officer?"

3. Say: "The Church also has offices, which are rooted in the Scripture. These offices have developed over the centuries, but what we have today began in the last part of the first century after the deaths of the first apostles."

4. Have the students read "Church Offices" and "The Bible in Context."

5. Ask: "Does your parish have a deacon? What is his role in the parish?" Have the students read Romans 16:1 and 1 Timothy 3:8–13. Your students will be interested in the biblical assumption that women are also deacons.

6. Examine the qualifications for deacons on page 251. Ask: "Do you think these are good qualifications for Christian leaders? Why or why not? What additional qualifications would you add?"

7. Have the students read 1 Timothy 5:3–16 about widows, and compare this passage with "The Office of Widows" in their text. Discuss why it was important for the Church to set up the Office of Widow. Is there need for the office still today?

SECTION ONE

50 C.E.–125 C.E.

Building for the Future

Rome, Catacomb of Priscilla, First Century?

The destruction of the Temple in 70 C.E., caused Christianity to begin its final move away from Judaism. Arguments between Christian and Jewish groups grew angrier. Because of these arguments, Rome recognized Christianity as a new and illegal religion, different from Judaism which was legal.

These changes produced many questions in the new Christian churches: how to respond to opposition from both Jews and Romans; how to settle arguments over teaching; how to maintain unity among various Christian communities? In this section, you'll study some of the ways Christianity responded to these challenges.

Learning Objectives for Section One

By the end of this section, you will be able to:

• Explain how the early Church developed the offices of deacon, presbyter, and bishop.

• Discuss the challenge of preserving apostolic teaching.

• Describe the nature of Roman persecution.

◆ Church Offices

In its earliest days, the apostles led the Christian community. Their authority came from their closeness to Jesus: they received his teaching directly. When disputes arose, the apostles resolved them, as at the Council of Jerusalem in 49 C.E. By the end of the first century C.E., however, most of the apostles had died. Peter and Paul died in the 60s in Rome. Tradition says that John was the last of the apostles, dying in the 90s. With their passing, new leaders for the Church had to be chosen with the authority to settle disputes and guide Christianity into the future. Several offices developed in response to these needs.

Deacons

The word *deacon* comes from the Greek term "diakonos," meaning "servant." We first hear of the office of deacon in the Book of Acts. Luke says that the growth of the church in Jerusalem was so rapid that the apostles were overwhelmed with the demands on their time and attention. They asked the community to appoint seven men who would care for the poor and distribute the community's resources. Luke describes the selection of the deacons:

> The proposal was acceptable to the whole community, so they chose Stephen, a man filled with faith and the Holy Spirit, also Philip, Prochorus, Nicanor, Timon, Parmenas, and Nicholas of Antioch, a convert to Judaism. They presented these men to the apostles who prayed and laid hands on them.
>
> (Acts 6:5–6)

Because of their Greek names, scholars believe the first deacons were all Hellenists. As you know from Chapter 12, the Hellenists left Jerusalem and spread the Gospel after Stephen was stoned to death by people angry at his teachings about the Temple. Philip, in Chapter 8 of Acts, makes an Ethiopian convert. These events show that the role of the deacons expanded to include preaching and teaching in addition to caring for the poor.

◆ MORE ABOUT THE LESSON

Deacons

Translations of the Greek word for deacon, "diakonos," vary, but the same word is used for men and in all the apparent references to women as deacons. Deacons today perform a variety of tasks, as this office has been reactivated in the Church since the Second Vatican Council. Today, a deacon's first responsibility usually is to take care of the poor and the sick. He also participates in the Mass, reads the Gospel and preaches the homily. He is empowered also to baptize, to witness marriages and preside at funerals.

Most dioceses have very stringent requirements for people who want to be deacons. A deacon candidate has to be male and at least 35 years of age. If married, a deacon candidate must have the permission of his wife.

Deacons are also mentioned several times in the letters, including references to several women deacons (See *Romans* 16:1 and 1 *Timothy* 3:11).

By the end of the first century, the office of deacon was well-established. The author of the First Letter of Timothy, a letter sometimes attributed to Paul but actually written after Paul's death, discusses the requirements and functions of the deacon. 1 Timothy mentions that the deacon:

- Must "hold fast" to the teaching of the apostles.
- Must have been married only once.
- Must be a good manager of his or her own household, before being entrusted with care of the church's resources.
- Should be put on probation before being confirmed in office.

The deacon was a leader of considerable importance within the local community. By the end of the first century C.E., however, the deacon's function was secondary to that of the presbyter and bishop.

Presbyter/Bishop

As the founding apostle, Paul held the highest position of authority in his local churches. Assisting Paul were people such as Silvanus, Timothy, and Sosthenes. They helped Paul in his missionary work, just as Paul had started out helping Barnabas. In times of trouble or conflict, these fellow workers

---

The Bible in Context

Married Bishops

It may surprise you to hear that the presbyter/ bishops had wives and children since Roman Catholic bishops and priests today take a vow of "celibacy" and do not marry. However, many of the original apostles were married. Paul even refers to Peter's wife in 1 Corinthians 9:5. The Jewish tradition did not have a history of a celibate priesthood.

The policy of priests and bishops not marrying developed over several hundred years as the Church began to place more emphasis on the unique nature of the priest's duties. This practice was not finalized until the Middle Ages.

---

spoke with the voice of the apostle. Similar relationships existed between other apostles and their fellow workers. The apostles and their helpers, however, could not remain forever in the local churches, and local leaders had to emerge.

In Paul's time, a member of a local community might be called to leadership because of:

- A personal connection to Paul or another apostle or fellow worker.
- A "gift of the Spirit," such as the ability to preach, teach, heal, or speak in tongues.
- Their wealth or social position in the community.

Lippi, *Crucifixion of St. Peter*, Fifteenth Century.

After the death of the apostles, new positions of leadership developed in the Church. This picture shows the death of Saint Peter. According to tradition, Peter was crucified upside-down because he did not feel worthy to die in the same way as Jesus died.

---

8. Lead the class discussion of the questions in "Have You Considered?"

9. Pray with your students. Offer a prayer of thanksgiving for the earliest officers of the Church and their willingness to serve the Christian community. Give thanks also for today's officers and their willingness to serve.

Practicing the Skills

Students will use the Bible to verify other written statements.

What to Do

Have the students read 1 Timothy 3:1–7, 5:17–22 about bishops and compare the qualifications given there with the bulleted list in the text on page 251. Ask: "Do you think these are good qualifications for Christian leaders? Is anything left out? Should any of them be changed? Why?"

Recall

Have the students write their answers to the "Chapter 14 Review Q/A," Section One questions 1–4.

Connect

Students will consider an early Church practice and evaluate it in light of today's practice.

What to Do

Have the students look again at the way leaders were chosen in Paul's time. Ask: "What do you think of these qualifications for leaders? Would they be good today? Do you think leaders are still chosen in the same ways? Why or why not?"

What's Next?

What to Do

Say: "You already know that Christians were sometimes persecuted. What character qualities do you think it takes to be willing to die for what you believe?" After the students talk about this, tell them that the effect of martyrdom on the early Church and its teaching will be discussed in the next lesson.

MORE ABOUT THE TEXT

Presbyter/Bishop

The Greek word "presbyteros" meant "elder" and sometimes is so translated. It is the root of our word "priest." The Greek for bishop, "episkopos" means "overseer." In the beginning, both terms apparently referred to a single function in the Christian community. As time went on and the Church's organization became more complex, the "presbyter" was in charge of the local community and the bishop became the "overseer" of the presbyters.

1. Students will present a variety of types of organizations. Focus on the main point, which is that no organization can survive and grow without some kind of leadership and structure (however unspoken or informal). Help students perceive organization that they may take for granted: for example, does the group generally meet at the same time and place? Do they have an accepted method for making decisions? Who is usually in charge?

2. Point out to students that in the Roman world, the head of a household was a position of importance with well-defined legal rights and privileges. To be the head of a household meant that one was a free male, with enough wealth to own a home and have charge of slaves and livestock. Such a person would command respect, both inside and outside of Christianity, in dealing with legal and religious authorities. For this reason, it was probably wise to require that the leaders of early Christianity were people with such legal and social status.

3. Bishops needed to be respected people because they represented Christianity to the world at large. No doubt, many people judged Christianity on the basis of their impression of its leaders, especially when Christians were a tiny minority facing persecution.

4. The purpose of the Office of Widow was to care for Christian women and children who had no one else to care for them. Religious Sisters today live as the letter of Timothy encourages.

Bonus Focus for You

Read 2 Timothy 4:1–5, hearing it within as if it were addressed to you. Reflect on the passage in relationship to your teaching and to your students. Write your reflections in your journal.

These leaders did not hold any defined office, they simply exercised authority because of their spiritual gifts, personality, or their social distinction. For example, a Christian wealthy enough to host meetings of a community in his or her home naturally assumed a position of leadership for that community. Paul may have designated certain individuals as leaders, but, more often, leadership emerged on its own.

As time went on, more definite offices began to develop. By the time of the First Letter of Timothy, at the end of the first century C.E., many local churches had a council of men, called the *presbyters*, who had the responsibility for leadership.

Presbyters were responsible for overseeing the affairs of the local church. The Greek term for an overseer is *episkopos*, usually translated into English as "bishop." In Paul's day, "presbyter" and "bishop" meant the same thing; both were terms for the leaders who guided the affairs of the local church. In the New Testament, presbyters and bishops almost always have the same functions.

The presbyter/bishop monitored the religious and ethical behavior of the local community, ensuring that people lived out their commitment to the Gospel, and did not bring shame upon the church. The presbyter/bishop also cared for the poor and sometimes presided at Christian worship. Their most important responsibility, however, was to preserve and defend the teaching of the apostles.

The author of 1 Timothy lists several requirements for anyone serving in this role. The bishop:

- Must be sensible, dignified, and moderate.
- Must be a model for other Christians, managing his own household well.
- Must be married only once, and his children must be well-behaved (the ability to guide his own family wisely was believed to be a sign that the bishop would guide the affairs of the church with wisdom).
- Must be someone respected by people outside Christianity, so that he could represent the community with confidence.
- Must be free from a love of money, not violent, and not a drinker.

In all things, the bishop must be able to command the respect of others and the obedience of his community.

The Office of Widows

Christian widows formed the final office in the early Church. In the Roman world, a widow who did not remarry was independent, but she had to live off what she inherited from her husband. If her husband had been wealthy, that could make her a very important and powerful person. Many early Christian converts were Gentile widows who were "God-fearers," or admirers of Judaism. Some of these widows were quite wealthy, and supported the Christian mission.

If a widow's husband had been poor and she had no family to support her, then the widow would have absolutely no means of support. As part of its care for the poor, Christians supported such widows with community resources. By the time of 1 Timothy, conditions were established to determine who qualified for such support.

First Timothy says that these widows:

- Had a specific duty to offer prayers.
- Must be of good character, meaning that she is hospitable and helps those in need.
- Must not engage in gossip or false teaching, giving herself "day and night" in prayer.

Along with the deacons and presbyter/bishops, the widows helped organize and expand the Christian mission in the last half of the first century.

Have You Considered?

1. Describe a club, activity, or other group to which you belong. Why is organization necessary in this group?

2. Do you think it's a good idea that a deacon had to be a good manager of his or her own household before he or she could manage the affairs of the community? Why or why not?

3. Why do you suppose it was so important to the early Christians that the bishop be someone whom those outside Christianity would respect?

4. What was the purpose of the office of Widows? What group of women today live as the letter of Timothy encourages?

MORE ABOUT THE TEXT

A Vacant Office

Few, if any, widows today are consecrated into the Office of Widow. Whether or not there remains a need for this office is a matter for discussion. The Office of Widow was established to care for the needs of those members of the Christian community who were unable to take care of themselves because of social restrictions. Government social services have replaced the Church in providing for many widows' needs in the western world, although the plight of widows is still desperate in much of Asia.

Although religious Sisters live today in a way similar to that described for the first widows, the status of nun or sister did not develop out of the Office of Widow, as the other offices developed from the earliest use. The Sisterhood was a monastic practice as such and often included virginity in the prerequisites.

◆ Defending the Faith

As long as Paul was alive, any arguments about his teaching could be settled with a letter from him. When he died, however, it was no longer clear how to resolve disputes over what Paul had said. The same was true for the other apostles. A need arose, therefore, to protect the apostolic teaching. The four gospel accounts serve this need, since they collect the shared memories of Jesus. The accounts themselves, however, were open to misinterpretation. The Church needed an office with the authority to teach the truths of the faith. This function soon became the role of the bishop.

Misinterpretation

In the first century, there were a bewildering variety of interpretations of Paul's letters. The author of 2 Peter (125 C.E.) refers to this problem:

> As our beloved brother Paul, according to the wisdom given to him, also wrote to you, speaking of these things as he does in all his letters. In them there are some things hard to understand that the ignorant and unstable distort to their own destruction, just as they do the other Scriptures.
>
> (2 Peter 3:15–16)

The specific belief in question in 2 Peter is Paul's teaching about the parousia (the second coming of Jesus). Because of its delay, some people became convinced that it was not going to happen at all, or that it had already happened. The author urges them to remember Paul's words.

A False Knowledge

Specific teachings such as the parousia could be misunderstood by people with the best of intentions. Such misconceptions were easily addressed by the bishops. The real challenge for them came not from ordinary people struggling to understand complex teachings, but from organized groups who claimed to possess superior knowledge: the Gnostics.

Using the letters of Paul as a point of departure, the Gnostics claimed to have special insight into salvation. Specifically, they claimed to know the names of the angels and spirits who controlled the universe, and, more importantly, how to manipulate them. Gnostics began to interpret Paul as a Gnostic, and Christianity as a Gnostic system of belief.

Scripture Workshop

The Meaning of "Faith"

In the gospel accounts and in Paul, "faith" referred to the believer's trust in Christ. In the later books of the New Testament, however, faith also came to refer to the teachings that came from the apostles. The following verses show this new meaning:

- 2 Timothy 2:18, 3:8
- 1 Timothy 4:1, 6:21

Read the passages surrounding these verses. Then write a paragraph explaining what "faith" meant for the author of these two letters.

What does 1 Timothy 4:16 mean when it says: "Attend to yourself and to your teaching: persevere in both tasks, for by doing so you will save both yourself and those who listen to you."?

The letter to the Colossians (75 C.E.) refers to such beliefs when it says that all things, including "thrones or dominations, principles or powers" were made through and for Christ. "Thrones and dominations," refers to types of angels, while principles and powers express astrological and cosmological ideas. The author says that all these things exist only to serve Christ. Christians, therefore, do not need to be worried about them, for in Jesus, Christians are in contact with an infinitely greater power.

The author of 1 Timothy urged Christians to focus on the goal of their faith, which is the salvation offered by Jesus and ignore the Gnostic influences:

> guard what has been entrusted to you. Avoid profane babbling and the absurdities of so-called knowledge. By professing it, some people have deviated from the faith.
>
> (1 Timothy 6:20–21)

Christian teaching then, is what has been handed down from the apostles. The Gnostics went wrong when they attempt to substitute their own knowledge for faith.

MORE ABOUT THE TEXT

Gnosticism

Gnosticism comes from the Greek word for knowledge. Saint Irenaeus referred to Gnosticism as a Christian aberration, a heresy. Gnosticism was a definite threat to Christianity with its emphasis on salvational knowledge and the quest for a higher spiritual life.

However, Gnosticism did not develop out of Christianity. Rather, it took ideas from outside of Judeo-Christianity and applied them to Christian thought. The main themes of Gnosticism are that: (a) God is totally unknowable and unconcerned with the world or humanity; (b) God and creation are complete opposites, but the spirit that animates creation is part of God; (c) The earth (and man) are governed by hidden evil powers; (d) Only the few who have been given special knowledge will be saved from this battle of good and evil.

---

2. Have the students read Colossians 1:15–20. Ask: "What does this passage say about Christ? What does it add to your text's comments about false knowledge?" Have the students read 1 Timothy 1:3–6.

3. Discuss Gnosticism.

4. Have the students complete "Scripture Workshop."

5. Lead the class discussion of the questions in "Have You Considered?"

Extend the Lesson   Have the class develop its own definition of faith along with what it would mean to live as a person of faith.

Have You Considered?

1. Different interpretations of Paul's statements would spring up in early Christianity because they are difficult to understand.

2. Students should realize that as the early Church developed, questions arose which Jesus and the Apostles had never addressed. Disagreement over such issues was a natural part of the "sorting out" process that any organization experiences.

3. Students should realize that healthy disagreement is what keeps the Church alive, because it means that it is growing and seeking new insights into God's will.

4. The answer to this question returns students to Paul's statement of "justification by faith." Faith for Paul meant saying "yes" to Jesus. A believer would then live according to the body of teachings. The later emphasis on faith as teaching is a return to a "following the law" mentality.

New Meaning of "Faith"

Gnosticism was not the only challenger to the apostolic teaching. Some Christians wanted to return to a strict obedience to the Law of Moses. This group, called the "Judaizers," were still active in the last part of the first century. Another group went to the opposite extreme and suggested getting rid of the Old Testament and Jewish traditions altogether. In the face of pressures such as these, the bishops were responsible for preserving the teaching they had inherited.

In the effort to preserve apostolic teaching, the term "faith" developed a new meaning. For the Gospel writers and for Paul, "faith" meant **being confident in the salvation offered through Jesus.** In the later part of the first century, the term also came to mean **the body of teachings handed down by the apostles.** Christians were to treasure and to preserve a body of teachings.

By the end of the first century, the Church, under the leadership of the bishops, had begun to organize the teachings that would later be expressed through the creeds (statements of belief, such as the one prayed by Catholics at Mass). The clarity of teaching became especially important when the faith came under attack, most notably by Romans who objected to Christianity as a "new religion" that seemed to threaten the empire.

Have You Considered?

1. Why might Christians disagree over what Paul meant in his letters?
2. Why do you think there were so many disagreements in early Christianity about what faith means?
3. What do you think about disagreements that occur in Christianity today? How should they be resolved?
4. For Paul, faith meant being confident in the salvation offered by Jesus. How is this understanding of faith different from the later teaching that faith was the body of teachings handed down by the apostles?

◆ Facing Persecution

Christians were not persecuted by the Romans immediately. Generally, the Romans were lenient with others' religions, since people were easier to govern when they were allowed to practice their own. When Rome turned against the Christian faith, Christians experienced the power of the Empire and longed for the deliverance that only God could offer.

Christianity and the Empire

Roman law was very tolerant of non-Roman religions. In part, this was for political reasons: it made people more likely to accept Roman rule. There was also a religious reason for Roman tolerance. The Romans were afraid of offending foreign gods and bringing trouble on themselves. Before a battle, the Roman army invited the gods of the other side to join their cause. Similarly, the Romans avoided offending the gods of a conquered people, allowing them to continue honoring these gods. That tolerance extended to the Jews and the Temple in Jerusalem.

Because early Christians were thought of (and mostly thought of themselves) as Jews, Rome extended same tolerance to them. After the destruction of the Temple in 70 C.E., however, Christianity and

The persecution of Christians began with the Emperor Nero. Christians were treated so harshly that even 30 years later the Book of Revelation remembered Nero as the hated beast.

MORE ABOUT THE TEXT

The Words of Jesus

For decades scholars have tried to sort out those parts of the Gospel which originated with Jesus—and truly were his words—from parts that were added later. The studies still go on and scholars do not agree about all possibilities. There is a general consensus, however, that while Jesus may have foreseen problems, the statements in the Gospels concerning persecution reflect later conditions.

The Gospel writers knew the principle that suffering could result from adhering to the Christian faith. Since Jesus suffered redemptively for all, they knew that any Christian might do the same. They developed these comments about persecution to support their first readers who were experiencing persecution. Here again, it is helpful to recall the dates of the writing of biblical books in order to best understand their content.

Judaism obviously began to separate from each other. Only then did Christians begin to attract the attention of the Romans, who suspected them of worshipping a "new" god, Christ.

The Romans were conservative in matters of religion, and regarded any changes in ancient practices as threatening to the "peace of the gods" which protected the empire. Although authors such as Luke showed the Romans that Christians continued to honor the God of the Old Testament, the Romans remained suspicious.

In addition, the Romans suspected Christians of being a "secret society" because they ate and worshipped by themselves. This, too, alarmed Roman officials. Because of these suspicions, Rome sometimes punished Christians on accusations of disloyalty or creating disorder. Such occasional crackdowns, however, did not amount to "official" persecution.

Nero

Christians were first persecuted during the reign of Emperor Nero. Nero was the emperor of Rome from 54–68 C.E. Nero used his power as emperor ruthlessly. He was so cruel as to murder both his mother and his wife to prevent them from plotting against him. Nero also had a reputation for scandalous living, offending even the "liberal" citizens of Rome.

In 64 C.E., Nero, wanting to build a monument to himself in Rome, started a devastating fire that destroyed a large part of the city. Needing someone to

Christians captured by the Romans suffered greatly. The persecution of Christians increased under the Emperor Domitian.

blame for this tragedy, Nero chose the Christians. Dozens of Christians were tortured and burned during this persecution including (according to tradition) Peter and Paul. Although Christians had not been popular in Rome prior to this time, the torture inflicted by Nero made people sympathetic to them. Christians remembered the experience all too well; references to it show up in the Book of Revelation (90 C.E.) and in other writings decades later.

Domitian

Roman criminal law was largely unwritten, so the judgment of whether or not something was a crime was largely left to the *magistrate*, the government official responsible for justice. For this reason, there was probably never any law which made Christianity universally illegal, although it was not officially legalized until 311.

After the destruction of the Temple in 70 C.E., Roman magistrates tended to pay more attention to Christianity, and were more likely to punish Christians who refused to worship the spirit of the Emperor. Refusal to honor the Emperor was considered an act of political disloyalty.

Nero's Persecution

The Roman historian Tacitus described the persecution of Christians under Nero. He said Christians were chosen because of their "antisocial" nature (which probably refers to their celebration of evening meals with one another rather than in mixed— Christian and non-Christian—company), and their unwillingness to participate in Roman religious festivals.

Whatever the reason, Nero inflicted horrible punishments. Tacitus says that some Christians were dressed in animal skins to be torn apart by dogs, and others were used as human torches to light Nero's garden parties. The shocking brutality of these acts created sympathy among the public, and eventually the persecutions came to an end.

◆ Facing Persecution

Development

What to Do

1. Have the students read "Facing Persecution" and "in the Spotlight."
2. Have the students examine the map on page 256 and compare it with the Roman Empire map on page 231. The colors on page 256 do not mean that the whole area was Christian, but that some Christian communities were spread around in those areas. We have no information about the actual number of early Christians.
3. Say: "Persecution is a theme that appears in a number of the New Testament books. The Gospel accounts are no exception. No one knows for certain whether Jesus predicted persecution as such, but by the time the Gospels were written, persecution had occurred and needed to be understood and endured. Let's read Mark 13:9–13; Matthew 5:11–12, 12:26–33; Luke 12:2–9, 21:12–19; John 9:22, 16:18–21."
4. Lead the class discussion of the questions in "Have You Considered?"
5. Pray with your students. Along with student intentions, pray for those people who are still suffering and dying for their faith. Close with the "Our Father" together.

Recall

Have the students write their answers to "Chapter 14 Review Q/A," Section One, questions 5–8.

Connect

What to Do

Discuss with the students what defending the faith and facing persecution might mean today.

What's Next?

What to Do

Have the students find the Letter to the Hebrews, the Letter of James, and 1 and 2 Peter, and put a marker at the beginning of each. Tell them that these are the subjects of the next lesson.

◆ MORE ABOUT THE LESSON

Martyrs

This discussion about modern people who suffered for their faith can include people like Oscar Romero or the Sisters killed in Latin America, or the many priests and other Catholics killed for their faith in Rwanda in 1994.

Feel free to discuss the kind of hurt they themselves may experience if they are open about their faith: social rejection, difficulties with unbelieving adults, and similar experiences. Let them mention as many types of suffering for the faith as they can before you give them hints.

The emperors were worried about Christian loyalty because Christian communities were located in all the key cities of the empire, including major ports and trading centers. An uprising led by Christians could easily develop into a serious challenge to Roman authority.

Have You Considered?

1. The Romans believed in maintaining the "peace of the gods." As the Romans understood it, this meant that they had an obligation to honor traditional religious practices, lest the gods become upset. Therefore, Rome always allowed conquered people the right to honor their gods. The Romans feared that new religions might anger the gods and upset the peace. For this reason, they were vary wary of any innovation.

2. Students should remember from Chapter 12 that the Holy Spirit used the events of history, including suffering, to guide the growth of Christianity. For example, the first missionary efforts outside of Jerusalem were the result of the martyrdom of Stephen. Luke, therefore, would likely explain the persecution of early Christians as part of the Holy Spirit's plan for the expansion of Christianity.

3. For Christians, there is only one Lord: Jesus, the Son of God. The refusal of early Christians to acknowledge the emperor as Lord was almost certainly not motivated by political considerations. Early Christian authors took great pains to emphasize the political loyalty of the Christian community. Remind students, however, that in the ancient world, there was no separation between religion and politics; a refusal was an act of political disloyalty.

Bonus Focus for You

Read John 10:7–18. Imagine what such an understanding must have meant to people facing death because of their faith in Jesus. What does it mean to you today? What price have you had to pay for your faith? Reflect on your experiences in your journal.

256

LEARN FROM THE MAP

Christianity at the End of the First Century
Notice all the places where Christians had established churches by the end of the first century. Given what you see on this map, why do you think the Roman emperors were so worried about Christian loyalty?

Magistrates rarely hunted Christians down. Usually, they waited until a Christian was denounced by someone else. Christians were given every opportunity to honor the Emperor, but if they refused to do so, they were put to death. Faced with this choice, some rejected their faith, while others held firmly to it.

Under the Emperor Domitian (81–96 C.E.), persecution of Christians heated up once more. Domitian viewed any potential disloyalty with suspicion. Like Nero, he targeted Christians for persecution.

Christians suffered greatly under this persecution although they were not the only ones; Domitian seemed more interested in promoting emperor worship than he was in stamping out other religions. Worship of the emperor was required of all Roman citizens. People could also worship as many other gods as they wished, as long as worship of the emperor came first. Failure to worship the emperor was a sign of treason, for which the penalty was death.

Christians and Jews both believed in the worship of Yahweh alone. They could not worship the emperor without violating the Covenant.

Such official hostility discouraged many Christians and prompted them to long for God's salvation, views expressed in the Book of Revelation. As you will see in the next section, Revelation offered a powerful message of hope to Christians facing the power of Rome.

Have You Considered?

1. Why do you think the Romans would tolerate members of "old" religions, but not members of "new" ones?
2. Given what you know about Luke's theme of salvation history, how do you think he would explain the persecution Christians faced?
3. Why do you think Christians would object to referring to the Roman Emperor as "Lord"? Do you think their refusal to do so was a political act, as the Romans felt?

MORE ABOUT THE TEXT

The Spread of Christianity

Students will remember that Paul's mission to spread the Gospel was made easier because of the success of the Roman Empire: there were good roads, regularly scheduled boat routes, a common language, and the enforcement of laws which made for safe travel. It is not surprising then that a map showing the spread of Christianity would look very much like the map of the Roman Empire.

There are two points to remember as you work with this map. First, Christianity would not become the dominant religion in the Empire until Constantine in the fourth century. Before that time, Christianity was a growing body with churches in most of the important cities. Second, Christianity was spread beyond the Empire with limited success by individual missionaries. The biblical letters are addressed to communities within the Empire.

Keeping the Faith

In the first section, you read about the two major challenges facing the Church in the last part of the first century: internal arguments over the faith, and external persecution from the Romans. In this section, you'll study how four New Testament authors responded to these challenges. In Hebrews, James, the letters of Peter, and the Book of Revelation, a wide variety of internal and external problems are discussed. In every case, however, the answer given by these authors is consistent:stay true to the faith, and God will not abandon you.

Learning Objectives for Section Two

By the end of this section, you will be able to:

* Explain the false teaching corrected in Hebrews, James, and the letters of Peter.
* Explain how the author of Revelation uses symbolism to respond to the problem of Roman persecution.
* Discuss the role of faith in Christian living.

◆ The Letter to the Hebrews

Although the Letter to the Hebrews (80 C.E.) has sometimes been attributed to the apostle Paul, modern scholars generally recognize it as the product of a later author. The letter, addressed to Jewish-Christians, is a long sermon explaining the consequences of their Christian faith. In Hebrews, the author corrects a false understanding among some Jewish-Christians, who felt that it was necessary to continue making Temple sacrifices to be on good terms with God. Hebrews reminds them that Christians need nothing but the sacrifice of Jesus to be saved.

Christ the High Priest

The Letter to the Hebrews sees Jesus as the divine Son of God, the image of God in the world.

The author calls Jesus the "image of divine glory," which was the same language used about Wisdom in the Wisdom literature (See *Book of Wisdom* 7:26). The author means that Jesus existed with God as a creative power before he became flesh and came to earth to make salvation possible by his death and resurrection. Christ suffered, but his suffering made him perfect.

Because Christ freed people from sins through his death, the author of Hebrews calls Jesus the "perfect high priest." In the Old Testament, the function of a priest was to make sacrifices which would rid people of sin and enable them to live in a right relationship with God. Jewish priests at the Temple made such sacrifices every day on behalf of themselves, private individuals, the king, and the nation. Because Jesus gave himself in sacrifice, and in so doing conquered sin, he achieved the goal of all those other sacrifices. For this reason, Hebrews says, Jesus deserves the title of high priest.

MORE ABOUT THE TEXT

Hebrews and the Temple

The Letter to the Hebrews was not only an attempt to answer Jewish-Christians who still wanted to keep the old laws and customs, but also an attempt to free Christians from internal attachments to the Temple and its rites—which were gone anyway. Every Jew would have been in sorrow over the loss of the Temple; it had been so precious to them for so long. With the destruction of the Temple both Jews and Jewish-Christians had to build a faith-expression without the Temple and free themselves from its priesthood and sacrifices. The writer of Hebrews is saying that the Temple, for all of its grandeur, has be superseded by Christ. Jewish-Christians have no more need for it.

LESSON THREE
(pages 257–262)

◆ The Letter to the Hebrews

Welcome

What to Do

Use water to help students remember their baptisms.

Introducing the Lesson

Teaching Objectives

By the end of this lesson students will be able to:
* Describe the key points presented in Hebrews and in the letters of James and Peter.
* Explain why these letters were important to the development of Christian faith.

What to Do

Have the students read the opening italics and Learning Objectives. Look at the picture on page 257. What can the students tell you about the importance of Baptism? What does it mean for them to be members of a parish community?

Development

What to Do

1. Begin by reading "The Letter to the Hebrews."
2. Have the students note on the timeline the relationship between the writing of Hebrews and the destruction of the Temple. Ask: "What reasons, in addition to those given in the text, might the writer of Hebrews have had to try and detach Jewish-Christians from worshipping in the Temple?"
3. Have the students read Genesis 18 to understand the subsection "Response in the Heart." Discuss their findings with them.
4. Have the students read Hebrews 13:1–17. Ask: "How do you think all these instructions apply to us today, just as they did to those who first read this letter?"
5. Lead the class discussion of the questions in "Have You Considered?"

Practicing the Skill

What to Do

Form small groups. Have the students complete "Bible Activity" number 1. If they have difficulty remembering where to find these stories, they should use a concordance. Have each group retell one or two of the stories and explain why the writer of Hebrews included it in his letter.

Have You Considered?

1. For the author of Hebrews, Jesus is the perfect high priest because the sacrifice he offered, his death on the cross, was the perfect, once-and-for-all offering which restored a right relationship for humanity with God. Allow students to talk about whether this title captures what is most important about Jesus to them. Encourage them to come up with their own titles expressing their views of Jesus' significance.

2. Jewish-Christians were Jews who expressed belief in Jesus as the Messiah. Many of them felt that the law of Moses was still in effect and binding on them. They looked to the example of the early apostles, who, according to Acts 2:46, continued to worship in the Temple. For these reasons, it is not surprising that many felt the need to continue offering Temple sacrifice. Of course, such discussion would have been purely academic after 70 C.E., since the Temple had been destroyed by the Romans.

3. Encourage students to be specific in their responses to this question. Ask them to consider scenarios from everyday life, such as encounters with the homeless on the streets, and appeals from charitable organizations in the mail or over the phone. Students should discuss how their responses to such situations might change if they regarded the poor as potential divine messengers.

No Other Sacrifices

According to the author of Hebrews, Jesus made one, perfect sacrifice for all people and all time. For this reason, no other sacrifices need to be made. Christ has accomplished the perfect sacrifice through his death. From this point forward, human beings are free from sin, and they no longer need the Temple or other rituals to restore their relationship with God.

Audience   Hebrews directs this message at Jewish-Christians who felt that God still wanted them to make sacrifices according to the Jewish law. The author tells such Christians that the death of Jesus is the only sacrifice necessary, and all Christians have to do is to accept it. To continue to rely on the traditional sacrificial system, the author says, would be a denial of the faith, suggesting that Christ's death was not sufficient to restore their relationship with God.

El Greco, *Christ Crucified*, Sixteenth Century.

The Letter to the Hebrews teaches that sacrifices according to the Jewish law are no longer needed. Jesus' death was the ultimate sacrifice and all we must do is accept it.

The belief that Christ's life and death are all Christians need is very important to the author of Hebrews. To underline this point, the author argues that God's revelation before Christ had always been partial and incomplete, while God was revealed in complete fullness through Jesus. Hebrews says:

> In times past, God spoke in partial and various ways to our ancestors through the prophets; in these last days he spoke to us through a Son, whom he made heir of all things and through whom he created the universe.

(Hebrews 1:1–2)

Heroes of the Faith   Hebrews does not reject the Old Testament or Jewish traditions. In fact, Chapter 11 of Hebrews is often called the "heroes of the faith" chapter, recounting the life stories of Abel, Noah, Abraham, Sarah, Jacob, Rahab, David, and others. All of these people, the author says, are examples of lives built on faith and obedience to God.

Response in the Heart

This perfect, once-and-for-all, gift from Jesus inspires a response from the heart. The author urges the readers to take care of each other, to encourage one another, and to continue meeting for support and growth.

Hebrews also advises Christians to show hospitality, saying that some have entertained angels that way without knowing it. (See the story of Abraham in Chapter 18 of Genesis.)

Above all, the author says, Christians must cling to true teaching. No one should be allowed to lead them astray from the faith. Hebrews reinforces correct teaching and defends the faith against possible misinterpretations. The author reminds Christians that faith in Jesus is all we need.

Have You Considered?

1. Why is Jesus called the "perfect high priest"? Does this title express your understanding of Jesus? Why or why not?
2. Why might Jewish-Christians have felt that Temple sacrifices were still necessary? Based on what you know about Jewish-Christians, explain why they might think this.
3. How might our behavior towards strangers and the poor change if we regarded them as potential messengers from God? Give two or three concrete examples of things we might do differently.

◆ MORE ABOUT THE LESSON

Understanding More About

The Letter of James was not the only New Testament book Luther objected to. He would like to have gotten rid of the Book of Revelation as well. However, none of the Protestant churches have followed his lead in this. There is no difference (other than possibly translation) between the New Testament as used in the Roman Catholic Church and the one used by all Protestant churches. The New Testament canon has remained the same for all Christian churches since the fourth century C.E.

This would be a good time to point out to students that churches such as the Jehovah Witnesses and the Mormons use a Bible different from that used by Christian churches. They have added books not found in the Christian Bible.

◆ The Letter of James

This brief letter, written around 65 C.E., has traditionally been attributed to James, the relative of Jesus, who governed the Church in Jerusalem. You may remember James from Chapter 12; he was present at the Council of Jerusalem and made the decision about the dietary rules for Gentile converts. Although the teaching in this letter may have come from James, the actual writing was probably done by a later author.

The letter is addressed to the "twelve tribes in the diaspora," probably referring to all of the Christian communities. James is concerned with another misunderstanding of apostolic teaching, one which says that because Christians are saved by faith, it is unnecessary for them to do any good works. James reminds Christians that acts of mercy and love go hand-in-hand with salvation, and they are part of being Christian.

Endurance

James begins by recognizing that many Christians are experiencing hard times. The author may have persecution in mind, or the "trials" may simply be the isolation from loved ones and social disapproval that often came with being a Christian. James argues that trials and temptations test our faith. By passing these tests, we bring our faith to perfection, and we assure

ourselves of the crown of life which Jesus has prepared for all of his loved ones.

James advises Christians experiencing difficulties to pray for the wisdom that comes from God. This prayer, however, must be offered in a spirit of trusting confidence that God will respond. One who prays in doubt must not expect anything from the Lord, James says, because such doubt shows distrust and instability. Only a heart full of faith can be open to the wisdom God offers.

An Important Christian Skill

One of the most important skills a Christian can have, according to James, is the ability to control one's tongue. "If anyone does not fall short in speech, he is a perfect man" (James 3:2).

Speech has great power. It can make another person feel wonderful. It can share about the glory and truth of God. It can express love. Speech can also cause harm through lies and gossip. As James puts it, "From the same mouth come blessing and cursing" (James 3:10).

James encourages all Christians to learn the skill of watching their tongues, so that their speech becomes like the pure fruit of a healthy tree. Everybody likes to hear good and true words. The Christian, James implies, should speak well at all times, especially when talking about another person.

The best way to learn this Christian skill is to look inside oneself and see one's own thoughts and feel-

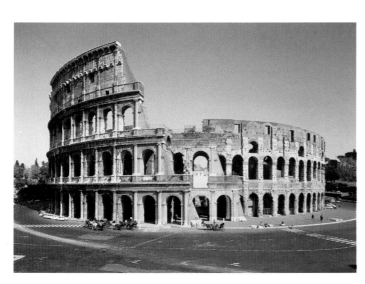

Christians were put to death in the Colosseum in Rome as entertainment. The Letter of James encourages Christians to persevere in their faith against all hardship, even if it meant their deaths.

◆ The Letter of James

Development

What to do

1. Have the students read "The Letter of James" in their text. They should also read James 1:1–8, to get the flavor of the author's approach.

2. Discuss with the students the importance of controlling one's speech. Have they ever tried? How do people talk about other people—kindly or unkindly? Do they say ugly things when they are suddenly frightened or angry? Do they ever wonder, "Why in the world did I ever say that?"

3. Have them read James 3:1–12. Ask: "Is the tongue as powerful as James says it is? Why do you think as you do?"

4. Have the students read and discuss James 2:1–9 and 5:1–6. How do their habits measure up to this standard of non-favoritism? How do they treat other teens who don't dress fashionably, don't own CD's, or can't buy tickets to an expensive show? What is their Christian relationship to social outcasts?

5. Have the students read "Understanding More About" on page 267. Discuss what would be missing from the Bible if James had not been included.

6. Have the students find the bulleted passages about virtues on page 261 in their Bibles. Ask for volunteers to read the passages aloud. After each reading, discuss students' responses to James's concerns.

7. Lead the class discussion of the questions in "Have You Considered?"

MORE ABOUT THE TEXT

James

The author of the Letter of James was almost certainly not one of the Twelve Apostles. He is never identified as an Apostle, but rather claims to be "a slave of God and of the Lord Jesus Christ." Some scholars think that the author may have been the James who is known as the "brother of the Lord" and who was the leader of the Christian community in Jerusalem. The

Jewish historian Josephus says that this James was stoned to death by the Jews in 62 C.E. (or around the time that Peter and Paul were martyred).

The letter is addressed to the "twelve tribes in the dispersion"; possibly the Jewish-Christian churches located outside of Palestine or to all Christians who are in exile from their true home with Jesus.

Have You Considered?

1. Given the intense adolescent sense of justice, most students will believe that they have experienced favoritism at some point. Allow them to describe their experiences, including what was done at the time and what could have been done differently. Remind students of the advice James gives, that favoritism is out of place in the Christian community.

2. What James says is that faith must include the will to help others. Thus, one cannot be authentically Christian without acting to meet the needs of others. Point out to students that historically, some interpreters saw here a conflict with Paul's teaching, as if James were saying that we somehow have to earn our salvation. What James is saying is that someone who authentically loves God will naturally seek to help others, not as a condition of salvation, but as a sign of faith.

3. Students will have different responses. Whichever virtue they select, encourage them to be specific as to why this would be difficult for them, based on their own personality and life-situation.

ings. James advises instilling wisdom and humility inside oneself. If everything inside is "pure, peaceable, gentle, compliant, and full of mercy," then one's speech will be the same.

Rich and Poor Alike

James also talks about relationships between Christians, especially between the rich and the poor. James emphasizes that everyone is welcome in the Christian assembly. In particular, no one is to be excluded because of their poverty or treated extra nicely because of their wealth.

The command for Christians is not to exclude the wealthy, but to treat rich and poor alike. No favoritism must be shown in the community based on someone's worldly status. The poor must be treated with the same decency and respect that any other member of the community enjoys.

The suffering of the poor will be rewarded in the last days, James says, while oppression and neglect of the poor will be punished. For that reason, the Christian is called to treat the poor, with special care (*James 2:1–9 and 5:1–6*).

Faith and Works

The special love Christians have for the poor is connected to one of the main themes in James: the need for Christians to perform good works. In the late first century, some Christians apparently had a dis-

torted reading of Paul's letters. They thought that simply by repeating slogans such as "God is one" they had done enough. Instead, James insists that their faith must not be simply a matter of slogans or theories. Faith must be reflected in the Christian's daily life.

James sums the idea up this way: we must be doers of the word, not just hearers. Our faith is meaningless unless we practice it. To make this point, James uses a very down-to-earth example: If someone comes up to you and says "I am hungry, and I have nothing to wear," and all you do is say, "Goodbye, and keep warm and well-fed," what good are those words without actions? In addition to being meaningless, they're insincere, since we do nothing to help the person. James says that "faith" has no power to save anyone unless used in obedience to God's commands.

The letter of James practically summarizes good Christian living. Against the false teaching that Christian faith is simply a matter of the mind, James insists that Christianity is a way of life, an active concern for the well-being of all, including those often forgotten in society.

Christian Virtue

The Christian way of life involves more than occasional acts of mercy. It also involves making our values part of our daily living. What does this mean in practice? James mentions several things:

*The Letter of James says that Christians should be known by their good works; how a person acts **is** ultimately important.*

MORE ABOUT THE TEXT

New Testament Wisdom

The Letter of James is not really written in the letter form that students have previously studied. It lacks all of the characteristic features of a real letter other than its greeting. The Letter of James is written in the literary genre of *parenesis* or exhortation with its great concern for ethical conduct.

The Letter of James most closely resembles the works found in the Wisdom literature of the Old Testament. It is similar in many ways to the books of Proverbs and Sirach. It also treats subjects that appear in the Synoptic accounts.

Scripture Workshop

The Man in the Mirror

A major theme in James is the importance of *doing* the word. In James 1:23–25, the author compares the Christian to a man who looks into the mirror. Read this comparison, and then answer the following questions:

- How is a person who hears the word but does not practice it like one who looks into the mirror?
- What do you think "freedom's ideal law" is?
- What does it mean to "peer" into it?

- Cultivating peacefulness (3:17–18).
- An unwillingness to judge others (4:11–12).
- Humility, and a refusal to boast of our accomplishments (3:13–14).
- Patience as we wait for the salvation promised by God (5:7–11).

James is a great help for people growing in faith and Christian living. James reminds us that Christian faith requires good actions, and that anyone who denies this is not a Christian.

Have You Considered?

1. Have you ever experienced favoritism in any group to which you belong? If so, what was done about it? Why or why not? What could have been done?
2. What does it mean to say that Christian faith must include good works? Do you think it's possible to be a Christian without acting to help others?
3. Review the list of virtues above which James says Christians should have. Which one do you think is hardest for you? Why?

◆ The Letters of Peter

Two letters in the New Testament are attributed to the apostle Peter. In all likelihood, neither were written by him. The first letter was written in Rome around 65 C.E., and came at the time of the first persecutions. This persecution included social prejudice as well as actual arrest and execution. 1 Peter urges Christians to stand fast, and tries to show that Christian life will continue in such circumstances. 2 Peter was written much later by another person. It is perhaps the last book written in the New Testament (possibly written as late as 125 C.E.). This book reaffirms traditional Christian teaching about the second coming of Jesus and calls on Christians to remain true to the faith.

Christian Exile

In the face of persecution and prejudice in the Roman world, 1 Peter urges Christians to consider themselves exiles in this life. Christians are just passing through, he says, on their way to their home in the kingdom with Jesus. Their lives will always be different and perhaps more difficult than others' lives. Christians should expect this as the price of living in exile.

Despite the hardships, Christians must continue to act in goodness and accept whatever experiences come their way. They must accept suffering in the same way that Christ accepted it, as part of God's plan for the salvation of the world. Despite enduring insults and punishments for their faith, Christians need feel no shame. Instead, they should feel pride, for the degree to which Christians now share in the suffering of Christ is the degree to which they will share in his glory when he returns.

Good Examples

The author urges Christians to live blameless lives so that non-Christians will have no cause to complain about them. They should live well, so that non-Christians will learn to give glory to God. Blameless living includes shedding envy, slander, and false pride. Christians should be compassionate and humble, and not be nasty to others. In all these ways, Christian behavior should be a model for their non-Christian neighbors.

◆ The Letters of Peter

Development

What to Do

1. Have the students read "The Letters of Peter" in their text. Raise questions about the four sub-points to see what students think about these teachings.
2. Have the students read 1 Peter 4:12–19. Ask: "What do you think of this view of life?"
3. Have the students read 1 Peter 2:11–17. Ask: "What is the value of being a good example for people who are not Christians?"
4. Form small groups. Have the students complete "Bible Activity" number 2 and share their results, especially their opinions about the meaning of these passages.
5. Lead the class discussion of the questions in "Have You Considered?"
6. Pray with your students. Have students offer their thoughts about how they can better live according to the guidance offered in these letters.

Recall

What to Do

Have the students discuss, then write their answers to "Chapter 14 Review Q/A," Section Two questions 1–6.

Connect

What to Do

Have the students review 1 Peter 3:13–17. Help them apply this to today: Are they so enthusiastic for their faith that people know they are Catholic Christians? Does anyone ever ask them about their faith? How do they respond?

What's Next?

What to Do

Say: "The last book in the Bible is the Book of Revelation. You have probably heard many different ideas about this book. If you already have questions about it, be sure to have them in mind for the next session."

Have You Considered?

1. The reference is to the Exile in Babylon. People should remember that the Jews returned from Exile strengthened in the Covenant and that God will act to end their suffering as well.

2. The second coming was important because their suffering would end, and would be replaced by the glory of life with God for which they all hoped. Encourage students to recognize why hope for the speedy return of Jesus has always helped Christians cope with difficult times.

Bonus Focus for You

Read 1 Peter 4:7–11. It is a beautiful summary of what may be expected of a teacher. Reflect on its application to yourself in your journal.

SECTION TWO ◀◀

LESSON FOUR
(pages 262–265)

◆ The Book of Revelation

Welcome

What to Do

Greet the students especially warmly today, and share your feelings for them.

Say: "Here is the greeting that opens the Book of Revelation." Read to them Revelation 1:4b–6.

Pray with your students. Offer thanks and ask for guidance.

Introducing the Lesson

Teaching Objectives

By the end of this lesson students will be able to:

• Explain the significance of the predictions in the Book of Revelation.

• Demonstrate an ability to work with apocalyptic language.

• Identify how the writers of the Bible were expressing faith themes.

What to Do

Ask the students to tell you everything they might know or have heard about the Book of Revelation (the Apocalypse). Put their contributions on the board. (This is the first question from "Have You Considered.")

Defending the Faith

1 Peter says that Christians must always be ready to defend their faith with gentleness and respect. The author reminds the presbyters that it is their duty to keep everyone on the right path. They should use their authority wisely and not abuse it in any way.

Ordinary Christians must remain solid in faith, 1 Peter says, because it is the same faith that believers are suffering for all over the world. God will give strength to those who endure, and their constancy will be rewarded when Christ returns.

The Second Coming

You already know that the *parousia*, or second coming, of Jesus had been expected by Christians from the very beginning. Many Christians, like those in Thessalonica, expected it to happen soon. As the years passed, the parousia was pushed further and further into the future. Some Christians began to doubt it was going to happen at all, and rejected the teaching altogether. 2 Peter (125 C.E.) is written to bring these Christians back to the true apostolic teaching.

Anyone who denies the parousia, according to 2 Peter, is a false teacher.

> For talking empty bombast, they seduce with licentious desires of the flesh those who have barely escaped from people who live in error.
>
> (2 Peter 2:18)

Christians should cling to the promises made by Jesus and not let anyone convince them to abandon hope in his return. We should wait patiently, however, because a thousand years is like a single day to the Lord. Even though Christians might want action immediately, they must trust God and be at peace.

Have You Considered?

1. When the author of 1 Peter compared Christian life to exile, what Old Testament event do you think his readers would have remembered? How might this help them endure their hardships?

2. Why would hope for the second coming of Jesus be important to Christians facing persecution?

◆ The Book of Revelation

Revelation (90 C.E.) is a book of fantastic—and sometimes horrible—visions and symbols. In it, we read about a huge red dragon with seven heads and ten horns, whose tail swept away a third of the stars; the four horsemen of the Apocalypse; and a woman wearing purple and scarlet who has become drunk on the blood of the Holy One. Some of these images sound like they come straight off the pages of a Stephen King novel!

Many of the symbols in Revelation are from the Old Testament and other Jewish literature outside the Bible. The original readers of Revelation would have recognized and understood these images immediately. Taken together, the symbols in Revelation give us a vision of Christian life and salvation. Addressed to people experiencing persecution and questioning the truth of their faith, Revelation offers hope that God's deliverance will come as promised.

Giotto, Last Judgment, Fourteenth Century.

Early Christians believed that Jesus would return again quickly to fulfill the kingdom. The Second Letter of Peter encourages people to stay true to the faith because Jesus would come again.

MORE ABOUT THE TEXT

Christian Examples

Not all of 1 Peter's notions of a "Christian example" would seem right to modern Christians. He does not object, for example, to slavery, but urges slaves to be submissive to their masters no matter how they are treated. He also urges that wives should be obedient and submissive to their husbands. Today, we simply do not agree with these saying, because culture has changed during these past 2,000 years.

Today, an author might illustrate the principles contained in 1 Peter, especially "Be good examples to non-believers," with an entirely different set of examples. Ask the students to come up with what they think 1 Peter would encourage today.

People of Note

The Beast

In general, you should not look for specific explanations for the symbols found in Revelation. They refer to events that occurred nearly 2000 years ago for which we have no evidence. We can only speculate on what they mean.

There is one case, however, where Revelation itself tells you what a symbol means. Revelation 13:8 says that the beast which forces people to be marked with its image stands for a man, and his identity can be determined from the number "666."

Ancient languages such as Greek and Hebrew did not have a system of numbers as we do, so each letter of their alphabet had a numerical value. In Hebrew, the letters in the name of the Roman Emperor Nero add up to 666, and most scholars today agree that this is the beast described. Nero had persecuted Christians, and some feared that he had escaped death and was coming back into power. The "image" of itself which the beast forced on people probably refers to Roman coins, which were stamped with the image of the Emperor.

God Is in Charge

Times are terrible, the author of Revelation says, and they're going to get worse. The violent images of destruction and chaos in the book communicate this belief. But no matter how it may appear from here, God is totally in charge. Believers in Christ, especially *martyrs*, Christians who die for their faith, will be granted a glorious life. Because deliverance is coming, however, Christians should accept these insults and injuries.

The book is written from the point of view of a *seer*, one who experiences a vision. Because this seer relates everything from God's point of view, the hearer may be sure that the present hardships are part of the divine plan. All of the difficulties Christians experience in the text have the same basic structure:

- The saints (Christians) suffer persecution.
- The coming judgment on the evil ones is described.
- A scene of salvation in heaven follows.

This structure shows the reader that the hardships Christians experience will inevitably lead to glory in heaven, so the only response is to endure with patience and confidence.

A New Jerusalem

Revelation ends with a final vision of what life will be like when the present age ends, and the kingdom comes in its fullness. The coming of the kingdom is captured in the vision of a "new Jerusalem."

Then I saw a new heaven and a new earth. The former heaven and the former earth had passed away, and the sea was no more. I also saw the holy city, a new Jerusalem, coming down out of heaven from God, prepared as a bride adorned for her husband. I heard a loud voice from the throne saying: "Behold God's dwelling is with the human race. He will dwell with them and they will be his people God himself will always be with them [as their God]. He will wipe away every tear from their eyes, and there shall be no more death or mourning, wailing or pain, [for] the old order has passed away.

(Revelation 21:1–4)

The seer goes on to describe what this New Jerusalem will be like. It will have no temple, because God will be the temple; it will have no sun or moon, for the glory of God provides the light.

For Christians experiencing harassment, punishment, and even death for their faith, this vision gave them hope to endure. The experience of these horrible things will pass away, and a new life with God awaits those who remain strong.

False Teachers

Along with the external persecution they faced, the readers of Revelation also were exposed to "false apostles and prophets" who were introducing new beliefs. The author of Revelation addresses these false teachers in the seven letters to different Christian churches which open the book. Some of these teachers claimed to have secret knowledge unavailable to ordinary Christians. Others, such as the *Nicolaitians*, were introducing elements of Greek and Roman religion and culture into Christian practice. The author rejects these teachings and commends his readers who have done the same.

MORE ABOUT THE TEXT

Revelation

Whether or not the writer of Revelation (who calls himself John) really experienced this long, complex series of visions, or whether he was an inspired, artistic writer who used symbols to communicate his meanings, is not important. We take the book seriously as it stands.

The text outlines the three basic thrusts of the Revelation. It leaves at least a hundred questions unanswered, largely because there are no reliable detailed interpretations of Revelation. However, that has not kept the Church and Christian artists from using its powerful images. We hear and see them everywhere, when we know enough of Revelation to recognize them. The symbols of Revelation fill an important niche in the Church's tradition: the four horsemen, for example, appear often. It is enriching for the students to meet as many of the symbols as they can.

Development

Students will recognize that the Book of Revelation, written in symbolic language, offers encouragement to people suffering persecution and does not predict literal events.

What to Do

1. Have the students read "The Book of Revelation" in their text, including "People of Note."
2. Have the students read Revelation 1:1–3,9–19. This gives them the setting of the book.
3. Say: "Revelation begins with letters to seven churches. Look in Chapters 2 and 3 to find their names, then see how many you can find on the map, page 256."
4. Have the students read Revelation 4; 6; 13:11–18; 15; 16; 21:1–22:5; and 22:20. Form groups to read these chapters aloud, as a choral reading.
5. Have the students do "Bible Activity" number 3. When they have shared their ideas, remind them that the Church uses part of this chapter as a Mass reading on the Feast of the Assumption. Ask: "Why do you think the Church has chosen these symbols for this Feast?"
6. Lead the class discussion of questions 2 and 3 in "Have You Considered?"

Practicing the Skills

What to Do

Have the students read Revelation 2–3. Say, "Make a list of the cities, and beside each city say why the Lord is happy with that one and why he is unhappy."

When the students have finished, use the following question to discuss what they've found: "Which of the admonitions of the Lord in these letters apply to us today? How?"

Have You Considered?

1. This question calls for "free association" on the part of the students. Once they have listed the images they have of Revelation, discuss the origin of those images. In many cases, they will be literary and artistic embellishments on the text.
2. Students should be aware that this is a distortion of the original

meaning of the text. Further, because many of the images in Revelation are violent and invite conflict, such interpretations can sometimes be abused and lead to destructive behavior. Students may be invited to discuss examples of such destructive behavior familiar to them.

3. This question also calls for a "free association" of symbols and images. You way want to encourage students to express their visions of such a "new world" artistically, in drawing, collages, or other media. Invite them to write an account of their own "visions" of the new world.

◆ The Importance of "The Faith"

Development

What to Do

1. Have the students read "The Importance of the Faith."

2. Discuss the importance of sharing beliefs. How did the books studied in this chapter help the Church come to a common belief?

3. Lead the class discussion of the questions in "Have You Considered?"

4. Pray with your students. Give thanks for this great moment: the last biblical book has been considered! Give thanks for all the effort that has been made, and the successes that have come. Give thanks especially for your students. Let them mention what they recall as being especially important in what they have learned, and include it in your prayer. After each prayer, respond "Thanks be to God."

Recall

Have the students write their answers to "Chapter 14 Review Q/A," Section Two, questions 7–8.

Connect

Students will experience using the Book of Revelation for prayer.

What to Do

Homework Assignment: Have students complete the Spiritual Reflection. Add these two references to those in the text: Revelation 3:20–21 and 21:17.

Problems of Interpretation

The general message of Revelation is clear: Things are bad now and getting worse, but salvation is on the way. The details of the images and symbols which contain this general idea, however, can be very difficult to understand. Sometimes, people have tried to find a specific meaning for each symbol, or tried to calculate the date of the end of the world on the basis of the description in Revelation.

Read Revelation as you would any book: let the symbols and images just be there, without trying to figure them out. Read to enjoy the book, not analyze it. When people draw mistaken conclusions about the end of the world or the identity of the "anti-Christ," they can cause harm to themselves and others. Instead, read Revelation for the feelings of amazement, wonder, thanksgiving, honor to God, threat, victory, and ultimately, hope, that the symbols provoke. Try to appreciate the book just as it is.

Have You Considered?

1. What have you heard about the book of Revelation? What images do you have of it?
2. Have you ever heard people who interpreted the symbols in Revelation as referring to people or events of today? What would you say about this kind of interpretation?
3. What images or symbols would you use to describe life in a "new world" created by God?

Unknown (N. France), Apocalypse. Thirteenth Century.

The Book of Revelation uses many types of symbolism. This picture shows the opening of the second seal (Revelation 6:3–4). The red horse and rider symbolize war that will "take away peace from the earth, so that people would slaughter one another."

◆ The Importance of the Faith

Despite the different interests of the authors you have studied in this section, they all agree on one thing: Christians must hold fast to the teaching of the apostles. As you know from Section One, the apostle's teaching and belief had, by the end of the first century, become part of what it meant to have faith.

You may be surprised by this emphasis on what Christians believe. After all, isn't it how we treat others that matters? Does it make any difference what we think about the Spirit, or about Baptism? Is it really important that we all hold the same beliefs?

What Christians Believe

The authors at the end of the first century C.E. remind us that what we believe **is** important. Our beliefs shape who we are and how we think about the world. Although sometimes people use the word "Christian" simply to refer to a kind act, Christianity also includes teachings about God, Jesus, the Spirit, and the purpose of human life.

The New Testament authors have given us several reasons why it is important that we share the same beliefs:

- **Our common beliefs link us to our tradition.** They connect us to our ancestors in the faith, and they ensure that we benefit from the wisdom of those who have gone before us in the Christian life.
- **What we believe influences our values and our attitudes towards life**. Our belief in the parousia, for example, gives us an optimistic and hopeful view in the face of difficulties we encounter.
- **Unity in belief helps to bring unity to the community**. When we remain united in what we believe, we remain united in other things as well. Our common beliefs give us a shared identity and sense of purpose.

For all these reasons, Christianity must include certain basic beliefs and teachings. However, we have to recognize that a person comes to this kind of faith only gradually, by studying and honestly encountering the teachings of the Church. One's faith has to be authentic.

◆ MORE ABOUT THE LESSON

Letter to the Churches

The letters to the various churches that are found in the Book of Revelation are quite understandable and a good introduction to the book as a whole because they introduce symbolic language that is fairly understandable.

On their map, the students will find Ephesus, Smyrna and Sardis. The other four cities are in the same general area and will likely be on a more detailed wall map of the ancient world.

How Christians Live

Even though faith includes right doctrine, its most important aspect is a "yes" to the love of God in our hearts. People who say "yes" to God may have more "faith" than Christians who have all the right beliefs, but shut themselves off from the love of God and others. We can never mistake what we believe to be the whole of our faith; this was the very mistake the letter of James was written to correct. This is also echoed in the Third Letter of John

> Beloved . . . . I rejoiced greatly when some of the brothers came and testified to how truly you walk in the truth. Nothing gives me greater joy than to hear that my children are walking in truth.
>
> Beloved, you are faithful in all you do for the brothers, especially for strangers; they have testified to your love before the church. Please help them in a way worthy of God to continue their journey . . . .
>
> Beloved, do not imitate evil but imitate good. Whoever does what is good is of God; whoever does what is evil has never seen God.
>
> (3 John 2–6,11)

The author of Hebrews defined faith as "the realization of what is hoped for, and evidence of things not seen" (Hebrews 11:1). With confidence in the Spirit and conviction about the truths of the faith, Christians face life with hope. As 1 Peter puts it:

> Once you were "no people," but now you are God's people; you had not received mercy for you, but now you have received mercy
>
> (1 Peter 2:10)

Have You Considered?

1. Do you think holding common beliefs is an important part of Christianity? Why or why not?
2. What do you think it means for someone to "honestly encounter" a particular teaching? Describe how you think this might happen.

Spiritual Reflection

The Book of Revelation

Read Chapter 19 of Revelation. In it, you will find the author's vision of the heavenly assembly. He hears two songs of praise of God sung by the angels in the assembly.

> "Alleluia! Salvation, glory, and might belong to our God, for true and just are his judgments. He has condemned the great harlot who corrupted the earth with her harlotry. He has avenged on her the blood of his servants."
>
> (19:1–2)

> "Alleluia! The Lord has established his reign, [our] God, the almighty. Let us rejoice and be glad and give him glory. For the wedding day of the Lamb has come, his bride has made herself ready. She was allowed to wear a bright, clean linen garment."
>
> (19:6–80)

For your reflection, do the following:

- Read over these songs carefully.
- Think about what the symbols might mean, but don't get hung up on whether you're right or wrong; just let the images flow in your mind, like you might for a daydream.
- Use the words of these songs, especially the second one, as the basis of your prayer. Add your own thoughts.
- When you're finished, offer a final prayer thanking God for this time. Jot a few notes in your journal and then go back to your day.

◆ MORE ABOUT THE LESSON

Choral reading

The images in the Book of Revelation are so powerful, they demand to be read aloud. If your students get fascinated with Revelation, they can read more than the chapters suggested in the text or lesson.

This can be an enjoyable event, for the symbols have their own power and will affect the students even though they might not be able to "explain" their meaning. Let the students decide where the breaks in subject or feeling come, where different groups or solo-reading would be effective. Let the reading be as intense and dramatic as is Revelation itself.

What's Next?

What to Do

Say: "We have come, finally, to the last book in the Bible, yet we have not looked at every single book of the Bible. Much remains for you to explore on your own. The next few lessons we will look back and realize how much you have learned and how important that learning could be for you."

Have You Considered?

1. Some students will stress that holding common beliefs is an important ingredient in church unity. Others will respond that it is not necessary or desirable for everyone to think exactly the same way. Point out that both responses are true: certain beliefs are the core of Christianity, and they must be upheld because they express the values and traditions of the Church. Beyond this necessary unity, however, expression and application of beliefs vary, and such diversity is healthy.

2. An honest encounter with a particular teaching is one in which we do not begin with our minds made up. Instead, we approach the teaching openly, trying in good faith to understand it, to appreciate the value it expresses, and to apply it in our lives. Encourage students to approach Church teachings, even those with which they disagree, in this manner. Point out that we do so because our leaders and ancestors in the faith are behind these teachings, and in humility (one of the marks of wisdom), and we give respect to what they have to say. This is not the same as blind obedience, but an authentic effort to understand the teaching. Ask students to express, in practical terms, how this might work in specific cases.

Bonus Focus for You ———

Read 1 John 4:16–21 and 5:1–5, pondering them for yourself. How do these complement the message of Revelation? What do these verses inspire in your own heart? Write your reflections in your journal.

CHAPTER 14 REVIEW

Q/A

Section One

1. At the end of the first century, the original Apostles, who had authority because they had followed Jesus personally, began to disappear. The question arose as to who inherited their authority.

2. A "deacon" was someone who had charge of the community's resources. The original deacons were the seven Hellenists mentioned in Acts.

3. A presbyter (in Greek, "elder") was a member of a council of men in charge of a local church community. A bishop (in Greek, "overseer") was also a leader of a local church. In the New Testament, these are not two distinct offices.

4. Widows offered prayers, and helped to organize and expand the Christian mission.

5. Gnostics attempted to substitute their own wisdom for the revealed truth about Jesus and his saving act.

6. "Faith" came to mean the collection of teachings handed down from the Apostles.

7. The Romans allowed religious diversity because they wanted to preserve the "peace of the gods."

8. Christians were likely to be persecuted if they were denounced or suspected of disloyalty.

CHAPTER 14 REVIEW

Q/A

Section One

1. Why did the question of leadership come up in the Church in the last part of the first century?
2. Define the term "deacon." Who were the original deacons?
3. Define the term "presbyter" and the term "bishop." How are they different from each other in the New Testament?
4. What was the function of the office of widows?
5. According to 1 Timothy, what was the problem with Gnosticism?
6. What was the new meaning of "faith" at the end of the first century?
7. Why was Roman law tolerant of foreign religions?
8. Under what circumstances were Christians likely to be persecuted?

Section Two

1. What audience does the Letter to the Hebrews address?
2. According to Hebrews, what value does the Old Testament have for Christians?
3. In the Letter of James, who are the "12 tribes in the diaspora"?
4. Explain James' teaching on faith and works.
5. What virtues does James say should be in the Christian life?
6. According to 1 Peter, how should Christians respond if they are questioned about their faith?
7. How should the Book of Revelation be read?
8. What does the Third Letter of John call Christians to do? Why is that important?

BIBLE ACTIVITY

1. In Chapter 11 of the book of Hebrews, the author lists several figures from the Old Testament who serve as examples of people of faith. Make a list of the names you recognize. Next to each name, write down the action which the author points to as a sign of that person's faith. What do these actions have in common? How do you think the author of Hebrews defines "faith" based on this chapter?

2. 1 Peter 2:1–9 quotes several verses from the Old Testament to urge Christians to grow in holiness. Make a list of these verses, and find out where they appear in the Old Testament, then look them up. Compare the original in the Old Testament with the version in 1 Peter. What changes do you find? What do you think they might mean?

3. Read chapter 12 of the Book of Revelation. What do you think the woman in this chapter might symbolize? There is no right answer; use your imagination, and remember that the author of Revelation was well-versed in the Old Testament.

BIBLE ACTIVITY

1. The people mentioned in Hebrews 11 are: (A) Abel, who offered a sacrifice greater than Cain's; (B) Enoch, whose belief was pleasing to God; (C) Noah, who built an ark based on warnings of things not seen; (D) Abraham, who obeyed his call not knowing where he was going; (E) Sarah, who conceived though she was past the age; (F) Abraham, who was ready to offer up Isaac; (G) Jacob, who worshipped God; (H) Joseph, who spoke of the Exodus to the Israelites; (I) Moses' parents, who hid him despite pharaoh's decree; (J) Moses, who preferred to be a Hebrew rather than the son of pharaoh's daughter, because he looked for God's reward; (K) Rahab, who received the Israelite spies.

In each case, "faith" refers to the willingness of these people to act on God's promises without receiving evidence or proof.

2. 1 Peter quotes Isaiah 28:16, Psalm 118:22, Isaiah 8:14, and Exodus 19:6. Important

GLOSSARY

- **Bishop:** From the Greek word "episkopos," meaning "overseer," a bishop is one who had responsibility for guiding the affairs of the early Christian churches.
- **Christian Exile:** Idea found in 1 Peter, which says that Christians are strangers in this life, and should expect their lives to be different from others' lives.
- **Deacon:** From the Greek term for a servant, a deacon was a leader in the early Church who cared for the poor, administered community resources, and preached the Gospel.
- **Faith:** Originally an acceptance of God's offer of love through Jesus; in the late first century C.E., it also came to mean the teachings handed down from the apostles.
- **Magistrate:** Roman official responsible for administering justice; the magistrate was the person who heard complaints against Christians and ordered punishment or execution.
- **Martyr:** A person who dies for his or her faith; in many late first century C.E. Christian books, martyrs are commended and praised.
- **Widow:** Office in the early Church of prayer and service; the early Church also offered protection to widows who were left without any means of support.

UNDERSTANDING MORE ABOUT:

"An Epistle of Straw"

The Letter of James was one of the last books to be accepted into the New Testament canon. Not until after 300 C.E. was James recognized universally within the Church. The struggle over the letter did not end there, however. It began again at the time of the Protestant Reformation.

Martin Luther (1483–1546) argued that James should not have equal standing with the rest of the letters in the New Testament. Luther felt that James' attitude on works contradicted what Paul had said about salvation coming from faith alone. He assigned James to the back of the New Testament, calling it "an epistle of straw."

Today, however, most Protestant and Catholic scholars agree that this debate over James was unnecessary. James did not mean to say that salvation is impossible without good works, but rather that a proper response to God's gift of salvation must include acting for the good of others. In this way, James did not contradict Paul, but corrected a misleading interpretation of the apostle's teaching.

Section Two

1. Hebrews is addressed to Jewish-Christians who felt that God still wanted them to make sacrifices according to Jewish law.
2. The Old Testament is valuable because it provides examples of lives built on faith and obedience to God.
3. The "12 tribes in the diaspora" are all the Christian communities.
4. James says that faith is not complete without works; a person of faith will naturally act to meet others' needs.
5. Peacefulness, an unwillingness to judge others, humility, and patience are virtues mentioned in James.
6. Christians should respond with gentleness and respect.
7. Revelation should be read for enjoyment and not analyzed. The images and symbols there should be appreciated for their emotional impact, not for their intellectual content.

changes are: (A) The word "approved" in the first citation, an important word in Hebrews referring to God's approval of Jesus' sacrifice on the cross. (B) The phrase "to both the houses of Israel" was removed from the third citation, so that it refers to 1 Peter's generation. (C) "To proclaim His glorious works" has been added to the fourth citation, emphasizing the missionary duty of Christians to share the good news about Jesus.

3. Many interpretations of Revelations 12 are possible. The *New American Bible* footnotes suggest that the woman represents the people of God in the Old and New Testaments. The "birth" in Chapter 12 would be the function of Israel in preparing the way for the coming of the Messiah. It is not necessary, however, to require students to arrive at this answer. Instead, let them use their imaginations, grounded in the imagery and content of the Old Testament.

Chapter Overview

This chapter, after reinforcing the Bible study skills learned throughout the text, focuses on the place of the Bible in the students' lives; both personally, as a source of growth in faith and prayer; and communally, as the heart of the Church's living tradition, liturgy, sacraments, and action.

Teaching Objectives

By the end of this chapter students will be able to:
• Recognize the academic and faith skills necessary for continued, individual Bible study.
• Understand the place of the Bible in the life of the Church and the importance of studying the Bible in their own lives of faith.
• Begin to explore ways they can continue to use the Bible to nourish their faith and help them in their daily lives.

Welcome

Greet the students with congratulations for all they have accomplished thus far. This is the last chapter; it will be a celebration of their learning.

What to Do

Form two or three teams. Alternating between the teams, asking each what it thinks are the benefits of the Bible. Write the answers on the board. Remind the students to think back over all they have learned so far. Reward the team with the most—or the best—answers.

Then, pray with your class in thanksgiving for all the blessings of the Bible, mentioning specifically some of the best answers your class came up with in the previous exercise. Offer thanksgiving also for all your students who have worked to learn what the Bible has to offer them.

CHAPTER

15

You and the Bible

100

135 C.E.
● Second Jewish War; Jerusalem burned

170
● Christians regard the four gospel accounts and Paul's letters as scripture

313
● Christianity adopted by Roman Empire

376
● Final canon of New Testament set

ca. 570
● Birth of Mohammed

1000

1099
● Crusaders capture Jerusalem

1520
● Protestant Reformation

1540
● Luther challenges the canon; canon ratified by the Council of Trent

1546
● The Council of Trent says that the Church must interpret the Bible

1948
● Modern state of Israel established

1965
● Vatican II calls for Bible study by all Christians

2000

Israel, *Dead Sea Scroll, Isaiah.* First Century B.C.E.?

Legend
● World History
● Regional History
● Biblical History
● Books written

Have you ever played the game "Marooned"? Which things would you want to have with you if you were stranded on a deserted island? A favorite CD, perhaps, or a particular movie, or even a special family member or friend. If you could have only one book, which one would it be?

When surveys have been taken that asked this question, the Bible is almost always placed at the top of the list. Why do you think this is? Before you answer, think about this true story.

> A man lived in Berlin just before World War II. He was wealthy, and his large house was filled with row upon row of books. One night the Nazis set fire to his home, and he had time to grab only a few items before he fled. The only book he packed was the Bible. When a friend asked him about his choice, he replied, "I already know what's in those other books. This book still has much to teach me."

◆ MORE ABOUT THE LESSON

Teaching Objectives

The material of this last chapter is intended to encourage your students to continue to read the Bible on their own. It is more important than ever that, as you work through this chapter, you affirm the students' insights, praise their efforts, and reward their accomplishments. At the end of each lesson, you might want to take a few moments to reminisce with your students over all that they have learned. Recall the humorous times and share the laughter with them again. Remember the significant contributions particular students made and reaffirm them. Try to find ways to remind your students of their achievements so that they feel confidant in their ability to read Scripture and to understand it on their own.

What is it about the Bible that keeps people coming back to it? Why is it that people feel the Bible never stops challenging them, teaching them, and filling them with a sense of God's presence? Consider these reasons:

- The Bible is really 76 separate books under one cover, each with its own style and message.
- The different cultures and experiences which lie behind the Bible make its books a challenge to understand and appreciate.
- Because the Bible is the Word of God, it is not merely interesting to read; it also nourishes our faith and helps us grow in our understanding of God.
- Whatever life's problems, the Bible helps us keep hope alive. As we read about the exile of the Israelites, and the persecution of the early Christians, we know that the People of God have triumphed over hard times.
- The Bible is the book of the Church, and through the tradition of the Church, the Bible plays an important role in shaping our beliefs and worship.
- Many people feel they actually meet and know God as they know a good friend through their reading of the Bible. For some, God can be heard in the Bible's words, like a partner in conversation.
- Praying with the Bible brings inner nourishment and contentment. It strengthens and deepens people's prayer and makes it vital and alive.

The Bible is a book in which every generation finds comfort and inspiration. The Bible is the all-time best selling book in the world, because it touches people's hearts and helps them grow in faith. Listening for what the Bible has to teach is an ongoing challenge.

In this course, you've taken several important steps towards becoming a lifelong Bible reader. You've encountered the leading people, places and events of the Bible story. You've also developed some important skills for Bible study. You may be wondering, however, where you go from here. What do you do with what you've learned? In this final chapter, you'll consider how you can continue to grow in your appreciation and understanding of scripture.

Introducing the Chapter
What to Do
Have the students read the opening spread, pages 268–269. Are there ideas in this section that point to the continued importance of the Bible? How many of them match up with the ideas you have listed on the board? Is there anything here not mentioned by the students? Add to the list as needed.

Development
Using the Timeline
Have the students look at the timeline. How is it different from those in earlier chapters? Discuss with them the importance of some of the events listed here. Focus your discussion on events related to Christians' acceptance of the gospel accounts and letters as Scripture and on the Second Vatican Council's call for all Christians to read and study the Bible. What have been the repercussions of these events? There are suggestions in "More about the Lesson" on page 269 that will help you with this discussion.

◆ MORE ABOUT THE LESSON

Using the Timeline
When discussing the timeline, encourage the students to consider the difference between Scripture and other writings about God. What is the significance of our belief in the inspiration of the authors of the New Testament? Be sure your students understand the change that came with the Second Vatican Council's call for all Christians to read and study the Bible (1965 C.E.). Your students not only are too young to remember the time before the Council—they may be totally ignorant of it. Help them realize that the Catholic Church has come a long way in the last 50 years regarding Scripture scholarship. The Council of Trent's declaration in 1546 C.E. was made from the concern that untrained readers might misinterpret Scripture. Even fifty years ago the idea of lay people reading Scripture for themselves was considered too dangerous to allow.

◆ Academic Skills

Teaching Objectives

By the end of this lesson students will be able to:

• Identify three academic and three faith skills for Bible study and explain how these skills help them understand Scripture.

• Use these skills effectively so that they can continue to study the Bible on their own.

Development

What to Do

1. Have the students read the opening italics and learning objectives, before going on to read "Academic Skills." Go over the three skills covered here, asking the students to remember times when each of these skills were used in studying the Bible.

2. Ask them to consider what they learned about the historical context that affected the writing of the four accounts. What can they remember about the influences that caused John to write so differently from the other authors?

3. Ask them to think over all the books that they have studied and name three that they think are dramatically different from each other. Encourage them to look back through their text or thumb through their Bibles to refresh their memories. Let a number of volunteers name their choices and explain what makes these books so diverse.

4. Form two or three teams again and have them list the different kinds of truth that can be found in the Bible. Then let them try to find examples of each.

5. Ask: "How have you developed other skills or special knowledge that will help you every time you pick up the Bible? Maybe you know things that aren't mentioned here in this lesson." Make a list of any additional skills or knowledge the students have (for example, the ability to use a concordance to find related passages, or specific references).

Bible Study Skills

*Think about your third or fourth grade English class. What do you remember? Can you recall the specific stories and poems you read? What about the textbook you used? If you're like most people, you won't remember much at all. But you probably **are** still using the skills you learned then: how to find words in the dictionary, pronounce them properly, and use them to write a paragraph. In most cases with education, you will carry with you the skills learned better than the specific content. You apply those skills repeatedly in other classes and situations in your life, and they stay with you.*

You have learned several skills during this course. In this section, you will review the skills for Bible study you've learned.

Learning Objectives for Section One:

By the end of this section, you will be able to:

• List six skills for Bible study.

• Explain the value of these skills and give examples of how they are used.

◆ Academic Skills

Reading any literature requires certain basic skills, such as concentration, attention to the author's use of language, and an ability to follow the plot or argument. Reading and understanding the Bible requires additional skills. Once you have mastered them, you will be better equipped to read the Bible and everything else you study as well.

Reading the Bible in Context

You know that the books of the Bible were written in times and places very different from today. In order to understand what a biblical author is saying, therefore, we must know about that work's background or *context*. Scholars try to understand both the historical and literary context of a work.

• **Historical Context:** When was the book written? What was happening at that time that might have affected the author's experience and point of view?

• **Literary Context:** What other books is this author familiar with? How do those books affect what the author wrote?

Understanding a biblical book often depends on knowing its context. For example, we are able to under-

The Bible in Context

Literary Context

As you have learned, it is easier to understand an author's message if you know the books with which he or she was familiar. In the case of the New Testament authors, this means, above all, knowing the Old Testament. The New Testament authors were all Jewish, and they relied heavily on themes, images, and characters from the Jewish Scriptures. The Old Testament character Rahab, for example, appears as a model of faith in Matthew, in the Letter of James, and in the Letter to the Hebrews. If you were not familiar with the Old Testament you would not have a clue as to why Rahab is so honored.

MORE ABOUT THE TEXT

Finding the Truth

The most important truth to be found in the Bible—New Testament or Old—is the truth of our salvation. Even if every other point were found to be false, the authors' statements regarding God's love for humanity, mercy, and forgiveness, and Jesus' role in our salvation would still be true. The truth or error in the details surrounding Salvation history matter little since our salvation was the main message of the authors, particularly in the New Testament: "But these are written that you may come to believe that Jesus is the Messiah, the Son of God, and that through this belief you may have life in his name" (John 20:31). Be sure this comes across clearly in your discussion with your students.

stand the Priestly writer's Creation story because we know its authors had lived through the Exile, were familiar with the Yahwist's Creation story, and belonged to the social class of priests. Knowing this context, we can recognize the authors' message clearly.

Recognizing Diversity

The books of the Bible developed over some 2000 years, shaped by oral tradition and the contributions of many authors and editors through the inspiration of God. This means that the Bible is incredibly rich in insight and experience. It also means that the Bible expresses many different points of view. For people who think the Bible, as the Word of God, should be free of all "contradictions," this discovery is unsettling. In fact, the diversity of the Bible is one of its greatest strengths, because God's inspiration is reflected through the wisdom of many different people.

You know that each author of the four gospel accounts in the New Testament had his own understanding of who Jesus was. For Mark, Jesus was the suffering Messiah, while Matthew saw Jesus as a great teacher and founder of the Church. These are not contradictions, merely four authors examining the same subject from different points of view. When you are comfortable with this degree of diversity, you will be open to all the insights the Bible has to offer.

Scripture Workshop

Diversity in the Bible

You know that an author's point of view reflects how he or she remembers events. An example of this occurs in Acts 15 and Galatians 2. In these two passages, Luke and Paul recount the events surrounding the Council of Jerusalem, where the Church decided to admit Gentile converts without making them first become Jews.

- Read these two passages, and make a list of all the differences you note.
- Write a paragraph explaining these differences, using what you know about Luke's and Paul's reasons for writing.

The Re-Harakhte Temple in Egypt was built during the reign of Ramses II, about the time of the Exodus. The Bible was written and refined for over 2000 years. Its incredibly rich message has continued to have value to its readers for the almost 2000 years since the last book was finished.

6. Have the students read "Scripture Workshop." Allow them to form small groups to complete this exercise. Encourage them to look back in their text to find the different reasons Luke and Paul wrote, rather than trying to remember everything on their own. They should choose a spokesperson for the group who will read their reasons to the class.

7. After the students have read about "Israel Today," have them find the map in Chapter 5 (on page 82) and compare it with the modern version on page 272. Discuss with them the importance to the Jewish people of the contested regions but be careful not to oversimplify: the history of that part of the world is complicated and many different peoples have historical ties to the land.

Have You Considered?

1. Responses will differ, but refer to the reasons listed in this chapter. Ask students to provide specific reasons for their selection.

2. Any number of examples are possible. For instance, knowing that *The Jungle* by Upton Sinclair was written during the early days of the Industrial Revolution in the United States helps to explain many of its images.

Scripture Workshop

1. Differences: *Why did Paul go?* In Acts 15, Paul and Barnabas were sent by the community, while in Galatians 2, Paul decided to go, prompted by a revelation. *What was decided?* In Acts 15, it was decided that Gentiles would follow Jewish dietary rules. Galatians 2 added nothing to this message.

2. Reasons: Luke wished to stress the harmony of the early Church, and thus presented the Council of Jerusalem as a perfect model of compromise. Paul, stressing his authority to the Galatians, presented the meeting as a complete triumph of his point of view.

MORE ABOUT THE TEXT

Respecting Diversity

The course of study presented in this text is designed to help students both develop a love for Scripture and develop the critical skills they need to read Scripture fully. If students learn the skills to critique the Bible without also learning to love and treasure it, they can badly misuse the skills that they have been given.

Help students to realize the importance of respecting the views of others, especially believers from other traditions who understand the Bible literally. Arrogance has no place in biblical study. Remember that the purpose of biblical scholarship is to increase one's knowledge of and love for God, not to debunk ideas or threaten the faith of others. The skills that students have learned should be used to enhance dialogue, not destroy it.

◆ Faith Skills

Development

What to Do

1. Have the students read "Faith Skills" and briefly discuss the three skills covered in the text.

2. Ask the students to give an example of someone in the Bible whose life might help them make a moral decision. Give a number of students the chance to respond, telling you how they would use that person's example. Provide an answer yourself, to get them started and to remind them that you, too, are learning with them.

3. Ask the students to name some of the different things they have learned about God as they studied this book. Be prepared to offer suggestions to get them started; you may want to have them put this list in their Spiritual Journals.

4. Ask the students to look through the Psalms until they find one that expresses a feeling they have or remember having recently. How can praying that Psalm help them to feel closer to God, or remember that God is with them no matter how they are feeling?

5. Close the lesson with a prayer of thanksgiving. Give thanks for the skills your students have learned, and for the wonderful students they are. Then, invite them to offer prayers of thanks. After each, the class can respond, "Thanks be to God."

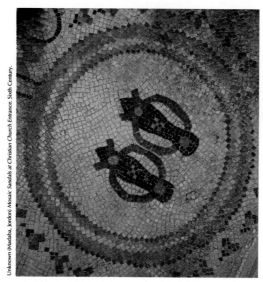

Unknown (Madaba, Jordan) Mosaic Sandals at Christian Church Entrance. Sixth Century.

In Exodus 3:4–5, God calls Moses to the burning bush and tells him, "Remove the sandals from your feet, for the place where you stand is holy ground." The same could be said about reading the Bible. To fully appreciate its gift, the reader must be aware that he or she is in the presence of God and act with humility.

Recognizing Different Kinds of Truth

Another skill you have learned in this class is to distinguish between the different kinds of truth a statement may have. For example, when your mother tells you she loves you, she isn't making a scientific claim or a historical statement. She can't prove her love using logic or the scientific method, but that doesn't make it any less true. In this case, the truth of your mother's love is personal, not scientific. In the same way, the authors of the Genesis didn't intend to write historical or scientific works. They communicated God's creation of humanity and love for us in the form of a story.

Have You Considered?

1. What do you think is the main reason so many people return to the Bible throughout their lives?
2. Give an example of how knowing the context of a literary work helps the reader to understand it.

LEARN FROM THE MAP

Israel Today

When the Temple was destroyed in 70 C.E., the Jewish nation ceased to exist. The diaspora of the Jews was complete. They were spread out across most of Northern Africa, most of Europe, and into Asia. Jews continued to live in the Middle East and Palestine (as Judah became known). Jews living in the Diaspora faced hardship and persecution. Although the Holocaust during the Second World War was the most systematic attempt, Jews have been put to death for their religion for close to 2000 years.

The Jewish people were without a homeland until the modern nation of Israel was formed by United Nations mandate in 1948. Israel's borders have changed since 1948 because of wars fought with its neighbors. Gaza, the West Bank, and the Golan Heights are known as the disputed territories and are part of the peace negotiations between Israel and its neighbors. Compare this map with the map of David's kingdom in Chapter 5. Why might these areas be of historic importance to Israel?

©1994 Magellan Geographix℠ Santa Barbara, CA.

MORE ABOUT THE TEXT

Learn from the Map

The areas of the West Bank and Gaza are of historic importance to Israel because they represent sites where the ancient nation was formed and where much of its national story took place. The West Bank includes many areas mentioned in the Old Testament. Golan was a city allotted to the Levites which functioned as a city of refuge. Gaza was a Philistine area eventually brought into the tribe of Judah, important because of its proximity to Egypt.

The Golan Heights area is not highlighted on this map but can be found around the Sea of Galilee on the border with Syria. As of this writing, Israel has turned over parts of Gaza and the West Bank to Palestinian rule. Update this information from a recent news source.

◆ Faith Skills

In order to truly understand what the Bible says, you need the academic skills discussed above. Ultimately, however, the challenge in reading the Bible is not just to understand it. Rather, the Bible's purpose is to help us grow in the love of God. The faith skills you've learned in this class will also help you to hear God's word in Scripture.

Making Moral Decisions

Paul and the other early Christian writers emphasized that being a Christian means trying to live in morally responsible ways. But how do you do this? Many people learn to make good choices by studying rules, codes, and moral principles. Others pick up values through stories which relate the experiences and choices of others. They are influenced, positively or negatively, by the examples around them.

Because the Bible contains the stories of so many faith-filled people, it is a great resource for learning values. The ultimate example for us, of course, is the life story of Jesus. By studying the choices Jesus made, and the reasons behind those choices, we begin to see the path of goodness God has marked out for us. The four gospel accounts help us follow the path through their unique interpretation of what it means to follow Jesus. As we practice following the example of Jesus in our own lives, we become moral people.

in the Spotlight

Negative Examples: Ahab

The Bible isn't just a source for positive examples. Its pages are also full of stories about those who made poor choices. Consider King Ahab from the Old Testament. (See *1 Kings 16:29 through 2 Kings 10:11.*) His fear of Assyria and Babylon (and of his wife!) prevented him from hearing the prophet Elijah. Because of his choice, Ahab was destroyed.

Ahab was afraid, and that fear paralyzed him when God called. His life story helps us learn two important lessons:

1. Our fears often keep us from making the right decisions.
2. Usually, the real consequences of wrongdoing are much worse than the imagined hardships of making the right decision.

Growing in Our Knowledge of God

A basic principle in relationships is that you can't love someone you don't know. Before you knew your best friend, you couldn't love that person. The same is true for your parents, your favorite aunt, and anyone else you love. To put it another way, getting to know people is the first step towards learning to love

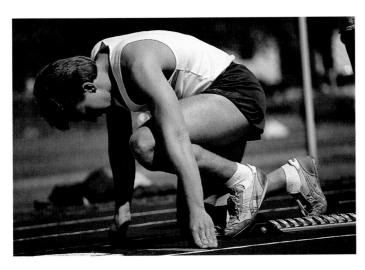

"Do you not know that the runners in the stadium all run in the race, but only one wins the prize? Run so as to win. Every athlete exercises discipline in every way. They do it to win a perishable crown, but we an imperishable one" (1 Corinthians 9:24–25).

Practicing the Skills

What to Do

Have the students complete "Bible Activity" numbers 1 and 2, individually. Give them plenty of time to complete the activities and keep things as quiet as possible so that they are not distracted. When they have finished, discuss their answers.

Recall

Turn to "Chapter 15 Review Q/A" and work through Section One, questions 1–8 with your class. Stay with each question as long as necessary, inviting input from many different students until you have reached the best and most complete answer and you are confident that the whole class has it clearly in mind.

Connect

What to Do

Have the students read "in the Spotlight" and the story of King Ahab in 1 and 2 Kings. Ask whether or not the students agree that his life story can teach us valuable lessons. Do they agree with the lessons suggested in the text? Are there other lessons that they see in the story?

What's Next?

What to Do

Ask the students to think about how we use the Bible in the Mass and at other Church celebrations. Start a list of all the times Scripture is quoted during Mass. Your students should easily come up with three places: during the Liturgy of the Word, in the Eucharistic Prayer, and at the Our Father. Continue the list with as many uses of Scripture as your students can generate. Save the list so that you can add it to the next lesson.

MORE ABOUT THE TEXT

Moral Development

Your students are at an age, developmentally, when they are seeking clear and definite answers about right and wrong. They may find it difficult to translate stories about a person's choices and lifestyle into the rules for conduct that they associate with making good moral decisions. For this reason, it may be difficult for them to think immediately of a person in the Bible whose example they would follow. It will help them if you suggest that they think of a person whom they admire (or despise), and then identify what character traits they find admirable (or despicable) in that person. Can they learn from that person's example what character traits they want to nourish (or avoid) in themselves? Developing moral character will ultimately help them make better decisions than if they merely learned rules.

1. Students may give any number of examples, but ensure that their choices are accompanied by specific references to the Bible. Also encourage students to place the character's actions in the context of the biblical story. For example, Samuel is a good moral example because he did God's will in anointing Saul and David, and in rebuking Saul. This is particularly impressive in light of the fact that prophets with negative messages in the ancient world were often abused and even killed. The value learned from Samuel's life might be the inner strength that comes from reliance on God's word.

2. Responses here will vary with the student, but be sure that their answers reflect a specific part of the Bible and specific, personal reasons for their selections. For example, a student might say that the most important thing she learned was that suffering is part of God's plan. She might point to the Deuteronomic history for this insight, and the reason for her selection might be the illness of a loved one.

Bonus Focus for You ————

Which of the skills listed in this lesson have you improved the most for yourself? What faith skills have been the most important to you in your own life? In which skills would you still like to grow? Write your reflections in your journal.

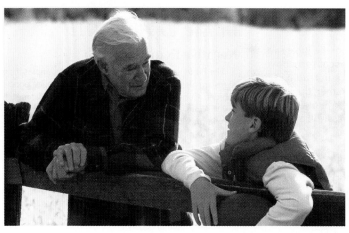

If we are willing to listen, we can learn much from our elders and from their traditions. The same is true concerning understanding the Bible. When we read the Bible we are guided by the tradition of the Church.

them. This principle holds true for God as well: we can't love God if we don't know God.

As Catholics, we learn about God from two main sources: the Bible and the tradition of the Church. In many ways, however, these two sources overlap, because the Church helps us to see God in the pages of the Bible, through its tradition of interpretation. The best way to grow in our knowledge of God, therefore, is to study the Bible in light of the tradition of Scripture study and understanding which the Church offers.

In this course, you've learned how to read the Bible for what it tells us about God. For example, you know that the gospel account of Luke and the Book of Acts are built on the theme of Salvation history. This theme tells us that God has been planning for our salvation from the beginning of time, and that God arranges the events of history to bring those plans about. The Church keeps this faith alive by helping us to see the events of our lives from the perspective of Salvation history. Knowing this, we can be confident that, in some mysterious way, things are happening as they should, and that God's love for us never fails. Reading the Bible helps us know and love God, who created us, guides us, and calls us to life in the kingdom.

Using the Bible in Prayer

Any good relationship is a two-way street, of course. Conversation is at the heart of a friendship

that is alive, growing, and filled with love. Friends talk to each other constantly about everything! The same is true with our relationship with God. If we are to be friends with God, then we must talk with God. Our conversation with God occurs when we pray. Praying with the Bible is an easy way to approach God.

Some parts of the Bible are written as prayers. As you know, many of the psalms are prayers that were used in the ancient Jerusalem Temple. You can pray these same psalms directly, connecting yourself to a tradition that's 3,000 years old.

Other parts of the Bible can also help us pray. When we read stories about our ancestors in faith, we can pray that God will give us the strength to follow their example. When we read Paul's teachings about grace and the Law, we can pray that the Spirit will grant us the grace to live as God requests.

Have You Considered?

1. Name one character from the Bible you think serves as a good example. What values or lessons do you learn from this person?
2. What do you think is the most important thing you've learned about God in this course? How did the Bible help you learn this?

◆ **MORE ABOUT THE LESSON**

What's Next?
Party time! You are rapidly approaching the end of this course of study with your students. Consider planning a closing celebration with them. Perhaps your students could plan a prayer service, choosing their favorite readings from the study they have done. Or, you could invite them each to bring in a treat or some (appropriate!) music to share, and have a class party.

Applying Your Skills

If you've ever played a sport or participated in the arts, you know that practice is the key to success. Behind that dramatic single in the bottom of the ninth inning are hours spent in the batting cage; that record-breaking lap comes from countless miles run around the track after school. The life-like statue or the perfectly rendered piano concerto reveal a dedication to practice. Reading the Bible requires no less dedication: the more you practice, the better you get.

The skills reviewed in the last section can be used to improve your understanding of the Bible and to grow in faith. In this section, you'll look at ways in which you can improve your Bible study skills.

Learning Objectives for Section Two

By the end of this section, you will be able to:

- Demonstrate your mastery of the six basic Bible study skills.
- Discuss several ways to apply these skills.
- Examine how the Bible is a part of the living tradition of the Church.

◆ The Bible in Society

One of the most consistent themes in the Bible is that how we live our faith affects society as well as our own spiritual lives. Amos, you will recall, said that religious ritual is useless unless people live justly. The Law of Moses contained provisions ensuring that the poor were cared for and that people had a chance to escape from debt. In the New Testament, Luke stresses the special love God has for the poor and those forgotten by society. As Christians, therefore, we should search the Bible for what it can tell us about the social problems we face today. Your Bible study skills can help you do this.

No Specific Solutions

Many of the problems we face today are unique to modern society. The Bible has nothing directly to say, for example, about nuclear war, since nuclear power was unknown in the time of the biblical authors. Problems such as poverty and homelessness are timeless, yet in neither case does the Bible offer specific solutions.

The Bible does not tell us how to run our economy or what our policies on taxes or foreign relations should be. The policies described in the Bible were appropriate for their time and place, and these circumstances have changed over time. We must develop our own solutions for every situation, guided by the principles offered in the Bible.

The Bible Offers Religious and Moral Values

The Bible provides directions and values which pertain to our problems. The Bible upholds the dignity of people living in poverty for example. Any proposal or program that treats the poor as objects or threatens their well-being is contrary to that biblical value. Similarly, the Bible upholds the sacred nature of human life. This value should influence the way we look at society and shape our political decisions. By carefully studying the various books of the Bible, we

---

MORE ABOUT THE TEXT

A Christian Nation?

The United States has been a haven for people of different nations, cultures, and religions for centuries, although its Christian majority has not always been hospitable. (The warning to Israel that it should be especially kind to exiles because it was once in exile, has often been ignored.)

There are many people in the United States of America who feel that the nation is built upon the Bible and is thus a Christian country. They then try to argue from Scripture how we should act and what we should do. While the Bible is misused in this way by some, your students should by now understand that using the Bible in this way is unproductive.

While the Bible can, and should, influence our discussion of public policy, it shares that role with the scriptures from other religious traditions.

LESSON TWO (pages 275–281)

◆ The Bible in Society

Welcome

What to Do

Greet your students individually as they come in and, once they are gathered, welcome the whole class and let them know how much you have enjoyed your time with them.

Remind the students of the "deal" you made in the first week of your study: you would try to be the best teacher you could, and they would give good effort to learning. Find out how they think this informal "covenant" has been kept.

Ask your students to think back over all that they have learned and studied. What was the most surprising thing they learned? What were their favorite stories, and why? Has their study of the Bible influenced their view of society in any way, or changed the way they think about things?

Invite your students to pray with you. Give thanks for the wonderful class times you have shared with your students, for what they have learned and what you have learned.

Introducing the Lesson

Teaching Objectives

By the end of this lesson the students will be able to:

- Explain the place of the Bible in society as a source of examples that show us the basic values that our solutions must uphold.
- Describe the place of the Bible in the life of the Church.
- Name ways that they can continue their own individual use of the Bible.

What to Do

Have the students read the italicized opening paragraphs and the Learning Objectives at the beginning of Section Two. Remind them that they have already completed the first objective in their previous lesson. Then, point out the list that you and they created at the end of the last lesson, and tell the students that they have already begun to fulfill the last objective. That only leaves one, and it's a good place to begin.

What to Do

Have the students read "The Bible in Society" and discuss the four skills listed on page 276. See how many examples your students can think of for each skill.

| People of Note |

Have the students read "People of Note." Discuss with them the significance of Chavez's actions. What gospel account would they guess he read a lot? Why do they think he received the Eucharist at the end of his hunger strikes? Then ask them to name other modern prophets.

Have You Considered?

1. The selection of the problem is up to the students. Whatever issue students choose, ask them to apply the model described in this section for getting a biblical perspective. First, they should study passages which apply to this problem in their original contexts. Second, they should seek a variety of biblical perspectives. Third, they should study the examples of biblical personalities. Finally, they should use the Bible to seek guidance in prayer.

2. Ensure that students have absorbed the definition of a prophet: one who speaks God's word in a specific historical and social situation. Ask students to seek examples in their own lives in which they could play a prophetic role.

People of Note

Cesar Chavez

Cesar Chavez was a modern prophet, someone who read the Bible intensely and applied the insights and strength he found there to the needs of his people. Chavez was the founder of the United Farm Workers of America, a union devoted to improving the working conditions and benefits of agricultural laborers.

Many of these workers speak little English, and often don't understand their rights. As a result, they can be mistreated and taken advantage of. Chavez helped the farm workers to organize to resist these abuses. One of his tactics was to protest unfair treatment of the workers with hunger strikes. The Eucharist was always the first food he would receive when he ended one of these fasts. Cesar Chavez died in 1993, a model for us of someone who was inspired by the Bible to address the injustices he saw.

Cesar Chavez, shown here with Senator Robert Kennedy, was inspired by the Bible to act for justice.

can discover the basic values they contain, and then apply these values in our own context.

Applying Your Skills

All too often, people jump to conclusions about what "the Bible says." Using your skills, you can carefully avoid this error. The following four points summarize what you've learned about reading the Bible.

1. **The Bible is to be read in context.** When biblical authors speak, their words are directed toward a specific historical, literary, and social situation.
2. **The Big Picture must be seen.** The Bible is multifaceted. To understand the real issues being discussed, read what a variety of authors have to say.
3. **The Bible teaches by example.** Biblical stories can shape our lives by their examples. These models can show us how people of faith reacted in situations similar to our own.

4. **The Bible is a book of prayer.** To discern what the Bible has to say on a particular subject, pray over it carefully, asking the Spirit to lead you in truth and consult the teaching of the Church, to be sure that you are staying on track.

Being Prophets

You have read the stories of many of Israel's prophets: Elijah, Elisha, Isaiah, Jeremiah, and Ezekiel. As you know, these courageous servants of Yahweh spoke God's word to the leaders of their society, calling the people back to their basic Covenant values. By applying your Bible study skills, you can hear God in Scripture. Once you have heard, you can proclaim God's message to others. In so doing, you can be a prophet for our age.

Our world needs prophets. We need people who can carefully discern the values of Scripture, and speak those values clearly and compassionately. Sometimes we are so overwhelmed by problems, that the situation seems hopeless. Prophets remind us that with God, there is always hope.

Whatever your situation, your Bible study skills can help you analyze the situations you experience, discover the important values at stake, and think about the choices you can make. In this way, the Bible can help you to discover and share God's word where it is most needed.

Have You Considered?

1. Name one social problem we face today, and describe how you would study the Bible to find out what it has to say about that problem.
2. Describe a situation in which you could imagine yourself acting as a prophet.

MORE ABOUT THE TEXT

Cesar Chavez

When Cesar Chavez is held up as an example of a modern day prophet, some people will shake their heads and wonder what the Church has come to. For them, Chavez was a pest and a nuisance who interfered with the business of farming. They wonder how the Church can hold up someone as an example who caused such discomfort for the business community.

This feature does not hold Chavez up as a saint. Whether he was or not remains to be decided. However, it is clear that he was a man who took seriously the Bible's underlying message to care for the poor and those who cannot take care of themselves. Chavez's life was dedicated to the migrant workers' struggle for justice; he always acted according to his understanding of the Bible.

◆ The Bible in the Life of the Church

As Catholics, we encounter the Bible in a variety of situations: in Mass, in the sacraments, during the Liturgical year, and in prayer. Another great application of the Bible study skills you have developed in this class is to participate more deeply in the life of the Church. If you do, the rituals and seasons of the Church will become more interesting and understandable.

At Mass

Mass is an important expression of the faith of the Church. Your Bible study skills can help you become a more informed and sensitive participant in the Mass. Knowing the Bible can revitalize your experience of the Mass and make it more enjoyable.

The Bible plays an important role in the Mass. The first major division of the Mass, called the *Liturgy of the Word*, is primarily taken from the Bible:

- A reading taken from the Old Testament
- A response, usually a psalm
- A reading from the New Testament, either from Acts or one of the letters
- A reading of the Gospel from one of the four accounts

Because many people don't know much about the Bible, they often don't appreciate the Liturgy of the Word. They wait for the priest's homily for things to make sense. The readings for each Mass were carefully selected to present a common theme. The

The Advent Wreath is used to celebrate the Liturgical season of Advent. The Liturgical year is organized around a three year cycle of readings from the Bible.

Scripture Workshop

The Readings for Mass

Find out what the readings are for this week's Sunday Mass, then, do the following:

- Look up each passage and read it. You may find the passage more understandable if you also read the entire chapter that contains the assigned passage.
- Try to identify the historical and literary context involved. Write a paragraph explaining your understanding of the passage.
- Reflect on what each reading says about God and yourself. Put these ideas into a paragraph also.
- After Mass, evaluate your work to see if this process helps your appreciation of the Liturgy of the Word.

Lectionary, the book containing the readings for Mass, has been organized so that a theme or an issue is seen in each set of readings and develops over the course of a few weeks.

One way to apply your biblical skills would be to study the Sunday readings in advance. Figure out what the authors were saying, and how their words help point us to God. Then put the readings together and try to determine the theme the Church saw in putting these particular selections together.

The Other Sacraments

Although the Eucharist is the sacrament that Catholics experience most often, other sacraments are also based on biblical teaching. The rite of baptism is based on actions performed by the disciples of Jesus (John 4:1–2), and our understanding of it has been shaped by Paul's teaching. Similarly, the rite of Holy Orders has been influenced by Luke's description of the coming of the Holy Spirit in Acts (*Acts* 2:1–41). The same passage in Acts is also part of the sacrament of Confirmation.

◆ The Bible in the Life of the Church

Development

What to Do

1. Have the students do the "Scripture Workshop." Ask for a volunteer to locate next Sunday's readings in a Missalette and tell the class what references to look up.

2. Have the students read "The Bible in the Life of the Church" and the references mentioned in "Holy Days and Seasons." Can they explain what these have to do with Lent?

3. Ask for volunteers to read the Scripture passages mentioned in "The Church in Prayer." Have them compare the two in Luke 1 with the words in the "Hail Mary."

Scripture Workshop

An example for one of the readings is:
- Reading: 1 Corinthians 8:1–13

1. Read this passage in light of chapters 5–10 in 1 Corinthians, a section on the moral problems experienced in the Corinth.

2. Context: The problem of meat offered to idols arose because Corinth was a Gentile community, and most meat available for sale had been sacrificed to Greek gods. Paul says that even though such gods are not real, Christians should abstain from eating such meat if it will offend their neighbor.

3. The reading is saying that just because we can do something doesn't necessarily mean we should do it. God wants us to use our freedom to build up the faith of others. Therefore, I should study myself to see if I'm using my gifts in a way that helps others and strengthens their faith.

1. Student responses will differ, but most students should recognize that the more they know about what's happening at Mass, the more they're likely to get out of it.

2. Lent is a period of time leading up to Holy Week. The more students know about the events of Holy Week, the more meaningful these celebrations will be. Similarly, the more students are familiar with the infancy narratives and the doctrine of the Incarnation, the more significant Advent will become. Finally, studying the Resurrection stories and the importance of the Resurrection in the preaching of the early Church will help students enter into the Eastern season more fully. Students should be directed to provide specific examples of how Bible study can help them to appreciate these seasons. For example, they might discuss how reading Paul's words in Philippians 2:6–11 about the Incarnation could help them appreciate the season of advent and the celebration of Christmas.

Just like the Mass, our interest in these sacraments, and our appreciation for them, will be enhanced if we reflect on the biblical passages that lie behind them. Maybe your own Confirmation is approaching, or your niece is being baptized soon. Maybe a friend or member of the family is being married or ordained. Whatever the case, you will get more out of the ritual surrounding the sacraments if you have used your Bible study skills to prepare.

Holy Days and Seasons

In the Catholic tradition, the Church year is divided into several seasons, each of which has a special importance in the life of the Church. The season of Advent, the four weeks before Christmas, opens the Church year. It is a time of preparation for the coming of Jesus. Christmas is then followed by the Christmas season. Later, the Church observes the season of Lent, leading up to Holy Week and Good Friday, followed by Easter Sunday and the Easter Season. In all of these periods, the Church focuses on specific aspects of the biblical story. How can your skills with the Bible help you to better appreciate these seasons?

Because Lent is a period of self-discipline and repentance leading up to the death and resurrection, you might prepare for it by reading the Bible stories that tie into this theme. Read the story of David's sin against Uriah and his sorrow when Nathan pointed out his evil deed in 2 Samuel 11 and 12. Read Psalm 51, often said to be David's prayer of repentance. Or you could read Jesus' comments on sin and forgiveness in the Gospel. Again, you would use your academic skills to figure out what these passages are saying. Then use your faith skills to hear God speaking to you through them.

The Church in Prayer

Catholics pray in many different ways. The rosary is a biblical prayer used by countless millions of Catholics every day. Maybe your family prays the rosary together. Catholics also pray at Mass, before meals, and in a wide variety of other situations. The formal prayers Catholics use are often formed around biblical passages and themes.

You already know that the Our Father is from the words of Jesus in the New Testament as they appear in Matthew 6:9–15 and Luke 11:2–4. Did you know that the Hail Mary is also biblical? The opening words of the prayer are from Luke 1:28, when the angel Gabriel appears to Mary and announces to her that she will give birth to Jesus. Elizabeth responds to Mary's visit with the next phrases of the prayer (*Luke 1:42*).

Sharing What You Know

Part of what makes us Catholic is our membership in the larger Church community. As you grow in your knowledge of the Bible, and use it to participate more deeply in the sacraments, seasons, and prayer of the Church, you should also share what you know with others.

- Take a few minutes to talk with your family about the Bible readings before you go to Mass.
- Explain the origins of the Hail Mary before you say the rosary together.
- During Lent, talk about the passion stories in the four gospel accounts.

Whatever the situation, when you share your skills with others, you respond to Jesus' call to focus on others first. You'll also keep coming back to Scripture because you're comfortable reading it.

The rosary is a vehicle for prayer and a source of great comfort for many Catholics. The rosary is based upon events mentioned in the Gospel and so is a biblical prayer.

Have You Considered?

1. Do you think you would participate better at Mass if you knew more about the Bible readings? Why or why not?
2. Describe a way in which using your Bible study skills would make Lent, Advent, or Easter more meaningful to you.

MORE ABOUT THE TEXT

The Interpretation of the Bible

On April 23, 1993, the Pontifical Biblical Commission presented the text "The Interpretation of the Bible in the Church" to Pope John Paul II. This document examines the features of modern biblical scholarship and reaches the conclusion that Catholics must be involved throughout the process, using all of the methods open to us, while canonizing none of them.

The Pope commented: "One will perceive the document's stress on the fact that the biblical word is at work speaking universally, in time and space, to all humanity. ... Biblical thought must always be translated anew into contemporary language so that it may be expressed in ways suited to its listeners ... faithful to the original and cannot force the texts in order to accommodate a fashionable interpretation."

◆ The Book of the Church

The relationship between the Bible and the Church is not a one-way street. It's not just that the Bible helps us to understand the Church; the Church also helps us to better understand the Bible. In fact, the Bible is the Church's book, and only through the tradition of the Church can we fully understand the message of Scripture.

The Church Gives Us the Bible

The Bible is the "book of the Church" in many senses. As you have seen, the Bible is central to the ritual and prayer of the Church. But there is another important way in which the Bible is the Church's book: the Church gave us the Bible. This statement is true in two ways:

1. The Bible was written by members of a faith community, who were writing on behalf of that community. The New Testament was written by early Christians and its contents reflect the beliefs and practices of those early communities.
2. Later, the Church decided which books deserved to be included in the Bible and which should be excluded. The list of books approved for the Bible is called the **canon.** The Church decided what the canon of the Old and New Testaments would be.

Taken together, these two points mean that the Bible originated in the Church and has been given its present form by the Church. In other words, the Church came before the Bible and the Church gave the Bible its importance.

The Church Interprets the Bible

Catholics recognize two primary ways in which God's will is revealed: (1) through Scripture and (2) through the tradition of the Church. Just as God inspired the authors of the Bible, we believe that God has also inspired the Church, and that both Bible and tradition are valid sources of revelation.

We have already seen that the Bible is a highly diverse collection of literature, containing many different points of view. How are we to know which points of view are valid for us today, and which have

to be revised in light of new experience? Our personal prayer and reflection are an important part of the answer, but an even more important source of guidance is the teaching of the Church.

Through the authority of the Pope and the bishops, the Church interprets the Bible for every generation. Because the Bible was given to us by the Church, it is only in light of the Church that we can truly understand its contents.

As Catholics, we believe that there is more to interpreting Scripture than our own, personal reaction; we are also members of a believing community, and our understanding of the Bible needs to be shaped by that community. As this process goes on, the Holy Spirit is with the Church, guiding it and protecting it. The second letter of Peter addresses this idea:

> Know this first of all, that there is no prophecy of Scripture that is a matter of personal interpretation, for no prophecy ever came through human will; but rather human beings moved by the Holy Spirit spoke under the influence of God.
>
> (2 Peter 1:20–21)

In other words, the biblical authors were not writing merely as individuals. Their efforts were guided by the Holy Spirit. To understand their work, we also need the guidance of the Spirit. This guidance is fully available through the Church.

The Dogmatic Constitution on Divine Revelation from the Second Vatican Council says,

> The Tradition that comes from the apostles makes progress in the Church, with the help of the Holy Spirit. There is a growth in insight into the realities and words that are being passed on. This comes about in various ways. . . . Thus, as the centuries go by, the Church is always advancing towards the plenitude of divine truth, until eventually the words of God are fulfilled in her.
>
> (Dei Verbum II, 8)

Have You Considered?

1. Which do you think is the most important sense in which the Bible is the "Book of the Church?" Why?
2. Give an example of how the Church helps us to understand the Bible.

◆ The Book of the Church

Development

What to Do

Give the students enough time to read "The Book of the Church." Go over the text to be certain your students have a good grasp of the material. Emphasize (once again) that the Bible both shapes the Church and was shaped by the Church. Review the Catholic approach to Bible study and how that approach differs from some other denominations.

Have You Considered?

1. Student responses will differ, but they should select from the list of senses provided in this section, and they should give specific reasons for their selection. For example, students might say that the Bible is the Book of the Church because it is used in ritual and liturgy. Their reason might be that since the Mass and the other sacraments are how they experience the Church in their lives, the role the Bible plays in these rituals makes it the book of the Church for them.
2. Many examples are possible. Historically, the Church has sometimes spoken on the meaning of specific passages, such as the Council of Trent's declaration that James 5:14f. refers to the sacrament of anointing the sick. More important than these specific interpretations, however, is the general point that as Catholics, we interpret Scripture within the context of our faith community.

MORE ABOUT THE TEXT

More on Biblical Interpretation

"The problem of the interpretation of the Bible is hardly a modern phenomenon, even if at times that is what some would have us believe. The Bible itself bears witness that its interpretation can be a difficult matter. Alongside texts that are perfectly clear, it contains passages of some obscurity.

"The problem is therefore quite old. But it has been accentuated with the passage of time.

Readers today, in order to appropriate the words and deeds of which the Bible speaks, have to project themselves back almost 20 or 30 centuries—a process which always creates difficulty. Furthermore, because of the progress made in the human sciences, questions of interpretation have become more complex in modern times" (The Interpretation of the Bible in the Church, Introduction).

◆ Personal Study and Prayer

Development

What to Do

1. Call students' attention to the last two paragraphs of "Life Situations" and discuss with them the different things in their lives that affect their character. Find and read Romans 5:3–5 and Sirach 15:14–19 for two examples of ways the Bible can influence their character.

2. Have the students look again at the last paragraph of "Prayer." Discuss it with them, adding to the discussion as needed from other sources.

Recall

Have the students work individually to answer questions 1–9 in Section Two of the "Chapter 15 Review Q/A." They can also complete this as a homework assignment if you need time.

Connect

Give the students a few minutes to think about how they have benefited from the Bible study they have now completed and how they might continue to benefit from reading the Bible on their own. Ask them to make some kind of resolution, or promise to themselves, about how they want to continue to use the Bible. They can write about these reflections and their final resolution in their Spiritual Journals.

What's Next?

What to Do

After your celebration (if you planned one) or the review, ask the students to become quiet once again and read the Spiritual Reflection, page 281. Use the suggestion here as your closing prayer with your students, offered with joined hands. Include also what you personally are thankful for; give the students a chance to add their personal thanks as well. Close by praying the "Glory Be" together.

280

◆ Personal Study and Prayer

This emphasis on the Church as the interpreter of Scripture does not mean that your personal Bible study is unimportant. Far from it! You can and should return to the Bible throughout your life to hear God speaking and to think and pray about how you want to respond.

Life Situations

All of us face difficult moments of choice. What ever your situation, choices require thought and prayer. They also require input from others. Here the Bible can help provide models; people who have overcome difficulty.

Consider the story of Ruth, who made the difficult choice to stay with her mother-in-law Naomi rather than return to her native country. Using your academic skills, you can figure out how to use this biblical situation to resolve an issue of your own. You can make a good decision grounded in prayer.

Of course, real life situations are not always filled with drama. Most of life requires that we make minor decisions and avoid insignificant obstacles. Through every choice we make, however, we develop our *character*. As a result, even seemingly minor choices we make are important.

Here, too, the Bible can help. Read something from the Bible every day, if only a few verses. Reflect on what they might mean. Think about those verses for the day. Decide on a goal you want to strive for in your behavior and your relationships with others. Over time, you will find that you have formed a character grounded in the Scripture and in the love of others.

Prayer

Your most important relationship is the one that holds you close to God. As we said above, this relationship cannot grow without conversation, and prayer is how conversation happens.

Many people today question the importance of prayer. They say, it seems weird to talk to someone (God) who doesn't talk back, and anyway, it's hard to know what to say. These feelings are natural, but they're also easy to avoid. You already know that God does speak to us—through Scripture. To hear God, however, you have to read the Bible carefully, using all of your skills to understand clearly and richly. Prayer is your chance to respond.

Pick a story or passage, and begin by using your academic skills to understand it. Then, use your faith skills to hear God's voice coming through the reading. Finally, respond in prayer in a way that makes sense for you. There's no one right way to do this. The important thing is simply to pray honestly and openly, whether you do it using words, or you just offer to God the thoughts and feelings you have inside. The Bible is the best way to develop a prayer life, and for that reason, it's the best way for you to grow in holiness and in faith.

The Bible is above all a book of prayer. We are called to pray constantly so that we might be prepared for what lies ahead of us. How can you use the Bible in your prayer?

Prayer

Praying with the Bible is as old as Christianity. Early Christians used the Old Testament for a springboard into prayer. Some passages were favorites, like the Psalms, the Wisdom literature, the stories of the great figures of the Old Testament, the Gospels and Paul's letters.

One of the most common ways people have prayed with the Bible is called "Lectio divina" or divine reading. It is something like what is described in the text, but with this added point: as you read, pay attention to your own response. Usually a sentence or a phrase—sometimes only a word—seems to "pop out" from the rest. You can accept that as God's pointer to the importance of this text for you for right now. So dwell on that phrase or sentence; squeeze all you can out of it, inside yourself, by repetition and pondering.

Through this study you have gained the skills you need to use the Bible fully for the rest of your life. You can only grow in those skills through practice.

The Word of the Lord

The three uses for your Bible study skills we have covered in this chapter are not the only ways to apply what you have learned. As you grow in your appreciation of Scripture, other uses will reveal themselves. Keep coming back. Understanding and applying the Bible is a lifelong adventure. The Bible is a source of hope, comfort, inspiration, and challenge. Ultimately, Scripture is God's gift to you.

Now, it's up to you to use this gift!

Have You Considered?

1. Describe a situation in your life in which you think Bible study might help.
2. Why do you think many people have difficulty with prayer? How can the Bible help one deal with those problems?

Spiritual Reflection

Words of Encouragement

Praying with the Bible is more than just gaining an understanding of it. It is savoring the words, just as you like to take your time enjoying the taste of your favorite food. It is repeating the words that touch your heart or wake you up inside—repeating them so they really sink in. Sometimes people like to memorize favorite verses that they discover. That, too, is prayer.

Prayer is reading the words as if they were being spoken directly to you. Listen to them well, then, act. Sometimes no physical action is called for, but only a response from your heart—in feelings, words, or thoughts.

When you read the Bible, use it as a springboard for prayer.

As you finish this course, your situation is similar to that of those early communities founded by Paul. You have the basis you need to grow in faith, but you have work to do in order to master it. Use this time to thank God for this start, and to ask for help along the rest of the way.

- Read Paul's words of encouragement to his community at Philippi in Philippians 1:3–11.
- Take this message personally, and ask God to help you finish the work you have started.

Q/A

Section One

1. People return to the Bible for many reasons: it is 76 separate books; it is a challenge to read and appreciate; it is the Word of God, nourishing our faith; it helps us cope with life's problems; it is the Book of the Church; it is a way to meet God; and it brings contentment when used in prayer.

2. The two aspects are the *Historical context*: what was happening at the time the passage was written, and the *Literary context*: what other literary works influenced this passage.

3. Diversity in the Bible is not a problem because God's inspiration is reflected through the wisdom of many different people.

4. There are at least five senses of truth: historical, scientific, moral, personal, and religious.

5. It is important to know these kinds of truth so that we don't misinterpret a particular passage.

6. The Bible not only provides rules of conduct, but also moral examples that help us face difficult choices.

7. God speaks to us through the inspired authors of the Bible, so it is a place to meet God.

8. The Bible can help us in prayer to build a dialogue with God.

Q/A

Section One

1. Why do people return to the Bible throughout their lives?
2. Describe two aspects of studying the context of the Bible.
3. Why is diversity in the Bible not a problem?
4. In which different ways could a part of the Bible be "true"?
5. Why is it important to know these different kinds of truth?
6. How can you use the Bible in making moral decisions?
7. How does the Bible help us to know God?
8. How can the Bible shape our prayer lives?

Section Two

1. Why is it necessary to practice your Bible study skills?
2. How does the Bible emphasize social issues?
3. How does the Bible offer specific solutions to these problems?
4. How can we apply the Bible to social problems?
5. How can the Bible help us to better appreciate the Mass?
6. What is the connection between the Bible and the seasons of the Church year?
7. How can you use the Bible in real life situations?
8. How does one form character?
9. Is there one right way to use the Bible in prayer? Why or why not?

BIBLE ACTIVITIES

1. Select one chapter from any Old Testament book, and one from any New Testament book. Practice your academic skills by doing the following:

- Write down the author of the book.
- Find out what was going on at the time. Write down how that history influences what the chapter means.
- Read the chapter to see if there are references to any other literary works. List them if there are, and write down what each reference means.
- See if there is more than one point of view in the chapter. If so, write down why and what they are.
- What kind(s) of truth does this chapter have? Write down your explanation of each.

2. Use these same two chapters and apply your faith study skills. Do the following:

- Write down how each chapter could help you in moral decisions. What principles or values does the chapter uphold? What positive or negative examples does it provide?
- What does each chapter tell you about God? How does each author view God and God's involvement with us? Write down your answer.
- How could you use this chapter in prayer? Write down 1 or 2 ideas.

You now have a completed study of two biblical chapters. Save them, and return to them now and then as reminders of how to use the skills you have developed.

BIBLE ACTIVITIES

1. An example of a completed activity:

- *Bible passage*—Genesis 1.
- *Author*—The priestly source "P."
- *References*—There are no direct references to other literary works, although there are some similarities with other ancient Middle Eastern creation myths.
- *Points of view*—The point of view in this chapter is consistently that of the "P" author.

- *Kinds of Truth*—Theological: That God created the world and cares for it; Cosmic: God created the world with order and purpose; Social: Men and women are equal, both created in the image of God; Moral: Humanity has a responsibility to care for creation.
- *Moral decisions*—This chapter communicates the values that all people deserve respect because they're made in the divine image, and that people should take responsibility for creation. This might help in moral

GLOSSARY

- **Advent:** The four weeks leading up to Christmas; a season of preparation for the coming of Jesus.
- **Biblical Truth:** The sense that the Bible is correct in what it says. Different parts of the Bible are true in different ways, such as historical, scientific, mythological, personal, or moral truth.
- **Canon:** List of books approved by the Church for inclusion in the Bible.
- **Character:** A moral identity built on choices made in a person's life.
- **Diversity:** The different ideas and points of view in the Bible because of the different authors who have contributed to it.
- **Historical Context:** The events happening at the time a Biblical book was written which influenced its content and point of view.
- **Lectionary:** The Church book which contains the biblical readings for the Mass.
- **Lent:** The season of Ash Wednesday to sundown on Holy Thursday. Lent is a time of self-discipline and repentance, commemorating the suffering, death and resurrection of Jesus.
- **Literary Context:** The earlier works of literature which influenced the content of a later biblical book.
- **Liturgy of the Word:** The first of the two major divisions of the Mass; it focuses on selected readings from the Bible, especially the four gospel accounts.
- **Social Context:** The social conditions in which the author of the biblical book lived and how those conditions influenced the author's point of view.

UNDERSTANDING MORE ABOUT:

Chiasm

Authors who wrote in ancient Greek used literary devices to embellish their writing. As someone familiar with Greek literature, Paul frequently used these techniques. One such device is called *chiasm:* the elements in one line or passage are flipped in the second.

An example of this is: **Moving too fast, too scared to stop.** "Moving" goes with "to stop," and "too fast" goes with "too scared." Their positions in the lines are switched around, however, which the Greeks believe sounded better.

Many Bible scholars believe that Paul's Letter to Philemon is an extended chiasm, made up of pairs like the one above. Much of the Gospel according to John also follows this pattern, especially John 13–17, though in John the chiasm is more difficult to follow. See if you can match up the 25 verses in the Letter to Philemon in this fashion. Hint: the pairs start at the beginning and end of the letter, and work their way into the middle.

Section Two

1. Like any other skill, practice is the key to success.
2. The Bible stresses social issues by stressing that our faith has an impact on the way we live and believe.
3. The Bible does not offer specific solutions, but rather general principles which provide guidance in selecting specific solutions.
4. We can apply the Bible through a four-fold process by: (A) recognizing its historical and literary context; (B) getting a variety of biblical perspectives; (C) studying biblical examples; and (D) using the Bible in prayer.
5. By studying the biblical passages for the Mass in advance, we are in a better position to appreciate their meaning. Also, a knowledge of Scripture helps us to appreciate how much of the liturgy of the Mass comes out of the Bible.
6. The seasons of the Church year focus on specific aspects of the biblical story.
7. We can apply biblical examples and principles to real life situations.
8. Character is formed through a series of individual choices.
9. No, the proper use of the Bible in prayer varies with the individual.

---

decisions dealing with how we treat other people and the environment.

2. The chapter tells me that God created the world and human beings, and that God loves us. Also, God is all-powerful and in supreme control of events, so I don't need to be anxious about whether or not things will work out as they should.

I could use this chapter in prayer in the following ways: praising God for the gift of creation, and asking God to help me treat the other people in my life as creatures made in God's image.

Review Questions

1. The "Jesus of History" is the flesh-and-blood person, Jesus of Nazareth. The "Christ of Faith" refers to Jesus as the Lord and Savior presented in the teaching tradition of the Church.

2. The Gospel was written to preach the risen Jesus and to express religious truth about him.

3. The future dimension refers to the coming of Jesus in glory and the completion of the kingdom. The present dimension refers to the kingdom available now.

4. Kingdom life is restful and contented, because it is the only path to true happiness.

5. Literal followers were people who abandoned their homes, families, and occupations to follow Jesus and receive his teaching. His wider circle were people who stayed in the community and supported him and the literal followers. Within the literal followers were the Twelve, who had special leadership responsibilities.

6. Jesus felt that the Law was good, but should not be placed before the needs of people.

7. The main interests of the gospel accounts are: *Mark*—Jesus as the Son of God with authority; discipleship as accepting suffering; *Matthew*—Jesus as teacher and new Moses; discipleship as belonging to the Church; *Luke*—Jesus created the new Israel; a disciple is one who spreads the good news; *John*—Jesus as the logos, the divine Son of God; a disciple is one who loves other and seeks unity with Jesus.

8. Agape is valuing and respecting others as people with integrity.

9. The Holy Spirit is the most important figure in Acts.

10. Converting Gentiles was controversial because the earliest Christians were all Jews, who kept the Law and looked upon Christianity as a form of Judaism.

11. The Holy Spirit filled the Apostles and inspired Peter to deliver a forceful sermon.

Review

Catching Your Breath

The six chapters which make up this unit have introduced you to the major people, themes, and events of the New Testament. At the center of the New Testament is Jesus, who filled his followers with a sense of God's love and blessing. The New Testament tells us about the life of Jesus, as seen from the faith perspectives of four different writers: Matthew, Mark, Luke, and John. The New Testament also includes Luke's story of the growth of Christianity, and Paul's letters to the mission communities he founded. We also read later letters which reflect the growing emphasis on doctrine and organization in the Church. All of this material helps us to grow in our knowledge and love of God.

Review Questions

1. What is the difference between the "Jesus of History" and the "Christ of Faith"?
2. Why were the gospel accounts written?
3. Explain the two dimensions of the kingdom.
4. What is kingdom life like?
5. Who were the different kinds of followers of Jesus?
6. What was Jesus' attitude towards the Law?
7. Describe the main interests of the four gospel accounts.
8. Define "agape."
9. Who is the most important figure in the book of Acts?
10. Why was the conversion of the Gentiles controversial in early Christianity?
11. Describe what happened on Pentecost.
12. How do we see the gifts of the Holy Spirit in the Book of Acts?
13. Why were first-century conditions in the Roman Empire ideal for Paul's missionary work?
14. Why did conflicts and confusion arise in Paul's communities?
15. What does it mean to say that Paul's letters are only one side of a conversation?
16. List and define four important themes in the letters of Paul.
17. Why did the question of leadership arise in the Church in the late first century?
18. Describe the key offices in the early Church.
19. Based on the book of James, what are the important virtues in the Christian life?
20. Why is it important for Christians to hold common basic beliefs?
21. Why is understanding Scripture a lifelong process?
22. Why is it never possible to simply answer "yes" or "no" when someone asks whether a particular passage in the Bible is "true"?
23. How does the Bible help us to grow in the love of God?
24. What does it mean to say that the Bible is the "gift of the Church"?

Bible Activities

Matthew's Genealogy

1. The five women are Tamar, Rahab, Ruth, wife of Uriah (Bathsheba), Mary.
2. Tamar disguised herself as a temple prostitute and slept with her father-in-law Judah; Rahab was the harlot in Jericho who assisted the Israelite spies; Ruth was the Moabite who married Boaz; Bathsheba was the woman who had an affair with King David, and whose husband was killed on David's orders.
3. The common element in each of these stories is that they all employed unusual behavior to advance the story of salvation.
4. The reason Matthew included the women is because it shows how God works through Gentiles to advance the story of salvation.

Paul and the Olive Tree

1. The root symbolizes the religious traditions of Israel.
2. The branches are Jews living in Paul's day.

Review

Bible Activities

Matthew's Genealogy

You know that genealogies, or "family trees," are important to the Bible. Matthew opens with a genealogy of Jesus, showing his descent from Abraham. Matthew normally mentions only the father's name, but five times he breaks this pattern and gives the mother's name as well.

- List the five women Matthew includes in his genealogy.
- Four of the five are from the Old Testament; look up their stories and summarize them.
- What do all five have in common?
- Why do you think Matthew mentions these women in his genealogy?

Paul and the Olive Tree

Read Paul's Letter to the Romans 11:11–24. This passage contains Paul's famous comparison to the olive tree. See if you can understand its meaning.

- What does the "root" of the tree symbolize?
- Who are the "branches"?
- What does it mean to be "grafted in" to the tree?

Revelation

As you know, the book of Revelation is highly symbolic. Among other things, the numbers in the book are not meant to be taken literally. They are symbolic, as are the beast, the seven seals, and the four horsemen. To get a sense of how this symbolism works, do the following:

- Read Chapter 21 of Revelation.
- Write down all the numbers that appear in this chapter.
- Which number appears most frequently? What do you think is its symbolic importance?

Praying With the Bible

Every day, members of the Catholic Church around the world pray a special set of prayers known as the Liturgy of the Hours. They include:

- Luke 1:46–50, the **Canticle of Mary.** The Canticle of Mary is sometimes called the "Magnificat."
- Luke 1:68–79, the **Canticle of Zechariah.** It is also called the "Benedictus."
- Luke 2:29–32, the **Canticle of Simeon.** The prayer is also called the "Nunc Dimittis."

Over the centuries, Christians have prayed these hymns in praise of God's gift of Jesus to humanity.

For your prayer experience, use these three hymns. Divide the class into three groups. Take a few moments of silent reflection. Then, do the following:

- Have the first group read Luke's infancy account up to the **Magnificat** (1:1–45). Each member of the group can take turns reading 1–2 verses.
- When you come to the Magnificat, have everyone in class recite it together.
- The next group will read up to the **Benedictus** (1:56–66).
- Again, the entire class will recite the prayer together.
- The third group will read up to the **Nunc Dimittis** (1:80–2:28). Again, all will recite the prayer in unison.
- Have one person finish reading chapter two aloud.
- Finish the experience by reflecting on the events of Jesus' life that follow. Allow a few minutes of quiet time for this to happen.

Finish the prayer experience by saying:

May the Lord bless us, protect us from all evil, and bring us to everlasting life. Amen.

12. Each gift is reflected in the actions of people in the book.
13. Paul's journeys were made easier by a good system for travel, general safety, and a common language.
14. Conflicts and confusion rose in these communities for many reasons, including their mixed Jewish and Gentile composition and the presence of other preachers and missionaries with different interpretations of the Gospel.
15. Paul was responding to problems and questions in his communities. We have only Paul's side of the conversation.
16. The themes are: (A) The importance of moral living; (B) Freedom from the law and sin; (C) Christian unity; (D) The grace of God.
17. The question of leadership arose because the original Apostles were dying.
18. The important offices were deacon, widow, and presbyter/bishop.
19. The important virtues are peacefulness, an unwillingness to judge others, humility, and patience.
20. It is important for Christians to hold common beliefs because they link us to our tradition, influence our values and attitudes towards life, and bring unity to the community.
21. Understanding Scripture is a lifelong process because it involves an ongoing dialogue with God.
22. The different senses of truth, including historical, scientific, moral, personal, and religious truth, prevent one from ever answering simply "yes" or "no."
23. The Bible helps us grow in God's love by inviting us to learn about God, to hear God's Word, and to join God in a conversation through prayer.
24. The Bible is the book of the Church because it was written by members of faith communities on behalf of those communities; the Church selected the list, or canon, of books which are included in the Bible; through the teaching authority of the bishops and Pope, the Church guides us in interpreting the Bible.

---

3. Gentiles were grafted onto the tree by virtue of their acceptance of Christianity.
4. The points of the comparison are to say that although it may appear that God has rejected the Jews, this rejection is only temporary, and that Jewish traditions remain holy. Further, Gentiles should be grateful to Jews for nurturing the tradition that now includes them.

Revelation 21

1. Here are the numbers that appear in Chapter 21: 7 angels, 7 bowls, 7 plagues, 12 gates, 12 angels, 12 names, 12 tribes, 3 gates (four times), 12 courses of stones, 12 apostles, 12,000 furlongs, 144,000 cubits, 12 courses of stones, 12 gates, and 12 pearls.

2. The number 12 (and multiples) appears most frequently. This number was viewed by ancient peoples as a symbol for fullness (12 signs of the Zodiac). In Israelite tradition, it stands for the 12 tribes. In Christian tradition, it represents the 12 Apostles. Putting all this together, 12 is a symbol for the fullness of the people of God.

Index